The Ge...

for
Emma and Justin

The Geographical Tradition

Episodes in the History of a Contested Enterprise

David N. Livingstone

Blackwell
Publishing

BLACKWELL PUBLISHING
350 Main Street, Malden, MA 02148-5020, USA
9600 Garsington Road, Oxford OX4 2DQ, UK
550 Swanston Street, Carlton, Victoria 3053, Australia

First published 1992
First publised in USA 1993

15   2008

Library of Congress Cataloging-in-Publication Data
Livingstone, David N., 1953–
The geographical tradition: episodes in the history of a
contested enterprise / David N. Livingstone.
p.   cm.
Includes bibliographical references (p.) and index.
ISBN 0-6311-8535-6 (acid-free paper). — ISBN 0-6311-8586-0(pbk. :
acid-free paper)
1. Geography — History. I. Title.
G80.L54   1993
910'.9 — dc20   92–15681

ISBN 978-0-6311-8586-4 (pbk. : acid-free paper)

A catalogue record for this title is available from the British Library.

Set in 10 on 12 pt Sabon
by Hope services (Abingdon) Ltd

For further information on
Blackwell Publishing, visit our website:
www.blackwellpublishing.com

Contents

A historian of ideas must go where his nose leads him, and it often leads him into chilly but not inhospitable regions whose borders are patrolled by men who know every square foot of it . . . A historian of geographic ideas . . . who stays within the limits of his discipline sips a thin gruel because these ideas almost invariably are derived from broader inquiries like the origin and nature of life, the nature of man, the physical and biological characteristics of the earth. Of necessity they are spread widely over many areas of thought.

Clarence Glacken *Traces on the Rhodian Shore*

Preface

This book has impossible aspirations. In a day when historians of science produce weighty tomes on single individuals or on a few years of scientific history, it seems more than foolish to try to write on a sequence of episodes in a half-millennium's history of a tradition – and to do so without lapsing into the manufactured narrative of what my good friend Henk Aay dismisses as 'textbook chronicles'. Still, in the aftermath of the micro-scale history that has come to typify revisionist history of science it is a pleasure to come upon Roy Porter's comments that overspecialization, narrowness, and fragmentation are high prices to pay for scholarly safety. 'Micro-studies are all very well,' he reflects, 'but without an adequate sense of scale and perspective, the real interplay of forces – intellectual, social, and political – cannot be grasped; history becomes impoverished, and our grasp of the present is thereby impaired by default.' I could not agree more.

If folly this project turns out to be, so be it. But if not, I am profoundly indebted to the numerous colleagues who have encouraged me in this enterprise. In its early days Derek Gregory, Peter Williams, Peter Jackson, and Roger Lee all took time to put comments on paper. Later conversations with Felix Driver have proven to be a constant source of encouragement. Denis Cosgrove's comments on an earlier version of chapter 3 provided some fertile lines of inquiry, and for generous permission to draw on their pre-published work I am grateful to Charles Withers, David Stoddart, and Mike Heffernan. Various chapters were also read and commented on by John Campbell, and by Frank Gourley, a philosopher of science, whose weekly conversations have kept me from at least some of the most foolish errors. Peter Gould and John Agnew read substantial portions of the manuscript and their gentle prodding in new directions is gratefully acknowledged. John Davey, Jan Chamier and Ginny Stroud-Lewis at Blackwell provided much encouragement and support while Jenitha Orr scrutinized the final text with her customary accuracy and precision. A travel grant from the History of Science Committee of the Royal Society enabled me to consult materials housed in the American Philosophical Society in Philadelphia. Yale University library has kindly given permission for me to use extracts from the Ellsworth Huntington Papers. To all these, and to Gill Alexander for her assistance with the figures, I express my gratitude. Yet despite their counsel and help, I could never have completed this project without the support and patience of Frances.

1

Should the History of Geography be X-Rated?

Telling Geography's Story

In March 1974, the prestigious weekly journal *Science* ran a cheeky article by the distinguished historian and physicist Stephen G. Brush, entitled 'Should the History of Science be Rated X?' The basic thrust of his argument, as he summarized it in his tongue-in-cheek subtitle, was that 'The way scientists behave (according to historians) might not be a good model for students.'

Brush's intention was simply to signal to his readers the new ways in which the story of science has been told by its recent historians. For the entire image of science has undergone a revolution as historians have highlighted thoroughly subjective – and thus what some people would call 'non-scientific' – elements at the very heart of the scientific enterprise. At the same time they have scotched the idea that data collection, experimental observation, and theory verification are the bedrock out of which good science is quarried. Take the celebrated case of Copernicus, for instance. As historians have raked over the ashes of the Copernican Revolution, they have shown that Copernicus's empirical observations for the rotation of the earth around the sun were actually no better than the evidence for the old geocentric model. What established the new astronomy, supposedly, was Copernicus's revulsion against the inelegance of Ptolemy's system compared with the simplicity, not to mention the theoretical scope and fertility, of his own.

Reconstructions like that of the Copernican Revolution are not unique in the history of science. For the conventional and comfortable image of science as the disinterested and objective pursuit of knowledge by way of experimental analysis and logical rigour has been similarly demythologized in the case of such scientific giants as Galileo, Kepler, Newton, Dalton,

Darwin, Mendel, and Einstein. Small wonder that practising scientists are suspicious of such historical work. It tends to undermine their efforts to inculcate in their students those very principles of 'proper procedure' that the 'greatest' scientists have ignored. Nor is it surprising that one philosopher has suggested that it would be in order to use fictionalized history of science to illustrate methodological propriety! As Stephen Brush caustically quips in the conclusion to his piece:

> I suggest that the teacher who wants to indoctrinate his students in the traditional role of the scientist as a neutral fact finder should not use historical materials of the kind now being prepared by historians of science: they will not serve his purposes . . . On the other hand, those teachers who want to counteract the dogmatism of the textbooks and convey some understanding of science as an activity that cannot be divorced from metaphysical or esthetic considerations may find some stimulation in the new history of science.[1]

Certainly, many find that a sanitized history of science which ignores so-called blind alleys, errors, and distortion in the past and pays little attention to broader intellectual and social movements is professionally and conceptually comfortable. And it is therefore not surprising that, judging by these standards, geography students have been only too well served by their own historians. Social context, metaphysical assumptions, professional aspirations, or ideological allegiances rarely feature in the textbook histories of the growth of geographical knowledge. This is not to denigrate the sterling work produced by historians of the subject working in traditional ways. But it is to urge that in the light of the new history of science, new things need to be said. During the course of this book, therefore, we will find ourselves asking rather different questions from geography's conventional historians. What role, for example, did geography play in past society? Was it used for political, or religious, or economic purposes by particular groups? Who benefited from the latest theory, and who lost out? We will, of course, try to ascertain just what theories were developed, and by whom; but we will pause to ask *why* they were generated, welcomed, or indeed outlawed. For accepting or rejecting any scientific theory is always and irreducibly a social act, by a specific social group, in particular cultural circumstances.[2]

---

[1] Stephen G. Brush, 'Should the History of Science be Rated X?', *Science* 183 (22 March 1974): 1170–1.

[2] Martin Rudwick, 'Senses of the Natural World and Senses of God: Another Look at the Historical Relation of Science and Religion', in A. R. Peacocke (ed.), *The Sciences and Theology in the Twentieth Century* (Henley and London: Oriel Press, 1981), pp. 241–61, ref. on p. 247.

Nor will we forget the practice of geography; that is, the expression of thought in action. Too often the practical outworkings of theory are overlooked. Indeed the 'applied' character of much geography – whether in imperial enterprises or planning programmes – makes it a prime candidate for teasing out the relationships between, say, political structures and intellectual puzzles, social forces and theoretical problems.

Let me emphasize at the outset that this book is not in any sense 'the', or even 'a', history of geography. Rather, I will proceed by identifying what I take to be some of the key chapters in the history of geography since around 1400, in the hope of uncovering some answers to the sorts of questions I have just been outlining. There will, certainly, be recognizable landmarks on the conceptual horizon. But readers will doubtless disagree with the way I want to draw the map. That is all to the good. Reconstructing intellectual history is never a once-and-for-all activity. Critics are free to tell geography's story in their own ways.

The importance of the task should not be undervalued, however, for its consequences are far-reaching. Practically, it will enable us to work with a more realistic picture of geographical knowledge as a cultural product and a political resource, without assuming that scientific knowledge is unique and therefore somehow immune to such forces. Conceptually it will prevent us from feeling that it is inappropriate to think about scientific research in the same way as we think about other sorts of human activity. History teaches us to be humble about any claims to knowledge. Moreover, by demonstrating that the nature of geography has always been contested and negotiated, historical awareness helps to keep the subject open to dialogue and debate. Pragmatically too, there are gains to be had from retrospection. Recognizing that the future is umbilically tied to the past, the United States Congressional *Report of the Task Force on Science Policy to the Committee on Science and Technology* emphasized in December 1984 that 'Proposals for new initiatives, new directions, or new emphases to be included in future science policies will be more effective and more likely to succeed if they are shaped against a background that includes an understanding of the forces and factors that shaped past policy developments. To achieve this the Task Force recommends that the Science Policy Study commission a history of American science and US science policy.'[3] Even if the triumphalist spirit of this appeal leaves something to be desired, the merit of learning lessons from the past – of, if you will, being wise after the event – is not to be sneered at.

---

[3] Cited in *History of Science Society Newsletter*, 14 (1985), p. 17.

Implicit in what I have been saying so far is the claim that the status of scientific knowledge in general (and by implication of geographical knowledge in particular) has been downgraded as philosophers, historians, and sociologists have plied the tools of their trade. To briefly reflect on the strategies of critics who have challenged conventional scientific wisdom will therefore be an initial concern. But before reflecting on their revised schemes, I want to turn to an assessment of the standard histories of geography – the 'textbook chronicles' as Henk Aay typifies them[4] – that have been issued over the years to initiate geography's apprentices into the mysteries of their chosen craft. But this will merely serve as a prelude to the altogether more difficult job of refashioning geography's history according to different principles of interpretation. My own scenario, let me repeat, is presented with the reminder that it constitutes an argument about the history of geography. It is, therefore, open to debate, to criticism, and to revision.

GEOGRAPHY'S STORYTELLERS

Stories are always told by people, about people, for people. Geography's story is no exception. The standard textbook surveys have been written by geographers, about other geographers, for still other geographers. They are, therefore, in-house reviews of disciplinary development for the geographical community. In most cases the underlying motivation is to furnish students with historical spectacles through which they can better see the present state of geography's affairs. The past, in other words, is only contemplated in terms of the present. The result is that history is written backwards – from the present to the past and this is what historians refer to as 'Whiggish' or 'presentist' history.

Elements of presentism, of course, are unavoidable. Historians of geography live in the present – and so do their readers. No purpose is served by pretending otherwise. And of course they have particular questions, queries, and assumptions in their minds as they encounter and peruse the documents of the past. So the historical task is inevitably implicated in historical creation. Inevitably historians are involved in selecting from the available sources the material they deem significant in the light of the problems under scrutiny. They never have access to all the facts anyway, and even

---

[4] Henry Aay, 'Textbook Chronicles: Disciplinary History and the Growth of Geographic Knowledge', in Brian W. Blouet (ed.), *The Origins of Academic Geography in the United States* (Hamden, Conn.: Archon Books, 1981), pp. 291–301.

those to which they do have access are selected to suit their own purposes. There is no history on a mortuary table. The 'facts' therefore do not simply 'speak for themselves'; the historian stage-manages their performance on the contemporary scene.

Selection, then, is inescapable. But manipulation is a quite different matter. The greatest evils of unrestrained presentism surface when partisans seek self-justification from the heroes of the past; when they suppress those parts of the story that do not enjoy contemporary respectability; and when they impose an altogether fabricated order on the past as it 'foreshadows' current orthodoxy. George Stocking summarizes these pitfalls rather well when he comments:

> As the degree of partisan involvement and historiographical effort increases, the author may attempt to legitimize a present point of view by claiming for it a putative 'founder' of the discipline, brushing out whigs and tories in the nooks and crannies of every century. Inevitably the sins of history written 'for the sake of the present' insinuate themselves: anachronism, distortion, misleading analogy, neglect of context, oversimplification of process.[5]

With these deadly sins in mind, Aay has recently scrutinized those 'textbook chronicles' most commonly served on the menu of history of geography courses. Sniffing out the infelicities with the skill of a practised heresy hunter, he has provided such a painstaking exposé that I can do no better than follow the broad contours of his critique filling out the picture here and there from my own survey.[6] This thumbnail inventory, let me emphasize, is not intended to gloat over past weaknesses. Instead my purpose is to argue that the preoccupation with 'great name' history and with plotting progress from an unenlightened past to a glorious present – pursuits characteristic of too much writing on the history of geography – need to be reassessed in the light of recent work in the history of science.

In their passion to achieve conceptual coherence and narrative continuity, historians of geography have frequently used their own definition of what constitutes geography as a lens through which to examine and reinterpret the past. Disciplinary definition then becomes a sort of criterion for discriminating heroes and villains, for arbitrating modern disputes about

---

[5] George W. Stocking, Jr., 'On the Limits of "Presentism" and "Historicism" in the Historiography of the Behavioral Sciences', *Journal of the History of the Behavioral Sciences*, 1 (1965): 215.

[6] What follows relies on Aay, 'Textbook Chronicles'; and D. N. Livingstone, 'Some Methodological Problems in the History of Geographical Thought', *Tijdschrift voor Economische en Sociale Geografie*, 70 (1979): 226–31.

methods, and for selecting the dramatis personae of the drama. In the case of Robert E. Dickinson's *The Makers of Modern Geography* (1969), for example, the leitmotif is the 'region'. So it is not surprising that his discussion of Alexander von Humboldt and Carl Ritter – figures conventionally regarded as founders of modern geography – is confessedly 'limited strictly to their contributions to the regional concept' which, Dickinson confidently and tellingly adds, 'they both regarded as the core of geography.' Nor is it surprising that past personalities are called into the dock to give testimony in the methodological feuds of Dickinson's own day. 'The history of the subject reveals,' he concludes, 'that the essential basis of geographical work lies in the study of the areal association of phenomena on the earth, not in the exclusive associations of man–land relationships in the traditional sense of environmental relationships. *Geography is fundamentally the regional or chorological science of the surface of the earth.*' This is not to be believed. A clearer case of the use of disciplinary history to justify the historian's own predilections can scarcely be envisioned. But just in case we should miss the thrust of the argument, Dickinson followed up this sketch with an even more focused volume, *Regional Concept*, in 1976. His message here is crystal clear: 'The true geographer is a regionalist, a categorical statement, that will undoubtedly raise a storm of opposition, but this is the main lesson derived from a historical evaluation . . . These conclusions are derived from ideas, procedures and achievements of the makers of modern geography in both western Europe and America.'[7] Just so.

Other similar, if less strident, examples are ready to hand. In Preston James's *All Possible Worlds* (1972), as Aay puts it, the 'concept of "occupied space" streamlines, engulfs, and ostensibly unifies geography's past.' Indeed James does affirm that 'occupied space on the face of the earth has provided the subject matter with which . . . geographical questions are concerned.'[8] Parallel conceptual manoeuvres can also be detected in such chronicles as *Breakthroughs in Geography* by Warntz and Wolff, Dickinson and Howarth's *The Making of Geography*, and the collaborative efforts of Fischer, Campbell, and Miller in *A Question of Place*.[9] To catalogue their

---

[7] Robert E. Dickinson, *The Makers of Modern Geography* (London: Routledge and Kegan Paul, 1969), pp. 22, 277–8; Robert E. Dickinson, *Regional Concept: The Anglo-American Leaders* (London: Routledge and Kegan Paul, 1976), pp. 382–3.

[8] Aay, 'Textbook Chronicles', p. 298; Preston E. James, *All Possible Worlds. A History of Geographical Ideas* (Indianapolis: Bobbs-Merrill, 1972), p. 457.

[9] William Warntz and Peter Wolff, *Breakthroughs in Geography* (New York: New American Library, 1971); Robert E. Dickinson and O. J. R. Howarth, *The Making of Geography* (Oxford: Clarendon Press, 1933); Eric Fischer, Robert D. Campbell and Eldon S. Miller, *A Question of Place* (Arlington, Va.: R. W. Beatty, 1967).

historical vices would be to unnecessarily multiply testimonials. And so one final illustration of the presentist procedure will suffice – Margarita Bowen's compendious survey of geographical scholarship from Bacon to Humboldt published in 1981. However scholarly her instincts, she has nevertheless not resisted the temptation to locate the roots of her own ecological vision of geography in a revivification of the spirit of Humboldt's early-nineteenth-century science. The holistic vision of nature that he espoused with its romantic and implicitly anti-positivist bias, Bowen finds more conducive to her purposes than the cold mathematics of those hard-nosed disciples of quantification. So it is no surprise that she concludes her treatise with the assertion that 'the task of geography, as for all science, is to make the most effective use of past traditions in responding to the issues of today'.[10] Indeed it is this very strategy that undermines the historical integrity of the volume and which was bitingly censured by her reviewer, Roy Porter, a historian of science. 'Her historical discussions', Porter concludes, 'are throughout commandeered to serve her reformist purposes, in the manner of the grand old Whiggish histories of science. Past geographers are dragooned into modern philosophical camps, and the analysis is studded with "precursors" and "echoes"; a reified geography "advances" and "retreats" depending on the philosophical system ordering it.'[11]

Whiggish history as conducted in this vein embodies a number of practices that serve to keep the past in bondage to the present. As Roy Porter's comments above imply, the search for precursors is a common ploy. This technique amounts to little more than a tireless ransacking of the documents of history in the hunt for what are variously called 'anticipations', 'premonitions', and 'foreshadowings' of current wisdom. At best this procedure distorts the significance of earlier practitioners; at worst it becomes a means of fixing 'one's own prejudices on to the most charismatic names, under the guise of innocuous historical explanation. History then becomes a pack of tricks we play on the dead.'[12] Of course it involves too the postulation of some 'ideal' version of the doctrine to which earlier writers were allegedly contributing. Region, environment, culture, landscape, and society are just some of the candidates that readily spring to mind as grand transcendental abstractions that are traced through one historical epoch after another. Plainly, to evaluate the work of past geographers as if they were

[10] Margarita Bowen, *Empiricism and Geographical Thought. From Francis Bacon to Alexander von Humboldt* (Cambridge: Cambridge University Press, 1981), p. 275.

[11] Roy Porter, Review of *Empiricism and Geographical Thought*, by Margarita Bowen, *British Journal for the History of Science*, 15 (1983): 301–2.

[12] Quentin Skinner, 'Meaning and Understanding in the History of Ideas', *History and Theory*, 8 (1969): 3–53, citation on pp. 13–14.

consciously closing their endeavours around a tradition as yet undeveloped would be profoundly misleading. On the one hand, such manoeuvres encourage the historian to filter out contradiction or dispute or inconsistency or sheer messiness, in the concern to tell a good story. Thus Tatham, for example, suppresses the genuine differences between the leading nineteenth-century German geographers Ritter and Humboldt in the hope of presenting geography as a unified, coherent intellectual tradition. The work of these founding fathers, he pleads, was 'really complementary'; together 'they provided an almost complete and modern programme for geography.'[13] And so we get no hint that, for example, for Ritter geographical patterns were the expression of divine providence, so much so that his entire geographical project was conceived as declaring the predestinarian will of a beneficent Creator. Humboldt, by contrast, constructed his geography on the more secular foundations of contemporary German idealism. Given such sentiments, it is not surprising that Crone candidly admits that these two men 'belonged indeed to different worlds.'[14]

If the historian's own definition of geography can thus result in harmonizing the past to a false consistency, it can, on the other hand, be used either to sit in judgement on history or to ignore the nastier elements in the story. Anuchin, for instance, does not hesitate to take up his own materialist conception of society to whip Humboldt. Because he 'failed to arrive at a correct understanding of geographical phenomena of a social character,' Anuchin insists, Humboldt's 'materialism was marred by inconsistency once it came to attempts to explain human society's qualitative differences from the rest of nature.'[15] At the same time, the pen portrait of the turn-of-the-century American climatologist Robert DeCourcy Ward in Dickinson's *Regional Concept* makes no mention whatsoever of Ward's fascination with racial differences and his major role in the affairs of the Boston Immigration Restriction League – pursuits that were the driving force behind much of his life's work, including his anthropo-climatology.[16]

To sum up, the assumption underlying the presentist channelling of history into favoured streams of thought is that tradition is normative, that the history of a discipline discloses its essential, unchanging nature. Thus when Hartshorne announced that 'If we wish to keep on the track – or

---

[13] George Tatham, 'Geography in the Nineteenth Century', in Griffith Taylor (ed.), *Geography in the Twentieth Century* (New York and London: Methuen, 1951), p. 58.

[14] G. R. Crone, *Modern Geographers. An Outline of Progress Since AD 1800* (London: Royal Geographical Society, revised edn 1970), p. 19.

[15] V. A. Anuchin, *Theoretical Problems of Geography* (Columbus: Ohio State University Press, 1977), pp. 90–1.

[16] Dickinson, *Regional Concept*, pp. 277–9.

return to the proper track. . .we must first look back of us to see in what direction that track has led,' he was in fact making a methodological statement about the character of geography rather than conducting a historical inquiry. What other explanation can there be for his insertion of an entire chapter in the celebrated *Nature of Geography* entitled 'Deviations from the Course of Historical Development'?[17] In Hartshorne's retelling, the history of geography merely becomes the handmaiden to its philosophy, or, more precisely, to Hartshorne's geographical philosophy. Such procedures serve to rule out the integrity of methodological discussion by putting it beyond the reaches of legitimate debate. For history has spoken.

Besides its presentism, Hartshorne's classic also alerts us to another not unrelated characteristic of much history of geography writing – internalism. By this I mean that the standard treatments pay scant attention to the wider context within which geographical theories and schemes were conceived, communicated, received, and implemented. Indeed too often contextual considerations only enter the scene to give biographical colour to the geographical superstars. As David Stoddart puts it: 'Hartshorne and subsequently many others have traced a development within geography from Kant through Humboldt and Ritter to Richthofen and Hettner. . . [I]t is hence not surprising that the names of Darwin, Marx and Freud are absent from Hartshorne's and similar works; that they give little or no attention to philosophical or epistemological issues; and that the history traced remains unrelated to social, economic and political conditions.'[18]

Internalist historians invariably present their material in a number of predictable ways. First, there is what I call the 'train timetable' approach. The tactic here is to provide a chronological scheduling of great names, key works, and important dates. T. W. Freeman's sketch of 'The British School of Geography' for the journal *Organon* in 1980 and his *History of Modern British Geography* of the same year, illustrate this nicely. British geography's route is followed through a succession of characters and institutions whose dates and publications are the whistle-stops along the track. A brief, though admittedly concentrated, extract will prove illustrative:

> In 1901, Oxford University awarded diplomas in geography to four successful candidates and in later years many of the country's professional geographers,

[17] Richard Hartshorne, *The Nature of Geography. A Critical Survey of Current Thought in the Light of the Past* (Lancaster, Pa.: Association of American Geographers, 1939), pp. 31, 102–29.
[18] D. R. Stoddart, 'Ideas and Interpretation in the History of Geography', in D. R. Stoddart (ed.), *Geography, Ideology and Social Concern* (Oxford: Blackwell, 1981), pp. 1–7, citation on p. 2.

including O. J. R. Howarth (1877–1954) (1902), Eva G. R. Taylor (1878–1966) (1908), C. B. Fawcett (1883–1952) (1912) and E. W. Gilbert (1900–73) (1924) took this examination. Others, including J. McFarland, A. G. Ogilvie (1887–1954) and P. M. Roxby (1880–1947) studied geography at Oxford without taking the examination.[19]

The amount of work involved in compiling such lists should not be underestimated even if it leaves the meaning of each component part unexamined.

Then there is the 'shopping catalogue' method – a compendium of portraits of the past masters pieced together with a series of contextless extracts drawn from their writings. We are left to take our pick. Dickinson's *Regional Concept* operates along these lines. His presentation of 'The Chicago Sequence' – to take a random example – proceeds by a series of vignettes of Rollin D. Salisbury, then Harlan H. Barrows, then J. Paul Goode, then Wellington Downing Jones, then Charles C. Colby, and on and on. All that is lacking is a picture of the product on offer.

Finally, the 'museum guidebook' presents a tableau of the subject's principal branches each illustrated with its own historical exhibits. As we are escorted into the several subdepartments of Geography – Social Geography, Economic Geography, Political Geography, Physical Geography, and so on – we are invited to view the specimens on display, namely, those pioneers who charted the once unfamiliar conceptual territory. E. H. Brown's *Geography Yesterday and Tomorrow* certainly favours this method.

Whatever the industry and utility of such internalist inventories, their inherent weaknesses are readily apparent. For one thing, they cut geography off from the wider currents of intellectual opinion and from the dynamic of social life. Without some sense of these broader movements of thought and action, it is difficult to grasp what was the meaning intended by the writer of any specific geographical text and, just as important, how that meaning was meant to be taken. If we ignore this context then we will fail to understand, for example, the fascination which geographers had with race during the nineteenth and early twentieth centuries. To grasp the significance of their racial geographies requires some awareness of the biological theories, the imperial forces, and the eugenic policies of the time. Or take the closely

---

[19] T. W. Freeman, *A History of Modern British Geography* (New York and London: Longman, 1980), p. 97. See also his 'The British School of Geography', *Organon*, 14 (1980): 205–16. Freeman's long essay on 'The Royal Geographical Society and the Development of Geography', in E. H. Brown (ed.), *Geography Yesterday and Tomorrow* (Oxford: Oxford University Press, 1980), pp. 1–99, and his *A Hundred Years of Geography* (London: Methuen, 1965) also favour the selfsame strategy.

related matter of acclimatization. The question, 'Can human beings or other animals adjust to new climatic settings?' was ordinarily posed in conjunction with the far more specific question, 'Can the white race settle in the tropics?' Here again the constitutive links between a 'scientific' question and its social setting are all-important. These are topics to which we will later return. Suffice at this point to say that they cannot be understood solely in terms of geography's internal history. Indeed, internalism has the added drawback that it tends to deflect attention away from the work of apparently minor figures. This is a grave weakness, for a perusal of the work of some lesser-known individuals might provide, to use the astute words of Wiener, 'a revealing key to the opinions of a larger cross-section of the contemporary population than the more advanced thinkers of the same era.'[20] Just because their significance seems to be small within the narrow confines of geography's disciplinary past it does not mean that they cast no light on the history of geography as a social phenomenon. I would venture the opinion that the very opposite is likely to be the case.

In the light of these limitations, a growing number of geographers have appealed for a contextual history of their subject. Stoddart, for example, calls for 'a history [that] will emphasize the development of problems and theories and the social and intellectual context of their protagonists, rather than the cataloguing of people, institutions and publications,' while Berdoulay, complaining that 'little interest is paid to historical contexts or intellectual climates,' has tried to elaborate his own 'contextual approach to the history of geography.' Glick too notes that an appropriate geographical historiography 'must fulfil the twin dictates' of internal, cognitive history and external, social history, but observes that these exacting standards have been met by all too few. Meanwhile Aay laments that the 'connecting links between the content of geographical scholarship and socioeconomic, technological, and cultural context are not systematically explored in reconstructing and, more importantly, explaining geography's past.'[21] What unites the critics raising this chorus of discontent is their familiarity with the new historical consciousness as it has surfaced in the writings of philosophers, historians, and sociologists. And since the few attempts by

[20] P. P. Wiener, 'Some Problems and Methods in the History of Ideas', *Journal of the History of Ideas*, 22 (1961): 531–48, ref. on p. 540. In certain circumstances internalism might arguably encourage the opposite, namely, over-attention to 'minor' figures by allocating to them an importance that, in the overall sweep of things, is unwarranted.

[21] Stoddart, 'Ideas and Interpretation', p. 3; V. Berdoulay, 'The Contextual Approach', in Stoddart (ed.), *Geography, Ideology and Social Concern*, pp. 8–16, ref. on pp. 9, 8; Thomas F. Glick, 'History and Philosophy of Geography', *Progress in Human Geography*, 8 (1984): 275–83, ref. on p. 280; Aay, 'Textbook Chronicles', p. 297.

geographers to push on beyond the purely programmatic to substantive research on the history of geography have drawn heavily on this body of literature, I want to turn now to a brief sketch of its salient features.

RETHINKING SCIENCE, HISTORY AND SOCIETY

The dislodgement of scientific knowledge from its privileged position of immunity to criticism has come about through the work of philosophers, historians, and sociologists. The corpus of literature embodying these reassessments is both complex and extended. All I can hope to convey in the few lines that follow is something of the flavour of these debates. But because the questions raised are crucially important in our science-dominated age, and because the currents of thought they represent are being registered more and more within geography, it is vital that we can begin to identify some of the major conceptual issues that are at stake. My sketch will certainly be altogether impressionistic; still, it will enable us to see the broad philosophical contours in this disputed territory.

In the past half century or so, revolutions in the philosophy of science have come thick and fast. Since the seventeenth century, science was typically, though not universally, regarded as knowledge derived from the empirical observation of the facts of nature. By dispassionately approaching the multitude of discrete data, painstakingly scrutinizing them, formulating hypotheses and testing them against reality, it was believed that the universal laws of nature could eventually be uncovered. The philosophical difficulties in actually achieving this vision, however, led a group of continental European philosophers in the 1930s to seek to give greater conceptual rigour to the empiricist vision and to spawn a movement known as logical positivism. Their principle was that the only statements that had any meaning were those which could be verified by scientific methods. A statement like 'Those rocks contain quartz' was thus a meaningful one in their eyes, because it could be tested scientifically without recourse to theoretical assumptions. The claims of metaphysics and theology by contrast were rapidly dismissed as meaningless. Here was another set of proposals in the attempt to procure knowledge untainted by personal beliefs, social attitudes, or political aspirations.

Or so it seemed. Logical positivism was soon to be scuttled when it was realized that the very observations themselves were not free of theory. Even the simple report about certain rocks containing quartz presupposes theories about what constitutes 'rock', what 'quartz' is, and what counts as an occurrence of quartz in rock. The setting up of a scientific experiment further illustrates the point. Clearly the whole procedure assumes distinctions between relevant and irrelevant processes – a theory-based demarcation right from the outset. And the situation gets worse when we remember that science is invariably interested in *universal* propositions; that is, in making general statements of the kind 'planets move in ellipses around their sun'. As Karl Popper made clear, these are the very propositions that can never be verified. But in recognizing the impossibility of verifying even a simple statement like 'all swans are white,' Popper came to realize that it could be *disproved*. Discovering a single black swan does the job. In other words, Popper suggested, science is not about verification, it is about falsification. And science is therefore the art of being precisely wrong!

The seeming elegance of Popper's principle, however, only obscured the fact that its simplicity was more apparent than real. The difficulty of finding cases of absolute refutation in theories above the level of the trivial concerned some of his critics. For science operates far more with notions of probability than with absolute certainty. Moreover, it suddenly became apparent that to say that a theory was false was not the same as telling which theories were closer to the truth. Still, Popper had opened up scientific discourse to the difficulties of establishing good criteria for claims to knowledge about the world. Was it indeed possible that the long-standing reverence for the scientific method had been misplaced, that scientific knowledge revealed as much about scientists as it did about the world itself?[22]

Any concern that Popper may have had to keep these questions in check was hastily jettisoned in Thomas Kuhn's *The Structure of Scientific Revolutions* (1962). In his idea of 'paradigms', historians, philosophers, and sociologists of science found a new toy to happily engage their imaginations. By 'paradigm' Kuhn roughly meant – and he was confessedly ambiguous, at least initially – a tradition with historical exemplars. In other words, a mature science is conducted within a social and conceptual framework that sets the standards for relevant research, specifies the puzzle-solving objectives, coordinates the disparate work of its member scientists, and initiates its students into the ways of the tradition. Now, Kuhn went on, scientific revolutions occur when the accepted paradigm is replaced by another which gives rise to a completely new programme. The changeover from Newtonian mechanics to Einsteinian physics is a classic case. It is like

[22] A useful introduction to these debates is A. F. Chalmers, *What is This Thing Called Science?* (Milton Keynes: Open University Press, 2nd edn. 1982). K. R. Popper, *The Logic of Scientific Discovery* (London: Hutchinson, 1968).

a Gestalt-switch; in other words, suddenly seeing an old familiar picture in a radically new way. We have all seen those pictures of a pile of boxes which when you look at it one way you see six boxes; look again and there are seven. A paradigm shift is rather similar, and the reasons for the changeover no less mysterious. The new model may accommodate more information; it may be more aesthetically pleasing, or more psychologically satisfying, or more theoretically fertile; it may even have greater explanatory scope. But – and this is crucial – there are no *independent* rational criteria for deciding between the old and new paradigms. This is simply because what counts as a rational explanation is determined by the paradigm itself. Indeed the problems in the new paradigm cannot even be expressed in the language of the old. The geological theory known as plate tectonics is a good instance. According to this theory the continents as well as the ocean floors are floating on giant plates and have substantially changed the configuration of the earth's landmasses over millions of years. This has led to a complete reinterpretation of, for example, the distribution of fossils, so much so that older theories about animal migration have had to be completely recast. Plainly the problems which engage geologists working within the new tradition simply would not make sense to the geologists of the nineteenth century.[23]

In the wake of Kuhn's treatise, a batch of historians working in various disciplines set out on a paradigm hunt, looking for paradigms, paradigm-shifts, and what not. Geographers were no exception. We will scrutinize their efforts presently. What is important in the present context, however, is that Kuhn had introduced a thoroughly relativist note into the philosophy of science. In other words, since the paradigm involves a set of criteria for determining what problems are worth solving and how solutions are to be recognized, there can be no mutually agreed basis for deciding which competing paradigm is best. The results of scientific investigation are therefore relative to the scientific community within which research is carried out, and not straightforward descriptions of the way the world really is.

The relativist temper of Kuhn's interpretation, moreover, has been pushed to the very limits by the anarchist philosopher Paul Feyerabend. To him, science is a completely freewheeling business. Without the availability of paradigm-free logic, implicit in Kuhn's model, literally anything goes. This, of course, means that everything goes. Indeed, Feyerabend rejects the notion that science is cognitively superior to any other form of knowledge,

---

[23] T. S. Kuhn, *The Structure of Scientific Revolutions* (Chicago: University of Chicago Press, 1962, enlarged edn 1970).

whether poetry or drama, or more fringe pursuits like astrology or voodoo.[24]

Following the broad contours of this critique, Richard Rorty has more recently maintained that we should give up the notion that science is travelling towards an end called 'correspondence with reality,' that science can, to use his own metaphor, 'mirror nature'. To Rorty, the scientific tradition has simply been the hunt for a vocabulary that helps us to predict the world better, and to control it. Some vocabularies work better for this purpose than others: Galileo used terminology that helped, Aristotle did not. But these languages are, to Rorty, emphatically not 'Nature's own vocabulary' – that is, the way nature would describe itself to us if it could. As he puts it: 'scientific breakthroughs are not so much a matter of deciding which of various alternative hypotheses are true, but of finding the right jargon in which to frame hypotheses in the first place.'[25] For students of human nature, sometimes a behaviourist language serves the purpose; on other occasions hermeneutic talk is better. So with geographers; sometimes quantitative vocabulary produces the best predictions, on other occasions the language of the humanities suits better, while for yet other purposes notions of human agency and social structure seem most appropriate. Either way, to Rorty, scientific method simply means having a good list of headings or vocabularies for tasks to be done – a good filing system. Scientific rationality, then, means obeying the conventions of your discipline, not fudging the data too much, and listening to your colleagues. It is what he calls 'epistemic good manners'. It certainly isn't Nature's own language. That is simply not a useful notion.[26]

What has provided even more ammunition for the relativist armoury has been the post-Kuhnian alliance between sociology and the history of science. There are, of course, many routes into this territory. The writings of Jurgen Habermas provide one access point, as does the work of the social anthropologist Clifford Geertz and the 'genealogical' investigations of systems of thought conducted by Michel Foucault. Their critique will ultimately have to be taken seriously into account by historians of geography. But here I shall focus on the so-called Edinburgh school because they are chief among the practitioners of this new art – the sociology of scientific knowledge – in Britain, and because their 'strong programme', as it has

---

[24] Paul K. Feyerabend, *Against Method: Outline of an Anarchistic Theory of Knowledge* (London: New Left Books, 1975).

[25] Richard Rorty, 'Method, Social Science, and Social Hope', in *Consequences of Pragmatism. Essays: 1972–1980* (Sussex: Harvester Press, 1982), p. 193.

[26] Richard Rorty, *Philosophy and the Mirror of Nature* (Oxford: Blackwell, 1980).

been christened, has substantially influenced writing in the history of science.[27] This group, focusing on the researches of David Bloor, Barry Barnes, Donald Mackenzie, and Steven Shapin, has increasingly made out a coherent case for scientific knowledge as a relativistic *cultural* product. Science, in other words, is merely the expression of social interests because social relationships insinuate their way into scientific pursuits at every level. One or two examples will illustrate the general approach.

Consider first the professional vested interests of the community of scientists. Typically, scientists acquire technical skills during the course of their training. These may include survey techniques, mathematical proficiency, laboratory expertise, or cartographical skills. In each case they represent a set of vested interests which are therefore valued and defended among the scientific fraternity. Now, the argument goes, these interests directly condition the content of scientific knowledge. The dispute among twentieth-century botanists over the correct classification of plants is illustrative. One group grew up on a diet of morphological studies and was therefore taught that species were to be delineated on the basis of their structure; a second, laboratory-trained, set claimed that experimental work, often of a biochemical sort, was of crucial importance. The result? Two different taxonomic schemes, because each group construed botanical reality differently. Other examples could certainly be provided. The so-called quantitative revolution in geography during the 1960s would seem to be a prime candidate. Having discovered mathematics, many geographers were only too ready to display their statistical wizardry to their non-quantitative colleagues; their new skill was a vested interest to be defended within the community of geographical scholars. Yet there is the suspicion that their findings were as much a reflection of the kinds of statistical techniques they employed as of the phenomena under scrutiny. Whatever, the argument here is that the content of scientific knowledge is a direct result of the craft competences of the investigators rather than a portrait of reality. Besides, an awareness of vested interests among professionals suggests that the practices of careerism, like the passion for novelty to advance one's own prospects, need to be taken far more seriously into account in the history of science. For here we come face to face with a politics of knowledge. The shape of the science-knowledge industry owes much to the primal drive to control intellectual property through publishing-outlet control, scientific censorship, establishment officialdom, and political sponsorship.

The cultural role played by professional scientists in society at large is also of crucial importance. Scientists, this argument runs, occupy a strategic, commanding niche in the modern world, and enjoy all the kudos such a position brings. Of course this was not always so. In earlier days the ecclesiastical hierarchy held the reins of cultural authority. From their vantage point, the religious leaders were able to exercise a large measure of social control. Thus, some argue that the professionalization of science in late Victorian England was merely part of an ideological transfer from religion to science as the basis of social validation. The new priests of science continued to wield the social power previously held by clergy; they merely used different language as they did so. Instead of the moral law, they spoke of natural law; instead of natural theology, they spoke of natural selection; instead of God, they spoke of Nature. Writing of an earlier period, Robert Mandrou has argued that the very emergence of the scientific enterprise at all required a variety of subterfuges in order to subvert established scholastic authority.[28]

So, as Shapin puts it, 'modern scientific representations of the natural world developed in the course of demarcation disputes with traditional sources of authority and intellectual expertise, such as religion.'[29] Here again, claims to scientific knowledge about the world are viewed less as descriptions about natural, or cultural, phenomena, than as manifestations of an ongoing *social* debate about where intellectual authority should reside in our society. The use of scientific equipment, know-how, and jargon to justify particular political policies or social interests – as in the case of racism, or geopolitics, or sociobiology – spring to mind. In all of these, critics would say, particular group interests are reinforced by the language of science.[30]

At this point it is tempting to allow the sociologists full rein in their historical explanations by arguing that they are providing helpful accounts of *false* knowledge; that is, of information that is tainted by non-scientific factors. But perhaps we might feel that these can be filtered out over time and the residue will be pure, unadulterated, scientific knowledge. The

[28] Robert Mandrou, *From Humanism to Science, 1480–1700* (Harmondsworth: Penguin, 1978).

[29] Steven Shapin, 'History of Science and its Sociological Reconstructions', *History of Science*, 20 (1982): 157–211, ref. on p. 172.

[30] See, for example, Steven Rose, Leon J. Kamin and R. C. Lewontin, *Not in Our Genes: Biology, Ideology and Human Nature* (Harmondsworth: Penguin, 1984).

Edinburgh sociologists of knowledge will have none of it. Theirs is no sociology of pathological belief, of deviant as opposed to true knowledge.
Their claim rather is that there is no independent means of discriminating
true and false science, because all science is, if you will, socially impregnated. The adoption or rejection of theories even in narrowly 'pure' sciences like physics, for example, are claimed to be as much the result of
social relationships between researchers, or of the overdetermining role of
theory, or of who controls the publishing outlets, as of the natural phenomena. Science is thus entirely relative to the culture or community in which it
is practised. Why? Because the criteria for evaluating different theories are,
to quote Mary Hesse, 'different for different groups and at different
periods.'[31]

Needless to say, these radical proposals have not found universal favour.
A number of strategies have been advanced to deflect at least the sharpest
of these critical arrows. Instinctively we may feel that the pragmatic success
of science in so many spheres is ample testimony to the truthfulness of its
theories. Surely the fact that aeroplanes can fly is evidence that we have
found out something about aerodynamics? Does landing men on the moon
not prove that our lunar theories are true? Unfortunately this is not necessarily the case. All sorts of pragmatically successful conceptions about
astronomical phenomena – for navigation, for example – were held by
people who believed that the earth was flat, static, and at the centre of the
universe, and about physics by those who believed that all space was filled
by an invisible ether. The instrumental success of a theory is therefore no
guarantee that it is a realistic depiction of the world. So other arguments
have had to be mounted by those who wish to defend realism against relativism. Again, the defence tactics are as diverse as the defenders. But to give
some sense of the possible escape routes from radical relativism that have
been tried, I shall focus on four key areas of debate: scientific rationality,
metaphor fertility, experiment, and theory resilience. These issues certainly
fall squarely within the philosophy of science, but because they each introduce in different ways a historical dimension into the arena they are important for any attempt to understand the history of geography.

Part and parcel of Kuhn's model of scientific change was his rejection of
any sufficient rational grounds for the shift from one paradigm to another.
This scheme has recently been challenged by Dudley Shapere who claims
that too much has been made of the discontinuities between succeeding par-

---

[31] Mary Hesse, *Revolutions and Reconstructions in the Philosophy of Science* (Sussex:
Harvester Press, 1980), chapter 2 on 'The Strong Thesis of Sociology of Science', p. 33.

adigms or research programmes (to use Lakatos's terminology). Even allowing that what counts as a legitimate theory, or problem, or solution, may
change radically over time, Shapere believes that there is nevertheless 'often
a chain of developments connecting the two different sets of criteria, a
chain through which a "rational evolution" can be traced between the two.'
Fundamental difference between scientific beliefs and criteria at two different epochs, therefore, 'does not automatically preclude the possibility of
connection, comparability, and progress.' What is needed here are empirical
case studies in the history of science to determine what really does happen
during the course of a scientific 'revolution'. Certainly what passes for legitimate or even observational evidence will change with time, but – and this
is crucial – there are always compelling reasons for the shift. Changes in
the standard of rationality, that is, of what constitutes reasonableness, can
itself be a rational process.

Plainly, in Shapere's scenario there is no guarantee that a current theory
truthfully depicts the world in any ultimate sense. So his strategy is no simple return to a naive realism. It does, however, recognize that, for all their
limitations on a broader scale, older theories often *are* successful at least to
some extent. Besides, it makes possible, though not inevitable, the situation
where a theory remains immune to reasonable doubt over a long period of
time.[32] Should this happen and should the theory be successful, of broad
scope, and uncontested, it would be difficult to remain sceptical about its
cognitive claims. As Shapere puts it, 'What else would count as discovery of
the way things are?'[33]

A second strand of anti-relativist argument has its roots in the notion
that scientific models are ultimately sophisticated metaphors. The argument
runs along the following lines. In their endeavours to come to grips with
some aspect of reality hitherto unexplained, scientists and social scientists
look around for some broadly similar process that they do understand, and
interpret the problem under investigation in the light of this information.
They construct, in other words, a sort of picture to represent what they
understand to be the nature of the processes at work. Pictures of this sort
are usually called models. But they are, for all that, analogies or metaphors
– looking at something *as if* it were something else. This metaphor in turn
becomes a kind of lens through which the subject is viewed; some aspects

[32] Shapere, of course, has in mind here the very specific doubts about a theory that surface
during scientific investigation, as opposed to the universal scepticism that he characterizes as
'Cartesian doubt'.

[33] Dudley Shapere, 'The Character of Scientific Change', in Thomas Nickles (ed.), *Scientific
Discovery, Logic, and Rationality* (Dordrecht: D. Reidel, 1980), pp. 61–116, refs on pp. 68, 83.

are ignored or suppressed while others are emphasized or organized in specific ways. So, for example, physicists tell us that light behaves *like* a wave, and that subatomic particles behave *as if* they are a miniature orbital system. Neurologists tell us that our brains function *like* computers. Geographers have told us that the state is an organism that grows, that the landscape is a text which has to be interpreted, or that the black inner city is a frontier outpost.

On the face of it, this might seem a thoroughly relativist conception of scientific models, because, as Mary Hesse develops the argument, there are no direct, corresponding links between our metaphorical talk about the world and the world itself. The links that exist are only analogical ones. Besides, a change from one metaphor to another would seem just as radical a break as a paradigm shift. To think of the world as a machine (that is, to employ mechanistic models) is radically different from regarding it as an organism (that is, to resort to organic analogies). But for Ernan McMullin the metaphor notion can be deployed as a realist strategy. For him the extension of a particular metaphor – suggesting new areas of investigation and predicting the discovery of novel facts – is a signal to its truth content. Plate tectonics is a notable case in the earth sciences. According to this theory, the continents as well as the ocean floors are carried on vast plates which move on the outer shell of the globe. Invoking the idea of 'plates' is, of course, a metaphorical move from the outset. Moreover, this original metaphor can be extended by asking, 'What happens when plates collide?' 'One is carried down under (subduction),' McMullin replies, 'the other may be upthrust to form a mountain ridge.' Now, McMullin goes on, here is a clue to the realist stake in metaphor. What best explains the predictive success of the metaphor 'is the supposition that the model approximates sufficiently well the structures of the world . . . for the scientist to take the model's metaphorical extensions seriously. It is because there is something like a floating plate beneath our feet that it is proper to ask: What happens when plates collide, and what mechanisms would suffice to keep them in motion?' That is to say, good metaphors have specific entailments and extensions that make them susceptible to testing procedures.[34]

A third tactic that has been employed to safeguard the realist ingredient in science is the renewed emphasis on the importance of experiment. For

---

[34] Ernan McMullin, 'A Case for Scientific Realism', in Jarrett Leplin (ed.), *Scientific Realism* (Berkeley: University of California Press, 1984), pp. 8–40, refs on pp. 32, 33. A full discussion of the plate tectonic example is available in Rachel Laudan, 'The Recent Revolution in Geology and Kuhn's Theory of Scientific Change', in Gary Gutting (ed.), *Paradigms and Revolutions* (Notre Dame: University of Notre Dame Press, 1980), pp. 51–89.

Ian Hacking, experimental physics provides the strongest evidence for realism – a realism not about theories or explanations, but about entities. In other words, the fact that in experiments, something out there in the world can be manipulated, whether electrons or atoms or whatever, is proof of their existence independent of what particular theory the researcher has in mind.[35] Hacking's use of experiment is therefore narrowly circumscribed, and it is difficult to see what bearing it could have on historical sciences like evolutionary biology, or geology, or for much of the human sciences, in which experimentation on historical or social processes is impossible. Besides, while it may get us to the point of being realist about mechanisms or entities in the world (that is, that they really exist), it does not answer the charge that our theories about them are relativist through and through. Nevertheless it does point the way towards putting some constraints on universal scepticism.

In Roy Bhaskar's hands, however, experiment is taken up as a tool with a wider range of possibilities. His argument runs something like this. Plainly, experiments are activities performed by human agents. People devise particular experimental situations which constitute, as closely as possible, the closed system appropriate for testing a particular law. There is, therefore, a sense in which the events observed in any experiment, whether flashes on a screen or the position of hands on a dial, are brought about by humans. If they had not intervened in nature, these events would not occur. But, at the same time, the laws which these events are designed to test are not produced by people. They exist independently of the agents investigating them. Clearly, there is a distinction between the sequences of events recorded in experiments and the actual laws of nature. This is because the laws themselves only pick out particular aspects of the object in question. For the objects or systems being scrutinized possess characteristics other then those specified by the law. Take, as an example, a moving ice sheet. It is at once a mechanical, hydraulic, chemical, and thermal system. Now if we want to specify the mechanisms of glacial motion, for example, we shall have to so control conditions as to allow the law to 'manifest' itself, as it were. So we endeavour to minimize those tendencies or forces or mechanisms that operate on the system beyond, and perhaps contrary to, the law of motion.

For Bhaskar, then, our knowledge of the world is socially produced. But at the same time 'it is the nature of objects which determines their cognitive

---

[35] Ian Hacking, 'Experimentation and Scientific Realism', in Jarrett Leplin (ed.), *Scientific Realism*, pp. 154–72.

possibilities for us.' Our theories are therefore *not* completely conditioned by social forces or personal predilections; there is a direct input from the material world that puts limits on what we can *say* about the world and – perhaps more important – what we can *do* in it. This latter point is crucial, because, for some realists, it is the 'practical adequacy' of a theory that points to its truthfulness. A theory is said to be practically adequate when it generates expectations about the world and about the results of our experiments that are realized. If this sounds suspiciously like mere instrumental success, the realist reply will have to be that useful knowledge is useful simply because it is true. Its usefulness, in other words, is not accidental, but is due to the nature of the world itself.[36]

Ernan McMullin's idea of the historical resilience of theories is the final realist strategy that will detain us here. To pass muster as a claim to knowledge, a theory must display a certain resilience with the passage of time. It needs to have a sort of survival quality in the face of changing scientific fashions. 'What counts, perhaps, most of all in favour of a theory is not just its success in prediction,' McMullin writes, 'but what might be called its resilience, its ability to meet anomaly in a creative and fruitful way.' The theory of evolution is a good illustration. Over the years since Darwin first put forward his version of the theory, there have been disputes and debates about the precise nature of the mechanisms involved, about the significance of genetic mutation, about the underlying social philosophy that it embodied and assumed, and so on. But the theory as held today is still recognizably Darwinian for all its modifications. Surely this provides some warrant for saying that the theory tells us something about the history of the organic world. Certainly there may have been social factors endemic to a theory's formulation, but over time such excrescences will simply be filtered out.[37]

These, then, are some of the ways in which philosophers have responded to the radical relativism of the earlier critics. It is noticeable, of course, that these defenders of realism are quite prepared to admit that social and other extra-scientific factors have insinuated their way into scientific theory and practice at many levels. They are only too ready to concede that political,

---

[36] Roy Bhaskar, 'Realism', in W. F. Bynum, E. J. Browne and Roy Porter (eds), *Dictionary of the History of Science* (London: Macmillan, 1981); Andrew Sayer, *Method in Social Science. A Realist Approach* (London: Hutchinson, 1984), p. 100. See also Roy Bhaskar, *A Realist Theory of Science* (Sussex: Harvester Press, 2nd edn 1978).

[37] Ernan McMullin, 'History and Philosophy of Science: A Marriage of Convenience?' in Robert S. Cohen and Marx W. Wartofsky (eds), *Methodological and Historical Essays in the Natural and Social Sciences. Proceedings of the Boston Colloquium for the Philosophy of Science, 1969–72* (Dordrecht: Reidel, 1974), pp. 585–600, ref. on p. 597.

social, metaphysical, and aesthetic concerns have conditioned the products of scientific knowledge. What they deny is that this provides grounds for a universal scepticism about the cognitive claims of science. To my mind, Martin Rudwick synthesizes matters pretty well when he writes:

> Scientific knowledge may indeed be a social construction . . . and therefore a cultural product, but it does also claim to have a more-than-random relation to the externality of the natural world. It has become a commonplace of current thinking about science that the natural world greatly under-determines the form that theories about it can take; but that insight should not lead us inadvertently into the position of implying that the natural world does not determine our theories at all . . . To put it more simply, to see scientific knowledge as a social construction does not rule out the possibility of cumulative scientific progress.[38]

The implications of these philosophical disputes are vital for any attempt to reconstruct geography's history. For one thing, history has played a key role in these debates themselves, having been called into the witness box to give evidence for relativists and realists alike. But they are vital too because both sides acknowledge the input from social forces and therefore reject the naive empiricism, not to mention the positivism, of the past. Thus even if we find ourselves convinced by the advocates of realism, we must concede that the 'strong programme' in the sociology of knowledge legitimately forces us to ask of any theory such questions as, Who propounded it? Who used it? What interests did it serve? These, however, are precisely the questions that conventional historians of geography have studiously ignored. What is needed, therefore, is an approach to geography's history that will do full justice to the intellectual and social context within which geographical knowledge was produced. The building blocks for a suitable historiography have been available for some time from the pens of intellectual historians; but the impact of their labours on historians of geography has been conspicuous by its absence. This is not to say that no efforts have been made. Indeed several of geography's recent historians have made valiant efforts to keep their endeavours abreast of the philosophical tides. And although their statements remain largely programmatic, to scrutinize them will serve as a prelude to sketching the outlines of my own approach.

[38] Rudwick, 'Senses of the Natural World', p. 252.

GEOGRAPHY'S NEW BIOGRAPHERS

Of all the new things to have come out of the recent history and philosophy of science, the paradigm concept has undoubtedly been the most fashionable among recent historians of geography. So, if only because the geographical literature has been liberally sprinkled with this new-fangled term, I want to pause briefly to reflect on how the concept has been deployed within the discipline and to consider the sorts of 'paradigm' spotted by geography's observers.

One of the earliest geographical rehearsals of the paradigm schema occurred in Haggett and Chorley's preface to their *Models in Geography*.[39] At this stage – in 1967 – their endorsement of Kuhnian principles was simply geared to exposing the difficulties of the 'classificatory' paradigm – traditional regional geography – and then to advocating a new 'model-based paradigm'. Since that initial flirtation with the Kuhnian model, geographers have remained fascinated by the promise of a paradigm-reconstructed geography. For some the intention was largely prescriptive; for others it was more consciously historical. Little needs to be said about the former group save that their appropriation of the Kuhnian perspective was propagandist in spirit and polemical in purpose. For them the paradigm seemed to amount to little more than a flag for rallying the troops. Haggett and Chorley commandeered the notion to advocate a mathematically based systems approach; Berry appealed for a systems-honed decision-making revolution; Harvey drew on Kuhn's notion of crisis to advance a positivist methodology.[40] The details of these (and other similar cases) need not be reviewed here. Suffice to say that their revolutionary gung ho spirit of triumphalism was scarcely what Kuhn had in mind as he portrayed the megalevel Gestalt-shifts in the history of science.

Such promotional hoopla, however, does not exhaust the repertoire of the advocates of geographical paradigms. Indeed it was almost inevitable that some of geography's historians would find in the paradigm idea the key to unlocking the historical shifts in the subject. What is immediately apparent from even a cursory survey of these various efforts is simply the

---

[39] Peter Haggett and Richard J. Chorley, 'Models, Paradigms and the New Geography', in Richard J. Chorley and Peter Haggett (eds), *Models in Geography* (London: Methuen, 1967), pp. 1–41.

[40] A discussion of the use of the Kuhnian model by these and other geographers is discussed in Andrew Mair, 'Thomas Kuhn and Understanding Geography', *Progress in Human Geography*, 10 (1986): 345–69. See also Anne Buttimer, 'On People, Paradigms, and "Progress" in Geography', in D. R. Stoddart (ed.), *Geography, Ideology and Social Concern* (Oxford: Blackwell, 1981), pp. 81–98.

diverse ranges of paradigm candidates that have been on offer. Berry conceived of the so-called quantitative revolution as geography's strategic initiation into full paradigm (and therefore scientific) status; Harvey and Holly isolated five sacred texts – by Ratzel, Vidal, Sauer, Hartshorne, and Schaefer respectively – as enjoying paradigmatic status; Johnston, though evidently increasingly suspicious of Kuhn's relevance for geography, none the less highlighted some half dozen disciplinary matrices; Martin, focusing more narrowly on geography in the United States, spotted no fewer than five different paradigms, some of which – like the 'eclectic pluralism' that he identifies for the period from 1957 to the present – hardly seem related to Kuhn's ideas even by the slightest family resemblance.[41]

When the first flush of paradigm enthusiasm died down, and a more measured consideration of Kuhn's relevance to geographical history was undertaken, it became plain that much of this writing amounted to misdirected effort. And so criticisms began to come thick and fast.[42] Yet what is remarkable is that, as Andrew Mair astutely observed, even among these critics the flavour of Kuhn's work still lingers. The Kuhnian ghost, it seems, is proving rather hard to exorcize from the history of geography.

Whatever the internal conceptual irresolutions within the corpus of Kuhn's writings, and the conceptual sloppiness of the manner in which it was imported into geographical history, there can be no doubting the benefit that a broadly sociological rendering of both science and geography has wrought. The disinclination among at least some of geography's historians to think in terms of conceptual cumulation, disciplinary progress, and

[41] B. J. L. Berry, 'Introduction', in B. J. L. Berry (ed.), *Perspectives in Geography 3: The Nature of Change in Geographical Ideas* (Illinois: Northern Illinois University Press, 1978); Milton E. Harvey and Brian P. Holly, 'Paradigm, Philosophy and Geographic Thought', in Milton E. Harvey and Brian P. Holly (eds), *Themes in Geographic Thought* (London: Croom Helm, 1981), pp. 11–37; R. J. Johnston, 'Paradigms and Revolutions or Evolution? Observations on Human Geography Since the Second World War', *Progress in Human Geography*, 2 (1978): 189–206; R. J. Johnston, *Geography and Geographers: Anglo-American Human Geography since 1945* (London: Arnold, 4th edn 1991); R. J. Johnston, 'Paradigms, Revolution, Schools of Thought and Anarchy: Reflections on the Recent History of Anglo-American Human Geography', in Brian W. Blouet (ed.), *The Origins of Academic Geography in the United States* (Hamden, Conn.: Archon Books, 1981), pp. 303–18; Geoffrey J. Martin, 'Paradigm Change: A History of Geography in the United States, 1892–1925', *National Geographic Research* (Spring, 1985): 217–36.

[42] Thus, for instance, N. J. Graves, 'Can Geographical Studies be Subsumed under one Paradigm or are a Plurality of Paradigms Inevitable?' *Terra*, 93, 3 (1981): 85–90; D. R. Stoddart, 'The Paradigm Concept and the History of Geography', in Stoddart, *Geography, Ideology and Social Concern*, pp. 70–80; P. B. Wheeler, 'Revolutions, Research Programmes and Human Geography', *Area*, 14 (1982): 1–6; R. Haines-Young and J. R. Petch, 'The Methodological Limitations of Kuhn's Model of Science' (University of Salford, Department of Geography, Discussion Paper 8, 1978).

internal chronology, has encouraged a number of 'contextual' readings of the discipline's history.[43] Any detailed inventory of these would certainly be impossible here. But a thumbnail sketch of some of the more sociologically grounded approaches that have been advocated within geographical historiography will perhaps be enlightening.

One move in this direction is the attempt to take far more seriously into account the various networks within which geographers have operated. The argument at work here is that these informal socio-scientific circles or, as they are sometimes called, 'invisible colleges' condition the shape and substance of natural knowledge. Such claims can come in a weaker or stronger mode. Advocates of the weaker version just see these informal networks as the diffusion tracks for ideas, as the 'external context' for the 'internal theories', or as the casual organizational structure in which a discipline's subgroups are embedded. Those supporting the stronger version press on to argue that these groupings – research schools, invisible colleges, scientific circles, and so on – directly shape knowledge itself. The relevance of the weaker version of this strategy for geography has been most clearly articulated in Elspeth Lochhead's investigation into the professionalization of British geography around the turn of the century,[44] while the stronger thesis surfaces in Horacio Capel's examination of the role played by various institutions in the crystallization of geography as a university discipline. As he puts it:

> [The] scientific community of geographers is an example of a scientific community constituted from clearly social factors, and not as a result of specific necessities in scientific knowledge . . . The presence of this science in programmes of primary and secondary education generated, from the nineteenth century, a need for geography teachers, which provoked in turn the university institutionalization of the science.[45]

[43] Notably Berdoulay, 'The Contextual Approach'; Olavi Granö, 'External Influence and Internal Change in the Development of Geography', in Stoddart, *Geography, Ideology and Social Concern*, pp. 17–36; Howard F. Andrews, 'The Durkheimians and Human Geography: Some Contextural Problems in the Sociology of Knowledge', *Transactions of the Institute of British Geographers*, n. s. 9 (1984): 315–36.

[44] On invisible colleges see Diane Crane, *Invisible Colleges: Diffusion of Knowledge in Scientific Communities* (Chicago: University of Chicago Press, 1972); J. Ben-David, 'Introduction', *International Social Science Journal*, 22 (1970): 7–27. For an application of this perspective to geography see: Elspeth Lochhead, 'Scotland as the Cradle of Modern Academic Geography in Britain,' *Scottish Geographical Magazine*, 97 (1981): 98–109; Elspeth Lochhead, 'On Socio-Scientific Circles and the History of Geography', unpublished typescript.

[45] Horacio Capel, 'Institutionalization of Geography and Strategies of Change', in Stoddart, *Geography, Ideology and Social Concern*, pp. 37–69, ref. on p. 65.

Scrutinizing geography's socio-scientific coteries and its institutional infrastructure, however, does not exhaust the scope of sociological interpretations of the subject's history. David Harvey, for instance, presses on towards a fully historical materialist account, urging that the structure, role, and function of geography has changed 'in response to shifting societal configurations and needs.'[46] The full import of this materialist rendition should not be glossed. For in Harvey's telling, the story of geography has been the tale of the geographical legitimation of the social conditions that produced it. Thus, for example, in the period that he calls the bourgeois era, geography merely provided one more scientific validation of the capitalist world economy. Accordingly, such standard Victorian geographical practices as exploration, cartographic survey, regional inventory, geopolitical taxonomy, and resource compilation can only be understood in the context of imperial manipulation, management, and exploitation. And so it is not just that the 'form' of geography has been a response to social circumstances; the 'content' of that knowledge is no less socially conditioned. Whether or not Harvey's recital turns out to be rather more socially reductionist than is warranted, his efforts to *situate* geographical knowledge in the social, economic, and political circumstances of its times is certainly to be commended. This can be said, let it be emphasized, without resorting to the crudest reductionism that sees ideas as nothing but the epiphenomena of social prejudices.

Of course an account that takes seriously the interpenetration of geographical knowledge and broader socio-intellectual circumstances need not be committed to a reductionist materialism. Another route that has been suggested centres on the cognitive role played by analogy and metaphor in human knowing. The idea here, as I have said, is that in our attempt to get a handle on the world's complexities we invariably turn for inspiration to processes that we *do* understand and then try to explain the phenomena under investigation in the light of that information. The heuristic potential of analogical thinking is very considerable, I would argue, even if it runs the risk of mistaking the metaphor for the thing, of confusing make-believe with belief. To repeat an earlier example, we can think of our brains *as if* they are computers; or we can think of light as waves or particles; or we think of atoms as if they are miniature orbital systems. In much the same way, it could be argued, geographers' visions of their self-appointed task have been metaphorically grounded. Thus Ratzel thought of the state as an

[46] David Harvey, 'On the History and Present Condition of Geography: An Historical Materialist Manifesto', *Professional Geographer*, 36 (1984): 1–10, ref. on p. 1.

'organism'; Davis thought of the landscape change as a 'cycle'; Marxist geographers tell us that the social world is actually a complex 'structure'; Rose says that the city is a 'text' to be read; and Samuels speaks of the 'biography' of landscape.[47] To be sure, to read the history of geography as a succession of metaphorical visions is not of necessity to adopt a sociologically embedded account. But it would certainly be instructive to investigate the social circumstances in which particular metaphors arise, survive, thrive, or decline.

IN DEFENCE OF SITUATED MESSINESS

I have no particular label to attach to the approach that I want to adopt in this book. In many ways it is just an amalgam of a range of those methods that now go under the rubric of the 'new historiography'. But I do have an aim, and that aim is – in the words of Steven Shapin and Simon Schaffer – to avoid 'preferring idealizations and simplifications to messy contingencies.'[48] The aspiration is simple; but the consequences are far-reaching. Let me spell out just a few of the implications.

First, it will require us to suspend judgement on the essential nature of geography. The idea that there is some eternal metaphysical core to geography independent of historical circumstances will simply have to go. Just as it does not make much sense to ask whether a particular belief is rational independent of specific conditions, so, I argue, it does not make much sense to think of the nature of geography as eternally fixed. Clearly what it is to be rational is different for a twelfth-century milkmaid, a seventeenth-century astrologer, and a twentieth-century university student. Similarly, what it was to be geography in sixteenth-century England was rather different from its counterpart in, say, Jeffersonian America, Enlightenment France, Victorian England, or inter-war Germany. Just as there can only be a *situated* rationality, so too can there only be a *situated* geography. For geography has meant different things to different people in different places and thus the 'nature' of geography is always negotiated. The task of geography's historians, at least in part, is thus to ascertain how and why particular practices and procedures come to be accounted geographically

---

[47] See David N. Livingstone and Richard T. Harrison, 'Understanding in Geography: Structuring the Subjective', in D. T. Herbert and R. J. Johnston (eds), *Geography and the Urban Environment: Progress in Research and Applications*, vol. 5 (Chichester: John Wiley, 1982), pp. 1–39.

[48] Steven Shapin and Simon Schaffer, *Leviathan and the Air-Pump. Hobbes, Boyle, and the Experimental Life* (Princeton, N.J.: Princeton University Press, 1985), pp. 16–17.

legitimate and hence normative at different moments in time and in different spatial settings.

Second, it will require us to depart from the traditional emphasis on the history of geographical thought. To be sure, we will be interested in developments in geographical theory and thinking, but we will always want to locate theory in social and intellectual circumstance. As with my rejection of an 'essential' geography, I shall want to speak of *situated* theory. And this will mean that it will never be wrong to ask of any theory: Why was it put forward? Whose interests did it advance or retard? In what kind of milieu was it conceived and communicated? How adapted was it to its cognitive and social environment? Certainly this is not to imply that these are the only ways in which theory may be cross-examined. But that these are legitimate questions is certainly the case I want to make. Moreover I shall want to suggest that the geographer's traditional craft-skills – such as cartographic and regional survey – turn out to be rhetorical devices of persuasion by which geographers have reinforced the authority of their assertions.[49] The cartographic and other methods of visual representation that I have employed in this text are, it goes without saying, no less susceptible to rhetorical analysis.

Third, it will require us to transcend the conventional distinction between text and context. As I see it, text and context are inextricably intertwined in disciplinary history. Contextual approaches to intellectual history, it seems to me, have frequently been little more than an apologia for a politicized reductionism that accords explanatory privilege – frequently in an unexamined fashion – to the socio-political side of the equation. What we need, rather, is something far more symmetrical, a greater sense of how texts and contexts are constituted reciprocally. For defining what constitutes geography's intramural domain – the text – in part determines what composes the extramural domain – the context. What too few historians of geography have engaged is this very question of just how the reciprocity of text and context is to be understood. And yet I believe that it is only as we grasp how they are interwoven that we can begin to understand the history of the geographical tradition. Thus it is not that in sixteenth-century England geography was practised in a magical context – astrology, alchemy, and all that; no, it is rather that geography just was part of magical discourse. Here, to separate out text from context and to explain one in terms of the other is to put asunder what was originally joined together.

[49] I owe my phrasing here to Jan Golinski, 'The Theory of Practice and the Practice of Theory: Sociological Approaches in the History of Science', *Isis*, 81 (1990): 492–505.

Moreover it is only as we grasp how what we might now think of as text and context were interlaced that we can begin to understand how the meanings of the very terms that geographers employ – map, region, landscape, social structure, human agency – change from context to context, trailing with them 'clouds of previous connotations', to use David Hull's words.[50] Indeed without a greater sense of conceptual and contextual shifts these labels conceal more than they reveal. The whole notion of the human agent or human subject is a case in point; without placing the term in the appropriate conceptual frame it is hard to know whether the user is referring to Augustine's image of God, to Descartes's mind and body sewn together at the pineal gland, to fundamentalist Marxism's flotsam and jetsam of economic history, or to Darwin's trousered ape. The cognitive content of the very terms we employ is subject to historical change and cannot be appropriated with uncritical essentialist assumptions. And this brings me back to my main claim: what is true of these terms is true, *a fortiori*, of geography itself.

As a rhetorical flourish to end this introductory chapter I want to risk suggesting that it might be helpful if we were to think of geography as a tradition that evolves like a species over time.[51] As I say, this is a risky analogy, for my colleagues are sure to sniff all the problems of earlier organic analogies or to suspect some underlying evolutionary epistemology. I eschew both. Nevertheless I judge the risk worth taking because I think the image helps us to see that ideas in general, and geographical ideas in particular, are historical entities that change, transform, evolve over time in different cognitive and social environments. As I see it, geography is a tradition that, like a species, has undergone historical transformation.

My aim in this book is thus to illustrate what geography was like at certain key points in the past. This means that the story I have to tell is far from complete. To the contrary, it is intentionally selective; I have chosen certain moments in geography's history to illustrate what the sort of history I advocate could begin to look like. Clearly a full treatment must await the outcome of numerous specialist studies. So, my account is biased. It is biased towards what I think of as important epochs. It is biased towards English-language geography, not because other traditions are unimportant,

[50] David L. Hull, *Science as a Process. An Evolutionary Account of the Social and Conceptual Development of Science* (Chicago: University of Chicago Press, 1988), p. 8.

[51] See Hull, *Science as a Process.* Also David L. Hull, 'Darwinism as a Historical Entity: A Historiographic Proposal', in David Kohn (ed.), *The Darwinian Heritage* (Princeton, N.J.: Princeton University Press, 1985), pp. 773–812. Of course I do not intend to endorse Hull's entire scenario; I merely suggest that there is heuristic value in the use of an evolutionary metaphor.

but precisely because they are too important to continue to be parodied in traditional textbook fashion. I simply do not know enough about these traditions to begin the task. For they too must be contextually interrogated and retold. Of course comprehensiveness is, I believe, quite irrelevant to the task I have set myself. Allow me to repeat. I have simply chosen what I take to be telling episodes in the history of the geographical tradition in the hope of illustrating what a fully-fledged account of geography's history might begin to look like. And no doubt this book is biased in other ways too. But now I shall have to await my readers' judgements, certain that reviewers will not hesitate to identify (with as much gusto as I would myself were I reviewing a work like this) the gaps that I have both purposely and unintentionally left unfilled.

2

Of Myths and Maps

Geography in the Age of Reconnaissance

The intellectual rigour of geography is often questioned nowadays by practitioners and observers alike. Some of the discipline's current leaders speak
of the 'vacuum' at the core of geography, of its formlessness, of its conceptual sickliness, while spectators from other subjects remind us of its lack of
intellectual repute.[1] However fashionable such judgements on modern geography may be, it would be entirely mistaken to assume that evaluations of
this sort have always characterized the geographical enterprise. For geography played a leading role in the evolution of the scientific tradition, not
least because of the tremendous intellectual significance of its emphasis on
sheer exploration. Accordingly we find historians of the 'Age of Discovery'
like J. H. Parry commenting:

> Geographical exploration, with its associated skills of navigation and cartog-
> raphy, was not merely the principal field of human endeavour in which sci-
> entific discovery and everyday technique became closely associated before the
> middle of the seventeenth century; except for the arts of war and of military
> engineering and (to a very limited extent) medical practice, it was almost the
> only field; hence its immense significance in the history of science and of
> thought.[2]

In the face of the intellectual crisis that some sense within modern geography, it is all the more important to remind ourselves just how crucial

[1] See the observations by David Stoddart, *On Geography and Its History* (Oxford:
Blackwell, 1986), pp. ix, x; Anthony Giddens, *The Constitution of Society: Outline of the
Theory of Structuration* (Oxford: Polity, 1984), p. 363.
[2] J. H. Parry, *The Age of Reconnaissance. Discovery, Exploration and Settlement 1450 to
1650* (Berkeley: University of California Press, 1981), p. 3.

geography's contributions have been to the emergence of modern science. Indeed I recall hearing the distinguished Dutch historian of science, Reijer Hooykaas, once saying (no doubt a little tongue-in-cheek) that if he had to isolate one individual who could be said to have inaugurated the so-called Scientific Revolution it would be neither Copernicus nor Galileo, neither Kepler nor Newton, but . . . Prince Henry the Navigator. On the face of it, to accord a fifteenth-century Portuguese prince, dubbed 'the Navigator', by a Victorian biographer, yet untravelled beyond Tangier, with such an accolade seems bizarre, even perverse. Yet the point of Hooykaas's diagnosis was to isolate the fundamental importance of real-world experience over against the 'authority' of the Greeks. Whether or not there was a southern landmass, or whether the earth was flat, or whether the Atlantic was navigable were questions that could not be resolved by rereading Aristotle; they could only be answered by honest-to-goodness experience. The fact that geography has always been a *practical* science is thus of central significance in its history, and all the more so because the triumph of experience over authority is seen by many as the fundamental ingredient in the emergence of experimental science in the West. The following words recently penned by Bernard Cohen nicely bring out the point I am making:

> The best way to assess the depth and scope of the Scientific Revolution is to compare and contrast the science that came into fruition in the seventeenth century with its nearest equivalent in the late Middle Ages . . . Traditionally, knowledge had been based on faith and insight, on reason and revelation. The new science discarded all of these as ways of understanding nature and set up experience – experiment and critical observation – as the foundation and ultimate test of knowledge. The consequences were as revolutionary as the doctrine itself. For not only did the new method found knowledge on a wholly new basis, but it implied that men and women no longer had to believe what was said by eminent authorities; they could put any statement and theory to the test of controlled experience. What counted, therefore, in the new science of the seventeenth century was not the qualifications or learning of any author or reporter but rather his veracity in reporting, his true understanding of the method of science, and his skill in experiment and observation.[3]

Certainly Cohen's evaluation may need to be more nuanced: sociologists of science have shown us that for all the anti-authoritarian rhetoric on the lips of its early practitioners, science itself soon assumed a position of immense

---

[3] I. Bernard Cohen, *Revolution in Science* (Cambridge, Mass.: Harvard University Press, 1985), pp. 78–9.

cultural authority in society; post-Kuhnian philosophers of science have shown that 'experience' just is not transparent – it is problematic; and historians of science have highlighted what would *now* be considered non-rational modes of discourse for the growth of science.

Yet in so far as the triumph of experience over authority is important in telling the story of science, geography had a critical part to play. For from the earliest days of the modern period, geography was profoundly implicated in the search for practical knowledge and infected by the zeal for testing received wisdom in the crucible of experience. Thus J. R. Hale was surely correct to remind us that the 'first scientific laboratory was the world itself' and O'Sullivan no less off target when he added that 'the voyages of discovery were in a way large scale experiments, proving or disproving the Renaissance concepts inherited from the ancient world.'[4] For some this unadulterated encounter with the real world left them breathless and intoxicated with new knowledge: 'Had I Ptolemy, Strabo, Pliny or Salinus here,' quipped the Portuguese historian of exploration João de Barros (1496–1570), 'I would put them to shame and confusion.'[5]

At least in part the story of geographical exploration therefore represented – if only rhetorically – a concern to move from myth to map, to convert cosmographical theory into cartographical reality. To take such claims only at face value would be profoundly misleading of course. The geographers and cartographers were themselves participants in myth-making through their own manufacture of imaginative, exotic geographies. In an important sense it was the replacement of one suite of myths by another. Yet for all that, in the century and a half between 1400 and 1550 most of the world's coastlines were for the first time reduced to map form. This was a truly 'scientific' achievement which set the fifteenth-century explorers apart from their predecessors. Indeed many of them consciously saw themselves as participating in a historical enterprise called 'discovery' – something that distanced them from medieval adventurers and travellers like Marco Polo and Sir John Mandeville, whom they saw as merely concerned to titillate readers with accounts of the weird and wonderful.

In the light of these developments it is perhaps not so surprising that the term 'discovery' soon came to be used to describe both the progress of geographical exploration and scientific breakthroughs. Even today the metaphor of mapmaking continues to be invoked as a means of describing

---

    [4] J. R. Hale, 'A World Elsewhere', in D. Hay (ed.), *The Age of Renaissance* (London: Thames and Hudson, 1967); Dan O'Sullivan, *The Age of Discovery 1400–1550* (London and New York: Longman, 1984), p. 3.
    [5] Quoted in O'Sullivan, *Age of Discovery*, p. 77.

scientists' attempts to get a handle on the world, and of social scientists' efforts to make sense of cultural multiformity. Stephen Toulmin, for example, devotes a whole chapter to unscrambling the relationship between theories and maps, and speaks of the laws of nature as a means of 'finding our way around' phenomena and of 'recognising where on the map' of knowledge a particular object of study belongs.[6] And yet if the desire to put meaning into what Boorstin calls the 'most promising words ever written on the maps of human knowledge . . . *terra incognita* – unknown territory'[7] was a driving force behind the voyages of discovery, as it was for the scientific enterprise more generally, the achievements were far from purely cognitive. For as we will presently see the whole enterprise was impregnated with non-scientific assumptions and to these 'contextual' factors we will now turn.

CONTEXTS

In the unfolding narrative of geography, 'myth' has performed a crucial role.[8] In its broadest terms a myth is a narrative in which some aspect of the cosmic order is manifest, and accordingly is an expression of the collective mentality of any given age through rendering 'intellectually and socially tolerable what would otherwise be experienced as incoherence.'[9] Myths frequently embody the deepest inclinations of a culture and provide patterns for human action by holding up prototypes for imitation. Besides this they also have epistemological functions that are both antecedent and analogous to scientific theory.[10]

In using the label 'myth' here, however, I want to refer fairly specifically to the various tales and legends about faraway places that flourished during the age of reconnaissance and do not intend to engage at this point the anthropological, psychological, or philosophical significance of myth-making, save to insist that mythologies of exoticism and 'otherness' were inti-

---

[6] Stephen Toulmin, *The Philosophy of Science* (London: Hutchinson, 1953), p. 94. Stuart Hall and Clifford Geertz also adopt the metaphor.

[7] Daniel J. Boorstin, *The Discoverers. A History of Man's Search to Know his World and Himself* (New York: Random House, 1983), p. xvi.

[8] See the discussion in Richard T. Harrison and David N. Livingstone, 'Meaning through Metaphor: Analogy as Epistemology', *Annals of the Association of American Geographers*, 71 (1981): 95–107.

[9] Alisdair MacIntyre, 'Myth', in Paul Edwards (ed.), *The Encyclopedia of Philosophy*, vol. 5 (New York: Macmillan and The Free Press, 1967), pp. 434–7.

[10] See Bernard J. F. Lonergan, *Insight: A Study of Human Understanding* (London: Darton, Longman and Todd, 1958).

mately intertwined with the construction of the modern European identity. In the history of geographical exploration, such fable-lore played the part of a double-edged sword. On the one hand there were many hardy seafarers who consciously distanced their task from the author of the *Travels of Sir John Mandeville*, a work which abounded with reports of headless men and women with horseshoe mouths or kneelength ears. And yet the myths of an opulent Christian kingdom in southern India, the lingering hopes of finding Prester John's glorious utopia in the heart of Africa or possibly the Far East, and the stories of El Dorado continued to inspire foreign travel. Magellan, for example, remained convinced of the existence of Patagonian giants, giants so tall that the tallest of his men only came up to their waists, while the French explorer Jacques Cartier, persuaded by local Indians that the Canadian interior was the home of a rich empire, recrossed the Atlantic in search of this kingdom.[11] Science and myth – to use two abstractions – have thus long been bound together in the history of geographical thought and practice.

Nowhere, perhaps, are these intertwining motivations more clearly displayed than in the case of Prince Henry the Navigator himself. Certainly the idea that it was his sole vision that launched Renaissance Portugal on a century of voyaging and discovery has had to be revised.[12] It is even questionable whether he established an observatory at Sagres in 1420 – as is commonly believed – designed for navigational research and sponsoring the work of cartographers, astronomers, and instrument makers. Nevertheless, a full two and half centuries before the founding of the Royal Observatory at Greenwich the royal house of Portugal *had* bestowed patronage on practitioners of navigational science. So by the time of Henry's death in 1460, his sailors – particularly the Venetian Cadamosto – had succeeded in exploring the coast of Africa at least as far south as Sierra Leone at about 8° North. No doubt Penrose was overenthusiastic when he affirmed that 'beside his forerunners, Henry stands out like a beacon, for it was he who for the first time in history laid down a definite geographical policy: he made a systematic and continuous campaign of exploration; he made discovery an art and science.'[13] Yet he did engage Mestre Jacome, an astronomical expert, to provide public instruction in navigational science. Still,

[11] Antonio Pigafetta, *Magellan's First Voyage Around the World*, translated by Lord Stanley of Alderney (Hakluyt Society, 1st series, vol. 52, 1874), p. 49; Richard Hakluyt, *Principal Navigations* 9 vols (1928), vol. 8, p. 440.
[12] See P. E. Russell, *Prince Henry the Navigator: The Rise and Fall of a Culture Hero* (Oxford: Clarendon Press, 1984).
[13] Boies Penrose, *Travel and Discovery in the Renaissance 1420–1620* (Cambridge, Mass.: Harvard University Press, 1952; 1967), p. 35.

uncovering his real motivations has proved to be an infernally stubborn problem. Yet his contemporary chronicler, Azurara, ascribes religious, strategic, even astrological motives to him. For having outlined Henry's interest in the commercial advantages of new markets, his desire to ascertain the extent of Moorish power in Africa, his quest of foreign political alliances, and his commitment to the missionary enterprise, Azurara concludes by noting that over and above all these was a motivation 'that would seem to be the root from which all the others proceeded: and this is the inclination of the heavenly wheels.'[14]

In the case of Henry the Navigator the production of geographical knowledge was thus all of a piece with a host of non-scientific interests. In this he was certainly not alone. With Columbus and Cortés, for example, the passion for fame was greater than either their missionary zeal or lust for gold. For others religious zealotry surpassed both glory and acquisitiveness as the inspiration for overseas voyaging, so much so that the voyages of discovery have frequently been regarded as a continuation of the crusades. And this serves to remind us that while there were significant links between voyaging and the embryonic 'scientific' spirit, they were neither immediate nor direct. Many of the voyagers were thoroughly practical men with little interest in contributing to the world of Renaissance scholarship. Besides, early modern science flourished best in those nations such as England and Holland that were least associated with these geographical discoveries. And yet the explorers' very concern with the world rather than the word, with the concrete rather than the abstract, with action rather than reflection, in sum, with the new rather than the old, itself serves to underscore their role in fostering the anti-authoritarian ethos that was so crucial to the coming of the new science. It was this spirit that brought news of new worlds and new peoples, and thereby challenged the assumption of the intellectual superiority of the Ancients. And it is well to remember that the cartographic knowledge they procured was gathered at great cost. Unspeakable privations and hardships often had to be undergone. On the voyage that gave practical demonstration that the earth was round, Magellan's men reportedly went for nearly four months without fresh food or water, many died of scurvy, and sailors were reduced to eating biscuit that had withered to powder and swarmed with worms, and rats that 'were sold for half a ducat apiece.'[15]

If the geographical knowledge of the voyages of discovery was ordinarily

---

[14] G. E. Azurara, *The Chronicles of the Discovery and Conquest of Guinea* (Hakluyt Society, 1st series, vol. 1, 1896), p. 27.

[15] Quoted in O'Sullivan, *Age of Discovery*, p. 42.

advanced at great personal cost, its production was no less dependent on numerous social factors.[16] By the early fifteenth century, for example, Europe was already undergoing rapid economic development in the form of commercial capitalism. Great international banking institutions, like the Fuggers of Augsburg, were providing facilities for borrowing and for the exchange of capital. The effects of these economic changes were two-way. On the one hand ships and sailors were expensive commodities and finance was clearly needed to provide the economic backing for exploration; Columbus, for instance, could not have embarked on his first voyage had not an international consortium of Castilian and Genoese merchants put money up front to underwrite the costs. On the other hand the need for metal to mint coin brought with it the necessity for locating new gold deposits and thereby a motivation for sending men to sea. The creation of wealth was thus both cause and condition of geographical discovery. These economic developments, married to the demand for labour in the aftermath of the Black Death, soon expressed itself in a burgeoning slave trade. Whether for use at home, on ships, or in the Atlantic islands, Portuguese slavers filled the new demands, building up barracoons in West Africa and keeping close ties with the local slave-dealing rulers. The lure of silk and the hunger for spices were further manifestations of these changes. Fifteenth-century governments threw their weight behind the search for pepper and cloves, once the preserve of the individual merchant, in the Far East. The lack of refrigeration together with the meaty appetites of what Braudel calls 'carnivorous Europe' only helped to reinforce a search that from time to time reached manic proportions. 'Everything depended on [pepper],' Braudel writes, 'even the dreams of the fifteenth-century explorers.'[17]

If the motivational mainsprings of exploration were commerical and evangelistic, the translation of these dreams into reality depended on the evolution of appropriate shipbuilding technology. The ships used for the great sea-going explorations were not, in fact, specifically designed for voyaging; they were built for everyday trading in the waters around western Europe. And yet the oceanic voyages undertaken during the fifteenth century just simply could not have been orchestrated a century before. For the fifteenth century was a period of intense and imaginative advance in ship-

[16] The following material draws on: O'Sullivan, *Age of Discovery*; Parry, *Age of Reconnaissance*; John R. Hale, *Age of Exploration* (Netherlands: Time-Life Books, 1966); Duncan Castlereagh, *The Great Age of Exploration* (London: Reader's Digest, 1971).

[17] Fernand Braudel, *The Structures of Everyday Life. The Limits of the Possible*, translated by Siân Reynolds (London: Collins, 1981), p. 220.

building technology. By and large, European ships tended to follow two patterns, one northern European, the other Mediterranean. The northern model, known as the cog (figure 2.1), was heavy, broad, and generally not very manoeuvrable. What further contributed to its clumsiness was its use of square sails; these certainly made it a safe vessel, but not particularly suitable for negotiating unexpected shoals and unfamiliar coastlines. Besides this, because the saw was apparently not in use in northern Europe, cogs were 'clinker-built', that is, with planking overlapped. The Mediterranean version was, all in all, more suitable for exploration. The caravel, as it was called, was built on a preconstructed frame and its smooth-sided planks

Cog

Single-Masted Lateen   Carrack

Figure 2.1   Fifteenth-century ships

were fitted edge to edge. It was a much lighter vessel, slimmer and faster, and used lateen rigging – an Arabic tradition in which a triangular sail is laced to a long yard hoisted obliquely to the mast. Not surprisingly, this was the vessel Prince Henry despatched on his reconnaissance exploits. But there were problems with the caravels as well. Lateen-rigged ships needed far larger crews than cogs of comparable cargo tonnage; the sails were difficult to furl aloft; and of course their small size made them unsuitable for the transport of bulk commodities like grain. To overcome the inherent problems of both cogs and caravels various hybrids were spawned, the most common of which was the carrack – a large, heavily built, square-rigged ship with a lateen on the mizzen-mast. At the same time, some explorers, like Vasco da Gama, sailed with balanced fleets incorporating several models: some heavy vessels with great carrying capacity, and accompanying caravels that could be used for more detailed coastal reconnaissance.

If developments in shipbuilding were at once a requirement and a result of the exploration experience, so too were the arts of pilotage and navigation. Pilotage, or the knowledge by sight of capes, rivers, and ports, was of course the stock-in-trade of any shipmaster worthy of the name. On the other hand, grand navigation, as Michiel Coignet called it in 1581, 'employs . . . several other very ingenious rules and instruments derived from the art of Astronomy and Cosmography.'[18] As Coignet's definition implies, there was for long enough a substantial gap between academic knowledge impinging on navigation and the everyday experience of seamen. And this was largely because practising mariners only gradually resorted to astronomical observations to calculate their position at sea. Rather they tended to use the age-old technique of deadreckoning: simply estimating the position of a ship by calculating the length, speed, and direction of its daily course. It was only after the Portuguese brought together a group of astronomers to deal with the problem that the idea of establishing latitude at sea from the position of the stars was given any real credence. Yet the success of even this depended on the availability of a set of tables for calculating the sun's angle, and the modification of instruments like the astrolabe for use at sea. The determination of longitude was a far more intractable problem which was not resolved until the middle of the eighteenth century. Indeed in 1714 the British government offered a handsome prize of £20,000 for anyone who 'could discover the longitude at sea.'[19]

[18] Quoted in Parry, *Age of Reconnaissance*, p. 83.
[19] Quoted in Hanbury Brown, *The Wisdom of Science* (Cambridge: Cambridge University Press, 1986), p. 24.

It is now clear that the geographical knowledge which was accumulated during the period of the 'Reconnaissance', as Parry describes it, was contingent on a host of contextual factors: economic, religious, technological, and so on. But before we turn to the content of this geography, it is important to recall that the science of geography as then understood, itself stimulated interest in exploration. Of key importance here was the translation of Ptolemy's *Geography* into Latin in 1410. This was truly a milestone in Renaissance scholarship, not least because Ptolemy had devised a system of geographical coordinates – in effect latitude and longitude – by which any point on the surface of the globe could be identified. The new availability of this work, together with the use of the compass since the eleventh century, and the idea that the ocean was not so much a barrier to movement but rather a waterway, stimulated a group of Florentine humanists to take seriously the possibility of westward exploration. And yet, as Parry puts it, Ptolemy's ideas 'were both stimulating and enslaving, and the advancement of knowledge . . . required that his theories should first be mastered and then superseded.'[20] The growth of geographical knowledge then, as now, depended on a thorough grasp of the classic texts as the first step toward transcending them.

ACHIEVEMENTS

Diverse though the motivations of the seafaring pioneers undoubtedly were, their achievements were none the less truly remarkable. Nor were these purely exploratory. For besides opening up the world to European consciousness for the first time, they also made substantial progress in the arts of cartography and navigation. A brief perusal of these accomplishments will therefore further highlight geography's strategic role in the evolution of Western culture.

The voyaging ventures of the Portuguese are the most natural place to begin, for the seamen of Portugal, as Daniel Boorstin puts it perhaps a touch deterministically, 'had an assignment from geography for their role in history.' Portugal's position on the western edge of the Iberian Peninsula, together with its long navigable rivers, favourable winds, and natural harbours only helped facilitate its 'long-term enterprise of discovery.'[21] But for all its natural advantages the translation of foreign dreams into reality depended on the vision of the royal household and a number of private

[20] Parry, *Age of Reconnaissance*, p. 14.
[21] Boorstin, *Discoverers*, pp. 156, 157.

nobles and merchants. Whatever the mainsprings of their logistic enthusiasm (and we have considered what some of these might have been in the case of Prince Henry), their feats were unmistakable. They built up the rudiments of a navigational research institute (whether at Sagres or not is much disputed); they despatched mariners to chart the coast of Africa in the hope of 'rounding' Cape Bojador, the seeming edge of the world, and were eventually rewarded with success in 1434 when Gil Eannes suddenly found it behind him. In Henry's case, his greatest legacy lies with the accomplishments of his most celebrated navigator, Cadamosto, whose voyages during the mid-1450s resulted in the discovery of the Cape Verde Islands and whose records revealed ravishing new botanical and anthropological specimens that tantalized readers and beckoned others to follow his trail.

The death of Prince Henry in 1460 brought no more than a mere hiccup to Portugal's roving enterprises. Certainly the zest for adventure was immediately carried on by Fernão Gomes who continued the African exploits. But it was in King João II, who succeeded to the throne in 1481, that the ghost of Prince Henry found a kindred spirit. Besides gathering together navigational experts in an endeavour to determine latitude at sea, he continued to sponsor voyages along Africa's western coast (figure 2.2). Diogo Cão, for example, found his way as far south as Cape Cross, reaching the mouth of the Congo *en route*, and establishing the practice of setting up *padrões*, stone pillars, on every conspicuous landmark to substantiate Portugal's discoveries. But King João II was also mesmerized by the legends of Prester John, and so he sent out expeditions both overland and by sea to reach India. Accordingly in 1487 Pero da Covilhã and Affonso de Paiva were secretly briefed, funded, and duly despatched to Alexandria and beyond to Cairo and Aden. There they parted company, Paiva heading for Ethiopia, Covilhã for India. Paiva dropped out of sight, but Covilhã eventually made it to Calicut, the heart of a flourishing trading empire, before wandering through Ethiopia in the continuing hunt for the elusive Prester John.

The latter stratagem, the search for a sea passage to India, was left in the hands of Bartholomeu Dias. In 1487 he set out and on 3 February 1488 he anchored in Mossel Bay having been driven by an only-too-auspicious storm right around the Cape, thereby achieving, as Boorstin remarks, 'what no planning could yet accomplish.'[22] Not too surprisingly Dias christened it the Cape of Storms, but later João II renamed it the Cape of Good Hope,

[22] Ibid., p. 172.

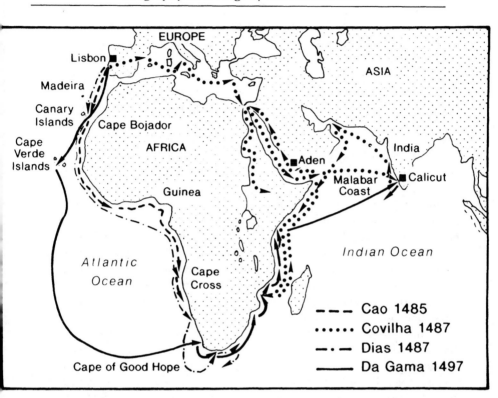

Figure 2.2   Portuguese voyages of reconnaissance

because it promised the way to India. Dias himself desperately wanted to press on into the Indian Ocean, but his men lost courage and the fleet limped back to Lisbon weather-beaten. They were welcomed with open arms. It was thus left to the indomitable Vasco da Gama to go all the way and stake Portugal's claim – now under Manuel I – in India. This he did in 1498 when on 22 May he touched the south-western coast of India, having displayed stunning navigational skills in his route around the Cape and across the Arabian Sea and Indian Ocean. When, with decimated crew, two of his ships returned to native soil in September 1499 he had accomplished something that would change the course of history. The Portuguese now sent every available ship and man to India and thereby came to dominate the Indian Ocean, eventually taking Malacca in 1511 and opening up trade links with Siam, the Spice Islands, and China. For a century and a half the Portuguese monopoly of Indian Ocean sea trade was to go unchallenged.

In the long run, of course, the maintenance of Portugal's overseas empire would prove to be too great a drain on domestic resources. The exploitation of timber supplies for shipbuilding would sooner or later bring its problems, as would the continuing selective migration of young males. Nor would Portugal's cavalier foreign policy prove the wisest course of action ultimately. Aggressive and disinclined to develop friendly commercial relations with non-Christians, Portugal for too long sowed the seeds of its own destruction. But in the meantime the riches of the East were beginning to flow to the West and Portugal could rejoice in its new-found power.

Not, of course, that Portugal remained totally unrivalled. The Spanish adventure in the new, still-to-be-named, America prevented absolute complacency. Although he was not Spanish by birth, it is with Christopher Columbus that this chapter of the story must begin. The broadest contours of his life and achievements are, of course, familiar, and yet interpreting his role in the history of geographical discovery has proved to be a notoriously ticklish problem. The standard view is that he was a truly far-sighted cosmographer who had visions of finding a new route to Asia by sailing due west and, having secured the financial backing of Spain, set out in 1492 for Cathay and was rewarded with the discovery of America. The received interpretation, however, has not gone uncontested. It has been suggested, for example, that he was a Jewish convert seeking a new home for persecuted Spanish Jews; some have speculated that he was really a secret agent for Portugal; others maintain that he was actually heading for the Caribbean, not Asia, because he had gleaned information on the New World from Scandinavian sources. Although these theories have been impossible to substantiate due to the signal lack of information about Columbus's early years, it has now been established that he was born in Genoa in 1451 and that in August 1492 he set sail from Spain with a letter from the Spanish sovereigns addressed to the grand khan of China.

On his first voyage, he reached San Salvador in the Bahamas, where he encountered an indigenous population only too willing to cooperate and frankly too friendly for their own good. Columbus's triumphal return to Spain quickly led to negotiations with the papacy to procure a Spanish monopoly on the navigation and settlement of the new lands which resulted in the famous line of demarcation running the length of the globe. Everything to the west of the line, which initially was set at 100 leagues to the west of the Azores and Cape Verde Islands, was to be granted to Spain; to the east was Portugal's share. The Portuguese, however, would have none of it and after tough bargaining on their part, the line was changed to the meridian of 370 leagues west of the islands at the famous treaty of Tordesillas in 1494. Even before the treaty was signed, however, Columbus was off again, this time carrying with him building equipment, farming tools, and somewhere between 1,200 and 1,500 men (and as before no women) in fourteen caravels. But the experience of revisiting colonies established on his earlier trip did not augur well for the future. At Hispaniola (Haiti), for example, all forty-eight of the men he had left there just over a year earlier had been murdered by natives pushed to the limit by colonial greed. These setbacks rather tarnished Columbus's prestige, for, although Spain granted him numerous privileges and rights, 'great hopes had been frustrated by the low level of profit that the distant posts had yielded.'[23] He had 'promised a gold mine', Boorstin writes, 'and only found a wilderness.'[24] On his third excursion Columbus had to take on convicts to man a substantially reduced fleet, and then the news of Vasco da Gama's Indian triumphs hit him hard. He died in 1506 without realizing the full potential of his discoveries.

For all that, Columbus was possessed of very considerable navigational skills and geographical awareness. His observations of various astronomical phenomena and his detailed knowledge of the wind circulation systems of the sea reveal his competence as a mariner; his profuse annotations on the margins of various contemporary geographical works, particularly the *Imago Mundi* and the travels of Marco Polo, demonstrate his scholarly commitments. And these skills were more than matched by his strategies for handling rough crews. He made a habit of misinforming his men about the distance actually travelled during the day – underestimating it – so that if the voyage was long they would not become unduly nervy, and therefore risky. Ironically his falsified estimates were actually more accurate than those he recorded in his 'true' ledger, for he was prone to overestimate the distance he had covered. Whatever, in the case of Columbus, the acquisition of geographical knowledge was thus both condition and consequence of his New World experiment. If, for example, he had not been vigilant enough to lay his hands on the chart of an alternative western route to the Spice Islands produced by the Florentine cosmographer Paolo del Pozzo Toscanelli – notwithstanding a colossal miscalculation of the actual distances involved – he might never have set sail to prove Toscanelli right, with all the consequences that that enterprising experiment entailed.

[23] 'Columbus, Christopher', *Dictionary of Scientific Biography*, supplement, pp. 87–91.
[24] Boorstin, *Discoverers*, p. 175.

Two other figures, at various times in the employ of the Spanish Crown, deserve mention among those whose voyages changed the course of history. The first is the Florentine businessman, Amerigo Vespucci, whose second expedition in 1501, now under Portuguese auspices, resulted in the casual naming of the New World after himself. Long held up in the doldrum belt, it took him sixty-four days to cross the Atlantic, and before returning to Lisbon in September 1502, he is said to have charted some 800 leagues of the South American coastline. In his journal he recorded everything from the childbirth practices to the religious customs of the peoples he encountered. Here the roots of geography's long-standing ties with the anthropological tradition lie clearly exposed.

The second worthy is, of course, Ferdinand Magellan. Although he did not live to complete it, he was responsible for the first circumnavigation of the globe. Little is known of his early career in India, but on his return he became fascinated by the possibility of discovering a faster route to the Spice Islands. Manuel of Portugal, to whom he submitted plans, was not impressed, and so, like many another, Magellan turned to Spain. In 1519 he set sail with five ships, and by October of the following year he had discovered, entered, and miraculously found his way through the straits that bear his name between the Patagonian mainland and the island of Tierra del Fuego. The nightmarish passage took over five weeks; indeed things were so grim that one of his ships, the *San Antonio*, mutinied and returned to Spain. Magellan, however, gritted his teeth, subjected himself and his men to terrible privations, and ended up in the Philippines. After drinking yellow water many days putrid, eating ox hides, and wolfing down anything that moved, the Philippines seemed paradise. It was not to be. Magellan quickly made friends with a local chief and insisted on joining his new ally in an intertribal war. It was a disastrously rash expression of solidarity. Magellan and four dozen of his men were hacked to death by 1,500 Mactan warriors on 27 April 1521. Still, by any standard, his feats cast the accomplishments of even da Gama, Columbus, and Vespucci in the shade, for the expedition that he orchestrated gave empirical demonstration that the world was round, and that it was navigable.

It goes without saying that these figures do not exhaust the list of explorers who helped, in Boorstin's words, to double the world during the sixteenth century. Men like Cortés who conquered the Aztec empire and Pizarro who obliterated the Inca civilization for Spain need to be recalled, as do John Cabot who 'discovered' Newfoundland in 1487 and Francis Drake who circumnavigated the globe a century later. The navigational exploits of the Arabs in the person of Ibn Majid, who continued a tradition which included figures like Ibn Batuta, Ibn Khaldun, and Al-Biruni, could also profitably be charted. As for the Chinese, the expeditions of Chêng Ho in the early fifteenth century were, until that date, probably the most extensive in history, numbering fleets of over 300. To recite their trials and tribulations in the present context, however, would be to multiply testimonials unnecessarily. Instead I want to devote a few words to those faceless seamen without whose guts and grit the geographical knowledge of the world acquired during the age of reconnaissance would never have been won.

The everyday life of the average able-bodied seaman in the late fifteenth and sixteenth centuries must have been anything but pleasant.[25] Conditions were often overcrowded and always cramped. The commanding officer, of course, had his own cabin aft and other officers had bunk beds against the sides of the vessel in the steerage section of the main deck; but the crew simply had to make do with the deck itself, except in fierce weather when they would have to shake down on the ballast below. The fact that the deck was cambered to allow water to run off scarcely made things better, even in mild weather. As for the menu, beef, pork pickled in brine, sardines or herrings, and ship's biscuit were staple diet. Fresh water was a perennial problem because most European ships stored it in casks and there it rapidly fouls. So large quantities of wine had to be carried, and often the casks had to serve as part ballast. For the ballast itself, sand was only too often used and that brought its own problems. For when filth of every description was washed down it simply clogged in the sand and turned it into a squelchy mess of putrefaction which then rolled with the ship in 'a semi-liquid state'.[26] And of course rough fare, gross insanitation, serious congestion, and frequent drenchings in an era of pre-waterproof clothing brought more than social embarrassment; it brought scurvy. A deficiency disease, it was the dread curse of every seafarer; scurvy claimed more men on Magellan's round-the-world voyage than any other cause.

However nasty the conditions, there were still jobs that had to be done. Unlike the captain, the master of the vessel had to be an accomplished seaman, for he had overall responsibility for the crew, the cargo, and the handling of the ship. The pilot and the mate were in charge of navigation, the steward had to see to provisions and various stores like lamps and sandglasses, while anchors, cables, rigging, and so on were in the hands of the boatswain or bos'n. Every ship carried a carpenter – a thoroughgoing do-it-yourself man who had to undertake most of the repairs. His skills were

---

[25] Here I have relied on chapter 4 of Parry, *Age of Reconnaissance*.
[26] Ibid., p. 74.

essential, as were those of the caulker, whose job was simply to ensure that the vessel was watertight, and the cooper, who had to keep all the casks in good shape. Lives depended on the skills of these crew members. Besides any specialized tasks like these, every sailor had to take his turn on watch. Ships' companies worked a two-watch system which changed every four hours, and during the shift decks would be scrubbed, the ship pumped, and rigging adjusted. Here again necessity was the mother of invention, for the need for accurate timekeeping kept producers of sand-glasses abreast of the latest techniques. Half-hour glasses were the norm and they were therefore turned eight times per watch. The best were manufactured in bulk in Venice and sold to ship chandlers all over Europe.

Human backbone, however, was not the only thing needed for fruitful seafaring; keeping up with the newest navigational technology also helped. The practice of dead reckoning, as we have already seen, was common procedure. But as more experience was gleaned and more thought exclusively directed to nautical problems, new advances were made.[27] Here, perhaps more than anywhere else save for the art of cartography, science, technology, accumulated lore, and naked experience were bound together. And yet the results were far-reaching, to put it mildly. Indeed D. W. Waters goes so far as to claim that 'civilization and science are the products basically of ship-borne trade . . . made practicable by the art and science of navigation – by the use made by seamen of the means provided by scientists to enable them to conduct ships about the seas in a safe and timely manner.'[28]

It was during the sixteenth century, for example, that rutters – pilot books – began to be printed in large numbers for the first time, as were various tide tables and almanacs. These certainly provided a wealth of hard-won wisdom indispensable for pilotage around familiar coastlines, but once in uncharted territory they were obviously useless. Thus the need for accurately plotting the whereabouts of some new island or stretch of coast became a real desideratum. Dead reckoning would help; but the position of the stars, particularly the Pole Star, was altogether more reliable. Solving this problem on land was one thing; in heaving seas it was quite another. So simplified versions of the quadrant and astrolabe had to be devised. The

---

[27] The following are useful sources of information about navigation in the period: D. W. Waters, 'Science and the Techniques of Navigation', in Charles S. Singleton (ed.), *Art, Science, and History in the Renaissance* (Baltimore: Johns Hopkins University Press, 1967), pp. 189–237; E. G. R. Taylor, *The Haven-Finding Art. A History of Navigation from Odysseus to Captain Cook* (London: Hollis and Carter, 1956); E. G. R. Taylor, *The Mathematical Practitioners of Tudor and Stuart England 1485–1714* (Cambridge: Cambridge University Press for the Institute of Navigation, 1954).

[28] Waters, 'Science and Navigation', p. 233.

seaman's quadrant was really a half protractor measuring angles of 1–90°, with a plumb line attached to the apex; two sights were located along a straight edge and when the star was aligned, the point at which the plumb line cut the scale gave the reading of its altitude angle. It was far from efficient, particularly in stormy weather and so the medieval astrolabe was modified again and again for use at sea. Its outer edge was divided into degrees while its movable central pointer was rotated to align with sun or star; the angle again told the user his latitude. Of course sailing by latitude produced new problems: chief among these were the need to follow true north rather than magnetic north and the need to compile various astronomical tables and nautical manuals giving the reading of solar declination for each day of the year. These were highly skilled operations and many pilots used a variety of methods. Still, the specific problems encountered in sea travel could lead to technological innovations that had far more general appeal. Take developments in timekeeping, for example. From 1530, according to Waters, 'all the great practical improvements in timekeeping, such as the gilding of watch parts against corrosion, introduced in the mid-sixteenth century, and the use of the pendulum and balance spring in the mid-seventeenth century, were inspired by attempts to perfect the means to find the longitude, primarily at sea.'[29]

If personal spunk and technological artistry thus underpinned successful voyaging, the emerging map of the world must rank among the finest intellectual achievements of the age of discovery.[30] And yet, as before, the cartographic encapsulation of geographical knowledge was both prerequisite and product of the reconnaissance undertaking. As Skelton observes, maps reflected 'the knowledge with which the explorer set out, his hopes and expectations, and the discoveries which he made. The chart or map was originally developed as a guide to travellers along frequented routes. As the limits of the world known to Europeans were extended, the critical effort

---

[29] Ibid., p. 195.

[30] On the developments in cartography in this period I have found the following works particularly useful: R. A. Skelton, *Explorers' Maps. Chapters in the Cartographic Record of Geographical Discovery* (London: Routledge and Kegan Paul, 1958); Charles Bricker and R. V. Tooley, *Landmarks of Mapmaking. An Illustrated Survey of Maps and Mapmakers* (Oxford: Phaidon, 1976); Leo Bagrow, *History of Cartography*, revised and enlarged by R. A. Skelton (London: Watts, 1964); Norman J. W. Thrower, *Maps and Man. An Examination of Cartography in Relation to Culture and Civilization* (Englewood Cliffs, N.J.: Prentice-Hall, 1972); John Noble Wilford, *The Mapmakers* (London: Junction Books, 1981); R. V. Tooley, *Maps and Map-makers* (New York: Crown Publishers, revised edn 1970); J. B. Harley and David Woodward (eds), *The History of Cartography. Volume One. Cartography in Prehistoric, Ancient, and Medieval Europe and the Mediterranean* (Chicago: University of Chicago Press, 1987).

of cartographers came to be concentrated at its periphery, on the uncertain boundary between knowledge and ignorance.'[31]

Maps with rather different purposes – expressing religious representations of the world – were common by the fifteenth century. The eighth-century Albi Map, the tenth-century Anglo-Saxon map of the world stretching as far east as the Persian Gulf and Red Sea, the thirteenth-century Psalter Map – a circular or cartwheel depiction of the world – and the Hereford Mappamundi are among the most celebrated examples of such early cartography. The purpose of the *mappaemundi* was multi-dimensional. Geographical accuracy, as we now understand it, was certainly not their prime function nor were they as Jerusalem-centred as is commonly supposed. Rather as 'cartographic representations of medieval culture' to quote David Woodward, they were 'primarily didactic and moralizing.' And so they symbolically projected onto a geographical base the major events in the Christian religion – Creation, Salvation, and Judgement, and as such they displayed the power of a clerical elite.[32]

But alongside these scholastic renderings of Christian cosmography were other maps very different from these medieval world-delineations, and altogether more practical. These were the portolanos or portolan charts that were made *by* seamen *for* seamen. As Tony Campbell observes: 'The Medieval *Mappaemundi* are the cosmographies of thinking landsmen. By contrast, the portolan charts preserve the Mediterranean sailors' firsthand experience of their own sea.'[33] At first they focused on the Mediterranean zone and although initially rudimentary they were so extensively revised and refined as to surpass the maps of the learned geographers. Typically these charts were covered with rhumb lines, that is, straight lines in the direction of winds intersecting in compass roses, and were often gathered together in portolan atlases of up to a dozen sheets. By the sixteenth century there were several famous chart-making families who produced works of technical excellence and stunning aesthetic appeal. Even allowing for the contingent nature of what would pass as accuracy, these charts depicted with remarkable precision the known coastlines, and the pictorial embellishments that covered *terra incognita* added to their charm. But while these heraldic symbols, albeit gradually, receded before 'solid geographical information', it would be mistaken to conceive of their history in unilinear evo-

---

[31] Skelton, *Explorers' Maps*, p. 325.

[32] David Woodward, 'Medieval *Mappaemundi*', in Harley and Woodward (eds), *History of Cartography*, pp. 286–368, ref. on p. 342.

[33] Tony Campbell, 'Portolan Charts from the Late Thirteenth Century to 1500', in Harley and Woodward (eds), *History of Cartography*, pp. 371–463, ref. on p. 372.

lutionary terms, for inherent conservatism from time to time prevented new information from achieving cartographic representation. Still, the world map of Henricus Martellus Germanus, for example, however crude, recorded Dias's voyage around the Cape of Good Hope; the 1500 chart of Juan de la Cosa portrayed the Columban discoveries and da Gama's expedition to India; and the Portuguese Cantino Planisphere of 1502 showed the most up-to-date information. And as more detailed exploration along the coastlines of North and South America, in the South Seas, and in the Far East proceeded, practical cartography kept pace with it.

Coincident with the beginnings of the age of reconnaissance, moreover, was the rediscovery of the work of Claudius Ptolemy; the influence of his *Geography* would be hard to exaggerate, for it stimulated great scholarly interest in the cartographic enterprise. Throughout the next two centuries the map-maker's craft was to achieve an ever-growing intellectual respectability, not merely for its inescapably functional character in a sea-going age, but also for the mathematical proficiencies and precision instruments that were to become the insignia of the accomplished cartographic draughtsman. Many of the great savants of the Renaissance, like Leonardo da Vinci and Peter Apian, thus interested themselves in the science and art of cartography. But there were others who practised cartography more single-mindedly. One of the most celebrated was the Belgian map maker Gerhardus Mercator, born in Flanders in 1512. He became an active instrument and globe maker, and an expert engraver, producing highly accurate maps of Europe in the 1540s and 1550s. But it was in 1569 that he produced a milestone in cartographic history. This was his world map produced on the projection that bears his name. Here all the compass directions and rhumbs are depicted in straight lines – a trick involving the squaring of the circle of the globe. Mercator achieved his objective by systematically increasing the distance between the parallels from the equator to the poles. It was a case of scientific distortion for specific purposes. He continued his work for a further quarter of a century and by the time of his death in 1594 he had issued the first two parts of a multi-volume atlas that was completed under the direction of his son Rumold Mercator. Subsequently many of his works were printed by Jodicus Hondius who acquired control of Mercator's stock and issued editions of the Mercator Atlas enlarged with maps of his own making.

Mercator's great friend and rival was Abraham Ortelius who was born in Antwerp of German parents in 1527. He began his career as a colourist of maps and then became a dealer. His unmatched experience, typified in the remarkable 87-name-long inventory of known cartographers that he drew up, sensitized him to the shortcomings in contemporary atlases and in 1570 he produced his own *Theatrum Orbis Terrarum* (plate 2.1). It has been described as the 'Atlas of the Renaissance' because it embodied the 'spirit of free inquiry that characterized the age.' Liberated from almost all lingering traces of the Ptolemaic cosmology, it has long been said to have heralded a new cartographic era in which every effort would be made to 'found the knowledge of the earth not on the writings of the ancients but on first-hand information and scientific investigation.'[34] And yet such portrayals smack rather too much of a naively progressivist vision of cartographic history. To speak of a shift from myth to map, from pre-scientific to scientific is to employ a narrative structure that is altogether too comfortable. What we are faced with here is something of far greater complexity. For at this point, the cartographic project finds itself profoundly implicated in an epistemological move of major proportions: representation as a way of knowing and, just as important, as a vehicle of conceptual and visual possession, is finding articulation. This trajectory needs some further perusal, and we will turn to it in the next chapter.

For the meantime we should recall that, as Ortelius's own list reminds us, there were many other cartographers whose accomplishments might readily be recorded. Among these we might mention Giacomo Gastaldi and a host of other cartographers and engravers from Italy, Petrus Plancius, William Janzsoon Blaeu (the 'Rembrandt of Geography' according to Paul Theroux), and Jan Jansson from the Low Countries, or Martin Waldseemüller and Sebastian Münster from Germany. But enough has been said just at this point to illustrate the revolution in map making that was inaugurated during the age of reconnaissance, an era that exemplifies *in excelsis* Paul Theroux's reminder that 'cartography, the most aesthetically pleasing of the sciences, draws its power from the greatest of man's gifts – courage, the spirit of inquiry, artistic skill, man's sense of order and design, his understanding of natural laws, and his capacity for singular journeys to the most distant places.'[35] Now it is time to consider some of the broader consequences of the voyages of geographical discovery on the lifestyle and consciousness of Europeans in the fifteenth and sixteenth centuries.

---

[34] Penrose, *Travel and Discovery in the Renaissance*, p. 261.
[35] Paul Theroux, 'Mapping the World', *The Hongkong and Shanghai Banking Corporation Annual Report* (1981), p. 12.

Plate 2.1   Theatrum Obis Terrarum by Abraham Ortelius, engraved TIP L.I.7 Art
Seld. Reproduced by kind permission of the Bodleian Library, Oxford

IMPACTS

However difficult it might be to figure out precisely what we ought to mean by the notion of an age of 'discovery' (could a fifteenth-century Italian 'discover' China?), and however fluid the definitions of key geographical terms in the late medieval period (for long enough 'India' meant no more than the East beyond the Muslim world),[36] the impact of overseas exploration both on Europe and on the lands Europeans encountered was unmistakable. Take the simple matter of diet, for example. From the New World came potatoes and peanuts, tomatoes and turkeys, kidney beans and maize, and in return it received wheat, poultry, and domesticated pigs. Other less pleasurable things were also exchanged: the conquistadors gave away measles, and got back syphilis. And of course tobacco spread like wildfire once it had gained a foothold in Europe, not least for its supposed medicinal qualities. The Asian impact was rather more quantitative. Europe had been in the grip of what Braudel calls a 'spice orgy' for centuries, and spice had been filtering through from the East both overland and via the Mediterranean; but the amounts increased dramatically as the Portuguese broke the stranglehold of the Egyptian–Venetian monopoly on the trade. Lisbon quickly became a major centre – at least for a period after da Gama's voyage – for spice distribution all over north-west Europe; by 1503 the cost of pepper in Lisbon was only a fifth of the Venice price. And although they were not widely consumed until the seventeenth century, coffee came to Europe from Arabia, tea from China, and chocolate from Mexico. At the other end of the social scale, rice from Egypt was, from time to time, shipped in to feed the poor in France.[37]

The geographical 'discoveries', however, did more than supplement routine diet and agriculture, titillate the fashion-conscious seekers after silk, or enlarge the apothecary's store; they brought economic and administrative problems of an altogether new order that needed urgent action. The European powers, of course, reacted differently in different places. And while the Portuguese in India and later the Dutch in the East Indies would equally deserve scrutiny, a few words on the fortunes of the Spanish in the New World must suffice to illustrate the methods of managing a sixteenth-

---

[36] See Wilcomb E. Washburn, 'The Meaning of "Discovery" in the Fifteenth and Sixteenth Centuries', *American Historical Review*, 68 (1962): 1–21; Charles E. Nowell, *The Great Discoveries and the First Colonial Empires* (Ithaca, N. Y.: Cornell University Press, 1954), p. 13.
[37] These impacts can be traced through Braudel, *Structures of Everyday Life*, pp. 249–60, and Owen and Eleanor Lattimore (eds), *Silks, Spices and Empire* (n.p.: Delacorte Press, 1968).

century overseas empire. Quite obviously repercussions were felt both in the New Spain and at home in Spain itself. The Spanish, in the shape of the *conquistadores*, established a permanent dominion in 'Spanish' America with stunningly little difficulty. They rapidly – and all too efficiently – disposed of chiefs and priests, and stepped into their dictatorial shoes. Thereby they easily won the sullen obedience of a people long tutored in the ways of servitude. But the Spanish did not leave the culture they had taken over unchanged. As new immigrants dribbled in 'there grew up, beside the Indian economy based on communal agriculture,' according to Parry, 'a new and characteristically Spanish economy, whose principal and most lucrative occupations were stock raising and silver mining.'[38] Indeed it was from the rapid success of the stock ranches that capital became available for large-scale mining projects, which in turn created a demand for local manual labour. This was not easily procured, and the indigenous Indians had to be forced into service. The working conditions in these mining camps were grim; overcrowding was the norm, infection was rife, and disease raged through local populations with the result that in central Mexico alone the population declined dramatically during the course of the century – from eleven million to two and a half million according to some estimates. As for administration, each province was in the semi-autonomous hands of a governor, semi-autonomous because, while he enjoyed the status of a viceroy, he was forever checked up on by judges (*audiencias*) acting for Spanish monarchs who never had complete confidence in their overseas administrators. Spain favoured a policy of strong centralization, a bureaucratic regime in which the judiciary held pride of place.

By 1550 this overseas empire, encompassing all the New World save for the coast of Brazil, had brought great international prestige to Spain. And yet it was only by that date that the New World investments began to pay, as gold, and more especially silver, began to float back from transatlantic mines. American revenue, O'Sullivan estimates, was contributing somewhere between a fifth and a quarter of the total by the end of Phillip II's reign. Still, as with Portugal, the long-term effects were enfeebling. The Castilian economy was incapable of capitalizing on its new-found fortunes and gradually degenerated into 'a *rentier* economy, buying from abroad what it failed to manufacture at home.'[39]

Of course the new geographical knowledge of the fifteenth and sixteenth

---

[38] Parry, *Age of Reconnaissance*, p. 228.
[39] O'Sullivan, *Age of Discovery*, p. 74.

centuries brought more than exotic merchandise, fresh reserves of precious metals, and bureaucratic innovation to western Europe; it brought an unprecedented *intellectual* challenge to the complacent consciousness of the Old World. To be sure, this psychological impact can too easily be overestimated. Only a small proportion of the books published in the period focused on the newly opened up Asian or American worlds. And it would be naive to see the voyages of exploration as, in any simple sense, the precursor of the Scientific Revolution. For there was always a substantial gulf between the achievements of sailors and scholarly progress in mathematics and astronomy. Besides, to repeat, early modern science flourished best in England and Holland, nations not especially associated with the geographical revelations. And yet the recognition of the superiority of experience over classical authority – to return to the theme with which this chapter began – did embody a methodological principle crucial to the new scientific enterprise.

Initially, of course, there was a theological flurry over the discovery of alien peoples. Where did they come from, and how was their existence to be accommodated to the Mosaic chronicles of creation? Soon problems like these resulted in the revival of an ancient heresy – Preadamism, the belief that human beings had existed before Adam.[40] Some wondered if they had escaped the reaches of Noah's flood; others, how they had migrated from the centre of creation in the Old World; still others worried about their soteriological status – were they human, had they souls, did they need conversion? Many answers were forthcoming. In some instances indigenous peoples were forcibly Christianized and their local religions obliterated; in others 'pagan' liturgies were given an ecclesiastical gloss that seemed to satisfy conqueror and conquered alike. In New Spain, for example, the sacerdotal ritual that evolved – infinitely more elaborate than anything at home – 'was an attempt to meet the Indians' longing for the old ceremonial life which they had largely lost.'[41] The cult of earth mother was overlain with the cult of the Virgin, and indigenous fertility rites were sacralized by the imposition of suitably tempered Christian vocabulary. Whatever the strategies deployed, the very presence of 'exotic' tribal customs exerted a lurid fascination. Who would not be held captive by tales of temple steps reeking with human blood as heathen priests carried out the grotesque ceremony of

---

[40] I discuss this in 'Preadamites: The History of an Idea from Heresy to Orthodoxy', *Scottish Journal of Theology*, 40 (1987): 41–66; and in *The Preadamite Theory and the Marriage of Science and Religion* (Philadelphia: American Philosophical Society, 1992).

[41] Parry, *Age of Reconnaissance*, p. 233.

manually ripping out the hearts of prisoners of war by the thousand, and all as worship to Aztec gods? Their portrayals thus created an imaginative geography of America in the fifteenth and sixteenth centuries as powerful as the mythologies of 'the Pacific', 'the Orient', and 'darkest Africa' in the eighteenth and nineteenth centuries. And with fascination went a sense of disquiet. The very fact of the existence of this 'new' world became a subject of what Pagden calls 'metaphysical unease'.[42] Because if the 'new world' brought, as we shall now see, challenges to the understanding of 'nature', it no less confounded standard conceptions of 'human nature'. Confronting America was as much a moral event as an economic or scientific one.

Revulsion at Aztec religious ritual, matched only by amazement at the sophistication of a legal system that manifestly owed nothing to classical antiquity, was symptomatic of an equally profound cognitive shock experienced among those intellectuals who sensed that a new era in the history of the world was being inaugurated before their very eyes.[43] From the outset it was clear that ancient science was incomplete; more, it was inaccurate. The very existence of America exposed the errors of Ptolemy's geography; its new species showed the deficiencies in Aristotle's taxonomy. In the long run this encounter would transform the very categories of natural history presentation. Consider one of the standard encyclopedic works cataloguing natural history specimens that were produced during the middle of the sixteenth century, namely, Konrad von Gesner's *Historia Animalium* which ran to more than 4,500 pages and included the famous woodcut of a rhinoceros – shipped from Asia to Lisbon – reputedly by Albrecht Dürer (plate 2.2). The style in which the work is cast has recently been depicted by William Ashworth as 'emblematic natural history'. By this he means that Gesner's entries for individual species incorporated a good deal more than a description of the animal's habits and characteristics; it also presented, for example, the creature's proverbial, mythological, etymological, hieroglyphical, and other associations. Now contrast this with Joannes Johnston's *Natural History* of 1650. Here the encyclopedic natural histories of New World animals are now fully incorporated. But because these animals were bereft of the emblematic associations that Old World creatures bore, the entire work is presented without what Ashworth calls the

[42] Anthony Pagden, '"The Impact of the New World on the Old": The History of an Idea', *Renaissance and Modern Studies*, 30 (1986): 1–11, ref. on p. 2.
[43] What follows is derived from the splendid survey by R. Hooykaas, *Humanism and the Voyages of Discovery in 16th Century Portuguese Science and Letters* (Amsterdam: North Holland Publishing Company, 1979).

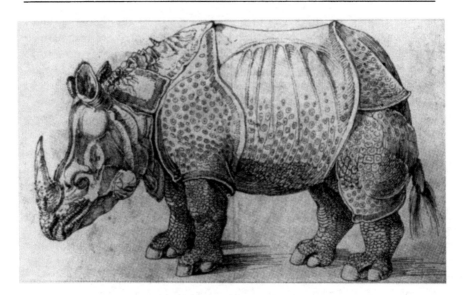

Plate 2.2   Albrecht Dürer, engraving of *Rhinoceros*

'emblematic garb' that clothed Gesner's presentation. A revolution in the convention of natural history communication had been effected.[44]

Still, even before this transformation had been accomplished, the end of the fifteenth century, as Wilma George has shown, had witnessed an explosive increase in knowledge of faraway faunas.[45] Small wonder that Diogo Gomes, a pilot on a ship approaching the equator, was already by the mid fifteenth century asserting the precedence of plain observation over scholastic prestige; for he already knew the ancient geographers Ptolemy, Strabo, and Pliny were as mistaken in claiming that the tropics were uninhabitable as were the poets Virgil and Ovid. The humble navigators, it was plain, were challenging the learning of the learned. As Hooykaas puts it:

> It was a particular satisfaction to the discoverers that unlettered seamen, travellers and merchants by simple observation gave the lie to the greatest philosophers of Antiquity. What they had seen with their eyes and touched

[44] William B. Ashworth, Jr., 'Natural History and the Emblematic World View', in David C. Lindberg and Robert S. Westman (eds), *Reappraisals of the Scientific Revolution* (Cambridge: Cambridge University Press, 1990), pp. 303–32.

[45] Wilma George, 'Source and Background to Discoveries of New Animals in the Sixteenth and Seventeenth Centuries', *History of Science*, 18 (1980): 79–104.

with their hands, they triumphantly proclaimed over against the logical deductions of the learned: simple facts weigh more heavily than acute reasoning.[46]

Naturally such enthusiasm was not universally shared. The humanists retained a profound love and admiration for all things antiquarian and so many of them tended either to play down the significance of the discoveries or to stress the indebtedness of contemporary navigation to the geometry and astronomy of the Ancients. Others were prepared to laud the explorers' empirical advances while continuing to revere the mathematical proficiency of the classical writers. In 1537, for example, Pedro Nunes declared that the descriptive part of Ptolemy's *Geography* was demonstrably deficient; but went on to insist that his mathematical equations remained unassailed. Still others lamented the hubris of modernity, castigating oceanic voyaging and modern technology as human arrogance run wild, audacious, irresponsible, reckless; they lamented the decadence in Portuguese life imported from an 'effeminate' India; and they bemoaned the depopulation of the rural landscape as young men drifted first to the towns and then from the capital to the colonies.

And yet the voyages of exploration had begun an irreversible history that could not be halted. The laicization of scientific culture followed, as Latin, the language of the cleric, was abandoned in favour of Portuguese in order to make the natural history of the New World and the heroic maritime feats of the nation available to a wider public. Besides, scholars like João de Castro were anxious to spread practical knowledge to the unlettered mariners and hence precipitated the vulgarization of science. Writing in Spanish as well as Portuguese, they soon realized, would also further this aim. But above all there was the feeling that modern discoveries were now eclipsing even the glories of the ancient world. The French historian Loys le Roy, for example, affirmed in 1579 that were Ptolemy to be resurrected he would have to stand in awe of modern progress in geography and astronomy, the very subjects he himself had fathered. Indeed his compatriot, the Huguenot Lancelot Voison de la Popelinière, was claiming by the end of the sixteenth century that the new geographical world must inevitably issue in a new scientific world. In this he was not alone. Looking back from their seventeenth-century perspective, commentators could recall the intellectual significance of the age of reconnaissance. As no less a figure than Francis Bacon claimed in the celebrated *Novum Organum* which first appeared in 1620:

[46] Hooykaas, *Humanism and the Voyages of Discovery*, p. 14.

> The reverence for antiquity, and the authority of men who have been esteemed great in philosophy, and general unanimity, have retarded men from advancing in science, and almost enchanted them . . . We must also take into our consideration that many objects in nature fit to throw light upon philosophy have been exposed to our view, and discovered by means of long voyages and travels, in which our times have abounded. It would, indeed, be dishonourable to mankind, if the regions of the material globe, the earth, the sea, and stars, should be so prodigiously developed and illustrated in our age, and yet the boundaries of the intellectual globe should be confined to the narrow discoveries of the ancients.[47]

Others agreed. In 1633, for example, when William Watts composed a Baconian appendix to *The Strange and Dangerous Voyage of Captain Thomas James, in His Intended Discovery of the North West Passage into the South Seas*, he took the opportunity to mount his case against conventional scholastic wisdom. He harboured no doubts, for example, that 'the careful reading of our *books of voyages* would more elucidate the *history of nature*, and more conduce to the improvement of *philosophy*, than anything that had been lately thought upon.' Aristotelianism could no longer 'like a Royal pass . . . carry a man all the world over.'[48]

It is precisely because of judgements of this sort that some historians of science have recently gone so far as to claim that the very origins of modern science are traceable to the forces of geographical discovery. Among these, emphasis has focused on the Portuguese experience and Florentine humanism.[49]

As far as Portugal is concerned crucial significance is attached to its encouragement of navigational science and mathematical practice. There, through the work of the Jewish map and instrument maker Mestre Jacome, the tradition of Mallorcan cartography, instrumentation, and nautical science was mediated to the West. Later, in the aftermath of the cataclysmic pogroms that swept through Spain in the early 1390s, Portugal became a haven for other Jewish-Mallorcan refugees who brought with them their cartographic skills. Thus when King João II revived the nation's earlier scientific tradition in the late fifteenth century, he turned to Abraham Zacuto and Joseph Vizinho – both Jewish practitioners of nautical science – to

---

[47] Francis Bacon, *Novum Organum* (London, 1620), § lxxxiv.

[48] Cited in R. Hooykaas, 'Puritanism and Science' in Open University, *Science and Belief: from Copernicus to Darwin. Block 3, Unit 6. Scientific Progress and Religious Dissent* (Milton Keynes: Open University Press, 1974), pp. 5–25, ref. on p. 20.

[49] Here I draw on my analysis 'Geography, Tradition and the Scientific Revolution: An Interpretative Essay', *Transactions of the Institute of British Geographers*, n.s. 15 (1990): 359–73.

resolve the problem of determining latitude at sea. Alongside these mathematical developments were other scientific achievements that were in part cause and consequence of Portugal's roving adventures. Francesco Faleiro (1480–1540), Garcia da Orta (1498–1568), and Pedro Nunes (1502–78) all made contributions to navigation, medicine, and cartography. Such accomplishments have recently been canvassed to substantiate the claim that this specifically Jewish style of science practised in sixteenth-century Portugal provided the template for English science in the period and the 'catalyst inducing the emergence of modern science in Western Europe.' Columbus himself admitted that cosmography, cartography, and astronomy were predominantly Jewish occupations.[50]

If the Jewish stimulus to modern science is central in the above scenario, an alternative emphasis – equally stressing the pivotal role of geography – focuses on fifteenth-century Florence. The rediscovery of Ptolemy's *Geography* caused a great stir among the intellectual coteries of Florence and this, along with rumours of Portuguese voyaging, stimulated Toscanelli and his circle to ponder the new data for their geographical significance. The mushrooming of geographical information, not least from Venetian travellers, and artistic mapping soon combined with commercial instincts to stimulate scientific growth. And it is for these reasons that Thomas Goldstein makes this Florentine geographical tradition his first port of call in his search for *The Dawn of Modern Science*.[51]

I certainly have no intention of trying to adjudicate between these competing claims. Nor do I mean to imply by what I have said that in geographical exploration we find exposed the very roots of modern science: all such monistic accounts are sure to founder on the plural rocks of history. When Sir George Thomson observed to Reijer Hooykaas that Henry the Navigator acted as 'the midwife of modern science' he was surely overenthusiastic.[52] And yet for Bacon, at least, geographical exploration was intimately bound up with the coming of modern science. This was no less true for Christopher Wren. In his inaugural lecture as Professor of Astronomy

[50] See Daniel Banes, 'The Portuguese Voyages of Discovery and the Emergence of Modern Science', *Journal of the Washington Academy of Sciences*, 28 (1988): 47–58, ref. on p. 58. A more careful assessment is given in David Goodman, 'Iberian Science: Navigation, Empire and Counter-Reformation', in David Goodman and Colin A. Russell (eds), *The Rise of Scientific Europe, 1500–1800* (Sevenoaks, Kent: Hodder and Stoughton, 1991), pp. 117–44.

[51] Thomas Goldstein, *The Dawn of Modern Science* (Boston: Houghton-Mifflin, 1988); Thomas Goldstein, 'Geography in Fifteenth Century Florence', in J. Parker (ed.), *Merchants and Scholars: Essays in the History of Exploration and Trade* (Minneapolis: University of Minnesota Press, 1965), pp. 9–32.

[52] Hooykaas, *Humanism and the Voyages of Discovery*, p. 15.

Elect at Gresham College in 1657 – a body from which the Royal Society would soon emerge – he affirmed that it was through astronomy and 'magneticks' that 'the Gates of true Science open'd, and the poor Philosophers Anaximander, Anaximenes, Leucippus, Empedocles are laugh'd at.' But these sciences did not arrive from heaven on tables of stone; they were delivered to Copernicus from the hands of those like Columbus and Vasco da Gama and other circumnavigators who first discovered 'the errors of the Ancients about Africk, and first open[ed] a Way to the Indies by sea.'[53] As Kepler himself confessed 'I am aware how great a difference there is between theoretical speculation and visual experience, between Ptolemy's discussion of the antipodes and Columbus's discovery of the New World.'[54]

To scrutinize geographical thought and practice during the period of the so-called Scientific Revolution will naturally be our next concern.

[53] Christopher Wren, *Oratio Inauguralis, in Parentalia: or, Memoirs of the Family of the Wrens; . . . But Chiefly of Sir Christopher Wren, Late Surveyor-General of the Royal Buildings, President of the Royal Society . . . compiled by His Son Christopher . . .* (London: Osborn and Dodsley, 1750, republished in 1965 by the Gregg Press), p. 203.

[54] J. Kepler, *Kepler's Conversation with Galileo's Sidereal Messenger*, translated by Edward Rosen (New York, 1965), p. 17.

3

Revolution, Celestial and Terrestrial

Geography and the Scientific Revolution

Europe in the sixteenth and seventeenth centuries was witness to revolution in almost every sense – ecclesiastical, intellectual, and political. The revolution of the celestial spheres, to which Copernicus attested, foreshadowed a more profound cognitive revolution in the heads of men and women, while the revolution in the religious consciousness of a Luther and a Calvin sowed the seeds of political unrest and social revolution. For this is the era of the Reformation and the Wars of Religion, the Dutch Revolt and the Puritan Revolution, the Copernican Revolution and the Scientific Revolution. All these cognitive jolts and political dislocations had profound implications for the geographical enterprise and it will be our task in this chapter to trace the history of geographical knowledge against the background of this 'revolutionary' world. Accordingly some reflections on the broader context of sixteenth- and seventeenth-century science will serve as a preface to the more specific growth of geographical knowledge in the period.

SCIENCE, AUTHORITY AND UTILITY

The spirit of intellectual anti-authoritarianism that the voyagers and circumnavigators had unleashed in intellectual Europe soon found more rigorous yet chastened expression among the founders of modern experimental science. Their concern was with truth rather than conceptual tidiness, with reality rather than scholarly rectitude. Nowhere is this more apparent than in the case of the early modern astronomers, Copernicus, Kepler, and Galileo. Certainly we now know that to speak of a Copernican 'revolution' is both linguistically and historically sloppy, for the publication of

Copernicus's *De Revolutionibus Orbium Coelestium* (On the Revolutions of the Heavenly Spheres) in 1543 caused anything but a stir at the time. He himself was dead within a few days of the publication of his book, and he had few dedicated disciples. The real impact of his theory did not grip many minds until some six or seven decades after his death. Indeed if there was something called the Copernican Revolution it was more associated with the names of Galileo, Kepler, and Newton. Moreover, Copernicus's empirical evidence for the rotation of the earth around a static sun was no better than that for the Ptolemaic system. Even with the invention of the telescope it was not until 1838 that the crucial observations could be made.

Copernicus's achievement lay in his handling of the conventional distinction between mathematical and physical explanations of astronomical phenomena. Here he was engaged in a major conceptual reform. The precise details need not concern us, save to explain that the Greeks had found it necessary to introduce into their astronomical systems numerous epicycles and eccentricities – essentially *ad hoc* mathematical arrangements – to explain the observed irregularities in planetary motion; but the truth of these mathematical hypotheses was irrelevant to the practical needs of astrology, navigation, or fixing the calendar. By contrast, Copernicus was far more concerned to provide a realistic depiction of the movements of the heavenly bodies that had more than mere instrumental value. To be sure, his empirical observations were little better than Ptolemy's; but his methodological project of establishing the earth's status as a planet from mathematical calculations transgressed the rules of Aristotelian physics.

In Kepler and Galileo this selfsame questioning of Aristotelian authority energized their scientific theorizing. In his *Astronomia Nova* of 1609 Kepler insisted that his purpose was to move astronomy from its fascination with 'fictitious circles' to natural causes and hence to jettison the Aristotelian system once and for all. Galileo, whose works were widely read in contrast to both Copernicus and Kepler, underscored the same point by insisting that 'sensate experiences' took precedence over philosophical and theological dogma. Of course Galileo's contribution cannot be restricted to mere philosophical principle: his own experiments with the newly invented telescope, which soon enabled him to combine lenses that magnified objects a thousand times, transformed the Copernican system from an intellectual oddity to a real theoretical possibility. Still, in his insistence on the 'worthlessness of authority in deciding any scientific question', Galileo reinforced perhaps the fundamental philosophical underpinning of the scientific enterprise.[1]

[1] Cohen, *Revolution in Science*. See also R. Hooykaas, 'The Rise of Modern Science: When and Why?' *British Journal for the History of Science* 20 (1987): 453–73.

If the questioning of authority was a prerequisite for the growth of the scientific spirit, the applicability of knowledge was for many its objective. Even the seemingly abstruse world of astronomy had implications for the arts of navigation, while medicine and agriculture had more immediately recognizable social virtues. In Francis Bacon the chief spokesman for this technological imperative is to be found. For him, practical inventions and improvements were the natural issue of true science; the knowledge of nature could, and must, lead to the control of environment. He thus lamented the disengagement of 'speculative men' from 'men of experience' and attributed to this cause alone the lack of advancement in learning. And Bacon was by no means a lone voice. During the interregnum following the English Civil War, for example, Samuel Hartlib and his scientific circle virtually conflated 'science' and 'technology', seeking for the application of everything from chemistry to mineralogy to the needs of life. Certainly to generalize about the scientific endeavour on the basis of individuals like these would be profoundly mistaken, for utility was not always and everywhere foremost in the minds of the practitioners of the new science. It has even been suggested that the stress on application and utility was often a public relations job promoted by a scientific community only too aware of external hostilities. Still, be that as it may, utility was heartily embraced by many, even if it was not always their top priority.[2]

The importance of this utilitarian impulse for the practice of geography in the period will presently attract our attention. For the moment we will do well to note just how widespread scientific application could be. Robert Boyle, for example, declared: 'I shall not dare to think my self a true naturalist till my skill can make my garden yield better herbs and flowers, or my orchard better fruit, or my field better corn, or my dairy better cheese.'[3] Boyle, admittedly, was only one voice, but the commitment of the Royal Society to the technological vision is clearly manifest in its project on the history of trades. The objective here was to gather together information about a host of technical practices, and so reports were presented on such topics as dyeing, tanning, salt making, cider brewing, and mining engineering. Alongside these the society also concerned itself with improvements in farming practice, with horticulture, and with silviculture. John Evelyn's celebrated *Sylva, or a Discourse of Forest-Trees and the Propagation of Timber in His Majesties Dominions* of 1664, for example, became a classic work,

[2] See Michael Hunter, *Science and Society in Restoration England* (Cambridge: Cambridge University Press, 1981), chapter 4 on 'Utility and Its Problems'; Charles Webster, *The Great Instauration. Science, Medicine and Reform 1626–60* (London: Duckworth, 1975).

[3] Quoted in Hunter, *Science and Society*, p. 91.

stimulating forest preservation and creation, and attesting to the success of collaborative research. New departures such as these marched alongside other more conventional concerns, like naval technology and the problems of establishing longitude at sea. So whether addressing practices long considered beneath the dignity of gentlemen, or tackling long-standing problems on the agenda of science, there was among many a concern to demonstrate the social utility of mathematical equations and the public value of apparently esoteric science. To be sure, too much can be made of this. The supposed public availability of knowledge and the attack on scientific secrecy did not diminish the agonies among scientists about whether to disseminate or withhold information. Besides, many of their suggestions for improvement often simply failed because they were utterly impractical, or were resisted by the conservatism of craftsmen, or were economically myopic. Still, in such an environment the traditional concerns of the geographer, ever practical, could not remain untouched. Before turning to these, however, a further contextual aspect must be addressed, namely, the role of religious and quasi-religious factors in the rise of modern science.

THE RELIGIOUS FACTOR

Crucial as they were in the so-called Scientific Revolution, the flourishing of intellectual anti-authoritarianism and innovative technology during the sixteenth and seventeenth centuries might too easily be taken to imply an altogether radical discontinuity between the new scientific mind and the thought-forms of an earlier generation. But this stance ignores the accumulating body of evidence that points to key magical and religious ingredients in the genesis of modern science. It is not surprising that science did not sweep away *popular* fascination with astrology, the occult, and magic of all kinds. But it has become clear that these esoteric forms of knowledge lingered long in the minds of many leaders in the new science.[4] Kepler, for

---

[4] The following materials provide useful insights into this topic: Frances A. Yates, 'The Hermetic Tradition in Renaissance Science', in Charles S. Singleton (ed.), *Art, Science, and History in the Renaissance* (Baltimore: Johns Hopkins Press, 1967), pp. 255–74; Frances A. Yates, *The Rosicrucian Enlightenment* (London: Routledge and Kegan Paul, 1986; first pub. 1972); Charles Webster, *From Paracelsus to Newton: Magic and the Making of Modern Science* (Cambridge: Cambridge University Press, 1982); Keith Thomas, *Religion and the Decline of Magic* (London: Weidenfeld and Nicolson, 1971); R. S. Westman and J. E. McGuire, *Hermeticism and the Scientific Revolution* (Los Angeles: William Andrews Clark Memorial Library, 1977); Allen G. Debus, *Man and Nature in the Renaissance* (Cambridge: Cambridge University Press, 1978).

example, was himself a practising astrologer and his scientific writings are suffused with what has been called 'number mysticism'; while Newton, himself champion of the mechanical philosophy, conducted secret alchemical experiments, maintained a lively interest in the occult, and devoted much energy to elucidating the symbolic apocalyptic of the biblical books of Daniel and Revelation.

For too long historians of science yielded to the temptation to suppress such magical elements in the corpus of writings produced by the scientific greats. But many now recognize that, far from being marginal or, worse, atavistic, these very ideas paid handsome scientific dividends. The interest in astrology, for example, stimulated and encouraged the use of mathematics to facilitate precise prophetic predictions. It is therefore not so surprising that in England some of the earliest defences of Copernicanism are to be found in the works of astrologers like Leonard Digges and John Field, and that most almanac makers just simply went over to the heliocentric model once it became scientific orthodoxy. And this is by no means an isolated case. It is now recognized that a whole tradition of mystical and quasi-magical thought that goes under the rubric of 'hermeticism' stimulated such crucial scientific discoveries as the circulation of the blood and a heliocentric solar system.[5] The diffusion of these hermetic texts during the period of the Renaissance helped foster a new conception of humanity's place in the cosmos and encouraged a magical *Weltanschauung* that saw mechanics as a branch of mathematical magic; through the use of number essential truths about the harmony of the world could be attested. This was undoubtedly so in the case of John Dee – to whom we will presently return – who saw in numerology the key to understanding the terrestrial and super-celestial worlds alike.

The world of hermeticism, magic, cabbalism, alchemy, in short, occultism, was of course highly diversified and the arcana of its practices changed over time.[6] Accordingly the relationship between 'magic' and 'science' (to employ two abstractions) was far from clear cut. Still, in two broad areas – astrology and natural magic – important conceptual resonances are clearly discernible. The fascination with the prophetic dimensions of astrology was deep and lasting, and permeated many scientific minds. We have already noted Kepler's long-term engagement with it.

---

[5] The term hermeticism is derived from the semi-religious writings thought to have originated in Egypt at the time of Moses and allegedly due to one Hermes Trismegistus.

[6] See Brian P. Copenhaver, 'Natural Magic, Hermeticism, and Occultism in Early Modern Science', in David C. Lindberg and Robert S. Westman (eds), *Reappraisals of the Scientific Revolution* (Cambridge: Cambridge University Press, 1990), pp. 261–301.

Tycho Brahe too, otherwise one of the founders of modern astronomy, did nothing to resist attributing astrological significance to the new star that appeared in the heavens in 1572; to him it presaged political turmoil in northern Europe and ultimately a new world order. Again Francis Bacon embraced aspects of astrology, as did his devotee John Bainbridge, who exploited to the full the comet of 1618 for anti-Catholic purposes. Later William Petty, whose geographical contributions we will presently consider, looked in 1647 for administrators 'skilled in the best rules of judicial astrology' in order that they could 'calculate the events of diseases and prognosticate the weather.'[7] Indeed in the wake of the Royal Society's investigation of comets during the mid-seventeenth century, detailed inventories were drawn up of correspondences between the appearance of comets and political events, natural disasters, and economic fortunes.

The emphasis on experience – a trait inherited from the navigators – that we have seen as crucial to the scientific experiment, also received impetus from the tradition of natural magic championed by Paracelsus (c.1493–1541), a polymath whose contributions to chemistry, medicine, and cosmology were all of a piece with his interest in theology and the occult arts. The belief that many secrets and mysteries, known to the ancient magi but long lost, lay hidden in nature and could be recovered, prompted an empirical approach to the natural world that rode in tandem with scientific advance. Paracelsus and his followers thus constantly opposed Aristotle on knowledge about everything from medicine to natural history. Many valuable chemical, pharmacological, and general medical findings were gained through the passion to release the magical properties buried in stones, herbs, and other plants. To many, this tradition of natural magic had an authentic role to play in the new age of science, unlike demonic magic which was often dismissed as the worthless cult of illiterate gulls. The latter had spawned esoteric sects, secret brotherhoods, and various brands of hocus-pocus, whereas the former reached towards the democratization of magic – an aspiration fully consonant with the scientific outlook of men like Bacon and Hartlib. Thus it was 'entirely consistent with the mentality of the Paracelsian type of natural magic' writes Charles Webster, 'that its practitioners should recognize the advantages of coordinated effort in the scientific field, and also apply their insights to planning in the wider social and political spheres.'[8]

My purpose in expanding on the role of magic in the evolution of modern science is not to make grandiose claims for the magical–mystical tradi-

[7] Quoted in Webster, *From Paracelsus to Newton*, p. 32.
[8] Ibid., p. 59.

tion. Rather it is to insist on the folly of separating the 'mystical' and the 'scientific' when they are both present in the thought and writings of an individual or community. In our perusal of geography's history in this period, then, it will be important to bear this particular context in mind, and not least because so many subjects close to geography's traditional concerns were deeply influenced by hermeticism. For example, natural history as it emerged during the period of the Scientific Revolution was the outgrowth, at least to some degree, of this earlier interest in natural magic. As Elias Ashmole put it at the time, 'true and pure Knowledge of Nature' was 'no other than what we call Natural Magick'; John Baptista Porta concurred, explaining that magic was no more and no less than the 'survey of the whole course of nature.'[9] Besides this, the earth was seen by the Paracelsians as a massive chemical receptacle, within which could be found the cause of volcanic eruptions, hot springs, and the formation of metals. Again the magical interest in herbals and the medicinal uses of the animal and vegetable kingdoms led to a renewed interest in botany, zoology, and phytogeography not known since the time of Pliny, and provided further stimulus to the quest for new botanical and zoological species across the face of the globe.

If the idea of conflict is unhelpful in understanding the relationship between science and magic during the sixteenth and seventeenth centuries, the notion of a warfare between science and religion is even less attractive. For too long the images of ecclesiastical condemnation, excommunication, and recantation, stemming from dramatic cases like that of Galileo, have been generalized to the whole period. In Galileo's case, in fact, it has now been shown that 'untoward political circumstances, personal ambitions, and wounded prides'[10] were crucially important in his running battle with the papacy. But books with titles like *History of the Warfare of Science with Theology in Christendom* (1896) or *History of the Conflict between Religion and Science* (1874), which did little to dispel the noise of battle, created the impression that the warfare metaphor best explained the history of the relations between science and religion – an impression that still lingers in many minds to this day.[11] Through ransacking the documents of the scientific

[9] Ibid., p. 64; Debus, *Man and Nature*, p. 13.

[10] William R. Shea, 'Galileo and the Church', in David C. Lindberg and Ronald L. Numbers (eds), *God and Nature. Historical Essays on the Encounter between Christianity and Science* (Berkeley: University of California Press, 1986), p. 132.

[11] I should point out, however, that in the latter work, John William Draper focused his attack on Catholicism while maintaining that science was the twin sister of the Reformation. John William Draper, *History of the Conflict between Religion and Science* (London: Henry S. King, 1875), p. 353.

past, however, many historians have come to see important relationships between religion and the rise of modern science. Certainly, pinpointing with needle-sharp precision the exact nature of these influences has proved to be far from easy. Still, two broadly related religious movements – the Continental Reformation and English Puritanism – have been the subject of numerous investigations to ascertain the correspondence between religious reorientation and scientific revolution.

Histories of the relations between Reformation and science come in a variety of interpretative styles, from those that take the Reformation as one of the causes of the Scientific Revolution to those claiming that its absence would have had no impact on the course of science. The literature on this subject is both vast and complex and hence the arguments and counter-arguments cannot be carefully weighed here.[12] Yet without denying for a moment the plural origins of science, I think it can be shown that there were significant conceptual reverberations between the two movements. This, I repeat, is not to locate the genesis of science in the Reformation. But it is to insist that there were many reformed scientists who saw no cognitive disjunction between their science and their theology; on the contrary, they saw them as mutually reinforcing. Right away, for example, it is clear that Protestantism embraced no naively literalistic interpretation of the Bible such as would inevitably conflict with, say, Copernicanism.[13] On the contrary, by various accommodationist strategies, followers of Copernicus had little difficulty in finding a suitable biblical hermeneutic.[14] Besides, the commitment of Protestantism to God's revelation in scripture *and* in nature underlay the scientific contributions of men like Robert Recorde, Bernard Palissy, Thomas Digges, and Philips van Lansbergen, while, to Robert Boyle, scientists more than anyone else glorified God in the pursuance of their tasks because it was given to them to interrogate his creation. At the same time, the radical individualism of the reformers, encapsulated in the

---

[12] The following works should be consulted: John Dillenberger, *Protestant Thought and Natural Science. A Historical Interpretation* (London: Collins, 1961); Eugene Klaaren, *Religious Origins of Modern Science* (Grand Rapids: Eerdmans, 1977); Richard Westfall, *Science and Religion in Seventeenth Century England* (New Haven: Yale University Press, 1958); R. Hooykaas, *Religion and the Rise of Modern Science* (Edinburgh: Scottish Academic Press, 1972); Gary B. Deason, 'Reformation Theology and the Mechanistic Conception of Nature', in Lindberg and Numbers, *God and Nature*, pp. 167–91.

[13] See B. A. Gerrish, 'The Reformation and the Rise of Modern Science', in Jerald C. Brauer (ed.), *The Impact of the Church Upon Its Culture* (Chicago: University of Chicago Press, 1968), pp. 231–75.

[14] Robert S. Westman, 'The Melanchthon Circle, Rheticus, and the Wittenberg Interpretation of the Copernican Theory', *Isis*, 66 (1975): 164–93; Robert S. Westman, 'The Copernicans and the Churches', in Lindberg and Numbers, *God and Nature*, pp. 76–113.

doctrine of the priesthood of all believers, tended to favour empiricism and anti-authoritarianism in scientific pursuits.[15]

Of course the most sustained influences of the Reformation on the scientific mind are likely to have been indirect. To understand just what is involved here, we need to recognize that the science of sixteenth-century Europe was born in a polemical context – the polemic between the new, mechanical philosophy and the old, Aristotelian philosophy.[16] By shifting the locus of authority from tradition and the church to scripture, the reformers paved the way for the Protestant questioning of the Aristotelian–Ptolemaic cosmology; and by seeking their theology inductively by what we could call 'biblical empiricism', they undermined the deductive rationalism of the scholastics. Such stances were entirely consonant with the empirical spirit of the new science, and it is no surprise that Thomas Sprat, the first historian of the Royal Society, could claim in 1687 that 'Protestantism and science . . . may lay equal claim to the word *Reformation*: the one having compass'd it in *Religion*, the other purposing it in *Philosophy*.'[17] Sensing this indirect influence of the Reformation at once allows for the practice of science (though to a lesser degree) in Catholic countries during the period, and sensitizes us to the need to locate geography's history in this selfsame intellectual context.

Narrowing the focus of their concerns historically, geographically, and theologically, some historians have sensed a specially close relationship between Puritanism and science in seventeenth-century England. It was through the work of the sociologist Robert K. Merton and later the historian Christopher Hill that attention was initially drawn to the disproportionately high numbers of Puritans involved with scientific pursuits during the seventeenth century. They had built on the work of earlier writers like Ernst Troeltsch, Richard Tawney, and Max Weber who had sought to clarify the cultural ramifications of the rise of capitalism and to locate its origin in the social ethic of religious groups. Since then, debate has raged about the precise nature of the relationship, about how we should understand the terms 'Puritan' and indeed 'science', and about what is to be made of any contingent correlation that might be found.[18] Here again the

---

[15] R. Hooykaas, 'Science and Reformation,' *Journal of World History*, 3 (1956): 109–39.

[16] Gary B. Deason, 'The Protestant Reformation and the Rise of Modern Science', *Scottish Journal of Theology*, 38 (1985): 226. See also Deason, 'Reformation Theology'.

[17] Thomas Sprat, *The History of the Royal Society of London for the Improving of Natural Knowledge* (London, 1687).

[18] For various perspectives on this, see Robert K. Merton, 'Science, Technology and Society in Seventeenth Century England', *Osiris*, 4 (1938): 360–632; Charles Webster (ed.), *The Intellectual Revolution of the Seventeenth Century* (London: Routledge and Kegan Paul, 1974);

literature is vast and daunting, not least because scientific 'revolution' and religious 'revolution' in the period were intimately connected with the political 'revolution' of the years between 1640 and 1660. During these revolutionary decades the established church was overthrown, the king executed, and a parliamentarian republic inaugurated. Besides, these events, as Charles Webster writes, 'initiated a remarkable phase of unbridled debate and experimentation over alternative forms of social and religious organization.'[19] Obviously it would be foolish to try to adjudicate this debate in the limited space available here; but a brief look at the topic is crucial to enable us to make sense of the history of geography during the period.

The Puritans, generally speaking, may conveniently be thought of as simply the hotter sort of Protestant, who held rigidly to the supreme authority of scripture, and remained cruci-centric in theology. They were never an entirely coherent or unified group; you could be a Puritan *and* a Presbyterian, or Anglican, or Congregationalist, or Quaker, or Digger, or Seeker, or Muggletonian! Clearly there was no single Puritan ideology, for while there were Puritans urging radical separatism from the established church, others were content with pushing for more moderate reform. And yet there were some common threads. The Puritan coalition, as it could be styled, was certainly sufficient for it to sustain at least for a period the stability of a republican regime. Many shared a profound belief in the priesthood of all believers, and this tended towards the democratization of religious institutions and an anti-authoritarian attitude in matters of civil and religious polity. Further reinforcement for this stance was forthcoming from their belief in the supreme importance of the individual, which in its turn led to an increased intellectual assertiveness among lower social orders.

When it came to science, Puritan practitioners were inclined to favour the more 'humble' sciences like chemistry, agriculture, forestry, medicine, marine technology, land-surveying, and so on. It is not so surprising therefore that many of them departed from scholarly convention by communicating their findings not in Latin, the language of the learned, but in English, the language of the people. Anti-authoritarianism, social utility, the

---

Christopher Hill, *The Intellectual Origins of the English Revolution* (Oxford: Clarendon Press, 1965); Westfall, *Science and Religion*; Webster, *The Great Instauration*; John Morgan, 'Puritanism and Science: A Reinterpretation', *The Historical Journal*, 22 (1979): 535–60; Douglas S. Kemsley, 'Religious Influences in the Rise of Modern Science: A Review and Criticism, particularly of the "Protestant-Puritan Ethic" Theory', *Annals of Science*, 24 (1968): 199–226.

[19] Charles Webster, 'Puritanism, Separatism, and Science', in Lindberg and Numbers (eds), *God and Nature*, p. 192.

ideals of personal edification and intellectual enrichment, and the democratization of learning were the sorts of beliefs and practices held by Puritans who expressed enthusiasm for science. Thus John Hall and Samuel Hartlib made pleas for less abstract learning and for greater use of maps, models, and experiments; John Webster looked forward to the time when 'the sound and *apodictical* learning of *Copernicus, Kepler, Tycho Brahe, Galilaeu* . . . and such like, might be introduced, and the rotten and ruinous fabric of *Aristotle* and *Ptolemy* rejected and laid aside';[20] and Thomas Digges devoted himself to the practice of applied mathematics in his concern for improved harbour fortifications. Most agreed with Calvin that *scientific* information was not to be gleaned from the pages of scripture, whatever they may have felt about the need for a thoroughly biblical conception of government and ethics. Institutionally too the Puritan presence was strongly felt, not least in the establishment of Gresham College, a body from which the Royal Society was subsequently to emerge. It had, among its chief objectives, the concern to bring together intellectuals and tradesmen in order to spread the virtues of science to a wider community.

Once again my claims for the relation between religion and science as exemplified by the English Puritans are not exclusivist. There were undoubtedly Puritan opponents of the new learning; science was certainly practised by other less 'orthodox' Protestant groups and of course by Catholics; and Puritans were obviously influenced by a wide range of philosophical opinion. In short, while it would be myopic to present the history of the emergence of English science as the result of any one particular group, it would be equally mistaken to rule out vital religious factors in the explanatory network. And what is true of science in general, I would argue, is also true of the science of geography in particular. So as we turn now to the practice of geography in the period we will see the integration of many of these contextual factors.

GEOGRAPHY IN AN AGE OF SCIENCE

As with the wider currents of scientific thought, the evolution of geography in the sixteenth and seventeenth centuries reveals a complex set of interrelationships between empiricism, social utility, natural magic, and Reformation religion. Perhaps the best way to map out this conceptual territory is to scrutinize the history of geographical knowledge against the

[20] Quoted in Hooykaas, 'Puritanism and Science', p. 21.

background of some of the key contextual social and intellectual movements of the era. My approach, while broadly chronological, is therefore more thematic in emphasis, although the themes, far from being discrete entities, merge and intertwine in important ways.

Magic and Astrology

The magical assumptions in which the intellectual world of Renaissance Europe was steeped found expression in the study and practice of geography no less than in the wider domain of natural science. Take, as a starting point, the contributions of William Cuningham, author of a work published in 1559 entitled *The Cosmographical Glasse, conteinyng the Pleasant Principles of Cosmographie, Geographie, Hydrographie or Navigation.* In this volume, Cuningham, employing the device of a dialogue between a teacher and pupil, outlined the major conceptual landmarks in these related disciplines. Accordingly he initiated beginners into the mysteries of latitude and longitude, the method of triangulation survey, and the globe's major climatic zones; into the arts of measurement by quadrant and astrolabe; and into definitions of key geographical terminology. Besides these, Cuningham took seriously the geography of the human race, for he expanded on the influence of climate on human physiology and on settlement, and later in his regional survey of the world's continents he dealt with such ethnographic matters as diet, religious and cultural behaviour, and weapons of war. Alongside these he included some remarks on the botanical and zoological characteristics of each region.

For Cuningham, the dignity of cosmography, as he styled this science of the globe, was grounded in its solidly utilitarian function, its practical use to a wide variety of interests. The military advantages, for instance, were immediately apparent, for the map was as crucial an implement of war as the sword; and its commercial benefits were no less clear through its capacity to guide merchants and seamen to the sources of the commodities for which they sought. And it had other uses too. Students of divinity were unable to proceed far in their study of the sacred writings without knowledge of the historical geography of the Holy Land; practitioners of medicine since the time of Hippocrates had sensed the need to inform themselves about regional climate, water quality, the diversity of racial constitution, and plant and animal biogeography; and students of law and classical literature could glean much from becoming informed about the geography of the world.

Important though these subjects were to Cuningham's conception of the science of geography, it would be mistaken, I believe, to abandon his contributions at this point. For in this selfsame volume Cuningham did not neglect to present his readers with a vision of the world system in its broader astronomic and astrological context. Thus he provided visual models of the globe surrounded by the heavenly spheres after the fashion of Ptolemy. Part and parcel of this cosmological scheme was the zodiac, the band in the celestial sphere in which the (apparent) motions of the sun, moon and planets take place, and which was divided into twelve sections (or signs) through which in the course of a year the sun was said to pass. This essentially astronomical construction had implications for judicial astrology, and it is no surprise that Cuningham proceeded in this volume to outline 'the Planets and signes governing every region . . . and adding furdermore unto Ptolomaeus the names both of Regions, and Cities, which ether were not knowne of hym, or els willingly omitted.'[21] Accordingly he drew up a detailed inventory of the known world's regions and cities as they came under the influence of each of the signs of the zodiac from Aries and Mars to Pisces and Jupiter.

Cuningham, as it turns out, was a practised astrologer. In 1558, just a year before the *Cosmographical Glasse* was published, he had issued *A New Almanacke and Prognostication*, in which he specified the unfortunate times of that year in which to buy or sell, take medicine, sow and plant, or undertake journeys – an exercise he repeated for the year 1565. These almanacs were based on detailed mathematical calculations of the position of the planets and attested to the essential compatibility of scientific astronomy and astrology. In 1560 he even published his own apologia for astrological practice under the title *An Invective Epistle in Defence of Astrologers*. For Cuningham, it is clear, no distinction was to be brooked between these various facets of his work. And as if to cement the links between astrology and geography he dedicated *The Cosmographical Glasse* to Lord Robert Dudley, whose enthusiasm for astrology was expressed in his close association with John Dee, a figure to whom we must now turn.

John Dee (1527–1608) truly played a monumental role on the intellectual stage of Renaissance Europe, although for long enough his contributions were ignored or suppressed because of his reputedly unsavoury occult dabblings.[22] In fact, Dee was a scholar-mathematician of great repute and a

[21] William Cuningham, *The Cosmographical Glasse, Conteinyng the Pleasant Principles of Cosmographie, Geographie, Hydrographie, or Nauigation* (London, 1559), p. 133.

[22] The following are useful sources about the life and geographical writings of John Dee: E. G. R. Taylor, *Tudor Geography 1485–1583* (London: Methuen, 1930); Frances A. Yates, *Theatre of the World* (London: Routledge and Kegan Paul, 1969); Yates, *Rosicrucian Enlightenment*; Peter J. French, *John Dee: The World of an Elizabethan Magus* (London: Routledge and Kegan Paul, 1972); Denis Cosgrove, 'Geography and the Mathematical Arts:

skilled map and instrument maker. After a distinguished career at St John's College, Oxford, Dee resorted to the University of Louvain where he studied with Gemma Phrysius, one of the greatest mathematical practitioners of the day. In turn, Dee was himself to attract as students such distinguished individuals as Frobisher, Gilbert, Ralegh, and possibly Drake, and to number among his friends and close associates men like Mercator, Ortelius, Leonard and Thomas Digges, and the Hakluyts. Nowhere, perhaps, were his intellectual capabilities more clearly displayed than in his 1570 'Mathematical Preface' to the first English translation of Euclid's *Elements of Geometrie*. Here Dee provided a definitive introduction to the common mathematical principles on which a diverse range of astronomical, navigational, cartographic, and surveying practices could be erected. Thereby he introduced a body of theoretical knowledge to the new, emerging class of mathematical practitioners, showing how it could readily be exploited for popular use in various arts and crafts. Thus such practices as surveying, navigation, and hydrography came under Dee's scrutiny as he introduced these to what might best be called the mathematical method.

Dee's geographical interests encompassed not only these subjects, but also the progress and implications of the voyages of discovery. *The Great Volume of Famous and Rich Discoveries*, which he wrote in 1577, for example, was specifically designed to show how the English could go about the task of exploiting the riches of the East, and it is therefore no surprise that it also included the evidence he had collected to date on a possible northeast passage to Cathay. But while this and other works bear witness to Dee's broad-ranging interest in the geographical enterprise, it is in the context of his mathematical pursuits that his conception of the nature of geography most clearly comes to the fore. In the preface to Euclid's *Elements*, then, Dee anchored geography's conceptual content in the notion of location; geography was the science that dealt with the 'situation' of cities, towns, villages, forts, castles, mountains, woods, rivers, and so on, across the face of the earth. Understandably the map was the centrepiece of this project, for the description and designation of these locations were crucially accompanied by cartographic depiction. Closely connected was a related science, that of chorography, the aim of which was to provide descriptions of small portions of the earth's surface without reference to the globe as a whole. Again cartography played a leading role in this essentially regional science and the maps contemporaneously being produced by Christopher

Considerations on Humanism, the Occult and Geography in the Late Renaissance'. Paper presented at the Annual Conference of the Institute of British Geographers, University of Leeds, 1985.

Saxton illustrated precisely what chorography amounted to. Such intense local description was dominated by a passion for naming and cataloguing, and stemmed perhaps from a belief that thereby the natural order could be established. 'Just as the Divine presence and purpose could be uncovered through the study of natural law in the political arena,' Lesley Cormack writes, 'so too could the proper classification of the countryside, that is the establishment of a natural order based on names and measurement, reveal the Divine Hand in English local affairs.'[23]

But just as geography could descend to the micro-scale, so too could it encompass the macro-scale; for Dee was no less concerned with astronomical geography and its ties with cosmography in order that the links could be clarified between the elemental or earthly world and the celestial or heavenly spheres. And it is with this latter concern that we come face to face with the mainspring of Dee's vision of the world. Profoundly implicated in the hermetic tradition of natural and ceremonial magic, astrology, and alchemy, Dee looked to mathematics as the cornerstone of the scientific-magical *Weltanschauung*; the intertwining relations between the elemental, celestial, and intellectual worlds – all based on numerology – were such that mathematics was the key that could unlock the mysteries of the universe.[24] It is therefore no surprise that Dee was profoundly influenced by Paracelsus and that, in his turn, he had a role to play in the emergence of the mysterious Rosicrucian brotherhood in continental Europe – a secret society whose members perpetuated the traditions of hermeticism. Nor is it surprising that Dee was attracted to the 'microcosm–macrocosm' analogy – a doctrine that emphasized the correspondences between the human individual and the form of the cosmos. For Dee, the geographical rendition of this ancient theory emerged in his spelling out the intimate relationships between human affairs and the celestial forces of the heavenly spheres. Not that human destiny was crudely determined by such forces; human beings had the capacity to transform the world by the mechanical arts of survey, cartography, land management, and architecture no less than by alchemy and natural magic.

It was at this point that Dee's mind-set took a profoundly political turn. Like many others he acknowledged a distinction between *malificarum* (witchcraft) and *magia* (natural magic). His sympathies were definitely with the latter; for Dee's magic was patriotic, Christian, well-intentioned. Thus he wanted to harness the microcosm–macrocosm notion for political ends

---

[23] Lesley Cormack, '"Good Fences Make Good Neighbours": Geography as Self-Definition in Early Modern England', *Isis*, 82 (1991): 639–61.
[24] Cosgrove, 'Geography and the Mathematical Arts'.

by arguing that the principle of 'as above so below' showed that the universe was linked up in a chain of continuous causation. So it was entirely natural that Dee should seek for both magical *and* political ways of achieving his grand constitutional vision – the restoration of Britain's ancient unity, and of advancing the cause of the 'Brytish Impire'. Exploration, colonization, Christianization, natural magic, and the cultivation of geographical learning were thus all part of his interest in the New World. Not surprisingly the frontispiece to his *General and Rare Memorials Pertayning to the Perfect Arte of Navigation* (1577) (plate 3.1) displays various hermetic symbols urging the queen to expand her overseas dominions.[25] With Dee, it is clear, the science of geography and the occult arts were intimately bound together.

Cuningham and Dee, I think, sufficiently illustrate that the practice of geography in the late sixteenth century was as deeply entangled in the network of magic as the other sciences. The late-sixteenth-century cosmographical writings of Thomas Blundeville further corroborate this contention. Blundeville was a broad-ranging essayist who composed numerous works on horsemanship, navigation, moral philosophy, logic, cartography, and cosmography. In the present context, however, it need only suffice to point out that Blundeville included 'Astronomie, Astrologie, Geographie, and Chorographie' as the 'speciall kindes of knowledge' that the science of cosmography encompassed. Thus for him geography (knowledge of the whole world) and chorography (knowledge of regions) were umbilically tied to astrology, 'a Science which by considering the motions, aspects, and influences of the starres, doth foresee and prognosticate things to come.' To be sure, Blundeville concentrated his efforts on topics which might best be summarized as the mathematics of the sphere – latitude, longitude, zones, climes, parallels, distances between places, and so on. But his geography also incorporated a thoroughly empirical component. When outlining the different climatic zones of the world he attributed the Ancients' error of supposing that three of the five zones were uninhabitable to their 'lacke of experiences, because they had never traveled into those regions.' And he displayed a characteristic passion for naming: topographic features, human inhabitants of particular zones, winds, and climes were all allocated specific terms usually deriving from the zodiac. Thus it is understandable that in his treatise entitled *A Plaine Description of Mercator his Two Globes . . . ,* which was designed to instruct his readers in the use of the globe, he did pause to explain the nature and further uses of the horoscope and to insist

[25] See Ian Seymour, 'The Political Magic of John Dee', *History Today*, 39(1989): 29–35.

Plate 3.1 Frontispiece to *General and Rare Memorials pertaining to the Perfect Arte of Navigation*

that 'there is nothing that chanceth to the inferiour bodies, but some cause thereof doth appear by meane of the Horoscope in heaven, and therefore the Astrologians have devided the whole heaven into 12 houres,' hours which 'doth shew the very secrets of nature.' A diagrammatic depiction of the significations of the hours for judicial astrology understandably accompanied his discourse.[26]

That astrological principles insinuated their way into the embryonic history of subjects cognate to geography is hardly surprising. The early cultivation of weather-forecasting, given its importance for navigation and agriculture, predictably demonstrates this association. Like the other figures we have just been considering, Leonard Digges (*c.*1520–59) was a mathematical practitioner specializing in surveying, navigation, and gunnery. He was, moreover, 'zealous for true religion', as was his son Thomas, a pupil of Dee's and a student of engineering and astronomy, who in the early seventeenth century closely associated himself with the Puritan cause. Their role in the cultivation of early English science has been charted elsewhere and need not detain us here.[27] Rather I want to focus briefly on the volume published by Leonard Digges and subsequently augmented by his son Thomas, entitled *A Prognostication Everlastinge* (plate 3.2). It was, at heart, a treatise on meteorology, as its fuller title indicates: *A prognostication everlastinge of righte good effecte, fruitfully augmented by the auctour, contayning plaine, briefe, pleasante, chosen rules to judge the weather by the Sunne, Moone, Starres, Comets, Rainebow, Thunder, Cloudes, with other Extraordinary Tokens, not omitting the Aspects of Planets, with a briefe judgement for ever of Plenty, Lacke, Sickness, Death, Warres . . .*[28] Clearly

[26] Thomas Blundeville, *M. Blvndevile, His Exercises, containing Six Treatises . . . Very Necessarie to be Read and Learned of all Yoong Gentlemen that Have not Bene Exercised in Such Disciplines, and Yet Are Desirous to Have Knowledge as Well in Cosmographie, Astronomie, and Geographie, as Also in the Arte of Navigation . . .* (London, 1594), pp. 134, 192, 232. The popularity of this work is attested by the fact that it had entered its seventh edition by 1636.

[27] See Hooykaas 'Puritanism and Science', pp. 9–32; F. R. Johnson and S. V. Larkey, 'Thomas Digges, the Copernican system, and the Idea of the Infinity of the Universe in 1576', *Huntington Library Bulletin*, 5 (1934): 69–117; A. Koyré, *From the Closed World to the Infinite Universe* (Baltimore: Johns Hopkins Press, 1957) pp. 34–9.

[28] The full title of the work is Leonard Digges, *A Prognostication Everlastinge of Righte Good Effecte Fruitfully Augmented by the Auctour, Contayning Plaine, Briefe, Pleasant, Chosen Rules to Judge the Weather by the Sunne, Moone, Starres, Comets, Rainebow, Thunder, Cloudes, with Other Extraordinary Tokens, Not Omitting Aspects of Planets, With a Briefe Judgment for Ever of Plenty, Lacke, Sickness, Death, Warres & c. Opening Also Many Naturall Causes Worthy to be Known. To these and other now at the last, are ioyned divers generall, pleasant tables, with manye compendious rules, easye to be had in memory, manifolde ways profitable to al men of understanding, published by Leonard Digges gentleman. Lately corrected and augmented by Thomas Digges his sonne* (London: Thomas Marsh, 1576). The significance of picturing as an epistemological device during the Renaissance is discussed in Robert S.

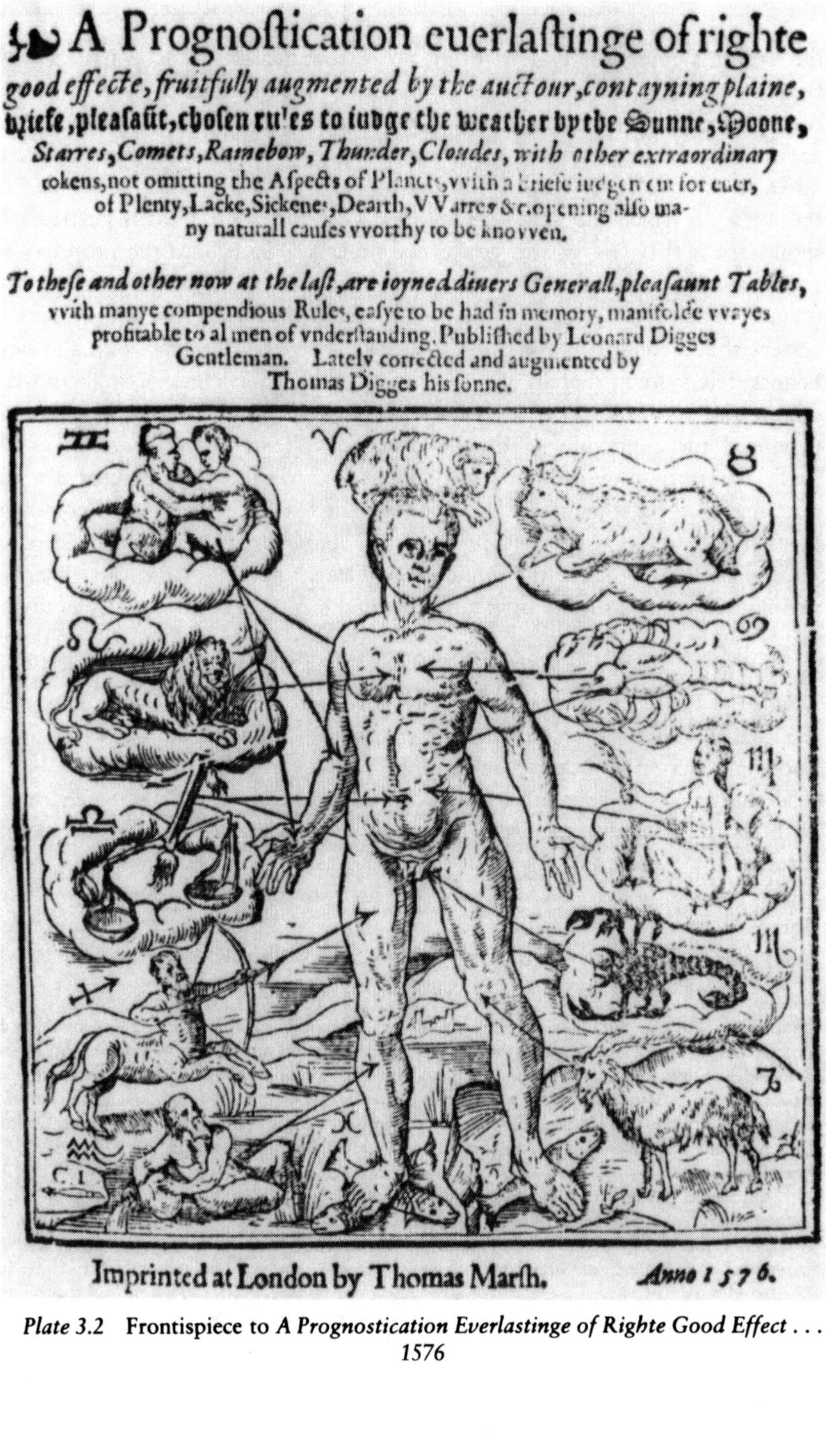

A Prognoſtication euerlaſtinge of righte good effecte, fruitfully augmented by the auctour, contayning plaine, briefe, pleaſant, choſen rules to iudge the weather by the Sunne, Moone, Starres, Comets, Rainebow, Thunder, Cloudes, with other extraordinary tokens, not omitting the Aſpects of Planets, vvith a briefe iudgement for euer, of Plenty, Lacke, Sickenes, Dearth, VVarres &c. opening alſo many naturall cauſes vvorthy to be knovven.

To theſe and other now at the laſt, are ioyned diuers Generall, pleaſaunt Tables, vvith manye compendious Rules, eaſye to be had in memory, manifolde vvayes profitable to al men of vnderſtanding. Publiſhed by Leonard Digges Gentleman. Lately corrected and augmented by Thomas Digges his ſonne.

Imprinted at London by Thomas Marſh. Anno 1576.

Plate 3.2 Frontispiece to *A Prognostication Everlastinge of Righte Good Effect . . .* 1576

the author's intention was to bring an astrological-scientific perspective to bear on weather-forecasting. So it is understandable that a typical micro-cosm–macrocosm engraving relating the signs of the zodiac to the different parts of the human body was strategically placed on the title page and that all sorts of 'rules' for weather-forecasting, like the significance of the day of the week on which the new year fell, were outlined. But what is particularly significant is that Digges was concerned no less to safeguard the propriety of astrology than to defend the rectitude of astronomy. And nowhere is this plainer than in his son's new edition of the work. Here the old Ptolemaic system that Leonard had relied on was replaced by Thomas with the new heliocentric system, thereby bearing out the claim that almanac makers were among the first in England to convert to Copernicanism. Yet, when Thomas produced his engraving of the heliocentric system, he presented it as 'A perfit description of the Caelestiall Orbes, according to the most ancient doctrine of the Pythagoreans' and embellished it with theological commen-tary. Indeed it is worth recalling in this very connection that Copernicus himself had come under the influence of Florentine neo-Platonism which, in neo-Pythagorean fashion, attributed spiritual significance to the sun as divine symbol. Accordingly Copernicus could elaborate his own heliocentric theol-ogy with explicitly hermetic talk of the personified sun as 'the Lamp, the Mind, the Ruler of the Universe.'[29] So yet again we have with the Diggeses, the intermingling – to use modern designations – of scientific knowledge and knowledge based on other 'non-rational' sources of belief.

Certainly there were other practitioners who conducted their geography with similar motivations. Denis Cosgrove, for example, has illustrated this through the writings of the Venetian Christoforo Sorte, an influential geog-rapher of the Italian Renaissance.[30] Then there were those like William Bourne who produced works, among many other subjects, on surveying alongside astrological almanacs; indeed he combined these two interests

---

Westmann, 'Nature, Art, and the Psyche: Jung, Pauli, and the Kepler-Fludd Polemic', in B. Vickers (ed.), *Occult and Scientific Mentalities in the Renaissance* (Cambridge University Press, Cambridge, 1984), pp. 177–229. Westman emphasizes that these visual epistemologists departed from Aristotelianism by treating occult qualities as intelligible. Their graphics were designed to provide accounts of how the visible and invisible worlds were interrelated. Various aspects of the influence of astrology on the early history of meteorology are discussed in H. Frisinger, *The History of Meteorology: to 1800* (New York: Science History Publications, 1977).

[29] Quoted in H. Kearney, *Science and Change 1500–1700* (New York: McGraw-Hill, 1971) pp. 99–100.

[30] See Denis Cosgrove, 'The Geometry of Landscape: Practical and Speculative Arts in Sixteenth-Century Venetian Land Territories,' in Denis Cosgrove and Stephen Daniels (eds), *The Iconography of Landscape. Essays on the Symbolic Representation, Design and Use of Past Environments* (Cambridge: Cambridge University Press, 1988), pp. 254–76.

when in 1567 he wrote a work entitled *An Almanack and Prognostication for iii Yeres, with Serten Rules of Navigation.* Again Robert Recorde, to whose enthusiastic commitment to vernacular science the English school of mathematical practitioners can be traced, and who very largely stimulated the study of cosmography at Cambridge, remained convinced that there 'was never any great changes in the world . . . but God by the signs of heaven did premonish men thereof.'[31] Rather than cataloguing the specific contributions of individuals like these, however, I want to turn now to the more specifically theological context of sixteenth-century geography, particularly as practised in Lutheran Germany.

Reformation Theology and Scientific Procedure

The evolution of German geography during the Reformation period cannot be understood in isolation from the currents of theological thought that swept through Europe in the sixteenth century.[32] No doubt this was largely because, in those days, almost all practitioners of geography were theologians and German institutions of learning were confessionally based. Fundamental shifts in the focus of geographical scholarship, then, were very largely attributable to the changing theological fashions. In pre-Reformation Germany the cognitive content of geography, judging by the standard of Vincenticus's *Speculum Naturae*, was a conventional Catholic synthesis of biblical cosmogony and Aristotelianism. Its emphasis was on interpreting the creation; but it amounted to little more than classical geography squeezed into a biblical mould. With the coming of the Reformation however, the theological thrust shifted from creation to providence – a doctrinal realignment that occasioned a move away from medieval deism towards more immanent divine action in the world. The geographical implications were dramatic. Philipp Melanchthon (1498–1560), for example, departed from the conceptions of his predecessors by insisting that geographical knowledge should not be gleaned from the pages of scripture, but from experience in the world. To be sure, this brand of geography was no less

---

[31] Quoted in Keith Thomas, *Religion and Decline of Magic*, p. 354.

[32] See Manfred Büttner, 'The Significance of the Reformation for the Reorientation of Geography in Lutheran Germany', *History of Science*, 17 (1979): 139–69; Manfred Büttner, 'Philipp Melanchthon 1497–1560', in *Geographers. Biobibliographical Studies*, vol. 3 (London: Mansell, 1979), pp. 93–7; Manfred Büttner and Karl H. Burmeister, 'Sebastian Münster 1488–1552', in *Geographers. Biobibliographical Studies*, vol. 3 (London: Mansell, 1979), pp. 99–106; Manfred Büttner, 'On the History and Philosophy of the Geography of Religion in Germany'. Paper presented at the XVth International Congress of the History of Science, Edinburgh, 10–19 August 1977.

designed to lead men and women to God; but the route was now via an awareness of his providential government of the world. Everything in the 'magnificent theatre' of the world was proof of the divine architect who was permanently engaged in preserving and protecting his creation. Accordingly, Melanchthon widened the sphere of geography to embrace the study of human culture by tracing the spread of Christianity and its influence on civilization across time and space.

If Melanchthon thereby opened up the subject to cultural-geographic themes, their full exploitation was left in the hands of other Reformation geographers. In 1556, for example, Caspar Peucer defined geography as nothing less than the science that is concerned with the visible dimensions of divine revelation. So, for him, any true geography must begin with the geography of Palestine – for that was where God's first self-revelation occurred – and then proceed to an outline of the expansion of Christendom. Thus it was that the historical geography of religion very largely conditioned the more general geographical tradition in Germany. This is clearly evident in the writings of Michael Neander, whose regional ecclesiastical history was firmly tied to geographical moorings. The same was true of Sebastian Münster, holder of theological professorships in various German universities, who also came under Melanchthon's spell. And this is nowhere more evident than in his *Cosmographia*, a work that went through some twenty-one editions between 1544, the year of its first appearance, and 1628. For he too saw the world-order as expressive of divine purpose and found therein the rationale for his regional interrogation of political, religious, and economic history. Throughout this corpus of literature everything from climate to culture was called upon to bear witness to the *Providentia*.

If one of the implications of the Reformation was the liberation of geography from a narrow biblicism, further 'secularization' of the subject was pursued by later Reformation geographers. It must be understood that these geographers were not attacking biblical religion or the Christian faith; rather they were convinced that if God had revealed himself in nature no less than in scripture, then the natural world could be interrogated independently of special revelation. The intellectual mainspring of this further course of development lies with the Reformed theologian, astronomer, and mathematician, Bartholomäus Keckermann (1572–1609).[33] Fundamental to Keckermann's posthumously published *Systema Geographicum* of 1611 was

---

[33] On Keckermann see Manfred Büttner, 'Bartholomäus Keckermann 1572–1609', in *Geographers. Biobibliographical Studies*, vol. 2, (London: Mansell, 1977), pp. 73–9; Paul Lawrence Rose, 'Keckermann, Bartholomew', *Dictionary of Scientific Biography* (New York: Scribner's, 1970); J. A. May, 'The Geographical Interpretation of Ptolemy in the Renaissance',

the distinction he drew between *geographica generalis* and *geographica specialis*. The former, and most substantial part of the *Systema* (163 pages), dealt with the measurement of the earth's subdivisions at the global scale. This project encompassed the earth's physical, climatological, and astronomical dimensions and also included observations on the earth's mathematical representations in maps and globes. Such a bias undoubtedly reflected Keckermann's astronomical inclinations, but he did supplement this treatment with a 31-page appendix on special geography – the study of the physical and human geography of particular regions. Whatever the relative significance Keckermann attached to each of these two components, and allowing for his own admission that the distinction was suggested by Ptolemy's separation of geography from chorography, he had introduced a new geographical terminology that would become the conventional wisdom of key figures like Varenius and Carpenter.

Keckermann's scholarly accomplishments were not restricted to his geographical contribution, however. Having studied philosophy and theology at Wittenberg, he moved to Heidelberg where he wrote on logic and dogma – works he supplemented by contributions on astronomy and mathematics. Indeed, during his short life he was to emerge as a leader in the German Reformed Church, and it is in his theological convictions that the philosophical roots of his geography are to be located. In the discrimination between the general and the special, already rehearsed in its geographical context, Keckermann found a concept that had theological value as well. For him, a fundamental distinction was to be made between the general and special workings of providence. The latter was purely soteriological in emphasis and was the special preserve of theology. By contrast, the former dealt with God's government of the world and could only be clarified by empirical investigation. It was thus entirely within the logic of Keckermann's reformed religion that geography should be emancipated from theology. As Büttner summarizes Keckermann's conviction: 'If God's intervention in nature is not or is no longer theologically interesting, geography can, at least as far as the physio-geographical branch is concerned, emancipate itself from theology. It no longer needs, as a servant of theology, to confirm the *Providentia*, but can construct its system on the basis of autonomous criteria, independent of theology and can set itself the goals of its own research.'[34]

Tijdschrift voor Economische en Sociale Geografie, 73 (1982): 350–61; Bowen, *Empiricism and Geographical Thought*, pp. 69–70.

[34] Manfred Büttner, 'Kant and the Physico-Theological Consideration of the Geographical Facts', *Organon*, 11 (1975): 237.

Within German geography Bernhard Varenius (1622–50) was the natural heir to Keckermann's enterprise. Indeed it was through his 1650 *Geographia Generalis* that the very terminology Keckermann had deployed found its way into geography's vocabulary. His training had been in mathematics and medicine, but when he moved to Amsterdam the recent discoveries of the Dutch navigators impelled him more and more in the direction of geography. And his geographical talents are nowhere more clearly displayed than in his book published in 1650, a work which established a framework for geography that was to last for more than a century. *Geographia Generalis* was typically mathematical and astronomical in impulse, and the special geography that he outlined as its accompaniment was to be grounded in thoroughly empirical investigations. Indeed his commitment to *geographia specialis* had already been seen in his regional account of Japan and Siam, published in 1649. In his hands, therefore, geography's status as a thoroughly empirical science was reinforced, because as he himself put it, 'the greatest part of Geography . . . is founded only upon the Experience and Observations of those who have described the several Countries.' With that Keckermann would have happily concurred. But more; through Varenius geography took its place in the science of the seventeenth century. It was precisely because he replaced Ptolemaic astronomy with that of Copernicus and Aristotle's physics with Descartes's, that Newton made use of Varenius's work in his own teaching of geography at Cambridge, issuing new Latin editions of it in 1672 and 1681.[35]

In some ways Keckermann's British equivalent was Nathanael Carpenter (1589–1628). His place in the history of English geography has been secured through the rehearsals of a variety of commentators: in 1901 H. R. Mill confirmed that Carpenter was 'the first British geographer to write on theoretical geography'; J. N. L. Baker scrutinized his *Geography Delineated Forth* in 1928 and shortly afterwards E. G. R. Taylor extolled its 'breadth of view and modernity of outlook'; while even more recently Bowen affirms that Carpenter 'provided in this period one of the most intelligent and mature attempts within the limitations of thought in his day, to clarify the theoretical position of geography.' Like Keckermann, Carpenter distinguished general and special geography and proceeded to delineate their particular conceptual territories. But he went further than earlier writers by insisting on the propriety of including chorography within the ambit of

---

[35] Vern L. Bullough, 'Varenius, Bernhardus', *Dictionary of Scientific Biography*; May, 'Geographical Interpretation of Ptolemy', p. 359; Bowen, *Empiricism and Geographical Thought*, pp. 77–90; William Warntz, 'Newton, The Newtonians, and the *Geographia Generalis Varenii*', *Annals of the Association of American Geographers*, 79 (1989): 165–91.

geography and thereby linked Ptolemy's geography and chorography with Keckermann's *geographia generalis* and *geographia specialis* respectively. Accordingly Carpenter's survey encompassed most of the topics that we have already seen as central to the geographical enterprise in the period: the motion and mathematics of the globe; the earth's zones, climes, and parallels; its topography and hydrography; the 'distinction of the inhabitants of the terrestriall spheare'; and distances between places.[36]

Once again, however, it would be mistaken to leave Carpenter's project at this point, perceiving him as a sort of Keckermann clone. For Carpenter went much further than Keckermann in his denunciation of Aristotelianism. Even in *Geography Delineated Forth*, for example, he inveighed against those who with 'prejudicate ignorance' were 'ready to lick up the dust under *Aristotles* feet, [and] with a supercilious look contemne all other learning, as though no flowers of science could growe in another garden.'[37] This robust rejection of scholastic authority and the espousal of experience has been noted in Bowen's survey. But the conceptual foundation for this theoretical innovativeness still needs to be exposed.

Carpenter was a Fellow of Exeter College and subsequently, at the invitation of Archbishop Ussher, schoolmaster of the king's wards in Dublin. He acquired a reputation in mathematics and geography equalled only by his renown as a student of divinity, his sermons on *Achitophel, or, the Picture of a Wicked Politician* attracting the attention of the most prominent divines of his day. And yet on his deathbed he is reported to have expressed regret that he had 'so much courted the maid instead of the mistress,' by which he meant, one writer observes, 'that he had spent his chief time in philosophy and mathematics and had neglected divinity.' Besides these interests, Carpenter produced a work on optics which was destined never to see publication. He discovered, to his great disgruntlement, the first printing of the preface encasing Christmas pies in his printer's house, and he himself eventually lost his only draft of the entire work in the Irish Sea![38]

---

[36] Hugh Robert Mill, 'On Research in Geographical Science', *Geographical Journal*, 18 (1901): 410; J. N. L. Baker, 'Nathanael Carpenter and English Geography in the Seventeenth Century', *Geographical Journal*, 71 (1928): 261–71; E. G. R. Taylor, *Late Tudor and Early Stuart Geography 1583–1650* (London: Methuen, 1934), p. 136; Bowen, *Empiricism and Geographical Thought*, p. 72; Nathanael Carpenter, *Geography Delineated Forth in Two Bookes. Containing the Sphaericall and Topicall Parts Thereof* (Oxford, 1625), chapter 10.

[37] N[athanael] C[arpenter,] *Achitophel, or, the Picture of a Wicked Politician* (London, 1627).

[38] W. P. C[ourtney,] 'Carpenter, Nathanael (1589–1628?)', *Dictionary of National Biography*; Thomas Fuller, 'Nathaniel [sic] Carpenter', in *The History of the Worthies of England* (London: Thomas Teff, new edn 1840), vol. 1, p. 424.

Such misfortune did not befall his first book, *Philosophia Libera*, published in 1622 under the pseudonym N. C. Cosmopolitanus. This volume was, in essence, an attack on Aristotelianism in support of a philosophy of science grounded in Calvinist theology. As a tract composed to oppose scholasticism and to foster a free science 'not adorned by great names but naked and simple,' *Philosophia Libera* stands as one example of the way in which Puritan theology could help nurture the empirical spirit.[39] And so Carpenter's rugged commitment to empiricism and to philosophical liberty, as fundamental to geography, was the scientific expression of his assurance that God was revealed in scripture and nature, but not in the human words of any scholarly authority. To ignore the basis for this foundational principle as historians of geography have done, diverts attention, I would suggest, from the thrust of Carpenter's geographical project. To acknowledge it brings the history of geography to a central position in the history of science in Puritan England.

Indeed I would contend that the dismissal of William Pemble's *A Briefe Introduction to Geography* of 1630 as a 'mediocre work', according to one commentator, and of Pemble himself as 'a conservative geographer [who] still held to the Ptolemaic theory,' according to another, stems from a failure to appreciate the vital methodological programme for science that some Puritans were engaged in.[40] Sure enough, Pemble did resist the Copernican model, but his rejection was based on his belief that the theory 'is contrary to experience' and not on any appeal to scriptural authority;[41] and this despite the fact, or perhaps because of the fact, that Pemble was a zealous Puritan divine and vigorous exponent of Calvinism.

The Puritan Social Programme

The Puritan engagement with the science of geography cannot be restricted to the fostering of a mere philosophical principle of procedure. On the contrary, geography's conceptual content occupied a strategic role in English Puritan society. Take for example the case of Samuel Hartlib. Hartlib had come from Elbing to study at Cambridge during 1625–6 and, having decided to settle in England, he quickly became a leading activist in the Puritan movement. Throughout his life he deeply involved himself in sci-

---

[39] R. Hooykaas, *Philosophia Libera. Christian Faith and the Freedom of Science* (London: Tyndale Press, 1957), pp. 20–21; [Nathanael Carpenter,] *Philosophia Libera* (Oxoniae, 1622).

[40] Bowen, *Empiricism and Geographical Thought*, p. 76; Edmund W. Gilbert, *British Pioneers in Geography* (Newton Abbot: David and Charles, 1972), p. 54.

[41] William Pemble, *A Briefe Introduction to Geography* (Oxford, 1630), p. 13.

ence education, social reform, and publishing and cultivated a network of associates who played a major role in the development of the Royal Society. Certainly Hartlib's own scientific discoveries were minor, but his vision for the role of science in Puritan social reform are important in the present context. For Hartlib was profoundly committed to establishing an Office of Public Address, a scheme designed to put the poor in touch with possible benefactors. Part and parcel of this scheme was Hartlib's appeal for the drawing up of a range of registers that would provide the public with basic economic and geographical information. Accordingly, he called for information on the situation 'of any of the Provinces, Shires, Counties, Cities, Towns, Villages, Castles, Ports,' to be amplified with details of their economic geography, and thereby drew the Baconian methods of natural history into the realm of regional survey. All this contributed to what he himself called political anatomy – a body of social knowledge which brought geographical, economic, and social data, organized on a regional basis, under the rubric of natural history.[42]

The social benefits of economic geography were not, of course, restricted to philanthropic purposes. Geography played a central role in the Puritan vision of science as a means of attaining national economic independence. John Webster in 1654 called for the overhauling of the higher education curriculum to 'equip the elite for an economically active role'; and Sir John Pettus in 1674 issued 'noble invitations to the Study of Geography, Hydrography and other Sciences,' because they would bring knowledge of 'the richest Minerals, Plants, and Precious Stones' and thereby improve merchandising. These concerns had long been part of the Puritan agenda, as Lewis Roberts's 1638 *Map of Commerce* reveals; for it was nothing less than a guide to the economic resources of every continent. At home this same motivation took the form of regionally biased natural history, often on a county basis. The tradition of county mapping was by now long established. Christopher Saxton's county maps of England and Wales, dating from 1574, were widely available and were used for every purpose from administrative control to decorating playing cards! His contemporary, John Norden, had also produced in 1607 a county-by-county topographical survey with accompanying maps. And of course John Speed's intensely patriotic maps of 1610–11 became the most famous of all; they 'were designed to proclaim an ideological belief about his country, about the course of its history, and about its political system and destiny.' In 1652 Gerard Boate took up the principle of economic survey in his regional description of

---

[42] Webster, *The Great Instauration*, p. 422.

Irelands Naturall History, in which he abandoned the antiquarian slant of earlier chorographic writings like those of Camden. Its strongly economic orientation reflected its purpose: to furnish settlers with basic regional information. This included reports on ports, river transport, fisheries, local marling techniques, and practices for the draining of bogs, together with an inventory of metals, minerals, marble, turf, 'and other Things that are taken out of the Ground.' Conceived on Baconian principles, Boate's resource compilation represented a major development in scientific economic geography. And it fitted hand in glove with the seventeenth-century mathematization of geography already in vogue among the nautical mathematical practitioners.[43]

If one figure representing these diverse interests were to be sought, an impressive case could be made for William Petty (1623–87) (Plate 3.3) 'a prominent virtuoso in an age of the many-sided genius.'[44] Petty's work ranged widely across many areas including anatomy, ship design, and 'political arithmetic'. His professional training was in medicine and he soon became part of an Oxford circle dedicated to experimental philosophy, from which the Royal Society was to emerge. The personal influence of Hartlib and his devotees was great. It has even been suggested that the 'unglamorous form of scientific activity undertaken by Hartlib's team of forgotten followers', which embraced the questionnaire method of gathering information, inspired Petty's scientific enthusiasms from the start of his career.[45] Whatever the precise sources of his inspiration, Petty found plenty of opportunity to deploy the Hartlib methodology in his various land-surveys of Ireland. The need for these had grown out of his position as physician-general in Ireland and the need to pay his troops with Irish land. Petty's first, and celebrated, effort was in the Down Survey, a project that he supplemented with a complete mapping of Ireland printed around 1685 which was envisaged as correcting the errors of Speed. His mathematical proficiency stood him in good stead and the resulting operation produced for the first time a reasonably accurate estimate of the shape and size of Ireland. Its bias again was quantitative, for Petty was interested in the statistics of rope, hemp, flax, and honey production; but it had administrative

---

[43] Ibid., pp. 334, 335, 350, 429. On the cartography of Saxton and Speed, see Ifor M. Evans and Heather Lawrence, *Christopher Saxton. Elizabethan Map-Maker* (London: Wakefield Historical Publication and the Holland Press, 1979); S. Tyacke and E. J. Huddy, *Christopher Saxton and Tudor Map-Making* (London, 1980); J. B. Harley, 'Meaning and Ambiguity in Tudor Cartography', in Sarah Tyacke (ed.), *English Map-Making. 1500–1650* (London: The British Library, 1983); Tooley, *Maps and Map-Makers*.

[44] Frank N. Egerton III, 'Petty, William', *Dictionary of Scientific Biography*.

[45] Webster, *From Paracelsus to Newton*, p. 62.

Plate 3.3   Engraving of *Sir William Petty, 1683*

purposes too, for it aimed to define 'the quantity, figure, and situation of all the Baronies, parishes and towne or farme lands, with the quantity of each.'[46]

[46] Webster, *The Great Instauration*, p. 442.

The cartographic venture begun in the Down Survey, however, did not exhaust Petty's contribution to geographical science. Indeed intrinsic to that scheme was the quantification of social phenomena that Petty would come to call *The Political Anatomy of Ireland* – essentially a treatise on economic policy and economic geography. Subsequently he widened the scope of this concern with his *Political Arithmetick* published in 1690, in which he helped lay the foundations of the science of demography. The first of these political arithmetic essays dealt with the 'People, Housing, Hospitals, &c., of London and Paris' and contained a wealth of demographic information quantitatively presented, but as he extended the geographical bounds of his concerns he demonstrated the even wider applications of the mathematical method. Earlier, in 1662, John Graunt had similarly brought what he called the 'mathematics of . . . shop-arithmetic' to bear on population questions, and used his findings, based on comparing the bills of mortality of London with the rural environment of Hampshire, to confirm the claims of natural theology. From his statistics he found it possible to extract the moral excellence of Christianity's monogamous precepts and the accuracy of post-diluvian biblical chronology.[47] For Petty and for Graunt such statistical exercises in economic geography were entirely consonant with their vision of social transformation along the lines of the Puritans and parliamentarians – a conviction that expressed itself both in the belief that universal education was the first priority in the social programme of the transformed state and in their advocacy of rational planning as practical politics.

Faraway places and faraway people

If the growth of geography in the sixteenth and seventeenth centuries owed something to the conceptual reverberations of hermeticism and of Reformation theology alike, and to the social policies of revolutionary Puritans, its roots in foreign travel still remained firm. Indeed it was precisely because of the immense significance of overseas exploration and the related arts of navigation and map-making that Richard Willis, in 1577, could assert, according to Christopher Hill, that 'geography had ousted grammar, poetry, logic, astrology and Greek in popular approbation.'[48] This strain of geographical endeavour manifested itself in many different ways and at both technical and popular levels of writing.

[47] Quoted in Hill, *Intellectual Origins*, p. 272. See the discussion in Clarence J. Glacken, *Traces on the Rhodian Shore. Nature and Culture in Western Thought from Ancient Times to the End of the Eighteenth Century* (Berkeley: University of California Press, 1967), pp. 398–99.
[48] Hill, *Intellectual Origins*, p.67.

Of the former, the writings of Edward Wright (1558–1615) are among the foremost. His *Certaine Errours in Navigation Detected* of 1598 revolutionized nautical science; but he had already by then made an enormous contribution both to navigation and cartography by providing a coherent theoretical method of constructing maps on the Mercator projection. Significantly, it was through the writings of his personal friend Thomas Blundeville that Wright's achievement was first made public, and its impact may be gauged from the fact that Jodocus Hondius employed Wright's tables in his cartographic work of the late 1590s. The close ties between geography, cartography, and navigation were to continue to characterize geography's history throughout the period of the Scientific Revolution as numerous writers produced works of practical nautical importance. Chronologies of this technical tradition have been provided elsewhere and in the present context it is only necessary to register its continuing vitality.[49]

But beyond this corpus of technical work, the interest in faraway places also spawned a popular literature designed either to make the stock-in-trade crafts of the geographer known to a wider public, or to keep readers abreast of global discovery and the most up-to-date international inventory. In 1573, for example, an anonymous author writing under the initials D. P. (possibly David Powell, Sir Henry Sidney's domestic chaplain and author of *The Historie of Cambria* in 1584) produced a pamphlet of around a dozen pages entitled *Certaine Brief and Necessarie Rules of Geographie, Seruing for the Vnderstanding of Chartes and Mappes*. It constituted an entirely elementary synopsis of the circles of the globe, latitude and longitude, climates and parallels, and distances. But the availability of such a miniature work attests to the significance of the popularization of geographical skills in the era.[50] As one commentator observes, this work was 'a popular tract on geography providing evidence of that phenomenal upsurge in interest in maps, geography and lands overseas inspired in Elizabethan England by the voyages of discovery and the expansion of trade.'[51]

Just as significant, however, for the spread of such knowledge were the activities of Thomas Hood (1556–c.1611), a medical and mathematical practitioner. Besides authoring works on the use of globes, astronomy, mathematics, and navigation, Hood did much to pass down the new

[49] See David W. Waters, *The Arts of Navigation in England in Elizabethan and Early Stuart Times* (London: Hollis and Carter, 1958); Taylor, *Mathematical Practitioners*.

[50] D. P., *Certaine Brief and Necessarie Rules of Geographie, Seruing for the Vnderstanding of Chartes and Mappes* (London: Henry Binneman, 1573).

[51] Quoted in *English Experience. Books Printed in England before 1640. A Descriptive Catalogue* (Norwood, N. J.: Walter Johnson Inc.), p. 210.

mathematics by public lecturing on the subject. In the 1580s, for example, he spoke in the Staplers' Chapel, Leadenhall, on geography, among other things, in a series of lectures that were sponsored by a group of London merchants. The content of these communications can be gleaned from *The Principles of Geometrie, Astronomie, and Geographie* specifically compiled by Francis Cooke in 1591, 'publiquelye to be read in the Staplers Chappell at Leaden hall, by the Wor. Tho. Hood, Mathematicall Lecturer of the Cittie of London.'[52] The contents amounted to a compilation of standard mathematical, geometrical, and astronomical information about the earth, and are another example of the importance of these subjects to the upwardly mobile social classes of the day. Indeed the continuing value of geography to mercantile interests is further underscored by the fact that when Hood's lectureship lapsed, the London coterie continued to support the cause of these same subjects as crucial to the reforming curriculum. Moreover public mathematical lecturing had apologetic purposes too. Because in post-Reformation England mathematics was from time to time accused of being a 'popish and superstitious activity, bound up with illicit and occult practices,' the mathematicalls – as they were called – strove 'to undermine and ultimately replace such perceptions.'[53]

The interest in faraway places was also to spawn another genre of geographical literature – the topographical compendium. Two popular works of the early seventeenth century are illustrative. George Abbot (1562–1633), an Anglican bishop 'stiffly principled in puritan doctrines' and subsequently Archbishop of Canterbury, brought out *A Briefe Description of the Whole World* in 1599. In essence the work was an international inventory providing its readers with synoptic information on the main countries of the world, a sort of universal catalogue which Eva Taylor promptly dismissed as an 'arid little compilation'. Arid it may have been, but that it served a useful function is plain from its continued popularity; a third and much enlarged edition appeared in 1608 and further editions were issued until 1664.[54] Its purpose was to keep the populace informed of the latest geographical information, as was, at least in part, that of the *Microcosmus* of

---

[52] Francis Cooke, *The Principles of Geometrie, Astronomie, and Geographie. Wherein is Breefely, Euidently, and Methodically Deliuered, Whatsoever Appertaineth unto the Knowledge of the Said Sciences. Gathered out of the Table of the Astronomicall Institutions of Georgius Henischius* (London, 1591).

[53] Stephen Johnston, 'Mathematical Practitioners and Instruments in Elizabethan England', *Annals of Science*, 48 (1991): 319–44, ref. on p. 320.

[54] 'Abbot, George', *Dictionary of National Biography*; Taylor, *Late Tudor and Early Stuart Geography*, p. 37; Edmund W. Gilbert, 'Geographie is Better than Divinity', in Gilbert, *British Pioneers in Geography*, pp. 44–58.

Peter Heylyn, first published in 1621. Certainly Heylyn, a High Church-man and opponent of Puritanism, had a broader geographical vision than Abbot, for he subtitled his work 'a treatise historicall, geographicall, politicall, theologicall' and thereby cemented links between geography and cultural history. Still, the appearance of numerous new editions again attests to a readership eager to be kept informed of the latest information on the resources and commerce of various regions of the world.[55]

Alongside these summary compilations was a travel literature altogether more serious in its intent. The writings I have in mind here will forever remain associated with the names of Richard Hakluyt and Walter Ralegh, and their successors. Obviously the broad-ranging achievements of these men cannot be rehearsed in detail here, but it is important to register the profundity of their contributions. Richard Hakluyt the younger (c.1552–1616) was the chief advocate and chronicler of English overseas expansion. Through his magisterial collections of voyages he inspired future generations of British seamen to chart the globe and colonial entrepreneurs to risk capital for creed and country. Hakluyt himself remained largely untravelled, but through him geography's ties with patriotism and expansionism were reinforced. His publishing ventures served to keep before the minds of the influential the conviction that the path of England's glory lay in exploits overseas. In *Divers Voyages Touching the Discoverie of America* (1582), for example, he sought to establish England's territorial rights through claims to a priority of discovery; in his *Discourse of Western Planting*, written in 1584, he looked to colonialism as a strategically vital means of making England self-sufficient; and in two separate editions of *The Principall Navigations* (1589 and 1598–1600) he recounted the history of England's navigational adventures and revealed his own vision of England's maritime destiny.[56] His work was thus replete with assumptions about the supremacy of English values, the Protestant religion, and the virtues of the Old World.

Hakluyt was joined in this ecstatic dream by Walter Ralegh (1554–1618), whose own ventures in Virginia, where he founded the first English colony, have made him a legend. But his achievements far exceeded even that. His *Discovery of Guiana* was a classic of exploration, and his final work, *History of the World*, written while imprisoned in the Tower, represented the culmination of his secular approach to history. Ralegh's career was nothing if not multi-faceted. During the course of his revolutionary life he

---

[55] Ibid.

[56] Helen Wallis, 'Hakluyt, Richard', *Dictionary of Scientific Biography*; Taylor, *Late Tudor and Early Stuart Geography*, pp. 1–38.

was involved with the ascendancy of parliamentary power over against the monarchy, the adoption of an aggressive foreign policy, and the redistribution of taxation. His specifically geographical contributions were no less notable.[57] Ralegh made each of his voyages a scientific expedition and helped foster science more generally by his patronage of a teaching academy in London in which cosmography, navigation, and cartography were among the subjects taught. Around him there blossomed a group of scientists whose refusal to defer to Aristotelian authority sprang at least in part from Ralegh's personal interests in magic. But just as important was his critical approach to historical explanation. To be sure his secularized history did not deny God as the prime mover. But his insistence that secondary causes were sufficient of themselves to explain the course of history had both intellectual and social consequences. Intellectually, it opened the door to new sorts of explanation: his recognition of the influence of climate, for example, and of the natural effects of population pressure had the possibly unintended consequence of diminishing the pre-eminence of divine agency in the world. Socially, it fostered the principle of self-help by taking seriously the human capacity to transform the world. Thus in Ralegh, no less than in his associate Hakluyt, we find geographical knowledge deeply implicated in a host of scientific, religious, patriotic, social, and economic projects.[58]

The travel writings of numerous others would also merit discussion. Thomas Hariot's *Briefe and True Report of the New Found Land of Virginia* (1588), for example, was an early case of statistical survey conducted on a grand scale. Robert Harcourt's 1613 narrative of his voyage to Guiana provided a detailed geographical description of the area. The account of Sir Richard Hawkins's 1593 voyage into the South Seas, with its description of the Indians of Florida, the Caribbean, and parts of South America, served to keep the ethnographical strain in the travel literature well to the fore. And Samuel Purchas, author of *Purchas His Pilgrimage* (1613) and literary executor of Hakluyt, surpassed even his mentor in his capacity to synthesize seemingly endless sources into a coherent survey of the peoples and religions of the world.[59] To pass over these for want of space is not to

[57] See R. A. Skelton, 'Ralegh as a Geographer', *The Virginia Magazine of History and Biography*, 71 (1963): 131–49.

[58] Hill, *Intellectual Origins*, pp. 131–224.

[59] Thomas Hariot, *A Briefe and True Report of the New Found Land of Virginia* (London, 1588); Sir Richard Hawkins, *The Observations of Sr. R. Hawkins in his Voiage into the South Sea 1593* (London: John Jaggard, 1622); Robert Harcourt, *A Relation of a Voyage to Guiana* (London: J. Beale for W. Welby, 1613); Samuel Purchas, *Purchas His Pilgrimage or, Relations*

deny their importance. Yet even these thumbnail sketches serve to remind us of geography's age-long ties with ethnography, a marriage whose success owed much to the earlier social theorizing of Jean Bodin (1530–96).

'Jean Bodin', writes Clarence Glacken, 'is the most important thinker of the Renaissance on the general subject of the relation between history and contemporary life and the geographic environment.'[60] Bodin's contribution was born of several diverse intellectual traditions. First and foremost there was the influence of classical and medieval thought in which he was well versed; Bodin was equally at home with Hippocrates' medicine, Plato's laws, Aristotle's politics, and Ptolemy's geography. But these classical sources were supplemented by his avid interest in contemporary travel literature which opened up new ethnological vistas to him. And finally there was the tradition of astrological anthropology which correlated the inhabitants of the world and their cultural traits with particular signs of the zodiac. Dwellers of the north-west quadrant of the globe, for example, coming as they did under the government of Aries, Leo, Sagittarius and the rule of Jupiter, were therefore independent-minded, liberty-loving, bellicose, pugnacious, and industrious. Combining these various sources, Bodin came to attribute the global patterns of ethnological diversity to the influence of environment, particularly climate.[61] His belief was that different environments brought about different combinations of the humours, which in turn manifested themselves in different physical and mental characteristics. Not that his environmentalism was crudely deterministic – other influences were allotted their roles. But the relativist implications were plain: religion, culture, and morality were all subject to environmental control and therefore in some degree relative to the particular geographical circumstances in which they developed. Certainly Bodin's thought was traditional through and through: his geography was firmly Ptolemaic, his explanations often astrological, his cultural evaluations thoroughly ethnocentric. But in his tying of history to geography, of culture to nature, he anticipated the later materialism and relativism of the 'harder' environmental determinists, while at the same time keeping human culture open to geographical scrutiny.

---

of the World and the Religions Observed in All Ages and Places Discovered, from the Creation unto this Present (London, 1613). Purchas, incidentally, was chaplain to George Abbot and was under his patronage.

[60] Glacken, *Traces on the Rhodian Shore*, p. 434.

[61] Joseph Hall's moral critique of the climatic determination of behaviour in 1605 is discussed in John Wands, 'The Theory of Climate in the English Renaissance and *Mundus Alter et Idem*', in I. D. McFarlane (ed.), *Proceedings of the Fifth International Congress of Neo-Latin Studies* (Binghampton, New York: Medieval and Renaissance Texts and Studies, 1986), pp. 519–25.

The Art of Representation

In the last few pages I have concentrated on the written productions and verbal descriptions of the overseas experience and their significance in the processes of scientific reform. But perhaps of even greater moment was the geographer's impulse toward mapping and picturing, namely, visual representation. When Blaeu produced his twelve-volume *Grand Atlas* in 1663, he explained to Louis XIV in his introduction that geography was 'the eye and the light of history.' The reason was simply because, he affirmed, 'maps enable us to contemplate at home and right before our eyes things that are farthest away.'[62] His atlas was a compilation of images of travel and exploration, and was thus designed to annihilate the space between near and far, and translate into visual form the hitherto unseen. In so doing, the map subverted the traditional authority of the word in history and reportage in favour of what Alpers calls 'the new testimony of the eye.'[63] Accordingly, the maps on map sheets increasingly came to be surrounded, in some cases engulfed, by pictorial representations of anthropological types, astronomical signs, historical events, floral specimens, urban morphologies, natural features, town plans, and so on. It was as if the graphic character of the map itself spilled over into the rest of human knowledge.

The triumph of representational modes of thinking in the seventeenth century owed a good deal to the philosophical moves that were afoot in the period. With the triumph of the mechanical philosophy and the disenchantment of nature that it accomplished, there emerged a radically new theory of scientific explanation. Nature now was no longer regarded as a self-revealing reality whose truth we just directly 'know'. Rather, as Charles Taylor puts it, the 'account of scientific knowledge which ultimately emerges . . . is a representational one. To know reality is to have a correct representation of things – a correct picture within of outer reality.'[64] In Descartes particularly this route to knowledge took a radical turn; it came to mean that the only knowledge any of us can have of the outside world is through the process of constructing a picture of it within the mind. This internalization need not attract our attention here, however; but what we do need to fasten on is the central importance that henceforth would be

---

[62] Johan Blaeu, *Le Grand Atlas* (Amsterdam, 1663), pp. 1, 3.

[63] Svetlana Alpers, *The Art of Describing. Dutch Art in the Seventeenth Century*, (Harmondsworth: Penguin Books, 1989), p. 159. The following draws on her account of 'The Mapping Impulse in Dutch Art', chapter 4 of this work.

[64] Charles Taylor, *Sources of the Self. The Making of Modern Identity* (Cambridge, Mass.: Harvard University Press, 1989), p. 144.

attached to picturing, or mirroring, or representing, or mapping, or modelling the world as the only reliable way of knowing it.

As far as the geographical tradition was concerned, the centrality of the picture-making impulse can be traced to the reappropriation during the Renaissance of Ptolemy's conception of geography as an enterprise essentially concerned with picturing (or representing) the world. Indeed as Alpers tellingly points out, Ptolemy himself clarified his distinction between geography and chorography by speaking of the former as a portrait of an entire head, the latter as a picture of individual features such as an eye or an ear. And here the links between cartography and art reassert themselves. For in both, the concern with the mirroring of nature appears as a cartographic-artistic correlate to the Cartesian epistemological project. Moreover, the coincidence between mapping and picturing is more than merely formal. Journeys were specifically undertaken for the purposes of mapping and description by artists in the sixteenth century. Besides, in the Dutch art of the seventeenth century, maps and mapping images were frequently portrayed as prominent features of works of art, and often as wall decorations in the scenes captured on canvas. Indeed the appearance of such maps in artistic works has suggested to some that they performed an authenticating role for the artists themselves. 'The map of the Netherlands reproduced by Vermeer,' writes Stephen Bann, 'is both an accurate diagram, and an internal metaphor of Vermeer's accuracy in notation which is equated with the excellence in the art of painting.'[65] The descriptive character of the map – Vermeer's map has the word *Descriptio* prominently displayed on it – serves to vindicate the painting's realism. It will not escape our notice that geography itself was, for Ptolemy, literally geo-graphic, earth-description. Ptolemy's term *grapho* thus merged verbal and pictorial description.

If the period of the Scientific Revolution evinces a movement towards representation as *the* epistemological procedure, it also discloses a shift in the locus of cultural authority. To use shorthand, authority comes to reside less and less in a monarchical hierarchy. The successive printings of Christopher Saxton's maps can be called as witness. As Richard Helgerson has pointed out, the earliest of Saxton's maps, which appeared in the 1570s, actually contain no reference whatsoever to Saxton himself, but rather carry the coat of arms of a certain Thomas Seckford. Seckford, it turns out, was the person who commissioned the maps, and in fact did so at the behest of the queen and her government. Accordingly, from the publication of the second map the royal insignia are also to be found along the map's margin.

---

[65] Stephen Bann, *The Inventions of History. Essays on the Representation of the Past* (Manchester: Manchester University Press, 1990), p. 201.

Saxton's own identifying mark, however, does not feature until much later re-engravings, but – and this is the crucial point – by the mid seventeenth century only Saxton's name appears on the maps. He has, as it were, eventually reappropriated the work of his own hands. Here, then, is displayed what Helgerson calls 'a momentous transfer of cultural authority from the patron and the royal system of government' and into the hands of the expert.[66]

Just as the authority of the representer assumes increasing importance in the seventeenth century, so too does the power of the represented. For parallel with this history of authorial attribution, from monarch and patron to surveyor, moreover, goes a shift in the *use* of representation. The earlier maps of the mid sixteenth century, for example, are conspicuously royalist in their claims: the cartographic image represents the queen's territory and her authority is confirmed by an overwhelming presence of the emblems of her rule. What is mapped is *her* land, and *her* people. By the seventeenth century, however, they show 'a diminution of the place accorded the insignia of royal power and a corresponding increase in the attention paid to the land itself.'[67] Small wonder that chorography and cartography, even when practised by royalists like Speed, were seen by those in power as threatening activities. Through highlighting the centrality of the land itself, cartographic representation manifested the inescapably ideological character of the undertaking.[68] The cartographer thus emerges as an agent of social change who subverts dynastic loyalty in favour of an identity earthed in local and national geography.

The evolution of geographical knowledge throughout the sixteenth and early seventeenth centuries, it is now plain, cannot be depicted in isolation from the rich intellectual and social contexts within which geographical ideas were enmeshed. Undoubtedly my portrayal is both sketchy and episodic. But through focusing on the interaction between geography and such important cognitive and social movements as hermeticism, Reformation theology, Puritan social policy, overseas expansionism, the art of map making, and ethnographic theory, we can begin to make sense of

[66] Richard Helgerson, 'The Land Speaks: Cartography, Chorography, and Subversion in Renaissance England', *Representations*, 16 (1986): 51–85, ref. on p. 54.

[67] Ibid., p. 56.

[68] This is in keeping with Harley's observation: 'Any cartographic history which ignores the political significance of representation relegates itself to an "ahistorical" history.' J. B. Harley, 'Maps, Knowledge and Power', in Denis Cosgrove and Stephen Daniels (eds), *The Iconography of Landscape. Essays on the Symbolic Representation, Design and Use of Past Environments* (Cambridge: Cambridge University Press, 1988), pp. 277–312, ref. on p. 303.

the ways in which a diverse range of geographies were forged. The geographical tradition, I would claim, has never been conceptually unified nor internally coherent simply because it has accommodated itself to the needs and interests of particular communities at particular times. And this is why a purely internalist account of geographical theory would lead us away from the underlying sources of geography's intellectual diversity, and therefore away from the realization that the history of geography is the history of a contested tradition.

4

Naturalists and Navigators

Geography in the Enlightenment

Strange as it may seem, many of the threads of thought weaving their way through late-seventeenth- and eighteenth-century geography are perhaps most clearly seen in the work of a singular individual who was not really a geographer at all, but rather a founding father of English physics and chemistry, Robert Boyle (1627–91). Consequent on the continuing Europeanization of the globe throughout the seventeenth century, all sorts of people had caught the travel bug. Indeed, at the age of twelve Boyle himself had taken the fashionable Grand Tour of Europe – an early experience that was to live with him for the rest of his days.[1] So it is not surprising that towards the end of his life 'many curious Gentlemen, Physicians &c.' thought it appropriate to resort to Boyle – now one of England's scientific elder statesmen – to inquire 'how they might improve themselves by their Travels to best advantage.' Because of their 'frequent Importunities' Boyle set about the task of drawing up a manual containing guidelines for how a natural history inventory of any region should be compiled, pausing to issue specific instructions for those travelling to the Far East, Turkey, Guinea, and the New World. It was a project, Boyle believed, of great intellectual and practical importance:

> Considering the great Improvements, that have of late been made of Natural History (the only sure Foundation of Natural Philosophy,) by the Travels of Gentlemen, Seamen, and others; And the gread [sic] Disadvantage many Ingenious Men are at in their Travels, by reason they know not before-hand, what things they are to inform themselves of in every Country they come to,

[1] R. E. W. Maddison, 'Studies in the life of Robert Boyle, F. R. S. Part VII. The Grand Tour', *Notes and Records of the Royal Society of London*, 20 (1965): 515–77.

or by what Method they may make Enquiries about things to be known there, I thought it would not be unacceptable to such, to have Directions in General, relating to all, and also in Particular, relating to Particular Countries, in as little Bounds as Possible, presented to their View.[2]

The topics Boyle chose to bring within the sphere of the inductive method were of considerable scope. Besides various features of the physical environment, Boyle insisted on the need to gather ethnographic data on native peoples and their traditions. The economic potential of regional reconnoitre did not escape his notice either: travellers were encouraged, for example, to be on the lookout for 'The Sign of Mines'. The resulting publication, enlarged by 'another hand', appeared in 1692, the year after his death, under the title *General Heads for the Natural History of a Country, Great or Small*.[3]

This latter-day concern of Boyle's serves to remind us of the close ties between voyaging, natural history, and regional geography. The expansion of Dutch trading routes, particularly in Southeast Asia through the offices of the Dutch East India Company, and the exploits of the English both in the Far East and in New England went hand in hand with the accumulation of ever more precise cartographic knowledge and the burgeoning of empirical data about the earth's surface. Boyle himself, we should recall, was director of the East India Company until 1677 and this, together with his governorship of the Society for the Propagation of the Gospel further underscores his economic and evangelistic interests in overseas ventures.[4] The conceptual and the commercial thus continued to serve each other's purposes throughout the seventeenth and eighteenth centuries in the accumulation of geographical knowledge no less than in other spheres of science.

If the drawing of the ageing Boyle into the realm of regional survey helped reinforce geography's long-standing ties with navigational concerns, so too did his commitment to the mechanical philosophy. To Boyle, the object of science was to give mathematical expression to natural law and thereby to advance a mechanistic conception of the natural order. For a considerable period of time geography had been taught in the universities in close association with astronomy and mathematics, largely because at least

---

[2] Robert Boyle, *General Heads for the Natural History of a Country, Great or Small; Drawn Out for the Use of Travellers and Navigators* (London, 1692), pp. 1–2.

[3] See also J. N. L. Baker, *The History of Geography* (Oxford: Blackwell, 1963), p. 23.

[4] John F. Fulton, 'The Honourable Robert Boyle, F. R. S. (1627–92)', *Notes and Records of the Royal Society of London*, 15 (1960): 119–35.

part of the geographical tradition – as we have seen – involved the search for precise knowledge of what we might call the 'mathematics of the globe'. And this had immediate practical consequences for navigators and cartographers whose very livelihoods depended upon the adequacy of their mathematical and technical competences. Thus geography's engagement with mathematical pursuits had both intellectual and practical implications: it kept geographical knowledge to the forefront of early science education in the university curriculum, while at the same time serving the commercial interests of the merchant classes. Indeed precisely because it was one of the very few subjects that maintained close ties between scholarship and craft skills – theory and practice – geography (as several recent historians have shown) had a crucial role to play in the rise of modern science.[5] As Lesley Cormack has put it:

> geographers, who were interested in increasing and developing their knowledge of the world, had to be theoretical, practical, and political. Geographers then were neither scholars nor craftsmen, nor even statesmen, but rather were a combination of all three . . . Geography thus stands as a model for the type of investigation which allowed its seventeenth-century practitioners to cast off the bonds of scholasticism and to enter a new, engaged era.[6]

Besides this, several of the other areas traditionally coming under the rubric of geography were beginning to experience the first flush of quantification. We have already noted that William Petty – an associate of Boyle's among the London scientific virtuosi and surveyor of Boyle's Irish estate – cultivated statistically based demography through his political arithmetic. But other areas were also receiving a mathematical baptism. In the early 1660s, for example, Christopher Wren (another of the Boyle scientific circle) invented one of England's earliest rain gauges, an altogether clever piece of scientific gadgetry by which rainfall could be recorded automatically on an hourly basis, while John Locke kept his own weather

[5] See, for example, Lesley Cormack, 'Non Sufficit Orbem: Geography as an Interactive Science at Oxford and Cambridge 1580–1620' (Ph.D. thesis, University of Toronto, 1988); Mordechai Feingold, *The Mathematicians' Apprenticeship. Science, Universities and Society in England 1560–1640* (Cambridge: Cambridge University Press, 1984); James McConica, 'Elizabethan Oxford: The Collegiate Society', in James McConica (ed.), *The History of the University of Oxford. Volume III. The Collegiate University* (Oxford: Clarendon Press, 1986), pp. 645–732.

[6] Lesley Cormack, 'The Social Context of Geography at Oxford and Cambridge, 1580–1620'. Paper presented at the Joint Conference of the British Society for the History of Science and the History of Science Society, Manchester University, July 1988.

and efficiency of an omnipotent and All-Wise Creator.' Ray's strategy, as implied in these words, was to work by analogy between the natural world and human contrivance, and so he elaborated eloquently and expansively the ways in which everything from the nesting habits of birds to the anatomy of camels afforded evidence of design. The whole edifice was erected on the belief that the world's human and animal inhabitants had been pre-adapted for conditions of life on earth.[10] And so from Ray's pen the notion of the earth as the planned abode of men and women received much impetus. But more than directing attention to the snug fit between the organic and inorganic worlds, the idea of divine design was a considerable spur to the empirical interrogation of nature. Experience, not scholarly erudition, was to Ray, as it was to many early advocates of science, the touchstone of knowledge. As he insisted:

> Let it not suffice us to be Book-learn'd, to read what others have written, and to take upon Trust more Falsehood than Truth; but let us ourselves examine Things as we have Opportunity, and converse with Nature as well as Books. Let us endeavour to promote and increase this Knowledge, and make new Discoveries . . . Let us not think that the Bounds of Science are fix'd.[11]

In the years following the appearance of Ray's classic, the selfsame viewpoint came through in the works of devotees like William Derham (1657–1735) whose *Physico-theology* – the Boyle lectures for 1711–12 – elaborated the evidence for divine benevolence that could be gleaned from the scrutiny of light, gravity, soils, landforms, human society, and the historical geography of the growth of Christendom. Again the emphasis was holistic, and the resort to organic ways of thinking has led some historians to suggest that physico-theology in this mode helped lay the foundations of ecological thinking.[12]

The theme of the fitness of the physical environment for its inhabitants also found its way into the more speculative cosmogonies that were issued during this period. The English clergyman Thomas Burnet (1635–1715) had already elaborated on the suitability of the earthly environment for human society in his *Sacred Theory of the Earth*, a work first published in Latin in 1681, but expanded and translated into English in 1684. Burnet's account assumed that the earth's present geomorphology was the consequence of its

---

[10] See John Hedley Brooke, 'Natural Theology in Britain from Boyle to Paley', in *New Interactions between Theology and Natural Science* (Milton Keynes: Open University Press, 1974), pp. 5–54.

[11] Quoted in Bowen, *Empiricism and Geographical Thought*, p. 110.

[12] So, Glacken, *Traces on the Rhodian Shore*.

having degenerated from a state of original perfection, and chief among the explanatory processes he invoked was the Noachian flood. Still, although the extremes to which he went in pursuing this line of reasoning drew forth censure from the Royal Society, his whole treatise was based on the latest statistical and geometric methods. Like Ray, Burnet rejected the 'dry philosophy' of Aristotle and the Schoolmen in favour of empirical investigation, thereby again revealing the mutual reinforcement natural theology and natural science received from each other.[13] Moreover, Burnet's treatise demonstrated the 'liberal' lengths to which physico-theology could stretch; for Burnet inveighed against the notion that 'this little planet . . . is the only habitable part of the Universe' and against the assumption of European superiority.[14]

The works of numerous other apologists for physico-theology might well be reviewed. For example, the theories of the earth advanced by John Woodward, which departed materially from Burnet's degenerative thesis, and by William Whiston, both published around the turn of the century, would merit scrutiny. But sufficient has been said to illustrate that numerous topics coming within the conventional reach of geography were to the fore in much physico-theological talk. Indeed it has been suggested that the idea of the hydrological cycle – a concept inexorably geographical in origin and evolution – was one of the most common vehicles for the communication of physico-theological principles throughout this whole era.[15] To be sure, this claim may be a bit extravagant; but it does nevertheless remind us of the particularly close marriage between geographical knowledge and natural theology in the early decades of the eighteenth century. And nowhere is this more clearly seen than in the evolution of German geography in the period.

The eleven-volume *Neue Erdbeschreibung* of Anton Friedrich Büsching (1724–93), for instance, was explicitly grounded in teleological convention. To him, geography's *raison d'être* lay in its investigation of the way in which the diversity of regions across the face of the earth, their political institutions, commercial relations, colonial history, and national identities all reflected the overriding rule of providence. Boundaries were thus 'grounded neither on chance, nor on the choice of the nations themselves, but on an almighty and all-wise Providence.' And alongside these political

[13] See G. L. Davies, *The Earth in Decay. A History of British Geomorphology 1578 to 1878* (London: MacDonald, n.d.), pp. 68–74.

[14] Quoted in Bowen, *Empiricism and Geographical Thought*, p. 109.

[15] Thus, Yi-Fu Tuan, *The Hydrological Cycle and the Wisdom of God: A Theme in Geoteleology* (Toronto: University of Toronto Press, 1968).

arrangements Büsching could detect an ecological economy that attested to providential overruling: the 'superfluity of one country abundantly supplies the wants of another.'[16]

Typical of the physico-theologists too, was Büsching's emphasis on first-hand experience, preferring the words of humble travellers to those of armchair scholars. The empathy that sensitive observers had with the objects of their scrutiny, moreover, not only produced better geography; it fostered humanitarianism. Büsching himself declared his conviction that racial differences were to be accounted for by environmental means – the influence of climate, soils, diet, and so on – and then went on to adopt what could be called an 'aesthetic relativism' by suggesting that what was considered beautiful differed from race to race and could not be objectively established. 'The inhabitants of the temperate Climates', he observed, 'have the whitest or fairest complexions. But whether these are the most beautiful among the species, or whether a well proportioned *Moor* or Black may not be reckoned as beautiful, I leave to the impartial determination of others.' Equally, he rejected the assumption of intrinsic cultural inferiority by asserting that an 'inhabitant of *Greenland* or *Lapland*, a *Moor* or a *Hottentot* is in his way as intelligent as one among the more civilized nations; and if the former had the same opportunities of improving his understanding and regulating his passions as the latter enjoys, he would not be inferior at all to him.'[17] Besides this, Büsching drew the newest statistical techniques into the realm of geographical discourse. Of crucial importance here was his reliance on the demographic work of Johann Peter Süssmilch, whose book *The Divine Order in the Variations of the Human Race* (1742) earned him, according to Margarita Bowen, 'recognition as the founder of population statistics in Germany.'[18] As the title of his treatise makes plain, Süssmilch was equally enthusiastic about natural theology and was therefore of special value to Büsching, whose own physico-theological conceptions continued to influence the German geographical tradition right through to the mid-nineteenth-century physical geography of K. F. R. Schneider.

The ways in which geography and natural theology served each other's interests were certainly not restricted to the scholarly realm. In the early

[16] A. F. Büsching, *A New System of Geography: In Which Is Given a General Account of the Situation and Limits, the Manners, History, and Constitution, of the Several Kingdoms and States of the Known World; And A Very Particular Description of their Subdivisions and Dependencies; their Cities and Towns, Forts, Sea-Ports, Produce, Manufactures, and Commerce*, 6 vols (London: A. Millar, 1762), vol. 1, p. 2.

[17] Ibid., vol. 1, p. 48.

[18] Bowen, *Empiricism and Geographical Thought*, p. 155.

eighteenth century clergymen and theologians used various means to spread knowledge of geography for religious purposes to their audiences. Edward Wells, rector of Cotesbach in Leicestershire, for example, issued in 1708 *An Historical Geography of the New Testament*, and later produced a comparable set of volumes for the Old Testament, which were intended to bring alive the biblical text by introducing readers to the geography and history of all the sites mentioned.[19] Again, the hymnwriter and doctor of divinity Isaac Watts published in 1726 *The First Principles of Astronomy and Geography*, a work devised for the instruction of the young in order to enhance their appreciation of scripture. Because the earth was 'the Theatre on which all the grand Affairs recorded in the Bible have been transacted,' Watts deemed it impossible to fully comprehend the salvation-history of Israel 'without some *Geographical* knowledge of those Countries.' The work had other purposes too. On the one hand Watts's compendium reinforced conventional values – the Hottentots were 'famous for their stupidity . . . as though they had little of human Nature in them beside the shape'; but on the other hand he raised the possibility that some of the planets were 'Habitable Worlds furnished with rich Variety of Inhabitants to the Praise of their great Creator.'[20]

There was, however, another medium of communication that reached a far wider audience than either elementary texts or scholarly tomes, a much neglected repository of geographical knowledge and ignored by historians of the subject, namely, the sermon. Ideas about nature and culture, wilderness and civilization were of course commonplace in preaching, not least among Puritans. To them the creation was the work of a rational, divine architect and its logical structure could therefore be disentangled by pious scrutiny; at the same time it was a place of mystery and ecstatic experience because it was the expression of an incomprehensible supernatural agent. The rational wing of Puritanism thus emphasized the orderly handiwork of the creator and this was accordingly a great incentive to Puritan science; Puritan pietism, by contrast, accented the mysteriousness of the natural world. Here I propose to illustrate some of these themes by the use of one

---

[19] Edward Wells, *An Historical Geography of the New Testament. In Two Parts . . . Being a Geographical and Historical Account of all the Places Mention'd, or Referr'd to, in the Books of the New Testament* . . . (London, 1708). See the brief discussion in Robin Butlin, 'George Adam Smith and the Historical Geography of the Holy Land: Contents, Contexts and Connections', *Journal of Historical Geography*, 14 (1988): 381–404.

[20] Isaac Watts, *The Knowledge of the Heavens and the Earth Made Easy: or, The First Principles of Astronomy and Geography Explain'd by the Use of Globes and Maps: With a Solution of the Common Problems by a* Plain Scale and Compass *as well as by the* Globe (London, 3rd edn 1736), pp. vi, 83, 103.

particular topic, the earthquake, in order to show the sort of role geographical knowledge could play in the moral economy.[21] Other themes, of
course, would do just as well. The love-hate relationship to the forest and
the wilderness among the New England preachers and scientists, or
Jonathan Edwards's mystic celebration of nature, for example, would
doubtless be every bit as instructive.[22] But with the earthquake we
encounter a phenomenon that nicely illustrates the tensions between the
rational and the mystic approach to nature.

In the period from around 1693 to 1755, the preachers of earthquake sermons favoured a rationalist account of the phenomenon, namely, that they
had natural causes and could be explained by the methods of scientific
investigation. Of course there were some who used the earthquake as the
launching pad for speaking of divine intervention, and to reinforce a sense
of the mystery of life. But what was far more common was the attempt to
use natural scientific explanations as the vehicles for moralizing. Thus in
the sermons of one Thomas Doolittle, numerous sophisticated scientific
explanations of earthquakes were advanced and the meteorological events
that were believed to herald earth tremors were also catalogued. And yet
interwoven with the scientific accounts that might be given of them, many
earthquakes were equally regarded as supernatural events; they were indicative of divine displeasure, and were therefore the grounds for moral reformation by the creative transformation of mortal dread into godly fear.
Earthquakes, in other words, were dramatic instances of the linkages
between God's physical and moral government of the world, while the ter-
ror they induced was regarded as a powerful agent of social change.
Throughout the length and breadth of the Puritan cosmogony, in which all
of creation served human purposes, preachers worked with a concept of
nature and culture, environment and society, that emphasized the interdependence of the rational and the moral.

From these reflections it is plain that geographical knowledge could be
used to subserve a variety of religious and moral purposes. And of course it
continued to further imperial interests too. Numerous geographies, amount-
ing to little more than commercial compilations and regional inventories,
were produced during the first half of the eighteenth century. To be sure,
this 'capes and bays' geography may seem arid to modern eyes; but the fact
that many of them were reissued again and again in new editions testifies to

---

[21] In what follows I have relied on Maxine Van de Wetering, 'Moralizing in Puritan
Natural Science: Mysteriousness in Earthquake Sermons', *Journal of the History of Ideas*, 43
(1982): 417–38.
[22] See Perry Miller, *Errand into the Wilderness* (New York: Harper Books, 1956).

the needs that they satisfied in society at the time. Laurence Echard's *Compendium of Geography*, for example, had already gone through some eighteen editions by 1713, while Pat Gordon's *Geography Anatomiz'd or, the Geographical Grammar* reached its twentieth edition by 1754. Works of this sort presented a bird's-eye view of the world, country by country, cataloguing the whole gamut of human activities from economy and religion to transport and government. The various later Universal Geographies and Geographical Grammars of writers like Thomas Salmon, Andrew Brice, John Payne, Alexander Adam, John Barrow, and William Guthrie, the specifics of which need not detain us, nevertheless demonstrate the continuing vitality of this tradition which kept the science of geography closely tied to commercial and imperial enterprises.[23]

Having sketched, albeit in outline, the features of the physico-theological geography that flourished in the eighteenth century and made some observations on the sort of social interests it could service, we should now pause to consider the philosophical moves that were afoot in this whole project. Let us recognize right away that the philosophical mainsprings of natural theology can be traced back to earlier figures like Aquinas, Augustine, and Scotus; but it was in the eighteenth century that scientific data were more explicitly drawn into the arena of debate. In order to get a handle on the sort of issues involved it will be profitable to distinguish between two different types of design argument: the argument *to* design, and the argument *from* design.[24] The argument *to* design goes something like this. Since the world is the creation of a supreme divine agent it will provide evidence of his design. Here the idea of design is premised on the existence of God and the argument moves as it were *from* God *to* design. By contrast the argument *from* design simply moves the other way: the evident instances of design in the world provide grounds for belief in the existence of God. Perhaps it could be said that the former is merely a confessional claim (belief in design follows from belief in God) whereas the latter is a philosophical argument (divine existence can be established from observed design in the world). It is, of course, difficult in reading any particular text to determine just which strategy is in operation, and both versions certainly stimulated much interest in the interrogation of the natural world in order to identify its marvellous design. But in so far as practitioners were seeking

[23] These are discussed in detail in Alan Downes, 'The Bibliographic Dinosaurs of Georgian Geography (1714–1830)', *Geographical Journal*, 137 (1971): 379–87; Bowen, *Empiricism and Geographical Thought*.

[24] See Thomas McPherson, *The Argument from Design* (London: Macmillan, 1972).

a philosophical justification for their religious beliefs there were indeed crucial conceptual manoeuvres in operation.

What was at stake in the construction of the argument *from* design, I believe, was a fundamental question about the proper grounds of rational belief. What was to count, in other words, as a rational claim about something? During the period with which we are concerned – for the sake of convenience it might be labelled the Enlightenment – one overwhelmingly influential answer was forthcoming, classical foundationalism, a principle insisting that all rational beliefs had to be erected on some indubitable foundation. Essentially, this meant that a belief was considered rational if, and only if, it was based on propositions that are self-evident or evident to the senses and therefore incorrigible for the holder. As it developed, the principle came to mean that the only beliefs that could be classified as rational were those based on either logic or science. And so it was plain that if belief in the existence of God was to pass muster as a rational belief, that is, beyond mere faith or conviction, it needed to be justified by the apparatus of scientific observation. Hence many turned to design in the world as providing an indubitable foundation for their theological claims. Implicit here was the idea that rational belief in God could not be the basis of knowing; rather it had to be the result of philosophical or scientific investigation. And so it was almost inevitable that those who accepted classical foundationalism would turn to the scientific investigation of nature for theological reasons. Subsequently, of course, the classical foundationalist model has crumbled as its philosophical inadequacies have been exposed. For one thing the principle itself is neither self-evident nor incorrigible! At this point, however, the details of that critique need not concern us. All we need to recognize is that the teleological geography that we have been examining had a hidden conceptual agenda that was every bit as far-reaching as its social one.[25]

THE KANTIAN TURN: GEOGRAPHY DE-THEOLOGIZED

Perhaps the greatest intellectual challenge to the design argument, and to conventional 'proofs' for the existence of God more generally, was to come from the pen of the Prussian philosopher, Immanuel Kant (1724–1804). We will come presently to the implications of Kantian philosophy for geography, but first it will be profitable to consider Kant's own views about the

[25] See the discussion in Alvin C. Plantinga, 'The Reformed Objection to Natural Theology', *Christian Scholar's Review*, 11, 3 (1982): 187–98.

nature of geography itself, for the great Enlightenment philosopher did deliver lectures on physical geography at the University of Königsberg for forty years from 1756 until 1796.[26]

The cognitive content of Kant's geography was conditioned substantially by his understanding of the conceptual territory it occupied within the structure of the sciences. For him a fundamental distinction was to be drawn between the rational sciences and the empirical sciences, the former encompassing those spheres of thought like philosophy and mathematics in which knowledge could be derived purely by the use of reason, the latter dealing with the world of experience and the senses and therefore subsuming both the natural and the human sciences. Understandably, physical geography was allocated its own niche in the empirical domain and, following the earlier prescriptions of Büsching, Kant described physical geography as that branch of learning dealing with the natural conditions of the earth, its mountains, rivers, plants, minerals, and so on. Moreover, as geographical commentators – ever with an eye to geographical apologetic and tireless of elaborating definitions of the field – have been at pains to point out, Kant included 'man' within the scope of the subject because human anatomy, culture, and moral patterns manifested themselves in the world of 'outer sense'. Certainly Kant considered that geography and history had resort to quite different modes of explanation, geography having to do with space, history with time; and yet his inclusion of the human within the orbit of physical geography serves to illustrate that the boundaries between history, anthropology, and geography were far from watertight.

Further elaboration of the precise content of Kant's geography need not detain us here, for in large measure the specifics of his teaching were culled from the conventional German geographical lore of the day, and from Büsching and Varenius in particular. More significant, I think, was Kant's conception of the role geography could play in human knowledge more generally, for he believed it provided a vehicle for unifying understanding of the world. As he saw it, geography could help break through the multitude of discrete data – the bits of piecemeal information of the world of experience – to a unity of knowledge. According to Hartshorne, this general framework for knowledge found its focus in Kant's idea of *Raum* (area or space), a holistic notion in which the findings of subjects ranging from

---

[26] On Kant's geographical work see J. A. May, *Kant's Concept of Geography and its Relation to Recent Geographical Thought* (University of Toronto, Department of Geography Research Publications, 1970); Bowen, *Empiricism and Geographical Thought*, pp. 206–9; Hartshorne, *The Nature of Geography*, pp. 35–40.

anatomy to zoology could be held together as parts of a single whole.[27] Indeed, it was just this idea that prompted Bowen to comment that Kant assigned 'to geography the function of Bacon's universal science.'[28] As Kant saw it, apparently, the notion of *Raum* provided a sort of organizing principle for holding together the multitudinous diversities of the natural world, and therefore he saw geography as a synoptic discipline synthesizing the findings of other sciences. In sum, Kant's allocation of the spatial realm to geography was part and parcel of his concern to carve out a set of permanent domains to be occupied by the various sciences. It was an 'essentialist', not an 'empirical', project, seeking for the intrinsic nature of disciplines rather than looking to see what geography was taken to be by its various practitioners.

The popularity of Kant's lecture course and his influence on Humboldt and, to a lesser degree, Ritter is no doubt sufficient justification for these brief observations on Kant's geography. But as Hartshorne himself has wryly commented, if our interest in Kant stops with his elucidation of geography's place in the sciences it would be wiser to 'return [it] to an historical footnote.' 'On other aspects of his role in the history of geography,' Hartshorne goes on, however, 'much more needs to be said.'[29] In my view, this judgement is entirely correct. For as I see it, it was Kant's assault on the various arguments for the existence of God that was to be of most significance, and accordingly I propose to turn now to that topic.

In order to grasp the nature of this dimension of Kant's thinking we need to appreciate the distinction he made between what he called the 'noumena' and the 'phenomena'. At the risk of oversimplifying I think it can be said that the 'noumena' refers to the world of external reality; for Kant, however, we never have direct access to this world because our knowledge of it is always mediated through our perceptual apparatus. All we know are the 'phenomena' or appearances – not things as they are in themselves, but rather as they appear to us. Space, time, number, causality, entities of all kinds – these are not to be thought of as belonging to the world itself; rather they are imposed on it by mind. It is the mind, then, that creates order and structure out of the confused flux of fragmentary data that are presented to it, and so, in a real sense, the human mind never *describes* the truth about how things are in the world; instead it *constitutes* that truth.

[27] Hartshorne, *Nature of Geography*, p. 44.

[28] Bowen, *Empiricism and Geographical Thought*, p. 208.

[29] Richard Hartshorne, 'On the Role of Immanuel Kant in the History of Geographic Thought'. Paper presented to the Association of American Geographers Annual Meeting, 23 April 1975, p. 16.

And so Kant opened up an unbridgeable chasm between mind and world, and cut knowledge adrift from the realm of external reality. Science accordingly is only valid within the 'phenomenal' sphere: it deals with observation, cause and effect relations, spatio-temporal properties. But science can never break through to the shadowy world of the noumena, for science's practitioners are never free from the mental spectacles that provide the very modes in which all of us actually conceive of entities and events. The world, as it were, mirrors the mind, not the other way round.

It was immediately apparent from this ontological bifurcation that the traditional arguments for the existence of God could never provide sure knowledge of a divine being. Evidently, if knowledge of the world itself is forever inaccessible to us, then ideas of cause and purpose in nature tell us only about our ways of conceiving. This, of course, is not to say that Kant necessarily rejected belief in the existence of God; it is to say that metaphysical knowledge could never be had from the scrutiny of science. Indeed Kant did tantalizingly quip that he had to deny *knowledge* of God in order to leave room for faith. Further elaboration of Kant's critique of the various arguments for divine existence need not be pursued here for the simple reason that their implications for geography are already plain: metaphysical conclusions about divine existence could never be had from the scrutiny of the sensible world. For science and religion occupy entirely different realms.[30]

It is precisely because Kant thus de-theologized the scientific study of the natural world that Büttner speaks of the Kantian 'emancipation of geography' from theology, and argues that Kant thereby returned to the earlier geographical position of Keckermann. As he writes:

> Kant joins the debate by making clear with inexorable poignancy (in doing so he goes decisively further than his teacher Wolff) that geography can help neither to prove the existence of God nor to furnish proof against his existence (as the advocates of the French Enlightenment especially tried to do). Geography is theologically neutral. Thus Kant returns to the view of Keckermann.[31]

In Kant, then, we see the disengagement of geography from providential teleology – 'perhaps his greatest service to our subject' according to Hartshorne.[32] Mountains are formed according to natural law and it is the

---

[30] S. Körner, *Kant* (Harmondsworth: Penguin, 1955); Ian Barbour, *Issues in Science and Religion* (New York: Harper and Row, 1966), pp. 74–8.

[31] Manfred Büttner, 'Kant and the Physico-Theological Consideration', p. 239.

[32] Hartshorne, 'The Role of Kant', p. 2.

geographer's duty to investigate these rather than speculating on their supposed role in the divine economy. And precisely the same holds true for the ebb and flow of tides, the course of rivers, the distribution of plants and animals, and the relationship between organisms and environment: divinity should not be sought here, for God is forever banished to the outer fringes of an unknowable noumenon. Of course this does not mean that teleological thinking cannot be a useful heuristic device. It has analogical value suggesting plausible modes of explanation and providing hints about which processes merit observation; but it emphatically does not tell us anything substantive about the things-in-themselves.

While I have dubbed this theological evacuation of geography the Kantian turn, it would be quite mistaken to think that Kant was its only or even primary exponent. Even before Kant had declared his own convictions on the subject, George Louis Leclerc, the Comte de Buffon (1707–88), had constructed a universal cosmogony along naturalistic lines – a scheme to which Kant himself resorted.[33] Buffon, director of the Jardin du Roi in Paris, crossed swords with the faculty of theology at the Sorbonne over his dating of the age of the earth and his bringing the human species within the ambit of the animal world. But arguably of even greater importance for the secularizing of science was the ridicule he heaped on the earlier cosmogonies of Burnet and Woodward, whose science he saw as the illegitimate offspring of a union between natural history and theology. To be sure, Buffon paid lip service in his multi-volume *Histoire Naturelle* to divine agency as the prime cause of phenomena; but he was determined to keep such physico-theological vagaries out of the science arena. So rather than looking to the biblical deluge as the cause of geological and geomorphological phenomena, he advanced naturalistic explanations of earth history, preferring to offer his own speculations about the earth's origination as a chunk of solar stuff chipped from the parent mass through collision with a fast-moving comet. Moreover, Buffon departed from the standard Linnaean classification system that took the boundaries of organic groupings as the steadfast and unchangeable expression of divine plan. Instead, he worked with the idea that classifications – far from being divine templates for creation – were rather tools that naturalists had manufactured to help them impose order on their experience of nature. In these ways, then, both

[33] See Stanley L. Jaki, 'Introduction', in Immanuel Kant, *Universal Natural History and Theory of the Heavens*, translated with Introduction and Notes by Stanley L. Jaki (Edinburgh: Scottish Academic Press, 1981).

cosmologically and taxonomically, Buffon engaged himself in the project of diminishing divine participation in the world of natural phenomena.[34]

The implications of Buffon's removal of providential intervention from nature for the study of topics coming under the rubric of geography are perhaps most immediately apparent in his thinking on questions of biogeographical distribution and on the relationship between human culture and environment. As far as the former were concerned, Buffon radically departed from the standard resort to an original post-deluge dispersal of all life from Mount Ararat as the explanation of organic distribution. Rather he looked to historical and ecological causes, explaining biogeographical patterns by reference to migration and climatic factors, and for this reason he has been widely regarded as the father of biogeography. More, the interrelationships Buffon postulated between organisms and their environments, together with his vitriolic rejection of Linnaeus's static taxonomic system, helped pave the way for the work of later evolutionists, even though he himself resolutely refused to countenance transformism.[35]

As for questions about the relationship between human culture and environment, Buffon had little patience with those romantic visionaries who traced the progress of civilization to genial physical environments, especially when these arguments were harnessed and put to physico-theological work. As Glacken has put it: 'In rejecting the idea of final causes, Buffon rejected also the old belief in a divinely designed earth; in emphasizing the power of man in changing nature he offered an alternative to an older environmentalism . . . To Buffon the changes which man had made on the earth were inextricably woven into the history of civilization.'[36] Through the arts of agriculture, animal domestication, migration, adaptation, and a host of other cultural practices, the human species had emancipated itself from the tyranny of nature and had transformed the world for its own purposes. Here, it is plain, the older theological teleology was replaced with what we might call an anthropocentric teleology.

This emphasis on the social utility of geographical knowledge also comes through in what has been described as the 'central document of the

---

[34] On Buffon, see Peter J. Bowler, *Evolution. The History of an Idea* (Berkeley: University of California Press, 1984), pp. 32–6, 67–72; Jacques Roger, *Les Sciences de la Vie dans la Pensée Français du XVIIIe Siècle* (Paris: Armand Colin, 1963).

[35] Ernst Mayr, *The Growth of Biological Thought: Diversity, Evolution, and Inheritance* (Cambridge, Mass.: Harvard University Press, 1982), pp. 341, 530–7.

[36] Clarence J. Glacken, 'Count Buffon on Cultural Changes of the Physical Environment', *Annals of the Association of American Geographers*, 50 (1960): 1–21, ref. on p. 20. It should be pointed out that Buffon did acknowledge that the soul sets humanity apart from the rest of organic life.

Enlightenment' – Diderot and D'Alembert's *Encyclopédie* (1751–66).[37] The materialism of these Enlightenment encyclopedists, stemming from the writings of figures like Julien Offray de la Mettrie, author of *L'Homme Machine* (1747), and Baron d'Holbach, whose *Système de la Nature* (1770) was regarded as the bible of atheism, surfaced in Diderot's increasing proclivity to incorporate everything from poetry to science within a materialist system. In this context it is not surprising that geography was allocated its place in that branch of the tree of knowledge that was concerned with the physical and mathematical sciences of nature. Even *géographie ecclesiastique, géographie civile ou politique* and *géographie historique* were similarly subsumed under the same rubric because these too had their social uses in Diderot's grand Baconian vision of material progress through the enlargement of science.[38]

NOT WITHOUT A PLAN

For all the philosophical attacks on the argument from design, and it has to be conceded that even Kant's assault was altogether half-hearted, teleological modes of thought lingered long in geographical theorizing during the final decades of the eighteenth century and on into the nineteenth century. The motivations for their retention were certainly many and diverse: social, scientific, theological, political. Some reflections on the structure and comprehensiveness of the teleological tradition as the eighteenth century drew to a close will therefore be valuable.

On the surface, it might seem that when James Hutton (1726–97), the putative founder of modern geomorphology, broke through the 4004 BC chronology of Archbishop James Ussher and reported that 'no vestige of a beginning – no prospect of an end' could be detected in nature, he was banishing God from the kingdom of earth science. Hutton had set out his thoughts on the subject in a presentation he made to the Royal Society of Edinburgh which appeared in its Transactions in 1788 and then in his two-volume *Theory of the Earth* of 1795. Here he argued that the earth's landforms were the result of the ordinary processes of uplift, erosion, and deposition, and were not due to catastrophic events like the biblical flood. Crucial to his scheme was his assumption that the earth's central heat

[37] Thomas. L. Hankins, *Science and the Enlightenment* (Cambridge: Cambridge University Press, 1985), p. 170.

[38] See Charles W. J. Withers, 'A Note on the Term "Historical Geography" in Diderot's *Encyclopédie*', unpublished typescript.

transformed eroded debris into sedimentary rocks which were in turn elevated to form dry land. To Hutton the history of the earth was thus the story of an unending series of cycles that kept everything in a steady state. Because Hutton would brook no recourse to preternatural agencies and consistently insisted in interpreting the history of the earth in terms of present-day processes and rates – that is, those currently observable – he earned the reputation as the founder of uniformitarianism.[39]

Jettisoning the Mosaic deluge and the catastrophist cosmogonies of the earlier physico-theologists certainly did not mean that Hutton broke free from teleological modes of thinking. To the contrary, he declared that the globe was 'evidently made for man.' The threat to orthodoxy that critics found at the heart of his cyclical theory thus became the very order that impressed on him the 'wisdom of the system.'[40] Now to be sure, Hutton's theology was far from Christian orthodoxy. He was a deist; but his deism underpinned his earth theory every bit as much as did the conventional theism of other natural theologians. As Laudan has neatly summarized it: 'the deity's perfection would be mirrored in a natural world that was so designed and balanced that it could maintain indefinitely a surface suited for God's creatures.'[41] Indeed we might well ask ourselves if it was not for theological reasons that Hutton wanted a cyclical theory of the earth. Be that as it may, there is little doubt that Hutton's scientifico-theological professions were themselves a product of Scottish culture during the period of what has been called the Scottish Enlightenment.

Of central importance to the philosophical architects of the eighteenth-century Scottish tradition was the perceived need to maintain links between moral philosophy and natural science. What they wanted was a comprehensive world-view in which nature and human existence had meaning within an overarching divine plan. In such a context science could be pursued without constant worries about transgressing the detailed authority of scripture, and yet also without the complete autonomy and ensuing recklessness that led along the dark path of Continental materialism. Hutton's earth science certainly played its part in the project of keeping natural the-

---

[39] For details of Hutton's work, see Rachel Laudan, *From Mineralogy to Geology. The Foundations of a Science, 1650–1830* (Chicago: University of Chicago Press, 1987), chapter 6; Davies, *Earth in Decay*, chapter 6; Bowler, *Evolution*, pp. 41–5.

[40] James Hutton, 'Theory of the Earth; or an Investigation of the Laws Observable in the Composition, Dissolution, and Restoration of Land Upon the Globe', *Transactions of the Royal Society of Edinburgh*, 1 (1788): 209–304, ref. on pp. 209–10; James Hutton, *Dissertations on Different Subjects in Natural Philosophy* (Edinburgh: Strahan and Cadell, 1792), p. 262.

[41] Laudan, *From Mineralogy to Geology*, p. 115.

ology, natural science, and social philosophy in conceptual equilibrium.[42] This is plainly revealed, for example, in his lifelong interest in agricultural improvement and in what we would today call demonstration farming; the betterment of society through the application of scientific procedures was the very stuff of Scotland's Enlightenment aspirations and that vision underlay the institution of a Society of Improvers in Knowledge of Agriculture. Take as just a single example the case of the Revd Dr John Walker (1731–1803). His teaching on agricultural economics was subsumed within his instruction in natural history, thereby again revealing how scientific investigation, philosophical speculation, and material improvement were all welded together. Here the institutional pursuit of environmental knowledge was all of a piece with the maintenance of the social order.[43]

However untouched Continental earth science remained from the Huttonian model – Continental geologists continued to follow Werner's principles – Hutton's resort to the idea of a designed world was shared by several major theorists of environment and culture across the English Channel. If the setting for the human drama, namely the earth's surface, was teleologically interpretable, well then, the history of human life on the globe was no less susceptible to the vocabulary of purpose and design. Nowhere is this more evident than in the writings of Montesquieu and Herder.

Although his originality has been questioned, Charles-Louis de Secondat, Baron de Montesquieu (1689–1755), undoubtedly exerted a tremendous influence on eighteenth-century thought, largely through his *magnum opus*, *The Spirit of the Laws*, published in Geneva in 1748. The book was an instant success, and not surprisingly, for Montesquieu had poured into it everything there was of himself: judge, historian, traveller, novelist. The volume's evident aim was to define the structure of law and to impose a coherence on the infinite range of social rules governing society. The way Montesquieu chose to approach his theme was to locate legislative regulation within the context of what he called 'the nature of things'. By so contextualizing law and custom he could show how they were related to the entire social and environmental conditions of which they were a part. At heart his thesis was that the cultural characteristics that shape and

[42] Arthur Donovan, 'James Hutton and the Scottish Enlightenment: Some Preliminary Considerations', *Scotia* 1 (1977): 56–68.

[43] See Charles W. Withers, 'Improvement and Enlightenment: Agriculture and Natural History in the Work of the Rev. Dr John Walker (1731–1803)', in Peter Jones (ed.), *Philosophy and Science in the Scottish Enlightenment* (Edinburgh: John Donald, 1989), pp. 102–16; Charles W. Withers, 'The Rev. Dr John Walker and the Practice of Natural History in Late Eighteenth Century Scotland', *Archives of Natural History*, 18 (1991): 201–20.

condition humanity were moulded by environmental factors, like climate and soil. Accordingly he presented evidence from far and wide, drawn from the burgeoning travel literature, that revealed to him how climatic conditions governed not only the degeneration or persistence of cultural traits, but also such universal experiences as pain and love-making. The hot climates of the East, he urged, explained its unchanging religion and customs; coldness and humidity precipitated drunkenness; slavery was a product of climatic zones inducing laziness; and so on. Thus arguing that everything from human physiology to social practices, from religious principles to moral judgements, was geographically conditioned, he presented the case for cultural relativism. For plainly if geographical circumstances differed from place to place, then so too would social mores. And yet while such professions were deeply disturbing to clerical readers, Montesquieu's schema was ultimately grounded in a deistic natural theology. For him, the very idea of law, whether natural or social, only made sense in the context of belief in a supremely intelligent being. Just as every artefact has a craftsman, and every machine an artisan, so every law has a legislator, whether human or divine. Certainly Montesquieu resisted any conflation of natural and human law, but as Shklar notes, 'Deism allowed Montesquieu to think that the laws of physical motion, animal instinct, and social rulers were somehow alike, except that we are able to refuse to follow the latter two.'[44]

One of the most trenchant criticisms of climatic determinism in the Montesquieu vein was to come from the pen of Johann Gottfried Herder (1744–1803), one of the two individuals (the other was Alexander von Humboldt) whom Glacken regards as 'representatives of ideas held toward the earth as a whole in the late eighteenth and early nineteenth centuries.'[45] The gist of his argument was simply that, granted that we humans are influenced by environmental conditions, it is just wrong to conclude that the effects are either uniform or universal; environmental determinists, to put it another way, invariably indulged in the pastime of overgeneralizing from one or two cases. Herder's own major work, *Ideas for a Philosophy of the History of Mankind* (1784–91), was itself a masterful synthesis laying out his thoughts on the reciprocity of nature and culture, environment and society. And synthesis indeed it was, for in it the contributions of dozens of geographical texts were reviewed: small wonder that Guthe named Herder as one of the three founding fathers of modern geography (the others were Humboldt and Ritter). Yet again teleological modes of thinking are plainly in evidence, for Herder spoke of the fitness of the earth for humankind,

[44] Judith N. Shklar, *Montesquieu* (Oxford: Oxford University Press, 1987), p. 71.
[45] Glacken, *Traces on the Rhodian Shore*, p. 537.

describing it as the stage on which the divine drama of history unfolded. Divine planning was, he believed, detectable in the location of particular physical features, the locus of the human race's origin, the patterns of world settlement, and the relative distribution of landmass in the two hemispheres. Throughout, he drew liberally on the writings of travellers, using their accounts of the different peoples they encountered to inform his speculations about racial history and to provide ethnographic sketches of various ethnic groups – the Eskimos, Lapps, Berbers, and so on. In this way Herder reinforced the long-standing links between the geographical tradition and the pursuit of anthropology.[46]

Just as Hutton's deism was philosophically domiciled in the context of Scottish Enlightenment values and Montesquieu's environmentalism in his efforts to keep social and natural law in conceptual tandem, so Herder's ethno-geography found its cognitive niche in the cultural nationalism movement of eighteenth-century Germany. This asserted, according to Gerald Broce, 'the equal worth of "authentic" German culture, so widely held in contempt for its political and literary backwardness, and aimed to throw off the foreign and especially the French models of "culture" that had permeated the upper classes. In other words, ideas forged in his [Herder's] early demands for equality and freedom of his own culture shaped his anthropology.' Each culture, to put it another way, could only be understood in terms of its own scale of values. If Broce is correct in this assessment, then the mainspring of Herder's insatiable fascination with cultural diversities and its ensuing cultural relativism is to be found in his concern to vindicate the legitimacy of his own cultural traditions. Accordingly, in his review of the cultural geography of South American Indians he extolled those travel writers who had the capacity to 'place themselves into the customs and culture' of the peoples they studied. The understanding of cultures was thus to be achieved not by rational analysis, general principles, natural laws, or classificatory devices, but by *Einfühlen* (empathy) and therefore with the qualities of the artist rather than the logician or the scientist. Imagination, reconstructive imagination – not analysis – was the key to grasping the life-world of an entire society. By this essentially ethnographic method, Herder found himself able both to empathize with and to

---

[46] On Herder, see H. B. Nisbet, *Herder and Scientific Thought* (Cambridge: The Modern Humanities Research Association, 1970); F. McEachran, *The Life and Philosophy of Johann Gottfried Herder* (Oxford: Clarendon Press, 1939); Robert T. Clark, Jr., *Herder: His Life and Thought* (Berkeley and Los Angeles: University of California Press, 1969). An introduction to certain aspects of Herder's geography is available in J. A. C. Birkenhauer, 'Johann Gottfried Herder', *Geographers. Biobibliographical Studies*, 10 (1986): 77–84.

impose coherence upon tribal practices that hitherto seemed utterly bizarre to European eyes, as well as to sanction a pluralism that gave his own Germanic heritage a rightful place in the scheme of things.[47] A profound respect for community, for difference, for locale thus characterized what might be christened the Herderian vision, with the result that, as Isaiah Berlin puts it, 'all regionalists, all defenders of the local against the universal, all champions of deeply rooted forms of life . . . owe something, whether they know it or not, to the doctrines which Herder . . . introduced into European thought.'[48] And yet world history was something more than just the collective doings of divergent cultural groups; it had a direction, a movement, a tendency towards an ultimate goal – a utopian kingdom of truth and cooperation of which divine providence was the architect.

If both the history of the earth and the history of its human inhabitants were subject to the presiding hand of divinity, it is scarcely surprising that the biogeographical distribution of plant and animal populations was commonly given a teleological gloss. Nor is it surprising that in the late eighteenth century there was substantial two-way traffic between the models of natural history and those of social theory. The economy and polity of nature was often spoken of, and spoken of moreover as revealing the theological purposes for which it had been created. In this way nastiness in nature – struggle, suffering, and death – no less than in society could be sanguinely welcomed as the price to be paid for higher purposes.

Still, it would be mistaken to assume that design arguments of this sort always surfaced in precisely the same way. The enterprise that I have just mentioned – the study of biogeography – amply illustrates this. For here there were frequent disputes about just how plant and animal distributions were to be explained – even within the context of natural theology. There was, for example, much disagreement as to whether they were to be accounted for by the processes of migration from a single centre or whether they were the product of a range of creations in several indigenous geographical zones. Could the plants found in the Alpine peaks and the Peruvian cordillera be equally the result of migration from an original location in Asia Minor? Migration versus environmental influence, single versus multiple creation all provided radically different answers. And of course before long there were those like Eberhard Zimmermann seeking for mediating positions between the Linnaean resort to migration and the Buffonian

---

[47] Gerald Broce, 'Herder and Ethnography', *Journal of the History of the Behavioural Sciences*, 22 (1986): 150–70, citations from pp. 151–2, 159.
[48] Isaiah Berlin, *Vico and Herder. Two Studies in the History of Ideas* (London: Chatto and Windus, 1976), p. 176.

emphasis on environment. Thus during the period when the world's major natural biogeographical regions were first beginning to be delineated, theological concerns insinuated their way right into the heart of the debate. So in the pioneering biogeographical works of men like K. L. Willdenow and Zimmermann, following in the wake of Linnaeus and Buffon, the idea that the world's geographical patterns of organic life had been ordained by the Creator was of crucial importance, and it was around this foundational conviction that debates about migration, adaptation, the permanence of species, and the role of environment, revolved.[49] Of course, what gave the greatest empirical stimulus to these theoretical questions were the various scientific voyages that were undertaken during the period. And it is to these that we must now turn.

NATURALISTS AND NAVIGATORS

The social theories of the armchair philosophers of environment and culture owed their very lifeblood to the scientific voyages that mushroomed during the eighteenth century. Previously, expeditions were fuelled by commercial and imperial zealotry, often tinged with evangelistic impulses. But during the Enlightenment, ostensibly more purely 'scientific' travel aroused greater and greater interest. Certainly it would be mistaken to take the travelling naturalists' apologetic rhetoric of 'science for science's sake' at face value; for geographical knowledge was geopolitical power. Still, the self-conscious objective of gathering data for scientific purposes heralded a much closer relationship between the pursuits of the naturalist and the navigator. The establishment of major natural history repositories like the London Kew Gardens and the Jardin du Roi in Paris under Buffon, both of which housed plants from all over the world, is only one illustration of this relationship. The patronizing of scientific missions by bodies like the Royal Society and the French Académie des Sciences is another. And on the more purely cognitive front the new classification schemes, like that of Linnaeus, which emerged to satisfy hitherto unprecedented taxonomic needs further reinforces the point. What with the development of new techniques of analysis, new instruments of surveying, new species of explorer, and new forms of organization, there is much justification for naming this era the

[49] See James Larson, 'Not Without a Plan: Geography and Natural History in the Late Eighteenth Century', *Journal of the History of Biology*, 19 (1986): 447–88; Gareth Nelson, 'From Candolle to Croizat: Comments on the History of Biogeography', *Journal of the History of Biology*, 11 (1978): 269–305.

second great age of discovery, as William Goetzmann has done. Throughout, a passion for precision characterized the whole enterprise: mathematical precision in astronomical observation, in cartographic accuracy, and in scientific illustration.[50] By these representational devices, the categories of European scientific ways of seeing came close to enclose – engulf – non-Western realms. These precision tools, indeed, became the very instruments used to cut the template on which the idea of the exotic was fashioned. Thereby the representation and constitution of 'otherness' went hand in hand.

The ramifications of the growth of scientific travel were evidently far-reaching, and it is clearly impossible here to exhaust the range and depth of its influence on the geographical tradition. Instead I hope to convey something of the flavour of the enterprise by restricting my comments to three subjects. First, I intend to focus on one or two specific expeditions in order to illustrate their logistic and informational achievements. Then I shall depart momentarily from scientific questions to reflect on the impact these travels made on the world of art, not least to illustrate geography's continuing links with the aesthetic realm. Finally, I hope to show just how crucial this whole endeavour was to what might be called the Humboldtian project.

Scientific Travel

The transformation of circumnavigation from hit-and-miss adventuring to orchestrated expedition owed much to the dedication of one man – Captain James Cook (1728–79). For from the start, Cook ensured that his crew comprised not only scientifically trained officers, but also landscape painters, natural history draughtsmen, and professional astronomers, surgeons and naturalists. Certainly Cook's engagement in scientific mission had its predecessors: in 1764 Commodore John Bryon was assigned the task of seeking for unknown lands in the Atlantic Ocean with climates conducive to commercial exploitation; similarly Louis Antoine, Comte de Bougainville – already with a substantial scholarly reputation for his *Treatise on Integral Calculus* – set out in 1766 with a fully equipped scientific crew to establish for the French Acadians a settlement bridgehead in one of the remaining American territories. In their cases, no less than with Cook, the integration of science and imperialism are only too clearly dis-

---

[50] William H. Goetzmann, *New Lands, New Men. America and the Second Great Age of Discovery* (New York: Viking, 1986).

played.[51] Still, it was with Cook's three expeditions between 1768 and 1780 that the tradition of scientific travel became firmly established.

According to Goetzmann 'all of the expeditions down through that of Bougainville formed . . . a prelude to the incredible work of Cook and his men.'[52] The son of a humble Yorkshire agricultural worker, Cook fled from a grocer's apprenticeship at the age of thirteen to sign on as a ship's boy. He spent the winter working in the yard, and, with the encouragement of John Walker the owner the collier, assiduously turned to the study of mathematics. With the outbreak of war with France in 1755, Cook soon found himself under the orders of Sir Hugh Palliser, the captain of the *Eagle*. It was to mark a turning point in his life. For Sir Hugh was deeply impressed with Cook's attempts at self-improvement through his efforts to acquire a working knowledge of geography, mathematics, and astronomy. And soon, under Palliser's patronage, he was engaging in various hydrographic missions, completing a four year survey of Newfoundland where Palliser himself had become governor. It was work of this sort, along with his personal account of an observed eclipse of the sun from Newfoundland, that brought him to the attention of the Royal Society, with the result that he was chosen to head an astronomical expedition to the South Pacific for the society in 1768. It was a trip that would later be simply known as Cook's first voyage.

Scientifically, it was a hugely successful venture. The transit of Venus was accurately observed and recorded, kangaroos were discovered, ethnographic studies of indigenous peoples carried out, the New Zealand coastline was charted, and a vast amount of material collected and shipped back to the Royal Society – thousands of plants, five hundred fish preserved in alcohol, five hundred bird skins, and hundreds of mineral specimens. Indeed Cook himself was to emerge as an ethnographer of no small talent, not least in his depiction of what seemed 'bizarre' burial customs and tattooing practices, for he combined observational patience with an empathetic understanding beyond the customary conventions of his day. But it was also successful in so far as it provided the launching pad for another meteoric career in natural science, that of Joseph Banks (1743–1820), who, as director of the ship's team of naturalists, personally engaged each member

[51] See Jacques Brosse, *Great Voyages of Discovery. Circumnavigators and Scientists, 1764–1843*, translated by Stanley Hochman (New York: Facts on File Publications, 1983); Numa Broc, *La Géographie des Philosophes. Géographes et Voyageurs Français au XVIIIe Siècle* (Paris, 1975).
[52] Goetzmann, *New Lands, New Men*, p. 38. Details of Cook's life and work are available in Brosse, *Great Voyages*, pp. 35–74; Hugh Cobbe, *Cook's Voyages and Peoples of the Pacific* (London: British Museum Publications, 1974); J. C. Beaglehole (ed.), *The Journals of Captain J. Cook*, 4 vols., (Cambridge: Cambridge University Press, 1955–61).

of the natural history corps and procured each and every item of scientific equipment. At this juncture Banks was not even twenty-five years old, but the voyage made him into a scientific celebrity, his fame culminating in his assumption of the presidency of the Royal Society.[53] But Banks also exerted an independent influence on the course of geographical history, for later from his Soho home in London he continued to support geographical exploration. He was a founder member of the Association for the Exploration of the Interior Part of Africa, established in 1788 – a body which was eventually incorporated into the Royal Geographical Society; he sponsored Mungo Park's travels; and he promoted exploration and development in Australia.[54]

For all its scientific success, however, the *Endeavour*'s triumphs were procured at no little cost. Cook himself was of a comparatively mild temperament by contemporary standards, but he felt compelled to flog his men for drunkenness from time to time, and for purloining nails with which they could purchase amorous favours from the Tahitian women. Moreover some of his officers did not hesitate to shoot down natives on impulse, while the rough-handed midshipmen, finding the captain's clerk in an alcoholic daze, whipped out their knives, cut the clothes from his back, and cropped his ears![55] Alongside these frictions, there were the disruptive effects of the impact of technologically superior Westerners on the hierarchical Polynesian society. The value of iron and steel to a society of canoe-making craftsmen and talented woodcarvers can scarcely be overestimated, and the theft of metal and tools from the ship's supplies spread like wildfire. Harsh reprisals soon alienated the once-friendly Tahitians and relationships rapidly degenerated. Besides all this, the peoples of the region were allocated a marginalized space on the Europeans' map of the 'natural' social order. Even as Cook and his draughtsmen represented their lands and limbs on paper, they constructed a world of fixed identities framed by the imperatives of European science.

For all that, Cook was soon in charge of a second scientific expedition (1772–5), now with two vessels at his command, the *Resolution* and the *Adventure*. On this occasion, however, he had to sail without Banks who could not be persuaded to join the team after he was told that the corpus of naturalists he had assembled was far too large. So Cook had to find a replacement and this time he ended up with two men, father and son,

[53] Patrick O'Brian, *Joseph Banks. A Life* (London: Collins Harvill, 1987); H. B. Carter, *Sir Joseph Banks, 1743–1820* (London: British Museum of Natural History, 1988).
[54] Crone, *Modern Geographers*, pp. 11, 12.
[55] O'Brian, *Banks*, p. 70.

whose influence on science and geography was no less far-reaching than that of Banks, namely Johann Reinhold Forster and Johann Georg Adam Forster. The elder Forster was crotchety to say the least: he was pedantic and prudish and got everybody's back up – not least Cook's. But his son was just the opposite and won the approval of all on board; moreover, his published narrative accounts of this round-the-world trip proved to be a great success and brought the expedition's achievements to a wide audience. Again Cook headed for the Pacific, visiting Tahiti, the Friendly Islands, New Zealand, Easter Island, and sighting Antarctica before returning home via South Georgia and Cape Town. But this time the emphasis was rather more on zoogeography than on botanical matters, for the Forsters were thus inclined, although anthropological questions were never far from their minds. J. R. Forster, for example, completed a study of comparative Tahitian anthropology, distinguishing two different human groups on the island. Cook shared this interest in the extension of Newtonian science into the realms of inductive human geography and later, on his third, and ill-fated, voyage, this time in search of the fabled Northwest Passage from the Atlantic to the Pacific, he himself collected native vocabularies, mythologies, and musical traditions. He even studied the population statistics of island peoples and traced their various patterns of migration.

Notwithstanding the scientific achievements of Cook's seafaring ventures, his three voyages were neither conceived nor executed in an ideological vacuum. Cook, in fact, sailed under secret orders of the British Crown. His circumnavigating instructions from the royal court included the specific objective of establishing British dominion on newly discovered soil and reporting on the natural resources, both organic and inorganic, that could be exploited for Great Britain. Of his second voyage Goetzmann writes: 'Clearly his most important duty was to establish the British empire on the bottom side of the globe. Science was seen as being of primary assistance in this imperial venture.'[56] It must not be imagined that in this respect Cook's geographical exploits were unique. The marriage of science and imperialism was so commonplace as to be conventional at the time. Nor was it restricted either to the British or to ocean-going expeditions. In France for example, Jean-François de la Pérouse followed in the wake of Bougainville. Supported by the French Academy of Sciences, he embarked with two ships at his command, the *Boussole* and the *Astrolabe*, to carry out an extensive natural history inventory between 1785 and 1788. But there were also political and commercial objectives at stake, particularly in the aftermath of the

[56] Goetzmann, *New Lands, New Men*, p. 44.

loss of many of France's North American fur-trading posts to the Hudson's Bay Company; in addition, La Pérouse was assigned the job of reporting on the situation in France's Russian establishments.[57] So far as non-maritime forms of scientific travel was concerned, Major James Rennell (1742–1830) instances the selfsame politico-intellectual alignments. Having joined the East India Company, he moved on to the position of surveyor-general in India, producing an *Atlas of Bengal* in 1777. He also issued an important *Memoir of a Map of Hindoostan* in 1783 – the first accurate map of India – and carried out detailed research on the oceanography of the Atlantic and Indian Oceans. To be sure, Rennell is today largely forgotten but his style of work linking mapping, discovery, and imperialism together serves to remind us of the vibrancy of a tradition of geographical practice that moulded the very shape of the geographical tradition at the end of the eighteenth century.[58]

Artistic Vision

If the global harvesting of the geographical facts of life reverberated throughout the reaches of science and politics, the world of artistic expression did not remain untouched. Cook, we need to recall, was among the first to make effective use of professionally trained artists, employing them on all three of his expeditions. Indeed it was largely courtesy of Cook's accomplishments that what Bernard Smith has christened 'the European vision of the South Pacific' was born.[59] In Smith's telling, this 'European vision', in which aesthetic judgement and epistemological procedure went hand in hand, was conditioned very substantially by European forms of knowing. And this represented a new turn of artistic events. For until then, Smith writes, 'the empirical approach to nature, despite its standing in philosophy and science, played little part in the history and practice of landscape-painting in England.'[60] Indeed where empirical artwork did exist was within science itself, where considerable graphic talents were required by draughtsmen for botanical, geological, zoological, and ethnological illustration. Soon, as on Cook's vessels, trained artists were working hand in glove with these scientific illustrators, with the result that the former acquired

[57] Brosse, *Great Voyages*, pp. 79–92.
[58] See Baker, *History of Geography*, chapter 9 on 'Major James Rennell and his Place in the History of Geography'; Simon Berthon and Andrew Robinson, *The Shape of the World. The Mapping and Discovery of the Earth* (London: George Philip, 1991), pp. 134–5.
[59] See Bernard Smith, *European Vision and the South Pacific* (New Haven and London: Yale University Press, 2nd ed 1985). The following few paragraphs owe much to Smith's analysis.
[60] Ibid., p. 2.

modes of illustrative practice and representational perspective that gradually prized them away from neo-classicism towards a more empirical perception. To be sure, this did not happen in the twinkling of an eye. But the seeds of what could be called the triumph of empirical vision were present right from Cook's first enterprise. In the long term, this trajectory would calibrate the shift from the transcendental to the material, from the numinous unity of the cosmos either to the ecological unity of the organic and inorganic or to an absorption with the individuality of discrete phenomena – the selfsame shifts that gave impetus to scientific theorizing.

As I have implied, talk of a changeover from classicism to naturalism is to use shorthand for a complex and lengthy historical transformation. Banks, for example, who devoted much of his life to the use of art in the service of geographical science, had been enthusiastic about the scientific illustration of exotic plants even before his voyage with Cook, and it is not surprising that he enlisted a landscape painter, Alexander Buchan, and a natural history draughtsman, Sydney Parkinson, as part of his scientific team. Rather than revealing the uniformity of nature, the purpose of their work, writes Smith, was 'to reveal her geographical variety.'[61] And yet Banks always felt a tension between the call of taste and that of pictorial reproduction, and so his painters did devote some of their energies to romantic topics like grottoes, exotic rituals, and so on because these suited the then fashionable rococo style. Moreover, even when accurate depiction of native peoples, like those models of documentary realism produced by Buchan, were provided, it just was very hard to bring an objective account of them before the British public. Engravers *would* dress up the original painting to keep them in line with their own philosophical predilections. Thus John Hawkesworth, for example, time and again allowed his enthusiasm for primitivism to come through in his illustrations, portraying as he did those 'noble savages' as modern exemplars of austere virtuousness. And thus was born the European vision of the Pacific as a world of primitive grace, free love, and paradisial geographies. Indeed Cook's entire enterprise of 'representation' facilitated the European appropriation of the peoples of the South Pacific. The very modes of conceptualization and inscription – Eurocentric as they were – that these 'interrogators' deployed became the tools of cultural subjection and the plundering of identity.

The scientific travels also had an impact on the methods of working and techniques used by artists. The way in which light, atmosphere, and meteorological phenomena were to be conveyed on canvas absorbed much time

[61] Ibid., p. 13.

and effort. On Cook's second voyage, for example, Parkinson devoted a great deal of energy to this pursuit, as did J. R. Forster, and efforts were made to come to terms with the effect of light on the colour of the sea – a topic, incidentally, of practical as well as artistic import. Besides this, through the increasing realism of William Hodges, who strove 'to contain new geographical knowledge within the framework of traditional classical forms'[62] and, on the third voyage, John Webber, naturalistic intrusions began to insinuate their way into the highest levels of academic painting. And so with the passage of time artists progressively subjected their own vision of reality to the service of science. The portrayal of 'primitive' peoples nicely reveals this shift. Thus, whether Polynesians instantiated the noble savage, so beloved of antiquity, or whether they were depraved and ignoble, as post-deistic Calvinists insisted, was a question that receded more and more before the 'empirical' depiction of various human groups as simply the cultural products of differing physical and social settings.

Taken overall, then, the 'scientific explorer-artist-writers,' to use Barbara Maria Stafford's words, 'in trying to break from the limits of solipsism, custom, and habits of representation, strained to be extra-referential'; what she means is that they sought to allow their art to be structured by reference to the world itself rather than by normative notions of the picturesque or the whisperings of a distant divine.[63] These traveller-artists made a determined effort to break out of the metaphorical mould of seeing the world of nature as something else, to just seeing it as it is. Besides, in the accompanying narratives within which these illustrations were set, men like George Forster and La Pérouse sought to talk straight talk, to use candid prose and unflowery language, and thus to match in words the plain copying of the illustrators. And yet all this cultivated respect for the thing itself could easily turn to worship of naturalism. Time and again the cultural came to be depicted in the idioms of the natural; nature, as it were, provided the metaphors in which the cultural could be understood – a move finding fulsome expression in the German scholar Samuel Witte, who, rhapsodizing over the triumphs of Enlightenment rationalism in the form of French geology, proclaimed that the Egyptian pyramids, the Inca temples, and the Ellora rock caverns were all mere basalt eruptions. Here the archaeological remnants of bygone cultures were well and truly naturalized. The apparent innocence of seeing nature as it is could thus become a hermeneutic tactic by which human culture could be naturalistically interrogated.

---

[62] Ibid., p. 107.

[63] Barbara Maria Stafford, *Voyage into Substance. Art, Science, Nature, and the Illustrated Travel Account, 1760–1840* (Cambridge, Mass.: The MIT Press, 1984), p. 2.

Whichever, in an epoch when spatial discoveries proceeded apace, the opening up of the geographical world meant the opening up of the artistic world as well. In both cases it was, again to use Stafford's words, a 'voyage into substance'. Thus it becomes clear that the geographical tradition of exploration, in tandem with its artistic accompaniment, was deeply implicated in the search for a scientific language, the advancement of empiricism, and the spread of naturalism. Small wonder that Andrew Sparrman could write: 'Every authentic and well-written book of voyages is, in fact, a treatise of experimental philosophy.'[64] And nowhere, perhaps, are these diverse strands of thought – artistic, philosophical, and scientific – more fully expressed than in the grand geographical testimony of Alexander von Humboldt (1769–1859) (plate 4.1).

Plate 4.1   Alexander Freiherr von Humboldt, George Friedrich Weitsch, oil on canvas, 126 × 92.5 cm, Nationalgalerie, Staatliche Museen, Berlin; photograph: Archiv Für Kunst und Geschichte

[64] Quoted in ibid., p. 47.

The Humboldtian Project

The Baconian empiricism of the naturalist-navigator in the Cook mould ('geography is facts,' Bougainville quipped),[65] the philosophical ideals of Kant's universal science, Georg Forster's passion for the beauties of nature, and Goethe's idealist search for a transcendental coordinating principle were all streams that flowed into Alexander von Humboldt's geography. Because for Humboldt, modern geography was first and last a synthesizing science and as such, if Goetzmann is to be believed, 'it became the key scientific activity of the age.'[66] Indeed, in crucial ways some of these particular individuals exerted a lasting influence on Humboldt. From his early days, for example, he dreamt of being another Cook; at the age of sixteen he first came under the influence of Marcus Herz, a devotee of Kant; in 1790 he travelled with the younger Forster through Europe; and later in 1794 he met Goethe and was initiated into the mysteries of German *Naturphilosophie*.[67]

While Humboldt always thought of himself as a scientific traveller, and emphatically not as an adventurous explorer, he was different in several crucial respects from Cook. For a start he was rich, and could therefore finance his own expeditions. Again, whereas oceanic discovery was Cook's forte, continental penetration was to be Humboldt's. Indeed he himself was only too pleased to be able to make this very comparison in his preface to *Cosmos*. Moreover their scholarly competences were different, for Humboldt's métier was geology and mineralogy rather than mathematics and astronomy. Humboldt had acquired his scientific education in a number of places. In 1789 he enrolled as a student at the University of Göttingen, having turned his back on Frankfurt where the library was poor and science was not part of the curriculum. But far more important than his university introduction to physics and chemistry was his time travelling with Forster and his experience in the early 1790s as an assistant inspector in the Department of Mines which allowed him to travel widely in what is now Austria, Czechoslovakia, Poland, northern Italy, and the Swiss and

[65] Quoted in Goetzmann, *New Lands, New Men*, p. 42.
[66] Ibid., p. 53.
[67] The following are useful English-language sources: Douglas Botting, *Humboldt and the Cosmos* (London: Sphere Books, 1973); Carl Troll, 'The Work of Alexander von Humboldt and Carl Ritter: A Centenary Address', *Advancement of Science*, 64 (1959–60): 441–52; Karl A. Sinnhuber, 'Alexander von Humboldt, 1769–1859', *Scottish Geographical Magazine*, 75 (1959): 83–101; L. Kellner, *Alexander von Humboldt* (London: Oxford University Press, 1963); Sonja Karsen, 'Alexander von Humboldt in South America: From the Orinoco to the Amazon', *Studies in Eighteenth-Century Culture*, 16 (1986): 295–302.

French Alps. These were the experiences that made him into a geographer, for through them he learned first-hand about the spatial distributions of organic life and its umbilical ties with environment, and this induced in him a lifelong respect for empirical methods.

But, as I have already implied, Humboldt was no narrow empiricist. His encounter with the transcendental nature philosophy of men like Goethe and Schelling impressed on him a sense of the harmony and beauty of the whole earth organism: all of its parts were delicately balanced, mutually interdependent, and intricately interlocked. Accordingly there was to Humboldt no incompatibility between the experimental method of probing the very secrets of nature – he himself conducted experiments on galvanism and animal chemistry – and an emotional appreciation of nature's sublimity. Indeed he derived great aesthetic satisfaction from the scientific analysis of the ways in which organisms on the earth's surface depended on one another. And it is no surprise that (in an age without the colour transparency) he was forever producing on-the-spot drawings of geographical phenomena, and later recommended that landscape painters could do worse than undertake detailed study of vegetable groups in their native splendour. Thus, even from these early days Humboldt constantly sought for the universal behind the particular, for underlying patterns and unities that tied nature together in such a beautiful, functioning system. It is noteworthy, therefore, that in the last years of his life the first topic he took up for discussion in his celebrated *Cosmos* was neither scientific method nor empirical findings, but the enjoyment of nature.

In 1799 Humboldt got the opportunity of a lifetime to translate these philosophical convictions into practical science. In June of that year, he and Aimé Bonpland set sail for the Spanish colonies on a research tour. They remained in South America until 1804, travelling by foot, packhorse, and native canoe through the Venezuela *llanos*, from the Caracas to the Orinoco, across the Andes and along the high valleys to Bogotá and Quito, ending up traversing the coastal plains and high plateaus of Mexico. In all, they explored portions of Venezuela, Cuba, Colombia, Peru, Ecuador, and Mexico, inveterately amassing plant specimens by the tens of thousands and accumulating vast amounts of information on local climate, geology, mineralogy, zoology, botany, and ethnography as they went.

Before returning to a tumultuous Parisian reception in August 1804, the two travellers dazzled scientific audiences in Philadelphia, where they met Jefferson, himself a passionate enthusiast for geography. But Humboldt was determined not to live off an adventurer's reputation and so, back in Paris, he set out to produce what would turn out to be a thirty-volume project detailing his findings in the New World. The story of the Orinoco expedition was published with luscious illustrations by various artists which aimed to combine detailed accuracy with romantic grandeur. Over the years various publications revealed the real scientific achievements of his South American expedition. And yet Humboldt was neither content nor at peace. For one thing, Napoleon suspected him of being a spy and in 1810 he was given 48 hours to leave Paris. Only the pleadings of a personal friend helped pour oil on troubled waters for the time being. In fact it was over a quarter of a century before he would leave the city. He made several abortive attempts to organize a second expedition, this time to Siberia and Tibet, Ceylon and the East Indies, but was prevented by political machinations. Indeed it was only in 1829, in his sixtieth year, that he was able to undertake the Siberian mission. Even in Berlin, where he moved in 1827, life was not carefree, for his liberal political views and his deep commitment to humanitarian causes, like anti-Semitism and abolition, were not shared by the ultra-conservative members of the Prussian aristocracy.

Even at the age of seventy, however, one dream lay unfulfilled: the production of a single work whose dimensions would range as broadly as the universe itself. Back in the high Andes so many years ago he had conceived of a project that even now he had hopes of bringing to fruition – a 'mad' project that he had outlined in 1834 in a letter to Karl Varnhagen:

> I have the crazy notion to depict in a single work the entire material universe, all that we know of the phenomena of heaven and earth, from the nebulae of stars to the geography of mosses and granite rocks – and in a vivid style that will stimulate and elicit feeling. Every great and important idea in my writing should here be registered side by side with facts. It should portray an epoch in the spiritual genesis of mankind – in the knowledge of nature . . . My title is *Cosmos*.[68]

It was, as he himself confessed, to be the work of his life in a race against death; for it was to encompass everything from surveying current theories of the structure of the universe, sketching the historical progress of science and geographical discovery, and expounding the content of the disparate sciences, to discussing nature poetry and landscape painting. *Cosmos* was truly envisioned as universal science; it was both the apex of Humboldt's own personal intellectual journey and the dynamic synthesis of the several

---

[68] Slightly varying renditions of this letter are available in Botting, *Humboldt and the Cosmos*, p. 257, and Kellner, *Humboldt*, pp. 200–2.

departments of the world of scientific learning.[69] As he explained in the preface:

> While the outward circumstances of my life, and an irresistible impulse to the acquisition of different kinds of knowledge, led me to occupy myself for many years, apparently exclusively, with separate branches of science, – descriptive botany, geology, chemistry, geographical determinations, and terrestrial magnetism, tending to render useful the extensive journeys in which I engaged, – I had still throughout a higher aim in view; I ever desired to discern physical phenomena in their widest mutual connection, and to comprehend Nature as a whole, animated and moved by inward forces.[70]

With such a self-appointed task, it is no surprise that Humboldt should presently avow that the very kernel of the undertaking lay in his single aim of 'manifesting the intimate connection of the general with the special.'[71] Thus the theme of unity in diversity reverberates throughout the length and breadth of his *magnum opus*.

Of course all this was just too grand a scheme for one pair of hands to hold. And this in itself may help account for the interminable and frankly tiresome debates among certain historians of geography as to whether Humboldt represents a beginning or an ending in geographical thought. Such a question is a historical misconstruction. The fact is the Humboldtian project progressively became diversified into many subjects, both human and academic. And yet despite this fragmentation, a number of identifiably Humboldtian practices continued to characterize a good deal of outdoor scientific doings throughout the nineteenth century.[72]

First, there was the emphasis on measurement. Humboldt himself had set the example by carrying with him on his American excursion more than four dozen measuring devices – chronometers, an achromatic telescope, several sextants, dipping needles, compasses, a cyanometer (for measuring the blueness of the sky), barometers, thermometers, rain guages, aerometers, theodolites, and on and on. Already he was convinced of just how crucial number was in scientific geography. Secondly, there was the regional dimension. Throughout the corpus of his writings, and nowhere more conspicuously than in his work on plant geography, Humboldt emphasized the

[69] The first volume of *Cosmos* was published in 1845, the second in 1847, the third in 1850, the fourth in 1858, and the fifth posthumously from his notes in 1862.

[70] Alexander von Humboldt, *Cosmos: Sketch of a Physical Description of the Universe*, translated by Edward Sabine, vol. 1 (London: Longman, Brown, Green, and Longmans, 1847), pp. xvii–xviii.

[71] Ibid., p. xxi.

[72] Susan Faye Cannon, *Science in Culture: The Early Victorian Period* (New York: Dawson and Science History Publication, 1978), chapter 3, 'Humboldtian Science'.

functional interrelationships between organic life and local environment. As he saw it, the world was divided into a series of natural regions, each with its own distinctive set of animals and plants. Indeed this idea of regionality proved to be so conceptually fertile for taxonomic and other purposes that, as Nicolson notes, 'botany itself became geographical' during the Humboldt era.[73] More, the strongly regional bias of Humboldt's vegetation studies can be seen as a crucial ingredient in the shift from systems of analysis based on observable, morphological features to a new *episteme* emphasizing the underlying ecological cohesiveness of nature. Thirdly, and closely related, was the Humboldtian mapping impulse, that is, the graphic recording of spatially distributed data. But Humboldt did not champion the use of just any old kind of map; rather, as Cannon has convincingly argued, he came to stand for the 'iso-map', namely maps with lines joining places of equal something – isobars, isothermals, isogons. By this comparative cartographic method the different climatic zones, magnetic fields, and biogeographic regions of the earth's surface could be delineated.

In all these ways, then, Alexander von Humboldt was engaged in advancing a form of scientific inquiry that made full use of the eighteenth-century geographical traditions of Europe and yet transcended that heritage by a new emphasis on the importance of accuracy, conceptual sophistication, and the use of the latest analytic instrumentation. Thus I can find no more fitting words with which to close this chapter of the story than Cannon's provocative evocation of Humboldtian science:

> the great new thing in professional science in the first half of the 19th century was Humboldtian science, the accurate, measured study of widespread but interconnected real phenomena in order to find a definite law and a dynamic cause. Compared to this, the study of nature in the laboratory or the perfection of differential equations was old-fashioned, was simple science concerned with easy variables. Insofar as you find scientists studying geographical distribution, terrestrial magnetism, meteorology, hydrology, ocean currents, the structures of mountain-chains and the orientation of strata, solar radiation; insofar as they are playing around with charts, maps, and graphs, hygrometers, dip needles, barometers, maximum and minimum thermometers; insofar as they spend much of their time tinkering with their instruments and worrying about error: they are not Baconian, they are not backward, they are not colonial, they are not doing that merely because they are amateurs and calculus is too difficult. They are eagerly participating in the latest wave of international scientific activity: they are being cosmopolitan.[74]

[73] See Malcolm Nicolson, 'Alexander von Humboldt, Humboldtian Science and the Origins of the Study of Vegetation', *History of Science*, 25 (1987): 171.
[74] Cannon, *Science in Culture*, p. 105.

5

Of Design and Dining Clubs

Pre-Darwinian Geography

For all his celebration of nature's unity, Alexander von Humboldt stead-fastly refused to allow his idealist inclinations to serve theological interests. His appreciation of the order of the cosmos was every bit as agnostic as it was aesthetic. With Carl Ritter (1779–1859) it was precisely the opposite. Everywhere he looked, Ritter would see evidence of God's design. And so it is no surprise that commentators writing in the first flush of positivist histo-riography should praise Humboldt at Ritter's expense, castigating him for his theological interpolations.[1] Such historical evaluations are profoundly misleading, however, for teleological modes of thought persisted in geo-graphical discourse right through to the end of the nineteenth century (in some cases later than that), even while the professionalizing impulse of the era impelled geography on its course towards institutionalization. These twin themes – teleological conviction and institutional infrastructure – thus provide the twin contextual tracks along which the arguments of the fol-lowing pages will run.

H. R. Mill, writing in 1929 on 'Geography' for the Encyclopaedia Britannica, observed:

---

[1] In 1951 George Tatham remarked: 'Later writers in the nineteenth century criticized this teleology as though it impaired the quality of Ritter's work, making it somehow unscientific. There is, of course, no basis for such criticism. Contemporary developments in science have shown that a teleological philosophy can be combined with most rigid scientific accuracy in research, and there is every indication that in Ritter it was so combined.' Presently Tatham goes on to add: 'What is the relationship between modern geography and present-day systems of philosophy? Is geography still so sensitive? If so, will the influence of writers like Bergson and Whitehead revive an interest in teleology reminiscent of that of Ritter, and for which Ritter has been so often criticized?' George Tatham, 'Geography in the Nineteenth Century', pp. 47–8, 69.

Teleology or the argument from design had become a favourite form of reasoning among Christian theologians and, as worked out by Paley in his Natural Theology, it served the useful purpose of emphasizing the fitness which exists between all inhabitants of the earth and their physical environment. It was held that the earth had been created so as to fit the wants of man in every particular. This argument was tacitly accepted or explicitly avowed by almost every writer on the theory of geography, and Carl Ritter distinctly recognized and adopted it as the unifying principle of his system.[2]

The Ritterian world-view clearly merits scrutiny, though its cardinal conceptual landmarks can be quite quickly sketched. But first a word about Ritter himself.[3] It was his greatest good fortune that as a child of five he was chosen to be what can only be described as a guinea pig in an educational experiment. In an effort to escape the traditional scholasticism of the German curriculum, and to practise the naturalistic methods of Rousseau and Pestalozzi, a certain C. G. Saltzmann had established a school at Schnepfenthal in which direct experience of nature replaced rote learning; here, to put it another way, the word gave way to the world. The young Ritter was chosen to attend the school and the experience was to have a profound impact on him. From it, he acquired a lifelong respect for the thing itself, for close observation, and for empirical methods. Subsequently he studied at the Universities of Halle and Göttingen and there his juvenile interests were reinforced through formal instruction in history and natural science. Then in 1819 he was appointed as a professor of history at the University of Frankfurt and the following year moved to Berlin to occupy Germany's first modern chair of geography. Here he also lectured regularly at the Military Academy, an appointment he held for thirty-three years.

The wellsprings of Ritter's efforts to construct a 'scientific geography' liberated from its enslavement to a 'lifeless summary of facts about countries and cities,' lay in his vision of unity in diversity.[4] Rather than conceiv-

---

[2] Hugh Robert Mill, 'Geography', *Encyclopaedia Britannica*, 14th edn (London: The Encyclopaedia Britannica Company, 1929), vol. 10, p. 147.

[3] Sources on Ritter include the following: Karl A. Sinnhuber, 'Carl Ritter, 1779–1859', *Scottish Geographical Magazine*, 75 (1959): 153–63; Dickinson 'Carl Ritter', chapter 3 in *Makers of Modern Geography*; James, *All Possible Worlds*, pp. 164–70; Manfred Büttner (ed.), *Carl Ritter: Zur Europaisch-Amerikanischen Geographie an der Wende vom 18. zum 19. Jahrhundert* (Paderhorn, FRG: Ferdinand Schoningh, 1980); M. Linke, 'Carl Ritter, 1779–1859', *Geographers. Biobibliographical Studies*, 5 (1981): 98–108.

[4] H. Bögekamp, 'An Account of Prof. Ritter's Geographical Labors', in W. L. Gage, trans., *Geographical Studies by the Late Professor Carl Ritter of Berlin* (Boston: Gould and Lincoln, 1863), p. 37.

ing of geography as the cold recitation of bits of information, he wanted to 'present a living picture of the whole land, its natural and cultivated products, its natural and human features, and to present these in a coherent whole in such a way that the most significant inferences about man and nature will be self evident, especially when they are compared side by side.'[5] What he was after, fundamentally, was a subject whose identity was to be found in its portrayal of the 'hanging-togetherness' of things (*Zusammenhang*), and here the Kantian roots of his aspirations are clearly visible. But even more specifically, Ritter, like Herder, consistently sought to preserve what he took to be the essential intercourse of culture and nature, history and geography. And so it is not surprising that twentieth-century partisans have seen in Ritter the legitimation for their conception of geography as a science of regions and of areal differentiation. Yet what gave philosophical muscle to Ritter's regional ideology was the teleological foundation on which the whole edifice rested. To study geography was to explore nothing less than the very laws of the Creator, who was the author of the human story, the architect of the world-plan, and the builder of humankind's earthly home. *Erdkunde*, according to one commentator, thus stands as perhaps 'the last great experiment in the providential tradition' of geography.[6] Accordingly Ritter could insist that the object of his *chef-d'oeuvre* was not 'merely to collect and arrange a larger mass of materials than any predecessor, but to trace the general laws which underlie all the diversity of nature.'[7]

The specific details of the unfinished nineteen-volume *Erdkunde*[8] – which was intended as a comprehensive world geography but in fact never advanced beyond Africa and Asia – need not be reviewed here. Suffice to note that Ritter sought to infuse the multitudinous data he had accumulated with a sense of grand purpose and cosmic unity. What is significant in the present context is that this teleological vision was nowhere nearly so moribund as is frequently thought; natural theology flourished in Britain as a context for science throughout the nineteenth century, and the Ritterian perspective in particular was championed in the United States through the writings of one of Ritter's greatest devotees, Arnold Guyot. And so I want

[5] Quoted in Tatham, 'Geography in the Nineteenth Century', p. 43.
[6] Hanno Beck, *Carl Ritter: Genius of Geography. On His Life and Work* (Bonn-Bad Godesberg: Inter Nationes, 1979), p. 121.
[7] Quoted in Dickinson, *Makers of Modern Geography*, p. 37.
[8] The full title of *Erdkunde* may be translated as: Earth science in relation to nature and to human history or a general comparative geography, as a secure foundation for study and teaching in the physical and historical sciences.

to turn now to the early history of the American geographical tradition, partly in order to illustrate the vibrancy of teleological geography in the New World.

From these few observations it might well seem that American geography was little more than a transatlantic offshoot of the Germanic tradition, with Guyot featuring as a sort of expatriate Ritter redivivus. Such images of geography as constitutionally a European enterprise have recently found support among modern historians of the subject.[9] Certainly there is much to be said for the view that such crucial devices as taxonomic classification and comparative methodology, adopted for the purpose of getting at the truth about how things are, were forged in late Enlightenment Europe. But to infer from this that American geography was a mere epiphenomenon, a pale shadow, of its European counterpart would be to ignore the vitality of an indigenous American geographical discourse.

The Jeffersonian Era

The period from 1780 to around 1830 – the Jeffersonian era – provides a good starting point. But even so, identifying the advent of Jeffersonian science as the point of departure is not a little arbitrary. A whole host of travellers, some, like Conrad Weiser, from the Old World, others born in America itself, had already trekked across the Alleghenies and into the margins of the western interior and provided raw data for naturalists like John Bartram, who in 1751 had produced a journal reporting on 'the inhabitants, climate, soil, rivers, productions, animals, and other matters worthy of notice' in trans-Allegheny.[10] It was a journal that was voraciously devoured in Europe. The mysteries of the Ohio also attracted a host of explorers. Thomas Hutchins, for example, surveyed not only the Ohio country but also the Mississippi and Gulf of Mexico coast before being engaged as geographer to Washington's Revolutionary army. Such exploits alone should be enough to substantiate the claim that American geography was born of – well – the geography of America.

Still, it was through Thomas Jefferson, who in 1801 assumed the presidency of the United States, that a real continental consciousness began to

---

[9] So, D. R. Stoddart, 'Geography – A European Science', *Geography*, 67 (1982): 289–96.
[10] Quoted in Goetzmann, *New Lands, New Men*, p. 79.

be aroused. Jefferson was, after all, the most scientific of America's presidents and certainly the only one who uttered the words 'science is my passion, politics my duty.'[11] Here before him lay a virgin continent open to scientific scrutiny for the first time, and so he was determined to transform its mythical images – what Goetzmann calls the hypothetical geography of the interior – into solid fact. Even into the eighteenth century California had appeared on some maps as an island! Thus Jefferson's desire was, so to speak, to scientize the traders' and trappers' geographies and reduce myth to map, much as the explorers of the great age of discovery had done. Accordingly it is no surprise that some have hinted that Jefferson, already dubbed 'The Father of Palaeontology,' 'The Father of Archaeology' and 'A Patriarch of American Natural History' might well have equally good claim to the accolade 'The Father of American Geography.'[12] Indulging in the pastime of creating a patriarchal lineage for American geography is certainly not my present aim, however. Yet locating the mainsprings of American geography in the symbolic figure of Jefferson, the only president who might legitimately be called a geographer, sensitizes us to the importance of the Jeffersonian context of American geography's scientific birth.

The Jeffersonian era in America had an ethos all its own.[13] To be sure, the major scientific context was still provided by Europe: the science of mechanics had been inaugurated by Newton; Laplace applied those principles to astronomy; Lavoisier launched oxygen chemistry; Werner developed a system of mineralogical classification; Hutton and Playfair laid the foundations of geology; Blumenbach and Prichard were reconstructing anthropology; Humboldt laid out the ground rules for biogeography; Lamarck and Cuvier overhauled the Linnaean classification scheme. Such were the European developments to which American science certainly owed its conventional wisdom.

And yet for all that, America's new experience of nationhood provided

[11] Cited in Silvio A. Bedini, *Thomas Jefferson. Statesman of Science* (New York: Macmillan, 1990), p. 1. See also Richard A. Van Orman, *The Explorers: Nineteenth Century Expeditions in Africa and the American West* (Albuquerque: University of New Mexico Press, 1984), chapter 5.

[12] See George T. Surface, 'Thomas Jefferson: A Pioneer Student of American Geography', *Bulletin of the American Geographical Society*, 41 (1909): 743–50; A. W. Greely, 'Jefferson as a Geographer', *The National Geographic Magazine*, 7 (1896): 269–71; Gary S. Dunbar, 'Thomas Jefferson, Geographer', *Special Libraries Association, Geography and Map Division, Bulletin*, 40 (April 1960): 11–16.

[13] In what follows I have learned much from John C. Greene, *American Science in the Age of Jefferson* (Ames: Iowa State University Press, 1984). See also Donald Jackson, *Thomas Jefferson & the Stony Mountains: Exploring the West from Monticello* (Urbana, Ill.: University of Illinois Press, 1981).

some additional compass points with which to orientate its scientific activity. In the immediate aftermath of the American Revolution, the emerging nation saw the need to cultivate the scientific spirit for both functional and prestigious reasons. Above all, knowledge for a nascent commonwealth had to be useful, and yet its very usefulness could demonstrate to the intellectual world the scholarly integrity of the republican régime. The power, prosperity, and prestige of the independent United States could all be served by practical knowledge. Even astronomy, a seemingly remote sphere of investigation, was grounded in its functional value to geographical and navigational questions. As the American Academy of Arts and Science noted in its first volume of *Memoirs*: the astronomical papers were 'chiefly of the practical kind' reporting 'such observations and deductions, as are subservient to the cause of geography and navigation.'[14]

Certainly this does not mean that political independence immediately issued in cultural emancipation – a point that did not escape the Jeffersonian patriots themselves. Too many members of the medical profession were still being trained in London and Edinburgh, they believed, and too many foreign students of botany, geology, and other sciences were seen to be exploiting the raw data and vast intellectual resources that a new continent could offer in the service of science. Besides this, the selfsame religious context that cradled European science surfaced in Jefferson's America. Again natural theology provided the mould in which so much natural science was cast. Of course there were internal debates about the extent of allowable supernaturalism: revelationists insisted on the propriety of miraculous intervention, while deists were chary of allowing any such disruption of the natural order. Jefferson himself stood firmly on the side of the deists, but there were many others – often clergymen – of more orthodox persuasion who showed that they could be as enthusiastic about science and its social benefits as any doubting Thomas. In American geography, as we shall presently see, this was certainly the case. Revd Samuel Miller, for example, was only too happy to report that the geographical discoveries of Captain Cook, Vitus Bering, and others corroborated biblical revelation, particularly regarding the common origin and historical migrations of the human species.[15] Later, William Woodbridge justified his commitment to monogenism by the formula 'The scriptures inform us,' and supported the case for providential government through a geo-determinism that typecast tropical peoples as 'indolent' and rarely

---

[14] Quoted in Greene, *American Science*, p. 6.
[15] Samuel Miller, *A Brief Retrospect of the Eighteenth Century* (New York, 1803).

exhibiting the same 'activity and enterprise, or the same skill in sciences, as those of more temperate climates.'[16]

Still, if the conceptual framework for Jeffersonian science was derived from the European tradition, its substantive content was conditioned by Jefferson's own patriotic, utilitarian, and empiricist enthusiasms and his delight in pondering the relationship between scientific, political, and religious discourse. But it is possible to go further than this and claim that it was Jefferson's personal fascination with the brute geography of the continent that provided the template for the science of the entire Jeffersonian era. Nowhere is this more clearly revealed than in the only book Jefferson himself ever authored: *Notes on the State of Virginia* published in 1780–1. It was, in essence, a regional geography of his beloved state, as is plain from its fuller title: *Notes on the State of Virginia, written . . . in answer to certain queries . . . respecting its boundaries, rivers, sea ports, mountains, cascades and caverns, productions, mineral, vegetable and animal, climate, population, military force, marine force, aborigines, counties and towns, constitution, laws, college, buildings and roads, proceedings as to Tories, religion, manners, manufactures, subjects of commerce, weights, measures and money, public revenue and expenses, histories, memorials, and state papers.* According to John Greene, this volume 'set the tone and foreshadowed the content of much of American science for the next three decades. It provided a preview of things to come.'[17]

Notes on the State of Virginia wore its author's patriotic heart on its sleeve. Again and again Jefferson paused to fire broadsides at Buffon's assertions about America's degenerate environment and inferior life forms. To refute the aberrant Frenchman's speculations, Jefferson – like Humboldt – measured just about everything he encountered: tree circumference, vegetable weight, animal height. In every case America's productions were, in both vigour and size, as good if not better than their Old World counterparts. And so Jeffersonian-style geography facilitated the ideological interests of national pride. As Greene puts it in his account of early American geography: 'Patriotism, economic interest, and scientific curiosity all dictated that the works of nature in the New World be described, catalogued, and placed at the service of the new nation.'[18]

Inspired by Jefferson's own work, numerous other geographical invento-

---

[16] William Channing Woodbridge, *A System of Universal Geography, on the Principles of Comparison and Classification* (Hartford: Oliver D. Cooke and Sons, 1824), pp. 155, 206.
[17] Greene, *American Science*, p. 29.
[18] Ibid., p. 188.

ries of different states were also published. Samuel Williams, for example, produced a patriotic, anti-Buffonian survey of Vermont in 1794; Jeremy Belknap did the same for New Hampshire. David Ramsay and John Drayton published accounts of South Carolina, and John Filson wrote about Kentucky. And so it soon became necessary to draw together these accumulating, if disparate, collections of data into a single work of reference, and a young Congregationalist clergyman, Jedediah Morse, rose to the task. Although neither a cartographer nor field geographer, he collected – largely by correspondence and the combing of secondary literature – a vast amount of material to produce in 1789 *The American Geography*, a thoroughly synthetic and derivative work. The volume dealt with astronomical geography, the discovery and settlement of the New World, theories about the origin of indigenous peoples and animals, followed by a survey of its physical geography as a prelude to a political account of each state and territory. Morse seemed bent on including every fragment of geographical information and so, like Topsy in *Uncle Tom's Cabin*, the book just 'growed'. It is no wonder that his friend and confidant Ezra Stiles wrote to him warning that other expansive geographical texts had become 'lost in oblivion' or were by self-enlargement 'on the road to death . . . like the Roman Empire to ruin and suicide.'[19] Still, all in all, it was a highly successful undertaking and the work was issued in one new edition after another. Indeed Morse also found time to produce *The American Universal Geography* in two volumes and *Geography Made Easy*, a text specifically designed for students. So, criticisms notwithstanding, Morse earned for himself the dubious title 'Father of American Geography', his only real contemporary rival being a German, Christoph Daniel Ebeling, who had published *Erdbeschreibung und Geschichte von Amerika: Die Vereinigten Staaten von Nordamerika*. But German was not widely read in America and so, despite Ebeling's rather more careful scholarship, his reputation suffered.

If Jefferson's scientific style snaked its way through these regional and sub-regional inventories, his greatest geographical legacy was born of his orchestration of the famous western territorial expedition undertaken by Meriweather Lewis and William Clark (figure 5.1). Earlier in 1793 he had planned a mission up the Missouri to be undertaken by the French naturalist André Michaux, but the project was still-born. However, in 1802, shortly after his assumption of the presidency of the United States, Jefferson hatched another scheme to bring the continental West under sci-

[19] Quoted in William Warntz, *Geography Now and Then: Some Notes on the History of Academic Geography in the United States*, American Geographical Society Research Series no. 25 (New York: American Geographical Society, 1964), p. 59.

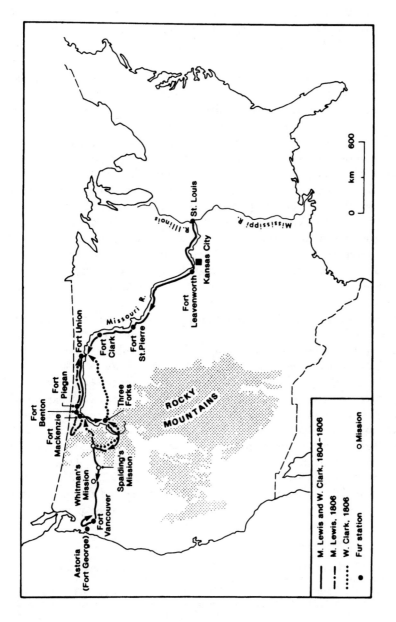

Figure 5.1 *Lewis and Clark's western territorial expedition*

entific scrutiny. This interior voyage of discovery was explicitly planned by Jefferson 'to enlarge our knowledge of the geography of our continent . . . and to give us a general view of the its population, natural history, productions, soil and climate.'[20]

In May 1804 Lewis and Clark began their ascent of the Missouri. It was to be well over two years before they were again to set foot in St Louis. As they went, they gathered large numbers of mineral and plant specimens which they shipped back along with scientific information of all kinds. Daily they were awed by the teeming wildlife of the northern prairies and their expedition provided a wealth of unrivalled ethnographic, ornithological, botanical, zoological, and mineralogical information about the West. But for all these undoubted contributions, John Greene reminds us that 'in the last analysis, however, any proper account of the scientific achievements of the Lewis and Clark expedition must stress its contributions to the geography of the North American continent.'[21] Apart from anything else it was a massive exercise in geographical self-education. For Lewis and Clark had set out with all sorts of assumptions that the West was a superabundantly fertile region perfectly suited for agricultural settlement. Their illusions were shattered as they compiled what has been described as a 'cartographic masterpiece', namely, Clark's map for the history of the expedition. In turn, their own depiction of the West as a great desert was to be challenged as the idea of the Great Plains was born.[22] But still, their cartographic and geographical achievements were substantial, as the Continental Divide and the great plain of the Columbia River were depicted for the first time.

Whatever the scientific achievements of Lewis and Clark's geographical inventory, imperial and political interests were never far below the surface. The economic possibilities of the West were soon realized and the rich upper Missouri country began to be opened up to traders and trappers. The West's geopolitical potential with its savour of Manifest Destiny was already being foreshadowed in the minds of Lewis and Clark. Besides this, the fact that their enterprise was a government-sponsored one meant that its broad-ranging discoveries were seen as belonging to the people of the

---

[20] Greene, *American Science*, pp. 196–7.

[21] Ibid., p. 211.

[22] On this see John L. Allen, *Passage Through the Garden: Lewis and Clark and the Image of the American Northwest* (Urbana, Ill.: University of Illinois Press, 1975); G. Malcolm Lewis, 'Early American Exploration and the Cis-Rocky Mountain Desert, 1803–1823', *Great Plains Journal*, 5 (1965): 1–11; G. Malcolm Lewis, 'Regional Ideas and Reality in the Cis-Rocky Mountain West', *Transactions of the Institute of British Geographers*, 38 (1966): 135–50; G. Malcolm Lewis, 'Changing Emphases in the Description of the Natural Environment of the Great Plains Area', *Transactions of the Institute of British Geographers*, 30 (1962): 75–90.

new democracy.[23] And thus geography played its role in the democratization of knowledge in the new republic as a whole clutch of entrepreneurs
and naturalists caught the exploring bug. Mountain men and government
officials, trailblazers and scientists, all swarmed to the West, making crude
maps, producing journals and reports, and, perhaps most of all, generating
an incredible oral tradition about the West right throughout the nineteenth
century. Their discoveries were to become part of the very fabric of the
nation's accumulated knowledge of its own environment. As for their
exploits, these have been chronicled elsewhere, and nowhere more elegantly
than in the writings of William Goetzmann, and so need not be surveyed
here.

Of course the lust for scientific knowledge and greedy visions of economic possibility were not the only ways in which the rise of the West
crystallized in both erudite and public minds. The West generated not only
an insatiable thirst for travelogues and guidebooks, but also for poems,
tales, and other works of fiction. James Fenimore Cooper's *The Pioneers*
(1823) and *The Last of the Mohicans* (1826) heralded a flood of publications
exploring what Gerald Kennedy calls 'the frontier of the imagination.'
Moreover there were a few individuals, and chief among them was a certain William Darby (1775–1854), in whom the poetic and scientific impulses
fused. Not only did Darby publish more than fifteen volumes on western
geography and history, but he also produced a whole series of border narratives in literary magazines.[24] Many of the latter were cram-full of eye-
catching detail on the geography of the West, and thus Darby's fascination
with the geography of fact *and* the geography of fiction were mutually reinforcing.

In the Jeffersonian and post-Jeffersonian era the American West was thus
a major stimulus to the development of American geography in both scientific and humanistic veins. At the same time the continuing vitality of
teleological thinking within geographical theory remained unimpeded. And
this is the subject to which we will now turn.

The Teleological Tradition

We have already noted that a good deal of Jeffersonian science was transacted within the context of natural theology. Now I want to show that in
the post-Jeffersonian period this selfsame discourse continued to provide

[23] Goetzmann, *New Lands, New Men*, p. 115.
[24] J. Gerald Kennedy, *The Astonished Traveler. William Darby, Frontier Geographer and Man of Letters* (Baton Rouge: Louisiana State University Press, 1981).

the common context for the pursuit of American geography. There are many individuals whose work would provide illustration of this claim; but I propose to restrict my observations here to two candidates whose influence on the American geographical tradition was both deep and lasting, namely, Arnold Henri Guyot (1807–84) and Matthew Fontaine Maury (1806–73).

It was through Guyot that American geography received its baptism in Ritter's philosophy.[25] For Guyot had grown up in Switzerland and had studied under Ritter before emigrating to the United States in the face of untoward political events. The Neuchâtel Academy in Switzerland, where he taught history and geography, was suppressed by the revolutionary council of Geneva in 1848. Jobless, Guyot had little option but to follow his old friend Louis Agassiz to the New World. It was a big change. For the Guyot family roots were deeply lodged in the Neuchâtel region. Guyot had studied at the local university before departing for Germany to complete his education. There, in Karlsruhe, he fell in with Louis Agassiz and Karl Schimper, both proponents of natural history in the great German idealist tradition. But it was later in Berlin, where he was preparing for the ministry of the church, that he came under the most formative influences of his career. The Berlin of the time was intellectually dazzling and Guyot soon found scientific diversion not only in the form of Humboldt and Hegel but also from Steffens in psychology and philosophy, Mitscherlich in chemistry, Hofman in geology, and Dove in physics and meteorology. But it was Carl Ritter who made the profoundest impression, for he more than anyone else captured Guyot's imagination through his integration of evangelical faith and geographical thought. Guyot found Ritter's near-beatific vision of the Creation as a grand organism animated by the will of an all-wise divine intelligence so overwhelming that he dedicated himself to the furtherance of the Ritterian philosophy. Indeed he sensed a special need to devote himself to this cause because, as he noted many years later in 1860, Ritter's work was not widely appreciated outside the German-speaking world.[26]

While Guyot found Ritter's rhapsodic geography captivating, he took

[25] On Guyot, see James D. Dana, 'Biographical Memoir of Arnold Guyot', *Annual Report of the Board of Regents of the Smithsonian Institution for 1887* (Washington: Government Printing Office, 1889), pp. 693–722; William Libbey, 'The Life and Work of Arnold Guyot', *American Geographical Society*, 16 (1884): 194–221; Albert V. Carozzi, 'Guyot, Arnold Henri', *Dictionary of Scientific Biography* (New York: Scribner's, 1970–81), vol. 5. I have discussed Guyot in my *Darwin's Forgotten Defenders* (Edinburgh: Scottish Academic Press, 1987), pp. 22–4.

[26] Arnold Henri Guyot, 'Carl Ritter: An Address to the Society', *Journal of the American Geographical Society*, 2 (1860): 28.

care, like his mentor, not to divorce sublime contemplation from mundane spadework. Prompted by Agassiz he spent some weeks of the summer of 1838 in the Alps making a series of fundamental observations on moraines, the differential flows of glaciers, and the banded nature of ice, all with a view to testing the glacial theories of Agassiz himself. His results were communicated orally, and it was with a mixture of pleasure and chagrin that he later saw his conclusions confirmed by Agassiz and Forbes, who received the accolade of scholarly acclaim. Besides this, Guyot was later to be engaged in the setting up of a series of meteorological observatory stations under the auspices of the Smithsonian Institution and produced an important volume on meteorology in 1851.

Guyot had been teaching at Neuchâtel some nine years when, as I have said, political events intervened to truncate his Swiss career. And so he followed Agassiz to the New World. It was a blessing in disguise, for no sooner had he arrived than he was delivering the prestigious Lowell lectures in Boston on 'Comparative Physical Geography'. They were presented to a large and appreciative audience, which evidently found Guyot's French no linguistic barrier, and were subsequently published as *The Earth and Man*. Fashioned on a Ritterian template, and conceived on a grand scale, the work was presented as a geographical testimony to the harmonies of nature and history that everywhere expressed the control of a beneficent providence. The text was rife with organic metaphors. Emphasizing the interplay of continental physiography and the course of human history, Guyot's *Earth and Man* revolved around the idea of development in earth history, organic growth, and social progress alike. It was a radical departure from the conventional geographical inventory. Rather it offered what can only be called an ecological perspective in which the interdependent relations within nature and between nature and humankind were expressed. And of course the whole vision was undergirded by Guyot's self-professed idealist natural theology:

> All is order, all is harmony in the universe, because the whole universe is a thought of God; and it appears as a combination of organisms, each of which is only an integral part o f one still more sublime. God alone contains them all, without making a part of any.[27]

It would be quite mistaken, I believe, to regard the teleological assumptions with which Guyot's geography was suffused as an unfortunate theological appendage to his substantive work. In fact his version of natural

[27] Arnold Henri Guyot, *The Earth and Man: Lectures on Comparative Physical Geography in its Relation to the History of Mankind* (1849; rep. New York: Scribner's, 1897), p. 82.

theology proved to be conceptually rich. In the inter-war years, for example, when W. M. Davis came to reflect on the progress of the American geographical tradition he reserved a special place for Guyot's contributions, commenting that *The Earth and Man* 'was pervaded by a spirit of rational correlation, and may therefore be regarded as having given us the first great impulse toward the cultivation of geography as a serious and independent science.'[28] Guyot's ecological geography, then, was the direct outgrowth of his reading of the design argument in its organic form. By the same token, if his natural theology was intellectually rewarding, it was also socially prescriptive. Immediate ideological implications were apparently to be drawn from a belief in the providential ordering of things. The geographical distribution of the different human races, for example, and their perceived place in an overall racial hierarchy could be accounted for by a fusion of environmental determinism and providential theology. So he explained the locus of civilization as a consequence of geographical circumstance and divine control:

> the Creator has placed the cradle of mankind in the midst of the continents of the North, so well made, by their forms, by their structure, by their climate, as we shall soon see, to stimulate and hasten individual development and that of human societies; and not at the centre of the topical regions, whose balmy, but enervating and treacherous, atmosphere would perhaps have lulled him to sleep, the sleep of death in his very cradle.[29]

Guyot was to retain this philosophico-theological perspective for the rest of his life, the challenges of Darwinism notwithstanding. Certainly there are hints in his later writings that he would allow some circumscribed version of the 'development theory', but again it had to be woven with suitable theological threads. In fact Guyot did regularly lecture to the Princeton seminarians on 'The Connection of Revealed Religion and Physical and Ethnological Science' while he occupied the position of geography professor at Princeton University. Later he published an elaborate harmonization of earth history with the early Genesis narratives in a volume entitled *Creation or The Biblical Cosmogony in the Light of Modern Science*, an expanded version of a paper he had originally read before the 1873 meeting of the Evangelical Alliance.[30] Such a project was, of course, not so outlandish then

---

[28] William Morris Davis, 'The Progress of Geography in the United States', *Annals of the Association of American Geographers*, 14 (1924): 165.

[29] Guyot, *Earth and Man*, p. 251.

[30] Arnold Henri Guyot, 'Cosmogony and the Bible; or, the Biblical Account of Creation in the Light of Modern Science', in Philip Schaff and S. Irenaeus Prime (eds), *History, Essays, Orations, and Other Documents of the Sixth General Conference of the Evangelical Alliance, held in New York, October 2–12, 1873* (New York: Harper and Brothers, 1874), pp. 276–87.

as it may appear to some today, and it was adopted as a means of harmonizing religion and science by a number of influential nineteenth-century scientists, notably James Dana, America's leading geologist at the time.[31]

Just as the organic analogy proved to be Guyot's inspiration, the machine metaphor best expressed the geographical natural theology of Matthew Fontaine Maury.[32] No doubt their radically different backgrounds conditioned the sorts of conceptual iconography to which they each turned. For while Guyot grew to intellectual maturity in the sophistication of Teutonic high culture and hence was drawn to holistic romanticism, Maury was brought up in backwoods Tennessee and, following his brother into a naval career, doubtless was absorbed with bits and pieces of machinery. His earliest scholarly work was, understandably, directly rooted in his navigational needs. As acting sailing master of the sloop of war, *Falmouth*, Maury searched high and low for reliable information on winds and ocean currents, all to no avail. So he decided to keep his own records in his rounding of Cape Horn. The results were published in the *American Journal of Science and Arts* for 1834. But sooner than he expected, or perhaps even hoped, Maury found himself permanently engaged in precisely this sort of paperwork. A knee injury in 1836 prevented him from returning to sea, and when in 1839 he received the appointment of superintendent of the Navy Depot of Charts and Instruments, he availed himself of the opportunity to carve out for himself a highly distinguished career in science.

When Maury was nominated to head the new US Naval Observatory he found himself in an ideal position to issue a series of pioneering reports on astronomical and oceanographical data. But he was not content to merely catalogue information; he sought to synthesize his material into a coherent system, and accordingly produced the widely known general model of atmospheric circulation depicting the equatorial doldrum belt, the trade winds, the mid-latitude and polar calms, and the Westerlies. Despite its flaws this scheme was almost universally adopted in school texts. And then

---

This was later expanded into *Creation or the Biblical Cosmogony in the Light of Modern Science* (New York: Charles Scribner's Sons, 1884).

[31] See James D. Dana's review, 'Creation; or, the Biblical Cosmogony in the Light of Modern Science', in *Bibliotheca Sacra*, 42 (1885): 201–24. Also Dana's *Memoir of Guyot* cited in note 25.

[32] Useful sources on Maury include Charles Lee Lewis, *Matthew Fontaine Maury, Pathfinder of the Seas* (Annapolis: US Naval Institute, 1927); Frances Leigh Williams, *Matthew Fontaine Maury: Scientist of the Sea* (New Brunswick, N.J.: Rutgers University Press, 1963); John Leighly, 'Introduction', to Matthew Fontaine Maury, *The Physical Geography of the Sea* (Cambridge, Mass.: Harvard University Press, 1963); Nathan Reingold, *Science in Nineteenth Century America* (New York: Hill and Wang, 1964), pp. 145–52.

in 1855 Maury issued a volume that was, according to Humboldt, to establish a whole new field of study, *The Physical Geography of the Sea*. That
Humboldt welcomed it is scarcely surprising, for those selfsame
Humboldtian practices of measurement, inventory, and social utility were
all part of the book's conceptual fabric.

Evaluations of Maury's significance in American intellectual life are
diverse. Some believed he had created a whole new science appropriate to
the period; others that he was an amateur, a dilettante, even a fake. Either
way, there were indeed things that kept him apart from certain key figures
in the emerging circle of professional scientists along what has been called
the Washington–Harvard axis. For one thing critics felt that he put the
cause of the naval service before scientific advancement when he was in
control of the observatory; again, some felt that his preparedness to theorize in advance of the data was evidence of a lack of professionalism. And
then his extremist advocacy of the South's regional causes distanced him
from Northerners who felt that he was only too willing to use his scientific
work in the service of political ideology. For Maury dreamed of advancing
Southern expansion right into South America and was forever finding
justifications for southern railroads, telegraph cables, and ocean vessels.

However his overall scientific contribution is to be judged, there can be
no doubting the popularity and significance of *The Physical Geography of
the Sea*. To be sure, it was laced with high-flown metaphysical speculations,
but these very speculations reveal the conceptual cast in which Maury's
whole science was shaped. The edifice was erected foursquare on the foundations of William Paley's natural theology. Maury's interpretation of the
land–water proportions of the globe; his idea of balancing compensations
in the inorganic and organic realms; his mechanistic model of energy trans-
fers between earth, sea, and air; and his understanding of atmospheric and
marine circulation systems – all were presented in terms of thoroughly
Newtonian natural law guided by providential design. The following
extract nicely captures the spirit of the entire undertaking:

> The sea, therefore, we infer, has its offices and duties to perform; so may we
> infer, have its currents, and so, too, its inhabitants; consequently, he who
> undertakes to study its phenomena, must cease to regard it as a waste of
> waters. He must look upon it as a part of the exquisite machinery by which
> the harmonies of nature are preserved, and then he will begin to perceive the
> developments of order and evidences of design which make it a most beauti-
> ful and interesting subject for contemplation.
>
> To one who has never studied the mechanism of a watch, its main-spring
> or the balance-wheel is a mere piece of metal . . . Take it to pieces, and

show him each part separately; he will recognize neither design, nor adaptation, nor relation between them; but put them together, set them to work, point out the offices of each spring, wheel, and cog, explain their movements, and then show him the result; now he perceives that it is all one design . . . So, too, when one looks out upon the face of this beautiful world, he may admire the lovely scene, but his admiration can never grow into adoration unless he will take the trouble to look behind and study, in some of its details at least, the exquisite system of machinery by which such beautiful results are accomplished. To him who does this, the sea, with its physical geography, becomes as the main spring of a watch.[33]

Again, let me repeat, such convictions are not to be regarded as just too precious; as Goetzmann remarks, the concept of the world as a 'mechanism controlled by God through design . . . [was] a concept that nearly every scientist in the America of Maury's time held to be true, including Joseph Henry, James Dwight Dana, Asa Gray, Benjamin Silliman, Louis Agassiz, and Alexander Dallas Bache.'[34]

The evolution of the American geographical tradition in the Jefferson and immediate post-Jefferson era, then, reveals at least two diverse though related strands of endeavour. First there was America's national love affair with its own environment, a love affair expressing the very unsizableness and extravagance of the continent itself. But more than that, this glory in the vastness of its continental data was, as often as not, gathered up into a chorus of devotion which found fulsome expression in the language of purpose, providence, and design. Enthusiasms, however, are rarely enough to establish a cognitive identity; what is frequently needed are institutional arrangements in which devotees can cultivate their mutual interests. In Britain, just such facilities began to emerge during the early decades of the nineteenth century, and to these we will now turn.

THE BRITISH SCENE

Geography in pre-Darwinian Britain was a pretty diversified affair, so much so that any mere chronology would rapidly degenerate into a stock-list of names, dates, and places. Rather than proceeding this way, however, I propose to organize our thinking about British geography in the period around four themes: its institutional framework, its expeditionary thrust, its

[33] M. F. Maury, *The Physical Geography of the Sea* (first pub. 1855, London: Nelson, 1874), pp. 44–5.
[34] Goetzmann, *New Lands, New Men*, p. 328.

imperial impulse, and its disciplinary aspirations. In this way something of the diversity of the tradition, its continuities and discontinuities, will, I hope, be glimpsed.

The Institutional Framework

Much British scientific endeavour in the early years of the nineteenth century was conducted by private individuals, many of whom were clergymen with the time and intellectual resources to engage in the pursuit of natural knowledge. But during these years a host of scientific institutions burst upon the cultural scene, drawing together like-minded investigators and providing a forum both for the communication of findings and for mutual encouragement. Such societies as the Geological, for example, had come into being in 1807, the Civil Engineers' in 1818, the Royal Astronomic in 1820 and the Zoological in 1826. These were London-based clubs and they each played key roles in the cultivation of the scientific professional. But there were important amateur societies, too, which exerted a particularly formative influence on the institutional fabric of British geography. The Newcastle Natural History Society, for instance, was founded in 1829 and was only one of a host of field clubs that mushroomed at the time. Under its auspices the mapping of the North Eastern Coalfield was carried out. Again there was the Berwickshire Naturalists' Club, formed in 1831, the ethos of which has been nicely captured by Colin Russell:

> [It was] an institution which owned no property, which opened membership widely to members of both sexes, and whose activities were far removed from the evening sessions of the so-called 'closet' naturalists. After suitable refreshment at a local hostelry early in the morning, members would spend whole days on the bracing uplands of the Cheviot or surrounding countryside, combining the sheer pleasure of open air exercise in congenial company with a serious attempt to study the natural history of the area and record it in a systematic manner.[35]

Besides providing outdoor diversion and scientific cultivation, many of these natural science societies had hidden ideological agendas, too. Those for working men, like the various mechanics' institutions, were frequently engaged in a programme of social management, if not control. Education was seen to have tremendous social advantages in that it could oppose such evils as sensuality, vice, crime, and alcoholism. And thus scientific knowl-

---

[35] Colin Russell, *Science and Social Change 1700–1900* (London: Macmillan, 1983), p. 184.

edge could be used both as a stabilizing force in society among conservative groups, or as a radicalizing tool among social reformers. Both shared a belief in the fundamental importance of education as a vehicle for social change, and the institutionalization of science aided that project. Hence movements for the diffusion of scientific knowledge frequently went hand in hand with advocacy for the democratization of education.

As far as the geographical community was concerned, the Royal Geographical Society (RGS), of which more presently, played the leading role in early-nineteenth-century Britain.[36] But it would be quite wrong to imagine that it was the sole representation of the institutional drive among geographical practitioners. Certainly there are those who take the RGS as the uncontested point of departure for the incipient professionalization of British geography. But this is to ignore the role played by the Ordnance Survey in the institutionalization of British geographical practice. Here I use the word 'practice' advisedly, not to disparage the Survey's very considerable theoretical and technical accomplishments in the field of cartography, but to indicate that its activities were more in the sphere of practical, rather than academic, geography.

Its official beginnings can be traced back to 1791, but its foundation owed much to the earlier impetus provided by the last Jacobite uprising, when the lack of reliable maps greatly hindered the pacifying operations carried out by the Duke of Cumberland after his defeat of Bonnie Prince Charlie at the Battle of Culloden in 1746. Later, the advent of the Seven Years' War interrupted operations and it was not until 1765 that William Roy was appointed to the new post of Surveyor General of Coasts and Engineer for Directing Military Surveys in Great Britain under the Board of Ordnance. 'Throughout cartographic history,' as Alan Hodgkiss comments, 'a threat of war has been necessary in order to provide the stimulus for mapmaking.'[37] Still, whatever the source, the Survey had produced by the beginning of the nineteenth century the first 1-inch to the mile sheets for Kent and parts of Essex and London. In Ireland the massive 6-inch survey, intended mainly for land valuation and hence for taxation purposes, was

---

[36] On the general theme of geography's institutionalization, see Capel, 'Institutionalization of Geography', pp. 37–69. Unfortunately Capel's treatment is laced with presentist and essentialist assumptions about what constitutes geography 'in the strict sense.'

[37] A. G. Hodgkiss, 'The Ordnance Survey One Inch to One Mile Map – An Outline History, with Special Reference to the Early Editions', *Bulletin of the Society of University Cartographers* (1969–70). See also Yolande O'Donoghue, *William Roy 1726–1790. Pioneer of the Ordnance Survey* (London: British Library, 1977); R. A. Skelton, 'The Origins of the Ordnance Survey of Great Britain', *Geographical Journal*, 128 (1962): 415–30.

instituted in the early 1830s.[38] That this was geographical practice is certainly beyond question, for vast amounts of regionally based information were gathered together and portrayed in cartographic form.

These observations are certainly not designed to decry the absolutely crucial role played by the RGS in the crystallization of geography as an independent discipline in nineteenth-century Britain. The society was formed in 1830, largely as the outgrowth of the African Association and the Raleigh Club, and its character for long enough reflected its origins in these societies.[39] For one thing, it perpetuated the prandial traditions of the Raleigh as a dining club for travellers. Of course this was in keeping with many of the other London-based scientific societies of the time like the Geological and, more colourfully, the Zoological, whose members were, as Stoddart gleefully notes, 'in the habit of eating whatever had recently died in the [Zoological] Gardens.'[40] The fare was truly rich and merits a brief gastronomic aside. The zoologists, for example, consumed from time to time such delicacies as zebra, yak, and canned rattlesnake, while the members of the Raleigh Club established the tradition of dining on specialities from whichever part of the world the host had been travelling in: accordingly diners on one occasion consumed reindeer from Spitzbergen, rye-cake from North Cape, crystallized berries from Lapland – all washed down by jars of Swedish brandy.[41]

Such private dining clubs, as might be expected, performed a vital social function among the London scientific set and the RGS certainly had more than its fair share of dignitaries. Most of the original members were men of high social standing or were drawn from the ranks of the military, and later Keltie could boast that 'everybody who was anybody was expected to belong.'[42] This alone made the RGS rather different from some of the other

[38] See J. H. Andrews, *A Paper Landscape. The Ordnance Survey in Nineteenth-Century Ireland* (Oxford: Clarendon Press, 1975).

[39] See Elspeth Lochhead, 'The Emergence of Academic Geography in Britain in its Historical Context' (Ph.D. thesis, University of California, Berkeley, 1980); Hugh Robert Mill, *The Record of the Royal Geographical Society 1830–1930* (London: The Royal Geographical Society, 1930); D. R. Stoddart, 'The R.G.S. and the "New Geography": Changing Aims and Roles in Nineteenth-Century Science', *The Geographical Journal* 146 (1980): 190–202; Ian Cameron, *To the Farthest Ends of the Earth. The History of the Royal Geographical Society, 1830–1980* (London: MacDonald, 1980).

[40] See Stoddart, *On Geography*, p. 22.

[41] Precisely the same was true of the Acclimatisation Society. In 1859 the gathered company enjoyed a 'zoological dinner to which each of the four points of the compass had sent its contribution.' At the head of the table sat Professor Owen, 'his scalpel turned into a carving knife, and his gustatory apparatus in full working order.' George C. Bompas, *The Life of Frank Buckland* (London: Thomas Nelson, n.d.), p. 95.

[42] John Scott Keltie, 'Thirty Years' Work of the Royal Geographical Society', *Geographical Journal*, 49 (1917): 350–72, citation on p. 350.

scientific societies and gave it a rather dilettantish, amateurish image, particularly as time went on and the number of members who were also Fellows of the Royal Society declined. Still, whatever the clientele, the RGS established itself as the cultural power base of the English geographical confraternity and reinforced its self-appointed hegemony by securing royal patronage and dispensing its own geographical benediction through the presentation of various medals. Thereby it could confer legitimation on the work of geography's practitioners. Yet all of this had to be fought for, for the society did not fall from heaven as a benign gift. The opposition of such a formidable figure as Sir Joseph Banks, for example, had to be circumvented, for he, as president of the Royal Society, jealously guarded the London scientific scene by acting as a kind of gatekeeper to the metropolitan scientific kingdom.[43] To Banks, dining clubs were all very well in their place, so long as their scientific aspirations did not get out of control, and so it was not until after his death that various of the societies could get going.

For all the gastronomic, social, and scientifico-political goings-on, the RGS did attract its share of serious-minded students of nature. Men like Darwin, Huxley, Wallace, Hooker, Bates, not to mention Sir Roderick Murchison, its chief architect during the mid-Victorian era, supported the venture to various extents. Darwin, for example, joined the society in 1838 soon after his famous *Beagle* voyage, frequently provided reports on papers submitted to the society, and published his celebrated study of coral reefs in the pages of its journal.[44] Wallace was, in due course, awarded the society's founder's medal for his biogeographical work and likewise contributed to the journal's proceedings.[45] Bates, assistant secretary of the society for some twenty-seven years, earned for himself a considerable scientific reputation for his work on entomology and his scientific travels with Wallace in South

---

[43] See Stoddart, *On Geography*, pp. 18–19.

[44] Mill, *Record of the Royal Geographical Society*, pp. 48–49. Darwin's paper appeared as 'The Structure and Distribution of Coral Reefs: Being the First Part of the Geology of the Voyage of the "Beagle", under the Command of Capt. Fitzroy, R.N., during the Years 1832 to 1836', *Journal of the Royal Geographical Society*, 12 (1842): 115–20. A full discussion of Darwin's coral reef theory is to be found in D. R. Stoddart, 'Darwin, Lyell, and the Geological Significance of Coral Reefs', *British Journal for the History of Science*, 9 (1976): 199–218. Darwin served on the council of the Royal Geographical Society for a few years in the early 1840s, but in April 1843 wrote to the secretary, Julian Jackson, informing him that he was no longer able to act in this capacity. See Frederick Burkhardt and Sydney Smith (eds), *A Calendar of the Correspondence of Charles Darwin, 1821–1882* (New York: Garland Publishing, 1985), No. 672.

[45] Mill, *Record of the Royal Geographical Society*, p. 132.

America.[46] J. D. Hooker, another founder's medal holder, supported the society's orchestration of various scientific expeditions.[47] And yet it would be true to say that these individuals did not find that the overall cast of the RGS was to their liking; Murchison's promotional efforts were distasteful to their scientific palates, the atmosphere too redolent with populism and pretension, and therefore many held themselves aloof. Joseph Hooker, for example, did not mince his words when he complained to Julius von Haast – surveyor-general of Canterbury, New Zealand – in 1864: 'I hate the clap-trap and flattery and flummery of the Royal Geographical, with its utter want of Science and craving for popularity and excitement, and making London Lions of the season of bold Elephant hunters and Lion slayers, whilst the steady, slow, and scientific surveyors and travellers have no honour at all.'[48]

The Expeditionary Thrust

The very way in which Hooker conveyed his revulsion at the propagandist pirouetting of the RGS's foremost chiefs-of-staff, however, still left room for considerable admiration for the genuinely 'scientific' products of its expeditionary forces. And indeed, whatever the activities of its well-positioned, publicity-conscious poseurs, the RGS did deliver a number of disciplinary motifs that substantially moulded the shape of British geography throughout the Victorian period. Chief among these were the long-standing concern with exploration, the passion to reduce *terrae incognitae* to cartographic enclosure, and the urge to catalogue the racial differences of the peoples of the earth.

The overseas adventure of expansionist Britain in the nineteenth century was, by and large, orchestrated through the agency of the Royal Geographical Society. Indeed, throughout the entire Victorian period, geography was the science of imperialism *par excellence*. We will turn presently to this catalytic impulse; but for the moment I only want to record that overseas exploration provided the society with its institutional identity. After all, as we have just noted, the RGS grew out of an interest group connected both with the Africa Association that had been established by

---

[46] Bates corresponded with Darwin about his work on mimicry in butterflies and provided Darwin both with zoological specimens and with books and atlases from the RGS's library. See *Calendar of the Correspondence of Charles Darwin*, nos 4800, 6214, 9275. On Bates see George Woodcock, *Henry Walter Bates. Naturalist of the Amazons* (London: Faber, 1969).

[47] See Mill, *Record of the Royal Geographical Society*, pp. 27, 80, 86, 154, 156, 160.

[48] Quoted in Robert A. Stafford, *Scientist of Empire. Sir Roderick Murchison, Scientific Exploration and Victorian Imperialism* (Cambridge: Cambridge University Press, 1989), p. 59.

Joseph Banks to further the exploration of the 'dark' continent, and with the Raleigh Club which itself was an offshoot of the Travellers Club. Given this heritage it is not at all surprising that the vast majority of communications to the society were first-hand accounts of travels and explorations.

Besides publishing in its journal travel chronicles like 'Narrative of a Journey from Mokha to Sana' by Mr T. Spratt (volume 8), 'Notes of a Journey to Kordofan' by Arthur Holroyd (volume 9), and 'Report of a Journey to the Sources of Amu Derya' by Lieutenant Wood (volume 10) – to take just one or two random samples – the RGS also provided sponsorship for numerous exploration ventures. The spectre of a Northwest Passage, for example, continued to haunt the society, and so with determined doggedness the RGS perpetuated a search that had captivated sea-going minds ever since the days of John Cabot. Thus, just the year after its formation, the RGS announced its interest in a 'land expedition across the territories of the Hudson's Bay Company' in search of Captain John Ross, with the added aim of extending 'knowledge of the Arctic shores.'[49] Although the enterprise – undertaken by Captain James Back – proved to be less than a spectacular success, it stimulated a sequence of similar treks over the next decade, the most significant of which was that led by Dr John Rae, the most tragic that of Sir John Franklin. His disappearance triggered a host of other expeditions to find him; these were sponsored not only by the RGS, but also the American government, the Hudson's Bay Company, the Royal Navy, and a clutch of private well-wishers.

The Arctic, of course, was not the only field in which the RGS sought to satisfy its appetite for exploration. The Australian outback was just an empty space on the map, and so the society also turned its attention in the early years to the southern antipodes.[50] Financial factors, however, not to mention commitments to other projects, prevented any sustained campaign of reconnaissance. And yet the society remained captivated by this ancient, unknown world and so sponsored a number of smaller-scale efforts and awarded its gold medal some eleven times to Australian explorers.

The first of these awards went to John Edward Eyre, who, in the early 1840s, experienced horrendous privations in his 1,000-mile trek from Fowler's Bay to King George's Sound. Eyre's reports appeared in the pages of the society's journal, as did his argument that the supposed existence of a great sea in the Australian interior was mistaken. Yet conjectures were not conclusive evidence, and so the challenge of removing the 'ghastly

[49] See Cameron, *Farthest Ends*, p. 29.
[50] For more on Australian exploration see Alan Moorhead, *Cooper's Creek* (London: Hamilton, 1963); Cameron, *Farthest Ends*, chapter 3.

blank' on the map of central Australia remained. It was taken up by Charles Sturt, who, despite poor health and failing eyesight, managed to come within a hair's-breadth of reaching the continent's centre. Certainly he dispelled the mists of ignorance that had lain over Australia's heartland, but they were replaced by the gloominess of a weary and desolate world, sterile, inhospitable, fly-infested. Of course, first-hand knowledge of the interior did not slake the thirst for expeditionary drama, and so in the decades following the race was on to win the accolade of being the first to complete the transcontinental trek. Foolhardiness, bravery, and boundless ambition all contributed to the succession of great Australian journeys that brought the RGS's benediction on exploration as the apogee of early Victorian geographical practice. As we shall subsequently see, this motif continued to reassert itself until well into the twentieth century.

Financial backing, institutional sponsorship, and a publication outlet for travel narratives, however, did not exhaust the RGS's lust for overseas lore. No less significant were the cartographic accompaniments that regularly complemented the travel prose. Indeed, during the first decade of its life, the 'London Geographical Journal', as *the Journal of the Royal Geographical Society* was sometimes called, published well over one hundred maps, sketches, and illustrations which attest to the draughting competences which were among the insignia of the incipient geographical professional. Expert cartographers like Arrowsmith, Petermann, Keith Johnston, Bartholomew, and Stanford worked with writers to provide graphic illustration of the regions they had traversed. The cartographic imperative to map the world can thus be seen on page after page of the RGS's journal and in the society's map room, which from 1854 received an annual government grant and which had accumulated by the early 1930s some 1,700 atlases, and 183,900 maps.[51] Besides this, patrons were kept fully informed of developments in the mapping of the homeland: reports on the progress of the Ordnance Survey and later of the Geological Survey were periodically issued. All in all the image of the geographer as the master of maps was amply reinforced.

To capture foreign and domestic topography on paper was just one prong of the RGS's assault on global ignorance; another was the cataloguing of racial divergence. Indeed, this ethnographic strain continued to survive in various strands of the geographical tradition for well over a century. The ethnic note was sounded right from the first issues of the RGS's journal when Scott Nind provided a 'Description of the natives of

[51] Mill, *Record of the Royal Geographical Society*, p. 240.

King George's Sound' in the inaugural volume, a refrain that was taken up in the next number of the journal in William Hillhouse's 'Notices of the Indians settled in the interior of Guyana', and the following year by W. D. Cooley in his 'Memoir on the civilization of the tribes inhabiting the highlands near Dalagôa Bay'. Of course this anthropological thrust is scarcely surprising in view of the fact that for many years certain key members of the Ethnological Society of London – men like John Crawfurd, Francis Galton, Frederick Hindmarsh, Richard Burton, William Spottiswoode, A. R. Wallace, and Thomas Hodgkin – were also Fellows of the RGS, and that at the British Association for the Advancement of Science, Section E was established in 1851 under the rubric of 'Geography and Ethnology'.[52] Moreover the published journals of travellers, like Captain Back, frequently contained ethnographic portraits of tribal peoples encountered.

The narrative detail provided by travellers in the publications of the RGS was only one source of fodder for the anthropological mind; another was the data that its funds generated through sponsorship of various expeditions. A. R. Wallace's free passage to the Malay Archipelago in the 1850s, courtesy of the RGS, enabled the co-discoverer of natural selection to sustain a substantial period of 'participant observation' in native huts, sharing food shortage, fever, and infection with the 'savages' who were the unwitting subjects of his reflections on the natural history of racial origins. Moreover, both geographical themes and the names of RGS-sponsored travellers also surfaced in the pages of the *Transactions of the Ethnological Society of London*. In the 1860s, for example, Dr John Rae shared his impressions of the Canadian Inuit with the ethnologists, Clements Markham provided an inventory of the indigenous peoples of the Amazon valley, and John Crawfurd spoke about the racial effects of climate and the relationships between ethnology and physical geography more generally in an address that provoked much comment from the audience.[53] Indeed

---

[52] It is true to say, however, that contributions specifically dealing with racial questions seemed to decline in the 1850s, perhaps as a consequence of the establishment of the ideologically racist Anthropological Society of London spearheaded by James Hunt and Robert Knox. On various aspects of anthropology in the Victorian period, see George W. Stocking Jr., *Victorian Anthropology* (New York: Free Press, 1987); Ronald Rainger, 'Race, Politics, and Science: The Anthropological Society of London in the 1860s', *Victorian Studies*, 22 (1978): 51–70; George W. Stocking, Jr., 'What's in a Name? The Origins of the Royal Anthropological Institute: 1837–1871', *Man*, 6 (1971): 369–90; Nancy Stepan, *The Idea of Race in Science: Great Britain 1800–1960* (London: Macmillan, 1982).

[53] Thus, Dr John Rae, 'On the Esquimaux', *Transactions of the Ethnological Society of London*, n.s. 3 (1865): 138–53; Clements Markham, 'A List of the Tribes in the Valley of the Amazon, Including those on the Banks of the Main Stream, and of all its Tributaries', *Transactions of the Ethnological Society of London*, n.s. 3 (1865): 140–95; John Crawfurd,

among the anthropologists, of both monogenetic and polygenetic persuasions, there spread a mode of discourse that might be described as 'moral climatology', in which certain regional climates were dismissed as degenerate, productive of dissolute and depraved living, in contrast with those zones conducive to the emergence of civilization. An analysis of the use of moralistic vocabulary in climatological talk throughout the entire Victorian era would be a project worthy of sustained consideration and we will peruse the subject in chapter 7. Thus the social evolutionary paradigm of the new anthropology, so indebted as it was to Wallace himself, as well as the flood of brute ethnographic data that flowed from naked Victorian expansionism, were at least in part a product of the RGS's lust for knowledge of exotic geographies.

The traffic between geography and anthropology, moreover, was not all one way. If anthropology benefited from the geographers' impulse towards faraway places and faraway peoples, the geographical fraternity had long been kept abreast of the latest findings and methods of ethnology by a number of partisans. Among those who kept these lines of communication open, special mention must be made of James Cowles Prichard, arguably the foremost student of race and ethnology in early-nineteenth-century Britain. Perhaps chief among his many anthropological interests were his investigations into the question of racial origins, a theme that runs like a high voltage current through his celebrated *Researches into the Physical History of Man*, which made its first appearance in 1813. Revealed here was Prichard's solid adherence to a monogenetic account of the history of the human species, namely, that all human races were descended from a single stock, not from a number of originally distinct strains as polygenists asserted.[54]

The sources of Prichard's anthropology were, predictably, many and diverse. But undoubtedly one of the most profound was his encounter with the travel literature of the late eighteenth and early nineteenth centuries produced by men like Cook, Banks, Foster, and Humboldt. So it is not surprising that in the early years of the RGS's existence Prichard's name

---

'On the Effects of Commixture, Locality, Climate, and Food on the Races of Man', *Transactions of the Ethnological Society of London*, n.s. 1 (1861): 76–92; John Crawfurd, 'On the Connection between Ethnology and Physical Geography', *Transactions of the Ethnological Society of London*, n.s. 2 (1863): 4–23. These issues are discussed in chapter 7.

[54] For a useful survey of Prichard's thinking, see George W. Stocking, Jr., 'From Chronology to Ethnology: James Cowles Prichard and British Anthropology, 1800–1850', in James Cowles Prichard, *Researches into the Physical History of Man*, edited and with an introductory essay by George W. Stocking, Jr. (Chicago: University of Chicago Press, 1973), pp. ix–cxviii.

should from time to time feature in the pages of its publications. In 1839, for example, he published a 24-page paper 'On the ethnography of High Asia' in the *Journal*, and over the years provided reviews of significant anthropological volumes for the geographers.

To my mind, one of the most interesting was his review of a work entitled *Crania Americana* by the celebrated American student of race, Samuel George Morton,[55] less because of the particular views expressed by Prichard than for the geographical community's engagement with the anthropological project that Morton's volume articulated. Morton's *bête noir* was the standard single-origin account of human races. To him there were actually different human *species* that had come into being in different geographical settings across the face of the globe.[56] Inevitably, Morton argued the case that human racial differences were permanent and therefore that racial differentiation could not have been produced by climatic or other environmental means. Racial factors were innate, not induced. His book was thus an attempt to provide hard statistical data that would substantiate a different created status for Europeans and Amerindians, a viewpoint he later extended with equal vigour to blacks and whites.

Given his Quaker background and evangelical leanings, not to mention his support for the causal role of cultural environment in the history of racial differentiation, Prichard's inclinations were understandably entirely different: as I have said, they were monogenetic. All humans were descended from a single primeval family unit, he believed. And so it is quite remarkable that in his review of Morton's treatise for the RGS one gets absolutely no hint of their divergence of views. Prichard's commentary was remarkably sanguine, even complimentary, in its lauding of 'the learning, ingenuity and skill manifested' by the author.[57] But what is significant for our purposes is less the similarities or differences between the two men, than the introduction of cranial measurements to the readers of the RGS Journal. That Morton's whole undertaking was geographically grounded is plain from the survey methods that he had employed, organizing his material on a regional basis and thus making observations on the physical and

[55] [James Cowles] Prichard, Review of *Crania Americana; or, a Comparative View of the Skulls of Various Aboriginal Nations of the North and South America: to which is Prefixed an Essay on the Varieties of the Human Species* by Samuel George Morton, *Journal of the Royal Geographical Society*, 10 (1841): 552–61.

[56] See the discussion in Stephen Jay Gould, 'Morton's Ranking of Races by Cranial Capacity', *Science*, 200 (5 May 1978): 503–59; also his *The Mismeasure of Man* (Harmondsworth: Penguin, 1984).

[57] Prichard, Review of *Crania Americana*, p. 561.

social characteristics of the inhabitants of particular locations. If there was a mathematics of cranial capacity, there was a geography of it as well.

The inferences to be drawn from any distributional pattern in skull size were hardly self-evident, of course; but that they were marshalled into the harshest of scientifico-racial ideologies is now well known. Indeed Morton's successors – Josiah Nott and George Gliddon – appended to their collaborative *Indigenous Races of the Earth* of 1857 a world chart tellingly entitled 'On the Geographical Distribution of the *Simiæ* in Relation to that of Some Inferior Types of Men'. The monkey-chart, as Gliddon himself styled it, contained portraits of Fifty-four monkeys and six human types, and was drawn up using such standard atlases as those of Schmarda, Berghaus, Johnston, Petermann, and Humboldt. The purpose of the undertaking was simple: it was to illustrate Agassiz's idea that monkeys and 'inferior' humans were connected in a specially intimate way with particular regional environments and that within the geographical bounds of what Gliddon termed 'the circumvalling line which surrounds the zone occupied by the *simiæ*, no "civilization" . . . has ever been spontaneously developed since historical times.'[58] This topic need not further be pursued just now; suffice, however, to note that here we encounter the beginnings of a geographical tradition of mapping – both literally and metaphorically – racial difference that continued to thrive within geography until well into the twentieth century.[59]

The Imperial Impulse

It is commonplace to find explorers, in the years around 1800, contrasting their own endeavours with the exploits of the overseas travellers of a century before. Earlier itinerants were hardly to be dignified with the title scientific traveller for – so people were told – they were more like buccaneers or pirates and were more consumed with reckless greed than with the thirst for knowledge exhibited by the sober, latter-day students of science and

---

[58] J. C. Nott and George R. Gliddon, *Indigenous Races of the Earth* (Philadelphia, 1857), p. 650.
[59] Even in 1988 anthropometric maps of Europe (hair colour, stature, cephalic index, and facial index) were still being published in geography textbooks using the mapping data of Renato Biasutti and Hans Günther. Of course the naked racism of earlier pronouncements are now expunged, but the cartographic project itself clearly has its roots in the nineteenth-century anthropometric tradition. See Terry G. Jordan, *The European Culture Area. A Systematic Geography* (New York: Harper and Row, 2nd edn 1988), chapter 3.

humanity.[60] Such characterizations are not to be believed. But they do nevertheless serve to draw attention to the changing *self-image* of explorers in the early nineteenth century. What had also changed – and this change no doubt had to do with explorers' self-proclamations – was public attitudes. Now the explorer was frequently seen as a heroic adventurer, a bearer of civilization, an agent of enlightenment. And yet in many ways the explorer was an outsider, the quintessential stranger both at home and abroad.

Just what was it that impelled these adventurers towards the unknown? Doubtless the lust for fame, a sense of patriotism, religious zealotry, hopes of fortunes, the desire for unfettered living, even the driving of the Devil and the sin-smorgasbord available abroad (if Richard Burton is to be believed) were all among the motive forces pushing them from hearth and home.[61] The motives were many and mixed and certainly were different for different people. The institutional engagement with exploration – if the RGS is in any sense representative – is perhaps more readily typified. And yet while it may be relatively easy to find a word – say, imperialism – under which to subsume institutional motives, it is undoubtedly true that the label masks a complex array of attitudes and practices regarding exploration.

For all that, the first issue of the RGS journal made plain the *raison d'être* of the newly instituted organization:

> That a new and useful society might be formed, under the name of THE ROYAL GEOGRAPHICAL SOCIETY OF LONDON.
> That the interest excited by this department of science is universally felt; that its advantages are of the first importance to mankind in general, and paramount to the welfare of a maritime nation like Great Britain, with its numerous and extensive foreign possessions.[62]

This submission makes plain the imperialistic undergirding of the institution's entire project and thereby reveals that Victorian geography was intimately bound up with British expansionist policy overseas. To be sure, these forces would become even more pronounced as the century wore on; but it is plain that from the earliest days of the society the imperial thrust was registered. Thus at the end of the first decade of the society's life it is

---

[60] James Bruce, for example, writing in the late eighteenth century rated William Dampier as little better than a pirate. See James Bruce, *Travels to Discover the Source of the Nile* (6 vols, Dublin, 1790–1), vol. 1, p. ii.

[61] See the analysis by Van Orman, *The Explorers*, chapter 7.

[62] *Journal of the Royal Geographical Society of London*, 1 (1831): vii.

not surprising to find the president, W. R. Hamilton, himself a diplomat and an FRS, reflecting on the scope of geography in militaristic, commercial, and imperialistic terms. Geography, he insisted,

> is the mainspring of all the operations of war, and of all the negotiations of a state of peace; and in proportion as any one nation is the foremost to extend her acquaintance with the physical conformation of the earth, and the water which surrounds it, will ever be the opportunities she will possess, and the responsibilities she will incur, for extending her commerce, for enlarging her powers of civilizing the yet benighted portions of the globe, and for bearing her part in forwarding and directing the destinies of mankind.[63]

It certainly was a stirring manifesto. Geography was not merely engaged in *discovering* the world; it was *making* it. What was more, this vision was altogether believable, largely due to the immense personal influence of one singular individual, Sir Roderick Murchison. Before we turn to what I would call the Murchisonian moment in Victorian geography, however, I want to illustrate something of the range of interplay between geographical knowledge and imperial prejudices by a brief consideration of a man who is rather less well known, Sir Henry Bartle Frere (1815–84).

Later in life, Frere served as president of the RGS, but his earliest geographical work dates from 1847 when he was serving as commissioner in Satara. From that vantage point he began issuing a range of surveys of various Indian excavations. The details need not concern us here. What is significant in the present context is the way in which Frere's field experience in the Deccan and in Sind were mobilized to confirm his conviction that human cultures were naturally segregated into the civilized and the savage. From the artefacts of material culture, from the practices of legal customs, and from religious teachings – namely, from the elements of historical, political, and cultural geography – Frere believed he could discriminate different levels of social achievement. Not, of course, that barbarous peoples were incapable of change; the civilizing powers of the Christian faith could redeem social structures. Thus Frere's vigorous promotion of the empire's various missionary endeavours was all of a piece with his geography, as was his engagement with frontier politics in South Africa and his advocacy of land reform to foster more intensive cropping on Indian farms. As assistant revenue commissioner in Bombay in the 1830s he obvi-

---

[63] William R. Hamilton, 'Presidential Address', *Journal of the Royal Geographical Society*, 12 (1842): lxxxviii–lxxxix. See also the discussion in Freeman, 'The Royal Geographical Society'.

ously had more than theoretical interests in this latter enterprise. All in all, as F. V. Emery has put it, 'a close and reciprocal bond existed between Frere's geographical attitude and his implementation of imperial policy.'[64] For Bartle Frere, geographical knowledge just *was* geographical praxis.

Given his imperialistic biases, it is not at all remarkable that Bartle Frere should reserve a special enthusiasm for the style of geography advanced by Sir Roderick Murchison. Thus, as president of the RGS, he was only too happy to announce, on the occasion of his conferring the society's gold medal on Murchison, that 'the history of Sir Roderick Murchison's connection with the Royal Geographical Society is, in fact, the history of the Society itself.'[65] If Frere is to be believed, Victorian geography was very largely cast in Murchison's own mould. For as Frere went on:

> he has become the common reference of geographers and scientific travellers of our own and of all other countries. It is no exaggeration to say that, during the past thirty years, no geographical expedition of any consequence has been undertaken in our own, or, I believe I might say, in any other country, without some previous reference to him for advice and suggestion.[66]

Under the watchful leadership of Murchison, the Royal Geographical Society emerged, to use the words of Robert Stafford, as 'a theatre of national suspense,' 'a company of talented adventurers purveying high drama in exotic settings,' and 'an extra-parliamentary venue for debate on empire and peripheral exploitation.' Small wonder that Murchison has been characterized as the 'scientist of empire' and 'the architect of imperial science.'[67] For through the agency of the RGS – which suited Murchison's scientific-colonial tastes perfectly – he almost single-handedly orchestrated the expansionist adventures of the institution that most comfortably represented British imperialism in all its many dimensions. Through its offices, Murchison sought to extend the cultural hegemony of his own scientific style in the antipodes, the Middle East, the Far East, and Africa. In these diverse arenas his robust patriotism, his prophetic scenarios for resource exploitation, his passion to translate *terrae incognitae* into the visual language of cartography, his political prurience in monitoring the commercial

---

[64] See F. V. Emery, 'Geography and Imperialism: The Role of Sir Bartle Frere (1815–84)', *The Geographical Journal*, 150 (1984): 342–50, ref. on p. 349. Frere's geographical vision comes through in H. B. E. Frere, 'Presidential Address, Section E (Geography)', *Report of the 39th Meeting, British Association for the Advancement of Science, Exeter* (1869): 152–9.

[65] Cited in Stafford, *Scientist of Empire*, p. 219.

[66] Ibid., p. 220.

[67] Ibid., pp. 211, 212.

potential of marginal economies, and his urgent advocacy of geographical exploration all found outlet.

Not that these activities were divorced from the cognitive side of his 'scientific' pursuits. On the contrary, he used whole continents as the laboratory in which to test his own Silurian theories (he was the discoverer of the Silurian strata) and as the sites over which his taxonomic control could be extended.[68] He was thus every bit as concerned to enlarge the empire of Siluria as to advance Britain's imperial interests abroad. Moreover geography satisfied Murchison's psychological proclivities too. The society's military clientele and the subject's logistic serviceability undoubtedly resonated with his own earlier exploits in the Peninsular War. Besides these, the imperial vocabulary in which he depicted the diffusion of the Silurian system resounded with pugilistic metaphors of territorial expansion – his taxonomy 'invaded' continents, 'enlisted recruits', and engaged in 'the field of battle' much like the ancient Romano-British tribe for which Siluria was named.[69]

Two additional observations on geography's complicity in Britain's imperial ventures are, I think, in order. First, while the encounter was hardly unique – numerous other sciences, from astronomy to zoology, were similarly implicated in overseas expansionism[70] – there is something to be said for the claim that geography was the science of imperialism *par excellence*. Exploration, topographic and social survey, cartographic representation, and regional inventory – the craft practices of the emerging geographical professional – were entirely suited to the colonial project. And this, together with the RGS's self-conscious cultivation of its public role as ser-

[68] See Robert A. Stafford, 'Roderick Murchison and the Structure of Africa: A Geological Prediction and its Consequences for British Expansion', *Annals of Science*, 45 (1988): 1–40.

[69] See the discussion in James A. Secord, 'King of Siluria: Roderick Murchison and the Imperial Theme in Nineteenth-century British Geology', *Victorian Studies*, 25 (1982): 413–42.

[70] See, for example, Roy MacLeod and Philip F. Rehbock (eds), *Nature in its Greatest Extent. Western Science in the Pacific* (Honolulu: University of Hawaii Press 1988); Roy MacLeod, 'On Visiting the "Moving Metropolis": Reflections on the Architecture of Imperial Science', *Historical Records of Australian Science*, 5 (1982): 1–15; Lucile Brockway, *Science and Colonial Expansion: the Role of the British Royal Botanical Gardens* (London Academic Press, 1979); G. Leclerc, *Anthropologie et Colonialisme: Essai sur l'Histoire de l'Africanisme* (Paris: Editions du Seuil, 1972); Lewis Pyenson, 'Astronomy and Imperialism: J. A. C. Oudemans, the Topography of the East Indies, and the rise of the Utrecht Observatory, 1850–1900', *Historia Scientiarum*, 26 (1984): 39–81; Robert A. Stafford, 'Geological Surveys, Mineral Discoveries, and British Expansion, 1835–71', *Journal of Imperial and Commonwealth History*, 12 (1984): 5–32; Terence Ranger, 'From Humanism to the Science of Man: Colonialism in Africa and the Understanding of Alien Societies', *Transactions of the Royal Historical Society*, 5th series, 26 (1976): 115–41; John M. MacKenzie (ed.), *Imperialism and the Natural World* (Manchester: Manchester University Press, 1990).

vant of empire, render altogether plausible Stafford's claim that in the early nineteenth century, national expansion provided the RGS with its leading unifying motif.[71]

Secondly, if the teleological vocabulary in the pages of the Royal Geographical Society's journal is conspicuous by its meagreness, the broader ideology of expansionism was bolstered by a providentialist theology that took colonialism as the vehicle of spiritual enlightenment. Nowhere, perhaps, is this more clearly displayed than in reflections on David Livingstone's missionary–imperial ventures in Africa. In his prefatory remarks to Livingstone's Cambridge lectures in 1858, for example, Adam Sedgwick, geologist and then vice-master of Trinity College, Cambridge, expressed his hope that the volume in hand would advance 'the great and good cause of civilization, brotherly love and Christian truth – and . . . encourage the Missionary of the Gospel in carrying the message of peace to poor benighted Africa.' Not surprisingly his commentary was replete with references to the workings of divine providence – a doctrine with religious, imperial, and scientific possibilities. For by it Sedgwick could legitimate both Livingstone's evangelistic engagements and the nation's imperial exploits, while at the same time claiming the approbation of Britain's favourite missionary on the integrity of the scientific enterprise by affirming that 'he [Livingstone] practically believed that no parts of true knowledge, whether sacred or profane, can, when rightly used, ever be in mutual antagonism.'[72] Moreover Sedgwick could support Livingstone's colonial project over against the Portuguese because he regarded them as 'slave-dealers and Papists, and therefore, on both accounts, adverse to any scheme bearing the diffusion of Christian light, and Christian protestant freedom.'[73]

Thus while what could be called the 'cognitive geographical teleology' of Guyot and Maury rarely surfaced among the dining club geographers – even from the numerous Fellows of the society who were members of the clergy – a providential theology of colonial praxis formed the common context for much of the discourse. Besides, while the former natural theology, whether in organic or mechanistic, homological or adaptationist modes, could be put to work in the service of theory, the latter, undergirding as it

---

[71] Stafford, *Scientist of Empire*, p. 218.

[72] Revd William Monk, *Dr Livingstone's Cambridge Lectures together with a Prefatory Letter by the Rev Professor Sedgwick, Edited with Introduction, Life of Dr Livingstone, Notes and Appendix* (London, 1858), pp. ii, vi.

[73] John Willis Clark and Thomas McKenny Hughes, *The Life and Letters of the Reverend Adam Sedgwick* (Cambridge, 1890), ii, 416–17.

did the rhetoric of colonialism, was frequently deployed for the purposes of political legitimation. Moreover as Alfred Sharpe reflected in the early years of the twentieth century, 'the first steps for occupation, civilization and development of our colonies were taken by the Church' – an observation reinforcing Bartle Frere's commentary some years earlier on the dozens of mission stations that collectively constituted 'an enormous agency for geographical and other scientific discovery.'[74]

Disciplinary Aspirations

In the expansive personage of Sir Roderick Murchison, Victorian geography's institutional framework, expeditionary thrust, and imperial impulse were almost seamlessly, not to say shamelessly, woven into the fabric of the subject. And yet it would be mistaken to take the Murchisonian style as the only geographical idiom of the period. There were those, and chief among them was Mary Somerville, whose concern was to spell out the central cognitive claims of geography as a branch of science and to keep it fully abreast of the latest advances in science rather than to view it as just an adjunct to exploitative commercialism or as the repository of travel diaries. To be sure, this does not mean that seeking for a piece of conceptual territory in the scientific scheme of things was incompatible with the imperial theme; it merely attests to another dimension in the incipient professionalization of geography.

Mary Somerville's concern in the various editions of her celebrated *Physical Geography* was to keep her readers informed of the geographical consequences of 'the recent rapid progress of science and the numerous expeditions by sea and land, not for mere amusement, but for high scientific research.'[75] This work won her the Victoria gold medal of the RGS, election to the American Geographical and Statistical Society and to the Italian Geographical Society, several medals, and personal praise from the ageing Alexander von Humboldt himself.[76] Indeed she was in an ideal position to act as a scientific go-between to the geographers, for she had already demonstrated her mastery of Laplace's celestial mechanics in *The*

[74] Sir Alfred Sharpe, 'The Geography and Economic Development of British Central Africa', *Geographical Journal*, 39 (1912): 1; Bartle Frere, 'On Temperate South Africa', *Proceedings of the Royal Geographical Society*, n.s. 3 (1881): 10.

[75] Mary Somerville, *Physical Geography* (London: Murray, 1848; 4th edn 1858), preface.

[76] For details see Elizabeth C. Patterson, 'Mary Somerville', *British Journal for the History of Science*, 4 (1969): 309–39; Elizabeth C. Patterson, 'Somerville, Mary Fairfax Grieg', *Dictionary of Scientific Biography*; Marie Sanderson, 'Mary Somerville: Her Work in Physical Geography', *Geographical Review*, 64 (1974): 410–20.

Mechanism of the Heavens (1831) and her proficiency in Newtonian mathematics in her 1834 volume *On the Connexion of the Physical Sciences.* Accordingly, the *Physical Geography* – her last book – was designed to keep the geographical community fully apprised of developments in astronomy, geology, zoogeography, terrestrial magnetism, botany, and oceanography.

In many ways, the *Physical Geography* was the conceptual culmination of her long-standing commitment to the Baconian ideal of universal integration. Thus the title page of several editions of her book *On the Connexion of the Physical Sciences* was adorned with Francis Bacon's words: 'No natural phenomenon can be adequately studied by itself alone – but, to be understood, it must be considered as it stands connected with all nature.' This theme of connectedness, of the hanging-togetherness-of-things, was precisely the geographical vision that men like Humboldt and Ritter had championed in continental Europe. It became Mary Somerville's too. For if geography had an independent disciplinary identity it was to be found here, in its capacity to integrate the disparate elements of world and life into a coherent whole. To be sure, in the long term, this unifying vision would become tarnished, as the professionalization and fragmentation of scientific knowledge rendered it increasingly obsolete or at least little more than mere rhetoric. Yet in Somerville's day such holistic aspirations seemed not only manageable, but essential, and the fact that the 'queen of science' should concern herself with the subject was greatly welcomed by the geographers.

Holistic comprehensiveness, however, did not exhaust Mary Somerville's conception of the geographical task. To her, geography reached beyond integrative description; it was a causal science of distributions. As she explained: 'Physical Geography is a description of the earth, the sea, and the air, with their inhabitants animal and vegetable, of the distribution of these organized beings, and the causes of that distribution.'[77] Those causes, moreover, were not merely environmental; they included the agency which the human subject exerted both on the natural order and on other living organisms. 'The effects of his [man's] intellectual superiority on the inferior animals, and even on his own condition, by the subjection of some of the most powerful agents in nature to his will,' she asserted, 'together with the other causes which have had the greatest influence on his physical and moral state, are among the most important subjects of this science.'[78] Accordingly, Somerville included within the rubric of physical geography

---

[77] Somerville, *Physical Geography*, p. 1.
[78] Ibid.

consideration of the geography of race, and the effects of human civilization on the earth's surface.

The ecological temper of Somerville's proposals were entirely in keeping
with the state of pre-Darwinian theoretical geography in the United States;
and the natural theological foundations on which American geography
rested was no less conspicuous in Somerville. This, of course, is not at all
surprising given her enthusiasm for the 'Physical Geography of the Ocean,
by Lieutenant Maury.' Accordingly, she insisted that the pattern of human
centres of civilization, mirroring as they did moral configurations of climate, exhibited 'the arrangement of Divine Wisdom'; the earthquake and
the torrent were 'the august and terrible ministers of Almighty Power'; irresponsible agricultural methods brought inevitable decline in yield because
the 'works of the Creator are nicely balanced, and man cannot infringe His
laws with impunity.'[79]

Pre-Darwinian geography in America and Britain was clearly a diversified
enterprise encompassing a range of vocabularies and practices, and arising
from a variety of social and cognitive interests. As for its idioms of communication, geographers variously resorted to the language of cartography, the
art of travel writing, scientific prose; their practices encompassed the para-
phernalia of exploration, the techniques of survey, the skills of draughts-
manship, not to mention the *in situ* implementation of administrative
policy; their motives ranged from the commerical thrust of an imperial era
and the concern to provide geography with a coherent cognitive identity, to
the impulse towards Christianizing the world and the desire to use geographical knowledge to confirm belief in God's design in the world.

And yet for all this diversity one can detect two strands that snake their
way through the geographical literature of the pre-Darwinian period,
emphases from which the title of this chapter is drawn. Those who predominantly concerned themselves with geographical *theory* almost invariably erected the discipline's conceptual edifice on the idea of design; on its
theoretical front geography was a teleological science. By contrast, those
engaged in geographical *practice* and who were associated with the dining
club set scarcely made reference to issues of this sort; teleological vocabulary, for example, is conspicuously missing from the contributions of geography's incipient professionals at the RGS where, as we have seen, business
centred on regional description and reportage, and the advancement of
Britain's colonial exploits overseas.

[79] Ibid., pp. 486, 2, 492.

Too much, of course, can be made of the divergence between the dining club set, as I have styled them, namely, those proto-professionals at institutions like the Royal Geographical Society, and the advocates of design, that is, those theoreticians who persistently detected the hand of divine superintendence in the patterns and processes of geographical agencies. As we have seen, the diners and the divines could find themselves in mutual reinforcement on the question of colonial expansionism. As explorers pushed back the cartographic 'darkness' that shrouded the inner reaches of continental landmasses like Africa and America, the interpreters of providential government sensed a celestial radiance 'enlightening' the spiritual gloom. Not only was the colonial adventure seen as a manifestation of the providential order, it was an opportunity for the enlargement of muscular science. As Felix Driver has recently observed: 'The iconography of light and darkness, which embodied powerful images of race, science and religion, portrayed the European penetration of the continent of Africa as *simultaneously* a process of domination, enlightenment and liberation.'[80] The ironies embedded in this coalition of religious rhetoric, scientific theory, and colonial praxis were, of course, manifold; but my purpose in referring to this episode is less to elaborate a moral commentary than to recall that the ideology of imperialism embraced both the teleology of the natural theologians and the expansionist practices of colonial politics. Geography, as we have seen, found itself directly implicated in both.

For all that, there was a substantial bifurcation in both substance and style between geography's out-of-door practitioners and its armchair philosophers. As to rhetoric, the former concentrated their endeavours on the inductive gathering of global data, though this was frequently an exercise in the fabrication of those facts best suited to the national interests of colonial power. By contrast, the theoreticians wanted to infuse such items of geographical particularity with a grander cosmic purpose and to identify in the agents of geographical change the hidden hand of divinity. Both in America and Britain, I would contend, these twin preoccupations helped structure the content and character of geographical science in the pre-Darwinian period.

The consequences of this bifurcation between theory and practice for later advocates of geography as a viable component in the university curriculum were far from inconsequential. For just how theory and practice

---

[80] Felix Driver, 'Geography's Empire: Histories of Geographical Knowledge', *Society and Space*, 10 (1992): 31.

were to be integrated in a time when Darwin had challenged the entire structure of teleological – or, as it has been called, doxological – science, and academic professionalization had rendered mere regional description as scientifically immature, posed very considerable challenges to geographers of the post-Darwinian era.

6

The Geographical Experiment

Evolution and the Founding of a Discipline

In the second half of the nineteenth century, geography's role as a mere adjunct to overseas rambling or as unscientific regional reminiscence, presented its advocates with considerable problems when it came to justifying its role as a university discipline. Such difficulties were exacerbated, moreover, in a day when the teleological undergirding on which its theoretical superstructure had long rested was beginning to crumble under the weight of naturalistic science. Allied to the break-up of the common context that had long been provided by natural theology was the incipient Balkanization of knowledge that accompanied the professionalization of scientific specialities.[1] In this intellectual environment, integrative subjects like geography seemed to lack the specialized scientific rigour that was required to provide a coherent disciplinary identity. It was clear, then, that if the newly professionalized geographers wanted to retain the subject's traditional concerns, some fresh conceptual foundations had to be found that would render their project intellectually plausible. Evolution theory domesticated to their needs, I contend, held out the best prospect. And so, as they turned from natural theology to evolution theory, the founders of professional geography embarked on what I propose calling the geographical experiment – an experiment in keeping nature and culture under the one conceptual umbrella.

In this chapter I want to examine the theoretical tools that a few strategically placed geographers took up in their effort to reconstitute, and thereby professionalize, their discipline in the face of academic atomization. These

[1] See Robert M. Young, 'Natural Theology, Victorian Periodicals and the Fragmentation of a Common Context', in Colin Chant and John Fauvel (eds), *Darwin to Einstein: Historical Studies on Science and Belief* (Harlow: Longman, 1980) pp. 69–107.

manoeuvres, however, turn out to be far from purely abstract; on the contrary, they appear again and again to be all too connected to political and social affairs and to display the 'stern practicality' that will be our focus in the following chapter. First, however, we need to pause and reflect on what is typically taken as the major scientific revolution of the nineteenth century – the coming of Darwinian evolution.

THE DARWINIAN DRAMA

Writing in 1966 David Stoddart claimed that 'much of the geographical work of the past hundred years . . . has either explicitly or implicitly taken its inspiration from biology, and in particular from Darwin' – a statement that might be taken as a geographical rendition of Ernst Mayr's later insistence that Darwinism 'caused a greater upheaval in man's thinking than any other scientific advance since the rebirth of science in the Renaissance.'[2] Even allowing for the overstatement of partisan enthusiasts, not to mention the more recent revisionist readings that play down the salience of the 'revolutionary' metaphor,[3] any serious engagement with the Darwinian corpus by geography's historians is frankly conspicuous only by its absence. Not only did various commemorative celebrations of key Darwinian moments go virtually unnoticed within the geographical literature, but one of the most highly regarded historical works of geographical apologetic – Richard Hartshorne's *The Nature of Geography* of 1939 – to all intents and purposes just simply ignored Darwin.

This lacuna in geography's chronicle has meant that the widespread mobilization of evolutionary motifs for professional (and practical) purposes has remained beyond the bounds of the subject's standard histories. Before turning to these manoeuvres, however, I want to focus momentarily on Darwin's personal involvement with the geographer's art.[4]

---

[2] David R. Stoddart, 'Darwin's Impact on Geography', *Annals of the Association of American Geographers*, 56 (1966): 683–98, ref. on p. 683; Ernst Mayr, 'The Nature of the Darwinian Revolution', *Science*, 176 (1972): 981–9, ref on p. 987.

[3] See for example Peter J. Bowler, *The Non-Darwinian Revolution: Reinterpreting a Historical Myth* (Baltimore: Johns Hopkins University Press, 1988).

[4] There are numerous biographical treatments of Charles Darwin. I have found the following useful: Peter Brent, *Charles Darwin* (London: Heinemann, 1981); Jonathan Howard, *Darwin* (Oxford: Oxford University Press, 1982); Wilma George, *Darwin* (London: Fontana, 1982); Roger G. Chapman and Cleveland T. Duval (eds), *Charles Darwin, 1809–1882: A Centennial Commemorative* (Wellington, New Zealand: Nova Pacifica, 1982); Peter J. Bowler, *Charles Darwin, the Man and his Influence* (Oxford: Blackwell, 1990).

Darwin and Geography

In many ways Charles Darwin (1809–82) (plate 6.1) stands in the grand tradition of geographical exploration stretching back at least to James Cook, and it is therefore no surprise that Alexander von Humboldt's *Personal Narrative of Travels to the Equinotial Regions of the New Continent* was one of his most treasured volumes. And though his formal education, first

Plate 6.1   Charles Darwin in 1840, by George Richmond at Down House. (By permission of the Darwin Museum, Down House, courtesy of the Royal College of Surgeons of England)

at Edinburgh studying medicine and then at Cambridge preparing for the Anglican ministry, did little to equip him for his five-year round-the world voyage on the *Beagle*, his engagement with Humboldtian geography, his friendship with John Henslow, and his inculcation in Paleyite natural theology – all encountered at Cambridge – stood him in good stead. So when on Tuesday 27 December 1831, the *Beagle* weighed anchor in Plymouth, it was with the twenty-two-year old Darwin, an amateur naturalist prone to sea-sickness, on board, travelling as the captain's table companion.[5]

It was during his time on board the *Beagle* that Darwin began to question much that he had been taught, and even more that he had assumed. The geographical distribution of the species he encountered, for example the different species of ostrich in South America, led him to question the standard creationist explanation that formed the warp and woof of Paley's natural theology. Had all the multitudinous varieties of organism come into being by special creative acts? Or was there, perhaps, some other, more naturalistic, interpretation? And just as significant as these dark musings was his encounter with what was to a hitherto untravelled English gentleman an exotic medley of the human species, notably in Tierra Del Fuego, which led him to ponder the question of human origins and the relationship between savagery and civilization. But it was not until his return to England that the idea of natural selection as an explanation for the transformation of species was born, probably at some point during the late 1830s.

In the meantime, Darwin published the first accounts of his circumnavigation in 1839, got married to his cousin Emma, and was elected to a Fellowship of the Royal Society. He became too, as we have seen, a Fellow of the Royal Geographical Society in 1838, no doubt in recognition of his scientific travels, and while he was never a particularly active member of the society, he did provide reports on papers submitted for publication, published his celebrated study of coral reefs in the pages of its journal, and had recourse to books and atlases from the RGS's library, all the while keeping up a sustained correspondence with its secretary, Henry Walter Bates.[6]

Darwin's impact on geography, however, cannot be restricted to his personal involvement with the geographical community. For it was, of course,

---

[5] Darwin apparently did not travel as the official naturalist; that position was occupied by Robert McKormick, the ship's surgeon. See Stephen Jay Gould, 'Darwin's Sea Change, or Five Years at the Captain's Table', in *Ever Since Darwin. Reflections in Natural History* (Harmondsworth: Penguin Books, 1980), pp. 28–33.

[6] See chapter 5.

the theory of evolution with which his name is so closely associated that was to have the profoundest reverberations. The precise moment of the birth of the principle of natural selection has – perhaps understandably – been a source of intense speculation among historians of biology.[7] The chronological details of its gestation period need not detain us here, however, for it is the more general impact of the evolutionary paradigm on geography that concerns us. Accordingly, I think it will be profitable to pause and consider the *structure* of Darwin's theory so as to get a handle on the ways it was called into service within geography.

Darwin's Multiple Metaphors

As Darwin pondered the puzzles of biogeographical distribution and the tantalizing analogies that were evident in animal morphology, it became increasingly clear to him that many of these problems might begin to unravel if different organisms turned out to share common ancestors. If, in fact, the received wisdom about the permanence of species was just plain wrong, and species could evolve and change over time, then observable differences might be traceable to some entirely natural cause. What Darwin needed to substantiate this speculation was a mechanism by which transmutation might be effected.[8]

Two different events provided him with the clues he needed. The first came from his love of pigeons. Darwin had a lifelong interest in pigeons and it was as plain as pikestaff to him that a skilful breeder could produce an almost infinite variety of pigeon forms. Here, he felt, was an inkling as to how the selective processes of nature might operate, and so he carried on a massive correspondence with pigeon fanciers all over the north of England, relentlessly extracting from them the information he needed.[9] It was from this source that Darwin's first metaphor emerged. If nature were to be thought of *as if* it were a breeder, then some light might be thrown on the principles of selection. Darwin, that is to say, developed an analogy between the breeder's selective activity and natural selection. The metaphor

---

[7] See M. J. S. Hodge and David Kohn, 'The Immediate Origins of Natural Selection', in David Kohn (ed.), *The Darwinian Heritage* (Princeton, N.J.: Princeton University Press, 1985), pp. 185–206; M. J. S. Hodge, 'Darwin as a Lifelong Generation Theorist', in Kohn (ed.), *Darwinian Heritage*, pp. 207–43.

[8] For more on Darwin's methodological procedures see Michael Ghiselin, *The Triumph of the Darwinian Method* (Berkeley: University of California Press, 1969).

[9] See James A. Secord, 'Nature's Fancy: Charles Darwin and the Breeding of Pigeons', *Isis*, 72 (1981): 163–86; James A. Secord, 'Darwin and the Breeders: A Social History', in Kohn (ed.), *Darwinian Heritage*, pp. 519–42. On the metaphorical character of natural selection, see Robert M. Young, 'Darwin's Metaphor: Does Nature Select?' *The Monist*, 55 (1971): 442–503.

certainly was suggestive, and so long as Darwin could remember that he was comparing an artificial process with a natural one, it had great explanatory power. It must be said, however, that the inherent danger of reading an anthropomorphic element into the workings of natural selection was a temptation that Darwin found hard to resist. Indeed, as the following gobbet makes clear, there were occasions when it seemed that the attributes of Paley's deity has been transferred to Darwin's nature and 'her' laws:

> It may be said that natural selection is daily and hourly scrutinizing, through-out the world, every variation, even the slightest; rejecting that which is bad, preserving and adding up all that is good; silently and insensibly working, whenever and wherever opportunity offers, at the improvement of each organic being in relation to its organic and inorganic condition of life.[10]

Even while Darwin was measuring the anatomical proportions of those newly hatched pigeons, he came across something else – Thomas Malthus's *Essay on the Principle of Population*, which had been published forty years earlier in 1798. There has certainly been much debate in recent years about precisely what the significance of this intellectual encounter was, and it would be fair to say that the myth of the Malthusian moment, as it might be termed, has been well and truly demythologized. Yet that the Malthus essay did have considerable impact is surely beyond question.

Revd Thomas Malthus, writing in the aftermath of the French Revolution, had identified the universal tendency of human populations to multiply exponentially, thereby exerting an increasing pressure on available resources, until stopped by the limits of food supply. The inevitable conse-quence of this run of events – so inevitable as to be regarded a law of nature – was the advent of a series of population checks such as starvation, famine, pestilence, and war.[11] Here was a pattern that Darwin could apply to all organisms – the idea of a struggle for existence. By transferring Malthus's social law to the natural world, Darwin realized that organisms must die if they multiplied beyond the carrying capacity of their environ-ments. Here, then, was the basis of another metaphor, that of a struggle for existence. Darwin did not mean by struggle, as Tennyson had earlier por-trayed it, that nature was 'red in tooth and claw'. It was rather a question of some organisms being better adapted to their environments, and in every

[10] Charles Darwin, *The Origin of Species by Charles Darwin: A Variorum Text*, edited by Morse Peckham (Philadelphia: University of Pennsylvania Press, 1959), pp. 168–69.

[11] See the discussion in Robert M. Young, 'Malthus and the Evolutionists: the Common Context of Biological and Social Theory', *Past and Present*, 43 (1969): 109–45; Dov Ospovat, 'Darwin after Malthus', *Journal of the History of Biology*, 12 (1979): 211–30.

case better adapted in the terms of leaving more descendants. It was a struggle *to reproduce*, that is to say, it was a theory of relative reproductive success. As he himself put it: 'I should premise that I use the term Struggle for Existence in a large and metaphorical sense including dependence of one being on another and including (which is more important) not only the life of the individual, but success in leaving progeny.'[12]

The key conceptual elements of the theory of natural selection were now in place, and it remained for Darwin to weld them together and publish the results – spurred on by a letter from A. R. Wallace in Borneo who seemed to have come to the selfsame conclusions – in *The Origin of Species* in 1859. Despite the length of the volume and the numerous changes it underwent from edition to edition, one passage in the book that remained virtually unaltered laid out the kernel of the theory:

> If under changing conditions of life organic beings present individual differences in almost every part of their structure, and this cannot be disputed; if there be, owing to their geometrical rate of increase, a severe struggle for life at some stage, season, or year, and this certainly cannot be disputed; then, considering the infinite complexity of the relations of all organic beings to each other and to their conditions of life, causing an infinite diversity in structure, constitution, and habits, to be advantageous to them, it would be a most extraordinary fact if no variations had ever occurred useful to each being's own welfare, in the same manner as so many variations have occurred useful to man. But if variations useful to any organic being ever do occur, assuredly individuals thus characterized will have the best chance of being preserved in the struggle for life; and from the strong principle of inheritance, these will tend to produce offspring similarly characterized. This principle of preservation, or the survival of the fittest, I have called Natural Selection . . . Thus the small differences distinguishing varieties of the same species, steadily tend to increase, till they equal the greater differences between species of the same genus, or even of distinct genera.[13]

It was over this biological theory, then, that the legendary encounter between Bishop Samuel Wilberforce (Soapy Sam, the bishop of Oxford) and Thomas Henry Huxley (Darwin's bulldog) reportedly took place at the 1860 meeting of the British Association for the Advancement of Science. Conventionally this encounter has been taken as symbolic of a warfare between science and Christianity. As historians have raked over the ashes, however, it has become clear that this conflict model is much too crude a

[12] Darwin, *The Origin of Species*, p. 146.
[13] Charles Darwin, *The Origin of Species* (London: Murray, 6th edn 1872), pp. 159–61.

historiographical device for understanding the encounter.[14] In fact, there was at the time a certain amount of support for at least some versions of Darwinian theory from segments of the religious fraternity.[15] These details are beyond our present concerns, however. I only introduce them to give context to what Darwin *did* challenge head on, namely, the old teleological mode of doing natural history. For he had advanced a way of understanding the development of the world's myriad organisms in a plain, casual, humdrum, naturalistic fashion. Besides – and this was of crucial importance – it became clear that the very evolutionary laws that explained organic change might be just as applicable to the human species. Indeed there is now evidence to show that Darwin had intended from very early on to include humanity within his explanatory scheme.[16] Henceforth human society might also be understood in the language of naturalistic evolution.

Evolution and Society

That human society could be brought within the orbit of evolutionary law is hardly surprising, given the conceptual sources of the theory of natural selection. Social Darwinism, as it is conventionally styled, is a catch-all term used to characterize a variety of social theories that emerged during the second half of the nineteenth century. What they all shared was a resort to the vocabulary of evolutionary biology. To consider this as an *extension* of biological theory might be a misconception, however. For as we have seen, Darwin's central ideas of selection and struggle were themselves *already* applications to nature from the realm of human behaviour. As Raymond Williams put it:

> In a sense, you can provide a very adequate analysis of Social Darwinism in terms of the errors of emphasis it makes in extending the theory of natural selection to social and political theory . . . But while that is true, I think it simplifies the matter a little too much, in that the biology itself has from the

---

[14] See the discussions in J. R. Lucas, 'Wilberforce and Huxley: A Legendary Encounter', *The Historical Journal*, 22 (1979): 313–30; Sheridan Gilley, 'The Huxley-Wilberforce Debate: A Reconstruction', in Keith Robbins (ed.), *Religion and Humanism* (Oxford: Blackwell, 1981), pp. 325–40; J. Vernon Jensen, 'Return to the Wilberforce-Huxley Debate', *British Journal for the History of Science*, 21 (1988): 161–79.

[15] See, for example, James R. Moore, *The Post-Darwinian Controversies: A Study of the Protestant Struggle to Come to Terms with Darwin in Great Britain and America, 1870–1900* (Cambridge: Cambridge University Press, 1979); David N. Livingstone, *Darwin's Forgotten Defenders*. See also John Hedley Brooke, *Science and Religion. Some Historical Perspectives* (Cambridge: Cambridge University Press, 1991).

[16] See Sandra Herbert, 'Man in the Development of Darwin's Theory of Transmutation: Part 2', *Journal of the History of Biology*, 10 (1977): 155–227.

beginning a strong social component. Indeed, my own position is that theories of evolution and natural selection had a social component before there was any question of reapplying them to social and political theory.[17]

Of course, social evolutionary concepts were in vogue prior to the appearance of Darwin's imaginative synthesis.[18] Spencer, for instance, had already outlined his own social evolutionary model in his *Social Statics* of 1851 in which he dilated on the metaphor of the body politic. Indeed he confessed that 'So completely . . . is a society organized upon the same system as an individual being, that we may almost say there is something more than analogy between them.'[19] Via his organic analogy Spencer transformed the static moral cosmos of convention into one of dynamic material progress. Nor was Spencer unique. Henry Maine, John Lubbock, and Edward B. Tylor had independently advanced developmentalist accounts of society in response to the earlier failure of positivism to found a social science on the conception of a quiescent human nature; while A. R. Wallace employed the notion of struggle in his interpretation of human society half a decade before the appearance of the *Origin of Species*.[20]

Besides this, there has been considerable debate about whether Darwin himself was a 'Social Darwinian'.[21] This precise issue does not need to be adjudicated here, however, in order to appreciate that the idioms of evolutionary biology were mobilized in the cause of various social and political programmes. We can even lay aside the question of whether the label Social Darwinism names any historical movement at all, for there are good grounds for supposing that it was an abstraction constructed by historians themselves and then read into the past. Apparently the phrase was not in

[17] Raymond Williams, 'Social Darwinism', in Jonathan Benthall (ed.), *The Limits of Human Nature* (London: Allen Lane, 1973), pp. 115–30, ref. on p. 115.

[18] See John C. Greene, 'Biology and Social Theory in the Nineteenth Century: Auguste Comte and Herbert Spencer', in Marshall Clagett (ed.), *Critical Problems in the History of Science* (Madison, Wis.: University of Wisconsin Press, 1959), pp. 419–46.

[19] Herbert Spencer, *Social Statics: or, the Conditions Essential to Human Happiness Specified and the First of Them Developed* (London: Chapman, 1851), p. 448.

[20] See John W. Burrow, *Evolution and Society. A Study in Victorian Social Theory* (Cambridge: Cambridge University Press, 1966); Peter J. Bowler, *The Invention of Progress: The Victorians and the Past* (Oxford; Basil Blackwell, 1989); George W. Stocking, Jr., *Victorian Anthropology*.

[21] See John C. Greene, 'Darwin as a Social Evolutionist', *Journal of the History of Biology*, 10 (1977): 1–27; Jim Moore, 'Socializing Darwinism: Historiography and the Fortunes of a Phrase', in Les Levidow (ed.), *Science as Politics* (London: Free Association Books, 1986), pp. 38–80; Steven Shapin and Barry Barnes, 'Darwin and Social Darwinism: Purity and History', in Barry Barnes and Steven Shapin (eds), *Natural Order: Historical Studies of Scientific Culture* (Beverly Hills: Sage Publications, 1979), pp. 125–42; Robert M. Young, 'Darwinism *is* Social', in Kohn (ed.), *Darwinian Heritage*, pp. 609–38.

vogue until around the end of the nineteenth century.[22] Moreover the way historians employed the term was morally loaded; it came to be used to depict *any* social application of evolution theory – so long as it was vile!

Accordingly, we do not need to agonize over the precise alignments of 'Social Darwinism' or to allow terminological tentativeness to obscure its impact on geography. In saying this I do not intend to seem skittish over the use of terms. All I mean is that ambiguous labelling should not blind us to the very considerable application of Darwinian-sounding language to social affairs. Walter Bagehot's *Physics and Politics* of 1872, for example, was tellingly subtitled 'Thoughts on the application of the principles of natural selection and inheritance to political society.' Saying this, however, certainly does not prejudge the issue of *how* evolutionary schemata were socialized.

That evolutionary talk could buttress *laissez-faire* individualism, as in the case of Herbert Spencer, is well known, as is its use in rationalizing nationalistic aggression, eugenic manipulation, and imperialistic impulses. In the 1880s, for example, Sumner argued that civilization was the social manifestation of the survival of the fittest; again John D. Rockefeller saw the growth of big business as the outcome of natural selection, judging that industrial monopoly was the next stage in society's evolution; John Fiske, John W. Burgess, and other patrician intellectuals saw their own American nation as in the vanguard of social evolutionary progress; and eugenicists like Arnold White found in evolutionary rhetoric justification for urging that the unfit should be prevented from weakening the social organism by transmitting hereditary deficiencies to future generations.[23] Such nasty things in 'Social Darwinism', however, can be overplayed. Greta Jones, for example, has shown that Darwinian motifs infiltrated every bit as deeply into the social outlook of political liberals. W. R. Greg and Francis Galton, for instance, used Darwinian language to make their assault on aristocratic privilege and landed property; in their eyes, aristocracy, 'by awarding social

---

[22] See Donald C. Bellomy '"Social Darwinism" Revisited', *Perspectives in American History*, n.s. 1 (1984): 1–129. Bellomy claims that the first reference in print to 'Social Darwinism' in America did not occur until May 1903. See also Robert C. Bannister, *Social Darwinism: Science and Myth in Anglo-American Social Thought* (Philadelphia: Temple University Press, 1979).

[23] See John Higham, *Send These to Me. Jews and Other Immigrants in Urban America* (New York: Atheneus, 1975); Mark Haller, *Eugenics: Hereditarian Attitudes in American Thought* (New Brunswick: Rutgers University Press, 1963); Kenneth Ludmerer, *Genetics and American Society. A Historical Appraisal* (Baltimore, Md.: Johns Hopkins Press, 1972); G. T. R. Searle, *Eugenics and Politics in Britain, 1900–14* (Leiden: Noordhoff International Publishing, 1976); Daniel Kelves, *In the Name of Eugenics. Genetics and the Uses of Human Heredity* (New York: Knopf, 1985).

status for reason of birth rather than achievement, protected the idle and unproductive in society.'[24] Moreover, significant segments of the political Left – Marxists and Fabians – continued to display great enthusiasm for the potential uses of eugenics.[25] George Bernard Shaw, for example, insisted that 'there is now no reasonable excuse for refusing to face the fact that nothing but a eugenic religion can save our civilization.'[26]

Further elaboration of such diverse 'Social Darwinian' motifs need not detain us here. Enough has been said, I believe, to indicate not only that biology was imported into social theory, but that Darwin's own evolutionary conceptions were conditioned by social factors. Science and society were always tightly interwoven in Darwinism's multiple metaphors.[27] Now I want to pause and reflect briefly on an alternative version of evolutionary theory that also had direct social ramifications and, if I am correct, even more immediate implications for geography in the Darwinian era.

The Neo-Lamarckian Alternative

Darwin's theory of evolution by natural selection certainly did not enjoy an uncontested consensus within the scientific community. In his day it was subjected to a series of criticisms from many quarters. There were, for instance, queries about just what the mechanisms of inheritance actually were, about what produced variation, and about the length of geological time that Darwin's theory presupposed.[28] As a consequence, by the decades around 1900 orthodox Darwinism was in eclipse as a host of competing alternatives surfaced,[29] perhaps the most widespread of which (and, as I shall argue, the most significant for geography) was the selective rejuvenation of the earlier evolutionary doctrines of Jean Baptiste Lamarck.

The precise relationship that this Neo-Lamarckian movement – as it came to be known – sustained with Lamarck's own doctrines is far from

---

[24] Greta Jones, *Social Darwinism and English Thought. The Interactions between Biological and Social Theory* (Brighton: Harvester Press, 1980), p. 36.

[25] See Diane Paul, 'Eugenics and the Left', *Journal of the History of Ideas*, 45 (1984): 567–590. Also Donald MacKenzie, 'Eugenics in Britain', *Social Studies of Science*, 6 (1976): 449–532.

[26] George Bernard Shaw, *Sociological Papers* (London, 1905), pp. 74–75.

[27] See Robert M. Young, 'Revolutionary Biology and Ideology: Then and Now', *Science Studies*, 1 (1971): 442–503.

[28] See David L. Hull, *Darwin and His Critics: The Reception of Darwin's Theory of Evolution by the Scientific Community* (Cambridge, Mass.: Harvard University Press, 1973); Peter J. Vorzimmer, *Charles Darwin: The Years of Controversy. The Origin of Species and its Critics* (Philadelphia: Temple University Press, 1970).

[29] See Peter J. Bowler, *The Eclipse of Darwinism. Anti-Darwinian Evolution Theories in the Decades Around 1900* (Baltimore: Johns Hopkins University Press, 1983).

clear cut. But that it perpetuated certain elements in his system and married them to the principle of natural selection as a secondary mechanism in a distinctively non-Darwinian way is the key issue that will concern us here. The Neo-Lamarckian scheme, broadly speaking, embraced two related mechanisms. Primarily, there was the doctrine of the inheritance of acquired characteristics. Basically this meant that qualities acquired by an organism during its own life-experience would be passed directly on to off-spring. Adaptive modifications could thus be built upon from one genera-tion to another and the evolutionary tempo greatly accelerated. Second, the Neo-Lamarckians attributed the directive force of organic variation to will, habit, or environment. The use or disuse of organs was thus crucial, contin-gent as they were on those altered habits, induced by environmental change, that produced different behaviour patterns. And so, despite its lack of empirical corroboration, the Neo-Lamarckian model seemed to possess theoretical resources to meet many of the problems facing the standard Darwinian scheme: it speeded up the whole evolutionary process by its insistence on direct organic modification; it outflanked the problem of new variations being 'swamped' in succeeding generations; and it provided an account of the origin of variations by insisting that they were attributable to environment and will in mutual cooperation rather than to the vagaries of some capricious variation. Indeed Darwin himself had increasing, if reluctant, resort to these very mechanisms in later editions of the *Origin*.[30]

Particularly in the United States, but also in Britain, this alternative evo-lutionary theory attracted widespread support: Cope and Hyatt spear-headed the movement among palaeontologists; Le Conte and King added their geological support; Argyll and Romanes in anthropology and psychol-ogy also helped swell the tide. Soon a loose coalition of dissident evolution-ary theory was available for those with a passion for socializing evolution. Of those conventionally labelled Social Darwinians – not least Spencer him-self – many drew more inspiration from Neo-Lamarckian dogma than from classical Darwinism. As Peter Bowler put it, 'Much of what has passed for Social Darwinism in the literature may be only Spencerianism – and thus based on Lamarckism with only a superficial gilding of Darwinian rhetoric.'[31] Thus many found in Neo-Lamarckian evolution grounds for looking to environment as the driving force behind social processes; others, more taken with the evolutionary significance Neo-Lamarckians attributed to mind and will, took a more idealist turn. Either way Lamarckism could

---

[30] These and related matters are treated in Bowler, *Evolution*.

[31] Peter J. Bowler, 'Darwinism and Social Darwinism Around 1900'. Paper presented to the 93rd Annual Meeting of the American Historical Association, December 1978.

be mobilized to justify the politics of interventionism.

The ramifications of engaging social Lamarckism were many and diverse. Lester Frank Ward, for example, was pushed by the controversies of the 1890s over Neo-Darwinism far into the Neo-Lamarckian camp and found there the justification for educating his children with the right values, for he believed they would then become part of the race's inherited repertoire.[32] Similarly the geologist Joseph Le Conte could only find firm scientific grounds for education in Neo-Lamarckian inheritance. All our hopes of race improvement, he insisted, 'are strictly conditioned on the efficacy of these factors – i.e., on the fact that useful changes, determined by education in each generation, are to some extent inherited and accumulated in the race.'[33]

Given these particular conceptual alignments it is not surprising, I would judge, that a number of geographers would find the Neo-Lamarckian construal of evolution to their liking. Because the environment played such a key directive role in the scenario, there seemed ample justification for shaping the newly professionalizing discipline on an environmentalist template. And this, as I will now argue, was crucial to the project of carving out some cognitive space in academia for geography as a scholarly discipline.

THE GEOGRAPHICAL EXPERIMENT

The story of how geography's academic institutionalization was eventually accomplished in the face of the educational reforms of the late nineteenth century is both long and complicated, and doubtless involved different strategies in different places. Yet for all that, my contention is that it was the inspiration of evolutionism, especially in its Neo-Lamarckian guise, that was perhaps the key ingredient. Not that numerous geographers were self-consciously Neo-Lamarckian in outlook; rather, when they filtered out of the evolutionary literature those themes least suited to their purposes, they were frequently left with a Neo-Lamarckian residue. This, I believe, can be illustrated from the activities and apologetics of three different personalities in three different locales: Halford Mackinder in Britain, Friedrich Ratzel in Germany, and William Morris Davis in America. I hope, however, that my

---

[32] Ibid.

[33] Cited in Cynthia Eagle Russett, *Darwin in America. The Intellectual Response 1865–1912* (San Francisco: W. H. Freeman, 1976), p. 11. An excellent survey of more general American impacts is available in George W. Stocking, Jr., 'Lamarckianism in American Social Science: 1890–1915', *Journal of the History of Ideas*, 23 (1962): 239–56; E. J. Pfeifer, 'The Genesis of American Neo-Lamarckism', *Isis*, 56 (1965): 156–67.

argument will not be read in terms of a single-factor cause; detailed studies of the academic-political machinations in these different arenas are still needed. But if my suspicions are well founded, the motifs of evolutionary theory do snake their way through the key theoretical pronouncements of these principal actors in the drama.

To Bridge An Abyss: Mackinder's Campaign

When, on the evening of Monday 31 January 1887, Halford Mackinder delivered his thoughts 'On the scope and methods of geography' to the Royal Geographical Society, he lamented that 'At the moment we are suffering under the effects of an irrational political geography, one, that is, whose main function is not to trace causal relations, and which must therefore remain a body of isolated data to be committed to memory. Such a geography can never be a discipline, can never, therefore, be honoured by the teacher.'[34] The fragmentariness of accumulated geographical data, owing to the absence of some coherent methodology, clearly troubled Mackinder, for the purpose of his lecture, as *The Times* reported it, 'was meant to show that the subject could be treated in a way that would make it worthy to take its place alongside of other departments of scientific research.'[35] The way out of the impasse, as Mackinder saw it, was to allocate to geography the task of reintegrating society and environment. Thus even as he passed judgement on 'one of the greatest of all gaps' – that 'between the natural sciences and the study of humanity' – he insisted that it was 'the duty of the geographer to build one bridge over [this] abyss which in the opinion of many is upsetting the equilibrium of our culture.'[36] This move is what I propose calling the geographical experiment – an experiment to keep culture and nature under one conceptual umbrella. So, when Mackinder confirmed that he proposed defining 'geography as the science whose main function is to trace the interaction of man in society and so much of his environment as varies locally,' this affirmation was in direct opposition to Sir Frederic Goldsmid's separation of scientific and historical understanding.[37] Certainly Mackinder was not the first to promulgate this unifying vision; as we have already seen, it had long been part of the geo-

[34] Halford J. Mackinder, 'On the Scope and Methods of Geography', *Proceedings of the Royal Geographical Society*, 9 (1887): 141–60, ref. on p. 143.

[35] *The Times* (18 February 1887), p. 14.

[36] Mackinder, 'Scope and Methods', p. 145.

[37] In the published version of the lecture, Mackinder appended a note indicating that Goldsmid had subsequently written to him claiming that he had misunderstood the import of his (Goldsmid's) comments.

graphical tradition. But with the natural theological foundation rapidly eroding, the casting of geography's integrative aspirations in the language of some alternative discourse seemed necessary.[38] Evolution theory, I contend, provided just such a vocabulary.

That Mackinder had succeeded in compellingly articulating his message was clear from the discussion of the paper that took place a fortnight later on 14 February. Douglas Freshfield – one of the most energetic of the RGS's campaigners for academic geography[39] – picked out as 'one great merit of Mr Mackinder's address' his adoption 'of the clear and liberal view of the functions of geography as the meeting-point between the sciences of nature and of man,' a vision that he himself had already upheld in Birmingham.[40] Almost precisely the same words had been uttered by James Bryce (then Regius Professor of Civil Law at Oxford and later Britain's distinguished transatlantic ambassador) the year before when he promulgated his own geographical rendition of universal history. 'Geography', he had said, 'is as a meeting point between the sciences of Nature and the sciences of Man,'[41] and it was thus only to be expected that he would throw his weight behind Mackinder's proposals. So he 'heartily agreed' with the twenty-six-year-old lecturer because, as he saw it, 'geography was not a science of description nor of distribution, but of causality, [and] that its function was to exhibit the way in which a variety of physical causes played, firstly upon one another, and secondly upon man.'[42] Besides these scholarly accolades, the address also helped earn Mackinder that same year (1887) the position of reader in geography at Oxford, a post sponsored by the RGS,[43] which launched his educational career – a career that would include the principalship of Reading College (1892–1903) and directorship of the London School of Economics (1903–08).

---

[38] See also D. R. Stoddart, 'The RGS and the "New Geography"'.

[39] See W. H. Parker, *Mackinder: Geography as an Aid to Statecraft* (Oxford: Clarendon Press, 1982), p. 107.

[40] Discussion, *Proceedings of the Royal Geographical Society* 9 (1887): 172.

[41] James Bryce, 'The Relations of History and Geography', *Contemporary Review*, 49(1886): 426–43, ref. on p. 426.

[42] Discussion, *Proceedings of the Royal Geographical Society*, 9 (1887): 169.

[43] The readership was established at a salary of £300 per year, half of which was contributed by the RGS. See John Scott Keltie, *The Position of Geography in British Universities*, American Geographical Society Research Series no. 4 (New York: Oxford University Press, 1921), p. 5. On the RGS's educational strategies at Oxford and Cambridge see D. I. Scargill, 'The RGS and the Foundations of Geography at Oxford', *Geographical Journal*, 142 (1976): 438–61; and D. R. Stoddart, 'The RGS and the Foundations of Geography at Cambridge,' *Geographical Journal*, 141 (1975): 216–39.

Mackinder's geographical experiment in keeping nature and culture umbilically connected, I believe, was ultimately grounded in his commitment to the social evolutionary paradigm. Tellingly, even as he lamented the 'irrational' geography under which the RGS was currently suffering, the social evolutionary underpinnings of his proposals emerge in his footnote affirmation that the intercourse of 'man' and 'environment' 'may best be considered on the lines of Bagehot's "Physics and Politics".' What this amounted to, he observed, was that the 'communities of men should be looked on as units in the struggle for existence, more or less favoured by their several environments.'[44] This predilection, actually, comes as no surprise when we recall that Mackinder's main training was in the biological sciences, particularly zoology; that he had absorbed the major tenets of evolution theory under the instruction of the Oxford anatomist H. N. Moseley who had been a member of the *Challenger* expedition; and that when he went on to read history in his final year at Oxford it was, as he later recalled, 'with the idea of seeing how the theory of evolution would appear in human development.'[45] Besides, he subsequently delivered extramural lectures on the social evolutionary theme of 'human communities as units in a struggle for existence.'[46]

None of this, however, is to be taken as evidence that Mackinder was an out-and-out Darwinian.[47] Later in life, for example, he did reject what he took to be the fatalism in orthodox Social Darwinian mechanisms. But his enthusiasm for social evolution Bagehot-style and his later allocating some conceptual space to the role of consciousness in human affairs, provide grounds for the suspicion that he was more inclined to Lamarckism.[48] For all that, his mid-life writings do convey an overwhelming impression of a deterministic construal of the relationship between nature and culture. To be sure it was, 'man and not nature' that was the initiator; 'but nature in large measure controls,' he affirmed in 1904. Thus he enthusiastically spoke of his search for 'a formula which shall express certain aspects . . . of geo-

---

[44] Mackinder, 'Scope and Methods', p. 143.

[45] Cited in Brian W. Blouet, *Sir Halford Mackinder 1861–1947: Some New Perspectives* (Research Paper no. 13, School of Geography, University of Oxford, 1975), p. 7.

[46] Halford J. Mackinder, *Oxford University Extension Lectures. Syllabus of a Course on Geography. Course II: Man and His Environment* (n.p., 1886).

[47] See Paul Coones, *Mackinder's 'Scope and Methods of Geography' after a Hundred Years* (School of Geography, University of Oxford, 1987).

[48] This has been argued in J. A. Campbell and D. N. Livingstone, 'Neo-Lamarckism and the Development of Geography in the United States and Great Britain', *Transactions of the Institute of British Geographers*, n.s. 8 (1983): 267–94.

graphical causation in universal history.'[49] The necessitarian bias in these words had long favourably disposed him towards John Richard Green's *Making of England*, because there he found 'a deduction from geographical conditions of what must have been the course of history.'[50] Elucidating the evolutionary laws of history inexorably led down the path of geographical compulsion. Either way, Mackinder's conception of the professional niche that geography could occupy in the academic scheme of things was evidently shot through with evolutionary motifs.[51]

To uncover the cognitive foundations of Mackinder's proposals, of course, does not imply that it was nothing but a question of evolutionizing geography. Intertwined with these were professional-political issues too. The desire to claw back conceptual territory from the geologists was one arena of engagement. His deliberations with the London University's board of studies for geography, for example, frequently led him into troubled waters with the geologists. They were, he recorded in his diary notes for 1902, 'a nuisance on a Geographical Board.' Indeed in the famous 'Scope and Methods' paper itself, he remarked that the rivalry between the two subjects 'has been productive of nothing but evil to geography.'[52] Another forum for playing professional politics was the faction-ridden RGS itself. Later in life he reflected that he himself had been a pawn in a 'battle royal that was being waged within the Council of the Society, between a hitherto dominant part of explorers, navigators, and mapmakers on the one hand, and on the other hand a small group of scientific men led by Douglas Freshfield and Francis Galton who saw in geography something more than a mere inventory of facts arranged upon a map.'[53]

The mobilization of evolution in the service of geographical theory and in the cause of academic – political infighting, however, were not the only practical uses he could find for geography's new evolutionary-inspired marriage of society and environment. Mackinder was, first and foremost, a man of action and he was not prepared to let his geographical musings lie buried in the pages of the RGS's journal. He wanted them translated into

[49] Halford J. Mackinder, 'The Geographical Pivot of History', *Geographical Journal*, 23 (1904): 421–37, refs on pp. 422, 421.

[50] Mackinder, 'Scope and Methods', p. 155.

[51] The same was true of H. R. Mill. In 1905 he spoke of the shift from Ritter's teleological views (which, he said, 'were substantially those of Paley') to those of Darwinian evolution. And in this context he considered that the ultimate problem of geography may perhaps be taken as the determination of the influence of the surface forms of the Earth on the mental processes of its inhabitants. Hugh Robert Mill, 'The Present Problems of Geography', *Geographical Journal* 1 (1905): 1–17, refs on pp. 4,15.

[52] See Coones, *Mackinder's 'Scope and Methods'*, p. 15.

[53] Cited in ibid., p. 10.

international political practice. Even in the 'Scope and Methods' paper, he confessed his belief 'that on lines such as I have sketched a geography may be worked out which will satisfy at once the practical requirements of the statesman and the merchant, the theoretical requirements of the historian and scientist, and the intellectual requirements of the teacher.' More, his vision of geography was specifically designed 'to attract minds of an amplitude fitting them to be rulers of men.'[54] The teaching of geography was thus itself an imperial task and the encouragement of what Mackinder called 'thinking geographically' part of a strategy to secure the 'maintenance and progress of our Empire.'[55]

Mackinder's strategic proclivities were a lifelong passion. During his student days he had been a member of the Oxford University Rifle Volunteers; in 1900 he ran for parliament and the following year joined the imperialist Victoria League; in 1903 he joined Joseph Chamberlain's crusade for tariff reform; and from 1910 until 1922 he was a Member of Parliament as a Conservative and Unionist.[56] Moreoever it was precisely during these years that *Britain and the British Seas* (1902), his famous 'Geographical Pivot of History' essay (1904), 'Man-Power as a Measure of National and Imperial Strength' (1905), 'The Teaching of Geography from an Imperial Point of View' (1911), and *Democratic Ideals and Reality* (1919) were written – pieces revealing how comfortably his brand of geography could facilitate the new imperialism.

Space does not permit any detailed rehearsal of the nuances in Mackinder's geopolitical writings during this period. Yet the thrust of it can be readily summarized. With a penchant for cartographic comparison on a world scale, and a fascination with the great scientific voyages of Huxley, Darwin, Wallace, and Bates, his geopolitical logistics were, predictably, conceived on a grand scale. In his mind, one key geographical zone existed on the earth's surface, which, if it were to come under the influence of a nation, would enable that people to take control of world political power. Mackinder urged that the maritime age had gone and that

[54] Mackinder, 'Scope and Methods', pp. 159, 143.

[55] Halford J. Mackinder, 'The Teaching of Geography from an Imperial Point of View, and the Use which Could and Should be Made of Visual Instruction', *Geographical Teacher*, 6 (1911): pp. 79–86, refs. on pp. 80, 79.

[56] Recent biographical accounts include, Parker, *Mackinder*; Brian Blouet, *Halford Mackinder: A Biography* (College Station, Texas: Texas A. & M. University Press, 1987); G. Kearns, 'Halford John Mackinder 1861–1947', in T. W. Freeman (ed.), *Geographers. Biobibliographical Studies*, vol. 9 (London: Mansell, 1985), pp. 71–86. See also Brian W. Blouet, 'The Political Career of Sir Halford Mackinder', *Political Geography Quarterly*, 6 (1987): 355–67.

in the future land-power would be decisive. The greatest land area was to be found in the Old World and at its heart lay a vast area, immune to sea attack, where resources and civilization could create a natural base of power. The political implications of controlling this 'Heartland' were plain. And he spelled them out in the famous jingle:

> Who rules East Europe commands the Heartland:
> Who rules the Heartland commands the World-Island:
> Who rules the World-Island commands the World.[57]

The threat inherent in this geopolitical vision was plain. For it was within the previous century, Mackinder explained, that man-power had become 'sufficient to threaten the liberty of the world from within this citadel of the World-Island.' Strategic planning was necessary, and the redrawing of the map of Europe in the aftermath of the First World War afforded the occasion to think hard about democratic ideals and geographical realities. As he put it:

No mere scraps of paper, even though they be the written constitution of the League of Nations, are under the conditions of to-day a sufficient guarantee that the Heartland will not again become the centre of a World-War. Now is the time, when the Nations are fluid, to consider what guarantees, based on Geographical and Economic Realities, can be made available for the future security of Mankind.[58]

These sentiments, in fact, were part of the British national debate on defence. The 'Geographical Pivot' essay and *Democratic Ideals and Reality*, for example, provided Lord Curzon of the Foreign Office with what was believed to be a 'scientific' basis for foreign policy. In his position as high commissioner to southern Russia beginning in 1919 – a post secured for him by Curzon himself – Mackinder thus sought to find ways to implement the policy of saving Great Britain from Bolshevik ideology and of dividing up eastern Europe in such a way as to prevent any one power seizing the world-scale politico-economic potential of the Heartland.

Mackinder's geography clearly cannot be isolated from the circumstances

---

[57] Halford J. Mackinder, *Democratic Ideals and Reality* (Harmondsworth: Penguin, 1944, First pub. 1919), p. 113. See the discussion in G. Kearns, 'Closed Space and Political Practice: Frederick Jackson Turner and Halford Mackinder', *Society and Space*, 1 (1984): 23–34; J. C. Malin, 'Space and History: Reflections on the Closed-Space Doctrines of Turner and Mackinder and the Challenge of those Ideas by the Air Age', *Agricultural History*, 18 (1944): 65–74.

[58] Mackinder, *Democratic Ideals*, p. 88.

that produced it. But it is not simply a case of separating out political context from geographical text. That is to assume closure on the precise issue at hand, namely, that Mackinder's was a politicized geography and a geographical politics. Certainly Mackinder tried, as a strategic device, to drive a wedge between them so as to use scientific geography to justify imperial politics; 'the extent of the red patches of British dominion upon the map of the world,' he insisted at one point, in an attempted depoliticizing and defusing move, was merely the 'cartographical expression of the eternal struggle for existence as it stands at the opening of the twentieth century.'[59] This neutralizing rhetoric is not to be believed. For Mackinder's geography was hammered out on a political anvil and his politics were forged in a geographical crucible. For after all, he could, at other moments, consider his whole life's work as a grand geographical mission, a biography all of a piece with the 'New Geography'.

The Fundamental Law of World History: The Ratzelian Programme

With his twin concerns to scientize geography and press it into the service of imperialism, it is not surprising that Mackinder should find kindred spirits in German geography. In 1895 during his presidential address to Section E of the British Association, he unfavourably compared the state of British geography with its German counterpart, a comparison extending to Germanic militarism and economics.[60] Institutionally, German geography was certainly far ahead of Britain, as Keltie's 1885 *Report on Geographical Education* had all too painfully revealed.[61] During the 1870s it had made great strides in the German universities: Oscar Peschel was appointed to a position in Leipzig, Alfred Kirchhoff to Halle, Friedrich Ratzel to Munich, and Ferdinand von Richthofen to Bonn.[62] These educational developments, of course, went hand in hand with the rise of the German empire and its acquisition of colonies in Africa and the South Pacific. For now geography became a compulsory secondary school subject and this fostered its expansion within the university sector. In such an atmosphere, geographers like Richthofen (1833–1905) with global preoccupations and colonial aspirations

---

[59] Halford J. Mackinder, *Britain and the British Seas* (Oxford: Clarendon Press, 1902), p. 343.

[60] Halford J. Mackinder, 'Modern Geography, German and English', *Geographical Journal*, 6 (1895): 367–79.

[61] John Scott Keltie, 'Geographical Education. Report to the Council of the Royal Geographical Society', *Royal Geographical Society, Supplementary Papers*, 1 (1882–5): 439–594. See also M. J. Wise, 'The Scott Keltie Report 1885 and the Teaching of Geography in Great Britain', *Geographical Journal*, 152 (1986): 367–82.

[62] Dickinson, The *Makers of Modern Geography*, p. 59.

were especially welcomed. As a scientist-traveller in the Humboldt mould, an expert on China, and a former surveyor for the Imperial Geological Office in Vienna, Richthofen could, with the support of the Prussian government and its Ministry of Culture, carve out for himself a distinguished career in university geography. The natural scientific inflection which he conferred on geography did much to establish the subject's scholarly reputation, while its political potential surfaced in his ultimately ineffective encouragement of German colonialism in the Far East.[63]

By making these observations, however, I have no intention of adjudicating on the question of whether Mackinder's geography was of German derivation, a subject on which several commentators have felt the need to voice an opinion.[64] For my purposes that question smacks too much of the tired hunt for precursors. Instead I want to show that the selfsame evolutionary forces that shaped Mackinder's geography were at work among the subject's first generation of German professionals. The legacy of Ritter's doxological geography was being dismantled as scientific materialism à la Haeckel gained ground, and new conceptual foundations were sought.[65] Recasting the subject's theoretical structure in the categories of evolutionary naturalism was the result – a manoeuvre effectively carried off through the efforts of Friedrich Ratzel (1844–1904).

Ratzel, like Mackinder, had been trained in the natural sciences – particularly zoology – and during his student days had been exposed to the evolutionary *Weltanschauung* then sweeping Germany.[66] This new philosophy of nature, which came to be known as Darwinismus, had its greatest European representative in Ernst Haeckel and, as a graduate, Ratzel sought out his courses at Jena during 1869 and thus early in his career became a devotee of his mentor's overweening evolutionism. His first published study on *The Nature and Development of the Organic World* was, according to

---

[63] Brief English-language treaments include Albert Kolb, 'Ferdinand Freiherr von Richthofen, 1833–1905', in T. W. Freeman (ed.), *Geographers. Biobibliographical Studies*, 7 (1983): 109–15; Dickinson, *Makers of Modern Geography*, pp. 77–88.

[64] For a sampling see Crone, *Modern Geographers*; Carl Troll, 'Halford J. Mackinder als Geograph und Geopolitiker', *Erdkunde*, 6 (1952): 177–8; Freeman, 'The Royal Geographical Society'; Coones, *Mackinder's Scope and Methods*.

[65] See Harriet Wanklyn, *Friedrich Ratzel. A Biographical Memoir and Bibliography* (Cambridge: Cambridge University Press, 1961), p. 17, where she points out that Oscar Peschel and others began 'to expose the weaknesses of the "Golden Age" of German geography'. Also W. L. Cage, *The Life of Karl Ritter* (Edinburgh: Blackwood, 1867), p. 191.

[66] The reception of Darwinism in Germany is discussed in William M. Montgomery, 'Germany', in Thomas F. Glick (ed.), *The Comparative Reception of Darwinism* (Austin: University of Texas Press, 1974), pp. 81–116.

Mark Bassin, 'based largely on Haeckel's *General Morphology*,'[67] at a time when the ferocity of Haeckel's Darwinism was even troubling Darwin himself. For all that, Haeckel's was never unadulterated Darwinism; for him *Darwinismus* encompassed a *mélange* of evolutionary theories prominent among which was Lamarck's principle of direct heritable adaptation. Thus when Ratzel turned more single-mindedly to the study of geography, consequent upon his visit to America in 1873–4 as a travel correspondent for the *Keolinische Zeitung*,[68] he was still under the influence of Haeckel's vision, although he would later temper the extremist tenor of that perspective, as did Haeckel himself as he moved more towards what has been labelled Darwinian pantheism.[69]

By the beginning of the following decade Ratzel had established himself in the Technical University in Munich and had published, amongst other things, his major two-volume *Die Vereinigten Staaten von Nord-Amerika*. Shortly afterwards, in 1881, the first volume of the monumental *Anthropogeographie* made its appearance. Here he sought to lay out the conceptual foundations of a new discipline – human geography. The human focus of this project betrayed his shift from the perspective of the natural sciences towards that of anthropology. His *Völkerkunde* (general ethnography) of 1885–8, the second edition of which was translated into English as *The History of Mankind* (1896–8) and introduced by E. B. Tylor, earned for him an acknowledged place in the history of ethnological theory. Tylor himself recommended it as 'a solid foundation in anthropological study' whatever his reservations over Ratzel's theoretical commitments;[70] Lowie identified it as 'unquestionably a significant work';[71] and Penniman

[67] Mark Bassin, 'Friedrich Ratzel 1884–1904', in T. W. Freeman (ed.), *Geographers. Biobibliographical Studies*, 11 (1987): 123–32, ref. on p. 124.

[68] See the discussion in C. O. Sauer, 'The Formative Years of Ratzel in the United States', *Annals of the Association of American Geographers*, 61 (1971): 245–54; Mark Bassin, 'Friedrich Ratzel's Travels in the United States: A Study in the Genesis of his Anthropogeography', *History of Geography Newsletter*, 4 (1984): 11–22.

[69] See Paul Weindling, 'Ernst Haeckel, Darwinismus and the Secularization of Nature', in James R. Moore (ed.), *History, Humanity and Evolution. Essays for John C. Greene* (Cambridge: Cambridge University Press, 1989), pp. 311–53.

[70] Edward B. Tylor, 'Introduction', in Friedrich Ratzel, *The History of Mankind*, translated from the second German edition by A. J. Butler, 3 vols (London: Macmillan, 1896–8), vol. 1, p. xi.

[71] Robert H. Lowie, *The History of Ethnological Theory* (New York: Holt, Rinehart and Winston, 1937), p. 122. Lowie praised the work's 'excellent illustrations [which] . . . far surpassed anything hitherto presented.'

described it as the greatest of several 'outstanding classics' on the general history of mankind.[72]

In the interim, Ratzel had formed an alliance with 'the highly respected, fatherly friend' who was to exert the profoundest influence on his life's work, the naturalist, explorer, and evolutionary theorist, Moritz Wagner.[73] Although Wagner had emerged as one of Germany's earliest devotees of Darwin's theory, he believed Darwin had failed to appreciate the significance of migration and geographical isolation in the processes of speciation. Without isolation, Wagner insisted, variations would become blended into the surrounding stock; but isolation would not only segregate incipient species, it would induce further divergence on account of changed nutrition, new climatic conditions, and other peculiarities of the environment. Captivated by the superorganic analogy, Wagner thought that species had fixed lifetimes and, therefore, that without the invigorating influence of migration and isolation, they would ultimately pass away. Throughout Wagner's account, as Sulloway shows, his predilection for Neo-Lamarckian mechanisms clearly surfaces. For he was convinced that direct organic modifications in response to environmental conditions could be effected and their benefits transmitted to succeeding generations. The act of migration was thus itself a mechanism inducing and preserving variation.[74] As William Coleman confirmed: 'The migration theory demanded the plasticity of the organism and its intimate relations with all natural phenomena. It shared and perpetuated the basic tenets of Lamarckian environmentalism.'[75] Migration, isolation, space, and environmental determinism were all part and parcel of the Wagnerian scheme of things. And it was precisely these themes that dramatically surfaced in Ratzel's new anthropogeography.[76]

Ratzel's *Anthropogeographie* can best be read as an attempt to situate the new science of human geography within the naturalistic framework of Wagner's *Migrationsgesetz*, which he portrayed as 'the [most] fundamental

[72] T. K. Penniman, *A Hundred Years of Anthropology* (London: Duckworth, 2nd edn 1952), p. 127. Penniman identified another geographer, Oscar Peschel, who had similarly authored a *Völkerkunde* (1874), as one of his other cited classics.

[73] Ratzel's words come from his lengthy dedication of *Anthropogeographie* to Wagner.

[74] Wagner's correspondence with Darwin on the matter, together with the vicissitudes of Darwin's response to the whole question of geographical isolation is treated in Frank J. Sulloway, 'Geographic Isolation in Darwin's Thinking: The Vicissitudes of a Crucial Idea', *Studies in the History of Biology*, 3 (1979): 23–65. Wagner's views on the role of isolation in evolution are also discussed in Mayr, *Growth of Biological Thought*, pp. 562–6.

[75] William Coleman, 'Science and Symbol in the Turner Frontier Hypothesis', *American Historical Review*, 72 (1966): 22–49, ref. on p. 39.

[76] On the relationship between Ratzel and Wagner, see Hanno Beck, 'Moritz Wagner als Geography', *Erdkunde*, 7 (1953): 125–8.

law of world history.'[77] Wagner's Lamarckian-honed evolution thus provided him with a voice in which to conjugate the grammar of his own anthropogeography. Accordingly the principles of diffusion, migration, and *Raum* were woven together to provide a network of natural laws within which the spatial arrangements, cultural characteristics, and social functionings of human society might be understood. Indeed it is for his fostering of the ideas of cultural diffusionism and migration that he is still remembered within anthropology.[78] The naturalistic bias in this vision is certainly clear, for Ratzel squarely positioned the human species within the orbit of secular evolution, and this, strongly reinforced by his Wagnerian-Lamarckian inclinations, disposed him towards an environmental determinist account of human geography which was, nevertheless, tempered from time to time by a greater ecological sensitivity.[79] For all that, he had elaborated on 'The Immediate Effects of Nature on the Spirit of the People' in his geographical portrait of the United States, and it was out of this naturalistic ethos that his concept of the *Lebensraum* was born, a theory which he most fully articulated in his *magnum opus*, the *Political Geography* of 1897.[80] Here, in Spencerian fashion, he dilated on the biological analogy of the state as an organism which inevitably underwent population enlargement to the point where resource exhaustion or territorial expansion was inevitable. For the state, to exist, was to extend. In expounding these Malthus-like principles, Ratzel believed he had disclosed the natural laws of the territorial growth of states and he happily located the contemporary colonial thrust of the European powers in Africa as the manifestation of their quest for *Lebensraum*. Imperial history was the spatial story of a struggle for existence.

There was, again, 'Stern practicality' inherent in the evolution-inspired human geography of Friedrich Ratzel. His vision of the state as an expand-

---

[77] Cited in Bassin, 'Friedrich Ratzel', p. 126.

[78] See Marvin Harris, *The Rise of Anthropological Theory. A History of Theories of Culture* (New York: Thomas Y. Crowell, 1968), pp. 382–3; Merwyn S. Garbarino, *Sociocultural Theory in Anthropology: A Short History* (New York: Holt, Rinehart and Winston, 1977), pp. 46–7; Bruce G. Trigger, *A History of Archaeological Thought* (Cambridge: Cambridge University Press, 1989), pp. 151–2.

[79] The literature on Ratzel's 'determinism' is controverted. While Hays commented that 'Ratzel taught that man was a passive creature rigidly ruled by climate and geography [and that] his point of view was dogmatic and, rejecting psychology, completely mechanical,' Lowie observed: 'Temperate on geographical causation, Ratzel was equally moderate in appraising biological heredity.' H. R. Hays, *From Ape to Angel. An Informal History of Social Anthropology* (New York: Knopf, 1958), p. 228; Lowie, *History of Ethnological Theory*, p. 121.

[80] On the intellectual history of *Lebensraum* see W. D. Smith, 'Friedrich Ratzel and the Origins of *Lebensraum*', *German Studies Review*, 3 (1980): 51–68.

ing organism led him to the conviction that the ideal towards which modern advanced states must aspire was *Grossraum* (large space). Impressed with the sheer territorial expansiveness of America's geographical space and equally certain that history revealed the cultural atrophy of *Kleinstaaten* (small-sized states), he came to believe that European states could only achieve *Grossraum* through overseas territorial acquisition. 'Since the areas of states grow with their civilization, people in a low state of civilization are naturally collected in very small political organization, and the lower their condition the smaller are the states,' he affirmed.[81] Here was a naturalistic theodicy that justified the imperial order in the language of scientific geography. In many ways, however, these convictions rubbed the grain of the standard political philosophy of the nation-state the wrong way, for that tradition presupposed social homogeneity and territorial circumscription.[82] But Ratzel's dissidence on this point was markedly in harmony with the prevailing mood of German empire-building, and they both resonated with the safety-valve theory that Frederick Jackson Turner was elucidating on the other side of the Atlantic. So it comes as no surprise to learn that Ratzel became intensely involved with colonial advocacy leagues early in his career and called upon the government to press ahead with overseas colonial enterprises. In the late 1870s he founded the Munich Association for the Defence of German Interests Abroad, and subsequently participated in the pan-Germanic league. And allied to this was his support for a competitive navy, which was predictably well received among the naval fraternity.[83]

The expansionist imperative inherent in Ratzel's advocacy of *Lebensraum* and *Grossraum* soon led some commentators to find in them sources for the later racist politics of the German National Socialists. Suffering guilt by a seeming association with the *Geopolitik* of Karl Haushofer, who appropriated Ratzelian vocabulary, his work was marginalized after 1945 for several decades. But, as the recent revisionist interpretations of Mark Bassin amply testify, Ratzel's environmentalist orientation was out of kilter with the genetic racism intrinsic to the Nazi worship of the *Volk*. For him,

[81] See, for example, Friedrich Ratzel, 'The Territorial Growth of States', *Scottish Geographical Magazine*, 12 (1896): 351–61, ref. on p. 352.

[82] See B. Shafer, *Nationalism: Myth and Reality* (New York: Harcourt, Brace and World, 1955).

[83] See Mark Bassin, 'Imperialism and the Nation State in Friedrich Ratzel's Political Geography', *Progress in Human Geography*, 11 (1987): 473–95. See also K. Hassert, 'Friedrich Ratzel: Sein Leben und Wirken', *Geographische Zeitschrift*, 11 (1905): 310–25, 361–80; J. M. Hunter, *Perspectives on Friedrich Ratzel's Political Geography* (Lanham: University Press of America, 1983).

Grossraum actually fostered the racial mixing that produced new ethnic blends. Accordingly he steadfastly distanced himself from the Aryanism emanating from the pens of Arthur de Gobineau and Houston Stewart Chamberlain and vigorously protested the biological unity of the human species against a resurgent anthropological polygenism,[84] though at times he seemed convinced of a human hierarchy when he distinguished between servile and sovereign peoples. Nevertheless he saw the whole project of ethnography as a moral enterprise to further the principles of justice. As he put it: 'The task of ethnography is therefore to indicate, not in the first instances the distinctions, but the points of transition, and the intimate affinities which exist; for mankind is one though very variously cultured.'[85] Thus, the impetus for Ratzel, as for *Anthropogeographie*, ever lay in external environmental circumstance, not in intrinsic genetic constitution.[86] And, as with Mackinder, Neo-Lamarckian evolution provided the theoretical sustenance on which the Ratzelian programme could thrive.

A Ripe Time: Davis's Strategy

In 1900, on the other side of the Atlantic, William Morris Davis (1850–1934) (plate 6.2) announced to the readers of the *Popular Science Monthly* that the 'spirit of evolution has been breathed by the students of the generation now mature all through their growing years, and its application in all lines of study is demanded.' Physical geography, Davis's lifelong passion, had apparently for too long ignored this evolutionary inspiration, and so he insisted that 'the time [was] ripe for the introduction of these ideas' into the conceptual fabric of the subject. Captivated, like Mackinder and Ratzel, by the organic analogy, he urged that conceiving the 'life of a geographical area' in terms of 'the life of a quick-growing plant' had enabled 'the many parts of a landform' to be depicted in the life-cycle vocabulary of a 'rapidly growing annual'.[87] Already by 1900 Davis had

---

[84] I have discussed the impact of this and other scientific racisms on geography in "Never Shall Ye Make the Crab Walk Straight": An Inquiry into the Scientific Sources of Racial Geography', in Felix Driver and Gillian Rose (eds), *Nature and Science, Essays in the History of Geographical Knowledge* (Historical Geography Research Series, no. 28, 1992), pp. 37–48. Ratzel's explicit monogenism is clear from his observation that 'wherever the earth is habitable by man, we find people who are members of one and the same human race. The unity of the human genus is as it were the work of the planet Earth, stamped on the highest step of creation therein. There is only one species of man; the variations are numerous, but do not go deep.' Ratzel, *History of Mankind*, p. 9.

[85] Ratzel, *History of Mankind*, p. 4.

[86] See the fine discussion in Mark Bassin, 'Race contra Space: The Conflict between German *Geopolitik* and National Socialism', *Political Geography Quarterly*, 6 (1987): 115–34.

[87] William Morris Davis, 'The Physical Geography of the Lands', *Popular Science Monthly*,

Plate 6.2   William Morris Davis, 1885, reproduced by permission of the Harvard
University Archives

been using biological terminology to portray the development of landforms for over a decade and a half. He had spoken, too, of an evolutionary 'cycle of erosion' and of a process he labelled 'inorganic natural selection', both of which conveyed the Darwinian-sounding character of his undertaking.[88]

It was in 1889 – in his investigation of the rivers and valleys of Pennsylvania – that Davis presented his first systematic exposition of the erosion cycle. It was an ideal typification of landform development, involving the several discrete phases of rapid initial tectonic uplift of a landscape, followed by the operation of destructive erosion agencies that sculpted the surface into a series of sequential forms, followed by the reduction of the land surface to its ultimate form – a low plain of imperceptible relief termed the peneplain. In the case of the Appalachian drainage system, as elsewhere, Davis argued that it had gone through several complete cycles and concluded that present-day ridges were merely the remnants of former base-levels.[89] The simplicity and elegance of the Davisian scheme was to mesmerize several generations of geomorphologists as he transformed the rudimentary suggestions of Powell and Gilbert on base-levels into a coherent geomorphological package.[90]

The evolutionary mounting onto which Davis nailed his landform theory could, however, serve even greater purposes. Like his German counterparts, Davis felt that Ritter's 'old doctrine of teleology' could no longer provide the necessary supports for the modern geographical enterprise and so he consciously turned to the 'modern principle of evolution'.[91] Thus, in enun-

---

57 (1900): 157–70, refs on pp. 169–70. See also the discussion in David R. Stoddart, 'Darwin's Influence on the Development of Geography in the United States, 1859–1914', in Brian Blouet (ed.), *The Origins of Academic Geography in the United States* (Hamden: Archon Books, 1981), pp. 265–78.

[88] William Morris Davis, 'Geographic Classification, Illustrated by a Study of Plains, Plateaus and their Derivatives', *Proceedings of the American Association for the Advancement of Science (33rd Meeting Philadelphia)* (1885): 428–32; William Morris Davis, 'The Development of Certain English Rivers', *Geographical Journal*, 5 (1895): 127–46.

[89] William Morris Davis, 'The Rivers and Valleys of Pennsylvania', *National Geographic Magazine*, 1 (1889): 183–253. A full statement of the ideal cycle appeared in W. M. Davis, 'The Geographical Cycle', *Geographical Journal*, 14 (1899): 481–504. The whole matter is discussed at length in Richard J. Chorley, Robert P. Beckinsale, and Antony J. Dunn, *The History of the Study of Landforms or the Development of Geomorphology. Volume Two: The Life and Work of William Morris Davis* (London: Methuen, 1973).

[90] See Charles G. Higgins, 'Theories of Landscape Development: A Perspective', in W. N. Melhorn and R. C. Flemal (eds), *Theories of Landform Development* (New York: State University of New York, 1975), pp. 1–29.

[91] William Morris Davis, 'Systematic Geography', *Proceedings of the American Philosophical Society*, 41 (1902): 235–59, ref. on p. 239. See the discussion in Richard Hartshorne, 'William Morris Davis – The Course of Development of his Concept of Geography', in Brian W. Blouet (ed.), *The Origins of Academic Geography in the United States* (Hamden, Conn.: Archon Books, 1981), pp. 139–49.

ciating the principle of 'geographical evolution' for the readers of the
School Review in 1900, he observed:

> In the days of Ritter . . . the relation between organic forms and their inor-
> ganic environment was explained, when explained at all, by the philosophy of
> teleology, – the philosophy which, among other things, regards the earth as
> prepared for man, – because no conception had then been gained of the dura-
> tion of the past time or of the development of the various forms of life. Since
> those days two great principles have been discovered, both of vast importance
> to geography. One is the evolution of land forms, contributed from geology;
> the other is the evolution of living forms, contributed from biology.[92]

For all that, though the foundations were new, the edifice itself was
remarkably familiar. For, as Herbst remarked in 1961, 'we find that but for
the substitution of the Darwinian theory of evolution for the teleological
interpretation of German natural philosophy, Davis did not diverge substantially from the path mapped out by Guyot.'[93]

The sanguine references to evolution which thus snake their way through
Davis's pronouncements on the new conceptual foundations for geography
have, for long enough, been taken as the codification of Darwinism within
the subject. But a closer attention to certain specifics in Davis's evolutionary talk reveals, I believe, the essentially Neo-Lamarckian undergirding of
his entire project. The deterministic thrust of his much publicized catch-
phrase 'the geographical relations of physiographic controls and onto-
graphic responses' (also rendered as 'inorganic controls and organic
responses')[94] is itself suggestive of Neo-Lamarckian inclinations. And this
suspicion is confirmed by a perusal of his 1903 exposition of the 'modern
principle of evolution.' Here he spoke of organic 'structures, processes, and
habits' as 'responses to physiographic causes'; of the 'torpidity of many animals during winter [as] a response to climatic conditions'; of the 'most
important inherited responses [being] those determined by long persistent

[92] W. M. Davis, 'Physical Geography in the High School', *School Review*, 8 (1900): 388–404,
ref. on p. 390.
[93] Jurgen Herbst, 'Social Darwinism and the History of American Geography', *Proceedings
of the American Philosophical Society*, 105 (1961): 538–44, ref. on p. 540.
[94] William Morris Davis, 'An Inductive Study of the Content of Geography', *Bulletin of the
American Geographical Society*, 38 (1906): 67–84. Reprinted in Douglas Wilson Johnson (ed.),
Geographical Essays by William Morris Davis (Boston: Ginn and Co., 1909), pp. 3–22, refs. on
p. 15. In 1920 Dryer referred to 'physiographic control and organic response' as 'the most
notable geographic phrase that has appeared in the English language in the 20th century.' C.
R. Dryer, 'Genetic Geography: The Development of the Geographic Sense and Concept',
Annals of the Association of American Geographers, 10 (1920): 3–16, ref. on p. 8.

conditions of environments'; and of characteristics being 'persistently inherited wherever the conditions under which they were developed have
endured.'[95] Given these convictions, it is hardly surprising that in seeking a
paradigm illustration of the ontography he envisioned – a neologism he
coined that came to describe human geography – Davis should specify
Ratzel's *Anthropogeographie*.

To read Davis's evolution as essentially Neo-Lamarckian is rendered all
the more plausible when we recall the conditions under which he was
exposed to the evolutionary synthesis. As a student at Harvard he had
come under the influence of Nathaniel Southgate Shaler, himself a student
of Louis Agassiz, and a founding father of modern American geography.
Agassiz was a staunch opponent of the Darwinian scheme of things and
emerged as Darwin's most implacable scholarly opponent in the New
World.[96] A number of his students and younger associates like Cope,
Hyatt, and Packard, however, came to feel that the charismatic Swiss naturalist's opposition to evolution was increasingly untenable and so they
themselves progressively moved in that direction. The influence of Agassiz
nevertheless lingered on, and so the Neo-Lamarckian school of biology that
they spearheaded retained certain continuities with Agassiz's idealist natural
history, though transforming it into a dynamic, historicized chain of being.
They also shared Agassiz's fascination with embryology, and speculated on
how it might serve as an analogy for evolution history; and so Haeckel's
idea that the life cycle of the individual (ontogeny) recapitulates that of the
race (phylogeny) spread among them like wildfire.[97] In this context, then, it
is surely significant that, as Stoddart puts it, Davis was 'profoundly more
impressed with the mystery of growth from egg or seed to adult than . . .
with the cumulated effects of small scale changes over many generations.'[98]
Life cycles evidently enchanted him a good deal more than linear evolution.
Small wonder that he devoted so many words to elucidating his own 'geographical cycle'.

Among the leaders of this Lamarckian renaissance was Davis's teacher,
Shaler, who independently exerted a profound influence on the character of

[95] William Morris Davis, 'The Progress of Geography in the Schools', *National Society for
the Scientific Study of Education. First Year Book* (1902), Part II, pp. 7–49. Reprinted in
Johnston (ed.), *Geographical Essays*, pp. 23–69, refs on pp. 51–2.

[96] The standard biography is Edward Lurie, *Louis Agassiz. A Life in Science* (Chicago:
University of Chicago Press, 1960).

[97] Stephen Jay Gould, *Ontogeny and Phylogeny* (Cambridge, Mass.: Harvard University
Press, 1977).

[98] Stoddart, 'Darwin's Influence on the Development of Geography in the United States', p.
272.

American geography. Shaler, who came to occupy the directorship of the Lawrence Scientific School at Harvard, was a geologist by profession, but a geographer by inclination.[99] He himself had been a student of Agassiz at Harvard during the days of the great debates over Darwinism in the early 1860s, and his own career illustrates his transitional stance in the intellectual drift from the older teleological science of Agassiz to the new evolutionary naturalism of Davis. Under Agassiz's tutelage Shaler might have learned to dismiss the new biology out of hand, but his personal friendship with Hyatt and his reading of the Darwinian heretics soon persuaded him of the truth of the theory of evolution, albeit in a decidedly Lamarckian vein. By the early 1870s he was a complete convert and retained the Lamarckian perspective on things for the rest of his life. In 1893, for example, he categorically insisted that organisms 'adapt themselves in an immediate manner to the peculiarities of their environment' and that those 'conditions which surround them make an impression on their bodies which is transmitted to their progeny.'[100] Lamarckism thus enabled Shaler to retain much that he had learned from his master, not least the broadly religious view of the cosmos to which Agassiz steadfastly adhered. So it was entirely understandable that Shaler should be invited to deliver the Winkley Foundation lectures at Andover Theological Seminary in 1891 and that he should choose as his subject 'Modern Science and Religious Beliefs'; they were subsequently published under the title, *The Interpretation of Nature*.

Shaler exploited the environmentalist strain in Neo-Lamarckian evolution to the full. His celebrated *Nature and Man in America* was an extended excursus on the intimate interrelationships between the natural and social worlds. So here he portrayed the transatlantic transfer of Old World institutions and traditions, and the ways in which they were domesticated by the American environment. And he reflected too on the cultural significance of the eastward range of the bison, on the process of prairie homesteading, and on the myth of the 'Great American Desert'. His historical portrayal of American character as the product of its own geography thus resonated profoundly with the frontier thesis of Frederick Jackson Turner, who was equally captivated by the Lamarckian metaphors of social plasticity, cultural recapitulation, and environmental compulsion.[101]

[99] Shaler's multifaceted career is charted in David N. Livingstone, *Nathaniel Southgate Shaler and the Culture of American Science* (London: University of Alabama Press, 1987).

[100] Nathaniel Southgate Shaler, *The Interpretation of Nature* (New York: Houghton Mifflin, 1893) p. 146.

[101] See Coleman, 'Science and Symbol in the Turner Frontier Hypothesis'; David N. Livingstone, 'Environment and Inheritance: Nathaniel Southgate Shaler and the American Frontier', in Brian Blouet (ed.), *The Origins of Academic Geography in the United States*,

But Shaler had other interests too that could be served by his geo-biological commitments. Towards the end of the century, and in the wake of the heaviest immigration in the nation's history, he concerned himself increasingly with racial questions. The *Atlantic Monthly*, the *North American Review*, *Scribner's Magazine*, and the newly established nativist weekly *America* all carried feature articles by him, as he seemed perfectly fitted to bring a 'scientific' perspective to the social problems unnerving genteel New Englanders. Believing that environment irresistibly impressed itself on racial character, he bemoaned the shifting patterns of United States immigration; the newcomers were no longer emanating from north-west Europe with its geographical conditions conducive to high civilization, and they thus lacked the racial credentials for making American citizenry. Accordingly, Shaler threw his weight behind the Immigration Restriction League of Boston during the last decade of the century by associating himself with the cause as one of its vice-presidents. Moreover, given the racial neurosis that currently dominated New England minds, Shaler presented his scientific judgement of the black race as 'a lowly variety of man,' and spoke of the need to 'separate blacks and whites in public conveyances'; he wrote of the American Indians' failure to attain 'an economic organization which deserves the name of civilization'; and he feared the coming of eastern European peasantry because it bore that indelible mark of inferiority that had been stamped on it by the institutions of Catholic Europe.[102]

Alongside these doctrinaire social prescriptions, Shaler published numerous monographs during his career as a geologist, both as a Harvard professional and in his practical role as director of the Kentucky Geological Survey and later in his capacity as director of the New England division of the United States Geological Survey under John Wesley Powell. And besides the survey reports that he regularly authored he also published on mineral resources, soil problems, and deforestation as well as on orogenesis, glacial theory, and fluvial action. Consequently Shaler always entertained a broad

---

pp. 123–38. The links between Turner and Shaler are discussed in Ray Allen Billington, *Genesis of the Frontier Thesis: A Study in Historical Creativity* (San Marino, California: The Huntington Library, 1971); Robert P. Block, 'Frederick Jackson Turner and American Geography', *Annals of the Association of American Geographers*, 70 (1980): 31–42.

[102] Nathaniel Southgate Shaler, 'Our Negro Types', *Current Literature*, 29 (1900): 44–5; Nathaniel Southgate Shaler, *The Neighbor: The Natural History of Human Contacts* (Boston: Houghton Mifflin, 1904), p. 183; Nathaniel Southgate Shaler, 'The Immigration Problem Historically Considered', *America*, 1, no. 30 (1888): 1–2; Nathaniel Southgate Shaler, 'European Peasants as Immigrants', *Atlantic Monthly*, 71 (1893): 646–55. See too the discussion in John S. Haller, Jr., 'Nathaniel Southgate Shaler: A Portrait of Nineteenth-Century Academic Thinking on Race', *Essex Institute Historical Collections*, 107 (1971): 173–93.

conception of geology; extant notes from his famous Geology 4 course for 1899–1900 reveal that he dealt with such subjects as the evolution of human society, the human species as an agent of geomorphological change, and the economic significance of natural resources. Yet the very broad-based approach that Shaler encouraged ultimately served to stifle geography's departmental independence at Harvard. 'Geography', he wrote in 1893, 'is commonly regarded as a matter somewhat distinct from geology. Experience however shows that although the political branch of the subject can in a narrow way be taught independently, any large consideration of the subject demands that it take account of the conditions which have given the earth its present aspect . . . We may indeed term geography the geology of the present.'[103]

With this conception of the nature of geography, Shaler at once championed the subject's cause as part of the university's scientific curriculum while placing it firmly within the sphere of geology. Thus if the subject's intellectual flourishing at Harvard owed much to Shaler, so too did its lack of a separate identity. And it was this that exercised W. M. Davis. Having learned his evolution from Shaler, and having been recruited by him to the geology department at Harvard, Davis nevertheless aimed at institutional independence. Accordingly, in an era witnessing rapid urbanization, industrialization, and the meteoric rise of the American university and thus more and more dominated by its concern for credentials and careers, Davis sought to map out the territorial boundaries between geography and geology.[104] As part of his strategy he wrote many elementary textbooks, popularized scientific geography on various committees and commissions, tutored numerous later leaders of the subject like Bowman, Huntington, and Jefferson, and deeply involved himself in the professionalizing activities of the nascent Association of American Geographers.[105]

Such aims, however, were only pursued at considerable cost. Consequent on his appointment to the research position of Sturgis Hooper Professor at Harvard in 1899, a promotion that Shaler himself insisted he had long tried to bring about, Alexander Agassiz perpetually carped to the university's president over Davis's activities. The appointment was, he told President Eliot in August 1890, 'a mistake'; in October he again wrote complaining that he had gone into a room only to find Davis 'instructing a class of

---

[103] Nathaniel Southgate Shaler, 'What is Geology?' *Chautauquan*, 18 (1893): 284–7.

[104] The story of professionalization is traced in Burton J. Bledstein, *The Culture of Professionalism: The Middle Class and the Development of Higher Education in America* (New York: Norton, 1976).

[105] Davis's strategies are discussed in Robert P. Beckinsale, 'W. M. Davis and American Geography: 1880–1934', in Blouet (ed.), *Origins of Academic Geography*, pp. 107–22.

women!' and found it necessary to remind Eliot of the same point that December. 'Instruction and not research is his great interest,' he lamented. For his part Davis felt it necessary to compose self-defensive missives (plate 6.3) to Eliot and pointed out in 1903 that

> Mr Agassiz has . . . little appreciation of the amount of really original work that these elementary books involve, and little interest in the relation of sound elementary work *today* to advanced and original work twenty years hence. I suppose he will be disappointed to see my name on the book of 'Laboratory Exercises' regarding which I spoke to you last spring. Yet I am convinced that such a book is of greater importance to the advancement of the *Science* of geography than would be the discovery of a new mountain, or island, or river . . . . My chief reason for writing you all this is a wish to avoid doing anything that you think would give Mr Agassiz just ground for serious disappointment with my work (I say 'serious disappointment', because *some* disappointment seems inevitable).[106]

As with Mackinder and Ratzel, Davis was engaged in what I have called the geographical experiment – a manoeuvre designed to hold together the natural and social worlds under one explanatory umbrella. Given their educational backgrounds in the natural sciences, the naturalistic turn that these key figures gave the geographical project was perhaps predictable. And in that context, I have argued, the vocabulary that best suited their purposes was provided by the Neo-Lamarckian construal of evolutionary theory. The difficulties inherent in sustaining such a vision were, however, far from inconsiderable. Perhaps Davis himself could already sense the incipient rupturing of the newly stitched sutures for he decidedly focused on the physiographic side of the dualism leaving ontography to others. Indeed, he confessed that he felt it necessary for students of geography to concentrate on the physical and human sides of the subject separately before embarking on the task of elucidating the causal effects of the former on the latter. Yet he warmly enthused over Ellsworth Huntington's strenuous efforts to read history through environmental spectacles. For his part, Huntington dedicated *The Pulse of Asis* to Davis, his former teacher, and, even needing

---

[106] Letter, W. M. Davis to President Eliot, October 6, 1903, Charles W. Eliot Papers, Harvard University Archives. I discuss this episode in 'A Geologist by Profession, a Geographer by Inclination: Nathaniel Southgate Shaler and Geography at Harvard', in Clark A. Elliott and Margaret W. Rossiter (eds), *Science at Harvard University. Historical Perspectives* (London: Associated University Press, 1992), pp. 146–66. These extracts are cited there.

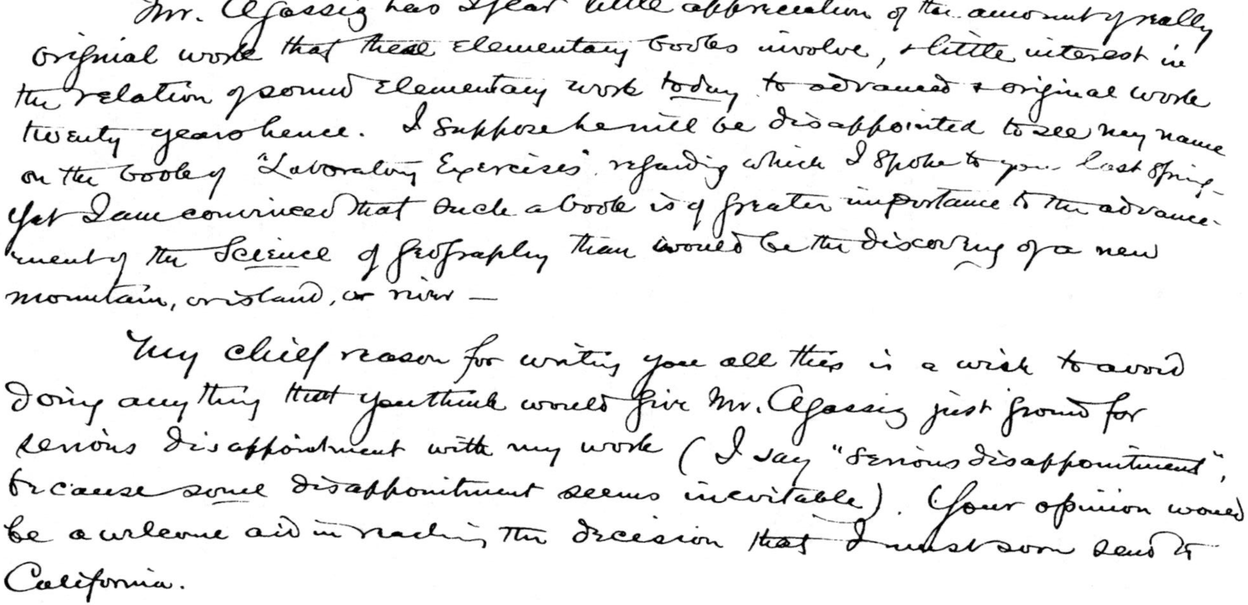

Mr. Agassiz has had little appreciation of the amount of really original work that head elementary books involve, — little indeed of the relation of sound elementary work today, to advanced + original work twenty years hence. I suppose he would be disappointed to see my name on the body of "Laboratory Exercises", refusing which I spoke to you last spring. Yet I am convinced that such a book is of greater importance to the advance of the Science of Geography, than would be the discovery of a new mountain, or river —

The chief reason for writing you all this is a wish to avoid serious disappointment with my work for Mr. Agassiz just found, for doing anything that you think would give Mr. Agassiz serious disappointment with my work (I say "serious disappointment" because some disappointment seems inevitable). Your opinion would be a welcome aid in reaching the decision that I shall soon send to California.

Plate 6.3   Extracts of a letter from William M. Davis to President Charles W. Eliot (6 October 1903) reproduced by permission of the Harvard University Archives

Davis's approval on a wife, confessed in a letter to his mentor that he had learned more from him 'than from any other man.'[107]

The geographical experiment in America, then, as I have portrayed it, was essentially a Lamarckian-derived attempt to couch geography's traditional concerns in the language of evolution during a time of professionalizing specialisms. Huntington, keeping up with the physiological research of prominent latter-day Lamarckians like Paul Kammerer,[108] found 'it hard to avoid the conclusion' that some organisms 'were themselves directly modified by the climatic conditions, and that they passed these modifications on to their descendants.'[109] His introduction of such precepts into the discourse on racial groups will presently attract our attention. Again, Ellen Semple, who popularized or − according to some − vulgarized Ratzelian *Anthropogeographie* in the New World, specifically took up Wagner's migration theory in her 1911 *Influences of Geographic Environment*.[110] And Albert Perry Brigham, another geographer in the Shaler–Davis succession, similarly perpetuated those selfsame principles of social plasticity, environmental causation, and cultural inheritance.[111] Thus the key players in the drama of professionalizing geography in America, as in Europe, found in the language of Neo-Lamarckian evolution foundations on which to rebuild the theoretical structure of the new geography.

THE NATURALIZATION OF LANGUAGE

By the early years of the twentieth century a dramatic change in the intellectual context of geographical theory had been effected. This, I think, can best be described as the naturalization of language, a shift effectively calibrated in the move, to use Davis's own words, from 'the old doctrine of

---

[107] Letter, Ellsworth Huntington to W. M. Davis, 3 October 1917, Davis Papers, bMS Am 1798 (245)–7, Houghton Library.

[108] Kammerer's career is the subject of Arthur Koestler's *The Case of the Midwife Toad* (London: Hutchinson, 1971).

[109] Ellsworth Huntington, *World Power and Evolution* (New Haven: Yale University Press, 1920), p. 243. Huntington claimed that this did not 'necessarily mean that there is any such thing as the inheritance of acquired characteristics,' though it is hard to construe his words in any other way. Moreover his belief that the germ-plasm was modifiable in response to environmental stimuli was diametrically opposed to the claims of the Neo-Darwinians.

[110] Ellen C. Semple, *Influences of Geographic Environment on the Basis of Ratzel's System of Anthropo-geography* (New York: Henry Holt, 1911), pp. 169–70.

[111] See, for example, Albert Perry Brigham, *Geographic Influences in American History* (Boston: Ginn and Company, 1903); Albert Perry Brigham, 'Problems of Geographic Influence', *Annals of the Association of American Geographers*, 5 (1915): 3–25.

teleology' to the 'modern principle of evolution.'[112] Stretching back through Ray and Derham to the founders of modern science like Boyle and Newton, the natural theology tradition had, as Yeo argues, 'provided a context for significant discussion of the methodological and epistemological features of both scientific and theological knowledge.'[113] Thus the nineteenth-century philosophical and scientific polymath William Whewell – famous for his original work on tides – could urge, in his treatment of the geography of plants, that he could find in the way that organisms were adapted to climatic conditions 'something well fitted to produce and confirm a reverential wonder.'[114]

In the previous chapter we traced this tradition through the writings of figures like Ritter in Germany, Maury and Guyot in the United States, and Somerville in Britain. In fact this set of teleological convictions permeated the geographical conversation of the time. A series of little-known volumes, but popular in their day, by a certain Robert Mudie illustrates this. In the final volume of the four-part set – *The Heavens*, *The Earth*, *The Air*, and *The Sea* – he informed his readers that he had tried to give 'that tone to the mind which irresistibly leads it from creation to the Creator, and thus makes scientific knowledge the handmaiden to true religion and sincere morality, without guile, lukewarmness, or hypocrisy.'[115] Indeed the contributions of the teleological geographers were from time to time used to inform the writings of theologians themselves. Robert Flint at the University of Edinburgh could, as late as 1883, observe that 'In Ritter's "Geographical Studies", Guyot's "Earth and Man", Kapp's "Allgemeine Erdkunde", . . . & c, will be found a rich store of teleological data as to the fitness of the earth to be the dwelling-place and the schoolhouse of human beings.'[116]

The coming of the evolutionary paradigm, I have argued, presented grave challenges to this whole way of proceeding.[117] Not that it instantly extracted God from scientific discourse. For a considerable period of time attempts were made to 'teleologize' evolution itself. Samuel Haughton

[112] William Morris Davis, 'Systematic Geography', p. 239.

[113] Richard Yeo, 'William Whewell, Natural Theology and the Philosophy of Science in Mid-Nineteenth Century Britain', *Annals of Science*, 36 (1979): 493–516, ref. on p. 495.

[114] William Whewell, *Astronomy and General Physics Considered with Special Reference to Natural Theology* (London: William Pickering, 1834), pp. 73–4.

[115] Robert Mudie, *The Sea. A Popular View of the Phenomena of Tides; the Inhabitants and Uses of the Ocean* (London: Ward and Co., 1835), p. iv.

[116] Robert Flint, *Theism* (London: William Blackwood, 4th rev. edn 1883), p. 376.

[117] I have discussed this in 'Natural Theology and Neo-Lamarckism: The Changing Context of Nineteenth-Century Geography in the United States and Great Britain', *Annals of the Association of American Geographers*, 74 (1984): 9–28.

observed in his 1876 treatment of physical geography that evolution 'by no means involves the denial of a creating and presiding mind'; David Thomas Ansted too spoke of the 'order and Law of the Creator' in his *Physical Geography* of 1881; Archibald Geikie insisted in 1886 that the object of science in general and physical geography in particular was to display 'more and more of that marvellous plan after which this vast world has been framed, to gain a deeper insight into the harmony and beauty of creation, with a yet profounder reverence for Him who made and who upholds it all'; Shaler still affirmed in 1891 his hope that 'our knowledge will reaffirm the old belief that our fathers had in the essential control of a beneficent Providence'; and the political geographer and president of Johns Hopkins University, Daniel Coit Gilman, noted in 1906 that 'evolution is regarded by many theologians as confirming the strictest doctrines of predestination.'[118] And yet for all that, such confessions, where they did surface, were now frequently presented as mere addenda to works that were thoroughly 'scientific' in spirit. It was a short step to jettisoning such theological observations altogether. From the time that Henry Walter Bates, the RGS's secretary, presented his thoroughly naturalistic, Darwinian account of his research on butterflies in 1861, until William Morris Davis's tellingly entitled Hector Maiben lecture to the American Association for the Advancement of Science in 1933, 'The Faith of Reverent Science', the discourse of geography had been progressively naturalized. Certainly this does not mean that all numinous language had been forever expunged. Ratzel, for example, moved away from his earlier materialism towards a more romantic spirituality, while a strong nature-mysticism surfaces in the environmental writings of Vaughan Cornish and in the holistic vitalism of Francis Younghusband.[119] But these were no longer sufficient foundations on which to erect a discipline; for that purpose, faith had to be placed in science. For his part, in that 1933 address, Davis mused that 'the ground for that forward-looking confidence is an optimism which . . . springs from a firm faith in the philosophy of evolution and the faith of reverent sci-

[118] Samuel Haughton, *Six Lectures on Physical Geography* (Dublin: Hodges, Foster and Figgis, 1880), p. 2; David Thomas Ansted, *Physical Geography* (London: W. H. Allen, 6th edn 1881), p. 362; Archibald Geikie, *Elementary Lessons in Physical Geography* (London: Macmillan, 1886), p. 356; Shaler, *Nature and Man in America* (New York: Scribner's Sons, 1891), p. vi; Daniel Coit Gilman, *The Launching of a University and Other Papers. A Sheaf of Remembrances* (New York: Dodd, Mead and Company, 1906), p. 132. See also John K. Wright, 'Notes on Early American Geopiety', in *Human Nature in Geography* by John Kirtland Wright (Cambridge: Harvard University Press, 1966), pp. 250–85.

[119] Bassin, 'Friedrich Ratzel', p. 128; David Matless, 'Nature, the Modern and the Mystic: Tales from Early Twentieth Century Geography', *Transactions of the Institute of British Geographers*, 16 (1991): 272–86.

ence.'[120] In geography, as in science more generally, 'the locus of the sacral,' as Jim Moore has written, 'moved from the noumenal towards the phenomenal, from the eternal towards the temporal, from another world towards this world.'[121]

In the preceding pages I have been elaborating on the theoretical building blocks out of which a number of geographers in pivotal positions believed their discipline could be reconstructed in the wake of specialist fragmentation. Now I want to turn from the interrogation of a few key individuals to illustrate some more general currents of 'sternly practical' thought and action that typified geography in the period. Here I plan working thematically, trying to tease out some of the assumptions pervading geographical discourse, while at the same time identifying some of the actions that gave teeth to geographical rhetoric.

[120] William Morris Davis, 'The Faith of Reverent Science', in Chorley et al., *Davis*, p. 791. Speaking of Davisian geography in the period, Herbst astutely remarked in 1961 that its 'philosophy no longer rested on the cosmological aestheticism of Humboldt or the teleological natural philosophy of Ritter and Guyot, but on the scientific dogma of evolution.' Herbst, 'Social Darwinism', pp. 540–1.

[121] James R. Moore, '"Engines of Empire, Energies of Extinction": Reflections on the Crisis of Faith'. Paper presented at a Conference on the Victorian Crisis of Faith, Victoria College, University of Toronto, November 1984.

7

A 'Sternly Practical' Pursuit

Geography, Race and Empire

To Hugh Robert Mill the study of geography was a 'sternly practical' pursuit. The reason was simple: geography, to him, was 'absolutely essential for our well-being, and even for the continuance of the nation as a Power among the states of the world.' Moreover it afforded 'an important clue to the solution of every problem affecting the mutual relations of land and people, enlightening the course of history, anticipating the trend of political movements, indicating the direction of sound industrial and commercial development.' With such persuasions, it is small wonder that Mill, one of British geography's most ardent publicists throughout the late Victorian era, should pause during his 1901 presidential address to the Geographical Section of the British Association for the Advancement of Science to lament that the 'passing of the nineteenth century was almost like the death of a friend.'[1] For during Darwin's century geography had exhibited *in excelsis* the 'stern practicality' with which Mill was so much smitten.

We have already seen how, in the pre-Darwinian era, British and American geography comfortably subserved the interests of nationalistic self-absorption both at home and abroad. In other places too the selfsame motive forces can clearly be seen. The production of geographical knowledge in France during the late eighteenth and early nineteenth centuries, for example, was intimately bound up with Napoleonic militarism and government.[2] And besides the strategic and bureaucratic services it rendered the

---

[1] Hugh Robert Mill, 'Research in Geographical Science', pp. 423, 416, 407.
[2] On French science in the period see Dorinda Outram, 'Politics and Vocation: French Science, 1793–1830', *British Journal for the History of Science*, 13 (1980): 27–43.; Maurice P. Crosland, *Science in France in the Revolutionary Era* (Cambridge, Mass: Harvard University Press, 1969).

state, it also satisfied nationalistic demands for civic information and the emblematic needs of an imperial civilization. Moreover, the geographical practices of this period mirrored, as Anne Godlewska has recently revealed, changes in the technology and logistics of warfare. Under Napoleon the passion for geodetic accuracy and human resource inventory, both for military purposes, spawned a corps of *ingénieurs-géographes*, as they were called, trained in the craft-skills of the regional surveyor. These military geographers produced – yearly – maps by the thousand, memoirs by the hundred, and atlases by the dozen. In Conrad Malte-Brun's journal *Annales des Voyages*, founded in 1807, for example, the glorification of the Napoleonic regime usurped much space. Thus as agents both of imperialism and modernity, the military geographers displayed their faith in the creed that 'what was local or regional or indigenous was demonstrably inferior [for] diversity was associated with degeneracy and uniformity with civilization.'[3] With such a confession of faith, French geography deeply implicated itself in the imperial imperatives of the era.

The various French excursions into Egypt (1798–1801) and Algeria (1839–42) were a major source of geographical intelligence. The Algerian expedition, for instance, was conceived as a civilizing conquest, and it is in this context that the shifting conception of the nature of French geography at mid-century has to be understood, and in particular the move away from the traditional geodetic emphasis on the determination of location.[4] As for the earlier Egyptian episode, the twenty-three-volume *Description de l'Égypte* that it spawned between 1809 and 1828 has been isolated by Edward Said as a turning point in the history of the representation of the unfamiliar.[5] Not only was it unique in its extent, it was also a self-conscious act of exotic interrogation in a fashion that domesticated the distant to the needs of European self-infatuation. By 're-orientating' Egypt's destiny *away* from the Orient, and *towards* the Occident, its artistic, scientific, and bureaucratic significance could thus be engulfed by the Napoleonic powers. The Egyptian fact-finding mission thereby turned out to be, in Said's

[3] See Anne Godlewska, 'Napoleon's Geographers: Imperialists or Soldiers of Modernity?' in Neil Smith and Anne Godlewska (eds), *Geography and Empire*, forthcoming.
[4] See Anne Godlewska, 'Tradition, Crisis, and New Paradigms in the Rise of the Modern French Discipline of Geography 1760–1850', *Annals of the Association of American Geographers*, 79 (1989): 192–213. See also Numa Broc, 'Les Grandes Missions Scientifiques Françaises aux XIXe Siècles (Morée, Algérie, Mexique) et leurs Travaux Géographiques', *Revue d'Histoire des Sciences et de leurs Applications*, 34 (1981): 319–58.
[5] See the discussion in Mike Heffernan, 'From Knowledge to Power: The Geography of Geographical Knowledge in Late Nineteenth-Century France'. Paper presented at the Annual Conference of the Association of American Geographers, Toronto, April 1990.

words, a 'great collective appropriation of one country by another.'[6] Moreover, the strategies that the French employed in these locales, aimed as they were at 'unlocking at last the intellectual treasures of these ancient lands and bringing them into the mainstream of world science,' as Dunbar puts it, were replicated on the other side of the Atlantic in the French scientific mission to Mexico in the mid-1860s.[7]

That these concerns continued to dominate French geography during the third quarter of the century is clear from the patriotic tincture of the Société de Géographie of Paris in the 1870s – sentiments that were echoed in the country's other geographical fraternities that soon came into being. The efflorescence of French geographical societies, as Said reminds us, rode in tandem with a 'powerfully renewed demand for territorial acquisition.'[8] In Paris, for example, a rejuvenated concern with the 'conquests of civilization over barbarism,' as one official put it, was needed to supplement what he took to be the subject's conventional self-limitation to scientific pursuits. So it was not surprising that the Second International Congress of Geographical Sciences that met in Paris in 1875 was dubbed a 'great international work in the pacific conquests of civilization over barbarism.' In this environment the cultivation of geography was promoted as 'one of the most imperative necessities of the present time.' Here again 'stern practicality' dramatically surfaced, for, as a contemporary commentator observed, 'geographic conquests do not have, as has been too long believed, a purely scientific and platonic interest' – rather they mapped the path to imperial exploitation. With the backing of the French government, it is thus scarcely surprising that the geographical expedition of Abbé Debaize through Africa was welcomed in the parliamentary chamber by George Périn expressly because 'aside from the scientific interest,' the whole project bore 'a practical economic interest.'[9] In the light of this liaison between French geography and French commerce it is entirely understandable why the new fields of commercial geography and colonial geography should be promulgated so widely and enthusiastically in France at the time. Indeed the initiative to

[6] Edward W. Said, *Orientalism. Western Conceptions of the Orient* (London: Routledge and Kegan Paul, 1978), p. 84.
[7] Gary S. Dunbar, '"The Compass Follows the Flag": The French Scientific Mission to Mexico, 1864–7', *Annals of the Association of American Geographers*, 78 (1988): 229–40.
[8] Said, *Orientalism*, p. 217. On French geography in the period, see Numa Broc, 'L'Establissment de la Géographie et Nationalisme en France: Diffusion, Institutions, Projets (1870–90)', *Annales de Géographie*, 83 (1974): 545–68; Vincent Berdoulay, *La Formation de l'École Française de Géographie (1870–1914)* (Paris: Bibliothèque Nationale, 1981).
[9] Cited in Donald Vernon McKay, 'Colonialism in the French Geographical Movement 1871–81', *Geographical Review*, 33 (1943): 214–32, refs on pp. 214, 222, 223, 227.

establish a geographical society in Lyon came from members of the business community, while the secretary of the Bordeaux Commercial Geographical Society insisted that geography 'must manifest the power of its utility and practical application.'[10]

None of this is intended to imply that in the French context either geography or imperialism were monolithic, uncontested entities. There were certainly profoundly contradictory currents of thought and practice, arising at least in part from the shifting fulcrum of imperial impetus after 1870 from the colonial periphery to the metropolitan core. Moreover, the emphases changed over time. In the 1830s, for instance, what Heffernan calls the 'utopian' imperialism of Enfantin and Duveyrier (who resorted to gender metaphors in their talk of a fruitful union between the masculine civilizations of Europe and their female African and Asian counterparts) was to decline in the wake of the more nationalistic version promulgated by Anatole Prévost-Paradol. In due course these cultural renditions of imperialism would take a more stringent economic turn. Yet for all that, geography in France was, as Mill would put it, 'sternly practical'. And it was sternly practical not just in the sense that, as Heffernan notes, 'French geographers were in the vanguard of the colonialist lobby and were among the more eloquent and sophisticated advocates of empire,' but also in the arena of domestic educational reform 'as a means of national rejuvenation in the wake of the Franco-Prussian war.'[11]

The interlacing of geographical knowledge and imperial drives that thus manifested itself in France, continued to typify a good deal of English-speaking geography during the decades around 1900. As Brian Hudson noted in 1977, there was a close temporal congruence between the emergence of the 'new geography and the new imperialism.'[12] At the inaugural meeting of the Scottish Geographical Society in December 1884, for example, H. M. Stanley hoped to excite his audience's 'regard for geography by showing . . . how it has been and is intimately connected with the growth of the British Empire.'[13] A decade and a half later, A. J. Herbertson would

[10] Cited in William H. Schneider, 'Geographical Reform and Municipal Imperialism in France, 1870–80', in John M. MacKenzie (ed.), *Imperialism and the Natural World* (Manchester: Manchester University Press, 1990), pp. 90–117, ref. on p. 106.

[11] See Michael J. Heffernan, 'Militant Geographers: the French Geographical Movement and the Forms of French Imperialism, 1870 to 1920', in Neil Smith and Anne Godlewska (eds), *Geography and Empire*, forthcoming.

[12] Brian Hudson, 'The New Geography and the New Imperialism: 1870–1918', *Antipode*, 9 (1977): 12–19.

[13] H. M. Stanley, 'Inaugural Address', *Scottish Geographical Magazine*, 1 (1885): 6. Stanley's comparable 1884 address to the Manchester Geographical Society is discussed in Hudson, 'The New Geography'.

expand on the 'Geographical Factor in Imperial Problems' in his presidential address to Section E of the British Association in 1910, calling for the training of geographers in the craft of economic forecasting and the establishment of an imperial intelligence department that would be serviced by university-trained geographers.[14]

This chapter in the story, of course, is not unconnected with the evolution-grounded geographical theory that, as we have seen, could provide 'scientific' warrants for the new imperialists' enterprise. In saying this, however, I do not mean to imply either that this was the only source of imperialism's scientific legitimation or that the relationship was either inevitable or straightforward. In fact, as we will see, evolutionary rhetoric could just as easily subserve entirely different political goals. But that the evolutionary world-view had a crucial role to play in the contract between the conduct of empire and late Victorian geographical theory is certainly the case. Apart from anything else, imbued with the spirit of social evolution, many imperialists felt they were acting in harmony with the prevailing *Zeitgeist*, and this bolstered their ideology of rulership.[15] Besides, the categories of social-evolutionary recapitulation provided a vocabulary that facilitated the depiction of non-European peoples in terms of retardation, atrophy, or decelerated growth. Race, gender, infancy, and criminality were thus frequently portrayed in interchangeable terms.

In making these assertions there is a danger of too narrowly typecasting both geography *and* imperialism, perceiving geography *just as* the scientific underwriter of overseas exploitation. To the contrary, the 'age of empire', as Driver has recently written, 'was constituted in complex ways, culturally and politically, as well as economically.'[16] So too was the geography. And it is therefore not simply a case of seeing geographical knowledge as an epiphenomenon of empire; rather it is again a matter of reciprocal constitution.

The way in which I want to treat this episode, however, is not via the provision of a catalogue of geographical practices and imperial exploits as they interpenetrated in a series of different regional arenas. This is a task that needs to be undertaken not least in order to get a grip on the key role played by those anonymous geographical practitioners – cartographers, surveyors, and the like – whose skills actually constructed the empire. The

---

[14] Herbertson, 'Geography and Some of its Problems', *Geographical Journal*, 36 (1910): 468–79.

[15] See M. E. Chamberlain, *The Scramble for Africa* (Harlow: Longman, 1974).

[16] Felix Driver, 'Geography's Empire'. Also Felix Driver, 'Henry Morton Stanley and his Critics: Geography Exploration and Empire', *Past and Present*, 133 (1991): 134–66.

social history of these geographical knowledges remains to be written and to be placed alongside the biographical treatments that we have of such high-profile figures as Burton, Grant, Livingstone, Stanley, and Speke.[17] So rather than providing silhouettes of their search for the sources of the Nile, their discovery of Lake Victoria or Lake Tanganyika, or their adventures into Dahomey, and charting their links with the RGS, I want instead to proceed by exploring some of the lingering refrains that persistently reverberated throughout the entire length and breadth of the geographical engagement with empire.

CLIMATE'S MORAL ECONOMY

I want to begin my investigation of the links between English-speaking imperialism and geographical knowledge by focusing on the conversation about climate. My claim here is that discussions of climatic matters by geographers throughout the nineteenth century and well into the twentieth century were profoundly implicated in the imperial drama and were frequently cast in the diagnostic language of ethnic judgement. To put it another way, the idioms of political and moralistic evaluation were simply part and parcel of the grammar of climatology. By focusing initially on climate, I thus hope to illustrate something of the way that scientific claims were constituted by, and then made to bear the weight of, moralistic appraisals of both people and places.[18]

Race and Region: Climate and Race Character

The idea that climatic regions on both global and local scales implied an ethnic moral topography was an idea that weaves its way throughout the corpus of nineteenth- and early-twentieth-century geographical writings.[19] Geography's mid-nineteenth-century links with anthropology helped facilitate such conceptual manoeuvres. As we saw earlier, there was a considerable membership overlap between the ethnological and geographical societies in the early Victorian period. So it was not surprising when, on 19 November 1861, John Crawfurd rose to address the ethnologists his subject

[17] A useful survey is available in Christopher Hibbert, *Africa Explored. Europeans in the Dark Continent, 1769–1889* (London: Allen Lane, 1982).
[18] In this discussion I have drawn heavily on my 'Climate's Moral Economy: Science, Race, and Place in Post-Darwinian British and American Geography', in Neil Smith and Anne Godlewska (eds), *Geography and Empire* (Oxford: Blackwell), forthcoming.
[19] I have discussed this topic more fully in my 'The Moral Discourse of Climate: Historical Considerations on Race, Place and Virtue', *Journal of Historical Geography*, 17 (1991): 413–34.

should be 'On the Connexion between Ethnology and Physical Geography.' His purpose was simple. It was to catalogue the effects of regional climate on racial constitution. The moralistic complexion of his project is clearly visible: Australia's inauspicious climates had only produced 'the feeblest . . . hordes of black, ill-formed, unseemly, naked savages,' while in Africa, 'the races of man . . . correspond with the disadvantages of its physical geography.'[20] To be sure, it was not clear whether climate had *produced* such racial degenerates, or whether they had been *placed* by nature or God in climatically appropriate regimes. No matter. Race and region were, in the eyes of Crawfurd and his colleagues, tightly – very tightly – tied together. Thus three months later, James Hunt could tell the same audience that in the tropical climates 'there is a low state of morality, and . . . the inhabitants of these regions are essentially sensual'; by contrast the 'temperate regions', he insisted, were characterized by 'increased activity of the brain.'[21]

Among geographers the idea that race and region were umbilically connected surfaced both in religious and naturalistic depictions of human racial history. The naturalization of geographical vocabulary thus had little effect on the legitimating moves that were afoot. The *context* changed; the *judgements* remained. This is nicely brought out when we compare Arnold Guyot's portrait of racial geography with those of the Michigan geologist Alexander Winchell. Guyot, we recall, had insisted that it was 'the Creator' who had 'placed the cradle of mankind in the midst of the continents of the North . . . and not at the centre of the tropical regions, whose balmy, but enervating and treacherous, atmosphere would perhaps have lulled him to sleep, the sleep of death in his very cradle.'[22] For Winchell, it was 'Nature, conscious of their [the blacks'] irremediable estrangement, [that] had contented herself to herd them in regions where they would never mingle in the stir and strife of social and national struggles.'[23] Either way, whether courtesy of creator or nature, racial constitution was moored to climatic circumstance.[24]

[20] John Crawfurd, 'The Connexion between Ethnology and Physical Geography', pp. 5, 6.

[21] James Hunt, 'On Ethno-Climatology; or the Acclimatization of Man', *Transactions of the Ethnological Society of London*, n.s. 2 (1863): 53.

[22] Guyot, *Earth and Man*, p. 251.

[23] Alexander Winchell, *Preadamites; or a Demonstration of the Existence of Men before Adam; Together with a Study of their Condition, Antiquity, Racial Affinities, and Progressive Dispersion over the Earth* (Chicago: S. C. Griggs and Company, 2nd edn 1880), pp. 156–7. A general history of the preadamite theory is available in David N. Livingstone, *The Preadamite Theory*.

[24] Of course such judgements did not necessarily occur in a climatic context. Daniel Coit Gilman, geographer and university president, simply insisted in an 1896 address to the

The construction of a moral-climatic idiom by which racial difference could be portrayed could operate at a much more localized scale as well. Consider, for instance, the analysis of the Edinburgh geologist, geographer, and explorer Joseph Thomson, who, during a short life travelled extensively in East Africa.[25] In 1886, during a period of convalescence between trips, he spoke to the Birmingham meeting of the British Association about his experience in Niger and Central Sudan, an address that appeared later that year in the *Scottish Geographical Magazine*. Here he paused to reflect on the moral-evolutionary impact of climatic conditions:

> It is a fact worthy of our attention that, as the traveller passes up the river [Niger] and finds a continually improving climate . . . he coincidentally observes a higher type of humanity – better-ordered communities, more comfort, with more industry. That these pleasanter conditions are due to the improved environment cannot be doubted. To the student with Darwinian instincts most instructive lessons might be derived from a study of the relations between man and nature in these regions.

Here the 'struggle for existence' had produced a 'higher type of man, both mentally and physically.' Evidently the changing topography of the moral economy could be mapped straight onto climatic regime. To be sure, he felt he must admit, in the upper reaches of the Niger,

> We are still dealing with negroes, but how different are they! Behind us are the unwashed barbarous *sans-culottes* of the Coast region, with fetishism, cannibalism, and the gin bottle in congenial union; before us lies a people astir with religious activity and enthusiasm, and wonderfully far advanced in the arts and industries.[26]

The intertwining of scientific and sermonic modes of speech are clearly to be heard here. And yet Thomson's fine-tuning of moral climatology on a sub-regional range did not prevent him from issuing moral imperatives on a far grander scale. That same year he also told the readers of the *Scottish Geographical Magazine* that the 'Negro . . . requires to be treated by the

---

Hampton Normal and Industrial Institute that the differences between black and white were 'natural and cannot be set aside by human action . . . differences of race are ineffaceable, by legislation or volition.' Daniel Coit Gilman, 'A Study in Black and White', in Daniel Coit Gilman, *The Launching of a University and Other Papers. A Sheaf of Remembrances* (New York: Dodd, Mead and Company, 1906), p. 338.

[25] See 'Thomson, Joseph', *Dictionary of National Biography*.

[26] Joseph Thomson, 'Niger and Central Sudan sketches', *Scottish Geographical Magazine*, 2 (1886): 582, 584.

State as a child is by the father, only, instead of years, the negro must undergo his moral and mental discipline for two or three generations before he can be trusted to rely upon himself.'[27] Echoes of the recapitulationist strain in biology are clearly audible.

Such moral obligations were at the same time political mandates too. Judgements about the present moral standing of ethnic groups had direct implications for their future in a new imperialist world economy. Tutelage under 'superior' races or, failing that, sweat equity, represented the policies that James Bryce, Britain's distinguished transatlantic ambassador and ally of Halford Mackinder, advocated at the inaugural meeting of the London branch of the Scottish Geographical Society in April 1892. Save for the Chinese, Bryce mused:

> none of these tropical peoples . . . has a native civilisation, or is fitted to play any part in history, either as a conquering or as a thinking force, or in any way, save as producers by physical labour of material wealth. None is likely to develop towards any higher condition than that in which it now stands, save under the tutelage, and by adopting so much as it can of the culture, of the five or six European peoples which have practically appropriated the torrid zone, and are dividing its resources between them. Yet the vast numbers to which, under the conjoint stimuli of science and peace, these inferior black and yellow races may grow, coupled with the capacity some of them evince for assimilating the material side of European civilisation, may enable them to play a larger part in the future of the world than they have played in the past.[28]

The idea that climate had stamped its indelible mark on racial constitution, not just physiologically, but psychologically and morally, was a motif that was both deep and lasting in English-speaking geography. Space does not permit a complete chronicle of this strain here, though such a survey would certainly be instructive. Suffice to note that in Austin Miller's standard textbook on *Climatology*, first published in 1931, he explained that 'Psychologically, each climate tends to have its own mentality, innate in its inhabitants and grafted on its immigrants.' And besides, there were direct behavioural correlates of climatic governance: 'The enervating monotonous

[27] Joseph Thomson, 'East Central Africa, and its Commercial Outlook', *Scottish Geographical Magazine*, 2 (1886): 74.

[28] James Bryce, 'The Migrations of the Races of Men Considered Historically', *Scottish Geographical Magazine*, 8 (1892): 420. The way Bryce moved the race debate from anthropology towards economics by his recognition of the emerging global economic system is discussed in Paul B. Rich, *Race and Empire in British Politics* (Cambridge: Cambridge University Press, 1986), pp. 20–4.

climates of much of the tropical zone, together with the abundant and easily obtained food-supply, produce a lazy and indolent people, indisposed to
labour for hire and therefore in the past subjected to coercion culminating
in slavery.'[29] What is remarkable here is the way moralistic terms – enervating, monotonous, lazy, indolent – were still being presented as settled
scientific maxims with the result that human mental and moral behaviour
was thoroughly naturalized through the deployment of what I have labelled
'climate's moral economy'.

The notion that ethnic constitution was riveted to climatic circumstance
implied that racial character was spatially referenced and could thus be presented in cartographic form. The whole business of what might be called
anthropometric cartography was a project that was taken up with varying
degrees of ideological gusto by anthropologists and geographers alike. We
have earlier examined aspects of this manoeuvre in the writings of
Gliddon.[30] The cartographic enterprise here turns out to be a rhetorical
device of persuasion to justify the authority of its practitioners' assertions,
and I believe this can be illustrated from a brief consideration of Ellsworth
Huntington's use of cartographic illustration in his 1924 *Character of Races*.

I shall want to say something more about Huntington in a moment, but
for the present I propose focusing on the maps he compiled to illustrate his
chapter on 'The Character of Modern Europe.' The details are easily
reviewed. Huntington drew up charts of the distribution of genius, health,
civilization, and so on, and correlated these with a chart of what he termed
'climatic energy'. The conclusion? The similarity, Huntington remarked, 'is
so clear that it speaks for itself. In each map there is the same dark area
around the North Sea.' How simple. Huntington's claim that 'climate
influences health and energy, and these in turn influence civilization' was
thus backed up by the traditional craft competence of the geographer – cartography – and the correlations were so plain that the suite of maps, well,
just 'spoke for itself'.[31]

Huntington's seemingly innocuous metaphor of those maps speaking for
themselves is not to be believed; in fact it was pernicious. He had to extract
the information for his map of the distribution of civilization – to isolate
one example – from numerous willing accomplices. Over fifty scholars –
geographers, anthropologists, historians, and so on – had assisted in the
exercise. Huntington, it turns out, had written to the intellectual elite of his

[29] A. Austin Miller, *Climatology* (5th edn London: Methuen, 1947. First pub. 1931), p. 2.
[30] See chapter 5, and Livingstone, 'The Moral Discourse of Climate'.
[31] Ellsworth Huntington, *The Character of Races, as Influenced by Physical Environment, Natural Selection and Historical Development* (New York: Scribner's, 1924), p. 232.

day asking them to rank whole countries on a graduated scale of civilization. Some, if J. Russell Smith is representative, relished the task. He apparently had taken 'a half day off to sit in judgement upon the world,' and confessed that it gave him 'a sense of a sort of tyrannic despotism to hold a country in his hand.'[32] Many a true word is spoken in jest! James Bryce was also predictably enthusiastic and found Huntington's idea 'ingenious'.[33] But others were not convinced. George Chisholm, for example, admitted to 'a peculiar incapacity for forming judgements about peoples' while A. L. Kroeber had to 'frankly confess that I believe you will obtain misleading results.'[34] Again, W. Z. Ripley wrote to him saying that he did 'not conceive that the method you suggest is possible of scientific results. One must choose between statistics which are definite and mere judgements which are general. To apply the geographic method to a compound of statistics and loose generalization may be productive of grave error.'[35] Even more telling was Franz Boas's eschewal of the cultural imperialism that undergirded Huntington's entire scheme in words that, paradoxically, demonstrate how dignifying to the human subject a positivist methodology could be!

> I feel . . . quite unable to comply with your request, for several reasons . . . It has been my endeavor, in my anthropological studies, to follow . . . the same principles that are laid down for natural sciences; and the first condition of progress is therefore to eliminate the element of subjective value; not that I wish to deny that there are values, but it seems to me necessary to eliminate the peculiar combination of the development of cultural forms and the intrusion of the idea of our estimate of their value, which has nothing to do with these forms. It seems to my mind that in doing so these obtain subjective values, which in themselves may be the subject of interesting studies, but which do not give any answer to the question you are trying to solve.[36]

[32] Letter from J. Russell Smith to Ellsworth Huntington, 3 July 1914, Huntington Papers, Box 6, Folder 34, Yale University Archives. The previous year Smith had written to Huntington praising his 'chart showing the relation of human output to temperature' as 'real geography'. Letter, J. Russell Smith to Ellsworth Huntington, Huntington Papers, Box 31, Folder 612, Manuscripts and Archives, Yale University Library.

[33] Letter, James Bryce to Ellsworth Huntington, 15 November 1913, Huntington Papers, Box 6, Folder 34, Manuscripts and Archives, Yale University Library.

[34] Letter, George G. Chisholm to Ellsworth Huntington, 13 November 1913, Huntington Papers, Box 6, Folder 34, Yale University Archives; letter, A. L. Kroeber to Ellsworth Huntington, 6 December 1913, Huntington Papers, Box 6, Folder 34, Yale University Archives.

[35] Letter, W. Z. Ripley to Ellsworth Huntington, 3 November 1913, Huntington Papers, Box 6, Folder 34, Manuscripts and Archives, Yale University Library.

[36] Letter, Franz Boas to Ellsworth Huntington, 5 November 1913, Huntington Papers, Box 6, Folder 34. It is significant, I think, that in his essay review of *The Character of Races*, George Chisholm observed that Huntington had ignored Boas's celebrated studies on the

Huntington's cartographic constructions were therefore just that – constructions, rhetorical devices by which he could legitimate what were even in his own time profoundly contested judgements about the moral economy of climate. Precisely the same moves, I would argue, undergirded the climographs Griffith Taylor prepared for the purpose of backing up his assertions about 'The Control of Settlement by Humidity and Temperature.'[37] At the centre of his graph of wet-bulb temperature and humidity was a composite white climograph – a shaded area – where conditions were 'close to the ideal.' This piece of graphic rhetoric, predictably, pleased Huntington enormously, and he asserted that 'as representation of the various effects of climate . . . Taylor's diagrams are much the best yet available.'[38] Yet if they were, at least to Huntington, intellectually rewarding, they were ultimately to prove political dynamite. For it was obvious from Taylor's schema that many places in Australia were unsuitable for white settlement. At this stage, Taylor was in the employ of the Meteorological Office in Melbourne and was advising the government on settlement prospects in tropical Australia at a time when the Weather Service was affiliated with the Home Office's intelligence branch. Later, in 1920, when he moved to the University of Sydney to establish the department of geography, he continued his work on climate and settlement, increasingly tying these investigations into questions of racial evolution. And so in the 1920s he came to voice the controversial opinion that, because they were brachycephalic, Chinese migration might help solve the settlement problem. Such views ran counter to the conventional White Australia policy, and Taylor found himself the subject of vituperative attacks in the press. In 1928 he left Sydney to take up a position at the University of Chicago.[39]

Besides providing cartographic rationale for their anthropo-climatic credo, both Taylor and Huntington also wanted to situate their theories within the deep historical framework of Darwinian theory. The role of climate in racial evolution thus occupied their attentions. I have only space here to briefly allude to their endeavours, again to illustrate the insinuation

modification of the immigrant head form. Geo. G. Chisholm, 'Perplexities of Race: a Review', *Scottish Geographical Magazine*, 41 (1925): 300.

[37] Griffith Taylor, 'The Control of Settlement by Humidity and Temperature', *Commonwealth Bureau of Meteorology. Bulletin No. 14* (Melbourne, 1914).

[38] Ellsworth Huntington, 'Graphic Representation of the Effect of Climate on Man', *Geographical Review*, 4 (1917): 401–3.

[39] See the discussions in J. M. Powell, 'Griffith Taylor Emigrates from Australia', *Geography Bulletin*, 10 (1978): 5–13; J. M. Powell, 'Thomas Griffith Taylor, 1880–1963', *Geographers. Biobibliographical Studies*, 3 (1979): 141–53; Marie Sanderson, *Griffith Taylor: Antarctic Scientist and Pioneer Geographer* (Ottawa, 1988).

of moral imperialism into their discourse. In his consideration of 'Climatic Cycles and Evolution' for the *Geographical Review* in 1919 Taylor repeatedly made reference to climates as 'strenuous', 'favorable', 'healthful', 'energy-promoting', and so on, and authenticated the whole undertaking with an impressive piece of coloured cartographic rhetoric depicting the 'Zones of migration showing the evolution of the races, based mainly on the cephalic indices of the most primitive tribes in each region' (figure 7.1).[40] Two years later he extended this analysis by attempting to correlate racial type and cephalic index with linguistic and cultural traits.[41]

Further commentary on such linguistic and cartographic ploys would be to merely multiply testimonials, however. Instead I want to mention three metaphors to which Taylor resorted that betray much about the ideological orientation of moral climatology. First was his use of the recapitulationist analogy of racial inferiority and infancy. This application of the youth/maturity/old-age scheme produced such racial stereotypes as the following:

> The childlike behavior of the negro has often been referred to as a primitive characteristic. The white races are versatile, gay, and inventive – all attributes of youth. The yellow races are grave, meditative, and melancholic – which possibly indicates their more mature position in the evolution of races.[42]

Secondly, Taylor elaborated an analogy between race migration and class-correlated crowd behaviour at a large sporting event.

> First come the lowest classes and pariahs, who wander freely over the ground long before the general public arrives. They have arrived there by the usual roads and tracks but ultimately are found perched in tree tops and in the least attractive positions. Then the proletariat advances along the same road and corridors. They are driven out of the best seats, which are reserved for the last comers.[43]

Some years later, in 1936, he returned to this subject when he produced for *Human Biology* his zones and strata theory. In a nutshell, Taylor urged that a sequence of migrations of ever-more-highly evolved stock out from a

---

[40] T. Griffith Taylor, 'Climatic Cycles and Evolution', *Geographical Review*, 8 (1919): 298, 299, 307.

[41] T. Griffith Taylor, 'The Evolution and Distribution of Race, Culture, and Language', *Geographical Review*, 11 (1921): 54–119.

[42] Taylor, 'Climatic Cycles and Evolution', p. 300.

[43] Ibid., pp. 300–1.

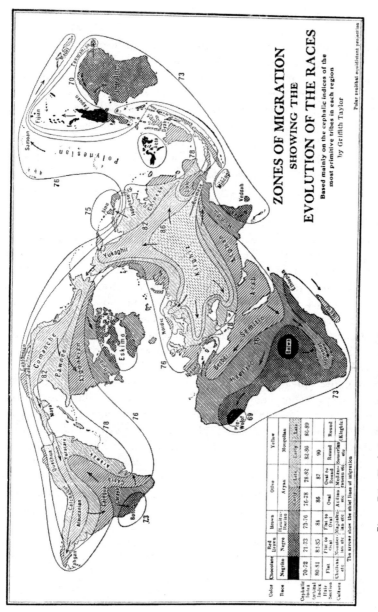

Figure 7.1 *Taylor's zones of racial migration*, reproduced by permission of the American Geographical Society from *Geographical Review* 8 (1921).

central core provided the key to unlocking race history. Hence his third metaphor – the geological one of zones and strata – which evoked the idea of racial groups diffusing over earlier cultures and in turn being subsumed under yet later migrant peoples. (Taylor had earlier developed a graphic stratigraphical metaphor of linguistic history with 'outliers', 'inliers', and 'transgressions')[44] The implication of this scheme (which had earlier been advanced by Gustav Fritsch, a disciple of Moritz Wagner, and more recently by W. D. Matthew)[45] was that the earliest expansion had not only spread farthest, but had encompassed the least evolved specimens. Assuming the cradle of humankind to have been somewhere in central Asia, Taylor elaborated his judgements. Climatic change had ushered out of south central Asia various early forms of primitive hominoid, the greater proportion of whom, in Taylor's reading, would have ended up in Africa. The conclusion was inevitable: blacks were a very ancient type of humanity akin to Neanderthal man.[46] As he was to put it in 1951: 'My suggestion is that a Neandertaloid type lived in southern Asia and gave rise to the negroes far back in the Pleistocene – perhaps in the Gunz-Mindel inter-glacial.' This is not, to be sure, polygenism, but it asserts such early racial differentiation that it might as well be. Moreover the moral censure associated with this proposal is clearly to be heard: 'The writer believes that it is precisely because the negro was thrust into the stagnant environment of the Tropics . . . that he preserves so many primitive features.' 'Racial evolution', he concluded, has left the Negro 'far behind'.[47]

The cumulative enregistration of climate on racial constitution over the aeons of human evolutionary history can finally be illustrated from Huntington's work. In 1924 he produced 'Environment and Racial Character' for an edited collection of essays on *Organic Adaptation to Environment*. That climate was 'a main determinant' of human activity was crucial to the story Huntington had to tell about race history and character. As he envisaged it, the human race had first come into being somewhere in Asia, probably not in its tropical zones, but rather further north. Enter now, a crucial environmental factor: climatic change in the form of glacial

[44] Taylor, 'Evolution and Distribution of Race, Culture, and Language'.

[45] Gustav Fritsch, 'Geographie und Anthropologie als Bundesgenossen', *Verhandlugen der Gesellschaft für Erdkunde zo Berlin*, 8 (1881): 234–51; W. D. Matthew, 'Climate and Evolution', *Annals of the New York Academy of Sciences*, 24 (1915): 171–318.

[46] T. Griffith Taylor, 'The Zones and Strata Theory: a Biological Classification of Races', *Human Biology*, 8 (1936): 348–67. See also Taylor's 'Racial Migration-Zones and their Significance', *Human Biology*, 2 (1930): 34–62.

[47] Griffith Taylor, 'Racial Geography', in Griffith Taylor (ed.), *Geography in the Twentieth Century* (New York: Philosophical Library, 3rd edn 1957), pp. 455, 454.

periodicity. This induced a series of migrations, which in turn exerted a profound and formative influence on human evolutionary history. Those who ended up in the tropics, where 'evolution . . . has stagnated', were psycho-biologically disadvantaged, because during all the hundreds of thousands of years of man's existence there have been few great changes, few *new* types of selection whereby mental specialization has been accelerated.' As a result, black Africans 'represent our primitive ancestors.' 'Their characteristic', he went on, 'are those which unspecialized man first showed when he separated from the apes and came down from the trees. It is not to be expected that such people should ever rise very high in the scale of civilization.' The tropical world was thus relegated to the moral margins of history and its people cast out from the mainstream chronicle of evolutionary advance.[48]

The same was true of the native Americans who had come to the New World via the wastes of northern Siberia and across the Bering Strait. Here they had been 'subjected to a repressive evolution.' Accordingly the American Indians forever carried with them the stamp of this subversive phase in their evolutionary past. Moreover, in the wilds of northern Siberia they had picked up 'arctic hysteria', an affliction to which women were apparently most susceptible. The overall result?

> The natural selection due to this disease together with the great premium which the Arctic environment places upon passive endurance may have been an important factor in moulding the mental quality of most of the people of America. If we compare the Amerinds with European races, one of the most striking differences is not only a lower degree of originality and initiative, but a certain passivity. The emotional types have been eliminated.[49]

In this extract, if my assessment is even in the neighbourhood of a correct analysis, we find a particularly clear instance of the discourse I have been tracking in post-Darwinian geography – namely, the deployment of climate's moral economy for the purposes of regionalizing racial character. A closely related issue centred on the question of human migration between different regional climates, and raised the whole matter of human acclimatization. The way in which the moral economy surfaced in this conversation will be our next concern.

[48] Ellsworth Huntington, 'Environment and Racial Character', in M. R. Thorpe (ed.), *Organic Adaptation to Environment* (New Haven: Yale University 1924), pp. 281–99. Reprinted in Earl W. Count (ed.), *This is Race. An Anthology Selected from the International Literature on the Races of Man* (New York, 1950), pp. 339–50, ref. on 346.
[49] Ibid., p. 350.

Mortality and Migration: The Acclimatization Question

With European penetration into the tropical and subtropical worlds, the whole question of human acclimatization assumed increasing importance towards the end of the nineteenth century.[50] Sir John Kirk, for example, reported to the Sixth International Geographical Congress, which met in London in 1895, that 'Climate is the most important of all considerations in the choice of a home for Europeans in Central Africa.'[51] E. G. Ravenstein concurred, insisting that the 'colonization and climatology of a country were closely connected.'[52] Besides, readers of the Scottish Geographical Magazine were kept informed of climatic-colonial matters by reports on the German experience in tropical Africa, the new British colony in South Africa, and reviews of various writers on the subject.[53] As I have argued elsewhere, the problem of – and attitudes towards – acclimatization crystallized a host of scientific, institutional, and imperial interests at the time. Moreover, the stances that participants in the debate assumed also reflected these interests.[54] Here, however, I want to focus specifically on the way in which the issue surfaced within the geographical coalition in the post-Darwinian era. It is important, however, to note in passing that the question of human acclimatization was not unconnected with agricultural questions about the domestication of foreign plants, zoological issues about animal naturalization, biological queries over the relationship between adaptation, inheritance and environment, and medical concerns over the physiological consequences of exposure to an unfamiliar climate.[55]

[50] For a discussion of earlier ideas about the subject, see Philip Curtin, '"The White Man's Grave": Image and Reality, 1780–1850', Journal of British Studies, 1 (1961): 94–110.

[51] Sir John Kirk, 'The Extent to which Tropical Africa is Suited for Development by the White Races, or under their Superintendence', Report of the Sixth International Geographical Congress, London 1895 (London, 1896): 526.

[52] E. G. Ravenstein, Discussion, Report of the Sixth International Geographical Congress, London 1895 (London, 1896) p. 547.

[53] 'German Colonisation in Tropical Africa', Scottish Geographical Magazine, 1 (1885): 263; anonymous, 'The New British Colony in South Africa', Scottish Geographical Magazine, 1 (1885): 383; anonymous, Review of Zur Klimatologie und Hygiene Ostafrikas, by Gerhard Rohlfs, Scottish Geographical Magazine, 2 (1886): 637.

[54] See my 'Human Acclimatization: Perspectives on a Contested Field of Inquiry in Science, Medicine and Geography', History of Science, 25 (1987): 358–94.

[55] Some of these issues are treated in the following works: Douglas R. Weiner, 'The Roots of "Michurinism": Transformist Biology and Acclimatization as Currents in the Russian Life Sciences', Annals of Science, 42 (1985): 244–60; Philip D. Curtin, Death by Migration: Europe's Encounter with the Tropical World in the Nineteenth Century (Cambridge: Cambridge University Press, 1989); Michael Osborne, 'The Société Zoologique d'Acclimatation and the New French Empire: The Science and Political Economy of Economic Zoology during the Second Empire' (Ph.D. thesis, University of Wisconsin-Madison, 1987); Alfred W. Crosby,

Accordingly, a whole spate of acclimatization societies emerged during the nineteenth century across Europe and in America to monitor different aspects of the question.[56] Besides this, there had been very considerable debate on the subject in the pre-Darwinian period too, particularly in view of Britain's interests in the Indian subcontinent and the death toll exacted on British troops and administrators there. Army surgeons reported on the statistics of disease and mortality in India, resident administrators were furnished with information on how to survive the Indian climate, and James Johnston's *The Influence of Tropical Climates on European Constitutions* – the medical bible for tropical travellers – went through six editions between 1812 and 1841. Besides, a tropical hygiene industry – largely to do with apparel – flourished, manufacturing such items as the cholera belt (a flannel strip worn around the abdomen to counter post-perspiration chills) and the solar topi or pith helmet to protect the head and neck from the tropical sun.[57]

As I have said, the details of these must remain beyond the bounds of my present concern. Instead I want to try and show how imperial interests and moralistic discourse were constitutive of late nineteenth and early twentieth century geographical treatments of the subject. My argument is simply put: it is that these issues provided a common framework of exegesis even among those who took up widely differing stances on the matter. That there was a moral economy of climate was a very largely uncontested presupposition among participants in the conversation.

For those who were sceptical about the possibility of white acclimatization to the tropics, there was, by the end of the nineteenth century, a substantial body of medical opinion providing support for their position and drawing on supposed evidence of racial degeneration, statistics of infant mortality, cases of hybrid sterility, the injurious physiological effects of heat, and so on. Geographers were certainly aware of this corpus of commentary. Thus E. G. Ravenstein simply took the judgements of the anti-acclimatization partisans as conventional wisdom when he came to draw up his map of 'Lands of the Globe still Available for European Settlement.'[58]

'Ecological Imperialism: The Overseas Migration of Western Europeans as a Biological Phenomenon', in Donald Worster (ed.), *The Ends of the Earth. Perspectives on Modern Environmental History* (Cambridge, 1988), pp. 103–17.

[56] Sir Christopher Lever is currently preparing a book on this subject.

[57] See E. T. Renbourne, 'The History of the Flannel Binder and Cholera Belt', *Medical History*, 1 (1957): 211–25; E. T. Renbourne, 'Life and Death of the Solar Topi', *Journal of Tropical Medicine and Hygiene*, 65 (1962): 203–18.

[58] E. G. Ravenstein, 'Lands of the Globe still Available for European Settlement', *Proceedings of the Royal Geographical Society*, n.s. 13 (1891): 27–35.

Demographic decline of the British in India, the Dutch in Java, and the Portuguese in Brazil simply clinched the argument for him. Moreover when Silva White produced in the same year, 1891, a comparable map 'On the Comparative Value of African Lands' he just built a climatic component into his assessment, for, he declared, it was only in the subtropical or temperate zones of Africa that European colonization was possible. White's map, we should note in passing, constituted another case of cartography as imperial rhetoric. After all, he himself described it as a graphic illustration of 'the relative value of African lands to any European power' and explicitly declared that 'all humanitarian motives may be set aside as not being pertinent to the present inquiry.'[59]

Medical and demographic concerns were certainly of crucial importance in the geographers' assessments of acclimatization. But as often as not the issue ultimately turned on the question of labour. Was the white race able to undertake physical labour in the tropics? *That* was the question. And if not, then what policy should be adopted? Thus Henry O'Neill, British consul in Mozambique and an RGS gold medallist, told the Edinburgh geographers in 1885 that coastal East Africa 'will not admit of the labour of the white.' This was an issue of first importance, he considered, and not least because the laws of England no longer tolerated 'coercion or compulsory labour in any shape or degree.'[60] In the same year the Scottish geographers also learned, courtesy of a certain Dr Fisher's work, that tropical Africa's climate was 'decidedly unsuitable for Europeans' and consequently that 'agriculture or other plantation work can only be done by Negroes or other natives.'[61] Ten years later the London geographers heard the same thing from Graf von Pfeil: 'Manual labour cannot be carried on [in tropical Africa] to any considerable extent by white inhabitants.'[62] And so, given this sad state of affairs, Sir Harry Johnston, an administrator in East Africa, acknowledged that the trick was to find out 'how a limited number of Europeans may *rule* the tropics . . . how, without unreasonable loss of life, our fellow-countrymen can govern tropical regions.'[63] That the tropics

[59] Silva White, 'On the Comparative Value of African Lands', *Scottish Geographical Magazine*, 7 (1891): 192. See also the concerns of Hugh Robert Mill, 'The Development of Habitable Lands: An Essay in Anthropogeography', *Scottish Geographical Magazine*, 16 (1900): 121–38.

[60] Henry E. O'Neill, 'East Africa, between the Zambesi and the Rovuma Rivers: its People, Riches and Development', *Scottish Geographical Magazine*, 1 (1885): 348.

[61] 'German Colonisation in Tropical Africa'.

[62] Graf von Pfeil and Klein Ellguth, 'On Tropical Africa in Relation to White Races', *Report of the Sixth International Geographical Congress, London 1895* (London, 1896), p. 542.

[63] Sir Harry Johnston, Discussion, *Report of the Sixth International Geographical Congress*, p. 603. As late as 1947 students of climatology were still learning from Austin Miller's text

needing ruling, of course, was just obvious to Johnston, for in his later 1920 volume *The Backward Peoples and Our Relations with Them* he made it clear that 'the chief and obvious distinction between the backward and the forward peoples is that the former . . . are of coloured skin, while the latter are white-skinned.'[64] It was precisely convictions of this sort that had prompted Benjamin Kidd, much earlier in 1898, to speak of rivalry for the *indirect* control of the tropics because their climate was only suited to the inferior black races and would ever remain an 'unnatural home' for whites.[65]

Among geographers, then, the medical queries about acclimatization were typically translated into imperial imperatives about white labour in the tropics. But what gave particular bite to the anti-acclimatization's crusade, I believe, was again the deployment of moralistic talk. The influence of the moral economy of climate, I contend, was not restricted to its role in the construction of race character; it also acted with relentless efficiency on trans-climatic migrants.

American treatments of the subject in the early decades of the twentieth century will serve to illustrate this claim. Huntington understandably provides our first port of call. Writing in 1914 for the *Journal of Race Development*, he spoke of the 'tropical inertia' that afflicted those who migrated to the tropics. What, then, was 'tropical inertia'? It was essentially moral degradation as manifest in a 'lack of will power', a 'lack of industry', 'irascible temper', 'drunkenness' and 'sexual indulgence'.[66] Nor was Huntington alone in such judgements, however much subsequent geographers have tried to portray him as marginal and atypical. For one thing, Arthur Balfour, director of the London School of Tropical Medicine from 1923 until 1931, used Huntington's research to support his judgements about degeneration and tropical climate. Besides, a few years earlier Ellen Churchill Semple had warned of the 'derangements in the physiological

---

book that 'India, with its excessive heat and moisture from the tropical monsoon, which is one of the danger-points in the British Empire, because it cannot be settled by Europeans . . . must be ruled by a transitory autocracy of British officials whose real home is elsewhere.' (Miller, *Climatology*, p. 3.) And in 1951 readers of *Geography in the Twentieth Century* heard from Karl Pelzer that the 'main problem of white settlement in the tropics is that of acclimatization, and closely related to this is the question of whether white settlers are able to perform manual labour in the tropics.' Karl Pelzer, 'Geography and the Tropics', in Griffith Taylor (ed.), *Geography in the Twentieth Century* (New York: Philosophical Library, 3rd edn 1957), p. 330.

[64] H. H. Johnston, *The Backward Peoples and Our Relations with Them* (Oxford: Oxford University Press, 1920), p. 9.

[65] Benjamin Kidd, *The Control of the Tropics* (New York: Macmillan, 1898), p. 51.

[66] Ellsworth Huntington, 'The Adaptability of the White Man to Tropical America', *Journal of Race Development*, 5 (1914): 199, 211.

functions of heart, liver, kidneys and organs of reproduction' because they induced 'intense enervation' in white settlers in the tropics. The consequences were truly far-reaching. 'The conquering white race of the Temperate Zone is to be excluded by adverse climatic conditions from the productive but undeveloped Tropics, unless it consents to hybridization' – presumably a cost too great to bear.[67] And then, writing in the *Geographical Review* for 1926, Glenn Trewartha took it upon himself to bring his colleagues up to date on recent medical work on the acclimatization question.[68] Noting again that the 'European cannot carry on sustained heavy muscular labor in the wet tropics' and that 'the brown man is superior to the white in his economy of sweating,' Trewartha went on to speak of the impact of a tropical regime on the nervous system. The terrible nerve exhaustion of the condition known as neurasthenia was certainly a direct effect of climate; but just as significant were the indirect effects. The moral topography of the white tropical experience was thus summarized:

> tendency towards excessive use of intoxicating liquor, altered social state, close association with so-called inferior races, with the temptation to sexual indulgence which this situation makes possible, and the difficulty of obtaining a correct and balanced diet make normal healthy living among whites in the tropics a difficult problem.[69]

Similar judgements had been issued a few years earlier on the climate of Liberia, when Emory Ross had dilated on the 'nervous strain of the tropics'. 'The odors, the mists, the sights, the sounds get on the nerves; the heavy, drooping, silent, impenetrable green forest everywhere shuts one in like a smothering grave; the mind grows sick, and the body follows. For these reasons, largely mental, no one should stay on the West coast longer than eighteen months at a time.' All of these convictions pointed to one inevitable conclusion: 'acclimatization at present is all but impossible.'[70]

[67] Ellen Churchill Semple, *Influences of Geographic Environment*, pp. 626–8.

[68] Among the sources he reviewed were Andrew Balfour, 'Sojourners in the Tropics', *The Lancet*, 204 (1923): 1329–44; Andrew Balfour, 'Problems of Acclimatisation', *The Lancet*, 205 (1923): 84–7, 243–7; Andrew Balfour and Henry Harold Scott, *Health Problems of the Empire: Past, Present and Future* (London and New York, 1924); C. Eijkman, 'Some Questions Concerning the Influence of Tropical Climate on Man', *The Lancet*, 206 (1924); 887–93; Sir Havelock Charles, 'Neurasthenia and its Bearing on the Decay of Northern Peoples in India', *Transactions of the Society of Tropical Medicine and Hygiene*, 7 (1913): 2–31; H. J. Spinden, 'Civilization and the Wet Tropics', *World's Work*, 45 (1922–3): 438–48.

[69] Glenn T. Trewartha, 'Recent Thought on the Problem of White Acclimatization in the Wet Tropics', *Geographical Review*, 16 (1926): 473, 472.

[70] Emory Ross, 'The Climate of Liberia and its Effect on Man', *Geographical Review*, 7 (1919): 402. Ross of course repeated the now standard axiom that in 'the humid tropics, the

The neurasthenia of which these writers spoke, and which supposedly scotched all hopes of acclimatization, however, turns out to have been a rather slippery piece of medical nomenclature. The term had begun life back in the 1870s to describe the condition of nervous exhaustion brought on by modern urbanization and industrialization. Originally identified in this context by George M. Beard, its application to the tropics was largely courtesy of Charles Woodruff, author in 1905 of *The Effects of Tropical Light on White Men.*[71] Woodruff had isolated what he termed actinic rays which were supposedly dangerous to fair-skinned Europeans. Exposure to these rays brought such perils as 'tropical inertia', 'tropical amnesia', and the condition that had long been described as 'Burma head' – a rag-bag assortment of ailments subsumed under the label 'tropical neurasthenia'. Soon the term had found its way into the conventional medical lexicon and a considerable literature on the subject was generated. But it was an exceedingly flexible concept, as Dane Kennedy has recently pointed out:

> Studies of the disorder described a bewildering range of symptoms: fatigue, irritation, loss of concentration, loss of memory, hypochondria, loss of appetite, diarrhoeas and digestive disorders, insomnia, headaches, depression, palpitations, ulcers, alcoholism, anemia, sexual profligacy, sexual debility, premature and prolonged menstruation, insanity, and suicide. What did this miscellany of afflictions share apart from an intangibility that placed it beyond the grasp of empirical investigation? Tropical neurasthenia, for all its aura of medical certitude, was exceedingly nebulous, a convenient repository for whatever bundle of obscure and often value-laden complaints otherwise eluded classification and explanation. It was precisely this feature of the diagnosis that made it prone to climatic interpretation.[72]

Given these neurasthenic ailments it is hardly surprising that Woodruff would soon produce a text on the *Expansion of Races* (1909) in which stan-

---

white man cannot do sustained manual labor' (p. 400). Much earlier there had been considerable debate about the acclimatization of American ex-slaves and free blacks in Liberia. See Amalie M. Kass, 'Dr Thomas Hodgkin, Dr Martin Delany, and the "Return to Africa"', *Medical History*, 27 (1983): 373–93. It was on account of 'the inertia which comes over white people living in an isolated community in the tropics' that E. Swayne recommended the establishment of hill station in British Honduras to which white settlers could resort. See E. Swayne, 'British Honduras', *Geographical Journal*, 50 (1917): 161–79.

[71] Charles E. Woodruff, *The Effects of Tropical Light on White Men* (New York, 1905). The book later appeared in an expanded edition under the title *Medical Ethnology* (New York, 1915).

[72] Dane Kennedy, 'The Perils of the Midday Sun: Climatic Anxieties in the Colonial Tropics', in John M. MacKenzie (ed.), *Imperialism and the Natural World* (Manchester: Manchester University Press, 1990), p. 123.

dard environmental determinism was integrated with Darwinian vocabulary to produce the paradoxical conclusion that, as Kennedy puts it, 'natural laws drove the white race to control, but prevented them from populating the tropics.'[73]

These discussions of acclimatization by geographers reveal how integral moral evaluations of the tropical world were. Indeed it became commonplace to actually build a moralistic component into the very definition of acclimatization, that is, to insist that successful acclimatization had to incorporate the maintenance of assumed white moral excellence. Robert DeCourcy Ward, for example, himself a leading light in the Boston Immigration Restriction League around the turn of the century, a student of Shaler's, and a distinguished climatologist at Harvard, believed that acclimatization 'in the full sense of having white men and women living for successive generations in the tropics, and reproducing their kind without physical, mental, and moral degeneration – i.e., colonization in the true sense – is impossible.'[74]

None of this should be taken to imply that the pro-acclimatization position found no representation within the geographical literature. In 1898, a certain Luigi Westenra Sambon, a medical practitioner from Rome who was to become a lecturer in the London School of Tropical Medicine and an advocate of the germ theory, addressed the RGS on the subject and repeated the arguments he had advanced the previous year in the *British Medical Journal.*[75] One by one Sambon picked up the 'superstitions' about the tropics that had dominated scientific discussion about acclimatization for too long, and relegated them to the slag heap of scientific folly. He exposed many of the problems in comparing death rate in England with mortality in India, not the least of which was the fact that such general comparisons ignored the sub-regional geography of demographic statistics.

[73] Ibid., p. 124. Kennedy also has a valuable discussion of Dr Aldo Castellani's discussion of neurasthenia in Castellani's *Climate and Acclimatisation* (London: J. Bale and Danielsson, 1931).

[74] Robert DeC. Ward, 'Can the White Race become Acclimatized in the Tropics?' *Gerlands Beiträge zue Geopolitik*, 32 (1931): 157. The previous year Ward had resorted to the new science of genetics to oppose the immigration of certain racial groups and to argue that no process of Americanization could make certain races 'true to the American type.' Robert DeC. Ward, 'Fallacies of the Melting Pot Idea and America's Traditional Immigration Policy', in Madison Grant and Chas Steward Davison (eds), *The Alien in our Midst or 'Selling our Birthright for a Mess of Industrial Potage'* (New York, 1930), p. 231. That the question of climate's influence on human culture was never far from his mind is evident from his discussion of Köppen's climatic classification scheme in which he included some reflections on Köppen's comments on climate and civilization. Robert DeC. Ward, 'A New Classification of Climates', *Geographical Review*, 8 (1919): 188–91.

[75] Luigi Sambon, 'Remarks on the Possibility of the Acclimatisation of Europeans in Tropical Regions', *British Medical Journal*, 1 (1897): 61–6.

And on the labour question he did not mince his words: 'The truth about the labour problem is that white men will not work; they go with a fixed resolve to gain wealth by coloured labour, which only too often is another word for slave-labour.'[76] Needless to say, his viewpoint did not go down well. Harry Johnston, in a characteristically anecdotal mode, reminisced on his experience of the atrophy of Britons born and brought up in India; J. A. Baines spoke about the degeneracy of white children in the tropics; and Robert Felkin found Sambon's arguments about rapid acclimatization frankly dangerous.[77] For all that, J. W. Gregory could, a quarter of a century later, report that Sambon's 'remarkable' paper had been endorsed by Sir Patrick Manson and was 'supported by the general trend of medical opinion during the past seventeen years.' Earlier prejudice about tropical climates, he announced, was without foundation.[78]

And yet even among pro-acclimatizationists, climate's moral economy could still surface. Gregory's own paper in 1924 certainly did not refrain from racial stereotyping: the 'affectionate, emotional Negro, the docile, diligent Asiatic, and the inventive, enterprising European' all made their appearance. Clearly there was still, to Gregory, a regional geography of ethnic character. Besides, there were immediate racial policies from such geographical realities. 'Close association' of the races was not successful, for intermarriage and inferior offspring were the inevitable outcome; 'co-residence' had been no more successful; only 'separate existence' remained as practical politics.[79]

Consider too in this regard the opinion of Robert Felkin, the Edinburgh expert on tropical diseases, who lectured on 'climatology and the diseases of the tropics' at Minto House School of Medicine and regularly authored articles on his African travel experiences for the *Scottish Geographical Magazine*.[80] Felkin was a fellow of both the RSGS and RGS and clearly

[76] L. Westenra Sambon, 'Acclimatization of Europeans in Tropical Lands', *Geographical Journal*, 12 (1898): 594. Sambon, however, was later to find Woodruff's theory about actinic rays convincing and actually produced a fabric supposedly impervious to them. See Luigi W. Sambon, 'Tropical Clothing' *Journal of Tropical Medicine and Hygiene* (15 February 1907), pp. 67–9. This is discussed in Kennedy, 'Perils of the Midday Sun', pp. 122–3.

[77] Discussion remarks, *Geographical Journal*, 12 (1898): 602–5.

[78] J. W. Gregory, 'Inter-Racial Problems and White Colonization in the Tropics', *Scottish Geographical Magazine*, 40 (1924): 270.

[79] Ibid., p. 281. The combination of views that Gregory held – that acclimatization and white labour in the tropics was certainly possible, and that races must develop in an apartheid fashion – meant that he was enthusiastic about the future possibilities that Australia held for white Europeans.

[80] Felkin's course was reported in the Geographical Notes section of the *Scottish Geographical Magazine*, 2 (1886): 124. He was the author of 'The Egyptian Sûdan', *Scottish Geographical Magazine*, 1 (1885): 221–38; 'Uganda', *Scottish Geographical Magazine*, 2 (1886):

saw it as his duty to keep the geographers informed about the medical aspects of acclimatization. His own position, spelled out at Section E of the British Association and in the *Scottish Geographical Magazine*, represented a half-hearted endorsement of acclimatization. What it amounted to was that acclimatization was only just possible over several generations, but that for the meantime European colonization needed to be restricted to upland areas. So he made proposals for a whole scheme of rapid trans- portation from the unhealthy coastal zone to temporary inland receiving stations, enabling emigrants to escape the pernicious effects of the coast within a single day of arriving in Africa. Besides, he did observe that tropi- cal uplands were better even for indigenous peoples than the swampy coastal belt. The inhabitants of coastal Bengal he thus stigmatized as 'timid, servile, and superstitious', while those living on the higher table land of Mysore were 'brave and courteous'.[81]

Finally, those who urged the possibility of acclimatization frequently pre- sented their advice on how to survive in the tropics in the moralistic lan- guage of prudence, abstemiousness, circumspection, and hygienic discipline. Here again was a moral economy of climate – not in this case that climate *conditioned* standards of behaviour, but rather *required* them. The ser- monic tincture of much of this 'travel-advice' literature would certainly merit closer inspection. All I have space to say here is that earlier medical works on how to survive conditions in tropical India included prophylactic advice on exercise, bathing, alcohol consumption, and the conduct of the 'passions'.[82] As H. M. Stanley, speaking of a different continent and to a different generation, and approvingly referring to this earlier medical litera- ture, concluded:

> with good food, with work to amuse or interest the mind, with due means to
> check the influences resulting from such a total change in life as the tropic cli-

208–26; *On the Geographical Distribution of Some Tropical Diseases, and their Relation to Physical Phenomena* (Edinburgh and London, n.d.).

[81] Robert W. Felkin, 'Tropical Highlands: their Suitability for European Settlement', *Transactions of the Seventh International Congress on Hygiene and Demography*, 10 (1892): 162. Felkin had also announced his findings in 'Can Europeans Become Acclimatised in Tropical Africa?' *Scottish Geographical Magazine*, 2 (1886): 647–57; and Robert W. Felkin, 'On Acclimatisation', *Scottish Geographical Magazine*, 7 (1891): 647–56. These articles were the written version of presentations he had made to the British Association for the Advancement of Science.

[82] James Johnson, *The Influence of Tropical Climates on European Constitutions; Being a Treatise on the Principal Diseases to Europeans in the East and West Indies, Mediterranean, and Coast of Africa* (London, 1821); James Ranald Martin, *The Influence of Tropical Climates on European Constitutions, Including Practical Observations on the Nature and Treatment of the Diseases of Europeans on their Return from Tropical Climates* (London, 1856).

mate demands, and with proper moral conduct, I maintain . . . the European [will be able] to thrive in a hot climate as well as in any climate under the sun.[83]

ON ACTIVE SERVICE

The 'sternly practical' services that geography could render the cause of empire were certainly not restricted to its cultivation of a moral discourse of climate. Even more directly instrumental were its ties with warfare and militarism.

From the earliest days of the campaign to professionalize geography in Britain, the stimulus of warcraft and logistics was plainly apparent. In his influential report on geographical education in 1885, John Scott Keltie noted the presence of geography within the academies of the various armed forces. In this regard, however, as in others, Keltie believed England lagged far behind conditions in continental Europe. A thorough knowledge of geography was required in the Kriegs-Akademie of Berlin, for example, while in the French Superior School of War, geography was 'the most important subject of education.' This situation was to be lamented, Keltie went on, for as Major Charles Wilson had recently reported at the Dublin meeting of the British Association, 'sufficient importance is not attached to a knowledge of geography in military sciences.' What with Wilson's diagnosis and the supporting comments of Chief Justice P. Daly, president of the American Geographical Society, who characterized the Franco-Prussian War as 'a war fought as much by maps as by weapons,' it was plain that the fostering of geography was a military necessity.[84]

The story of geography's professionalization in the decades around the turn of the century was thus not unrelated to the militaristic needs of imperial Britain, and the mobilization of such arguments frequently coincided with calls for curricular reform. A. J. Herbertson, for instance, voiced the opinion in 1904 that the 'extraordinary omission of a systematic study of the possible theatres of war from the recent programmes for military cadets' was precisely because geography had for too long been considered

---

[83] Henry M. Stanley, *The Congo and the Founding of its Free State: A Story of Work and Exploration*, 2 vols (London, 1885), vol. 2, p. 294. That such were still live issues among geographers in the late 1930s is evident from A. Grenfell Price, *White Settlers in the Tropics*, American Geographical Society Special Publication no. 23 (New York: American Geographical Society, 1939).

[84] John Scott Keltie, 'Geographical Education', p. 473.

mere 'gazetteer knowledge'.[85] The sort of military geography that did exist, moreover, if T. Miller Maguire's *Outlines of Military Geography* was at all typical, was criticized for making geography too subservient to history.[86] Clearly there was need for the reform of officer training and appeals of this sort regularly accompanied moves for the overhauling of college geography. Thus Clements Markham, lamenting the state of curricular geography in some of the universities, was only too pleased to announce to the RGS in 1905 that 'the best military opinion' now favoured geographical education. 'We have the War Office with us' he gladly declared.[87] A few years earlier the *Scottish Geographical Magazine* had been pleased to report that the War Office's own committee on the education of officers had recommended that 'the main facts of the geography of the British Empire' should in future be a '*compulsory* subject of examination of *first* importance.'[88] Indeed the relationship geography sustained with war was to become so tight in the minds of some pugnacious enthusiasts that, as Sir George Goldie quipped in his 1907 speech to the Royal Scottish Geographical Society on receiving the Livingstone medal, it was 'a moot point whether war is more useful to geography or geography to war.' After all, he mused, 'War has been one of the greatest geographers.'[89]

Understandably, military men were primarily drawn to geography's cartographic flank. That association was both deep and lasting. The great trigonometrical survey of India, for example, can be traced back to the alliance between the commercial interests of the East India Company and the military expertise of Captain Colin Mackenzie and Captain William Lambton during the first years of the nineteenth century. On that early

[85] A. J. Herbertson, 'Recent Discussions of the Scope and Educational Applications of Geography', *Geographical Journal*, 24 (1904): 417–27, p. 423.

[86] 'Military Geography: A Review', *Scottish Geographical Magazine*, 16 (1900): 138–60. T. Miller Maguire, *Outlines of Military Geography*, Cambridge Geographical Series (Cambridge: Cambridge University Press, 1899). See also Major-General E. F. Chapman, *Physical Geography in its Relation to Military Operations* (Aldershot: Aldershot Military Society, No. xxvii, 1890). A recent commentator observes that Maguire's text 'was mainly a chronological account of various field campaigns and a history of fortification which made little attempt to contribute to either strategy or tactics.' G. L. Ashworth, *War and the City* (London: Routledge, 1991), p. 3. By the same token, the historian H. B. George told the readers of his volume on *The Relations of Geography and History* (Oxford: Oxford University Press), first published in 1901, that 'War, in the modern sense of the word, is altogether based on geography' (p. 95).

[87] C. R. Markham, 'Address to the Royal Geographical Society, 1905', *Geographical Journal*, 26 (1905): 1–28, ref. on p. 6.

[88] 'Geography and the War Office', *Scottish Geographical Magazine*, 18 (1902): 423–5.

[89] George T. Goldie, 'Geographical Ideals', *Geographical Journal*, 29 (1907): 1–14, ref. on p. 8.

morning of Saturday 10 April 1802, when Lambton was to be found on a flat plain near Madras adjusting his measuring chains, the objective of bringing a subcontinent under imperial jurisdiction took a leap forward as the project of covering the country with triangles took its first step.[90] Speaking a century later and of a different continent, the same military absorption with maps was evident in Colonel D. Johnston's announcement to the Scottish geographers in 1907 that 'Topographical maps are . . . of the utmost military value even in peace time for training and manoeuvre purposes and for military problems connected with the defence of the country.'[91] And as a *de facto* observation on cartographic history, Major E. H. Hills declared in 1908 that 'We may first note the somewhat curious fact that the production of a map of a country, useful as a work is for many purposes, has almost always been embarked upon because the imperative necessity of maps of the theatre of operations in war has been brought home to the people and government of a nation.'[92] Francis Younghusband's expedition to Lhasa a few years earlier bore ample testimony to such claims. The British troops had entered Tibet's capital under Younghusband's command in August 1904, and before their departure had carried out the basic triangulation survey of 45,000 square miles of territory, engaged in detailed quarter-inch mapping, and completed large-scale plans of Gyantse and Lhasa. In western Tibet Captain Rawling and Lieutenant Hargreaves had surveyed 35,000 square miles. These accomplishments, and others like them, were routinely chronicled in annual progress reports to the RGS.[93]

But perhaps the chief advocate of the subject's military potential within the company of geographers was Sir Thomas H. Holdich, himself a founder's medallist and president of the RGS (1917–19). A veteran of frontier campaigns and Anglo-Indian demarcation survey, and arbitrator in the Chile–Argentina boundary dispute in Patagonia, Holdich confessed in his *Political Frontiers and Boundary Making* of 1916 that 'War has been in the world's history the first and greatest civilizing agent.' Moreover, imbued as he was with the naturalistic spirit of Lamarckian evolutionary determinism, he wanted to locate the inexorably geographical expression of political

[90] See Simon Berthon and Andrew Robinson, *The Shape of the World*, chapter 8, 'Measuring India'.

[91] D. Johnston, 'A Brief Description of the Ordnance Survey and Some Notes on the Advantages of a Topographical Survey of South Africa', *Scottish Geographical Magazine*, 22 (1906): 18–27, ref. on p. 18.

[92] E. H. Hills, 'The Survey of the British Empire', *Scottish Geographical Magazine*, 24 (1908): 505–19, ref. on p. 506.

[93] Markham, 'Address, 1905', p. 9.

development in the human species' boundary-making impulse. This he regarded as the consequence of 'hereditary nomadic instincts' which, in an era of closing global space, had fostered the recent upsurge in territorial delimitation. As a consequence, national and international conflict was naturalized in the bio-demographic categories of a 'fierce struggle . . . for the survival of the fittest, which we must regard as the heritage of the world's overgrowth of population.'[94]

Holdich had long emphasized the 'sternly practical' character of geography for the resolution of the empire's political and military dilemmas. While the incipient geographical professionals in the universities were cultivating theory, he remarked, various of the armed forces were attesting to the *practical* value of geographical knowledge. Thus in an 1899 address to the society, he pronounced judgement on the restrictive scholasticism that characterized academic geography and waxed eloquent in his portrayal of the 'absolutely immeasurable cost of geographical ignorance' to military, commercial, and national interests.[95] In a short space of time he was speaking of the need to establish what he called a school of practical geography to service the military's topographical corps.[96]

The disconnected character of traditional university geography also exercised the mind of a certain Lieutenant-Colonel Charles A. Court Repington, who initiated a campaign of assault in a piece he published in the pages of *The Times* on 19 November 1904 entitled 'Geography and War'. In recounting the details of this episode, David Stoddart observes that Repington's apologia for the formal incorporation of geography into the educational process 'was at least as eloquent as anything written by Mackinder.'[97] The lamentable state of military cartography and geographical knowledge within the army had been driven home as a consequence of a whole series of military engagements around the turn of the century – the

[94] Thomas H. Holdich, *Political Frontiers and Boundary Making* (London: Macmillan and Co., 1916), pp. 15, 44, 245. Holdich's Neo-Lamarckism is discussed in Campbell and Livingstone, 'Neo-Lamarckism and the Development of Geography'.

[95] Thomas Holdich, 'The Use of Practical Geography Illustrated by Recent Frontier Operations', *Geographical Journal*, 13 (1899): 465–80, ref. on p. 477. In the discussion following the paper, Mackinder felt he could not agree with Holdich's depiction of English university geography as too academic. Ibid., p. 479. See also Thomas Holdich, 'Some Aspects of Political Geography', *Geographical Journal*, 34 (1909): 593–607.

[96] T. H. Holdich, 'The Progress of Geographical Knowledge', *Scottish Geographical Magazine*, 18 (1902): 504–25. See also T. H. Holdich, 'Some Geographical Problems', *Geographical Journal*, 20 (1902): 411–27.

[97] David R. Stoddart, '"Geography and War": The New Geography and the New Army in England, 1899–1914', *Political Geography*, 11 (1992): 87–99. The following paragraph and citations are drawn from Stoddart's excellent account.

Afghan Wars, the Burma Campaign, and the Boer War. The 'practical utility' that geography could offer the War Office and Civil Service, Repington insisted, was simply conspicuous only by its absence. Their strategy was 'on the whole . . . either not to teach it [geography] at all, which has the merit of simplicity, or to pass it round to geologists, economists, historians, or perhaps even to topographers, and to consider we have done something of which we may worthily be proud.' But Repington was scathing in his condemnation of the universities' capacity to meet the demand. Those 'cold cloisters of useless archaism' were simply impotent to provide 'the trained minds that we require for the national service of a world-wide Empire.'

The story of the specialization and curricular reform of geography in Britain around the turn of the century is thus connected to the move towards a more professionalized army. The call for reform embraced both, and for both 'stern practicality' was the watchword. Elsewhere, the biological metaphors to which figures like Holdich had resort were also of decisive importance in the building of a sternly practical geography. And nowhere, perhaps, is this more dramatically revealed than in the case of German *Geopolitik* as it developed under the aegis of figures like Karl Haushofer and Richard Hennig.[98]

Like Ratzel before him, Haushofer had a passion to decode what he regarded as the immutable laws of political life, a task requiring as its cardinal principle the reconstitution of the natural and political sciences in the categories of evolutionary biology. With such persuasions it is hardly surprising that Haushofer should revere Mackinder as a 'geopolitical genius', and that Hennig should produce in 1928 a volume with the organicist-sounding title, *Geopolitik: The Theory of the State as a Living Being.*[99] After all, Rudolf Kjellén, the Swede who minted the term *Geopolitik* around the turn of the century, had himself authored in 1924 a volume tellingly entitled *The State as a Life Form.*[100]

Recently much revisionist writing, both in German and English, has been

---

[98] General histories include Geoffrey Parker, *Western Geopolitical Thought in the Twentieth Century* (London: Croom Helm, 1985); S. D. Brunn and K. A. Mingst, 'Geopolitics', in Michael Pacione (ed.), *Progress in Political Geography* (London: Croom Helm, 1985), pp. 41–76; J. Klein, 'Reflections on Geopolitics: From Pangermanism to the Doctrines of Living Space and Moving Frontiers', in C. Zoppo and C. Zorgbibe (eds), *On Geopolitics: Classical and Nuclear* (Dordrecht: Martinus Nijhoff, 1985), pp. 45–76. The standard work on Haushofer is H.-A. Jacobsen, (ed.), *Karl Haushofer: Leben und Werk*, vols 1 and 2 (Boppard-am-Rhein: Harald Boldt, 1979). See also P. Schöller, 'Die Rolle Karl Haushofers für die Entwicklung und Ideologie Nationalsozialistischer Geopolitik', *Erdkunde*, 36 (1982): 160–7.
[99] See Mark Bassin, 'Race contra Space'.
[100] Klaus Kost, 'The Conception of Politics in Political Geography and Geopolitics in Germany until 1945', *Political Geography Quarterly*, 8 (1989): 369–85.

devoted to 'demythologizing' the role that figures like Haushofer played in the history of the Third Reich and the Nazi party. The result has been, very largely, to diminish their significance, but in so doing to reveal just how pervasive the politicization of German geography actually was.[101] Walter Christaller, for example, further developed his original 1933 dissertation on central place theory during the 1940s in association with National Socialist regional planning; by that stage the Nazi regime – because of the significance it attached to area research and spatial planning – were already incorporating his theory into their plans for the building of new German cities in eastern Europe.[102] I do not propose, however, portraying this German episode in anything but an impressionistic fashion or entering into debates on the precise intellectual and social genealogy of *Geopolitik*. For my purpose is different. It is merely to illustrate something of the form that instrumentalist geography took in another national context.

The myths surrounding the person of Karl Haushofer are legion.[103] The so-called new German science – *Geopolitik* – that he was said to have inaugurated fuelled a scare article in the July 1941 issue of *Reader's Digest* which spoke of 'The Thousand Scientists Behind Hitler' and of the way that the ideas of 'Dr Haushofer and his men dominate Hitler's thinking.'[104] The reality was entirely different. According to Henning Heske, there never was an institute of geopolitics in Munich, nor any close relationship with Hitler. The myths sprang from the fact that Haushofer was a First World War high commander, a leading geopolitician, and the editor of the *Zeitschrift für Geopolitik* between 1924 and 1944.

To Haushofer, geopolitics was a science of world politics in which Ratzel's notion of the near mystic *Lebensraum* played a crucial role. Geopolitics, of course, was not a monolithic movement, and various strands have been isolated by recent historians of the subject.[105] Yet it did

[101] For an introduction see Gerhard Sandner, 'Recent Advances in the History of German Geography 1918–1945. A Progress Report for the Federal Republic of Germany', *Geographische Zeitschrift*, 76 (1988): 120–33.

[102] See M. Rössler, 'Applied Geography and Area Research in Nazi Society: Central Place Theory and Planning, 1933 to 1945', *Environment and Planning D: Society and Space*, 7 (1989): 419–31.

[103] I have relied on the analysis of Henning Heske, 'Karl Haushofer: His Role in German Geopolitics and in Nazi Politics', *Political Geography Quarterly*, 6 (1987): 135–44.

[104] See J. H. Paterson, 'German Geopolitics Reassessed', *Political Geography Quarterly*, 6 (1987): 107–14.

[105] See especially K. Kost, *Die Einflüsse der Geopolitik auf Forschung und Theorie der Politischen Geographie und Ihrer Terminologie unter besonderer Berücksichtigung von Militär- und Kolonialgeographie*, Bonner Geographische Abhandlungen 76 (Bonn: Ferd, Dümmler-Verlag, 1988)

embrace a number of related purposes – to inculcate a more expansive sense of 'space-consciousness' in the German people, to effect revision of the terms of the Treaty of Versailles, and to provide practical guidance in the process of Germany's internal territorial reorganization. To Haushofer, geopolitics thus provided the rationale for an enlargement of Germany's *Raum*, and he himself dilated on the strategic possibilities inherent in a Mackinder-like continental Heartland stretching all the way from Germany via Russia to Japan.[106] But he wanted to go beyond Mackinder, and proposed a global political model in which the map of the world was carved up into three grand regions: Pan-America, Eurafrica, and East Asia. Haushofer, however, always intended his geopolitics to be applied science, a geologistics and a geopragmatics, in which policy would be gleaned from the study of the ways in which political processes were bound by earth-realities.

Given the Ratzelian roots of this vision, it is clear that whatever practical purposes Haushofer envisioned for his new applied science, in principle it sat uneasily with the genetic racism of the growing Nazi ideology and its cultivation of racial hygiene in stern opposition to Lamarckian environmentalism.[107] Unreformed geopolitics was regarded by the Nazi fraternity as placing an overemphasis on space and environment at the expense of inherent racial constitution. Such differences of principle, however, did not prevent certain mergings of these different intellectual streams: the rationalistic, causal, law-bound, scientific, environmental determinism, *and* the romantic, subjectivist, Herder-like fascination with the *Volk*. The extent to which this was achieved, if only as a rhetorical strategy in a threatening political environment, surfaces in the fact that Hennig's staunch rebuttal of the racial obsessions of the Nazis was actually the subject of censure in Haushofer's own journal. And yet explaining this incoherence as a mere tactical strategy is scarcely sufficient to account for the enthusiasm with which *Rassenlehre* (race-theory) came to be developed as a category within *Geopolitik*. In the 1930s the *Zeitschrift* included statements, from Louis von Kohl and others, that depicted geopolitics as specifically integrating *Volk*

---

[106] An analysis of the shifting meanings of some of the key terms associated with this way of thinking is provided in Hans-Dietrich Schultz, 'Fantasies of *Mitte*: *Mittellage* and *Mitteleuropa* in German Geographical Discussion in the 19th and 20th Centuries', *Political Geography Quarterly*, 8 (1989): 315–39.

[107] On these subjects see Benno Müller-Hill, *Murderous Science. Elimination by Scientific Selection of Jews, Gypsies, and Others, Germany 1933–45* (Oxford: Oxford University Press, 1988); Robert N. Proctor, *Racial Hygiene. Medicine Under the Nazis* (Cambridge, Mass.: Harvard University Press, 1988).

and *Raum*.[108] In the transformed National Socialist geopolitics that emerged, then, the emphasis shifted from the physical environment itself towards a *Kulturlandschaft* which centred on the way human culture transformed nature rather than lying as the victim of a necessitating environmentalism. And yet this trajectory, for all the seeming incoherence of its twin commitment to geo-determinism *and* genetic determinism, environment *and* eugenics, might have been predicted from the fact that Kjellén himself had elaborated an *Ethnopolitik* as part of his original geopolitical system.

Besides all this, geopolitics had its own sternly practical expression in *Wehregeopolitik* (defence geopolitics), an important subfield of the movement which Haushofer himself advanced. The legitimacy of such a development Haushofer saw as entirely in keeping with the Ratzelian tradition. He was only too aware that Ratzel himself (in one of the master's volumes over which he had editorial oversight) had commented that 'In the life of a nation, war is a moment of enhancement, of elevation.'[109] Recently described as standing 'in the tradition of German military sciences established by Clausewitz's *Vom Kriege* (On War) (1832) and continued through the intimate links between geography and the military,'[110] German defence geopolitics thus evinces the selfsame militaristic roots that undergirded certain strands of geography in Victorian Britain.

Sentiments of this kind were not restricted to those specifically engaged in *Geopolitik*.[111] Nor were the conceptual nuances of genetic and environmental determinisms, so central in Hennig's early prescriptions, elsewhere so clearly perceived. The messiness of this chapter in geography's intellec-

---

[108] This is discussed in David T. Murphy, 'Space, Race and Geopolitical Necessity: A Critique of Geopolitical Rhetoric in German Colonial Revanchism, 1919–1933', in Neil Smith and Anne Godlewska (eds), *Geography and Empire*, forthcoming. Wilhelm Volz, Murphy points out, combined Volkish and geopolitical ideas in the mid-1920s.

[109] Cited in Paterson, 'German Geopolitics Reassessed', p. 112. The phrase comes from Friedrich Ratzel, *Erdenmacht und Völkerschicksal*, edited and introduced by Karl Haushofer (Stuttgart: A Kröner, 1940).

[110] John O'Loughlin and Henning Heske, 'From "Geopolitik" to "Geopolitique": Converting a Discipline for War to a Discipline for Peace', in Nurit Kliot and Stanley Waterman (eds), *The Political Geography of Conflict and Peace* (London: Belhaven Press, 1991), pp. 37–59, ref. on p. 41. It should be recalled that Ritter had lectured for some thirty-three years at the Military Academy in Berlin under Karl von Clausewitz.

[111] On the basis of a content analysis of German geography serials in the period, Heske writes: 'Geography, more than any other established science in Germany, consciously and unconsciously supported National Socialism and, even more, was active in its support before the Nazi seizure of power in 1933.' Henning Heske, 'German Geographical Research in the Nazi Period: A Content Analysis of the Major Geography Journals, 1925–1945', *Political Geography Quarterly* 5(1986): 267–81, ref. on p. 279.

tual history is remarkably illustrated in Gerhard Sandner's studies of Siegfried Passarge. The final chapter of Passarge's volume on *Beobachtungen über Tier und Mensch* (Observations on Animal and Man), Sandner reports, was entitled *Erdkundliche Weltanschauung*. Here he elaborated a determinist geography precisely as a means of coming to grips with the breakdown of the German *Volk*. It was, in essence, a combination of the concepts of *Lebensraum* and *Volk* in a manner reminiscent of an earlier prophetic volume *Germania Triumphans!* (1895), which used these very notions to forecast global war in the early years of the twentieth century. The heart of Passarge's own message was that the apogee of human culture could only be achieved in particular geographical settings, and thereby he could account for Aryan superiority through correlation with Nordic climate. Besides this, he elucidated his 'law of development of the character of peoples' in which, Sandner writes, 'determinism, Darwinism, folkish nationalism, racism, antisemitism and cultural pessimism amalgamate.' In this coalition, as Sandner himself concedes, 'it is difficult to separate the many "isms" involved.' Still, the perceived role of geography as non-reversible diagnostic knowledge is dramatically revealed.[112] Passarge urged, for example, that for the good of biological selection, public health provision, social security, and so on should be abolished, *and* that urban and industrial environments were the active agency in determining moral degeneration. Geography was thus resorted to, to both diagnose and treat the sicknesses of the German *Volk*. The idea that the moral properties of human beings are genetically or environmentally determined, and thus subject to scientific prophylaxis, has always been essential to the racists' programme,[113] for only in this way could Passarge at once speak of his scientific objectivity *and* of 'moral cripples', 'degenerated bourgeoisie', and the 'poisoning effect of the Jew.'[114]

Throughout this episode, geography was intimately connected with the militaristic will to power. Penck, for example, speaking on geography and war declared that since 'Knowledge is power, geographical knowledge is world-power.'[115] The American political geographer Isaiah Bowman was in entire agreement with this sentiment, even if he did insist that he was

---

[112] I owe my phrasing here to Stephen Bann, *The Inventions of History*, p. 16.

[113] The implications of the racist debate for moral philosophy are the subject of an arresting paragraph in Charles Taylor, *Sources of the Self*, p. 8.

[114] Gerhard Sandner, 'The *Germanic Triumphans* Syndrome and Passarge's *Erdkundliche Weltanschauung*: The Roots and Effects of German Political Geography beyond *Geopolitik*', *Political Geography Quarterly*, 8 (1989): 341–51, on p. 347.

[115] A. Penck, 'Der Krieg und das Studium der Geographie', *Zeitschrift der Gellschaft für Erdkunde zu Berlin* (1916): 158–76, 222–48, ref. on p. 227.

deeply 'disturbed by the rapid growth in Germany of the pseudo science of geopolitics and alarmed by its territorial theories.'[116] For not only did he urge universal military training but he laid his geographical skills at the feet of the American Council on Foreign Relations and the State Department.[117] Indeed he himself emerged as an apologist of the American war effort in the 1940s.[118]

Bowman had been a student of Shaler and Davis at Harvard's Lawrence Scientific School during the first decade of the twentieth century and remained a devotee of both for the rest of his days. He wrote to Davis in 1912, for example, saying that 'there seems to be something semi-religious in nature in my attitude toward your work.'[119] By that stage he had been in the Yale geology department for some eight years and the experience only served to reinforce in him environmentalist geography on the Shaler–Davis model. He found Brigham's and Semple's geographical expositions of American history fascinating, taught a course on that very theme, and shared another with Ellsworth Huntington on 'Geographical Controls in History'. Small wonder that he strove to convey to his own students the contagion of his enthusiasm for the anthropogeography emanating from Germany: Ratzel, Kirchhoff, Peschel, and Hettner were all required reading. To be sure, later in his career, in elaborating his thoughts on *Geography in Relation to the Social Sciences* (1934), he would insist that 'Contemporary geographical knowledge and thought have abandoned the mechanistic determinism of older schools. Earth facts do not *determine* the form and nature of human society in development. They *condition* it.' And yet a certain equivocation lingered even in this dismissal, for in the same volume his uneasiness at Franz Boas's culturalism surfaced as he claimed that the Boasian critique was 'applicable only to that sketchy "environmentalism" or "determinism" which was early rejected by all but a handful of writers who were seduced by pretty phrases about "influences" or "controls".'[120]

Bowman remained at Yale for eleven years until he assumed the position

[116] Isaiah Bowman, 'Geography vs Geopolitics', *The Geographical Review*, 32 (1942): 646–58.

[117] Geoffrey J. Martin, *The Life and Thought of Isaiah Bowman* (Hamden: Archon Books, 1980), pp. 169–70.

[118] See his review of N. J. Spykman's *American Strategy in World Politics*, in Isaiah Bowman, 'Political Geography of Power', *Geographical Review*, 32 (1942): 349–52.

[119] Letter, Isaiah Bowman to W. M. Davis, 17 August 1912, Davis Papers, bMS 1798 (60)–2, Houghton Library of Rare Books and Manuscripts.

[120] Isaiah Bowman, *Geography in Relation to the Social Sciences* (New York: Scribner's, 1934), pp. 225, 70.

of Director of the American Geographical Society in 1915. So began his meteoric rise to national prominence during the period of the American preparation for post First World War reconstruction and the recarving up of Europe. In his capacity as director of the AGS, he provided cartographic resources for President Woodrow Wilson's use at the Paris Peace Conference of 1919. Moreover, he sought out articles for the *Geographical Review* – the AGS's journal – that were of particular significance for that purpose, paying several hundred dollars to Jovan Cvijić, for instance, for a piece on the Balkan peoples and an ethnographic chart.[121] This active service in international affairs brought its own rewards. On his return to the US he published *The New World* (1921), a work in which he surveyed the global scene in the aftermath of the Great War as a basis for future policy. During the next decade he attained conspicuous prominence in various science policy and advisory capacities, and then in 1935 was appointed president of Johns Hopkins University. Indeed the National Research Council, of which Bowman became chairman in 1933 – a position for which he had been groomed – had in the 1920s specifically set out to restructure science so as to achieve national goals through cultivating a network of relationships among the major American power centres of finance, education, and government.[122]

Besides these administrative positions, Bowman carried out research on pioneer settlement, tackling subjects like *The Pioneer Fringe* in 1931 and *The Limits of Land Settlement* in 1937. The instrumental function of these studies is surely plain. For the purpose of Bowman and his contributors was to identify settlement possibilities across the world where relief from population pressure could be achieved, and 'to plan out measures in advance if colonization is to be rational.'[123]

It was these latter pursuits, as Neil Smith has shown, that brought Bowman the request from Franklin D. Roosevelt to undertake a survey of the refugee resettlement potential on a global scale.[124] Just after the 1937

---

[121] Martin, *Bowman*, p. 63. The article referred to is Jovan Cvijić, 'The Geographical Distribution of the Balkan People', *Geographical Review*, 5 (1918): 345–61.

[122] See, for example, Robert Kargon and Elizabeth Hodes, 'Karl Compton, Isaiah Bowman, and the Politics of Science in the Great Depression', *Isis*, 76 (1985): 301–18.

[123] Isaiah Bowman (ed.), *The Limits of Land Settlement. A Report on Present-day Possibilities* (New York: Council on Foreign Relations, 1937), p. 3. Here again under the guise of scientific neutrality Bowman pleaded that it was 'not out of such material that policies are made. These grow chiefly out of political, social, and economic conditions and situations. Once a policy has been determined upon, however, its form will be guided largely by the data presented in studies of this type.' p. 5.

[124] Neil Smith, 'Isaiah Bowman: Political Geography and Geopolitics', *Political Geography Quarterly*, 3 (1984): 69–76.

book appeared, US Senator E. K. Cubin wrote to Bowman saying that he had 'recommended it as a "must" to be read by all legislators interested in land settlement for European refugees.'[125] Soon he was more and more drawn into foreign policy on territorial dimensions of reconstruction. And here the 'sternly practical' character of Bowman's political geography ever more clearly surfaces. As I have said, Bowman affected to disdain geopolitics as pseudo-scientific ideology. But this was an apologetic move designed to out-manoeuvre the danger of witnessing himself cast as the American mirror image of Haushofer. After all, there were those who dubbed him the American geopolitician, and even suggested that German Geopolitik had aped the transatlantic variety.

Of course this does not mean that Bowman was committed to the political and military aspects of empire. On the contrary, he eschewed them. But he did retain empire's economic and cultural correlates even as he threw his weight behind the US assault on the British empire's colonies. Acknowledging that the United States was among the few nations ruling the globe 'by virtue of economic power', he tried to argue that the 'American habit of thought in relation to international things is not imperialistic; it is commercial and it seeks above all commercial equality.'[126] With such casuistry it is hardly surprising that he could, at once, defend the rights of native peoples and speak of the 'plastic and imitative temperament' of the 'pure-blooded negro [who] never exercised any self-originating political influence.' Or again, looking inwards on America's domestic scene, he could express concern at the changing patterns of American immigration which, no longer 'Anglo-Saxon by race', was affecting 'not merely our political forms and social institutions, but also the quality of our people.' The Italians, Poles, Hungarians, and the like were 'peoples far more ignorant and restless in disposition than the immigrants from northwestern Europe' and thus had 'become an ever-increasing problem.' So whether it was on account of 'lack of opportunity or racial character or historical experience', Bowman remained convinced that the black was 'undoubtedly inferior'.[127] As Neil Smith, writing of Bowman's later activities for the State Department in the 1940s, has astutely observed, they displayed all the 'shades of a Tocquevillian paradox. All of the high sounding morality concerning independence and trusteeship and the earnest desire to unyoke the

[125] Cited in Martin, Bowman, p. 125.
[126] Isaiah Bowman, The New World. Problems in Political Geography (London: George G. Harrap, revised and enlarged edition, 1926), supplement, pp. 57, 56.
[127] Bowman, New World, p. 534, supplement pp. 12, 15, 17.

"natives" from European imperialism was not matched by a concern for equality.'[128]

Bowman's political geography, then, was every bit as conditioned by social circumstances as the German variety. In his case it was first the democratic idealism of the Woodrow Wilson vision and later a more reactionary harshness that was the undergirding; but the pledged nature of Bowman's political geography vitiates his own uneasy claims to scientific objectivity. His political geography was as political as it was geographical. The tensions of handling claims to scientific neutrality and retaining political partisanship thus appear again and again in his writings. On the one hand, he made the strongest case for the scientific status of geography in the hope of avoiding the 'horrid examples' of confused thinking which 'affect chiefly the human side of the subject' where practitioners had been seduced by 'new social philosophies'. On the other hand, reflecting on political geography and its mobilization in the cause of international relations, he was forced to concede that here 'there is no "science" of geography'. Certainly as he penned these words he clearly had in mind the German situation where philosophical systems had been 'devised which are nothing more than apologia for policies based on military necessity or the logic of "high culture requires more space,"' and as such could comfortably be dismissed as 'ideology, not science'. And yet he did begin his treatise with an epigraph from Strabo to the effect that the 'greater part of geography subserves the needs of states; for the scene of the activities of states is land and sea, the dwelling place of man.'[129] The territorial border between science and politics was one boundary Bowman just could not map.

STERN PRACTICALITY?

The way that I have sought to narrate this chapter in geography's story has been via an extended commentary on those words of H. R. Mill with which I began, namely, that geography was a 'sternly practical' science. In a variety of national settings – imperial Britain, Nazi Germany, and postwar America – I have emphasized geography's instrumentalist function, and throughout have eschewed the project, which I take as misconceived, of separating out the science of geography from practical politics. For the sub-

---

[128] Neil Smith, 'Shaking Loose the Colonies: Isaiah Bowman's Role in the U. S. Assault on the British Empire', in Smith and Godlewska (eds), *Geography and Empire*, forthcoming.
[129] Bowman, *Geography in Relation to the Social Sciences*, pp. 227, 212, 1.

ject's leading advocates were only too happy, as some of their recent successors have been, to speak of geography's social relevance.

Yet it would be mistaken to assume that it was only in the cause of stern practicality that geographical knowledge was mobilized. There were those, of different political persuasions, who sought to humanize the new scientific geography for altogether different ends. Whether their aims were more or less laudable than those I have been scrutinizing I leave purposely to one side. My point is, rather, that those who found radicalism more congenial were just as keen to read their geography though political spectacles.

Nowhere perhaps is this conceptual fusion more clearly evident than in the writings of Petr Kropotkin (1842–1921), the Russian *émigré*, who exchanged his aristocratic heritage for deep personal involvement in anarchist politics.[130] The visionary conception of geography that Kropotkin championed was, predictably, profoundly at odds with those we have just been considering. 'What Geography ought to be' was an essay composed in a prison cell in 1885 after he had been arrested on charges of complicity in the attempt to establish the International in France, and has been described as 'a moving plea for the injection of social relevance into the content and methodology of geographic education.'[131] Kropotkin evidently saw geography as a practical enterprise that could render 'important service':

> It must teach us, from our earliest childhood, that we are all brethren, whatever our nationality. In our time of wars, of national self-conceit, of national jealousies and hatreds ably nourished by people who pursue their own egoistic, personal or class interests, geography must be . . . a means of dissipating those prejudices and of creating other feelings more worthy of humanity . . . It is the task of the geographer to bring this truth, in its full light, into the midst of the lies accumulated by ignorance, presumption, and egotism.[132]

Despite the challenges inherent in these words to the imperialist-driven new geography in England, Kropotkin's links with Keltie, forged in the 1870s, continued through his years of active anarchism; in fact, this very plea for geographical humanitarianism was heard at the Manchester Geographical

---

[130] Biographical treatments include G. Woodcock and I. Avakumović *The Anarchist Prince: A Biographical Study of Peter Kropotkin* (London: T. V. Boardman, 1950); Martin A. Miller, *Kropotkin* (Chicago: University of Chicago Press, 1976).

[131] Myrna Margulies Breitbart, 'Peter Kropotkin, the Anarchist Geographer', in David R. Stoddart (ed.), *Geography, Ideology and Social Concern* (Oxford: Blackwell, 1981), pp. 134–53, ref. on p. 145.

[132] P. Kropotkin, 'What Geography ought to be', *Nineteenth Century*, 18 (1885): 940–56, ref. on pp. 942–3.

Society on his release from prison, and he himself was the guest of honour at a banquet hosted by the RGS in 1890.[133]

That Kropotkin's geography was of the engaged variety, recent commentators have not tired of informing us. Nor have the pedagogical implications of Kropotkin's vision been overlooked, for in his concern to provide education free from ideological domination he called for the integration of the mental with the manual, for practice as well as precept, and for the value of the age-old tradition of apprenticeship.[134] Yet for all that, the moral crusade on which Kropotkin was embarked involved, I would argue, a naturalization of morality that was tantalizingly analogous in its conceptual structures to that of the Darwinian imperialists. Kropotkin was just as anxious to earth his idealist vision in the mundanity of evolutionary naturalism. He may have read a different social theory out of evolution, but that evolution could exegete the moral principle in nature he had no doubt. Indeed, throughout the Kropotkin corpus, a biologization of political categories is only too apparent. Biological functionalism, for example, was canvassed as an integrative rejoinder to the atomization of society that the division of labour had precipitated,[135] and as an explanation for altruism both in the social insects and in human society. Small wonder that in his article on 'Anarchism' for the 1910 edition of the *Encyclopaedia Britannica*, he himself should write that 'Peter Kropotkin for many years endeavoured to develop the following ideas: to show the intimate logical connections which exist between the modern philosophy of natural sciences and Anarchism; to put Anarchism on a scientific basis . . . and to work out the basis of Anarchist ethics.'[136] This integration of the moral and the material was equally vital for his conception of geography. 'I cannot conceive of Physiography from which Man has been excluded,' he told the Teacher's Guild Conference in Oxford in 1893. 'A study of nature without man is the last tribute paid by modern scientists to their previous scholastic education.'[137]

It was his time spent as a military officer on an expedition into Siberia during the early 1860s that had stimulated Kropotkin's sociobiological

---

[133] See Stoddart, *On Geography*, pp. 136–41.

[134] See P. Kropotkin, *Fields, Factories and Workshops* (Boston: Houghton Mifflin, 1899); P. Kropotkin, *Memoirs of a Revolutionist*, 2 vols (London: Smith, Elder, 1899). See the discussion in Miller, *Kropotkin*, pp. 102–3.

[135] See the discussion in Bob Galois, 'Ideology and the Idea of Nature: The Case of Peter Kropotkin', *Antipode*, 8, 3 (1976): 1–16.

[136] Kropotkin, 'Anarchism', *Encyclopaedia Britannica* (1910), vol. 1.

[137] Krapotkin [sic], 'On the Teaching of Physiography', *Geographical Journal*, 2 (1893): 350–9, ref. on p. 355.

outlook. There he had become profoundly impressed with the ways in which intra- and inter-specific cooperation in an austere environment might have survival value. Kropotkin thus came to question the competitive element in Darwinian natural selection, and later in *Mutual Aid* (1902) he sought to highlight the significance of acquired sociability as an evolutionary determinant. He had been encouraged in this revisionist stance by the zoologist Karl Kessler, who had, in 1880, addressed the Russian Congress of Naturalists on the very subject, and by the appearance of books like Büchner's *Liebe und Liebes-Leben in der Thierwelt* and Henry Drummond's *Ascent of Man*, works which were intent on reconstructing evolution on a more benign foundation.

Accordingly Kropotkin distanced himself from what he called Huxley's 'Struggle-for-Life' manifesto, claiming that it actually failed to do justice to the subtleties of Darwin's own viewpoint, and of course from the current vogue of political Darwinism championed by Spencer. But he was certain that moral precepts could be extracted from scrutiny of evolutionary processes because mutual aid was its chief driving force. Sociability was a law of nature, he insisted, and thus governed 'the progressive evolution of both the animal species and human beings.'[138] As he put it in the final sentences of the volume:

> In the practice of mutual aid, which we can trace to the earliest beginnings of evolution, we thus find the positive and undoubted origin of our ethical conceptions; and we can affirm that in the ethical progress of man, mutual support – not mutual struggle – has had the leading part. In its wide extension, even at the present time, we also see the best guarantee of a still loftier evolution of our race.[139]

All this, of course, resonated with the spirit of equality and self-sufficiency that he witnessed among the Russian peasantry, whose lives were evidently more in harmony with nature's inherent morality than was the misery-producing regime of czarists. It inevitably led him into conflict too with the official geographers' organization, the Imperial Russian Geographical Society.[140]

The dissatisfaction that Kropotkin thus voiced over classical Darwinism was indicative of his own increasing predilection for the Lamarckian alter-

---

[138] Petr Kropotkin, *Mutual Aid. A Factor of Evolution* (Harmondsworth: Penguin, 1939, first pub. 1902), p. 18.

[139] Ibid., p. 234.

[140] See John Slatter, 'The Kropotkin Papers', *Geographical Magazine*, 53, 14(1981): 917–21.

native in which acquired characters could be passed from generation to generation.[141] Organic cooperation had thus convinced him that 'in some respects Lamarck had been unjustly passed over,' and so he later published, in the half decade prior to the outbreak of the First World War, a sequence of articles in the *Nineteenth Century* with titles like: 'The Direct Action of Environment on Plants', 'The Response of Animals to their Environment' and 'The Inheritance of Acquired Characteristics.'[142] Kropotkin's anarchistic humanism, with its focus on mutuality, decentralism, and community self-government, therefore, was grounded in his naturalistic interpretation of acquired sociability which was thoroughly suffused with Neo-Lamarckian principles. These links, moreover, were entirely comprehensible, for Lamarckism had a history of close association with radical groups in the pre-Darwinian era. Among the dissident medical practitioners in London who flagrantly imported with Continental morphology French revolutionary republicanism, for example, Lamarckism flourished because it provided a model of transformation 'from below'. By resonating with extremist calls for the dissolution of the church and the subversion of aristocracy, it directly appealed to the insurrectionary working classes. And this, as Desmond writes, 'was far more radical than anything Darwin envisaged.' Agitators had for long enough been 'using a social Lamarckian science of progressivism, materialism, and environmental determinism to underwrite the change to a democratic, cooperative society.'[143]

Clearly Kropotkin found it no more difficult than contemporary reactionaries to harness evolution theory in the service of politics.[144] But while they dilated on the evolutionary grounds for subjection, Kropotkin elaborated a biological basis for freedom. It would be mistaken, however, to assume that evolution theory, whether of Darwinian or Lamarckian stripe, was the only foundation on which a more radically relevant geography

[141] Kropotkin, it should be noted, also found Wagner's criticisms of classical Darwinism persuasive.

[142] This is discussed in J. A. Campbell and D. N. Livingstone, 'Neo-Lamarckism and the Development of Geography'.

[143] Adrian Desmond, *The Politics of Evolution. Morphology, Medicine, and Reform in Radical London* (Chicago: University of Chicago Press, 1989), pp. 4, 329.

[144] The project of finding legitimacy for social and political action in evolutionary theory is eschewed by some modern radicals, like the libertarian Marxist Bob Young. Yet there has been a long tradition within radicalism that found in evolution the basis of Marxism itself, notably Karl Kautsky, the leading nineteenth-century intellectual of German socialism, the English Fabians, G. Plekhanov, and, perhaps most dramatically, Soviet Lysenkoism. Indeed this ambivalence reverberates through the writings of Marx and Engels themselves: Marx saw in Darwinism a natural scientific basis for his historical analysis, whereas Engels regarded it as a 'conjuring trick' in which social categories were transferred to the natural order.

could be raised. In the case of Elisée Reclus, associate of Kropotkin and fellow anarchist, it was the lingering strains of German *Naturphilosophie* in the form of a pervasive romanticism that was decisive. For Reclus had come under the spell of Karl Ritter, whom he had encountered at the University of Berlin in the early 1850s, and even though he later abandoned Christian orthodoxy he retained much of Ritter's holistic geography, and even transformed it into a near-mystic nature philosophy.[145] Radicalized in the aftermath of the Paris Commune, Reclus's secularized millenarianism produced an anarchistic outlook even more sweet than Kropotkin's. Accordingly, his ecological geography, reminiscent of Guyot's, presented a holistic vision of *La Terre* which, together with his *Nouvelle Géographie Universelle* (1876–1894), Kropotkin himself regarded as 'the geographical work which is most representative of our times.'[146] With his emphasis, as Dunbar has written, 'on those matters that are of perennial concern to the *engagés* – social ills and their solutions,' Reclus's geography evinces his concerns with 'the unequal distribution of wealth and . . . the importance of the study of geography in making an inventory of the world's resources and suggesting a plan for their equitable spread.'[147]

Similarly non-evolutionary, equally practical, and correspondingly synthetic in his approach to the relations of nature and culture, was the American George Perkins Marsh, whose wise-use approach to nature, encapsulated in his celebrated *Man and Nature* of 1864, brought him into contact with Reclus.[148] In fact Marsh greatly warmed to Reclus's *La Terre* and urged an English translation, Reclus reciprocating by giving his support to a French translation of *Man and Nature*. To be sure, there were differences between their respective commitments, Marsh emphasizing humanity's destructive engagement with nature, Reclus preferring instead to focus on the mystical bond between the two that issued in the humanized landscape. Yet both, like J. F. Schouw and Nathaniel Shaler in different contexts, were groping for new ways of conceptualizing the relationship between society and nature that was philosophically nuanced and ecologically practical.[149] So too was the Marxist critic of geopolitics, Karl

---

[145] See Gary Dunbar, *Elisée Reclus. Historian of Nature* (Hamden: Archon Books, 1978).

[146] Krapotkin [sic], 'On the Teaching of Physiography', p. 355. See also the discussion in Stoddart, *On Geography*, p. 131.

[147] Gary Dunbar, 'Elisée Reclus, an Anarchist in Geography', in David R. Stoddart (ed.), *Geography, Ideology and Social Concern* (Oxford: Blackwell, 1981), pp. 154–64, ref. on p. 161.

[148] The standard biography remains David Lowenthal, *George Perkins Marsh. Versatile Vermonter* (New York: Columbia University Press, 1958).

[149] Kenneth Robert Olwig, 'Historical Geography and the Society/Nature "Problematic": The Perspective of J. F. Schouw, G. P. Marsh, and E. Reclus', *Journal of Historical Geography*, 6 (1980): 29–45; Livingstone, *Shaler*, chapter 7.

Wittfogel, who underscored Marx's own assertion that by transforming external nature through labour, human beings simultaneously changed their own nature. Drawing from traditions as diverse as Montesquieu, Herder, and Ritter to fashion a reconditioned materialism, Wittfogel emphasized the ways in which society's dependence on natural conditions took on an increasingly mediated character. As he put it himself, his stance was to be characterized as '*Active* materialism? Yes! But also: active *materialism*.'[150]

Although some of these latter traditions were, by and large, ignored as *stern* practicality became increasingly embedded within the Western geographical establishment, their stance has become something of a beau ideal for a later generation of geographers seeking a heritage in which to domicile their own version of radicalism. Yet, as I have tried to argue in this chapter, the impetus towards relevance, practicality, and engagement, bolstered wherever possible by the vocabulary of scientific objectivity, typified the geographical enterprise throughout the political spectrum during the decades around 1900. For as A. J. Herbertson, underscoring geographical utility, proudly announced in 1902: 'Ignorance of geography produces frequent friction and occasional wars, stupidity in commercial enterprise, hasty and reckless counsel in our journals, and loss of life . . . Be it politics, finance or commerce, missionary zeal or the mere pursuit of pleasure or health, an end will be more effectually obtained if we have studied environments.'[151] That geography should be made to subserve social purposes was not only typical of the era, it was a shared assumption that remained inviolate across the ideological reaches of the tradition.

[150] Karl Wittfogel, 'Geopolitics, Geographical Materialism and Marxism', translated by G. L. Ulmen, *Antipode*, 17, 1 (1985): 21–72, ref. on p. 59. Wittfogel's critique was originally published in 1929 as 'Geopolitik, Geographischer Materialismus und Marxismus', *Unter dem Banner des Marxismus*, vol 3 (1929): nos 1, 4, 5.

[151] A. J. Herbertson, 'Geography in the University', *Scottish Geographical Magazine*, 18 (1902): 124–32, ref. on p. 127.

8

The Regionalizing Ritual

Geography, Place and Particularity

It is December 1940. The Association of American Geographers has convened at Baton Rouge, Louisiana. Its president, Carl Sauer, now at the height of his powers, finds himself in the awkward position of having to deliver a presidential address to an audience for whom he has little esteem, and probably a good deal of contempt. 'I can live advantageously by disregarding almost completely the work they turn out,' he would soon confide to an associate.[1] The problem was their obsession with disciplinary definition. This 'lingering sickness of American academic geography,' Sauer lamented, looked as if it might be a terminal illness. For when 'a subject is ruled, not by inquisitiveness but by definitions of its boundaries, it is likely to face extinction.'[2] Curiosity had gone, party spirit flourished.

Sauer attributed these definitional neuroses to what he called the 'great retreat' of the subject during the 1920s and 1930s. Utterly simplistic formulas had been concocted, he believed, in 'the attempt to devise a natural science of the human environment, the relationship being gradually softened from the term "control" to "influence" or "adaptation" or "adjustment", and finally to the somewhat liturgical "response".' But this was, to Sauer at any rate, a contingent state of affairs attributable to the subject's earlier struggle 'to gain administrative independence in the universities and colleges.' Institutional visibility had been tangled up with a particular vision of disciplinary identity. So whatever its practical utility, the geographical experiment in holding nature and culture together in causal evolutionary

---

[1] Quoted in Michael Williams, '"The Apple of My Eye": Carl Sauer and Historical Geography', *Journal of Historical Geography*, 9 (1983): 1–28, ref. on p. 11.

[2] Carl O. Sauer, 'Foreword to Historical Geography', *Annals of the Association of American Geographers*, 31 (1941): 11–24, ref. on p. 4.

terms was collapsing as an academic enterprise. And the consequence was that American geography faced a personality crisis as it repeatedly 'failed to locate the uncontested field in which only professionally certified geographers may be found.'[3]

To Sauer, the way the modern geographical experiment had been set up in America was just deeply flawed. And the reasons why it had to be abandoned were diagnosed some years later by Sauer's longtime colleague at Berkeley, John Leighly. Reflecting on Davis's attempt to refashion Guyot's predestinarian structure on an evolutionary template, he observed: 'It is ironic that precisely in the years when Davis was maturing at Harvard a group of thinkers at the same institution was tearing down the intellectual structure that Herbert Spencer and the social Darwinists had erected.' What Leighly had in mind was the challenge of the Harvard pragmatists to the facile monisms of evolutionary naturalism and their manifestation in mechanistic readings of psychology, anthropology, and economics.[4] The irony was that 'environmentalism burgeoned in American geography at a time when specialized students of cultural phenomena had abandoned it.' And when at last 'the link of assumed causation between these sets of incommensurable phenomena [nature and culture] was finally recognized as being hopelessly weak,' Leighly observed, 'the two halves of Davis's structure of geography fell apart, and the two sets of phenomena toward which it was directed retained only their empirical association in space.'[5]

Since, according to these critics, the geographical conversation had confined itself too narrowly to the idioms of causal mechanics, it seemed only too obvious that allowing other voices to be heard would be an altogether good thing. Sauer himself had complained that the American geography of his day was 'essentially a native product; predominantly it is bred in the Middle West; and in dispensing with serious consideration of cultural or historical processes it reflects strongly its background.' Aping the very thing he disdained, he thereby accounted for the great commercial civilization of the Midwest as 'shaped' rapidly, simply and 'directly out of the fat of the land and the riches of the subsoil.'[6] The cure, however, was obvious; American geographers needed to escape their ingrained anti-culturalism and

[3] Ibid., pp. 2–4.

[4] See Morton White, *Science and Sentiment in America: Philosophical Thought from Jonathan Edwards to John Dewey* (New York: Oxford University Press, 1972); Philip P. Wiener, *Evolution and the Founders of Pragmatism* (Cambridge, Mass.: Harvard University Press, 1949).

[5] John Leighly, 'What Has Happened to Physical Geography?' *Annals of the Association of American Geographers*, 45 (1955): 309–18, ref. on pp. 312–13.

[6] Sauer, 'Foreword to Historical Geography', pp. 2–4.

turn elsewhere for inspiration. Sauer recommended that a thorough soaking in the history of geography's European heritage would do a deal of good. The meaty regional 'monographs of the French and German type' were thus held up as examples of good practice in the hope that a massive exercise in the reappropriation of an alternative tradition could be pulled off.[7]

THE CONTINENTAL CONNECTION

In nineteenth-century Germany, methodological debate had been both intense and protracted. Ritter's geography, for example, had been subjected to a series of critiques, first from Julius Fröbel and later from Oscar Peschel in the effort to exorcize its teleological animus. Ritter, of course, found the naturalism of these criticisms, especially when focused on his near-mystical conception of 'terrestrial units', far from palatable, and in response asserted geography's need to embrace an 'ethical purpose' and a motivation 'directed towards ends higher than merely natural ones.' The sense of irresolution about its central cognitive commitments continued to dog German geography during the mid nineteenth century. Various protagonists issued appeals for the reconditioning of the discipline along natural science lines in the attempt, to use John Leighly's words, 'to disburden geography of the load that Ritter's example had laid on it.' In consequence, some, like Gerland, thought the problem could be solved by amputation; so he proposed departing from tradition by simply sloughing off the human component as incompatible with geography as the science of the earth. Others, like Ratzel, endeavoured to overcome such a dualistic bifurcation through the mobilization of biological evolution; Hermann Wagner, sensing that the emerging geophysical emphasis was vitiated in any case by its inclusion of plant and animal distribution, also saw in biology the grounds for keeping the human subject within geography's bounds.[8]

By the end of the century, the way in which the geography-dualism might be overcome increasingly took the form of an appeal to a reformulation of the subject as a science of regions. Alfred Hettner, for example, in his inaugural address at Tübingen in 1898 happily relinquished the geophysical component as too remote from the subject's traditional concerns and urged regional synthesis along the lines of a de-theologized return to Ritter. His departure from the predestinarian character of Ritter's undertaking thus did

---

[7] Leighly, 'Physical Geography', p. 316.
[8] John Leighly, 'Methodologic Controversy in Nineteenth Century German Geography', *Annals of the Association of American Geographers*, 38 (1928): 238–58, refs on pp. 245, 251.

not prevent him from reasserting the centrality of *Länderkunde* (regional study) as better expressing 'the content of the discipline than the term *Erdkunde*.'[9] Accordingly Hettner tenaciously and dogmatically propounded in the pages of his own *Geographische Zeitschrift* the principle of chorology – the explanatory investigation of terrestrial reality divided into a series of component regions – as geography's only *raison d'être*, backing up his philosophical assertions by appeals to historical exemplars.[10] Given this absolutism it is not surprising that grand theorizing rubbed Hettner's grain the wrong way. The Davisian cycle of erosion thus grated because it tended to ignore local variations in lithology, structure, and climate. Deductive schemes could never take precedence over inductive particularities, and so Hettner remained convinced that only on the chorological principle could geography retain both its physical and human components because it was precisely in their dialectic that particular places acquired regional character.

This geographical agenda, however, might all too easily lapse into an unsystematized regional impressionism that could scarcely be dignified by the label science. Consequently, in order to achieve some coherence in the regionalizing ritual, Hettner reasserted a long-established procedure for investigation, the *Länderkunde Schema*, which consisted of a seriatim listing of items needing sequential treatment – geology, relief, climate, natural resources, zoogeography, settlement, and so on. While Hettner from time to time equivocated on the issue, this chain of geographical causation, as he himself styled it, revealed the fundamentally necessitarian bias of the undertaking. For Hettner was convinced that everything from health and hygiene to cultural and spiritual life were the legitimate subjects of geographical inquiry in so far as they were dependent on natural conditions. Herein too lay the grounds of his impatience with those who strove to segregate the natural and human sciences on hermeneutic grounds.[11]

Whereas for Hettner the balance of regional explanation lay with the 'physical basis', others radically shifted the fulcrum towards culture by asserting the transformative dominance of human agency. Perhaps it was

[9] Cited in T. H. Elkins, 'Human and Regional Geography in the German-Speaking Lands in the First Forty Years of the Twentieth Century', in J. Nicholas Entrikin and Stanley D. Brunn (eds), *Reflections on Richard Hartshorne's The Nature of Geography* (Washington, DC: Occasional Publications of the Association of American Geographers 1, 1989), pp. 17–34. See also Hans-Dietrich Schultz, *Die Deutschsprachige Geographie von 1800 bis 1970: Ein Beitrag zur Geschichte Ihrer Methodologie* (Berlin: Free University, 1980).

[10] See Alfred Hettner, *Die Geographie: Ihre Geschichte, Ihr Wesen und Ihre Methoden* (Breslau: Hirt, 1927). This volume grew out of a series of methodological pieces in the *Geographische Zeitschrift*.

[11] See Ernest Plewe, 'Alfred Hettner, 1859–1941', *Geographers. Biobibliographical Studies*, vol. 6, pp. 55–63.

because of his abiding interest in Kantian philosophy that Otto Schlüter, a student of Richthofen and Kirchoff, came to champion the view that the essential object of geographical inquiry was landscape morphology as a cultural product. Any idealist inclinations that he may have gleaned from his philosophical mentor Benno Erdmann, were doubtless confirmed in his early studies of the settlement patterns in the Unstrut Valley. Here in areas of similar physical geography Schlüter came to see the importance of the different cultures of German and Slav settlers in transforming the landscape. Thus rather than conceiving of human society as invariably controlled by environment, Schlüter emphasized humanity's cultural imprint on the land. In order to understand human settlement, then, it was necessary to acknowledge 'the totality of human life, the social as well as the individual, the physical as well as the mental, the intellectual as well as the sphere of feelings and wilful intentions.' Thereby Schlüter emerged as a major exponent of the significance of the cultural landscape (*Kulturlandscahft*) in contrast to the natural landscape (*Naturlandschaft*). And even though he insisted that the geographical focus was the *visible* landscape, he was convinced that, because the concrete was the expression of the immaterial, 'the circle of concepts within which settlement geography operates is immediately considerably enlarged.'[12] Not surprisingly his German followers went on to investigate the influence of the non-material – like religion – on the terrestrial: H. Lautensach worked on 'Religion and Landscape in Korea'; P. Fickeler examined 'The Imprint of Religion on the Landscape Throughout the World'; closer to home, H. Hand tracked 'Denominational Influence in Hansrück', H. Bleibrunner considered 'Religious Influence in Lower Bavaria', and W. Tuckerman traced 'The Imprint of Protestantism on a Part of the Black Forest'.

Schlüter's redrawing of the bounds of geography was the subject of intermittent assault from Hettner during the first quarter of the twentieth century. He felt, for example, that his own chorological principle was being assailed by Schlüter's landscape focus, and that Schlüter's exclusivity in restricting the subject's scope to the *material* expressions of culture meant an unwarranted expulsion of 'the mental element' to the detriment of 'political geography, ethnic geography, and effectively the geography of transport and trade, for which the study of visible transport means is no substitute.'[13] And yet this feud – one on which geography's historical apol-

[12] Cited in Manfred Schlick, 'Otto Schlüter, 1872–1959,' in *Geographers. Biobibliographical Studies*, vol. 6, 115–22, ref. on p. 117, from Otto Schlüter, *Die Siedelungen im Nordöstlichen Thüringen. Ein Beispiel fur die Behandlung Siedelungsgeographischer Fragen* (Berlin, 1903).

[13] Hettner, *Die Geographie*, p. 129, translated in Elkins, 'Human and Regional Geography', p. 28.

ogists have felt compelled to take sides – must be seen as an intramural fracas between devotees of the regional model. Indeed the exegetical fussiness
of those who energetically distinguished between *Landschaftskunde* and
Länderkunde has been exposed by Schultz, who has demonstrated that the
terms were in fact used synonymously as a methodology for interrogating
geographical areas.[14] Here, no doubt, academic interests were at stake in
the bid to control conceptual territory by linguistic stricture.

If this turn of events was not innocent of a struggle to secure a monopoly on disciplinary discourse, neither was it politically inviolate. Within the
German school system the principles of *Landschaftskunde* were mobilized
in the cause of liberating the subject from its enslavement to statistical enumeration. The ideological interests at work here turn out to have been far
from inconsiderable.[15] For as it subsequently developed, the *Landschaft*
model moved more and more in the direction of a holistic, organicist conception of the relations between a people and its land, or, to put it more
menacingly, between blood and soil. After all, Mecking confessed in 1934
that the '*völkish* renovation catchwords such as "blood and soil" sound in
our ears as being at close range with the content and aim of geographic
research, with its synthesis of soil and man.' As a recent set of commentators observe: 'Now the external was thought to be only a reflection of
deeper spiritual forces. The body mirrored the soul. Landscape and geography were considered indispensable to the soul of the *Volk*.' Moreover,
when this emphasis was supplemented by an enthusiasm for *Heimatkunde*
(local study), a coalition of ideas was produced that could – and did –
encourage the cultivation of a powerful rhetoric for opposing the growing
sense of class-based solidarity and internationalism. Political conservatism
and landscape geography could thus be mutually reinforcing. In this political environment the cultural landscape could be transmuted all too easily
into a 'völkish-created scenery . . . a *volk*-space reality and the whole
complex . . . interpreted as racial anthropocentrism.'

In France the cultivation of 'le régionalisme' had also been implicated in
the political arena.[16] Local fealty had been used by early-nineteenth-century
social theorists like Louis de Bonald to provide a pluralist critique of the
centralized state which had usurped the authority that had long resided in

[14] Schultz, *Die Deutschsprachige Geographie*.
[15] This paragraph, and its citations, rely on Michael Fahlbusch, Mechtild Rössler and
Dominik Siegrist, 'Conservatism, Ideology and Geography in Germany 1920–1950', *Political
Geography Quarterly*, 8 (1989): 353–67.
[16] The imperial, educational, and republican impulses in the emergence of the modern
French school of geography are traced in Berdoulay, *La Formation de l'École Française*.

family, church, and local institutions. Equally it contested the radical individualism that ignored the formative influence of society. De Bonald himself
repudiated any idea of a system of territorial representation in government,
preferring instead to conceive of the ideal society as 'a society of societies',
that is, as constituted by an amalgam of intermediate associations like the
church, parish, or guild. This was, so to speak, a structural rather than a
spatial localization of political authority. But this conception of society suggested to others, like Hugues Felicité de Lamennais, that regionalism could
advance provincial interests over against the unifying impositions of the
centralized state. Conceived as an antidote both to corporatism and atom-
ism, regional attachment could help resist state encroachment through the
reinstitution of decentralized government. This commitment to a strong
family system, to the historic provinces, and to the restoration of the local
commune all reveal the profoundly conservative, not to say medieval, thrust
such regional thinking could encourage.[17]

Subsequently the ideology of regionalism was supplemented and transformed as novelists and historians came to revere the significance of the
particularities of place. And its political associations eventually widened to
encompass advocates from both the Right and the Left. In the midst of
these developments, academic geography flourished as a consequence of the
enlarged role assigned to it in the school system during the early 1870s. In
the aftermath of the Franco-Prussian War (1870–1) and the establishment of
the Third Republic, and at a time when the university sector was redirect-
ing its energies toward national regeneration, the minister for education,
Jules Simon, took steps to revitalize geography teaching in the schools.
Convinced that national salvation lay in education, he established a
Commission de l'Enseignement de la Géographie in November 1871 to
inspect the current state of affairs. The result was an appeal for the overhauling of the geography curriculum in the direction of a much greater
focus on the local region. Instead of beginning with an abstract recitation
of celestial mechanics, the new programme began 'in the youngest years
with a study of the immediate vicinity of the child's home, school and
commune.'[18]

These circumstances, enabling if not determining, facilitated Vidal de la
Blache's career move from classical studies to geography on his return to

[17] See Robert Nisbet, 'Conservatism', in Tom Bottomore and Robert Nisbet (eds), *A History of Sociological Analysis* (London: Heinemann, 1978), pp. 80–117.
[18] Howard F. Andrews, 'The Early Life of Paul Vidal de la Blache and the Makings of Modern Geography', *Transactions of the Institute of British Geographers*, n.s. 11 (1986): 174–82, ref. on p. 178.

France from Athens in 1870. Precisely what role they played in conditioning the cognitive content of Vidal's geography is uncertain. Nevertheless his conception of geography as 'the scientific study of places' was clearly in keeping with the prevailing *Zeitgeist*. For Vidal was determined to depart from both traditional encyclopedism and Ratzelian necessity in the forging of his own *géographie humaine*. As he saw it, the geographical task lay in the investigation of how, in particular places, a variety of natural realms provided the milieux in which human life-styles (*genres de vie*) were shaped.

These *genres de vie* Vidal understood as the functionally patterned modes of living – nomadic, agricultural, and so on – that constituted an integrated web of physical, social, and psychological threads. The ecological-organic tincture of this vision is conspicuous – just as conspicuous as in its Ratzelian counterpart. But whereas Ratzel dilated on the moulding power of environment, Vidal stressed society's role in modifying nature. To him the very label *genre de vie* was a signifier for a methodical, continuous, and powerful transformation of environment. This was particularly so in the later phases of social evolution when engrained customs – agricultural practices, building traditions, settlement types, transportation modes – were ever more deeply etched on the land.[19] Just how Vidal thought the physiognomy of the earth, at once the product of nature and culture, should be painted is amply displayed in his own *Tableau de la Géographie de la France* (1903).

Yet it would be mistaken to consider Vidal's as an altogether radical voluntarism. He was convinced that habits of life were themselves reflective of nature even as they transformed it. Again and again he paused to elucidate the various ways location and climate influenced the history, anthropology, and physiology of the human species. Hence Vidal did not pursue what Buttimer terms the 'internal dynamism of a *genre de vie*,' preferring instead to call upon it as the explanans of a region's humanized landscape.[20] The reasons are readily apparent. Vidal, never psychologistic, always conceived of human geography as a *natural*, not a *social* science. To him the regional articulation of life-style consisted in the material expressions of human–land relationships. Human geography thus had the task of elucidating a socialized nature. Its 'special mission' was to ascertain how the laws

[19] Paul Vidal de la Blache, 'Les Genres de Vie dans la Géographie Humaine', *Annales de la Géographie*, 20 (1911): 193–212, 289–304.
[20] Anne Buttimer, *Society and Milieu in the French Geographic Tradition* (Chicago: Rand McNally, 1971), p. 53. See also Anne Buttimer, 'Charism and Context: The Challenge of *La Géographie Humaine*', in David Ley and Marwyn Samuels (eds), *Humanistic Geography: Prospects and Problems* (London: Croom Helm, 1978), pp. 58–76.

of physics and biology had conspired in different regional arenas to produce the specificities of locality – 'It has for its special study the changing
expression which, according to the locality, the appearance of the earth
assumes.'[21]

Indeed it was this reluctance to venture into deeper sociological waters
that called forth censure from an otherwise admiring Lucien Febvre. With
Vidal he insisted that 'natural regions are simply collections of possibilities
for society which makes use of them but is not determined by them.' But
even while celebrating the Vidalian impulses within the *Annales* school of
history, which liberated French historical consciousness from the 'string-of-
events' mentality, Febvre nevertheless remained chary of the 'relapse into a
kind of unconscious "naturalism"' characteristic of too many of those who
best knew 'of man and human society and of their activity on the surface
of the earth.'[22]

Vidal evidently conceived of the essays that were posthumously drawn
together in *Principes de Géographie Humaine* (1921) as a manifesto. 'Our
science', he wrote, 'offers a new conception of the interrelationships
between earth and man,' one based on 'a more synthetic knowledge of the
physical laws governing our earth and of the relations between the living
beings which inhabit it.[23] And yet, perhaps because of the way the text was
assembled, perhaps because the project was incomplete, there is little sense
in the volume of any systematic articulation of a code of 'principles' for the
nascent enterprise. Rather, it reveals Vidal's inclination to proceed on a
more inductive basis elucidating the particulars of the great population
agglomerations in Africa and Asia, Europe, and the Mediterranean.
Moreover the essays are conspicuously bereft of the epistemological
manoeuvring that one might expect of a pronunciamento for a new science.
Instead what comes clearly through is the naturalistic drift of Vidal's
thought *from* ecology *to* human geography. Zoogeographers, he remarked,
'use such expressions as "community of life" or even "faunal association"'.
These truly were 'significant terms' and prompted him to ask how far they
were 'applicable to human geography.' With such proclivities it is entirely
understandable that the volume should resort to earthy metaphors (Vidal

[21] Paul Vidal de la Blache, 'Les Caractères Distinctifs de la Géographie', *Annales de
Géographie*, 22 (1913): 289–99.

[22] Lucien Febvre, *A Geographical Introduction to History*, translated by E. G. Mountford
and J. H. Paxton (London: Kegan, Paul, Trench, Trubner, 1932), pp. 171, 364. Febvre's appreciation of Vidal is discussed in Paul Claval, *Essai sur l'Évolution de la Géographie Humaine*
(Paris: Les Belles Lettres, 1976), pp. 55–7.

[23] Paul Vidal de la Blache, *Principles of Human Geography*, translated by Millicent Todd
Bingham (London: Constable and Company, 1926), pp. 4, 10–11, 16.

speaks, for example, of the deposition of 'human alluvium') and that it should focus on the transformative activities of cultivation and domestication – predominantly nature occupations. A profound sense of historical dynamic thus pervades the project. Population growth, migration, isolation, race history, colonization, acclimatization, evolution, progressivism, circulation: it is from these that Vidal's querying of determinism is culled rather than from the enunciation of an abstractly possibilist philosophical creed. It was left to his disciple and systematizer, Jean Brunhes, to infuse a more logically articulated possibilism into the Vidalian spirit. Though at the same time he earthed the geographical project even more firmly in the material artefacts of human culture.[24]

Given the attention it devoted to the material forms of social life, the question of what relationship *géographie humaine* should sustain with the social morphology of Emile Durkheim was almost bound to arise. In his earlier encounter with Ratzel's geography, Durkheim had proposed welcoming *Anthropogeographie* – a potential ally of the new social science – by engulfing it. This was, however, an altogether partial appropriation. Because he conceived of social differentiation in essentially morphological terms Durkheim was drawn to the geographical scrutiny of the different settlement forms societies assumed across the surface of the earth. What he spurned was the reductionism implicit in explaining the political in terms of the physiographical. To lay out social morphology by mapping spatial patterns was one thing; to explain social forms as constituted by environment was to confuse constraint with causality.[25] For Durkheim, the character that societies assume was the result of the nature and arrangements of their constituent elements.[26] The political was not reducible to the pedological.

With these sentiments, Durkheim, seeking for a science of society that likewise shunned a reductionist naturalism *and* a disengaged psychologism, was understandably drawn to Vidal's *genres de vie*. Yet their parallel interests in society and milieu, and their twin insistence on thinking collectively rather than individually about society, did nothing to prevent certain hostil-

[24] See Jean Brunhes, *La Géographie Humaine: Essai de Classification Positive* (Paris: Alcan, 1910). Brunhes insisted that '*primary and fundamental human geography . . . should be first the geography of the material achievements of man*, thus preparing the way for the *geography of groups and races of men*, particularly as these groups and races translate their specific and different forms of activity into material achievements.' This passage is taken from Ernest F. Row's translation, *Human Geography* by Jean Brunhes, abridged edition by Mme M. Jean-Brunhes Delamarre and Pierre Deffontaines (London: George G. Harrap, 1952), p. 47.

[25] See the discussions in Derek Gregory, *Ideology, Science and Human Geography* (London: Hutchinson, 1978), pp. 84–9; Buttimer, *Society and Milieu*, pp. 30–40.

[26] See Tom Bottomore and Robert Nisbet, 'Structuralism', in Tom Bottomore and Robert Nisbet (eds), *History of Sociological Analysis* (London: Heinemann, 1978), pp. 557–98.

ities between these masters and their disciples. The issue focused on the relative merits of sociological and human geographical accounts of the terrestrial aspects of social life. For while the former proceeded in a 'structural' fashion by identifying institutional frameworks and collective consciousness as causal factors of social morphology, the latter was more taken up with regional case studies, historical particulars, and landscape characteristics. Such commitments, it has been argued, crystallized divergent epistemological orientations that subsumed different assumptions about the nature of science, different conceptions of explanation, and different appropriations of neo-Kantian philosophy.[27]

To recount the cardinal features of social morphology's encounter with *géographie humaine* in purely intellectual terms is, however, a question-begging enterprise. For one thing the very terms employed – *géographie humaine* and social morphology – are arguably bloodless abstractions, as indeed are the collectives 'Vidalians' and 'Durkheimians'. Moreover, since the conversation, however it took place, was situated in the context of the institutionalization of two academic disciplines, and clearly underwent evolution in the light of these circumstances, the arguments and counter-arguments cannot be divorced from the academic goals and career ambitions of the interlocutors. Besides, as with Kepler's laws of planetary motion, it has been perhaps too easy to extract static formulations from the documents of the past, and thereby to produce a 'debate' with a precision that imposes contemporary clarity on historical opacity. The non-polemical character of Vidal's remarks on the whole issue, and Durkheim's own declared tentativeness in advancing his social-structural explanation, should themselves temper bellicose interpretations.[28] And yet these circumstances can scarcely be used to disqualify our interest in intellectual history. For indeed even if commentators have been too ready to read these events through the 'idiosyncratic' spectacles of the rhetorically articulate historian Lucien Febvre,[29]

---

[27] See Vincent Berdoulay, 'The Vidal-Durkheim Debate', in David Ley and Marwyn Samuels (eds), *Humanistic Geography: Prospects and Problems* (London: Croom Helm, 1978), pp. 77–90; Vincent Berdoulay, 'French Possibilism as a Form of Neo-Kantian Philosophy', *Proceedings of the Association of American Geographers*, 8 (1976): 176–9. See also Fred Lukermann, 'The "Culcul des Probabilités" and the École Française de Géographie', *Canadian Geographer*, 9 (1965): 128–37.

[28] See Paul Vidal de la Blache, 'Rapports de la Sociologie, avec la Géographie', *Revue Internationale de Sociologie*, 12 (1904): 309–13. Durkheim remarked that he had 'never dreamed of offering the preceding observations as a complete theory of the concept of causality. The question is too complex to be resolved thus.' Emile Durkheim, *The Elementary Forms of Religious Life*, translated by Joseph Ward Swain (London: Allen and Unwin, 1915), p. 369.

[29] So Andrews, 'The Durkheimians and Human Geography'.

the way in which his reconstruction has itself shaped subsequent history is undeniable.

Whatever the specificities of *géographie humaine*'s altercation with social morphology and whatever the criticisms levelled at it for its scientific imprecision, these serve only to underscore the regional vitality that characterized the Vidalian tradition. Certainly their resolution of the dilemmas of disciplinary identity needs to be seen in the context of the way the French geographers chose to negotiate their way around a series of problems: how to hammer out a non-determinist geography that retained traditional links between society and environment without encroaching on the territory of the social morphologists. But whatever their source, the energies of Vidal's successors were devoted primarily to elucidating, in terms of contingency rather than necessity, 'the complex web of relationships binding society and milieu' through their production of a suite of small-scale regional monographs of particular French *pays*.[30] Just how this motif surfaced across the channel will be our next concern.

THE GEDDESIAN CIRCLE

In Great Britain, the articulation of regionalism in the French mode owed much to the activities of the Scottish polymath Patrick Geddes (1854–1932) and the circle of geographers who came under his spell.[31] Scientific links between Scotland and France were both deep and lasting, for the Edinburgh–Paris axis, around which Geddes's own intellectual life revolved, had been in service since the early nineteenth century as a means of importing French political and scientific radicalism into Britain.[32]

During Easter 1878, Geddes had spent a convalescent few weeks working with the marine biologists at Roscoff. But it was during his time in Paris the following winter that he made the crucial intellectual encounter, via Edmond Demolins, with the social theories of Frédéric Le Play. Here Geddes found a model for the scientific study of society that would enable him to translate the natural science that he had been studying with Huxley in London into practical politics.

---

[30] Buttimer, *Society and Milieu*, p. 42.
[31] The standard biography is now Helen Meller, *Patrick Geddes. Social Evolutionist and City Planner* (London: Routledge, 1990). See also Philip Boardman, *The Worlds of Patrick Geddes. Biologist, Town Planner, Re-Educator, Peace-Warrior* (London: Routledge and Kegan Paul, 1978).
[32] See Desmond, *The Politics of Evolution.*

In his capacity as a mining engineer, Le Play had had the opportunity of travelling extensively throughout Europe during the middle decades of the nineteenth century. A twenty-year exposure to the regional variety of European social organization eventually issued in *Les Ouvriers Européens* which he published in 1855. From that point in his career until 1870 Le Play gave his support to the Napoleonic regime, and the schemes of social reform that he advocated were thus tempered by a concern to preserve the status quo. To him the restoration of a rich variety of intermediate associations would both overcome state interventionism and hasten a revivification of family, religious, and local life. Thus undergirding Le Play's project was a set of moral-political principles derivative of de Bonald and every bit as traditionalist, Catholic, and critical of the Enlightenment *mentalité*. So, while he perceived the links between economic change, cultural conventions, and the means of production, Le Play resisted the Marxist materialist analysis of historical transformation with its revolutionary imperatives. Instead he focused on particular communities, the variations between them, and how they were conditioned by geographical circumstances. In the Le Play scheme, social structures were thus intimately bound up with physical environments and it is understandable that in the hands of devotees, like Demolins, it was embroiled in a deterministic reductionism. Accordingly it came under the whiplash of Febvre's tongue for the 'mechanical fury' with which Demolins had extracted universal inevitabilities from his survey of racial and social types.[33]

The thoroughgoing regionalism that permeated his analysis of social structure encouraged Le Play to seek for some systematic method of probing the particularities of place. Taking the family as the basic social unit, Le Play organized his account around the key elements of family, place, and work. By elucidating the interrelationships among these components, he believed the inner dynamic of regional life could be disclosed: the modes of livelihood (work), produced by specific environments (place), conditioned the mores of the fundamental social element (family).[34] This scheme was widely promulgated by his admirers, frequently, though not invariably, in the rigidly determinist formulation of the Demolins model.

The regional insights that Geddes was gleaning from the Le Playists found reinforcement from the first volumes of Reclus's *Géographie Universelle* which had begun to make their appearance in the late 1870s. In

---

[33] Febvre, *Geographical Introduction*, p. 15.
[34] See M. Z. Brooke, *Le Play: Engineer and Social Scientist. The Life and Work of Frédéric Le Play* (London: Longman, 1970); Robert E. Dickinson, 'Frédéric le Play', in *The Makers of Modern Geography*, pp. 197–207.

fact Geddes became so profound an admirer of Reclus that later, in the 1890s, he brought him to his own Edinburgh summer school. In time he came to believe that Reclus had perhaps 'too much lost sight of the inter-mediate categories of the city and state, of the nation and empire' in the grand sweep of his canvas.[35] Yet his own commentary on the development of civilization – the so-called 'Valley Section' – in which physical environment and nature occupations featured prominently, was imbued with Reclus's categories.[36] For all that, Geddes sensed something missing in the works of these regional apologists. They had not registered the force of evolutionary currents. For Geddes was only too aware, as he later put it, that 'the place occupied by Paley's theological and metaphysical explana-tion has simply been occupied by that suggested to Darwin and Wallace by Malthus in terms of the prevalent severity of industrial competition.'[37]

The sociology of Auguste Comte – which Geddes had encountered earlier in London, and now found propagated with renewed enthusiasm in the Paris of the late 1870s – promised a way out of the impasse. For Comte had presented as the foundation of the science of society a positive theory of social progress which, even if it was in its essentials a synthesis of a long Western tradition of progressivist thinking, nevertheless gave impetus to the search for laws regulating the social development of the human race.[38] The developmental scheme of social progress that he outlined, in which society moved inexorably along the path from the theological via the metaphysical to the scientific or positive, was thus appealing to Geddes.[39] Through the Comtists, then, he came to see that in an evolutionary sociology the abstract and the concrete were intimately connected. Even the pure sciences were not socially detached: 'logic and mathematics, physics and chemistry, biology and psychology,' Geddes insisted in 1919, 'are none of them inde-pendent of social life . . . they are, on the contrary, direct products of the social conditions and changes of their times.'[40]

Geddes's evolutionizing of social theory, however, was not exclusively

[35] Patrick Geddes, 'A Great Geographer: Elisée Reclus 1830–1905. An Obituary', *Scottish Geographical Magazine*, 21 (1905): 490–5, 548–55, on p. 552.

[36] Geddes's 'Valley Section' or 'Valley Plan of Civilization' was a diagrammatic portrayal of the interconnections between physical environment and economic life. Along the cross section of the river valley from source to sea Geddes placed Demolins's 'natural occupations' – wood-man, hunter, shepherd, peasant, fisherman, and so on – at appropriate locations. See Patrick Geddes, 'Civics as Applied Sociology. Part I', *Sociological Papers*, 1 (1905): 103–18.

[37] Patrick Geddes and J. Arthur Thomson, 'Biology', *Chambers Encyclopedia* (London and Edinburgh: W. and R. Chambers, new edn 1925), vol. 2, pp. 157–64, ref. on p. 164.

[38] See Robert Nisbet, *History of the Idea of Progress* (New York: Basic Books, 1980).

[39] See Frank E. Manuel, *The Prophets of Paris* (Cambridge: Harvard University Press, 1962).

[40] Cited in Meller, *Patrick Geddes*, p. 44.

dependent on his espousal of Comtean positivism. The philosophy of
Herbert Spencer was just as decisive. Of course, Spencer himself had built
on Comtean foundations as he hunted for a scientific law of progress
stripped of any happiness component or moral principle.[41] Geddes's own
translation of social progress into the idioms of Spencerian evolution thus
facilitated his frequent repudiations of the all-sufficiency of Darwinian natural selection as the exclusive mechanism of transformism. Moreover, it
enabled him to misrepresent Le Play's trilogy of *lieu, travail, famille* as the
functional equivalents of Spencer's environment, function, and organism,[42]
an equation, nevertheless, that Lewis Mumford was later to regard as of
quite fundamental importance.[43] From Spencer, then, and indeed from
Haeckel with whom he studied at Jena, Geddes came to appreciate the typically Lamarckian insistence on organic adaptation as the product of active
rather than passive responses to environmental stimuli.[44] Humankind's
capacity to escape the fatalism of an evolutionary environmentalism thus
lay in Geddes's psycho-biological account of organic change, with its con-
comitant dedication to the *élan vital* as a creative force. These judgements,
which surfaced in the emergent evolution that Geddes and C. Lloyd
Morgan championed, plainly resonated with the creative evolutionism of
Henri Bergson.[45]

Geddes thus conceived of the human species as a new evolutionary
'emergent' experiencing the greatest freedom from the constraints of environmental fate. Acknowledging his intellectual debts to 'the older and more
directly practical and economic' Le Playists as well as to their 'younger and
more geographical and evolutionary' representatives, he told the London
geographers in May 1898 that

> while circumstances modify man, and that in mind as well as body, man,
> especially as he rises in material civilization, seems to escape from the grasp
> of environment, and to react, and that more and more deeply, upon nature;

---

[41] See Kenneth Bock, 'Theories of Progress, Development, Evolution', in Tom Bottomore
and Robert Nisbet (eds), *A History of Sociological Analysis* (London: Heinemann, 1978),
pp. 39–79.
[42] See Patrick Geddes, 'Man and his Environment: A Study from the Paris Exposition',
International Monthly, 2 (1900): 169–95. This is discussed in Campbell and Livingstone, 'Neo-
Lamarckism and the Development of Geography'.
[43] Lewis Mumford, 'Introduction', in Jaqueline Tyrwhitt (ed.), *Patrick Geddes in India*
(London: Lund Humphries, 1947), pp. 7–13.
[44] J. Arthur Thomson and Patrick Geddes, *Life: Outlines of General Biology*, 2 vols
(London: Williams and Norgate, 1931), vol. 1, p. 28.
[45] Geddes, however, chose to depict his own position as *neo*-vitalism to distinguish it from
the Bergsonian version.

at length, as he develops his ideas and systematizes his ideals into the philosophy or religion of his place and time, he affirms his superiority to fate, his moral responsibility and independence; his escape from slavery to nature into an increasing mastership.[46]

Understandably, the possibilism of French geography was especially appealing; it seemed to articulate a geographical translation of his own biological juxtaposition of materialism and idealism. Thus biological and social Lamarckism formed the warp and woof of Geddes's outlook, explaining as it did both organic inheritance and social heritage in a progressivist way and holding out hope for the future by permitting the intervention in human affairs, by environmental and educational planning, that other versions of Social Darwinism outlawed.

If it was in France that Geddes was exposed to the possibilities of regional synthesis and to the reinterpretive impulses of Continental scientific philosophy, it was in Scotland that his thinking and influence flourished. The Edinburgh to which he returned late in 1879 – and where for a decade he taught zoology prior to taking up the chair of botany at Dundee in 1889 – was host to an emerging community of geographers whose very existence evidenced a decentralizing challenge to the hegemony hitherto exerted by the metropolitan set at the London-based Royal Geographical Society. A number of independent factors converged in Edinburgh to encourage the formation of this geographical circle.[47]

On the publishing front, for example, Edinburgh had long been the home of Britain's two largest map-making companies – Bartholomew and Son, and W. and A. K. Johnston – and was the centre for the production of a range of encyclopedias. It had too a strong natural scientific tradition. In geology the earlier contributions of Fleming, Playfair, Hutton, and Miller, were supplemented by the Geikies, Archibald and James, who focused more exclusively on earth surface geology in contrast to the stratigraphical and palaeontological emphases of their English counterparts. Then the *Challenger* expedition of 1872–6 – the aim of which was to determine the physical conditions of the great ocean basins – had its offices located in Edinburgh under the directorship first of Wyville Thompson and then of John Murray.[48] A range of figures who would later become prominent

[46] Patrick Geddes, 'The Influence of Geographical Conditions on Social Development', *Geographical Journal*, 12 (1898): 580–7, refs on pp. 581, 585.
[47] See the discussion in Lochhead, 'Scotland as the Cradle of Modern Academic Geography'; Elspeth N. Lochhead, 'The Royal Scottish Geographical Society: The Setting and Sources of its Success', *Scottish Geographical Magazine*, 100 (1984): 69–80.
[48] See Eric Linklater, *The Voyage of the Challenger* (London: John Murray, 1972).

members of the geographical fraternity, like H. N. Dickson, H. R. Mill, and A. J. Herbertson, were involved with this oceanographic enterprise. The same was true of meteorology: several geographers served as assistants at the high and low-level observatories on Ben Nevis and at Fort William. All this, together with a vibrant, indigenous tradition of exploration and travel – David Livingstone, Mungo Park, and Joseph Thomson were all Scottish – helped foster a taste for geography.

It was in this cultural matrix that the idea of a national geographical society for Scotland was conceived and, in 1884, born. Understandably the aim of the Royal Scottish Geographical Society (RSGS) was both to advance knowledge of local geography and to see the subject develop within commercial, scientific, and political spheres.[49] But compared with the RGS, this institutional project attracted a larger proportion of members directly involved in academic and scientific careers. This difference between the Edinburgh and London geographical scenes, in fact, was symptomatic of the long-lasting divergence between the scientific cultures of the two cities. For example, throughout the century the Royal Society of Edinburgh had drawn in the city's leading cultural figures – university professors, lawyers, and medical men, whereas at the Royal Society of London 'the gentry, clergy and military officers were trying to ensure that the dominant ethos remained dilettante and amateur.'[50]

The disciplinary pluralism that characterized the RSGS's clientele, together with the strong environmental emphasis that its chief advocates had gleaned from their oceanographic and meteorological experience, not to mention their interest in global-scale distributions, were all features attractive to Geddes on his return to Edinburgh. He soon gathered around him a coterie of individuals attracted, in all probability, less by his scientific competences than by his magnetic personality and reforming zeal manifested in environmental, planning, and educational initiatives. What they all shared was a fascination with the region as a geographical unit.

In Geddes's case, it was only in the delineating of regional particularities that the 'evolutionist's promise of scientific synthesis' could be delivered via the elucidation of the interaction between geographical factors, social forces, and evolutionary trends. This was simply because regional character was the accumulated record of social evolution. Evolutionists therefore needed to 'descend from the region of philosophic abstraction to co-ordinate and inter-

[49] See *Prospectus of the Royal Geographical Society* (Edinburgh: Royal Geographical Society, 1884).

[50] Jack B. Morrell, 'Individualism and the Structure of British Science in 1830', *Historical Studies in the Physical Sciences* (1971): 183–204, ref. on p. 193.

pret the whole facts of geography and history,' Geddes affirmed.[51] Yet for him, regionalism was never to be conceived of as a mere academic formula. The holistic, vital, evolutionary underpinnings of his own regional ideology were typically translated into a critique of the moral and cultural shallowness of the planning enterprises of his day. He repudiated the functional, dehistoricized idealism of the 'garden-city' school of Ebenezer Howard. Because Geddes conceived of the planning process as an evolutionary science,[52] he believed such ventures failed to take with sufficient seriousness the inner historical dynamic of regional life. To Geddes, the city was, as a later admirer put it, 'an evolving organism charged with influences from the past, some bearing promise for the future and some merely persisting as useless vestiges.'[53] Yet this reverence for tradition never led Geddes into a nostalgic sentimentalism or to a static memorialism. Living history was vitiated by such gestured monumentalism. So, later in India, he arraigned Gandhi's token cultural conservation when he reverted to the spinning wheel at the precise moment that rural poverty required a more mechanized agriculture.[54]

The 'diagnostic survey' and 'conservative surgery' – both medical metaphors – that Geddes advocated as a means of urban reform were thus designed at once to preserve the historical integrity of a city's 'collective soul' *and* to foster community change at the local level. They were the very antithesis of totalitarianism.[55] As Mellor has put it: 'Planning was not a matter of ironing out the technical and physical problems of modern city life. It was a matter of opening people's eyes to their biological nature, treating with respect the interaction of human organism and environment, and engaging people in their own development activities, since the only objective of importance was the social evolution of the species.'[56] Geddes's

[51] Geddes, 'Influence of Geographical Conditions', p. 586.

[52] Geddes wrote, for example: 'First it [the method of diagnostic survey] seeks to unravel the old city's labyrinth and discern how this has grown up. Though, like all organic growths, this may at first seem confused to our modern eyes, that have for so long been trained to a mechanical order, gradually a higher form of order can be discerned – the order of life in development. This is the method of all evolutionary science and hence the method of the latest and youngest of all social sciences – and yet the most ambitious and most necessary of them all – the science of the city survey.' Patrick Geddes, *Town Planning in Kapurthala. A Report to H.H. the Maharaja of Kapurthala* (Lucknow: Murray's London Printing Press, 1917), p. 2.

[53] R. N. Rudmose Brown, 'Scotland and Some Trends in Geography: John Murray, Patrick Geddes and Andrew Herbertson', *Geography*, 33 (1948): 107–20, ref. on p. 111.

[54] Mumford, 'Introduction', p. 9.

[55] See Patrick Geddes, *Cities in Evolution. An Introduction to the Town Planning Movement and to the Study of Civics* (London: Williams and Norgate, 1915).

[56] Helen Meller, 'Cities and Evolution: Patrick Geddes as an International Prophet of Town Planning before 1914', in Anthony Sutcliffe (ed.), *The Rise of Modern Urban Planning, 1800–1914* (New York: St Martin's Press, 1980), pp. 199–223, ref. on p. 205.

own voluntary work in the slums of Edinburgh's James Court was a practical articulation of the principle. And with such activist inclinations it is understandable that Geddes found himself more drawn to Kropotkin and Reclus than to either the imperialist geography of Halford Mackinder or the theoretical socialism of the Fabians.

For Geddes, then, regional survey was no dry stocktaking exercise; it was the very stuff of political reform and educational transformation. Politically, he hoped the fostering of regional awareness would prove to be the first stage in civic rehabilitation through popular involvement in decision making.[57] His holistic approach to community on the small scale ('Civilisation', he wrote, 'has flourished best in small aggregates') was tailor-made to encourage local participation. It fostered decentralization.[58] 'The true city', to Geddes, was 'that of a burgher people, governing themselves from their own town halls and yet expressing also the spiritual ideals which govern their lives.'[59] The effective democratization of the planning process, moreover, required curricular reform. So, convinced that 'Education, if real, begins with a Regional Survey, as action with a regional usefulness,' Geddes energetically threw his weight behind the nature-study movement[60] and organized his Outlook Tower in Edinburgh (described by some as the first sociological laboratory) as an educational museum in which the world could be encountered through a hierarchy of regional levels. Such projects were intended to take education out of the classroom and into life, to replace bibliolatry with first-hand experience, and to involve local people in the making of their own history. The synthesis of knowledge at which Geddes aimed was therefore, as he put it in 1917, 'no longer that of arts and sciences but of Place and People . . . no longer an abstract classification . . . but a concrete one. It is that of geography instead of philosophy.'[61]

The reformist spirit that Geddes had breathed into regional survey, however, was to be compromised by his successors in both planning and geography. Too often the dry husks of regional survey persisted without the crusading kernel. In planning, the professionalization of the enterprise did much to warp the Geddesian vision. It tended to substitute a static physi-

[57] On Geddes's contributions to civics, see Helen Meller, 'Patrick Geddes: An Analysis of his Theory of Civics, 1880–1904', *Victorian Studies 16*, (1973): 291–315.

[58] Patrick Geddes, *Town Planning Towards City-Development. A Report to the Durbar of Indore*, 2 vols (Indore: Holkar State Printing Press, 1918), p. 178.

[59] Geddes, *Cities in Evolution*, p. 254.

[60] Geddes, 'Influence of Geographical Conditions', p. 586; Patrick Geddes, 'Nature Study and Geographical Education', *Scottish Geographical Magazine*, 18 (1902): 525–36.

[61] Quoted in Meller, 'Cities and Evolution', p. 212.

calism for social dynamism, technical skills for civic vision, scientific precision for political passion. The 'liberal, humanitarian, and social reform element,' writes Cherry, 'was partly squeezed into a professional frame.'[62] Similarly in geography: as Robson has put it, 'His [Geddes's] social crusade, his goal of social awakening and betterment, evaporated in the general descriptive accounts which came from this geographical translation of his method.'[63] C. W. Fawcett, for example, an enthusiastic advocate of regional survey, produced in 1919 the *Provinces of England* as a geographical resolution to the question of political devolution. It was, certainly, an effort at operationalizing the rather vague talk of regions. Yet, as Stevenson notes, it 'lacked some of Geddes's *élan* and almost all of his humanism.'[64] Still, the economic, rather than cultural, concerns that undergirded the question of land utilization, and which lay at the headwaters of Fawcett's campaign to strengthen regional autonomy, was to become ingrained in British geographical practice. L. Dudley Stamp's orchestration of the Land Utilization Survey in the 1930s, in which the mapping of British land use was undertaken with 22,000 field assistants, was symptomatic of the unleashing of the new regionalism, as was the strong emphasis on fieldwork that this tradition enshrined.[65]

The Geddesian legacy within geography, however, cannot be restricted to the mechanistic production of provincial compendia. Something more of the spirit of Geddes came through in the contributions of his disciple A. J. Herbertson (1865–1915). The intellectual influences on Herbertson were, of course, manifold. He had studied natural history with P. G. Tait, and geology with James Geikie, both in Edinburgh; in Paris he encountered Demolins and the Le Playists; at the University of Freiburg-im-Breigsau he studied heredity with August Weismann during the winter of 1889–90. Yet for all this, it was Geddes who had the profoundest impact.[66] In the early

[62] G. E. Cherry, *The Evolution of British Town Planning: A History of Town Planning in the United Kingdom during the 20th Century and of the Royal Town Planning Institute 1914–74* (Leighton Buzzard: Leonard Hill, 1974), p. 61.

[63] See the discussion in Brian Robson, 'Geography and Social Science: the Role of Patrick Geddes', in David R. Stoddart (ed.), *Geography, Ideology and Social Concern* (Oxford: Blackwell, 1981), pp. 186–207, ref. on pp. 202–3.

[64] W. Iain Stevenson, 'Patrick Geddes 1854–1932', *Geographers. Biobibliographical Studies*, 2 (1978): 53–65, ref. on p. 59.

[65] See Stanley H. Beaver, 'The Le Play Society and Fieldwork', *Geography*, 47 (1962): 226–39; C. Board, 'Field Work in Geography, with Particular Emphasis on the Role of Land-Use Survey', in R. J. Chorley and P. Haggett (eds), *Frontiers in Geographical Teaching* (London: Methuen, 1965), pp. 186–214; Stoddart, *On Geography*, chapter 3 'Geography, Education and Research', and chapter 7 on 'Geography, Exploration and Discovery'.

[66] E. W. Gilbert observed that 'One cannot exaggerate the great influence that Geddes exercised on Herbertson's thought.' E. W. Gilbert, 'Andrew John Herbertson 1865–1915. An

1890s he enthusiastically threw himself into the activities of Geddes's Outlook Tower, worked as his demonstrator in botany at Dundee, and later modelled his own summer schools at Oxford on the Geddesian prototype.

The major conceptual forces in Herbertson's thinking thus resonated with those of Geddes himself. Most conspicuous, perhaps, was the role that Herbertson accorded to natural regions in his geographical pronouncements. Reflecting on the scope of geography in 1904, for example, he distanced himself from Davis's characterization of the subject as 'the relationship between physical environment and the organic responses to it,' preferring instead to emphasize the 'geographical units we may term regions.'[67] His programmatic statement the following year on the major natural regions of the world was to become a classic statement of the genre. Dudley Stamp, with E. W. Gilbert's approval, was later to assert that 'it would be difficult to cite any other single communication which has had such far-reaching effects in the development of our subject.'[68] Here Herbertson called for the delimiting of regions on the naturalistic basis of their 'unity of configuration, climate, and vegetation.'[69] This sense of regional holism clearly evinces Geddes's organicism; and yet one gets the impression in Herbertson, and certainly in later practitioners of regionalism, that regional delineation had become an end in itself rather than the prelusive identification of the natural unit within which evolutionary processes, both natural and social, could be grasped.

Again, Herbertson's encounter with the Le Play model of society and the central role accorded there to family life, was tempered by Geddes's suspicions that more could be learned about cultural transmission through analogical investigations of the botanical relationships between organism and environment. It was precisely this problem that Geddes packed Herbertson off to tackle with Charles Flahault in Montpellier in 1893.[70] Given this naturalistic impetus, it is understandable that Herbertson's own extremely popular *Man and His Work*, which purported to constitute an application of Le Play's sociology to human geography, turned out to be a bio-environmentalist caricature of that perspective. The celebrated differentiation of family types – 'patriarchal', 'stem', and 'unstable' – that were constitutive

Appreciation of his Life and Work', *Geography*, 50 (1965): 313–31, ref. on p. 316. See also L. J. Jay, 'A. J. Herbertson: his Services to School Geography', *Geography*, 50 (1965): 350–61.

[67] A. J. Herbertson, 'Recent Discussions', refs on pp. 421, 423.

[68] L. Dudley Stamp, 'Major Natural Regions: Herbertson after Fifty Years', *Geography*, 42 (1957): 201–16, ref. on p. 201; Gilbert, 'Herbertson', p. 322.

[69] A. J. Herbertson, 'The Major Natural Regions of the World: An Essay in Systematic Geography', *Geographical Journal*, 25 (1905): 300–12, ref. on p. 309.

[70] Meller, *Patrick Geddes*, p. 126.

of the Le Playan scheme, for instance, are conspicuous only by their absence. If anything they were subverted into a system of racialized categories over which, Herbertson claimed, 'no circumstance has a greater influence . . . than climate.'[71] Regional character mediated via ethnic 'modes of life' – nomadic, hunting, pastoral, agricultural, and so on – were just 'read off' the world's major biome categories – tundra, temperate forest, hot desert, equatorial rainforest, savannah, and suchlike. It is therefore not difficult to appreciate why later, when dilating on 'The Social Factor in General Geography' he should take the opportunity to redraw attention to 'the biological factor.'[72]

If the naturalism in Herbertson's output thus owed much to Geddes's influence, his geographical determinism doubtless reflected both his familiarity with Demolins and his close association with Mackinder who recruited him to Oxford in the spring of 1899. Certainly there was much in the transatlantic transfer of geographical ideas to confirm Herbertson's determinism. At his own summer schools in Oxford, Davis, Semple, and Brigham – all Neo-Lamarckian determinists – were among those featured. Yet, in the long run, Herbertson must not be mistaken for a materialistic reductionist. This is amply demonstrated in his posthumously published and tellingly entitled article on 'Regional Environment, Heredity and Consciousness.' Here, Neo-Lamarckian motifs structure the entire narrative. Criticisms of exclusionary hereditarianism, a partiality for embryological recapitulation, and convictions that social heritage were irreducible to germ plasm, all make their appearance. Moreover a holistic sense of the indissolubility of 'man' and 'environment' – to separate them was 'a murderous act' he said – had ultimately encouraged him to widen out the notion of environment to encompass the non-material. Because Herbertson had become convinced that there was 'a mental and spiritual environment as well as a material one,' he could urge, in language reminiscent of Geddes himself, that 'to grasp the idea of region' required 'a feeling of regional consciousness.' Accordingly, the regionalizing ritual involved

> no purely materialistic interpretation of history or of geography. The geographer is no more confined to materialistic considerations than the historian.

[71] A. J. and F. D. Herbertson, *Man and His Work. An Introduction to Human Geography* (London: A. and C. Black, 1920, first published 1899), p. 2. The same was true of his wife's volume on Frédéric Le Play, which, until the appearance of Brooke's study in 1970 was the only English-language introduction to Le Play. See F. D. Herbertson, *The Life of Frédéric Le Play*, edited by V. Branford and A. Farquharson (Ledbury: Le Play House, 1946).

[72] A. J. Herbertson, 'The Social Factor in General Geography', *Educational Bi-Monthly*, 1 (1906): 137–8, ref. on p. 137.

There is a *genius loci* as well as a *Zeitgeist* – a spirit of a place as well as of a time. No social psychology is worth much that is not also regional psychology, and no regional psychology is possible without a loving familiarity with the region . . . No simple chronicle suffices for the historian, no superficial geographical inventory suffices for the geographer.[73]

Here then, to use perhaps an anachronistic modern designation, we find expressed a poetics of place. Like Geddes, who himself articulated a synthesis of scientist and romantic, Herbertson came to suspect that 'each place has its *genius loci*, of which the poet is usually the best interpreter.'[74] So, just as the mainsprings of Herbertson's Neo-Lamarckian commitments – notwithstanding his early exposure to the Neo-Darwinism of Weismann – are to be located in Geddes's legacy,[75] so too are the humanistic sentiments to which Herbertson increasingly gave voice in the early years of the twentieth century.

Although he was perhaps more inclined to rework the Geddesian credo, there is, I think, much to be said for the view that Herbert John Fleure (1877–1969) more profoundly absorbed the essentials of Geddes's vision than any other of his geographical enthusiasts. Fleure's experience of assisting Geddes run a school of civics in Dublin in 1914, his recruitment of Geddes as a visiting lecturer at his own Aberystwyth summer schools for geography teachers, his intimate involvement with both the Regional Survey Association and Le Play Society, and an extensive correspondence during the war years, were just some of the diffusion tracks along which the Geddes outlook migrated. Besides, on several occasions Fleure made public his indebtedness to the flamboyant Scotsman. When writing on 'Geography and Evolution', for example, he spoke of the power exerted by the 'sparkling mind of Sir Patrick Geddes,' and later wrote an appreciative biographical sketch for the *Sociological Review*.[76] For reasons such as these, J. A. Campbell felt constrained to focus his penetrating evaluation of the

---

[73] A. J. Herbertson, 'Regional Environment, Heredity and Consciousness', *Geographical Teacher*, 8 (1916): 147–53, refs on pp. 149, 152, 153.

[74] A. J. Herbertson, 'On the One-Inch Ordnance Survey Map, With Special Reference to the Oxford Sheet', *Geographical Teacher*, 1 (1902): 150–66, ref. on p. 166. In the same issue of this journal M. W. Keating called for the cultivation of the 'geographical imagination', suggesting that the use of travel and fictional literature would be of great service. M. W. Keating, 'Geography as a Correlating Subject', *Geographical Teacher*, 1 (1902): 145–9.

[75] See the discussion in Campbell and Livingstone, 'Neo-Lamarckism and the Development of Geography'.

[76] H. J. Fleure, 'Geography and Evolution', *Geography*, 34 (1949): 1–9, ref. on p. 7; H. J. Fleure, 'Patrick Geddes (1854–1932)', *Sociological Review*, n.s. 1/2 (1953): 5–13.

sources of Fleure's humanism very largely on what he called the 'Geddesian Fugue'.[77]

Like Geddes, Fleure had originally pursued studies in the natural sciences, particularly zoology, and even during his undergraduate days at Aberystwyth came to question the all-sufficiency of the Darwinian natural selection mechanism.[78] Certainly he absorbed the profoundly ecological cast of Darwin's theory – its emphasis on the complex interplay of the organic and inorganic – and later spoke of the 'vision' he had there glimpsed 'of the stream of change, all-embracing change, flowing through space-time.'[79] Yet as early as March 1899 he was using Spencerian apparatus to undermine Weismann's Neo-Darwinism. And within a couple of years he was clearly feeling the draw of Lamarckian principles. To be sure, 'the balance of evidence' might currently be 'against the transmission of . . . acquired characters,' he confessed; but recent experiments were beginning to 'show the peculiar susceptibility of the germ, and embryo, to influence of its environment.'[80] These early suspicions followed Fleure's career shifts from geology, botany, and zoology to geography and anthropology, moves disclosed in the succession of positions he occupied at the University of College of Wales, Aberystwyth. Between 1908 and 1910 he was in charge of the geology department; in 1910 he was appointed professor of zoology; and then in 1917 he took up the chair of geography and anthropology.[81] Those early zoological qualms over Neo-Darwinism thus found anthropological expression in a series of convictions: that there was a correlation – as a consequence of the 'interplay of heredity and environment' – between anthropological type and regional environment in Wales; that cultural atrophy might be understood in terms of organic degeneration; that in racial evolution 'fitness' was necessarily relative to social circumstance; and that the pygmies in Africa could be degenerate remnants in a climate where 'debilitation makes achievement difficult.'[82] This latter turning to biological

[77] J. A. Campbell, *Some Sources of the Humanism of H. J. Fleure* (School of Geography, University of Oxford, Research Paper no. 2, 1972).

[78] That this hesitancy was lifelong is clear from the following: H. J. Fleure and Harold Peake, *Apes and Man – The Corridors of Time, Volume 1* (Oxford: Oxford University Press, 1927), p. 31; H. J. Fleure, 'Geographical Thought in a Changing World', *Geographical Review*, 34 (1944): 515–28.

[79] Fleure, 'Geography and Evolution', p. 2.

[80] H. J. Fleure, 'The Factors of Organic Evolution', *University College of Wales Magazine*, 24 (1901): 71–3, ref. on p. 72. See also Campbell and Livingstone, 'Neo-Lamarckism and the Development of Geography', p. 283.

[81] See the biographical sketch by T. W. Freeman, 'Herbert John Fleure, 1877–1969', *Geographers: Biobibliographical Studies*, 11 (1987): 35–51.

[82] H. J. Fleure and E. Davies, 'Physical Character Among Welshmen', *Journal of the Royal Anthropological Institute*, 88 (1958): 45–95, ref. on p. 75; H. J. Fleure, 'The Geographical

degenerationism to explain cultural decline had its sources in Fleure's uneasiness with unilinear portraits of social evolution, and he used it to account for the occurrence of chronologically later but less elaborate cultural artefacts. His resort (notwithstanding the critiques of functionalists like Malinowski) to the idea of 'survivals' – persistent cultural forms to be found in remote geographical districts – was also indicative of his disinclination to see human culture as treading a predetermined evolutionary path, as was his willingness to acknowledge the possibility of parallel cultural developments in different places.[83]

If Fleure's evolutionary leanings mirrored those of Geddes, so too did his emphasis on the region. Whereas Herbertson had more than flirted with determinism, Fleure resolutely repudiated such a construal of the relations between environment and society. So, while he applauded the ecological thrust of Herbertson's natural regions, he later confessed that he had always entertained doubts about his 'mapping of the world in a large number of regions based on climate in the main. The idea of fitting the human story into a physical frame seemed to me open to criticism.'[84] Similarly, in an early review of Semple's *Influences of Geographical Environment*, he subverted any absolutist implications of her project by wryly observing: 'If the book claimed to be an account of the life-work of man, it might well be criticised for leaving out too completely the unceasing influence of what Bergson has named the "Elan Vital", whether in the great man or in the more average citizen, but the aim is the more confined and fragmentary one of tracing environmental influences.'[85] For reasons such as these, Fleure was not especially sympathetic to Geddes's 'Valley Section', which smacked too much of Demolins-style determinism. Thus he felt the need to augment Herbertson's naturalistic system with a more humane set of categories, and produced in 1917 a paper on 'Régions Humaines', appropriately published in the Vidalian *Annales de Géographie*. The impact of the message first articulated there was to reach English-language geography through a

---

Study of Society and World Problems', *Reports of the British Association for the Advancement of Science* (1932): 103–18, ref. on p. 107. These extracts are cited in Campbell and Livingstone, 'Neo-Lamarckism and the Development of Geography', p. 284.

[83] These issues are insightfully examined in the second half of Campbell's monograph.

[84] H. J. Fleure, 'Recollections of A. J. Herbertson', *Geography*, 50 (1965): 348–9, ref. on p. 348.

[85] H. J. Fleure, 'The Influence of Geographic Environment. A Review of Miss Semple's Work', *Geographical Teacher*, 35 (1911): 65–8, ref. on p. 66. Fleure was also highly critical of Griffith Taylor's *Environment and Race*. See his review in *Geographical Journal*, 70 (1927): 587–8.

revised version which appeared in the *Scottish Geographical Magazine* two years later.[86]

Here Fleure sought to reconceptualize the region by taking with much greater seriousness lived experience. He thus spoke of regions of difficulty, of privation, of increment, of nomadism, and so on. And these were not just the product of a symbiotic union of people and place; they were also the consequence of the shifting relationships between people and people. The 'civic sympathy' and 'social reintegration', on which Geddes had elaborated, became for Fleure crucial processes in social evolution guided by mutual aid. Indeed this emphasis on cooperative evolutionary mechanisms – derived in large measure from Kropotkin – both undergirded the 'Biological Socialism' of which Fleure spoke and impressed on him the significance of the intercourse of cultures in regional consciousness.[87] These contact zones in fact were of momentous consequence in the unfolding human drama and persuaded Fleure that a humanized regionalism could not traffic in cartographic precision. The 'linear boundary', he insisted, 'however necessary it may be under our outworn system of aggressive states in politics, is an artificiality when applied to the study of peoples.'[88]

Moreover contact zones played a crucial role in Fleure's accounts of key moments in human cultural history. The emergence of monotheism, for instance, he attributed to the 'presence side by side of diverse cosmogonies and schemes of ritual with attendant mythologies' – consequent upon the subjugation of Bronze Age agriculturalists by the horsemen of the steppes – and the ensuing quest for cosmic coherence.[89] Because it was along such *zones de bordure* that ideas, beliefs, skills, and artefacts were shared, they played a major part in the processes of cultural evolution.

Throughout the corpus of Fleure's geography a moral stance, muted but audible, is clearly discernible. It surfaces, for example, in the moral topography that he elaborated in his musings on the region. Aware of the precariousness of biological overspecialization, and enthralled with Geddesian organic analogies, he applauded the virtues of regional economic diversification.[90] Again he conceived of the geographical task as bound up

[86] H. J. Fleure, 'Régions Humaines', *Annales de Géographie*, 26 (1917): 161–74; H. J. Fleure, 'Human Regions', *Scottish Geographical Magazine*, 35 (1919): 31–45.

[87] J. A. Campbell points out that Fleure delivered a paper on 'Biological Socialism' to a joint meeting of the Fabian Society, University College of Wales, and the Aberystwyth Women Students Social Reform League on 5 November 1901. See Campbell, *The Humanism of H. J. Fleure*, p. 41.

[88] H. J. Fleure, *The Peoples of Europe* (London: Oxford University Press, 1922), p. 28.

[89] H. J. Fleure, 'Ritual and Ethic: A Study of a Change in Ancient Religions about 800–500 BC', *Bulletin of the John Rylands Library*, 22 (1938): 435–54, ref. on p. 437.

[90] See Fleure, 'Human Regions', p. 100.

with the inculcation of a *morale planetaire* because it fostered cultural diversity and encouraged international understanding and peace.[91] Such persuasions would be worthy of more detailed consideration. Here, however, I want to turn to the more subtle, but arguably more profound, moral posture that formed a kind of sub-text for the anthropometric mapping that Fleure carried out in the early part of the twentieth century.

As we have already noted, links between geography and anthropology were both deep and lasting. But they had more recently been reinforced with the publication of A. H. Keane's *Man: Past and Present* in the Cambridge Geographical Series in 1900 and in the lectures on anthropogeography that the Cambridge ethnologist, A. C. Haddon, delivered to the university's geographers between 1903 and 1917. Indeed, both authors were required reading for a degree in geography in several universities.[92] As for Fleure it was both his geographical and his anthropological competences that earned him a Fellowship of the Royal Society, an award largely based on his cartographic survey of Welsh anthropometric types. In this study, as he himself was later to observe, his methods were 'geographical in a higher degree than such work has usually been.'[93]

Fleure certainly set his face steadfastly against racism in every shape and form, fiercely criticizing the Nordic myth and other schemes of racial purity.[94] Yet in his 1918 investigation into the racial history of Britain he applied Ripley's threefold taxonomy of 'Nordic', 'Alpine', and 'Mediterranean' to European ethnic groups. This classification scheme was already well known to British geography, for it had been used in Marion Newbigin's *Modern Geography* of 1911.[95] While the Nordics were presented as a significant element in the landed aristocracy and in overseas colonial expansionism, the Mediterranean race type, although contributing much to church life, medical expertise, and poetic imagination, were maladapted to town life and rapidly degenerated in slum conditions. In Britain,

[91] H. J. Fleure, 'The Teaching of Geography', in A. Watson Bain (ed.), *The Modern Teacher: Essays on Educational Aims and Methods* (London, 1921), pp. 173–94, ref. on p. 179.

[92] Dickinson observed that both 'these ethnologists were friends of geography, and their works, as I know from personal experience, were required reading forty years ago for an honours degree in geography in several British universities.' Dickinson, *Makers of Modern Geography* p. 62.

[93] H. J. Fleure, 'Ancient Wales – Anthropological Evidence', *Transactions of the Honourable Society of Cymmrodorion* (1915–16): 75–164, ref. on p. 75.

[94] See H. J. Fleure, 'The Nordic Myth: a Critique of Current Racial Theories', *Eugenics Review*, 22 (1930–1): 117–21; H. J. Fleure, 'Racialism and Toleration', in E. Ashworth Underwood (ed.), *Science, Medicine and History. Essays on the Evolution of Scientific Thought and Medical Practice* (London: Oxford University Press, 1953), vol. 2, pp. 401–8.

[95] See Marion I. Newbigin, *Modern Geography* (London: Williams and Norgate, 1911), chapter 8 'The Races of Europe'.

the question of the cultural relationships between these two racial types, which Fleure labelled the English and Welsh traditions respectively, was a major issue. His hope was that 'instead of looking upon the Celtic tradition as the poor keepsake of a conquered people, all but exterminated by the Anglo-Saxon conquerors, we might with more truth look upon it as an heirloom, a precious ancient phase of our own tradition, to lose which would be to impoverish the British peoples forever.' When the 'fever of industrialism' and the spirit of war-mongering had finally subsided, Fleure hoped that the riches of the Celtic tradition would be rediscovered.[96] In this way he advanced what Rich calls 'a liberal paternalism that in the colonial context frequently expressed itself in a form of benevolent segregation.'[97]

Suspicious of urban industrial societies, Fleure thus harboured a moral enthusiasm for those rural values that persisted among the racial remnants of the more remote western areas of the Welsh principality. A sort of bio-social psychology snakes its way through much of his writing, so much so that his conviction that the Celtic fringe acted as the 'ultimate refuge' of 'old thoughts and visions that had been lost to the world' merged with Cyril Fox's observations on the 'survival of the Celtic language [and] the persistence in the west of very old racial stocks,' though it stopped short of the more racist Continental Celticism promoted by Numa Denis Fustel de Coulanges and Maurice Barrès.[98] Fleure, it is clear, was sure that the 'little dark people' – the fundamental Welsh type – had cultivated music, poetry, literature, and religion, leaving commercial activities to the coastal Nordic types.[99] Here the moral economy could, to one degree or another, be mapped onto regional and racial characters.

To sustain these judgements, Fleure found it necessary to insist that head forms displayed considerable persistence over time, and that human types were not entirely cosmopolitan, for, as he observed, 'wherever different climatic zones have been invaded, the intruders have failed to secure a permanent footing, perished outright, or disappeared by absorption.'[100] Such sentiments were entirely in keeping with John Beddoe's conviction – and

[96] H. J. Fleure, 'The Racial History of the British People'. *Geographical Review*, 5 (1918): 216–31, refs on pp. 230–1.

[97] Rich, *Race and Empire in British Politics'* p. 111.

[98] H. J. Fleure, *Wales and Her People* (Wrexham: Hughes and Son, 1926), p. 1; Cyril Fox, *The Personality of Britain: Its Influence on Inhabitant and Invader in Prehistoric and Early Historic Times* (Cardiff: National Museum of Wales, 1932), p. 32.

[99] On this I have learned much from reading parts of Pyrs Gruffudd's doctoral dissertation, 'Landscape and Nationhood: Tradition and Modernity in Rural Wales, 1900–1950' (Ph. D. thesis, Loughborough University, 1989).

[100] Cited in Stepan, *The Idea of Race in Science'* p. 106.

Fleure drew substantially on Beddoe's earlier 1885 British survey, *The Races of Britain* – that race traits displayed remarkable fixedness.[101] But the very fact that he had to look *back* to Beddoe was, perhaps, symptomatic of the increasing distrust of anthropometry that surfaced in the early decades of the twentieth century, although Fleure himself had a considerable personal influence on anthropology in the 1920s.[102] Still, he had no option but to contest Franz Boas's latest findings on the modification of the European head-form in America because he felt they 'would destroy the foundations of anthropological research for the elucidation of race history.'[103]

Fleure certainly had little intention of elaborating a Celticized racism. He *did* explicitly affirm that there were dangers in applying the term 'Celtic' – a linguistic designation – to physical anthropology, and that 'very little is as yet known as to the correlation of physical and psychical type.'[104] And yet he would shortly announce that it was 'highly probable' that 'physical type and mental characteristics are correlated in some way.'[105] After all, he had for long enough been mapping correlations between anthropological type and behavioural traits. Recall his conviction, articulated in 1918 and now repeated in 1951, that the dolichocephalic, dark-haired inhabitants of western Britain – particularly in Wales and western Scotland – had provided the country with important 'elements in medicine and surgery'. He still suspected that while the preponderance of singing, oratory, and religious zealotry in Wales might be the result of environment, it was a real 'possibility that racial characteristics may play a part too.'[106]

The suspicion that Fleure was elaborating (albeit as a textual substratum) a moral geography, is, I think, confirmed in other ways too. In 1922, for instance, he amplified on what he took to be the links between linguistic geography and political achievement: 'whereas the peoples of Roman and Teutonic speech have built up the organization known as the nation-state,'

---

[101] In 1922, for example, he insisted that the 'facts of Mendelian inheritance' had confirmed 'the maintenance of types very little changed even through thousands of years.' Fleure, *Peoples of Europe*, p. 9.

[102] See for example, A. H. Keane's *Man. Past and Present* (Cambridge: University Press, 1899), pp. 522–4; A. C. Haddon, *The Races of Man and Their Distribution* (Cambridge: Cambridge University Press, 1924), p. 57.

[103] H. J. Fleure and T. C. James, 'Geographical Distribution of Anthropological Types in Wales', *Journal of the Royal Anthropological Institute of Great Britain and Ireland*, 46 (1916): 35–153, ref. on p. 37.

[104] Ibid., pp. 118, 152.

[105] H. J. Fleure, *The Races of England and Wales. A Survey of Recent Research* (London: Benn Brothers, 1923), p. 180.

[106] H. J. Fleure, *A Natural History of Man in Britain, Conceived as a Study of Changing Relations between Men and Environments* (London, 1951), pp. 195, 197.

he affirmed, 'in most cases on a basis of linguistic unity, the peoples of the Slavonic regions . . . have hardly achieved this.'[107] The following year he confirmed that 'the little dark long-head better resists factory conditions, mining conditions, and town overcrowding than the big fair type. It would thence seem possible to argue that industrialism has increased greatly the importance of this element in our population.'[108] And finally, in 1951, he lauded the peoples occupying the Welsh moorland, an 'unfavourable environment' that had 'somehow drawn to itself a self-conscious community of miners of remarkable intellectual and moral power, diluted with flotsam and jetsam from many distant areas.'[109] To be sure, Fleure's moralistic geography is not to be thought of as a surface feature of his vast output; but that there was some intertwining of his scholarly enthusiasms – regional character, anthropometric localization, rural preferences, cultural survivals, and behavioural traits – is, I think, beyond doubt. For Fleure the regionalizing ritual was an exercise in moral retrieval 'even as it had been a political crusade for Geddes.

The regional strain within British geography could, of course, be charted via the careers of other practitioners. In the Fleure vein we might consider the work of his successor at Aberystwyth, Darryl Forde, whose anthropology merged with the French historical geography of Febvre and Vidal, or Estyn Evans's luminous studies of the personality of Ireland. In an effort to counterbalance geography's traditionally environmental concerns, Forde insisted that 'human geography demands as much knowledge of humanity as of geography.'[110] For his part, Evans expressed his gratitude to 'Professor H. J. Fleure, who taught me to study regional social evolution as a continuous interaction between people and their environment.'[111] In a different vein, J. F. Unstead's more naturalistic system of regional classification, P. M. Roxby's delimitation of agricultural regions in England, and H. C. Darby's painstaking historical reconstruction of a Domesday geography of England would all merit scrutiny in order to ascertain precisely what factors were at work here.[112] But my objective has not been to

[107] Fleure, *Peoples of Europe*, p. 88.
[108] Fleure, *Race of England and Wales*, p. 107.
[109] Fleure, *Natural History of Man in Britain*, p. 13.
[110] C. Darryl Forde, *Habitat, Economy and Society. A Geographical Introduction to Ethnology* (London: Methuen, 1934), p. 465. See also his 'Values in Human Geography', *Geographical Teacher*, 13 (1925): 216–21.
[111] E. Estyn Evans, *Irish Folk Ways* (London: Routledge and Kegan Paul, 1957), p. xvi. See also E. Estyn Evans, *Irish Heritage* (Dundalk: Dundalgan Press, 1942); E. Estyn Evans, *Mourne Country* (Dundalk: Dundalgan Press, 1967); E. Estyn Evans, *The Personality of Ireland* (Belfast: Blackstaff Press, 1981).

present an exhaustive survey; rather it has been to convey something of the range of intellectual, political, and moral interests that certain key theorists brought to their investigation of regional character. Now I want to turn finally to the United States to identify some of the forces that advocates of geographical particularism, especially Carl Sauer, mobilized to oppose what they considered to be a vulgar environmentalism.

HISTORICAL PARTICULARISM AND AMERICAN GEOGRAPHY

In the early years of the twentieth century a good deal of American geography, as we have seen, found itself implicated in what was described by opponents as an increasingly unsophisticated environmental determinism under the influence of figures like Davis, Semple, Brigham, and Huntington. Yet even as the canons of geographical causation were becoming enshrined as American geography's *raison d'être*, the entire tradition of positivist anthropogeography, as it was dubbed, was elsewhere being dismissed as a hollow dogma. The mono-causal character of environmentalism was subjected to anthropological critique in 1928 and discarded, because 'geographical conditions by themselves have no creative force and are certainly no absolute determinants of culture.' Besides, as this anthropologist put it, advocates of the theory failed to take with sufficient seriousness culture's historicity (the 'overlaying of geographical by historical factors' as Lowie later expressed it)[113] which meant that the environment never created a culture *de novo*, and that in any case 'many different types of culture are found adjusted to similar types of environment.'[114]

Earlier in an investigation of *The Mind of Primitive Man* (1911), this same critic had already expressed his preference for historical idealism over environmental reductionism as a means of understanding cultural forms. 'No matter how great an influence we may ascribe to environment,' he wrote, 'that influence can become active only by being exerted upon the

---

[112] J. F. Unstead, 'A System of Regional Geography', *Geography*, 18 (1933): 175–87; P. M. Roxby, 'The Agricultural Geography of England on a Regional Basis', *Geographical Teacher*, 7 (1913–14): 316–21. H. C. Darby (ed.), *An Historical Geography of England before AD 1800* (Cambridge: Cambridge University Press, 1936); this and subsequent volumes in the series were entirely in keeping with E. W. Gilbert's vision of historical geography as presenting a picture of the regional geography of the past. E. W. Gilbert, 'What is Historical Geography?' *Scottish Geographical Magazine*, 48 (1932): 129–36.

[113] *History of Ethnological Theory*, p. 144.

[114] Franz Boas, *Anthropology and Modern Life* (New York: W. W. Norton, 1928), pp. 240, 242.

mind; so that the characteristics of the mind must enter into the resultant forms of social activity.'[115] Indeed the conceptual roots of this anti-environmental determinist stance are traceable to the article on 'The Study of Geography' that he had published in 1888 and which expressed his sense of irresolution about the geographical enterprise. Here the contrast was drawn between a physicalist anthropogeography which conceived of its task as the search for general laws, and a historicist cosmography that focused on the description of particular terrestrial phenomena. The methods of natural science thus provided the model for the former, those of the historian the latter. Juxtaposing Comte's positivism and Humboldt's 'Cosmos', he contrasted the logical needs of the physical scientist with the 'affective' impulse of the cosmographer.[116] But it was not just a matter of allocating items to either of these realms. What the essay disclosed was its author's 'inner-tension', as Stocking calls it, over the very nature of scientific inquiry – a tension with which he had been struggling for nearly a decade.[117] Its resolution takes us to the heart of American anthropology's repudiation of determinist geography, and its espousal of historical particularism.

Both this article, and the volumes from which I have been quoting, were written by the distinguished anthropologist Franz Boas (1858–1942), who conducted for fifty years a polemical crusade against crude environmental determinisms and, as one observer puts it, 'indoctrinated several generations of students in the historicist mode of conceptualizing environment.'[118] Boas's academic career at the university of Kiel in the late 1870s had begun with the study of physics and geography.[119] Shortly after receiving his doctorate for work on water colour in 1881, Boas decided to concentrate more single-mindedly on geography, and turned his attention to Eskimo migration as a means of determining the relationships between culture and environment. Thus began Boas's intellectual journey from physics to ethnology via geography.

[115] Franz Boas, *The Mind of Primitive Man* (New York: Macmillan, 1911), p. 192.

[116] Franz Boas, 'The Study of Geography', *Science*, 9 (1887): 137–41.

[117] George W. Stocking, Jr., 'The Basic Assumptions of Boasian Anthropology', in George W. Stocking, Jr. (ed.), *A Franz Boas Reader. The Shaping of American Anthropology, 1883–1911* (Chicago: University of Chicago Press, 1974), pp. 1–20, ref. on p. 9.

[118] William Speth, 'The Anthropogeographic Theory of Franz Boas', *Anthropos*, 73 (1978): 1–31, ref. on p. 9.

[119] I have used the following sources: Melville J. Herskovits, *Franz Boas. The Science of Man in the Making* (New York: Scribner's, 1953); George W. Stocking, Jr., 'From Physics to Ethnology: Franz Boas' Arctic Expedition as Problem in the Historiography of the Behavioral Sciences', *Journal of the History of the Behavioral Sciences*, 1 (1965): 53–66. See also Marshall Hyatt, *Franz Boas. Social Activist: The Dynamics of Ethnicity* (New York: Greenwood Press, 1990).

When Boas undertook his 1883 expedition to Baffinland he was thoroughly versed in the historical geography of Carl Ritter, especially as mediated through the teachings of his disciple Theobald Fischer. Through Fischer he came to appreciate the spirit of romantic idealism. At the same time his studies in physics were pushing him in the direction of a monistic materialism. The merging of these diverse strands in German thought comes through in his monograph, *Baffin-land*, which was published a year after his return. For the volume was replete with the leitmotifs of what he called physicalist anthropogeography and its determinist-naturalistic thrust. But over the next few years he came increasingly to question that perspective. Later he reflected that the environmental influences he had traced were too obvious and the study too intellectually shallow to cast any real light on the forces that lay behind human behaviour. So by the time he embarked in 1886 on his second field trip, this time to British Columbia, where he would encounter with the Kwakiutl of Vancouver Island, he was turning from anthropogeographical towards historical modes of thinking.

In large part Boas's anthropogeographical defection was a consequence of his encounter with Wilhelm Dilthey's philosophy of history. During the 1880s Dilthey had endeavoured to free history from enslavement to the presuppositions of positivistic natural science. Distinguishing between the *Naturwissenschaften* and the *Geisteswissenschaften* – that is, between sciences dealing with the physical world and those dealing with human culture – Dilthey urged that while the former strove for 'explanation', 'understanding' was the aim of the latter. Historical periods and cultural traditions just could not be reduced to some mechanistic, law-like formula. Analytical generalities simply failed to take account of historical and cultural particularity. Armed with such convictions, it is entirely understandable that Boas should question the idea of unilinear cultural progress based on some inexorable evolutionary law. The 'orgy of evolutionary and diffusionist speculation had nauseated him', Harris writes, 'so that he could never again feel at ease in the presence of a generalization.'[120] Besides, the neo-Kantian philosophy to which he had been exposed under the influence of Benno Erdmann (who, as we have seen, had a significant impact on Schlüter) began to find expression in his growing conviction that the interpretative activity of the human mind largely conditioned the nature of observed objects in the 'external' realm. The idealist thrust of the Kantian undertaking in which cognition preceded experience thus reinforced the lessons Boas was learning from Dilthey.

[120] Harris, *The Rise of Anthropological Theory*, p. 260.

The radical dualism that Dilthey propounded was to find its way into Boas's 1888 scrutiny of the geographical project, and his increasing sympathy with Dilthey's way of seeing things later found expression in his affirmation that 'We may be able to *understand* social phenomena. I do not believe we shall ever be able to *explain* them by reducing one and all of them to social laws.'[121] Boas's critique of environmental determinism and his particularistic conviction that 'In ethnology, all is individuality'[122] thus drew philosophical sustenance from Dilthey's philosophy of history. The 'concrete particularity of the specific historical case,' as Parsons was later to describe it, was to become the fulcrum of Boas's historicist anthropology.[123] Accordingly Boas always preferred to work from the actual distribution of empirical phenomena rather than from conceptual abstractions and ideal taxonomic categories.

Yet none of this must be taken to imply that Boas entirely dismissed the conditioning power of environment. On the contrary, he again and again reiterated its importance;[124] what he repudiated was its elevation into a monistic account only too typical of the newly professionalized geographical fraternity. This repudiation, moreover, was matched only by his antipathy for the racial prejudice that he saw displayed in both physical and cultural anthropology. On the former front, he set out to provide a critique of the hierarchical racial formalism of his day by urging a nominalist approach to racial typecasting. The very categories that anthropologists and geographers were using in racial cartography – the mapping of dolichocephalic and brachycephalic crania, for instance – were regarded by Boas merely as arbitrary systems of classification that anthropologists had imposed on a statistical spectrum. What reinforced this judgement was his conviction that no one individual instantiated all the 'typical' traits of the supposed racial type. His study of the environmental (both physical and social) modification of the bodily forms of immigrants was thus designed to undermine the idea of racial fixity and to replace the notion of racial type with statistical distributions.[125] This Lamarckian-inclined project effectively

---

[121] Boas, *Anthropology and Modern Life*, pp. 215–16.

[122] Franz Boas, 'Museums of Ethnology and their Classification', *Science*, 9 (1887): 587–9, ref. on p. 589.

[123] Talcott Parsons, *The Structure of Social Action* (New York: McGrawHill Book Company, 1937), p. 477.

[124] See Speth, 'Anthropogeographic Theory of Franz Boas'.

[125] See Franz Boas, 'Race,' in Franz Boas (ed.), *General Anthropology* (Boston: D. Heath, 1938), pp. 95–123. Here he noted: 'If we describe individuals composing a population by a number of measurements . . . it appears that only very few are what we might call typical specimens of the population.' p. 99.

took the wind out of the sails of those still mesmerized by essentialist ideas of a pure race. Indeed Boas's statisticizing assured him that so-called racial hybrids displayed greater fertility than parent stocks and, contrary to many, he urged that intermixture was biologically favourable.[126] On the cultural front, his firm belief in cultural particularities led him to advocate a mild cultural relativism that insisted that cultures could only be understood in their own terms and therefore that ranking on a hierarchical scale was impossible.[127] Imbued with the mystical view of nationality that his teacher, Bastian, had espoused, Boas urged that culture had to be thought of as a self-contained whole.

Boas's anthropological historicism was mediated to a new generation of students largely through the work of such dedicated disciples as Robert H. Lowie and Alfred L. Kroeber, who were students of his at Columbia. And it was through them that Carl Sauer (plate 8.1) later glimpsed the Boasian vision at Berkeley.[128] That Sauer was drawn into this conceptual orbit is hardly surprising. For the Boasians at once retained a robust interest in the geographical enterprise even as they dismissed geographical determinism. Kroeber, for example, was described – with adjectival exuberance – by Feldman as 'an idiographic, anti-cultural materialist historical particularist.'[129]

The sense of cultural particularism that Sauer imbibed from Lowie and Kroeber quickened his dismissal of the American geographical tradition as an unsophisticated transatlantic offshoot of Ratzelian anthropogeography. Indeed he observed that it was in England and the United States that Ratzel's categorizations were most widespread.[130] Semple, for example, he depicted as a mere American mouthpiece for her German master, and at one point confessed that he could see little that Ratzel had contributed to human geography beyond the notion of the culture area.[131] In these

---

[126] See George W. Stocking, Jr., *Race, Culture and Evolution. Essays in the History of Anthropology* (Chicago: University of Chicago Press, 1982), chapter 8 'The Critique of Racial Formalism'. Among other things, Stocking discusses Boasian statistics in the context of the debate between the biometricians and Mendelians over blending versus particulate inheritance.

[127] A Marxist evaluation of the anthropogeographic materialism and cultural relativism that characterized Boas's anthropology at different times is available in Maurice Bloch, *Marxism and Anthropology: The History of a Relationship* (Oxford: Oxford University Press, 1983).

[128] See Roger T. Trindell, 'Franz Boas and American Geography', *Professional Geographer*, 21 (1969): 328–32.

[129] Douglas A. Feldman, 'The History of the Relationship between Environment and Culture in Ethnological Thought: An Overview,' *Journal of the History of the Behavioral Sciences*, 11 (1975): 67–81, ref. on p. 74.

[130] Carl O. Sauer, 'Geography, Cultural', in E. R. A. Seligman (ed.), *Encyclopedia of the Social Sciences* (New York: Macmillan, 1934), vol. 6, pp. 621–4.

[131] Later, in his 1971 assessment of Ratzel's time in America, Sauer found rather more to praise. See the discussion in Sauer, 'Formative Years of Ratzel in the United States'.

Plate 8.1   Carl Sauer, reproduced by kind permission of the Department of Geography, University of California, Berkeley.

judgements he was – consciously or not – following the contours of Boas's critique and it is therefore not surprising that they appeared in the multi-volume *Encyclopedia of the Social Sciences* that was published in 1934.[132] Boas himself headed the list of the board of directors and the commissioning of Sauer to write biographical entries on Ratzel and Semple ensured that the battle lines Boas himself had drawn up would remain firm. That frontier precision, however, could only be maintained by a good deal of typecasting in the portrayal of the environmental determinists. In a later encyclopedia of the social sciences Mikesell took the trouble to emphasize that Ratzel was not such an extreme environmentalist as stereotypes had frequently suggested, and Spate was at pains to point out that Huntington 'gave considerable weight to heredity . . . and to the persistence of traits through endogamy.'[133] As for Semple, who seems to have been characterized on all sides as the archetypal environmental determinist, she was not so single-sighted as might be thought. In the Anglo-Saxons of the Kentucky Mountains, for example, Semple believed a pure racial stock – notwithstanding the disadvantages of its local environment – continued to exhibit 'the inextinguishable excellence of the Anglo-Saxon race.' The 'natively strong and acute' intellects of which she spoke, her reference to 'the prevalence of that democratic spirit,' and her discussion of linguistic and cultural survivals, are hardly what one would expect from an author ordinarily portrayed as a determinist who never once allowed cultural factors to play any causal role in social evolution.[134]

Whatever the reasons, it does seem that Sauer's fierce assault on American geography in the Ratzelian vein, and his willingness to trade in the historical abstractions, possibilism and determinism, owed something to the antipathy to environmentalism and the enthusiasm for comparative culture history that he had learned from Kroeber.[135] In Berkeley anthropology,

[132] Carl O. Sauer, 'Friedrich Ratzel', in *Encyclopedia of the Social Sciences*, vol. 13, pp. 120–1; Carl O. Sauer 'Ellen Churchill Semple', in ibid., vol. 13, pp. 661–2.

[133] Marvin W. Mikesell, 'Friedrich Ratzel', in David L. Sills (ed.), *International Encyclopedia of the Social Sciences* (New York: Macmillan and Free Press, 1968), vol. 13, pp. 327–9; O. H. K. Spate, 'Ellsworth Huntington', in ibid., vol. 7, pp. 26–7.

[134] Ellen Churchill Semple, 'The Anglo-Saxons of the Kentucky Mountains: A Study in Anthropogeography', *Geographical Journal*, 17 (1901): 588–623, refs on pp. 609, 619, 623. Gregory astutely remarks that she 'had a more qualified understanding than a first reading might suggest . . . [but that] her "rhetorical flourish" virtually invited caricature.' Derek Gregory, 'Environmental Determinism', in R. J. Johnston, Derek Gregory and David M. Smith (eds), *The Dictionary of Human Geography* (Oxford: Blackwell, 2nd edn, 1986), pp. 131–3, ref. on p. 132. See also Gordon Lewthwaite, 'Environmentalism and Determinism: A Search for Clarification', *Annals of the Association of American Geographers*, 56 (1966): 1–23.

[135] See Carl O. Sauer, 'The Morphology of Landscape', *University of California Publications in Geography*, 2, 2 (1925): 19–54. Here (p. 52) he cited Kroeber's *Anthropology* (1923) in sup-

Sauer thus found reinforcement for the mordant anti-environmentalism that he had entertained since his Michigan days when he encountered the earlier polemics of German geography.[136] From Hettner, for example, he learned that to identify the core of geography in terms of some abstract *relationship* (as the environmental determinists did) was fundamentally misconceived. A field of science needed substantive *content*, for without a 'category of objects' to call its own, geography had only, in Hettner's words, a 'parasitic existence'. Sauer's exposure to the German tradition, however, did more than provide sources for an anti-environmentalist tirade; it encouraged him to promote the Germanic 'transformation of the natural landscape into the cultural landscape' as 'a satisfactory working program' for geography. Moreover, because such landscape transformations were what 'functionally differentiated' cultural areas from each other, he found Richthofen's 'term "chorology", the science of regions' intellectually congenial.[137] His celebrated monograph on 'The Morphology of Landscape', first published in 1925, had already given voice to Passarge's *Landschaftskunde* as providing a coherent statement of geography's goals that was entirely compatible with the anthropology of Clark Wissler – another of Boas's students. Indeed, at this point he believed that 'a gradual coalescence of social anthropology and of geography may represent the first of a series of fusions into a larger science of man.'[138]

From Boasian anthropology *and* German *Kulturlandschaft* Sauer thus came to conceive of geography as culture history in its regional articulation. To him, regional geography really had 'meaning only as a study of culture areas.' Thus correspondence during the 1930s reveals his denunciation of

port of his assertion that 'environmentalism has been shooting at neither cause nor at effect, but rather it is bagging its own decoys.' In the light of this direct reference to Kroeber in 1925 it is startling to read Martin Kenzer's efforts to deny intellectual connections between Kroeber and Sauer. Kenzer finds it 'difficult to see Kroeber's hand in either of Sauer's early "methodologic works," (and especially in the "Morphology").' Moreover, because the first personal communication between them did not occur until about a month after the publication of the 'Morphology' he asks: 'Was this intellectual relationship by osmosis?' No. It was by conventional scholarly means – publication. See Martin S. Kenzer, 'Tracking Sauer Across Sour Terrain', *Annals of the Association of American Geographers*, 77 (1987): 469–74, ref. on p. 471.

[136] See Earl W. Kersten, 'Sauer and "Geographic Influences"', *Yearbook. Association of Pacific Coast Geographers*, 44 (1983): 47–73. Earlier intellectual influences are discussed in Martin S. Kenzer, 'Milieu and the "Intellectual Landscape": Carl O. Sauer's Undergraduate Heritage', *Annals of the Association of American Geographers*, 75 (1982): 258–70; and Martin S. Kenzer, 'Like Father, Like Son: William Albert and Carl Ortwin Sauer', in Martin S. Kenzer (ed.), *Carl O. Sauer. A Tribute* (Corvallis, Oregon: Oregon State University Press, 1987), pp. 40–65.
[137] Sauer, 'Geography, Cultural', p. 622.
[138] Sauer, 'Morphology of Landscape', p. 53.

undisciplined regional description but at the same time show an enthusiasm for 'really get[ting] into the problems of one region.'[139] What he abhorred were the trite regional descriptions that he believed too many American colleges accepted as dissertations. And while he became less taken up with its regional manifestation, the particularism inherent in the idea of the culture area, which had its roots in Ratzel's anthropogeography, continued to dominate his thinking. This orientation, and his corresponding commitment to cultural diversity, however, were not incompatible with a holistic organicism. 'I don't think one can have a community [that] is a real social organism without cultural particularism' he wrote to Joseph Willits, director of the social science division of the Rockefeller Foundation, in 1948. Indeed it was precisely that particularism, he said, that was 'necessary to social evolution if it bears any resemblance to organic evolution, which I think it does.'[140] But the fact that Sauer resisted unilinear, orthogenetic, schemes of cultural evolution did not prevent him from conceiving of culture from time to time in organic terms, or from taking with profound seriousness the evolutionary motifs of gradualism and diversity in his accounts of cultural change.[141] The landscape, he mused, had 'an organic quality' and, like Bluntschli, he felt that 'one has not fully understood the nature of an area until one "has learned to see it as an organic unit"'.[142]

While Sauer's cultural geography thus merged with the anthropology of Boas's students, the emphasis on the material manifestations of cultural diversity that he championed might serve to modulate any tendency to see him in solely humanistic mode. Because Boas and Kroeber had found inspiration in the neo-Kantianism of Richert and the *Geisteswissenschaftern* of Dilthey, it certainly does not follow that Sauer had exclusively adopted that perspective. Let us recall that he insisted in 1934 that 'in the proper sense all geography is physical geography.' Why? Certainly it was 'not because of an environmental conditioning of the works of man, but because man, himself not directly the object of geographic investigation, has given physical

[139] Cited in John Leighly, 'Carl Ortwin Sauer, 1889–1975', in *Geographers: Biobibliographical Studies*, 2 (1976): 99–108, ref. on p. 103.

[140] Cited in John Leighly, 'Scholar and Colleague: Homage to Carl Sauer', *Yearbook, Association of Pacific Coast Geographers*, 40 (1978): 117–33, ref. on p. 121.

[141] Whether or not Sauer adopted the idea of the 'superorganic' has been the subject of debate. See James Duncan, 'The Superorganic in American Cultural Geography', *Annals of the Association of American Geographers*, 70 (1980): 181–98; Michael Solot, 'Carl Sauer and Cultural Evolution', *Annals of the Association of American Geographers*, 76 (1986): 508–20.

[142] Sauer, 'Morphology of Landscape', p. 26. Sauer's citation came from Hans Bluntschli, 'Die Amazonasniederung als Harmonischer Organismus', *Geographische Zeitschrift*, 27 (1921): 49–68. On Sauer's use of ecological metaphor see John Leighly, 'Ecology as Metaphor: Carl Sauer and Human Ecology', *Professional Geographer*, 39 (1987): 405–12.

expression to the area by habitations, workshops, markets, fields . . . Cultural geography is therefore concerned with those works of man that are inscribed into the earth's surface and give to it characteristic expression. The culture area is then an assemblage of such forms as have interdependence and is functionally differentiated from other areas.' The works of Camille Vallaux and Otto Schlüter were understandably held up as instances of good practice over against American environmentalism. Geography was thus 'an observational science' – even if it did encompass historical-cultural *Verstehen*.[143]

As Entrikin has forcibly reminded us, the thoroughly naturalistic undertaking of Sauer's project must not be underestimated.[144] Leighly had earlier stressed this natural science heritage when he reflected on Sauer's exposure to the geology of Rollin D. Salisbury and the plant ecology of H. C. Cowles.[145] But Entrikin has extended the significance of these early scientific encounters by arguing for their crucial philosophical impact on Sauer. His empiricist tendencies, his distrust of grand theory, and his willingness to countenance multipleworking hypotheses, it seems, were derived at least in part from an instrumentalism mediated from such sources. Again, the ecological principles of diversity, equilibrium, disturbance, and habitat, crucial terms in Sauer's culture history, were biologically grounded idioms.[146] Indeed he wondered if there was in 'human societies something like an ecologic climax.'[147] Moreover when he suggested that 'this theory about migration' might have 'something to say about cultural diversity,' it

---

[143] Sauer, 'Geography, Cultural', pp. 622, 623. On the congruences between Sauer's historicism and German *Geisteswissenschaften*, see William W. Speth, 'Historicism: The Disciplinary World View of Carl O. Sauer', in Martin S. Kenzer (ed.), *Carl O. Sauer. A Tribute* (Corvallis, Oregon: Oregon State University Press, 1987), pp. 11–39.

[144] J. Nicholas Entrikin, 'Carl O. Sauer, Philosopher in Spite of Himself', *Geographical Review*, 74 (1984): 387–408.

[145] John Leighly, 'Introduction', in John Leighly (ed.), *Land and Life. A Selection from the Writings of Carl Ortwin Sauer* (Berkeley: University of California Press, 1963), pp. 1–8; Leighly, 'Carl Ortwin Sauer'.

[146] And this, despite the fact that he railed against Harlan Barrows's 'human ecology', saying that there were dangers in forcing 'into geography too much biological nomenclature' and that the 'name ecology is not needed.' Sauer, 'Morphology of Landscape', p. 342. The appearance of Barrows's article 'Geography as Human Ecology' (*Annals of the Association of American Geographers*, 13 (1923): 1–14) he described as marking the beginning of geography's 'Great Retreat'. Carl O. Sauer, 'Foreword to Historical Geography', in Leighly, *Land and Life*, p. 352. On Barrows, see William A. Koelsch, 'The Historical Geography of Harlan H. Barrows', *Annals of the Association of American Geographers*, 59 (1969): 632–51. Here Barrows's departure from an early environmental determinism learned from Semple is recorded. See also H. Roy Merrens, 'Historical Geography and Early American History', *William and Mary Quarterly*, 22 (1965): 529–48.

[147] Sauer, 'Foreword to Historical Geography', p. 375.

was on the basis of a Wagner-sounding conviction that any 'organism which stays "at home" has little chance of varying.'[148] Given such commitments, his comment (to Frank Aydelotte in 1938) that he wished 'more social scientists would come along who go at their work in the way in which anthropologists or paleontologists or other natural historians do' becomes entirely understandable.[149]

I have dwelt for the past few paragraphs on the theoretical side of Sauer's geography. It is well to remember, however, that Sauer himself affected to disdain methodological pronouncements. Such protestations are not to be taken at face value. Apart from anything else it takes considerable philosophical acumen to argue against deductive theorizing or to make the case for the conceptual coherence of an empiricist particularism. Moreover philosophical activism is arguably as potent medicine as philosophical discourse. Boas's massive zeal for data gathering (so large was it that the modern Kwakiutl are rediscovering their own culture via the Boasian collections!)[150] can hardly be taken as evidence for a lack of interest in theory. Neither can Sauer's enthusiasm for fieldwork. Indeed there is much to be said for the view that fieldwork Sauer-style was itself a demonstration of the explanatory power of the historical imagination – reconstructing 'from within' behaviour as revealed in material objects.[151]

For all that, it would be too easy to allow the intellectual sources of Sauer's philosophical particularism to deflect us from the substantive particulars with which he himself was concerned. Indeed, inasmuch as the label 'the cultural landscape' in the English-speaking world is associated with Sauer and the Berkeley School, it conjures up a set of empirical associations – Latin America, animal and plant domestication and diffusion, and landscape transformation since prehistoric human occupance.[152] Such were the subjects to which Sauer himself was persistently drawn, and it is for these –

---

[148] Carl O. Sauer, Plant and Animal Exchanges between the Old and the New World: Notes from a Seminar Presented by Carl O. Sauer, at UCLA in 1961, edited by Robert Newcomb (privately printed, 1963), p. 5. Indeed, when he rejected Isaiah Bowman's invitation to take up the headship of geography at Johns Hopkins University, he made the observation that his fondness for the provinces and his 'emotional attitude that the better world will come through the strengthening of local centers of culture, not from the great capitals' were themselves expressions of his conviction that 'the whole geography of evolution shows arguments uniformly in favour of partial isolation'! Cited in Williams, 'Sauer and Historical Geography', p. 14.

[149] Cited in Entrikin, 'Sauer', p. 398.

[150] See Helen Codere's abridged edition of Boas's work in a volume entitled *Kwakiutl Ethnography* (Chicago: University of Chicago Press, 1975).

[151] See Williams, 'Sauer and Historical Geography', p. 5.

[152] So, R. J. Johnston, *Geography and Geographers*, pp. 45–6.

rather than any methodological pronouncements on geography – that he is remembered within anthropology.[153] Closely allied was the recurrent attention he devoted to the early history of exploration and discovery.[154] I do not propose surveying the specifics of each of these areas, however. Instead I want to turn to one particular theme in which Sauer's moral commitments persistently reasserted themselves, and which thereby reveals something of the ethical impetus behind his entire project.

Like his teacher, Thomas C. Chamberlin, whose Wesleyan background encouraged him to strive for a philosophy integrating the material and the spiritual,[155] Sauer's writings frequently convey what Estyn Evans described as a 'Quakerish quality of "concernment"'.[156] That 'concernment' very largely centred on Sauer's revulsion against the exploitative commercialism under exchange economies that wreaked environmental havoc. Given his profound awareness of the landscape's cultural metamorphoses, it soon became clear to him that resource depletion was a major consequence of humanity's geomorphological agency. Such views, articulated in the 1930s, were only reinforced when Leighly introduced him to the work of George Perkins Marsh towards the end of that decade.[157] Thus began Sauer's polemical assault on the devastation caused by the Europeanization of the globe. Its commercial imperialism had precipitated the extermination of large numbers of species. Human civilization had been achieved at the expense of colossal biological impoverishment. Besides, mono-agriculture had caused widespread soil devastation – perhaps the 'most serious debit to be entered against colonial commercial exploitation.'[158] Sauer's philippic was thus directed at those modern agricultural techniques which were

[153] See, for example, Lowie, *History of Ethnological Theory*, pp. 165, 259–60.

[154] For example, Carl O. Sauer, *The Early Spanish Main* (Berkeley: University of California Press, 1966); Carl O. Sauer, *Northern Mists* (Berkeley: University of California Press, 1968); Carl O. Sauer, *Sixteenth Century North America: The Land and the People as Seen by the Europeans* (Berkeley: University of California Press, 1971). See also James J. Parsons, 'Carl Ortwin Sauer, 1889–1975', *Geographical Review*, 66 (1976): 83–9.

[155] See Herbert C. Winnik, 'Science and Morality in Thomas C. Chamberlin', *Journal of the History of Ideas*, 31 (1970): 441–56.

[156] E. Estyn Evans, Review of *Land and Life*, by Carl O. Sauer, edited by John Leighly, *Geographical Review*, 54 (1964): 596–7.

[157] In a letter to the author, 18 December 1980, John Leighly wrote: 'I introduced Sauer to Marsh sometime in the late 1930's. My attention was called to him by the late J. O. M. Broek, who was in our department here at Berkeley at the time. Broek had found Marsh in Mumford's *Brown Decades*. I had read that book, but had not absorbed the meaning of Marsh. Sauer, so far as I know had not read it.'

[158] Carl O. Sauer, 'Destructive Exploitation in Modern Colonial Expansion', *Comtes Rendus du Congrès International de Géographie*, 2 (1938): 494–9; see also Carl O. Sauer, 'Theme of Plant and Animal Destruction in Economic History', *Journal of Farm Economics*, 20 (1938): 765–75.

umbilically tied to the growth of wealth in the modern era. But unlike Marsh, who depicted primitive society as a 'warfare of extermination, a series of hostilities against nature,'[159] Sauer even went so far as to question whether the impact of the hoe or the effects of customary burning could be rightly termed exploitative.[160]

With such sentiments Sauer's anti-modernist preferences clearly manifest themselves. What he deplored was the shift in values that had accompanied the move from a culturally diverse rural society towards homogeneous industrial urbanism.[161] And thus Sauer's geographical project of elucidating the cultural landscape was, as much as anything else, an exercise in moral recovery. It was a double-directed vision – back to the wisdom of the past, and forward to posterity – and found ample expression in the symposium and volume of collected essays on *Man's Role in Changing the Face of the Earth* in which he was deeply involved in the mid-1950s. With its international roster of contributions, its multi-disciplinary character, and its 'holistic, integrative interpretation of the past, present, and future,' it suited Sauer's cast of mind to perfection.[162]

If the figures I have selected to illustrate the regional episode in geography's modern history are in any sense representative – and I have certainly made no claims to comprehensiveness – a number of refrains are clearly discernible among those geographers whose focus was on the particularities of place and period. To start with, there is their vocabulary. Throughout, there was a characteristic resort to the ecological metaphors of holism or organicism in the attempt to articulate the configurational unity of the region. This serves to remind us of the naturalistic character of their enterprise. To be sure, many endeavoured to humanize the natural region by incorporating the significance of human factors, *genres de vie*, or cultural areas. Yet this widening of the empirical circle to encompass the human subject was only rarely permitted to extend to the psychological realm;

[159] See George Perkins Marsh, *Address Delivered before the Agricultural Society of Rutland County, 30 September, 1847* (Rutland, Vt.: Agricultural Society of Rutland County, 1848).

[160] See the discussion in William W. Speth, 'Carl Ortwin Sauer on Destructive Exploitation', *Biological Conservation*, 11 (1977): 145–60.

[161] Hooson observes that Sauer 'always maintained an incurably romantic vision of his "country-bred" origins and "the native virtues of rural life".' David Hooson, 'Carl O. Sauer', in Brian Blouet (ed.), *The Origins of Academic Geography in the United States* (Hamden, Connecticut: Archon Books, 1981), pp. 165–74, ref. on p. 166. Sauer's anti-modernism is discussed in Kent Mathewson, 'Sauer South by Southwest: Antimodernism and the Austral Impulse', in Kenzer (ed.), *Sauer*, pp. 90–111.

[162] Michael Williams, 'Sauer and "Man's Role in Changing the Face of the Earth"', *Geographical Review*, 77 (1987): 218–31, ref. on p. 218.

instead human regions were regularly sought through the manifestation of culture in material artefacts. By this strategy, geography could retain its natural science image, its observational methods, and its field orientation. To recall that its chief practitioners in France, Germany, Britain, and America were all trained in the natural sciences should serve to temper the suspicion that because regionalists dealt in specificities rather than universals they could make no claim for the scientific status of their enterprise. On the contrary, they regarded it as the highest form of scientific synthesis.

For all these naturalistic aspirations, advocates of regionalism typically found in it a vehicle for the expression of their social and moral commitments. For those with a historical and rural bias, the reconstruction of past geographies could become a project in moral recovery. Those more politically motivated could champion the raising of regional consciousness as a prelude to political reform, or as a means of bolstering ethnic loyalty. So even if there were those who rested content with a checklist approach to regionalism, or who dashed off regional compositions in the fulfilment of degree requirements, the architects of the regional synthesis model were only too aware of their enterprise's social, moral, political, scientific, and philosophical overtones.

9

Statistics Don't Bleed

Quantification and its Detractors

To have command of definition is to have control of discourse. For this reason it is not surprising that exegetical fussiness over the precise meaning of terms is characteristic of those apologetic works that aim to fix disciplinary identity. The fact of the matter is, however, that key words frequently have a certain plasticity about them which means that their meaning can be expanded or contracted to serve the purposes of their users. Success in managing vocabulary – and thereby solidifying conceptual slipperiness – therefore brings considerable advantages in attempts to map out conceptual territory. For scientific endeavour is not just 'a conversation with nature'; it is also, as David Hull has reminded us, 'a conversation with other scientists.'[1] 'Species', 'atom', 'social class', 'ego' are all labels whose meanings have been the subject of internecine warfare among biologists, physicists, sociologists, and psychoanalysts. The adjudication of definitions is, of course, an inherently boundary-marking, or boundary-making, enterprise designed to demarcate the true from the false, the legitimate from the illegitimate, the relevant from the irrelevant. Accordingly, the ownership of terminology is of enormous consequence in dialogue, for by it both ideas and people can be positioned on particular sides of debates. To dictate definition is to wield cultural power. Definitions of a discipline's cognitive domain are thus frequently less an ontological exercise about the piece of reality that the subject has a rightful claim upon, than a strategy for delimiting the scope of vocabulary that will be allowed as good currency within that professional division of labour. And so with these reflections in mind I want to turn now to the magisterial statement of disciplinary definition provided for geography in 1939 by Richard Hartshorne.

[1] Hull, *Science as a Process*, p. 7.

HARTSHORNE, SCHAEFER, AND THE TYRANNY OF TERMINOLOGY

As things were to turn out, 1938–9 was not the best year to enjoy a leave of absence with a research grant to investigate the problems of European boundaries. Such was Richard Hartshorne's experience. But world-scale political events joined forces with a personal irritation to encourage him to spend a good deal of his European sojourn inside the walls of the library at the University of Vienna and interviewing leading European geographers.[2] Even before he had left America's shores, however, Hartshorne' mind had been turning from land frontiers to cognitive boundaries. In 1937 – during a decade in which methodological discussion was rife in American geography – John Leighly had published a philosophical tract that greatly irked him.[3] Over a luncheon meeting Hartshorne reportedly told Derwent Whittlesey, the editor of the *Annals of the Association of American Geographers*, in no uncertain terms just exactly what he thought of Leighly's paper. And thus began an antipathy between Midwestern and Berkeley geography that was to last for decades. Whittlesey encouraged him to put his criticisms in publishable form.[4] And so, before heading for Europe, Hartshorne had already embarked on a historical, boundary-making enterprise that, spurred on by encouraging letters from Whittlesey, would usurp much of his time abroad. In succeeding communications Hartshorne's reflections expanded to the point where the resulting monograph of nearly 500 pages took up two issues of the *Annals*.

If the Leighly incident provided the proximate cause of the raising of Hartshorne's pen, there were factors of a more general nature that rendered it an opportune moment to provide geography with a philosophical apologia. With the disapproval of environmental determinism, geographers had resigned themselves to seeking their disciplinary identity in the subject's synthetic claims to bridge the gap between the natural and social sciences.

---

[2] See James, *All Possible Worlds*, p. 417–18. Hartshorne had already written on aspects of boundaries in Richard Hartshorne, 'Upper Silesian Industrial District', *Geographical Review*, 24 (1934): 423–38.

[3] The paper was John Leighly, 'Some Comments on Contemporary Geographic Methods', *Annals of the Association of American Geographers*, 17 (1937): 125–41. During the 1930s commentaries on geography's nature were prepared by Almon Parkins, Isaiah Bowman, Vernor Rinch, Glenn Trewartha, Preston James, and Robert Platt, among others. See Fred Lukermann, 'The Nature of Geography: Post Hoc, Ergo Propter Hoc?' in J. Nicholas Entrikin and Stanley D. Brunn (eds), *Reflections on Richard Hartshorne's* The Nature of Geography (Washington: Association of American Geographers, 1989), pp. 53–68.

[4] See Preston E. James and Geoffrey J. Martin, *The Association of American Geographers: The First Seventy-Five Years, 1904–1979* (Washington: Association of American Geographers, 1978), p. 81.

It was, according to Neil Smith, a period in geography's history that 'marked a withdrawal from the competition to establish academic turf, an isolation from the contemporary ferment in social, economic and political theory, and a growing resignation that geography occupy the fragmented interstices between the more dominant social sciences.' Some intellectual muscle, however, was needed to rationalize for the first generation of professional geographers their subject's occupancy of such an uncomfortable academic niche, and it was 'into this frustrating intellectual vacuum that Hartshorne launched *The Nature.*' A grand historical and philosophical conspectus, it provided a generation with 'unprecedented self-justification', but at the tremendous cost of bequeathing to the discipline a thoroughly internalist and, it has to be said, partisan reading of its historical sources.[5]

Whatever its stimulus, the book's aim was crystal clear. It was to specify the *nature* of geography from an examination of its *history*. As Hartshorne himself insisted, his concern was 'to present geography as other geographers see it – or have seen it in the past . . . If we wish to keep on the track – or return to the proper track . . . we must first look back of us to see in what direction that track has led. Our first task will be to learn what geography has been in its historical development.'[6] That this indeed was his purpose was reiterated in the 1941 review that J. K. Wright published in *Isis* – the only review to appear in the history of science literature so far as I have been able to determine. Here Wright observed: 'He sensibly maintains that one cannot arrive at any acceptable concept of geography through "logical reasoning from *a priori* assumptions." To define or describe the field it must be examined objectively, which is a problem in research and not one of rationalization, a problem that involves careful investigation of the ways in which geographers in this country and abroad have actually developed and are developing their subject.' Indeed Hartshorne's strategy for determining what Wright called 'the inherent nature of geography' was to provide 'a critical survey of current thought in the light of the past.'[7]

At this point we perhaps need to pause briefly to reflect on just what moves were afoot here. As I have said, Hartshorne's project was to determine the nature of geography from scrutinizing its history. But there is surely a distinction to be drawn between normative questions (what geogra-

---

[5] Neil Smith, 'Geography as Museum: Private History and Conservative Idealism in *The Nature of Geography*', in Entrikin and Brunn, pp. 91–120, refs on p. 95.

[6] Hartshorne, *The Nature of Geography A Critical Survey of Current Thought in the Light of the Past* (Lancaster, Pa.: Association of American Geographers, 1939), p. 31.

[7] John K. Wright, Review of *The Nature of Geography* by Richard Hartshorne, *Isis*, 33 (1941): 298–300.

phy *ought to be* about) and the empirical *contingencies* of intellectual history (what geography *has been* about). And this raises the question of whether Hartshorne was ultimately making – rhetoric notwithstanding – a philosophical claim about geography's conceptual territory, or a historical claim about its evolution. As I see it, it is just very difficult to see how Hartshorne hoped to determine geography's 'essential nature' – and that is what he was after – from historical inquiry, for the deliverances of history are certain to be anything but monolithic.[8] The investigation of historical contingencies, I would contend, just cannot be dragooned into serving essentialist philosophical apologetics.

It is for this reason, then, that in reading Hartshorne's treatise we get little sense that geography – like science – is a negotiated entity. The volume just was not an inquiry into the contextual evolution of ideas, but was rather a sophisticated series of testimonial elaborations – a static, de-historicized history. Accordingly, it is understandable that Lukermann should observe.

> One can only conclude that *The Nature* was not history . . . The 'light of the past,' in this sense, is not a search for history . . . but a search for authority to validate the conclusions drawn from selected premises – largely formulated by Hettner, who had philosophical associations and leanings rather than historical associates.[9]

The authority to which Hartshorne ultimately appealed was German geography, especially as seen through the interpretative spectacles of Alfred Hettner. Just whether Hettner was the arch-regionalist that Hartshorne's emphasis on his chorological statements implied has certainly been questioned.[10] I do not intend to adjudicate on that scholastic point, however, nor on the validity of Hartshorne's restricting his investigations to the recent Germanic tradition, rather than to, say, Elizabethan England, or Enlightenment France, or Jeffersonian America. What *is* clear is that in order to retain the authority of his assertions, Hartshorne sought to expose the incoherences in alternative definitions of the field by dilating on their terminological inexactitudes. Thereby he was able to manufacture for a

[8] Hartshorne, *The Nature*, p. 27.

[9] Lukermann, p. 58. In my view Lukermann's judgements are correct, even though Hartshorne quoted Hettner to the effect that 'The system of the sciences has been an historical growth; abstract designations of the sciences that tend to take no account of the historical development – unfortunately the methodological literature has been particularly rich in such *a priori* conceptions – are foredoomed to unfruitfulness.' Hartshorne, *The Nature*, p. 30.

[10] See Karl W. Butzer, 'Hartshorne, Hettner, and *The Nature of Geography*', in Brunn and Entrikin, pp. 35–52.

generation of American students a tradition with an apparently crystal clear focus – chorology – to which they could give allegiance. By controlling the terms of debate he found it possible to pass judgements on the legitimacy of what had hitherto circulated as good currency within the tradition, and therefore to speak of 'Deviations from the course of historical development.'[11]

Nowhere is Hartshorne's concern with exegetical precision more evident than in his interrogation of the notion of landscape or, better, *Landschaft* in its various connotations, and not least in Carl Sauer's programmatic statement *The Morphology of Landscape*. On the surface it might seem that Hartshorne's chorological focus and his enthusiasm for the Germanic tradition would have resonated with Sauer's similarly inspired enthusiasm for the probing of areal specificities. (At one point Hartshorne even noted that Sauer had inspired a younger generation 'to think of geography in terms of the study of material landscape features, both natural and cultural, and to consider these features according to their chorographic, or regional, interrelations.')[12] Nothing, however, could be further from the truth. What might seem on the surface as a trivial difference of opinion on the precise methodology of regional investigation became for both an issue of tremendous import. What was at stake was nothing less than what geography's cardinal watchwords were – and who had control of them. Hartshorne maintained he just could not understand how Sauer could operate with the conceptual vagaries of the seemingly sloppy notion of a 'cultural landscape'. The very label 'landscape', he declared, had introduced 'unnecessary confusion into our language,' and so he elaborated on its myriad nuances both exuberantly and exhaustively.[13] For his part, Sauer was tremendously impatient with Hartshorne's dealing in definitions and resented the terminological tyranny of such armchair methodologists. Thus, however much they may have agreed on geography as the study of areal differentiation – Hartshorne cited collectively Hettner, Richthofen *and* Sauer on this precise point[14] – Hartshorne's philosophical semantics and Sauer's anthropological empiricism served to bolster their distaste of each other's choice of vocabulary.

In order to avoid the self-referential gambit, Hartshorne realized that because his self-appointed task centred on what he called the 'justification

---

[11] This was the title of chapter 3.

[12] Hartshorne, *The Nature*, p. 24.

[13] Ibid., p. 149. It is interesting to note that while Hartshorne was willing to expose the conceptual plasticity of 'landscape' by showing how it was used differently in different contexts, he never considered applying the selfsame strategy to the label 'geography'.

[14] Hartshorne, *The Nature*, p. 237.

for the historical concept of geography as a chorographic science'[15] it was necessary to elaborate on the precise meaning of his cardinal principle – the region. Ironically it turned out to be a remarkably insubstantial entity. In typical fashion he began by deconstructing the anatomical, organic, and musical metaphors to which other regionalists were drawn. Obst and Geisler's '*Raumorganismus*', Sauer's areal 'anatomy', Finch and Trewartha's regions as 'functioning organisms', Volz's suggestions about regional 'rhythm', and Creutzburg's *Landschaft* 'harmony' were all dissected and dismissed as lacking any concrete unitary objectivity.[16] To be sure, areas might be *encountered* as organic wholes, or harmonies, or Gestalts; but these were merely subjective experiences having no ontological status. Such existential unities could never provide the basis of geography without transforming the discipline into 'a psycho-geographic subject'.[17] The region, it seemed, was a noetically constructed entity – a thoroughgoing Kantian conception. As he put it:

> The most that we can say is that any particular unit of land has significant relations with all the neighboring units and that in certain respects it may be more closely related with a particular group of units than with others, but not necessarily in all respects. The regional entities which we construct on this basis are therefore in the full sense mental constructions; they are entities only in our thoughts, even though we find them to be constructions that provide some sort of intelligent basis for organizing our knowledge of reality.[18]

And again:

> From the point of view of the areal divisions with which we are commonly concerned in regional geography, we conclude that it is not possible to define sections of the earth surface as regions that form units in reality, that we cannot correctly consider them as concrete individual objects.[19]

For Hartshorne regions just did not exist as all-embracing units. Specific regions were 'not inherent in the world which the geographer studies – neither in the world of nature nor in the actual world which nature and man together have made.'[20] But this did not mean that doing regional geography

---

[15] This was the title of chapter 4.
[16] Hartshorne, *The Nature*, pp. 255, 258, 260, 261.
[17] Ibid., p. 266.
[18] Ibid., p. 275.
[19] Ibid., p. 281.
[20] Ibid., p. 362.

was an incoherent enterprise. On the contrary; for him the regional project consisted in determining how 'particular elements and complexes of elements within regions are related to those in others.'[21] Such particulars included relief, vegetation, climate, land use, and so on; but it was a confusion to regard any one of these as synonymous with a 'geographical region'. Moreover the choice of which elements to map, which criteria to employ in the construction of regions, was inherently arbitrary and implied that, as Hettner had put it, 'one cannot speak of true and false regional divisions, but only of purposeful and non-purposeful.'[22] The task was, it might be said, akin to library cataloguing; a catalogue can be more or less useful, but it just doesn't seem correct to speak of it as 'true' or 'false'. Thus expunging any conceptual fertility that might reside in metaphorical expression – organic regions, regional personality, and the like – Hartshorne revealed a positivistic inclination towards a formalism that accorded ontological privilege only to discrete geographical facts.[23] As he insisted, 'A comparative division of the world into generic types arranged in a logically sound system can be based on any one single natural element or element-complex . . . but only on one.'[24]

While a subsequent generation may have lacked Hartshorne's philosophical acumen, the principles of areal differentiation rapidly became enshrined as geography's primary article of faith. When Wooldridge and East issued their volume on *The Spirit and Purpose of Geography* in 1951, for example, they supported their contention that geography essentially addressed the question 'how and why does one part of the earth's surface differ from another' by calling upon the testimony of Hettner, Vidal, Hartshorne, and Sauer. With such a confession they insisted (and this despite Wooldridge's own thoroughly geomorphological inclinations) that a 'cleavage' between physical and human geography was 'wholly antithetic' to the spirit and purpose of the subject. Moreover, their conviction that the 'nature of man and of human evolution ensures that each region which we study is in large measure unique' did nothing in their eyes to undercut its scientific status. On the contrary, it was precisely where the discipline was furthest removed from formal categories and universal principles – namely, human geography – that its complexity, subtlety, and flexibility was most displayed.[25]

---

[21] Ibid., p. 282.
[22] Ibid., p. 290.
[23] See Smith, 'Geography as Museum', p. 113.
[24] Hartshorne, *The Nature*, p. 326.
[25] S. W. Wooldridge and W. G. East, *The Spirit and Purpose of Geography* (London: Hutchinson, 3rd edn 1966), pp. 25, 29, 27.

For all the grand rhetoric of its philosophical and scientific advocates, however, the manner in which the regional undertaking was conducted by and large failed to deliver the subject from its definitional neuroses. For too many practitioners it degenerated into a plodding, enumerative exercise lacking both the intellectual vigour and moral zest of its earlier champions. In America, as Stoddart later observed, a generation 'following Hartshorne in his quest for "areal differentiation", committed themselves to what was at worst, an exercise in the classification of areas, involving as an after-thought problems of organization and function.[26] A lack of intellectual pro-fundity, however, was one thing; the threat of institutional annihilation quite another. When the geography programme was terminated at Harvard in 1948 a new sense of crisis swept through the profession. It was, as Jean Gottmann later recalled, "a terrible blow", one from which American geog-raphy "never completely recovered." '[27]

The leading figure in the expansion of the geography programme at Harvard during the second quarter of the century was Derwent Whittlesey, the very individual who, as editor of the *Annals* had encouraged Hartshorne in the production of his magisterial text, and later supported Hartshorne's rebuttal of Fred Schaefer's critical reading of *The Nature*. By the late 1940s, however, the claim that regional synthesis constituted geog-raphy's essential identity gave the subject a dilettantish image among the practitioners of ever more specializing sciences. James Conant, the Harvard president, had reportedly come to the view by 1948 that 'geography is not a university subject.'[28] Indeed, Edward Ullman, reflecting on those years at Harvard, was shortly to confess in a letter to Glenn Trewartha, that 'Instead of having the backing of a lot of good works to recommend to my colleagues, I felt almost alone in fighting the battle for geography.' It was, he mused, 'rather hard to fight honestly for something that has not pro-duced.'[29] Moreover when *human* geography was cultivated in relative isola-tion from the physical components of the regional synthesis, it seemed to

---

[26] Stoddart, 'Geography and the Ecological Approach', p. 242.

[27] Quoted in Neil Smith, ' "Academic War over the Field of Geography": The Elimination of Geography at Harvard, 1947–1952', *Annals of the Association of American Geographers*, 77 (1987): 155–72. The following paragraph relies on Smith's analysis and on Rita M. Morris, 'An Examination of some Factors Related to the Rise and Decline of Geography as a Field of Study at Harvard, 1638–1948' (Ph.D. thesis, Graduate School of Education, Harvard University, 1962). See also Geoffrey J. Martin, 'On Whittlesey, Bowman and Harvard', *Annals of the Association of American Geographers*, 78 (1988): 152–8.

[28] Cited in Smith, 'Academic War', p. 159.

[29] Edward Ullman to Glenn Trewartha, 19 March 1953, cited in Edward Ullman, *Geography as Spatial Interaction* edited by Ronald R. Boyce (Seattle: University of Washington Press, 1980), p. 126.

some – including strategically placed geographers like Isaiah Bowman – that the subject's scientific aspirations were being relegated to the sidelines. At Harvard, Whittlesey's background in history and his orientation towards the social perspective of the French tradition, had encouraged him to consider the construction of a human geography erected on its own, albeit evolutionary, principles.[30] Bowman found this vision unappealing; he felt that an autonomous human geography could never be anything but 'descriptive, fragmentary and "easy".'[31] He himself retained a lifelong commitment to the Davisian programme modulating only the shrillest tones of its determinism. Given this naturalistic orientation he insisted that a detached *human* geography lacked both scientific principle and scholarly standing – merely skimming off the top of the other sciences, as he put it – and so from his position as the country's most strategically placed geographer, he did little to support its cause at Harvard during the very months when its life was petering out.

Of course the assassination of geography at Harvard is doubtless attributable to several factors. Intramural feuding between the geology and geography factions over curricular interests, Whittlesey's less-than-scholarly reasons for bringing Harold Kemp to the Harvard campus, questions about financial viability with which the administration had to deal, a lack of quality work from some of the Harvard personnel, not to mention Bowman's alleged revulsion at Whittlesey's sexual preferences and his suspicions about the leftist political slant of social science, are all believed to have contributed. Whatever the reasons, Bowman's failure to raise his voice in support of the subject at Harvard, even while he was promoting its interests in the academy more generally, did little to help the cause. His silence spoke volumes.

It was just shortly after geography's demise at Harvard that, in May 1950, Richard Hartshorne drove out to Iowa City to give a public lecture in Harold McCarty's department and to speak to a seminar on the history of geographic thought that Fred Schaefer was running. According to Hartshorne the meeting was entirely cordial and certainly did nothing to alert him to the attack on *The Nature* which Schaefer would shortly publish in the 1953 issue of the *Annals*.[32] Hartshorne's version is entirely differ-

---

[30] Incidentally Whittlesey's historical bias encouraged him to adopt a more enthusiastic posture towards historical geography than Hartshorne. See Derwent Whittlesey, 'The Horizon on Geography', *Annals of the Association of American Geographers*, 35 (1945): 1–36. Here too Whittlesey's awareness of Lamarckian biology is evident.

[31] Letter, Isaiah Bowman to J. Russell Smith, 15 November 1948, cited in Smith, 'Academic War', p. 162.

[32] Richard Hartshorne, 'Hettner's Exceptionalism – Fact or Fiction?' *History of Geography Newsletter*, 6 (1988): 1–4.

ent from some of the rumours that circulated around what came to be regarded as a crucial altercation between the two men. William Bunge, for example, who considered Schaefer's a classic work, thought it necessary to make assertions about Hartshorne's position in the Office of Strategic Services during the Second World War and to claim that Schaefer – himself a refugee from the Third Reich – was the victim of a calculated campaign of persecution.[33] This grapevine tattle is repeatable here only because it has achieved wide circulation within the discipline, and because – irrespective of the facts of the case – prominent members of the profession sided with one or other of the two figures in the fracas. Whittlesey, Edward Ullman, Stephen B. Jones, and Henry Madison Kendall all had severe reservations about the Schaefer piece. William Warntz, by contrast, believed that Schaefer had been subjected to vilification – including the signal absence of obituary notices – because his viewpoint presented a challenge to 'the vested intellectual interests' of the geographical establishment; William L. Garrison felt excited by the article because Schaefer, in however crude a way, had some 'sense of the world of science of which geography is a part.'[34] Regardless of the precise issues involved, Hartshorne and Schaefer became symbols for alternative visions of the geographical enterprise.

Precisely what had moved Schaefer to launch his attack may be difficult to discern; but the broad thrust of his message was plain. Basically he wanted a more scientific geography. (After all he had worked for the Institute of Social Biology in London during 1936.) To this end he vigorously opposed what he took to be geography's ingrained historicism – its focus on the unique – in favour of searching for law-like statements that could explain spatial patterns. While this tended to prioritize systematic geography, Schaefer nevertheless believed that 'knowing such laws one can ideally predict the whole course of history in a region.' For Schaefer, then, spatial *explanation* was what geography should be about, and that *always* meant recognizing phenomena 'as instances of law.'[35] To sustain this vision he found it necessary to conduct a two-pronged operation.

First, Schaefer juxtaposed scientific and historical modes of explanation –

---

[33] See William Bunge, *Fred K. Schaefer and the Science of Geography* (Harvard Papers in Theoretical Geography, Special Papers Series A, 1968). A condensed version of this paper appeared as 'Fred K. Schaefer and the Science of Geography', *Annals of the Association of American Geographers*, 69 (1979): 128–32. See also Derek Gregory, *Ideology, Science and Human Geography*, p. 31.

[34] Cited in Geoffrey J. Martin, '*The Nature of Geography* and the Schaefer-Hartshorne Debate', in Brunn and Entrikin, pp. 80, 77.

[35] Fred K. Schaefer, 'Exceptionalism in Geography: A Methodological Examination', *Annals of the Association of American Geographers* 43 (1953): 226–49, refs on pp. 248, 227.

'the scientific approach and historicism', as he termed them.[36] Because the latter had been mesmerized by Wilhelm Dilthey's ambiguous talk of 'empathetic understanding' as the appropriate means of comprehending individual events, Schaefer felt it was mistaken to model geographical explanation on a historical template. This would be to favour an idiographic (describing the unique) over a nomothetic (searching for laws) approach. The blame for the relegation of both geography and history to this 'exceptional' position within the structure of the sciences was to be laid at the door of Immanuel Kant. And it was essentially his vision, according to Schaefer, that was perpetuated by Hartshorne. Almost immediately the tyranny of the struggle for terminological control surfaced. Hartshorne vigorously contested the claim that he was 'essentially idiographic' – a point he reiterated on numerous occasions, gladly parading the names of those, like Norman Graves, who conceded that he had not neglected the nomothetic perspective.[37] Charges and counter-charges aside, it is clear that the label 'nomothetic' named something that both combatants wanted to possess, for in intellectual property, as elsewhere, possession is nine-tenths of the law.

Secondly, sensing like Hartshorne the power of heritage, Schaefer felt the need to bolster his own conception of geography with the names of figures looming large in the traditional hagiography of the discipline. This inevitably forced him to dispute Hartshorne's account, to accuse him of selective citation of key sources like Hettner, and to claim that such figures as Humboldt, Ritter, and Kraft considered geography 'a science trying to discover laws.'[38] Hartshorne was incensed and wrote to Kendall, now editor of the *Annals*, describing Schaefer's piece as 'a palpable fraud, consisting of falsehoods, distortions, and obvious omissions.' Later, in correspondence with Kendall's successor, Walter Kollmorgen, he observed: 'In whatever sense it is possible for a learned journal to commit a crime . . . *The Annals* has committed a crime unparalleled in its history.'[39]

In a series of rebuttals, which appeared during the second half of the 1950s, Hartshorne descended into ever more detailed exegesis of the sacred texts.[40] With hindsight, however, it is clear that Schaefer was basically

[36] Ibid., p. 236.
[37] Hartshorne, 'Hettner's Exceptionalism'. See Norman Graves, 'Can Geographical Studies be Subsumed', and his later letter in *Terra*, 96, 3 (1984): 229.
[38] Schaefer, 'Exceptionalism', p. 228.
[39] Both citations appear in Martin, 'The Schaefer-Hartshorne Debate', pp. 73, 76.
[40] Richard Hartshorne, '"Exceptionalism in Geography" Re-Examined', *Annals of the Association of American Geographers*, 45 (1955): 205–44; Richard Hartshorne, 'The Concept of Geography as a Science of Space, from Kant and Humboldt to Hettner', *Annals of the Association of American Geographers*, 48 (1958): 97–108; Richard Hartshorne, *Perspective on the Nature of Geography* (Chicago: Rand McNally, 1959).

indifferent to historical detail; his prime concern was philosophical and his use of past heroes was little more than a naked appeal to authority. In Henk Aay's view, Schaefer's paper was thus a vivid example of 'how historical material may be presented in a misleading fashion to sustain philosophical arguments.'[41] Moreover, if what John Hook wrote to William Bunge in 1961 is true, Schaefer himself entirely appreciated the distinction between normative questions and the contingencies of conceptual history. According to Hook, Schaefer was fully aware 'that the historical development of the field was one thing, its logical structure quite something else; and he was primarily concerned with the latter.'[42] But then, if what I have been arguing is correct, the same was, to one degree or another, true of Hartshorne. Fundamentally both were seeking for essentialist definitions precisely where they could not be found – in history. For if the history of geography reveals anything, it is the shifting nature of its own conceptual boundaries. Indeed Bunge himself fastened on this very point when he wrote to Hartshorne in 1959 insisting: 'I do not care about historical scholarship. I consider it irrelevant. History, as conducted in geographic methodological discussions in general, can prove anything and therefore proves nothing.'[43] In England advocates of geographical quantification would either take Bunge's attitude to history or would present variant readings of the tradition. Thus Stan Gregory, for instance, in his 1976 presidential address to the Institute of British Geographers in which he insisted that the new quantification had at last come of age, confessed that he had 'never been enamoured of returning to Humboldt and Ritter, let alone the Greeks, in every consideration of the history of geography,' while Alan Wilson presented his own alternative history in which the names of mathematically inclined economists and sociologists loomed large.[44] Whatever the strategy, the need to come to terms with history persistently reasserts itself.

For all the talk of a bitter feud between Hartshorne and Schaefer, however, it is clear that when the 'debate' is stripped of its stereotypical accretions, there was considerable consonance between the protagonists. Apart from anything else they both retained an allegiance to the importance of the regional project while rejecting holistic metaphors of regions as

[41] Henry Aay, 'Conceptual Change and the Growth of Geographic Knowledge: A Critical Appraisal of the Historiography of Geography' (Ph.D dissertation, Clark University, 1978), p. 331.

[42] Cited in Martin, 'The Schaefer-Hartshorne Debate', p. 81.

[43] Ibid., p. 79.

[44] S. Gregory, 'On Geographical Myths and Statistical Fables', *Transactions of the Institute of British Geographers*, n.s. 1 (1976): 385–400, ref. on pp. 385–6; A.G. Wilson, 'Theoretical Geography', *Transactions of the Institute of British Geographers*, 57 (1972): 31–44.

organisms. More significantly, Sack notes that both revealed 'a common commitment to empiricism and a shared interest in the physical geometric relationships of facts' – thereby effectively excising any notion of process from geography's purview; and Gregory comments that it 'is certainly hard to see how Hartshorne's "simple correlations" differ from Schaefer's "morphological laws", given that they can both be reduced to spatial patterns.'[45] Yet for all these continuities, the politics of definitional discourse was such that Hartshorne felt the need to reassert his own authorial intentions and to spill a good deal of ink in reiterating just precisely what he meant to say. No doubt disciplinary integrity requires such efforts at scholarly adjudication. Yet from the perspective of the subject's historical evolution it might be well to ponder David Hull's provocative quip that 'too much emphasis in communication is put on the intentions of the sender . . . What the receiver thinks the sender intended is what matters.' Besides, there is good evidence to suggest that scientists frequently 'do not know what they intended to say until they discover what it is that other scientists have taken them to be saying. Scientists show great facility in retrospective meaning-change.'[46] Irrespective of what was said, how it was said, or why it was said, advocates of a more scientific geography found in Schaefer a hero, and in Hartshorne the personification of, as one observer puts it, 'what we struggled against.'[47]

THE QUANTITATIVE (RE)TURN

The precise impact of the Schaefer–Hartshorne debate on the subsequent history of geography is extremely hard to ascertain. My own feeling is that rather too much has been made of the wrangle. Certainly, many, craving for a more scientific geography, found in Schaefer's piece the sort of philosophical symbolism their campaign required. Just how formative an influence it actually was is a different matter, however. Indeed, when Peter Gould came to reflect on the subject's developments at the time, Schaefer's

[45] Robert David Sack, 'Chorology and Spatial Analysis', *Annals of the Association of American Geographers*, 64 (1974): 439–52; Gregory, *Ideology, Science and Human Geography*, p. 31. See also Derek Gregory, 'Solid Geometry: Notes on the Recovery of Spatial Structure', in Peter Gould and Gunnar Olsson (eds), *A Search for Common Ground* (London: Pion, 1982), pp. 187–219.

[46] David Hull, *Science as a Process*, p. 7.

[47] Richard L. Morrill, 'Recollections of the "Quantitative Revolution's" Early Years: The University of Washington 1955–65', in Mark Billinge, Derek Gregory and Ron Martin (eds), *Recollections of a Revolution. Geography as Spatial Science* (London: Macmillan, 1984), pp. 56–72, ref. on p. 59.

name is conspicuous only by its absence. Instead Gould spoke of how 'much of the original inspiration . . . came from theoretical and methodological developments in Germany, Sweden and Finland.'[48] From Germany impetus came from the writings of Walter Christaller and the spatial economist August Lösch, while from Sweden Edgar Kant, S. Godlund, Torsten Hägerstrand, and K. E. Bergsten had all produced 'scientific' geography prior to the appearance of the Schaefer piece.[49] In the United States, Edward Ullman had drawn attention in 1941 (in an article written at the request of the Chicago sociologist Louis Wirth) to J. H. von Thünen's *Der Isolierte Staat* of 1826 and Christaller's 1933 work on central places in southern Germany, while readers of the *Geographical Review* were exposed to the Princeton astronomer John Q. Stewart's social physics in 1947.[50] Besides, it seems that Ullman had grasped, quite independently of Schaefer, the deterministic implications of a causal geography, for as he wrote to Stephen B. Jones in 1953, 'there is nothing new in geography save perhaps a return to environmentalism if one wants to state it that way – in my case and Isard's an environmental determinism of just one element: space.'[51] Moreover Leslie King, reflecting in 1979 on his years at Iowa, observed that Schaefer's 'paper was not accorded the recognition within the Iowa department that others since have given it. No reference was made to it in publications by the Iowa geographers at the time,' he recalled, even if 'it was a

[48] Peter R. Gould, 'Methodological Developments since the Fifties', in Christopher Board, Richard J. Chorley, Peter Haggett and David R. Stoddart (eds), *Progress in Geography. International Reviews of Current Research. Volume 1* (London: Edward Arnold, 1969), pp. 1–49, ref. on p. 3.

[49] Walter Christaller, *Die Zentralen Orte in Süddeutschland* (Jena: Gustav Fischer, 1933); Edgar Kant, 'Umland Studies and Sector Analysis', *Studies in Rural-Urban Interaction, Lund Studies in Geography, Series B, Human Geography*, 3 (Lund: Gleerup, 1951), pp. 3–13; S. Godlund, 'Bus Services, Hinterlands, and the Location of Urban Settlements in Sweden, Specially in Scania', in *Studies in Rural-Urban Interaction, Lund Studies in Geography, Series B, Human Geography*, 3 (Lund: Gleerup, 1951), pp. 14–24; Torsten Hägerstrand, *The Propagation of Innovation Waves, Lund Studies in Geography, Series B, Human Geography*, 4 (Lund: Gleerup, 1952); K. E. Bergsten, 'Variability in Intensity of Urban Fields as Illustrated by Birth-Places', in *Studies in Rural-Urban Interaction, Lund Studies in Geography, Series B, Human Geography*, 3 (Lund: Gleerup, 1951), pp. 25–32.

[50] Edward Ullmann, 'A Theory of Location for Cities', *American Journal of Sociology*, 46 (1941): 835–64; John Q. Stewart, 'Empirical Mathematical Rules Concerning the Distribution and Equilibrium of Population,' *Geographical Review*, 37 (1947): 461–86; John Q. Stewart, 'Suggested Principles of Social Physics', *Science*, 106 (1947): 179–80. Shortly afterwards Zipf introduced his 'principle of least effort' as a cardinal principle of social physics. See G. K. Zipf, *Human Behavior and the Principle of Least Effort* (New York: Hafner, 1949).

[51] He went on: 'perhaps you can state why the "new" environmentalism is more respectable. I can't.' Cited in Ullman, *Geography as Spatial Interaction*, p. 184.

methodological milestone in the development of a positivistic approach to human geography.'[52]

King's mention of Schaefer's methodological inclinations suggests that he had facilitated positivism's entrée into the geographical conversation. Other commentators concur. Derek Gregory, for example, speaks of Schaefer opening 'the door for the formal admission of logical positivism into geography,' while Bunge stresses the paper's 'introduction to geography of modern philosophy of science.'[53] Such judgements only seemed confirmed by Schaefer's close association with the logical positivist mathematician-philosopher Gustav Bergmann, also at Iowa, who had participated in the Vienna Circle in the 1930s and was later to author volumes on *The Philosophy of Science* and *The Metaphysics of Logical Positivism*. As is well known, Bergmann had, on the death of Schaefer, taken over the task of proof-reading his 'Exceptionalism' article for the *Annals*. Indeed, according to some, Bergmann had an independent influence on the Iowa geographical fraternity. Leslie King, for instance, recalled that in the Iowa department, if 'Schaefer's paper was not . . . required reading, Bergmann's book on the philosophy of science certainly was!'[54] Again Duane Knos, remarking on Iowa's statistical turn, considered that Bergmann, who 'had a tendency to integrate himself with the geographers, sociologists and economists,' had an 'important' influence on the geographical community. For Knos, statistical procedures were 'just a very handy way to play that type of philosophy out.'[55] Nor was Bergmann's influence restricted to personal encounters at Iowa. In his *Theoretical Geography*, for instance, Bunge expressed his indebtedness to Bergmann for his philosophical assistance, while Amedeo and Golledge had liberal resort to his writings in their later introduction to scientific reasoning in geography.[56]

Yet for all these claims it is hard to see just precisely what Schaefer, and his successors, gleaned from their flirtation with logical positivism. Certainly there was a dissatisfaction with Diltheyesque *verstehen*, an ambition to bring geographical data within the bounds of natural law, and a

[52] Leslie J. King, 'Areal Associations and Regressions', *Annals of the Association of American Geographers*, 69 (1979): 124–8, ref. on p. 128.

[53] Derek Gregory, *Ideology, Science and Human Geography*, p. 32; Bunge, 'Fred K. Schaefer', p. 131.

[54] King, 'Areal Associations', p. 128.

[55] Duane Knos in 'American Geography in the 1950s', in Anne Buttimer (ed.), *The Practice of Geography* (London: Longman, 1983), pp. 196–208, ref on pp. 198, 199.

[56] Reginald G. Golledge and Douglas Amedeo, 'On Laws in Geography', *Annals of the Association of American Geographers*, 58 (1968): 760–74; Douglas Amedeo and Reginald G. Golledge, *An Introduction to Scientific Reasoning in Geography* (New York: John Wiley and Sons, 1975); William Bunge, *Theoretical Geography* (Lund: Gleerup, 1962).

sense of the need to construct either deductive-nomological or inductive-statistical models. But it is only in so far as both logical positivism *and* quantitative geography were absorbed into a contemporary mood of international empiricism that any significant links can be established. Logical positivism, as championed by such members of the Vienna Circle in the 1920s and early 1930s as Herbert Feigl, Hans Hahn, Moritz Schlick, Otto Neurath, Rudolph Carnap, and Ernst Mach, was concerned with extending the range of science over the entire gamut of systematic knowledge, and in so doing it spearheaded an antimetaphysical assault on traditional philosophy. To the logical positivists, transcendental metaphysical claims just had no meaning because there was no possible way of testing them in experience. Hence the verification principle, as it was called, became – for a short time – a methodological tool by which meaningful and meaningless sentences could be discriminated. Epistemologically this meant that since there was no conceivable way of verifying even the assertion that there was an external world independent of our experience, debates between realists and idealists were just meaningless. And it is for such reasons that Kolakowski specifies the rule of phenomenalism – restricting knowledge to sense data – as one of positivism's cardinal criteria.[57] The logical positivist task, so to speak, was to translate long-standing philosophical questions – like the relations between mind and body – into empirical language that made some sense. The philosophers' traditional 'riddles of the universe' were thus portrayed as conceptual confusions or misuses of language. As characterized by a focus on the analysis of language and meaning in the manner of Wittgenstein, on elucidating the implications of the Humean distinction between analytical and synthetic propositions, and on a reductionist physicalism (of the type that reduced the laws of chemistry to atomic theory and thermodynamics to the kinetic theory of heat), logical positivism scarcely penetrated the geographical literature.[58]

If geography's ties with logical positivism thus turn out to have been little more than implicit, the same, I think, has to be said of its connections with the earlier positive philosophy of Auguste Comte. To be sure, there were *resonances* between the practices of 'causal geography' and the

[57] L. Kolakowski, *The Alienation of Reason: A History of Positivist Thought*, translated by N. Guterman (New York: Doubleday, 1938), pp. 3–10.

[58] Useful brief introductions include John Passmore, 'Logical Positivism', in Paul Edwards (ed.), *The Encyclopedia of Philosophy* (New York: Macmillan, 1967), volume 5, pp. 52–7; Herbert Feigl, Positivism in the Twentieth Century (Logical Empiricism),' in Philip P. Wiener (ed.), *Dictionary of the History of Ideas* (New York: Scribner's, 1973), vol. 3, pp. 545–51. See also O. Hanfling, *Logical Positivism* (Oxford: Basil Blackwell, 1981).

Comtean project. Their twin concentration on the factual, on the provisional nature of scientific knowledge, on the importance of technological control, on the need to expunge value judgements, and perhaps most of all on the cultivation of a natural science of society, are undeniable. Yet we do need to recall that Comte rejected the essential idea of 'Enlightenment', and nurtured his own progressivist *mentalité* on the writings of what he himself called the 'retrograde school' of traditional apologists for Catholicism such as Bonald, Lamennais, de Maistre, and Chateaubriand. This was a move entirely consistent with his own more or less secularized Catholicism that asserted the centrality of tradition, of family and of social inequality over against that 'disease of the Western world' – individualism.[59] Comte's was thus a progressivism that undercut the more radical rationalism with which the Enlightenment project is typically associated.[60] Nor indeed should the rhetoric of the Comtean unity of scientific method be taken too simply at face value. As Manicas has recently observed, 'Comte's views on the "hierarchy of the sciences" . . . are emphatically *not* those of the twentieth-century unity of science movement. Against that view, Comte held that the sciences were *stratified* and *non-reducible*.'[61]

In the light of all this, Comte's influence on the logical positivist tradition, conventionally interpreted as mediated via Mach, cannot be read in too chronologically teleological a fashion. To be sure, the general spirit of the Comtean ideal was certainly transmitted to the twentieth-century positivists. But it is well to recall that the early logical positivists drew much more heavily on German experimental physics and on those intellectual sources concerned with the significance of logic and symbolic representations in scientific thought. This encouraged their concentration on the centrality of language – a theme taken up in rather different ways by different members of the circle. For Carnap it meant that psychological claims – about, say, mental states – could "be translated into a language which refers to physical events in the body of the person or persons concerned." Psychology, in other words, was simply a species of physics.[62]

---

[59] See George Boas, *French Philosophies of the Romantic Period* (Baltimore: Johns Hopkins University Press, 1924).

[60] See Robert Nisbet, 'Conservatism'; also Anthony Giddens, 'Positivism and its Critics', in Tom Bottomore and Robert Nisbet (eds), *A History of Sociological Analysis* (London, Heinemann, 1978) pp. 237–86.

[61] Peter T. Manicas, *A History and Philosophy of the Social Sciences* (Oxford: Blackwell, 1987), p. 61.

[62] Giddens, 'Positivism and its Critics', p. 275. See also David Oldroyd, *The Arch of Knowledge. An Introductory Study of the History of the Philosophy and Methodology of Science* (New York and London: Methuen, 1986), chapter 6.

As it turns out, then, the label 'positivist' within the geographical tradition has simply been used as a convenient term of reference under which to subsume its modern scientific aspirations, namely as a designator for a parsimonious orientation towards a mathematized account of the distribution of observable entities. Geography rarely engaged in any profound way the positivist epistemological programme. Now given my earlier strictures on terminological tyranny it would certainly be churlish to complain about the use of the term 'positivist' within the geographical tradition. My reason for questioning just how tight the bond between geography and positivist philosophy actually was, however, is to warn against the danger of manufactured history. Accordingly, Gregory's otherwise penetrating exposition of 'positivist explanation in geography' must be appropriated with care. For however telling his exposé of an *implicit* positivist legacy in the geographical search for spatial 'laws', this must not be taken to imply any clear intellectual lineage between Comtean philosophy and the modern geographical experiment – save for the bland reverberations of empiricism. As he himself tellingly observes, the naturalistic thrust of Victorian geography was simply reaffirmed in the mid twentieth century when geography reasserted its confidence in the methodology of natural science – a commitment the subject's Victorian champions would have readily embraced. 'This meant a tacit allegiance to a positivist philosophy of science,' Gregory writes, 'which in its original Comtean form grounded all knowledge in the direct experience of an immediate reality: from this could be derived the laws regulating both man and his material universe.'[63]

All this suggests that geography's contract with positivist vocabulary was a means of ratifying the subject's renewed infatuation with scientific aspiration; and the work that this empiricist mood inspired revealed a discipline increasingly smitten with the language of mathematics. To be sure, later works of geographical theory, like Bunge's *Theoretical Geography* (1962) and Harvey's *Explanation in Geography* (1969) drew substantially on positivist reasoning, ironically at a time when positivism was entirely outmoded in the wider intellectual world. Besides, Hägerstrand's earlier studies of innovation diffusion which were irresistibly connected to communicative functions were, if Gregory's account is to be believed, imbued with the physicalist principles of positivism.[64] Through Froberg, a physicist friend at Lund, Hägerstrand was introduced to Monte Carlo simulation methods,

---

[63] Gregory, *Ideology, Science and Human Geography*, p. 19.
[64] See Derek Gregory, 'Suspended Animation: The Stasis of Diffusion Theory', in Derek Gregory and John Urry (eds), *Social Relations and Spatial Structures* (London: Macmillan, 1985), pp. 296–336.

and his comments on the structural properties of 'social atoms' serve as analogues to Froberg's use of the selfsame technique to investigate the absorption of atomic particles into the concrete shielding surrounding an atomic pile. Thereby the naturalistic bias of Hägerstrand's undertaking is exposed, a bias incidentally supplemented by his expressed desire to incorporate bio-ecological principles into social-geographical theory.

Nevertheless, despite these various appropriations, I still think there are good grounds for supposing that quantitative geography's early encounter with positivism was altogether *implicit*. The personal testimony of some of those nurtured on the quantitative paradigm bear this out. Johnston, for example, confessed that even by the time he had acquired a reputation as a 'quantifier' he still had 'no coherent philosophy of the discipline' and was 'an empiricist' even though he 'didn't know it',[65] while Bennett explicitly eschewed any equation of quantitative geography with positivism.[66] Again Leslie King described his own characterization of positivism, though reflecting its general connotation in the social sciences, as 'less formal than is usually ascribed to the school of "logical positivism".'[67] Comments such as these suggest that the mainsprings of geography's most recent quantitative turn should not be located in the realm of an abstract theoretical positivism. If there are links here they are more likely to have been mediated via the spread of the *practices* that positivism fostered. Instead we should perhaps look towards a more sociological account of the rejuvenation of geographical quantification.

In trying to get a handle on the statistical encroachment on geography during the 1950s and 1960s, it might be wise to recollect that it was, in some ways, a quantitative *return*. Let us not forget that the quantification of economic and social life can be traced back to the early seventeenth cen-

---

[65] R. J. Johnston, 'A Foundling Floundering in World Three', in Mark Billinge, Derek Gregory and Ron Martin (eds), *Recollections of a Revolution. Geography as Spatial Science* (London: Macmillan, 1984), pp. 39–56, ref. on p. 44. Elsewhere Johnston concedes that 'Whatever the general attraction of the positivist approaches, it is clear that in most cases these were not fully assimilated into geographical training. There was little evidence of courses in philosophy of science or even in positivist scientific method . . . the main impression is one of only partial appreciation of the details of the positivist arguments.' R. J. Johnston, *Philosophy and Human Geography. An Introduction to Contemporary Approaches* (London: Edward Arnold, 2nd edn) 1986, p. 31.

[66] R. J. Bennett, 'Quantification and Relevance', in R. J. Johnston (ed.), *The Future of Geography* (London: Methuen, 1985), pp. 211–24.

[67] Leslie J. King, 'Alternatives to a Positive Economic Geography', in Stephen Gale and Gunnar Olsson (eds), *Philosophy in Geography* (Dordrecht: Reidel, 1979), pp. 187–213, ref. on p. 197.

tury.[68] The merchant John Graunt, for example, had constructed life-expectancy tables in his *Observations on the London Bills of Mortality* in 1662, Edmund Halley had prepared his own life-tables, and William Petty advocated the establishment of a state statistical department to conduct what he called 'political arithmetic'. Such exercises, we recall, were part of a Puritan social agenda in which geographical practices loomed large. Moreover, that these statistics were also 'state-istics' has not escaped the notice of critical commentators, not least because the later flourishing of statistical knowledge paralleled the expansion of industrial capitalism in England.[69] Of course there were other contexts too. Numerology could and did subserve the needs of the astronomers, the astrologers, and the alchemists. But these only serve to underscore the fact that the role of num-bering in our approach to the natural and social worlds is a historical prod-uct, rather than some eternal analytical principle.

More specifically, however, the emergence of statistical *theory*, aside from the practices of statistical enumeration, can very largely be traced to the efforts of figures like Francis Galton and Karl Pearson working on eugenics during the decades around the end of the nineteenth century. Because these leading eugenic statisticians embraced a class-based social philosophy that presupposed a hierarchy of innate physical excellence and intellectual talent, it has been argued that the techniques they evolved for the handling of population data – like regression and correlation – were suffused with their practitioners' ideological orientations.[70] Of crucial importance in Galton's formulations, for example, were the ideas he gleaned from Adolphe Quetelet's observations on the error law (or the nor-mal distribution curve, or, simply, the bell-shaped curve, as it later became known) in his presentation of the moral statistics of crime, suicide, and marriage. Working by analogy from observational astronomy, Quetelet thus hoped to model his social physics on celestial physics. Significantly Galton, it seems, first came across Quetelet's law of distribution in a paper that his friend William Spottiswoode, a geographer, published in 1861 on the

[68] See Peter Buck, 'Seventeenth-Century Political Arithmetic: Civil Strife and Vital Statistic', *Isis*, 68 (1977): 67–84.

[69] Martin Shaw and Ian Miles, 'The Social Roots of Statistical Knowledge', in John Irvine, Ian Miles and Jeff Evans (eds), *Demystifying Social Statistics* (n.p.: Pluto Press, 1979), pp. 27–38.

[70] See Donald Mackenzie, 'Eugenics in Britain'; Donald Mackenzie, 'Statistical Theory and Social Interests: A Case Study', *Social Studies of Sciences*, 8 (1978): 35–83; Donald Mackenzie, 'Eugenics and the Rise of Mathematical Statistics in Britain', in Irvine et al. (eds), *Demystifying Social Statistics*, pp. 39–50; Donald Mackenzie, *Statistics in Britain, 1865–1930: The Social Construction of Scientific Knowledge* (Edinburgh: Edinburgh University Press, 1981).

application of probability theory to physical geography. Spottiswoode's immediate interest was to do with the way in which the orientation of Asian mountain axes might be governed by the error law; but he did conceive of his paper as a methodological tract, and certainly Galton enthusiastically embraced its statistical procedure as a means of defining population types. It was to become a cornerstone in Galton's volume on *Hereditary Genius*, published in 1869 – only one of a series of notorious statistically based projects which included a mathematical method of cutting a cake, a quantitative map of the distribution of female beauty in Britain, and a statistical test on the efficacy of prayer![71] But Galton also later proposed in his presidential address to the Geographical Section of the British Association in 1872 that geography's 'highest problem' in dealing with land configuration, soil type, vegetation characteristics, climatic conditions, animal and human populations, and so on, was 'to analyze their correlations and to sift the casual from the essential.'[72]

The early history of quantification thus reveals that social and political interests evidently underlay the enterprise. This, of course, should not be taken to mean that quantification was *just* ideological crystallization. But it does serve to remind us that its claim to objectivity simply cannot be taken at face value. And it is for reasons such as these that David Harvey has recently accounted for the quantitative move in modern American geography as a strategic manoeuvre to escape the political suspicion falling on social science during the McCarthy era. The repression of commentators like Owen Lattimore, Harvey concludes, 'led many progressivist geographers thereafter to express their social concerns behind the supposed neutrality of "the positivist shield".'[73] Commentators from other disciplines provide accounts similarly based on political grounds. The libertarian Marxist historian of science, Robert Young, for example, suggests that the reductionist metaphysical and methodological assumptions that pervade quantitative analyses have made it all too easy to adopt what he calls 'the

[71] William Spottiswoode, 'On Typical Mountain Ranges: An Application of the Calculus of Probabilities to Physical Geography', *Journal of the Royal Geographical Society*, 31 (1861): 149–54. This episode is treated in Theodore M. Porter, *The Rise of Statistical Thinking 1820–1900* (Princeton, N. J.: Princeton University Press, 1986). On the question of prayer, see Francis Galton, 'Statistical Inquiries into the Efficacy of Prayer', *Fortnightly Review*, n.s. 12 (1872): 125–35. The issue of what came to be known as the prayer-gauge debate is treated in Frank Miller Turner, 'Rainfall, Plagues and the Prince of Wales: A Chapter in the Conflict of Religion and Science', *Journal of British Studies*, 13 (1974): 46–65; and David N. Livingstone, 'Darwinism and Calvinism: The Belfast-Princeton Connection', *Isis*, 83(1992).
[72] Francis Galton, 'Address as President of Geography Section', *Annual Reports of British Association for the Advancement of Science*, 42 (1872): 198–203, ref. on p. 199.
[73] David Harvey, 'History and Present Condition of Geography', ref. on p. 5.

diverted gaze', namely one in which social criticism is muted. 'By represent-ing variations in numerical forms', he writes, 'the quantitative approach tends to direct our attention away from the evaluation of the concepts and variables themselves'.[74] In a threatening political environment, such moves have an obvious appeal. Still, this is hardly a recent turn of events. Galileo's conviction that the language of nature is mathematics resulted in his isolation of those phenomena most translatable into quantitative vocab-ulary, and then, having performed this operation, to devalue descriptive appearances as having at most secondary value and to regard mathematical representation as constitutive. As Price has written, in Galileo 'the mathe-matical geometry of matter in "space" is given ultimate status.'[75]

Alongside the ontological reductionism inherent in this vision of the sci-entific enterprise has gone a style of communication which, particularly when applied to the social sciences, has further contributed to a mode of discourse from which value judgement has been exiled. Taking up this issue within geography, David Mercer – drawing on the critique of the Radical Statistics Group which regards statistics not as 'findings' but as 'creations' – portrays what he calls technocratic geography as a means of suppressing humankind's 'existential awareness' and 'moral nature'. Not surprisingly, in Mercer's reading such technocentrism easily 'became the intellectual arm of western imperialism'[76] – an achievement effected through its capacity to close scientific language around such terms as manipulation, control, pre-diction, and efficiency. That this move – crystallized in the application of control engineering to geographical systems – is itself ideological has not been ignored by critics.[77]

If drawing attention to the political dimensions of recent geographical quantification provides a corrective to a too comfortable official story of progress, it can hardly be the whole explanation for the quantitative return. For while quantification could bolster political conservatism, we should recall that key advocates of scientific geography were not infrequently of an actively leftist orientation. Schaefer, as Bunge has reminded us, involved himself with a variety of socialist organizations both before and after his

---

[74] Robert M. Young, 'Why are Figures so Significant? The Role and Critique of Quantification', in Irvine et al. (eds), *Demystifying Social Statistics*, pp. 63–74, ref. on p. 68.

[75] Geoffrey Price, 'Reductionism and the Differentiation of Consciousness', in Arthur Peacocke (ed.), *Reductionism in Academic Disciplines* (Surrey: Society for Research into Higher Education and NFER-Nelson, 1985), pp. 125–42, ref. on p. 129.

[76] David Mercer, 'Unmasking Technocratic Geography', in Billinge et al. (eds), *Recollections of a Revolution*, pp. 153–99, ref. on p. 181.

[77] See for example Derek Gregory, 'The Ideology of Control – Systems Theory and Geography', *Tijdschrift voor Economische en Sociale Geografie*, 71 (1980): 327–42.

arrival in the USA, and while Bunge later immersed himself in a participatory geography, his own politics did not prevent him from embracing the scientific vision with not a little enthusiasm. A narrow political interpretation is thus sure to founder on the plural rocks of the historical record.

What I want to suggest is that in the wake of geography's demise at Harvard and the ensuing sense of disciplinary marginalization in an increasingly specialist academy, numerical language was adopted by practitioners lusting after scientific credibility.[78] Consider, for instance, the judgements of Peter Gould. For him the label 'quantitative revolution' was just simply 'a disastrous misnomer'. 'It was not the numbers that were important,' Gould confessed, 'but a whole new way of looking at things geographic that can be summed up in Whitehead's definition of scientific thought, "To see what is general in what is particular and what is permanent in what is transitory".'[79] Johnston concurs, noting that by becoming 'more scientific' geographers could thereby advance 'disciplinary and personal esteem'.[80] So, in their encounter with Lösch, Christaller, and Walter Isard's recently published *Location and Space Economy*, figures like W. L. Garrison, Richard Morrill, and Brian Berry at Washington came face to face with more than statistics; they found what they believed was scientific theory. Because the subject seemed bound up with description, enumeration, even intuition, it was, as Morrill later recalled, 'no wonder that geography was being eased out of prestigious institutions'. The only alternative was to seek scientific standing. 'Our vision', according to Morrill, 'may have seemed radical to those satisfied with an inferior status, but was actually conservative in the sense that we wanted to save geography as a field of study and to join the mainstream of science.' This was altogether desirable because he believed that it was science that had 'liberated so many from superstition, and made possible through technology and organisation an escape from slavery, poverty and disease.'[81]

Seen in this light, the quantitative methods that geographers espoused turn out to have been rhetorical devices of persuasion by which the scientific authority of their assertions could be reinforced. Like graphs, plans,

---

[78] Perhaps this too is a political interpretation; but if so, it is of wide remit.

[79] Peter Gould, 'Geography 1957–1977: The Augean Period', *Annals of the Association of American Geographers*, 69 (1979), pp. 139–51, ref. on p. 140.

[80] Johnston, *Philosophy and Human Geography*, p. 31.

[81] Morrill, 'The "Quantitative Revolution's" Early Years', pp. 67, 68. Davies makes a similar judgement when he speaks of geography 'being pushed down the path of modern science.' Wayne K. D. Davies, 'Theory, Science and Geography', in Wayne K. D. Davies (ed.), *The Conceptual Revolution in Geography* (London: University of London Press, 1972), pp. 31–41, ref. on p. 38.

models, maps, and diagrams, equations are contrivances that investigators construct to represent real world circumstances. But they are not 'pictures' of those events. They rather purport to go below the surface, so to speak, and unveil the underlying principles of organization.[82] Just how successful the operation is taken to be depends on the support the account is able to muster from the best-aligned authorities.[83] In geography's case, appeals were made to the scientific powers. Thus, because statistical competence provided what Taylor calls 'prestige by association', there was more than a little temptation to obfuscate; the quantitative moment supplied the opportunity to generate a methodological complexity that could all too easily camouflage conceptual superficiality; and it facilitated the 'creation of a generation gap' through the manufacture of an old orthodoxy to attack.[84]

The rising generation were thus socialized in a different intellectual setting, with the result that by 1960, according to Burton, the 'quantitative revolution' was over, in the sense that the 'revolutionary' ideas had by then become conventional wisdom.[85] How accurate Burton's date is may be questionable, but there certainly was already a growing sense that the aspiring geographical professional simply had to acquire, as a craft competence, elementary mathematical techniques for the handling of spatially distributed data. In the British context, this newest of the new geographies was promulgated in a series of books that emanated from two geographers at Cambridge, Peter Haggett and R. J. Chorley, whose concern, at least in part, was to reinforce the image of the subject as a model-building enterprise through the continuing transformation of geographical education.[86] Henceforth the spatial language of surfaces, diffusion, movement, nodes, channels, and the like became geographical vernacular, while regression methods and principal components and factor analyses became, at least for

[82] Gould, for example, writes that there are occasions when 'algebraic languages take over as the *only* forms capable of describing complexity with any degree of depth.' Peter Gould, 'Signals in the Noise', in Gale and Olsson (eds), *Philosophy in Geography*, pp. 121–54, ref. on p. 133.

[83] See the essays by Michael Lynch and Steve Woolgar, 'Introduction: Sociological Orientations to Representational Practice in Science' (pp. 1–18) and Bruno Latour, 'Drawing Things Together' (pp. 19–68) in Michael Lynch and Steve Woolgar (eds), *Representation in Scientific Practice* (Cambridge, Mass.: The MIT Press, 1990).

[84] Peter J. Taylor, 'An Interpretation of the Quantification Debate in British Geography', *Transactions of the Institute of British Geographers*, 1 (1976): 129–42, ref. on p. 136.

[85] Ian Burton, 'The Quantitative Revolution and Theoretical Geography', *The Canadian Geographer*, 7 (1963): 151–62.

[86] So Peter Haggett, *Locational Analysis in Human Geography* (London: Edward Arnold, 1965); Peter Haggett and R. J. Chorley (eds), *Frontiers in Geographical Teaching* (London: Methuen, 1965); Richard J. Chorley and Peter Haggett (eds), *Models in Geography* (London: Methuen, 1967).

some, the insignia of the scientific geographer. And yet for all that, if Leslie King's diagnosis is in the neighbourhood of a correct analysis, the 'so-called quantitative revolution changed mainly the research techniques' but did little to channel the subject away 'from a traditional concern' with static locational patterns.[87]

STATISTICS DON'T BLEED

Geography's confrontation with the vocabulary of logical positivism, I have suggested, was a *post hoc* means of rationalizing its attempt to reconstitute itself as spatial science. However, this exposure, mediated through such works of philosophical apologetic as Bunge's *Theoretical Geography* (1962) and Harvey's *Explanation in Geography* (1969), came – as I have said – at a time when logical positivism was already largely discredited in the wider scholarly world. The problem of verifying induction, the theory-ladenness of observation, and the challenges of Kuhnian and post-Kuhnian philosophy of science, for example, had all been aired. Moreover the criticisms of positivism's imposition of strict limits on moral reason that emanated from the Marxist-inspired Frankfurt philosophers, and the sociological reappropriation of Dilthey's *Geisteswissenschaften*, provided further inspiration for those reaching towards a post-positivist conceptual framework.

But the quantitative reassertion in twentieth-century geography was perhaps flawed in an even more fundamental way. Its significance, I suggest, cannot be restricted to its concern with number. Rather it instantiated – using algebraic codes – a way of thinking that, in its most pernicious form, could represent qualitative issues about worth – such as, say, virtue and vice, nobility and baseness, courage, pusillanimity, alienation – as confused perceptions of the real bases of human behaviour. Spatial scientists, with their Newtonian aspirations, sought to uncover a few foundational axioms by which the patterns and processes of human interaction could be explained. Similarly utilitarians had, for long enough, sought to evacuate language of value judgement and to replace it with a formal calculus. This was, if I can borrow the words of Charles Taylor, an attempt 'to do away with strong evaluation' and to replace it with 'calculation'. Now, if Taylor's reading is correct, this is not just an aberrant philosophical move; it is actually subversive of human agency, because, as he sees it, the capacity to make morally robust evaluation is 'an essential feature of the mode

---

[87] King, 'Alternatives to a Positive Economic Geography', p. 187.

of agency we recognize as human.' To succeed in substituting calculation for evaluation would therefore be, in Taylor's view, a thoroughly dehumanizing achievement.[88]

For both conceptual and, I suggest, moral reasons, positivism in geography rapidly came under severe attack from several quarters. Certainly geographical *practice* continues to be profoundly implicated in the technical revolution that quantification ushered into the tradition. But the positivist credo has been the subject of theoretical censure from those of both radical and humanist leaning. Temporal propinquity and publication profusion over the past two decades, however, render it impossible to investigate in any detail the multifarious ways in which geographical critics have expressed their revulsion at positivism's pretended neutrality, its atomistic conception of the social, its devaluation of the intuitive, and its failure to recognize that statistics don't bleed.[89] Indeed in some ways it is still much too early to attempt any rigorous contextual elucidation of these most recent moves. All I can hope to present in the remaining pages at my disposal is an outline map of this contested terrain.

It is perhaps no surprise that the very figures who had acted as godfathers at geography's positivist baptism – Bunge and Harvey – were among the first to express their disaffection. Yet while their philosophical acumen doubtless alerted them to logical positivism's philosophical fragility, in both cases a political awakening was decisive, and represented a realignment with Marxist social theory.[90] For Bunge this engagement took the form of a return to the geographical motif of exploration, not this time to the heart of remote jungles, but into the ethnic no-go areas of Detroit. Thus the very individual who had issued one of the most articulate and, as he himself puts it, 'unmitigated attack[s] on uniqueness' found himself pressed by the experience of his own political struggles in Detroit's Fitzgerald to issue a public retraction.[91] Yet while Bunge considered his project as an express

[88] Charles Taylor, 'What is Human Agency?' in *Human Agency and Language. Philosophical Papers, Volume 1* (Cambridge: Cambridge University Press, 1985), pp. 15–44, refs on pp. 17, 16.

[89] See Alan M. Hay, 'Positivism in Human Geography: Response to Critics', in D. T. Herbert and R. J. Johnston (eds), *Geography and the Urban Environment: Progress in Research and Applications Volume 2* (Chichester: John Wiley, 1979), pp. 1–26.

[90] On this general association, see Richard Peet 'The Development of Radical Geography in the United States', *Progress in Human Geography*, 1 (1977): 240–63; Richard Peet (ed.), *Radical Geography* (London: Methuen, 1978); Derek Gregory, 'Marxist Geography', in R. J. Johnston et al. (eds), *The Dictionary of Human Geography* (Oxford: Blackwell, 2nd edn 1986), pp. 287–92.

[91] William Bunge, 'Perspective on *Theoretical Geography*', *Annals of the Association of American Geographers*, 69 (1979): 169–74, ref. on p. 173. See also William Bunge, *Fitzgerald: The Geography of a Revolution* (Cambridge, Mass.: Schenkman, 1971).

rejection of what he called '"nice" geography or *status quo* geography' – and it certainly did constitute an angry call for a refocusing of the object of geographical study through an impassioned plea for a particular kind of social relevance – his *analytical* apparatus remained firmly that of the spatial science brigade.[92]

In David Harvey's case the turn to Marxism went far deeper. It began with his 1972 consideration of ghetto formation, appropriately enough published in the recently established radical journal *Antipode*. But this empirical moment served as the occasion to enunciate a revolutionary manifesto for geography as a whole. And this revolution was not just of the conceptual variety; it appealed for revolutionary action because, as Harvey now saw it, theory and practice were inextricably intertwined. Geography was thus to be conceived of as itself a social practice needing transformation; to continue to produce further empirical studies of wretched social conditions without reformist commitments would be counter-revolutionary.[93] Within the year, he had brought out his *Social Justice and the City* – a collection of work-in-progress essays in which he sought to connect justice, space, and theory in the idioms of Marxist historical materialism.[94] An integral ingredient of this conceptual re-evaluation was Harvey's recognition of the ideological captivity of science – a topic he explicitly took up the following year. Here he rejected the logical positivism that had 'provided a general paradigmatic basis for scientific enquiry' in general and for the conventional Malthusian analysis of global resource questions in particular. The assumption of science's ethical and cognitive neutrality was now simply untenable, given the constitutive 'connections between method, ideology and substantive conclusions'. Scientific explanation just *was* ideological, and the sooner this was universally acknowledged the better.[95] For Harvey himself 'a

---

[92] William Bunge, 'The First Years of the Detroit Geographical Expedition: A Personal Report', in Richard Peet (ed.), *Radical Geography: Alternative Viewpoints on Contemporary Social Issues* (London: Methuen, 1978) (first published 1969), p. 35.

[93] David Harvey, 'Revolutionary and Counter-Revolutionary Theory in Geography and the Problem of Ghetto Formation', *Antipode*, 4, 2 (1972): 1–13.

[94] David Harvey, *Social Justice and the City* (London: Arnold, 1973). The volume drew forth fierce criticism from Brian Berry. See the discussion in Paul Cloke, Chris Philo and David Sadler, *Approaching Human Geography. An Introduction to Contemporary Theoretical Debates* (London: Paul Chapman, 1991), pp. 38–9.

[95] In keeping with this perspective were the investigations of geography's past ideological captivities. Thus Brian Hudson, 'The New Geography'; Richard Peet, 'The Social Origins of Environmental Determinism', *Annals of the Association of American Geographers*, 75 (1985): 309–33. Given such realignments it is understandable that the earlier perspectives of radical figures like Kropotkin, Reclus, and Wittfogel also began to be reappropriated.

properly constituted version of dialectical materialism' provided the only compelling option.[96]

Of course much of the geographical academy remained untouched by these early statements of Marxist avowal. Systems analysis, for example, of problems in both physical and human geography persisted,[97] while producers of spatial statistics continued to investigate diffusion patterns and to engage in spatial forecasting.[98] Still, in the aftermath of Harvey's programmatic statement, the task of inserting the spatial into the standard Marxist model was undertaken with the objective of fashioning a historical-*geographical* materialism. Massey, for instance, reworked industrial locational theory, at once exposing its ideological biases and drafting a spatial account of the division of labour.[99] To understand the spatial transformations of industrial change, she insisted, it was necessary to go beyond observable surface patterns and examine those changes in production that were the driving force behind shifts in locational requirements. As she later reflected, this recasting of location theory crucially understood 'spatial change . . . as being an outcome of production change.' The relations of ownership and production, it turned out, were what were 'stretched out over space.'[100] And then Harvey, having continued to work on housing markets, set himself the task of rewriting classical Marxism in geographical terms. *The Limits to Capital* was the result. A complex theoretical argument which devoted special attention to the dynamics of urbanization, it injected space at various scales into the Marxist conceptualization of capitalism.[101] Thus in his continuing efforts to theorize the historical geography of capitalism Harvey has continually sought ways of overcoming the spatial deficiencies of social theory:

> The issue of space and geography is a sadly neglected stepchild in *all* social theory . . . Marx, Marshall, Weber, and Durkheim all have this in common:

[96] David Harvey, 'Population, Resources, and the Ideology of Science', in Gale and Olsson (eds), *Philosophy in Geography*, pp. 155–85, refs on pp. 183, 157, 183. This essay first appeared in *Economic Geography*, 50 (1974): 256–77.

[97] Earlier S. R. Eyre had expressed the hope that an eco-systems approach would enable geographers to free themselves from naive determinism. S. R. Eyre, 'Determinism and the Ecological Approach to Geography', *Geography*, 49 (1964): 369–76.

[98] The work of such figures as Bennett, Chorley, Cliff, Haggett, Haining, Johnston, Kennedy, Wrigley, and Wilson, working in this tradition are reviewed in R. J. Johnston, *Geography and Geographers*. A sociological account of this tradition is a real desideratum.

[99] See, for example, Doreen Massey, 'Towards a Critique of Industrial Location Theory', *Antipode*, 5, 3 (1973): 33–9; Doreen Massey, *Spatial Divisions of Labour: Social Structures and the Geography of Production* (London: Macmillan, 1984).

[100] Doreen Massey, 'New Directions in Space', in Derek Gregory and John Urry (eds), *Social Relations and Spatial Structures* (London: Macmillan, 1985), pp. 9–19, refs on pp. 13, 15.

[101] David Harvey, *The Limits to Capital* (Oxford: Blackwell, 1982).

they prioritise time and history over space and geography and, where they treat of the latter at all, tend to view them unproblematically as the stable context or site for historical action.

Just how the particulars of specific geographical spaces are to be stitched into 'the universal and abstract determinations of Marx's theory of capitalist accumulation' remains, for Harvey, geography's grand project.[102]

To speak, as I have just done, of geography's realignment with Marxism in such unqualified terms is, of course, to risk the charge of caricature. For the intellectual genealogy of Marxism reveals it to be both a complex and diversified tradition. In the West, the critical theory of the Frankfurt school, for example, markedly differs from both the structuralist version advanced by Althusser and the more humanistic Marxism of figures like Raymond Williams and E. P. Thompson.[103] Still, I think it would be fair to say that geography's espousal of Marxist categories of interpretation facilitated an exposure to the canons of structuralism. To be sure, those earlier practitioners who absorbed Spencerian evolution had come face to face with a functionalism that explained organic (and superorganic) structures as arising to achieve certain functions.[104] But now a more explicitly socio-political, less instrumentalist, version presented itself.

A family of beliefs united by the conviction that observable phenomena are the manifestations of some underlying set of mechanisms,[105] structuralism of Althusserian-Marxist stripe accounts for the political and ideological elements in civil society (the superstructure) as the surface expressions of the economic modes of production (the infrastructure) – the precise antithesis of Hegelian philosophy. It would, however, be mistaken to read this account in an overly deterministic fashion, for the mediations between economic structure and superstructure are, according to Althusser, both intricate and indirect. To achieve geographical articulacy, this version of Marxian structuralism required translation into spatial categories. And it was largely through Manuel Castells that the various levels of social formation and modes of production were provided with spatial analogues – the

---

[102] David Harvey, 'The Geopolitics of Capitalism', in Gregory and Urry, *Social Relations and Spatial Structures*, pp. 128–63, refs on pp. 141, 144. See also Nigel Thrift, 'On the Determination of Social Action in Space and Time', *Environment and Planning D: Society and Space*, 1 (1983): 23–57.

[103] See Tom Bottomore (ed.), *Modern Interpretations of Marx* (Oxford: Blackwell, 1981).

[104] See Derek Gregory, 'Functionalism', in R. J. Johnston et al. (eds), *Dictionary of Human Geography*, pp. 165–7.

[105] See E. Kurzweil, *The Age of Structuralism* (New York: Columbia University Press, 1980).

institutional and symbolic representations of space at the superstructural level, and the spatial organizations of production, consumption, and exchange at the economic level.[106] In this reading of things, spatial arrangements have come to be seen as the realization of economic and social relations: spatial structure, so to speak, articulates social structure. Accordingly, as recent commentators frequently remind us, 'spatiality' is to be thought of as a social *production*. The spaces in which we transact the affairs of our daily lives – local, regional, and beyond – are thus themselves the products of social forces; in turn, these family, educational, employment, religious, and a host of other, spaces become the arenas in which social life is reproduced. As Soja, drawing on the work of Henri Lefebvre, has written of it: 'The production of space . . . can thus be described as both the *medium* and the *outcome* of social action and relationship.'[107]

In their efforts to theorize these relationships, some geographers have flirted with other forms of 'deep' structuralism, notably of the linguistic, psychological, and anthropological varieties. Accordingly, the names of Chomsky, Piaget, and Lévi-Strauss from time to time surface in these deliberations. What unites these thinkers is their search for deep, universal structures at the neural level – focused, for Chomsky, on a generative theory of language, for Piaget on a universal sequence of mental stages, for Lévi-Strauss on forms of prohibition and exchange.[108] Yet thus far these seem to have held out little more than a promissory geographical note. Johnston, for instance, confesses that the 'search for deep structures does not characterize work in human geography' save perhaps for the tacit biologization of such behavioural traits as territoriality, a sense of place, and spatial orientation.[109] Again, Gregory, having dilated on Lévi-Strauss's exploration of kinship systems in grammatical terms, and urging the need to examine its implications for contemporary geography, ultimately moves off to an

---

[106] See Derek Gregory, *Ideology, Science and Human Geography*, pp. 118f.

[107] Edward W. Soja, 'The Spatiality of Social Life: Towards a Transformative Retheorisation', in Gregory and Urry (eds), *Social Relations and Spatial Structures*, pp. 90–127, ref. on p. 94. Here Soja explicates Lefebvre's *La Production de l'Espace*.

[108] See G. C. Lepschy, *A Survey of Structural Linguistics* (Oxford: Oxford University Press, 1982); John Sturrock (ed.), *Structuralism and Since: From Lévi-Strauss to Derrida* (Oxford: Oxford University Press, 1979).

[109] Johnston, *Geography and Geographers*, p. 221. A genetic account of mapping as an inherited trait linked to 'the structural as well as the functional foundations of language' is espoused in G. Malcolm Lewis, 'The Origins of Cartography', in J. B. Harley and David Woodward (eds), *History of Cartography, Volume One. Cartography in Prehistoric, Ancient, and Medieval Europe and the Mediterranean* (Chicago: University of Chicago Press, 1987), pp. 50–3.

interrogation of structural Marxism, leaving the connection between these various structuralisms at best implicit.[110]

Although structural explanation in the Marxist vein has arguably been more theoretically and empirically productive, it would be mistaken to assume that radical geography has had a monopoly on such projects. Earlier, tantalizing flirtations with structural categories surfaced in William Kirk's portrait of the 'behavioural environment' and in David Lowenthal's 'geographical epistemology'. Because both fastened on the structuring processes of the human mind in its encounter with the outside world, they can – implicitly at least – be joined up to the epistemological programme of Immanuel Kant.[111] In Kirk's case this took the form of a separation of the 'external' world of natural and culturally constructed things, from the 'internal' world of perception. Between these he interposed what he called the 'behavioural environment', a realm in which external stimuli were ordered into conceptual patterns or 'structures' (figure 9.1). The results of these ordering processes, moreover, turned out to be relative in both time and place. This meant that, as he put it, 'the same empirical data may arrange themselves into different patterns and have different meanings to people of different cultures, or at different stages in the history of a particular culture.'[112] And so Kirk conceived of the geographer's task as elucidating locational decisions through reconstructing 'the environment not only as it was at various dates but as it was observed and thought to be, for it is in this behavioural environment that physical features acquire values and potentialities which attract or repel human action.'[113] With this move, Kirk hoped at once to close the gap between mind and nature, and widen the scope of geographical inquiry. To achieve this goal he turned to the Gestalt psychologists Max Wertheimer, Wolfgang Köhler, and Kurt Koffka (from whom he acquired the label 'behavioural environment'), who had been con-

---

[110] Indeed he comments on the lack of development of 'a formalist conception of spatial structures' – derived from linguistic structuralism – within geography, save for hints in the writings of David Lowenthal. These are discussed below. Gregory, *Ideology, Science and Human Geography*, pp. 102–3.

[111] See the discussion in chapter 4, and in D. N. Livingstone and R. T. Harrison, 'Immanuel Kant, Subjectivism and Human Geography: A Preliminary Investigation', *Transactions of the Institute of British Geographers*, n.s. 6 (1981): 359–74.

[112] William Kirk, 'Problems of Geography', *Geography*, 48 (1963): 357–71, ref. on p. 366.

[113] William Kirk, 'Historical Geography and the Concept of the Behavioural Environment', *Indian Geographical Journal*, Silver Jubilee Volume (1952): 152–60, ref. on p. 159. This original formulation is reprinted in Frederick W. Boal and David N. Livingstone (eds), *The Behavioural Environment: Essays in Reflection, Application, and Re-Evaluation* (London: Routledge, 1989), pp. 18–30. See also the discussion in Harold C. Brookfield, 'On the Environment as Perceived', *Progress in Geography*, 1 (1969): 51–80.

FACTS   VALUES

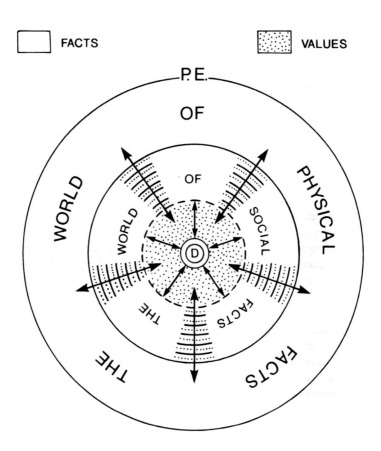

Figure 9.1   William Kirk's behavioural environment. P.E. = Phenomenal Environment; D = Decision-taker

ducting various experimental studies on colour perception and pattern recognition.[114] And indeed he subsequently incorporated Gestalt terminology into his very portrayal of the behavioural environment when he depicted it as 'a psycho-physical field in which phenomenal facts are arranged into patterns of structures (*Gestalten*) and acquire values in

[114] Their rejection of logical positivism should not be taken to mean that Kirk found no time for the methods of natural science. See John A. Campbell, 'The Concept of "The Behavioural Environment"', and its Origins, Reconsidered', in Boal and Livingstone (eds), *The Behavioural Environment*, pp. 33–76.

cultural contexts.'[115] With such intellectual associations it is entirely understandable that he should subsequently make overt acknowledgement of the
resonances between his own convictions and the respective structuralisms of
Lévi-Strauss and Piaget.[116]

In like manner David Lowenthal appealed, in 1961, for geographers to
take with greater seriousness the images contained within the minds of different human groupings. Because the 'geography of the world is unified
only by human logic and optics, by light and colour of artifice, by decorative arrangement, and by ideas of the good, the true, and the beautiful,'
Lowenthal affirmed, 'the relation between the world and the pictures in our
heads' was a project of considerable moment.[117] Indeed, he hoped to, but
ultimately despaired of, uncovering a 'psychology of environment'.[118]
Lowenthal's aspirations, and his call to chart the *terrae incognitae* of the
human psyche call to mind the earlier writings of J. K. Wright who likewise wanted to plumb the mental geography – 'geosophy' as he termed it –
of different cultures. Given their shared enthusiasm for the subjective, it is
entirely understandable that Lowenthal should later, in 1972, collaborate in
editing a collection of essays dedicated to Wright under the title
Geographies of the Mind.[119] In Wright's case, this 'geosophical idealism'
had earlier taken the form of a reconstruction of the geographical 'lore'
held by medieval Europeans during the time of the crusades and an appeal
for a far broader conception of what the history of geographical ideas
might mean. To him the history of 'error' was every bit as enlightening as
the history of 'truth'.[120] For Clarence Glacken, similar concerns undergirded his monumental survey of the history of culture and nature from
ancient times to the end of the eighteenth century.[121]

[115] Kirk, 'Problems of Geography', p. 366.

[116] William Kirk, 'The Road from Mandalay: Towards a Geographical Epistemology',
Transactions of the Institute of British Geographers, n.s. 3 (1978): 381–94.

[117] David Lowenthal, 'Geography, Experience, and Imagination: towards a Geographical
Epistemology', *Annals of the Association of American Geographers*, 51 (1961): 241–60, refs on
pp. 241, 260.

[118] David Lowenthal and Hugh Prince, 'Transcendental Experience', in S. Wapner, S. Cohen
and B. Kaplan (eds), *Experiencing the Environment* (New York: Plenum, 1976).

[119] David Lowenthal and Martyn J. Bowden (eds), *Geographies of the Mind: Essays in
Historical Geosophy* (New York: Oxford University Press, 1976).

[120] J. K. Wright, *The Geographical Lore of the Time of the Crusade: A Study in the History of
Medieval Science and Tradition in Western Europe* (New York: American Geographical Society,
1925); J. K. Wright, A Plea for the History of Geography', *Isis*, 8 (1926): 477–91. See also his
collection of essays *Human Nature in Geography*.

[121] Clarence Glacken, *Traces on the Rhodian Shore*. In 1979 Ludmilla Jordanova and Roy
Porter, historians of science, applauded the methodological creativity adopted by such writers.
See L. J. Jordanova and Roy Porter, 'Introduction', in L. J. Jordanova and Roy S. Porter (eds),

The idealist thrust of this corpus of work has meant that these geographers have frequently been cast as precursors of a more consciously articulated humanism that found voice in geography during the 1970s.[122] But it would be wise to recall that Kirk himself was not unfavourably disposed to positivist methods,[123] and that others with a behavioural interest could, and did, migrate in an altogether computational direction. It was entirely feasible, for instance, just to extend the scope of positivist methodology beyond its traditional emphasis on observable entities, and to apply numerical measures to the components of mental construction in the hope of creating a behavioural spatial science. Successive projects on charting mental maps, scaling locational choice preferences, and so on, could thus easily connect up with the stimulus–response mechanisms of the behaviouristic psychologists. Certainly this was neither invariably nor inevitably so; but behavioural geography – especially in mathematical voice – could certainly exude the aura of positivist science.[124]

Similarly recognizing the importance of reasserting the salience of the human subject, though explicitly culling from a different set of philosophical traditions, a number of geographers began issuing a series of 'humanistic' critiques of positivist spatial science during the 1970s. To speak of this revolt as 'humanistic', of course, is to use shorthand for the diverse range of proposals that were canvassed to give shape to the chorus of discontent that was sounded. What united these critics was what they opposed, namely, the disappearance of the human agent as a thinking, feeling, subject from the geographical conversation. The human had been elided in 'human' geography, and had been replaced by rational economic actors,

---

Images of the Earth. Essays in the History of the Environmental Sciences (Chalfont St Giles: British Society for the History of Science, 1979), pp. v–xx, ref. on pp. x–xi.

[122] The same might be said of J. Wreford Watson's early call to incorporate the subjective and non-material into social geography. See J. Wreford Watson, 'The Sociological Aspects of Geography', in T. Griffith Taylor (ed.), *Geography in the Twentieth Century: A Study of Growth, Fields, Techniques, Aims and Trends* (London: Methuen, 1951), pp. 463–99.

[123] See the comments in Frederick W. Boal and David N. Livingstone, 'The Behavioural Environment: Worlds of Meaning in a World of Facts', in Boal and Livingstone, *Behavioural Environment*, pp. 3–17.

[124] See Reginald G. Golledge and G. Rushton (eds), *Spatial Choice and Spatial Behavior: Geographical Essays on the Analysis of Preferences and Perceptions* (Columbus, Ohio: Ohio State University Press, 1976); Reginald G. Golledge and Helen Couclelis, 'Positivist Philosophy and Research on Human Spatial Behaviour', in T. F. Saarinen, D. Seamon and J. L. Sell (eds), *Environmental Perception and Behavior: An Inventory and Prospect* (University of Chicago, Department of Geography, Research Paper no. 209, 1984); Peter R. Gould and Rodney White, *Mental Maps* (Harmondsworth: Penguin Books, 1974); Reginald G. Golledge and H. Timmermans (eds), *Behavioural Modelling in Geography and Planning* (London: Croom Helm, 1988).

statistical equations, stimulus–response mechanisms, and dotted distributions. But because these were sucked dry of desires, meanings, and emotions, they represented what Entrikin described as an 'overly objective, narrow, mechanistic and deterministic view' of the human agent.[125] Moreover, the realization that the precise language of 'scientific' social science could certainly cope well with such dehumanized abstractions, but at the cost of assassinating ambiguity and veiling the investigators' values, led some geographers, like Olsson and Buttimer, in different ways, to look seriously at linguistic conventions.[126] The appearance of the collection of essays drawn together by David Ley and Marwyn Samuels under the title *Humanistic Geography* in 1978 constituted an important moment in the consolidation of this mood, particularly as advocates sought to connect their endeavours to the earlier French tradition, though in their reappropriation Vidal's natural science aspirations for *géographie humaine* are conspicuous by their absence.[127]

For all that, the label 'humanistic geography', as I have implied, imposes a greater sense of conceptual coherence than is warranted on a heterogeneous miscellany of philosophical styles. United chiefly by their dissatisfactions, the humanists' positive proposals have been anything but cohesive. Early on, Leonard Guelke, pursuing and paralleling some of Cole Harris's concerns, turned for inspiration to the idealist philosophy of historical explanation put forward by R. G. Collingwood. As Guelke saw it, the task of historical geography was to reconstruct the thoughts behind action in the attempt to get 'inside the minds' of past actors and thereby to explain their spatial behaviour.[128] Yet, while his aspirations were evidently thoroughly

---

[125] J. Nicholas Entrikin, 'Contemporary Humanism in Geography', *Annals of the Association of American Geographers*, 66 (1976): 615–32, ref. on p. 616.

[126] See the essays in Gunnar Olsson, *Birds in Egg/Eggs in Bird* (London: Pion, 1980); Gunnar Olsson, 'Social Science and Human Action or on Hitting your Head Against the Ceiling of Language', in Gale and Olsson (eds), *Philosophy in Geography*, pp. 287–307; Anne Buttimer, *Values in Geography* (Association of American Geographers, Commission on College Geography, Resource Paper no. 24, Washington DC, 1974).

[127] David Ley and Marwyn S. Samuels (eds), *Humanistic Geography: Prospects and Problems* (London: Croom Helm, 1978). Others have sought to root the methodology of humanistic geography in versions of neo-Kantianism and pragmatism. See Susan J. Smith, 'Practicing Humanistic Geography', *Annals of the Association of American Geographers*, 74 (1984): 353–74; Peter Jackson and Susan J. Smith, *Exploring Social Geography* (London: George Allen and Unwin, 1984); J. Nicholas Entrikin, 'Robert Park's Human Ecology and Human Geography', *Annals of the Association of American Geographers*, 70 (1980): 43–58.

[128] Leonard Guelke, 'An Idealist Alternative in Human Geography', *Annals of the Association of American Geographers*, 64 (1974): 193–202; Leonard Guelke, *Historical Understanding in Geography: An Idealist Approach* (Cambridge: Cambridge University Press, 1982).

anti-positivist, in the last analysis his proposal could be read as little more than an attempt to widen the scope of scientific investigation; empathetically rethinking thoughts might just amount to a methodological strategy for throwing up hypotheses that could be explained by some covering law. Again, in his sensitive ethnography of Philadelphia's black inner city, David Ley certainly used conventional cartographic techniques, albeit to map the affective landscape of stress.[129]

Geography's newest encounter with the realm of the subjective, however, has gone a good deal further. Some turned more explicitly, though not always in the same way, to the phenomenological philosophy of Edmund Husserl. At its most basic, phenomenology constituted a call for a way of doing philosophy in which the way that the world is disclosed to us – *prior* to theoretical or scientific enquiry – is recovered. Thus rejecting the objectivizing thrust of contemporary positivism, Husserl's was an appeal for a new means of encountering the world in a presuppositionless way. In geography, this aspiration took various forms. Ley, for example, used Alfred Schutz's version as a means of grasping the everyday meanings of individual's and society's life-worlds; Tuan found in it inspiration for his conviction that geographies disclosed the psychological essences and emotional attachments of their human creators; Relph emphasized the way in which human subjects create their worlds by virtue of their constituting (rather than merely perceiving) the objects of geographical scrutiny.[130] At the same time, others have turned to the categories of existentialism to depict the sense of loss and alienation at the heart of humankind's experience of being-in-the-world, to Wittgenstein's linguistic philosophy to find the geographical significance of links between various 'forms of life' and ordinary language, to fictional literature as a repository of geographical sensibility, or to Geertz's interpretative anthropology to reconstitute geography as a hermeneutic endeavour engaged in the semiotic decoding of verbal and

---

[129] David Ley, *The Black Inner City as Frontier Outpost: Images and Behaviour of a Philadelphia Neighborhood* (Washington DC: Association of American Geographers, 1974).

[130] Thus, David Ley, 'Social Geography and the Taken-for-Granted World', *Transactions of the Institute of British Geographers*, n.s. 2 (1977): 498–512; Yi-Fu Tuan, 'Geography, Phenomenology and the Study of Human Nature', *Canadian Geographer*, 15 (1971): 181–92; Yi-Fu Tuan, *Space and Place: The Perspective of Experience* (London: Edward Arnold, 1977); Edward Relph, 'An Inquiry into the Relations between Phenomenology and Geography', *Canadian Geographer*, 14 (1970): 193–201; Edward Relph, *Place and Placelessness* (London: Pion, 1976). See also John Pickles, *Phenomenology, Science and Geography: Spatiality and the Human Sciences* (Cambridge: Cambridge University Press, 1985); David Seamon and R. Mugerauer (eds), *Dwelling, Place and Environment: Towards a Phenomenology of Person and World* (Dordrecht: Martinus Nijhoff, 1985).

non-verbal texts.[131] The details of these encounters have been surveyed elsewhere.[132] I have only gestured here towards their broadest contours to
reaffirm the turn towards the subjective realm characteristic of geographers
of humanist leaning.

As yet at least some of these perspectives remain little more than personal predilections, and for that reason, as Ley himself has admitted, some
already seem *passé*. Just how significant they will turn out to be remains to
be seen – bearing in mind that intellectual survival is the outcome of more
than genuine cognitive insight; the power networks that operate through
the control of publishing outlets, not to mention sheer faddishness, are also
history-forming factors. For all that, the humanistic insurrection against the
deterministic credulity of a fundamentalist structuralism,[133] served to keep
human agency firmly on geography's agenda. At the same time, the disconnected, idealist tinge of much humanistic endeavour just seemed
insufficiently earthed in the material realities of economy and society. The
concern to find ways of keeping the human agent *and* social structure – or
humanism and Marxism, if you will – in some sort of conceptual equilibrium thus found expression in a move towards the theory of structuration
most forcefully articulated by the Cambridge social theorist, Anthony
Giddens. On the one hand, Giddens wants to take with profound seriousness the structures and systems within which we all play out our daily lives;
these include the various rules of social interaction which we as individuals
and, more importantly, through institutions routinely implement and in
turn reproduce; they also incorporate the resources by which certain groups
can exercise power over others. Yet, on the other hand, human subjects do
not lie passive in the iron grip of social structure; they are agents whose
actions have both intended and unintended consequences. And thus in the
interplay of the individual and society – structuration as he calls it –
Giddens advances his resolution to the tensions between voluntarism and
necessitarianism.[134] Through figures like Gregory, Thrift, and Pred this

[131] So, for instance, Marwyn Samuels, 'An existential Geography', in Milton E. Harvey and
Brian P. Holly (eds), *Themes in Geographic Thought* (London: Croom Helm, 1981), pp. 22–40;
Trevor Barnes and Michael Curry, 'Towards a Contextualist Approach to Geographical
Knowledge', *Transactions of the Institute of British Geographers*, n.s. 8 (1983): 467–82; Douglas
C. D. Pocock (ed.), *Humanistic Geography and Literature: Essays on the Experience of Place*
(London: Croom Helm, 1981); Denis Cosgrove, *Social Formation and Symbolic Landscape*
(London: Croom Helm, 1984).
[132] Most recently, Cloke et al., *Approaching Human Geography*, chapter 3.
[133] See, for example, James Duncan and David Ley, 'Structural Marxism and Human
Geography: A Critical Perspective', *Annals of the Association of American Geographers*, 72
(1982): 30–59.
[134] Among the key sources are Anthony Giddens, *Central Problems in Social Theory: Action*,

vision of social systems (and spatial structure) as both the condition and the consequence of the very practices that constitute them has been introduced (though not always uncritically) to human geography.[135] Indeed Giddens himself has found explanatory mileage in the time-geography of Hägerstrand, and this has served to further cement the connections between human geography and social theory. Because it is in specific arenas that the engagements between the individual and social structure – places, locales, time–space stations and domains, whatever – are played out, some now assert that geographical concerns necessarily lie at the very mainsprings of social theory.

If Giddens has cast a long shadow over geographical theorizing in the recent past, the writings of the Continental theorist Michel Foucault have also begun to be registered within the tradition. Of course there are significant divergences between these critics, but what unites them is their concern with issues of power and modernity.[136] In Giddens's case, social systems of interaction mediate power relations and manifest themselves in structures of domination. For Foucault, the broad systems of thought that undergird the ways in which we conceive of the world, and their practical expression in regulative institutions like clinics, prisons, and so on, are, when unmasked, exposed as the conductors of social power. The truth-claims that these 'discourses' (as Foucault depicts them) embody are thus revealed for what they are – strategies of moral manipulation. The 'strategic' metaphor here, moreover, is more than merely decorative. Indeed it was precisely because 'tactics and strategies of power', 'control of territories and organizations of domains' were so central to Foucault's analyses that he could concede at one point that 'geography must necessarily lie at the heart of my concerns.'[137] At least one implication of this diagnosis is immediate: overall explanatory theories – totalizing discourses or grand narratives as they are also called – can no longer enjoy any privileged status, for

Structure and Contradiction in Social Analysis (London: Macmillan, 1979); Anthony Giddens, *The Constitution of Society.*

[135] So, Derek Gregory, 'Human Agency and Human Geography', *Transactions of the Institute of British Geographers*, n.s. 6 (1981): 1–18; Derek Gregory, 'Presences and Absences: Time-Space Relations and Structuration Theory', in D. Held and J. B. Thompson (eds), *Social Theory of Modern Societies: Anthony Giddens and his Critics* (Cambridge: Cambridge University Press, 1989); Thrift, 'The Determination of Social Action'; Allan Pred, 'Place as Historically-Contingent Process: Structuration and the Time-Geography of Becoming Places', *Annals of the Association of American Geographers*, 74 (1984): 279–97.

[136] For a recent geographical introduction see Cole Harris, 'Power, Modernity, and Historical Geography', *Annals of the Association of American Geographers*, 81 (1991): 671–83.

[137] Michel Foucault, *Power/Knowledge: Selected Interviews and Other Writings, 1972–1977* (Brighton: Harvester Press, 1980), p. 77.

the 'truth' they purport to proclaim is at base a human construction. In this scenario, epistemology is transmuted into intellectual genealogy as itself a prelude to social criticism.[138]

Certainly this position has been criticized from such different viewpoints as those of Jürgen Habermas, whose own theory of communicative action is advanced as a general scaffolding on which to pin his analysis of modernity, and Charles Taylor, who questions the internal coherence of some of Foucault's proposals.[139] For Habermas, Foucault is caught on the horns of a dichotomy between an irrationalism derived from Nietzsche and a 'crypto-normativism' that assumes but cannot explain standards for judgement. Taylor, similarly, doubts whether the regime-relativity of truth in Foucault's analyses can sustain the sort of revolt/resistance that his unmasking requires. Still, one can profoundly appreciate the potency of Foucault's own genealogical unveilings – about discourses as mediations of an insidious modern system of surveillance and power, for example – without assuming that this is a universal trait. Besides, it is surely possible to follow Foucault in seeing the wisdom of sticking close to the particular, to the local, to lived experience without adopting his Nietzschean model of truth.[140] Yet, what has given force to Foucault's critique, and that of others like Richard Rorty, has been the collapse of foundationalism within epistemology.

At base, classical foundationalism is a normative thesis about the conditions that must be met by anyone whose system of beliefs is to be credited as rational. To be rational, the argument went, is to exercise one's epistemic powers properly. Now, in order to pass muster as rational, it was asserted, any claim to knowledge had ultimately to be based on statements that are either self-evident or evident to the senses, and therefore incorrigible for the holder. Under the influence of men like Descartes, Leibniz, and

[138] A useful introduction is Paul Rabinow (ed.), *The Foucault Reader* (New York: Pantheon, 1984).

[139] See the essays in David Couzens Hoy (ed.), *Foucault: A Critical Reader* (Oxford: Blackwell, 1986).

[140] Other thinkers, from entirely different traditions, could concur. Because, according to Alisdair MacIntyre, for example, narrative and situation are crucial to the forging of human identity, we cannot characterize ourselves 'independently of the settings which make . . . intentions intelligible both to agents themselves and to others.' Questions of place thus approach central questions of moral philosophy. Alisdair MacIntyre, *After Virtue: A Study in Moral Theory* (London: Duckworth, 2nd edn 1985), p. 206. As yet, however, there seems to be little discussion within geography about the nature of the human agent and the changing meanings of the self. A first step in this direction may be Chris Philo (compiler), *New Words, New Worlds: Reconceptualising Social and Cultural Geography* (Department of Geography, St David's University College, Lampeter, 1991).

Locke, this principle came to mean that rationality could only be conferred on beliefs that were either self-evident or founded upon the procedures of logic, mathematics, or science. And this conviction was chief among the crucial building blocks out of which 'modernity' was constructed.

The criticisms of classical foundationalism are many and diverse. For one thing, the normative theory of rationality that it espouses is highly suspect. We are clearly rational to believe many things which cannot be inferred from some set of foundational certitudes. Deductivism, probabilism, and falsificationism have all failed to provide general rules for warranted theory acceptance and rejection. In short, the foundationalist procedure has not given us the epistemological certainty that it was designed to provide. But perhaps the most telling philosophical criticism is the simple realization that it is not at all obvious how the principle (that we should only accept as rational, statements that are self-evident or incorrigible) can *itself* be rationally established.

At least in part this collapse has been seen as a crucial ingredient in the ushering in of what is now frequently called postmodernity.[141] The modern rationalist project is said to have failed, and a pluralist relativism judged to be inevitable. The prestige of scientific precision has gone, only to be replaced by a delight in ambiguity, an uncertainty that only seems confirmed by the experimental research of the quantum physicists; consistency is neither possible nor desirable and different styles can be juxtaposed in playful ways; the idea of texts revealing authors' intentions – or indeed of there being an authorial 'self' at all – is being subverted by deconstructionist literary critics; and the architectural functionalism of Le Corbusier's modernist movement recedes before pastiche and nostalgia. Beyond the academy, this postmodernist mood seems reflected in a television generation seemingly bred for the short attention span, a yuppie culture characterized by too much money without moral moorings, and a global shopping centre in which high consumption capitalism puts a premium on surface glamour.[142] Ironically any sense of a universal coherence in social life seems to be gone even as the worldwide dissemination of the technologies of Western culture proceeds apace. Yet whether all this is genuinely *post*modern or simply yet another inflection of modernity is hard to judge. Certainly

---

[141] J. F. Lyotard, *The Postmodern Condition. A Report on Knowledge* (Manchester: Manchester University Press, 1984).

[142] Useful popular introductions are Todd Gitlin, 'Postmodernism Defined, At Last!' *Unte Reader*, 34 (1989): 52–61; Robert A. M. Stern, 'The Doubles of Post-Modern', *Harvard Architecture Review*, 1 (1980): 75–87.

much of what passes for postmodernism seems not unlike the kind of world of which Nietzsche spoke last century.

Geographers, it seems, have been interacting with this corpus of commentary and conduct in a number of different, though related, ways. The inherent relativism of the postmodern challenge, for example, has encouraged geographers to think hard about their own writings as 'representations' of the subjects of their inquiry.[143] For some – where they are not enamoured of an out-and-out relativism – this has taken the form of a challenge to think of ways of retaining something of a realist stance.[144] For others the very *sequential* nature of writing has proven problematic when the concern is to convey, in 'thicker' ethnographic idioms, spatial *simultaneity*, and has prompted some speculations about the cultivation of a geographical 'poetics'.[145] Then again, if there indeed is a condition of postmodernity, it too becomes an empirical state of affairs that has its own geography and genealogy. To elucidate these configurations is the task that Harvey recently set himself, analysing the postmodern situation as itself the outcome of the workings of advanced capitalism over the past two decades or more.[146] The way in which production and consumption have come to be organized has encouraged a certain Western cultural condition characterized by confusion, complexity, messiness, and difference. Thus the contrasting landscapes of modernity and postmodernity as expressions of diverse political cultures have become the objects of geographical scrutiny.[147] And finally, postmodernism's celebration of difference, of juxtaposition, of fragmentation, has further reasserted the importance of the specific, the local, the placebound.[148] And it is for this reason that Derek Gregory, speaking of areal

[143] The whole question of geographical 'writing' is prominent in the collection of essays edited by Trevor J. Barnes and James S. Duncan, *Writing Worlds: Discourse, Text and Metaphor in the Representation of Landscape* (London: Routledge, 1992).

[144] For example Sayer, *Method in Social Science*; also see Michael Dear, 'The Postmodern Challenge: Reconstructing Human Geography', *Transactions of the Institute of British Geographers*, n.s. 13 (1988): 262–74.

[145] Derek Gregory, 'Areal Differentiation and Post-Modern Human Geography', in Derek Gregory and Rex Walford (eds), *Horizons in Human Geography* (London: Macmillan, 1989), pp. 67–96.

[146] David Harvey, *The Condition of Postmodernity. An Enquiry into the Origins of Cultural Change* (Oxford: Blackwell, 1989).

[147] See, for example, David Ley, 'Styles of the Times: Liberal and Neo-Conservative Landscapes in Inner Vancouver, 1968–1986', *Journal of Historical Geography*, 13 (1987): 40–56.

[148] Recent reconceptualizations of place include J. Nicholas Entrikin, *The Betweenness of Place* (London: Macmillan, 1991); and the essays in John Agnew and James Duncan (eds), *The Power of Place: Bringing Together Geographical and Sociological Imagination* (Boston: Unwin Hyman, 1989).

differentiation, has urged geographers to engage again with their own history, though armed with a new set of analytical categories.[149]

The past few pages, I realize, have moved at a considerable pace. To readers actively engaged in these debates, I am fully aware that my whistle-stop tour may seem an unreflective dash through a labyrinth of assertion and argument. And yet even if such a judgement is correct, I believe that at the very least my portrait, lacking in nuance as it is, has revealed that the geographical tradition continues to be embedded in a wide range of conversations about the nature of human identity, society, and place.

For the future, if I may be permitted a diagnostic observation, I suggest that the geographical community urgently needs to address the challenges that 'postmodernity' has raised. For myself, I think it will be mistaken to give up the notion of rationality altogether, even in the face of classical foundationalism's philosophical dissolution. Indeed those who tell us that this is the way of wisdom are just as open to the charge of self-referential incoherence as were the classical foundationalists. Why we should listen to their counsel is hard to see, for eradicating rationality cuts both ways. If the idea of things being some way has no meaning, indeed if meaning itself has become unhinged, well then, it's hard to know what to say, and just as important, who to listen to. Rather, as I see it, we need to acknowledge that discovering how classical foundationalism has failed to provide us with a criterion for warranted knowledge is altogether different from claiming that the idea of true and justified belief is just an illusion. Whether we must now turn to non-foundationalist epistemology or to a weaker notion of rationality is not easy to say.

Nevertheless, it is now clear that classical foundationalism is in bad shape and had better be given up for dead. In this context geographers will have to acknowledge that warranted knowledge is relative to a body of *beliefs*, not to a body of certitudes. Pluralism in the geographical academy is thus an inevitability. We have no option but to live with positivist geography, Marxist geography, humanistic geography, Islamic geography, structurationist geography, Christian geography, a people's geography, and on and on. Each will be within their cognitive rights to hold to theories that comport with their system of control beliefs. We now need to realize that non-foundationalist discourses – in the political, the affective, the moral, the artistic, the cultural, the aesthetic, the religious, and doubtless a host of

---

[149] Gregory, 'Areal Differentiation'. See also Edward W. Soja, *Postmodern Geographies: The Reassertion of Space in Critical Social Theory* (London: Verso, 1989).

other spheres – are as legitimate now as they were in the fifteenth and sixteenth centuries, where my story began. This has far-reaching consequences. And the consequences for geography of acknowledging *this* postmodernist claim is the task that confronts the present generation.

10

The Geographical Tradition

A Conversational Conclusion

'A living tradition', writes Alisdair MacIntyre, 'is an historically extended, socially embodied argument, and an argument precisely in part about the goods which constitute that tradition.' This means that while a university, or a hospital, or a farm is the bearer of a tradition of practices, it is also constituted by a continuous argument about what good scholarship, or good medicine, or good farming, actually is. 'Traditions, when vital', according to MacIntyre, 'embody continuities of conflict.'[1]

That geography has been just such a tradition – a contested and pluralist tradition – is the case I have tried to sustain in the preceding pages. Because geography has meant different things to different people in different settings my intention has been to look at what people have taken geography to be over the years and thereby to acknowledge the transformations that the geographical tradition has undergone. For the heart of my argument is simply that geography changes as society changes, and that the best way to understand the tradition to which geographers belong is to get a handle on the different social and intellectual environments within which geography has been practised.

Yet the narrative form in which this history has presented itself may have obscured the diverse range of conversations in which geographers have engaged since the age of reconnaissance. In the few lines that follow I therefore want to try to highlight again some of these major discourses. My list is certainly not exhaustive, and it will recap something of the story I have had to tell. It will also again take something of a chronological shape. But now I want to suggest that these conversations have, to one degree or

[1] Alisdair MacIntyre, *After Virtue*, p. 222.

another, persisted within the tradition and that the pluralism they bespeak is not just a desirable state of affairs, it is diagnostic of a living tradition.

For generations, geography has been intimately involved in a conversation about exploration. At least since the time of Muslim scholar-travellers like Ibn-Batuta and Ibn-Khaldun, and the voyages of the Scandinavians, the Chinese, and medieval Christian adventurers, first-hand knowledge of the world contributed to geographical lore. But it was with the European voyages of reconnaissance, during the fifteenth and sixteenth centuries, that these earlier fragmentary gleanings began to be marshalled into something of a coherent body of knowledge about the terrestrial globe. Besides the crypto-Baconianism of their data acquisition, these enterprises made a not insignificant contribution to the development of science in the West through challenging both classical learning and the Renaissance style of natural history presentation. Certainly it is too simplistic to portray those early seafarers as participating in global experiments to test Renaissance dogmas inherited from the ancient classical world. But the information they gathered certainly helped challenge the scholarly authorities of the day by demonstrating that there were people inhabiting the southern hemisphere, that there were varieties of plant and animal which just did not fit into Aristotle's or Erasmus's taxonomies, and that standard accounts of the history of languages would have to be rethought. Moreover, the conventional world-chronologies of Christendom could not remain immune from the challenges that anthropological encounters raised and from questions about the settlement of the New World.

Alongside all this, the geographer-as-explorer was drawn into conversations about the solution to the technological and scientific problems of navigation – how to determine a ship's position at sea and, more important, to chart the way back to safe havens. Certainly too much can be made of the navigational institute that Prince Henry 'the Navigator' supposedly established at Sagres in the early fifteenth century – and which drew together experts in cartography, astronomy, and nautical instrumentation – as a crucial early move in the development of Western science. Yet it is true that by the early sixteenth century, Portugal had established itself as a nation of cartographic experts, and as a centre for work on commercial arithmetic, medicinal botany, and astronomical instrumentation – all largely on account of a worldwide empire centred on Lisbon.

Of course geography's engagement with exploration did not come to an end in the sixteenth century. Voyages of reconnaissance continued to expand geographical knowledge of the globe throughout later centuries and special mention might be made of the eighteenth-century journeys of James Cook and Joseph Banks into the South Pacific and the nineteenth-century circumnavigations of such naturalists as Charles Darwin and Thomas Henry Huxley. At the same time the significance of scientific travel was being championed by men like Alexander von Humboldt, Henry Walter Bates, and Alfred Russel Wallace through their own explorations in the Far East or South America. Moreover, the Royal Geographical Society, which did so much to promote overseas exploration in the Victorian era, continues to sponsor expeditions of this sort right up to the present day. Indeed this expeditionary motif has become so engrained in the subject's collective memory that geographers have continued to speak of it in other contexts: expeditions into the urban jungle, ethnic ghettoes, and other threatening environments. The vocabulary of exploration has thus long continued to capture the spirit of certain aspects of the geographical tradition.

MAGICAL GEOGRAPHY

Even while new geographical knowledge was challenging accepted scholarly traditions, there were ways in which geographical lore continued to confirm long-held beliefs. Thus, just as other nascent sciences were deeply implicated in various magical practices, so too was geography. This is plain, for example, in the early development of modern astronomy. Much interest in the stars was stimulated by astrological concerns and among the earliest Copernicans there is evidence of a continuing interest in that enterprise. Again, the belief that various plants possessed hidden occult powers that could be harnessed for medicinal purposes led to important pharmacological and chemical findings. The writings of such giants of the Scientific Revolution as Kepler, Bacon, and Newton reveal a substantial interest in such seemingly arcane practices.

Geography, I have urged, was no less involved with astrology and natural magic than these other fields of discourse. Numerous early writers on geography, like William Cuningham, Thomas Blundeville, John Dee, and Thomas and Leonard Digges were engaged in various aspects of magic. For some, like Dee, the key lay in the mystical significance of number – the celestial and terrestrial worlds were held together in certain mathematical relationships in such a way that changes in one directly influenced the other. For others, like the Diggeses, astrology was of first importance, and their early meteorological efforts were all of a piece with astrological knowledge; to them weather forecasting required acquaintance with the significance of celestial changes in the moon, the stars, and the planets. For still others, notably Jean Bodin and Cuningham, the diversity of the world's peoples and cultures was closely bound up with which sign of the zodiac governed the particular region they inhabited.

However bizarre all this may seem to modern eyes, this episode – for too long ignored or suppressed by historians of geography – demonstrates the role of apparently non-rational discourse in the evolution of the discipline. But more. Some recent revisionist work is beginning to disclose a geographical involvement with the numinous right up to the twentieth century. Various mystical elements in the history of the modern conservation movement – displayed in late nineteenth and early twentieth century figures like Francis Younghusband and Vaughan Cornish, for example – persist today among those who call for the re-enchantment or spiritualization, even divinization, of nature.

A PAPER WORLD

The knowledge explosion occasioned by the European voyages of exploration soon brought new cartographic challenges and accomplishments. To be sure, the science of cartography was not born in the sixteenth century. Around the Mediterranean, portolano sea charts had been circulating for long enough, and of course there already existed numerous symbolic depictions of the world in the form of various *mappaemundi*. But the new worlds that Europeans encountered had to be reduced to paper and this task was seen as geographers' business. Gerard Mercator solved some of the mathematical problems associated with transferring a sphere to a flat surface with his famous map projection. And soon a series of Dutch and Belgian cartographers like De Jode, Jodocus Hondius, and Petrus Plancius charted the course of overseas discovery. Closely associated with this enterprise was the further cultivation of the skills of surveying and instrument making, which were taken as the craft competences of the early cartographer. Map making, of course, was as artistic a practice as it was scientific. Frequently maps were elaborately decorated and skilfully executed, so much so that they often became *objets d'art* in their own right. But more, it was philosophical, in the sense that it traded on 'representation' as *the* mode of communicative comprehension.

In the following centuries, geography's close links with cartography continued to be maintained. The progress of the Ordnance Survey's work in nineteenth-century Britain was regularly reported on at the Royal Geographical Society; geographers frequently involved themselves in the thematic mapping of drift geology, soils, disease, populations, and so on; now in our own day geographers maintain this tradition when they turn to remote sensing and computer mapping. The mapping drive has thus always been strong in geography; so much so that Carl Sauer believed that if a geographer was not fascinated by maps to the extent of always needing to be surrounded by them, then that was a clue that he or she had chosen the wrong profession. And even while the power relations that the map's semiotic systems embody are now being exposed by students of cartographic iconography, the map, as both graphic language and visual representation, continues to be used as a standard item of geographical apparatus.

A CLOCKWORK UNIVERSE

In the wake of the mechanical philosophy that came to dominate science in the seventeenth century, there were numerous efforts to retain the integrity of religious discourse in the face of the apparently naturalistic implications of a mechanistic world picture. One of the most common strategies, defended by men like Newton and Boyle, was to argue that the world was essentially like a grand clock, comparable to that at Strasbourg, and that by investigating the world machine, scientists were interrogating the very mind of the Great Designer. This logistic move played a key role in the evolution of the geographical tradition. Numerous writers during the period of the Enlightenment developed a style of natural history called physico-theology. Regarding the world as teleologically designed and providentially controlled, they interpreted the world environment as a functioning revelation of divine purpose. In the writings of Thomas Burnet, John Ray, John Woodward, William Derham, as later in the works of William Paley, the world's geography – its physical and organic forms – was seen as pointing beyond itself to nature's divine architect.

Of course these practitioners of natural theology frequently differed among themselves on both detail and strategy; but between them they delivered to history a vision of nature as a holistic system, a sort of ecological picture, that emphasized the interrelationships and interdependence between organisms and environment. Here the image of a warfare between science and religion turns out to be something of a historical fiction. Indeed earlier geographers like Bartholomaus Keckermann in Germany and Nathanael Carpenter in England found in the theology of the Reformation the resources to *reject* ecclesiastical authority in matters of science and to argue for the liberation of science from scholastic censure.

This particular intellectual trajectory persisted within the geographical tradition over the following centuries. In the nineteenth century Carl Ritter exemplified the same stance, and the Ritterian vision was propagated in the United States by his disciple-devotee Arnold Guyot. Besides these, physico-theology lingered on in the works of Mary Somerville and David Thomas Ansted in England, and Matthew Fontaine Maury and Daniel Coit Gilman in the United States, confirming H. R. Mill's 1901 comment that teleological modes of reasoning were tacitly or explicitly espoused by almost every writer on geographical theory during the nineteenth century. Even more recently, the selfsame teleological vision comes through in the writings of the Dutch geographer, De Jong. Here geography continues to operate as the handmaiden to theology.

AN INSTRUMENT OF IMPERIALISM

Besides subserving theological ends, geography could, and did, serve other interests too. Throughout its history, geography has frequently cast itself as the aide-de-camp to militarism and imperialism. Maps, it was long known, were as vital implements of warmongering as gunnery, and it is therefore no surprise that institutional geography first flourished in military schools. Indeed the prehistory of the Ordnance Survey can be traced back to military needs during the Jacobean era. In the twentieth century, geographers like Isaiah Bowman played their parts in America's involvement with post-war European reconstruction. And at the level of geographical practice, numerous geographers made their skills available to government during the two world wars, while terrain evaluation and land classification continue to be carried out by military engineers and surveyors.

By the same token, British expansion overseas aroused a renewed interest in geography for its functional purposes. At the inaugural meeting of the Royal Geographical Society of London in the early 1830s, the need for such a society was defended, we recall, on the grounds that geography was vital to the imperial success of Britain as a maritime nation. Accordingly there was, and continued to be, considerable debate in British – not to mention German and American – geography on the subject of acclimatization because the question of white adaptation to the tropical and subtropical worlds was of pressing international significance. Here geographers worked closely with medical experts to delineate the significance of climatic factors. Indeed in so doing they kept alive an ancient tradition, rejuvenated by Montesquieu, that kept the cultural and the natural in close association.

Such aspects of geographical theory could easily be manipulated to serve a range of purposes. Some found in environmental determinism the justification for a racial ideology; indeed racial questions were commonplace in geography texts around the turn of the century and in some cases long after that. Others saw in it a doctrine with strategic potential. Halford Mackinder's theory of world political power crucially depended on the control of a particular piece of territorial space in the Old World. Friedrich Ratzel in Germany erected an organic theory of the state on his notion of *Lebensraum*, urging that the character and destiny of a *Volk* was umbilically tied to a definite area or *Raum*. In the United States the Ratzelian viewpoint was propagated by Ellen Semple who used it to chart the necessitarian course of American history, while Ellsworth Huntington turned to climate as the great mainspring of civilization. In all of these, as in the stop-and-go determinism of Griffith Taylor – the constitutive links between geographical theory and social outlook are clearly displayed. This is not to say, of course, that geographical determinism as a precept was *just* social ideology writ large. But it *is* to remind us that geographical ideas and practices have a social history as well as a cognitive one.

THE REGIONAL RECITATION

Even while environmental determinism in one form or another was spreading like wildfire among professionalizing geographers, there were those, initially in Germany, whose conversation centred on the capacity of human culture to transform its natural milieu rather than remaining in nature's deterministic grip. In Britain H. J. Fleure emphasized the importance of human agency in modifying environment and in so doing turned away from the conventional concentration on natural regions towards the significance of transitional zones of culture contact down through history. Moreover, even those like A. J. Herbertson, for whom the concept of natural region occupied a strategic place, nevertheless recognized the subtle interplay of environment, heredity, and consciousness in producing the geographical patterns of human diversity across the face of the globe. For both, the idealist strain in Lamarckian evolution – an evolutionary model stressing the significance of life-force and will – was of crucial importance. A related strain of environmentalist critique was forthcoming from the vibrant tradition of French cultural geography associated with Vidal de la Blache. For Vidal and the Vidalians, environment came to be seen, not as a determinative force, but rather as a limiting factor setting limits on cultural possibilities. The 'possibilisme' that the historian Lucien Febvre found at the core of this French school promoted geography as the science of human regions, because it was in specific physical milieux that distinctive *genres de vie* (modes of life) found expression.

A related strand of determinist criticism emanated from Carl Sauer and the Berkeley school of cultural geography in the United States. Here inspiration was derived less from evolutionary biology than from German geography and the cultural particularism of the anthropologist Franz Boas. Boas's questioning of environmental determinism, consequent on his anthropological work among the Canadian Inuit, induced a mild cultural relativism that was mediated to Sauer through anthropological colleagues at Berkeley. Sauer consolidated this discourse as he closed geography's endeavours around the treatment of residual material culture as historical artefacts of cultural diversity. Whatever their differences of approach, these geographers shared a conception of geography as a study of areal differentiation, a stance enshrined in Richard Hartshorne's influential monograph *The Nature of Geography*. An apologetic history argued from a partisan review of German sources, it established its author as regionalism's chief English-speaking advocate. Moreover, the notion of geography as regional recitation provided a paradigm that still governs much geographical work, whether in the qualitative contributions of writers of regional personality or in the more quantitative emphasis of the practitioners of regional science.

THE GO-BETWEEN

Alongside these efforts to delineate for geography a piece of cognitive territory — a sector of conceptual space in the academic scheme of things — there were those who were rather more inclined to speak of its environmental value in taking with equal seriousness physical and human systems. Certainly this 'go-between' function also had instrumental value in the search for institutional identity and so it was appealed to to justify geography as a coherent and independent academic discipline both in Britain and the United States. Frequently the case was made that geography was the integrating discipline *par excellence* that kept the study of nature *and* culture under one disciplinary umbrella. In Britain, Halford Mackinder considered it was the only foundation on which geography as a causal science could be built, while in the United States, W. M. Davis, otherwise remembered for his elucidation of the cycle of erosion, nevertheless felt that physical geography was incomplete without its human counterpart.

But as often as not, geography's bridging role between nature and humanity frequently took the form of a strenuous engagement with questions of resources. In America the roots of this geographical tradition go back to such figures as Nathaniel Southgate Shaler and George Perkins Marsh, and later J. Russell Smith, whose contributions were resurrected by early-twentieth-century geographers seeking the recovery of an ethic of environmental sensitivity. For some, this emphasis led to a historical reassessment of 'man's role in changing the face of the earth'; for others, the needs of the future fostered an engagement with environmental systems analysis or with ecological energetics in the attempt to model the changing human-nature interface. In our own day, as the resource crisis has bitten even more deeply, environmental geographers have done much to keep this conversation at the forefront of the geographical tradition.

SPACE SCIENCE

If some identified geography's essence in its focus on regional integration, there were those who found the emphasis on the particularity of places lacking in methodological rigour. To them, all the talk of bridging the gulf between the sciences and the humanities seemed little more than academic-political rhetoric, and the idea of regional personality frankly unscientific. Even while geographers were independently encountering the spatial economic models of von Thünen, Weber, Christaller, Lösch, and Isard, Fred Schaefer spearheaded a conceptual assault with his article on 'Exceptionalism in geography' published in the *Annals of the Association of American Geographers* in 1953. Schaefer's attack was designed to transform geography into a true science by urging that it become a law-seeking, explanatory discipline concerned with universal laws, not regional specifics. Schaefer's paper, it is commonly believed, heralded the introduction of logical positivism into the discipline, and its curriculum was defended in William Bunge's *Theoretical Geography* of 1962 and David Harvey's *Explanation in Geography* published at the end of the decade. These served to further reinforce an already vigorous conversation about geography as the science of spatial distribution, or locational analysis, as it was frequently styled.

As figures like W. L. Garrison in America and Peter Haggett in Britain introduced to geography various theorems seeking to explain the location of economic behaviour, the tradition received its newest initiation into statistical technique. Not, of course, that geography had been utterly innocent of quantification hitherto. The roots of geography as a mathematical practice can be traced back at least to the period of the Scientific Revolution in the seventeenth century, and doubtless before that to the mathematical geography of classical figures – Thales, Anaximander, Herodotus, Strabo, Ptolemy. Nor does it mean that all of geography was quantified; plainly, many areas of the tradition remained statistically immune. Still, the scientific ideal, bolstered by the vocabulary of logical positivism, has made substantial inroads into geographical theory and practice since the 1950s and a variety of reasons for geography's relatively late baptism in positivist practices have been put forward. Was it a strategic move by geographers to escape the political suspicion falling on social science in the post-McCarthy era by retreating into the safety of number-crunching? Or was it an attempt by geographers to accrue to themselves a set of craft competences that could bolster their professional vested interests in creating a spatial *science*?

FIGURING PEOPLE OUT

Whatever the causes of geographical quantification may have been, recent decades have witnessed a sequence of attacks on positivism from different perspectives. From the radical side comes the complaint that the whole quantitative procedure is ideologically laden from the start. The argument here is that by keeping geography as just a sort of spatial calculus, a geometric technique for depicting distributions, fundamental questions of justice and political involvement are simply – and too comfortably – ruled out of court. Accordingly, various contemporary radical geographers see themselves in a geographical lineage stretching back to figures like Reclus, Kropotkin, and Karl Wittfogel who strenuously advocated social engagement. In this scenario, and it has to be admitted that it is far from unified, there is something of an emphasis on the determinative role of economic structure. Whether investigating the significance of residential segregation, the vicissitudes of the world economic system, or the historical change from feudalism to capitalism, this selfsame motif regularly reasserts itself.

On the other hand, there are those humanistic geographers who insist that the quantitative tabulation of economic data and other activities has dehumanized geography by ignoring, not to say suppressing, human agency.

Because whole acres of human experience – fear, imagination, emotion – were ignored, real people were simply 'figured' out of the picture altogether. So these geographical humanists have seen it as their task to keep the tradition open to the artistic side of its history by their interrogation of literary texts and their championing of the importance of the subjective. Yi-Fu Tuan's meditations on 'topophilia' and 'topophobia', David Ley's excursion into the mind of the inner city ghetto, and Leonard Guelke's turning to Collingwood's idealist philosophy of history are just some of the currents to have recently swept through the discipline. Again partisans are quick to point out that this is not a wholly new departure; some claim that the earlier behavioural geography of J. K. Wright, David Lowenthal, and William Kirk accorded a key role to subjective experience, while others – ignoring his natural science aspirations for *géographie humaine* – speak of the revivification of the Vidalian tradition. Either way a conversation about emotion, meaning, and value has served to keep the subjective within geography's realm.

EVERYTHING IN ITS PLACE

These respective emphases on the role of social structure and human agency in accounts of geographical phenomena have most recently led some to wonder if explanatory privilege ought to be accorded to either one or the other. In the attempt to find a way out of the impasse, some geographers have turned to the theory of 'structuration' advanced by the Cambridge sociologist Anthony Giddens. This account of social formation and transformation highlights the interplay of both forces; human beings find themselves in structural circumstances not of their choosing, but through the exercise of their own agency can do something to effect change. The never-ending ebb and flow of agent-structure intercourse provides the engine power of social transformation. Where geography enters the picture is in the need to 'earth' this general model of historical change. Just how the relations between social structure and human agency fall out is evidently different from place to place and depends crucially on the particular arena of encounter. In this scenario, it is the interplay of subject and structure that gives both character and texture to places because they are at once the medium and outcome of social reciprocity. Hence geographers – arguing for the prime significance of locale – increasingly call for the geographizing of social theory.

What has given further encouragement to this renewed emphasis on the significance of place is a whole series of philosophical and social developments typically subsumed under the inscription 'postmodernism'. Now, it seems, cultural and epistemological pluralism are just inevitable. Fragmentation of knowledge, social differentiation, and the questioning of scientific rationality have all coalesced to reaffirm the importance of the particular, the specific, the local. And in this social and cognitive environment a geography stressing the salience of place is seen as having great potential.

If my story approaches accuracy – and I am certainly aware that traditions can as easily be fabricated as delineated – the geographical tradition has certainly been an extended argument embodying a range of conversational substances and styles. This tradition, I have urged, has evolved as it has adapted to different social and intellectual environments. Because it has connoted rather different things to different people at different times and in different places, it has employed a range of vocabularies to suit different purposes – from magic and theology to science and art. On occasion these discourses have been in conflict, at other times they have been mutually reinforcing. Sometimes the conversations have admitted a range of geographers, from time to time only a select group were equipped, or permitted, to take part. Yet recognizing the intelligibility of these diverse discourses in their own terms is to acknowledge the essentially contested character of the geographical tradition. I will venture two opinions. To concede the historically situated nature of the tradition will mean admitting that its standpoint can only be articulated in the midst of the particularities of time and place. To disregard its contested character will mean sacrificing the history and future of geography to partisan apologists who strive to monopolize the conversation in order to serve their own sectarian interests.

Bibliography

Aay, Henry, 'Conceptual Change and the Growth of Geographic Knowledge: A Critical Appraisal of the Historiography of Geography' (Ph.D dissertation, Clark University, 1978)

——'Textbook Chronicles: Disciplinary History and the Growth of Geographic Knowledge', in Brian W. Blouet (ed.), *The Origins of Academic Geography in the United States* (Hamden, Conn.: Archon Books, 1981), pp. 291–301

Agnew, John and James Duncan (eds), *The Power of Place: Bringing Together Geographical and Sociological Imagination* (Boston: Unwin Hyman, 1989)

Allen, John L., *Passage Through the Garden: Lewis and Clark and the Image of the American Northwest* (Urbana, Ill.: University of Illinois Press, 1975)

Alpers, Svetlana, *The Art of Describing. Dutch Art in the Seventeenth Century*, (Harmondsworth: Penguin Books, 1989)

Amedeo, Douglas and Reginald G. Golledge, *An Introduction to Scientific Reasoning in Geography* (New York: John Wiley and Sons, 1975)

Andrews, Howard F., 'The Durkheimians and Human Geography: Some Contextural Problems in the Sociology of Knowledge', *Transactions of the Institute of British Geographers*, n.s. 9 (1984): 315–36

——'The Early Life of Paul Vidal de la Blache and the Makings of Modern Geography', *Transactions of the Institute of British Geographers*, n.s. 11 (1986): 174–82

Andrews, J. H., *A Paper Landscape. The Ordnance Survey in Nineteenth-Century Ireland* (Oxford: Clarendon Press, 1975)

Anonymous, 'The New British Colony in South Africa', *Scottish Geographical Magazine*, 1 (1885): 383

Ansted, David Thomas, *Physical Geography* (London: W. H. Allen, 6th edn 1881)

Anuchin, V. A., *Theoretical Problems of Geography* (Columbus: Ohio State University Press, 1977)

Ashworth, G. L., *War and the City* (London: Routledge, 1991)

Ashworth, William B. Jr., 'Natural History and the Emblematic World View', in David C. Lindberg and Robert S. Westman (eds), *Reappraisals of the Scientific Revolution* (Cambridge: Cambridge University Press, 1990), pp. 303–32

Azurara, G. E., *The Chronicles of the Discovery and Conquest of Guinea* (Hakluyt Society, 1st series, vol. 1, 1896)

Bacon, Francis, *Novum Organum* (London, 1620)

Bagrow, Leo, *History of Cartography*, revised and enlarged by R. A. Skelton (London: Watts, 1964)

Baker, J. N. L., 'Nathanael Carpenter and English Geography in the Seventeenth Century', *Geographical Journal*, 71 (1928): 261–71

——*The History of Geography* (Oxford: Blackwell, 1963)

Balfour, Andrew, 'Problems of Acclimatisation', *The Lancet*, 205 (1923): 84–7, 243–7

——'Sojourners in the Tropics', *The Lancet*, 204 (1923): 1329–44

——and Henry Harold Scott, *Health Problems of the Empire: Past, Present and Future* (London and New York, 1924)

Banes, Daniel, 'The Portuguese Voyages of Discovery and the Emergence of Modern Science', *Journal of the Washington Academy of Sciences*, 28 (1988): 47–58

Bann, Stephen, *The Inventions of History. Essays on the Representation of the Past* (Manchester: Manchester University Press, 1990)

Bannister, Robert C., *Social Darwinism: Science and Myth in Anglo-American Social Thought* (Philadelphia: Temple University Press, 1979)

Barbour, Ian, *Issues in Science and Religion* (New York: Harper and Row, 1966)

Barnes, Barry, *Interests and the Growth of Knowledge* (London: Routledge and Kegan Paul, 1977)

Barnes, Barry and Steven Shapin (eds), *Natural Order: Historical Studies of Scientific Culture* (Beverly Hills and London: Sage, 1979)

Barnes, Trevor J. and Michael Curry, 'Towards a Contextualist Approach to Geographical Knowledge', *Transactions of the Institute of British Geographers*, n.s. 8 (1983): 467–82

Barnes, Trevor J. and James S. Duncan, (eds), *Writing Worlds: Discourse, Text and Metaphor in the Representation of Landscape* (London: Routledge, 1992)

Barrows, Harlan H., 'Geography as Human Ecology', *Annals of the Association of American Geographers*, 13 (1923): 1–14

Bassin, Mark, 'Friedrich Ratzel's Travels in the United States: A Study in the Genesis of his Anthropogeography', *History of Geography Newsletter*, 4 (1984): 11–22

——'Friedrich Ratzel 1884–1904', *Geographers. Biobibliographical Studies*, 11 (1987): 123–32

——'Imperialism and the Nation State in Friedrich Ratzel's Political Geography', *Progress in Human Geography*, 11 (1987): 473–95

——'Race contra Space: The Conflict between German *Geopolitik* and National Socialism', *Political Geography Quarterly*, 6 (1987): 115–34

Beaglehole, J. C. (ed.), *The Journals of Captain J. Cook*, 4 vols (Cambridge: Cambridge University Press, 1955–61)

Beaver, Stanley H., 'The Le Play Society and Fieldwork', *Geography*, 47 (1962): 226–39

Beck, Hanno, 'Moritz Wagner als Geograph', *Erdkunde*, 7 (1953): 125–8

——*Carl Ritter: Genius of Geography. On His Life and Work* (Bonn-Bad Godesberg: Inter Nationes, 1979)

Beckinsale, Robert P., 'W. M. Davis and American Geography: 1880–1934', in Brian Blouet (ed.), *Origins of Academic Geography in the United States* (Hamden: Archon Books, 1981), pp. 107–22

Bedini, Silvio A., *Thomas Jefferson. Statesman of Science* (New York: Macmillan, 1990)

Bellomy, Donald C., ' "Social Darwinism" Revisited', *Perspectives in American History*, n.s. 1 (1984): 1–129

Ben-David, J., 'Introduction', *International Social Science Journal*, 22 (1970): 7–27

Bennett, R. J., 'Quantification and Relevance', in R. J. Johnston (ed.), *The Future of Geography* (London: Methuen, 1985), pp. 211–24

Berdoulay, Vincent, 'French Possibilism as a Form of Neo-Kantian Philosophy', *Proceedings of the Association of American Geographers*, 8 (1976): 176–9

——'The Vidal-Durkheim Debate', in David Ley and Marwyn Samuels (eds), *Humanistic Geography: Prospects and Problems* (London: Croom Helm, 1978), pp. 77–90

——'The Contextual Approach', in D. R. Stoddart (ed.), *Geography, Ideology and Social Concern* (Oxford: Blackwell, 1981), pp. 8–16

——*La Formation de l'École Française de Géographie (1870–1914)* (Paris: Bibliothèque Nationale, 1981)

Bergsten, K. E., 'Variability in Intensity of Urban Fields as Illustrated by Birth-Places', in *Studies in Rural-Urban Interaction, Lund Studies in Geography, Series B, Human Geography*, 3 (Lund: Gleerup, 1951), pp. 25–32

Berlin, Isaiah, *Vico and Herder. Two Studies in the History of Ideas* (London: Chatto and Windus, 1976)

Berry, B. J. L., 'Introduction: A Kuhnian Perspective', in B. J. L. Berry (ed.), *Perspectives in Geography 3: The Nature of Change in Geographical Ideas* (Illinois: Northern Illinois University Press, 1978), pp. vii–x

Berthon, Simon and Andrew Robinson *The Shape of the World. The Mapping and Discovery of the Earth* (London: George Philip, 1991)

Bhaskar, Roy, *A Realist Theory of Science* (Sussex: Harvester Press, 2nd edn 1978)

——'Realism', in W. F. Bynum, E. J. Browner and Roy Porter (eds), *Dictionary of the History of Science* (London: Macmillan, 1981)

Billington, Ray Allen, *Genesis of the Frontier Thesis: A Study in Historical Creativity* (San Marino, California: The Huntington Library, 1971)

Birkenhauer, J. A. C., 'Johann Gottfried Herder', *Geographers. Biobibliographical Studies*, 10 (1986): 77–84

Biswas, Asit K., 'The Automatic Rain-gauge of Christopher Wren, F. R. S.', *Notes and Records of the Royal Society of London*, 22 (1967): 94–104

Blaeu, Johan, *Le Grand Atlas* (Amsterdam, 1663)

Bledstein, Burton J., *The Culture of Professionalism: The Middle Class and the Development of Higher Education in America* (New York: Norton, 1976)

Bloch, Maurice, *Marxism and Anthropology: The History of a Relationship* (Oxford: Oxford University Press, 1983)

Block, Robert P., 'Frederick Jackson Turner and American Geography', *Annals of the Association of American Geographers*, 70 (1980): 31–42

Bloor, David, *Knowledge and Social Imagery* (London: Routledge and Kegan Paul, 1976)

Blouet, Brian W., *Sir Halford Mackinder 1861–1947: Some New Perspectives* (Research Paper no. 13, School of Geography, University of Oxford, 1975)

——*Halford Mackinder: A Biography* (College Station, Texas: Texas A. & M. University Press, 1987)

——'The Political Career of Sir Halford Mackinder', *Political Geography Quarterly*, 6 (1987): 355–67

[Blundeville, Thomas], *M. Blundevile, His Exercises, containing Sixe Treatises... Very Necessarie to be Read and Learned of all Yoong Gentlemen that have not bene Exercised in Such Disciplines, and Yet Are Desirous to Have Knowledge as Well in Cosmographie, Astronomie, and Geographie, as Also in the Arte of Navigation. . .* (London, 1594)

Bluntschli, Hans, 'Die Amazonasniederung als Harmonischer Organismus', *Geographische Zeitschrift*, 27 (1921): 49–68

Boal, Frederick W. and David N. Livingstone (eds), *The Behavioural Environment: Essays in Reflection, Application, and Re-Evaluation* (London: Routledge, 1989)

Board, C., 'Field Work in Geography, with Particular Emphasis on the Role of Land-Use Survey', in R. J. Chorley and P. Haggett (eds), *Frontiers in Geographical Teaching* (London: Methuen, 1965), pp. 186–214

Boardman, Philip, *The Worlds of Patrick Geddes. Biologist, Town Planner, Re-Educator, Peace-Warrior* (London: Routledge and Kegan Paul, 1978)

Boas, Franz, 'Museums of Ethnology and their Classification', *Science*, 9 (1887): 587–9

——'The Study of Geography', *Science*, 9 (1887): 137–41

——*The Mind of Primitive Man* (New York: Macmillan, 1911)

——*Anthropology and Modern Life* (New York: W. W. Norton, 1928)

——'Race', in Franz Boas (ed.), *General Anthropology* (Boston: D. Death, 1938), pp. 95–123

Boas, George, *French Philosophies of the Romantic Period* (Baltimore: Johns Hopkins University Press, 1924)

Bock, Kenneth, 'Theories of Progress, Development, Evolution', in Tom Bottomore and Robert Nisbet (eds), *A History of Sociological Analysis* (London: Heinemann, 1978), pp. 39–79

Bögekamp, H., 'An Account of Prof. Ritter's Geographical Labors', in W. L. Gage, trans., *Geographical Studies by the Late Professor Carl Ritter of Berlin* (Boston: Gould and Lincoln, 1863)

Bompas, George C., *The Life of Frank Buckland* (London: Thomas Nelson, n.d.)

Boorstin, Daniel J., *The Discoverers. A History of Man's Search to Know his World and Himself* (New York: Random House, 1983)

Botting, Douglas, *Humboldt and the Cosmos* (London: Sphere Books, 1973)

Bottomore, Tom (ed.), *Modern Interpretations of Marx* (Oxford: Blackwell, 1981)

——and Robert Nisbet, 'Structuralism', in Tom Bottomore and Robert Nisbet (eds), *A History of Sociological Analysis* (London: Heinemann, 1978), pp. 557–98

Bowen, Margarita, *Empiricism and Geographical Thought. From Francis Bacon to Alexander von Humboldt* (Cambridge: Cambridge University Press, 1981)

Bowler, Peter J., 'Darwinism and Social Darwinism Around 1900'. Paper presented to the 93rd Annual Meeting of the American Historical Association, December 1978

——*The Eclipse of Darwinism. Anti-Darwinian Evolution Theories in the Decades Around 1900* (Baltimore: Johns Hopkins University Press, 1983)

——*The Non-Darwinian Revolution: Reinterpreting a Historical Myth* (Baltimore: Johns Hopkins University Press, 1988)

——*Evolution. The History of an Idea* (Berkeley: University of California Press, 1984, revised ed 1989)

——*The Invention of Progress: The Victorians and the Past* (Oxford: Basil Blackwell, 1989)

——*Charles Darwin, the Man and his Influence* (Oxford: Blackwell, 1990)

Bowman, Isaiah, *The New World. Problems in Political Geography* (London: George G. Harrap, revised and enlarged edition, 1926)

——*Geography in Relation to the Social Sciences* (New York: Scribner's, 1934)

——'Geography vs Geopolitics', *The Geographical Review*, 32 (1942): 646–58

——'Political Geography of Power', *Geographical Review*, 32 (1942): 349–52

——(ed.), *The Limits of Land Settlement. A Report on Present-day Possibilities* (New York: Council on Foreign Relations, 1937)

Boyle, Robert, *General Heads for the Natural History of a Country, Great or Small; Drawn Out for the Use of Travellers and Navigators* (London, 1692)

——'A Free Inquiry into the Vulgarly Received Notion of Nature', in Marie Boas Hall (ed.), *Robert Boyle on Natural Philosophy* (Bloomington: University of Indiana Press, 1965), pp. 150–3

Braudel, Fernand, *The Structures of Everyday Life. The Limits of the Possible*, translated by Siân Reynolds (London: Collins, 1981)

Breitbart, Myrna Margulies, 'Peter Kropotkin, the Anarchist Geographer', in David R. Stoddart (ed.), *Geography, Ideology and Social Concern* (Oxford: Blackwell, 1981), pp. 134–53

Brent, Peter, *Charles Darwin* (London: Heinemann, 1981)

Bricker, Charles and R. V. Tooley, *Landmarks of Mapmaking. An Illustrated Survey of Maps and Mapmakers* (Oxford: Phaidon, 1976)

Brigham, Albert Perry, *Geographic Influences in American History* (Boston: Ginn and Company, 1903)

——'Problems of Geographic Influence', *Annals of the Association of American Geographers*, 5 (1915): 3–25

Broc, Numa, 'L'Establissment de la Géographie et Nationalisme en France: Diffusion, Institutions, Projets (1870–1890)', *Annales de Géographie*, 83 (1974): 545–68

——*La Géographie des Philosophes. Géographes et Voyageurs Français au XVIIIe Siècle* (Paris, 1975)

——'Les Grandes Missions Scientifiques Françaises aux XIXe Siècles (Morée, Algérie, Mexique) et leurs Travaux Géographiques', *Revue d'Histoire des Sciences et de leurs Applications*, 34 (1981): 319–58

Broce, Gerald, 'Herder and Ethnography', *Journal of the History of the Behavioural Sciences*, 22 (1986): 150–70

Brockway, Lucile, *Science and Colonial Expansion: the Role of the British Royal Botanical Gardens* (London: Academic Press, 1979)

Brooke, John Hedley, 'Natural Theology in Britain from Boyle to Paley', in *New Interactions between Theology and Natural Science Block Four of Science and Belief from Copernicus to Darwin* (Milton Keynes: Open University Press, 1974), pp. 5–54

——'Newton and the Mechanistic Universe', in *Towards a Mechanistic Philosophy, Block Two of Science and Belief from Copernicus to Darwin* (Milton Keynes: Open University Press, 1974), pp. 45–95

——*Science and Religion. Some Historical Perspectives* (Cambridge: Cambridge University Press, 1991)

Brooke, M. Z. *Le Play: Engineer and Social Scientist. The Life and Work of Frédéric Le Play* (London: Longman, 1970)

Brookfield, Harold C., 'On the Environment as Perceived', *Progress in Geography*, 1 (1969): 51–80

Brosse, Jacques, *Great Voyages of Discovery. Circumnavigators and Scientists, 1764–1843*, translated by Stanley Hochman (New York: Facts on File Publications, 1983)

Brown, Hanbury, *The Wisdom of Science* (Cambridge: Cambridge University Press, 1986)

Brown, R. N. Rudmose, 'Scotland and Some Trends in Geography: John Murray, Patrick Geddes and Andrew Herbertson', *Geography*, 33 (1948): 107–20

Bruce, James, *Travels to Discover the Source of the Nile* (6 vols, Dublin, 1790–1)

Brunhes, Jean, *La Géographie Humaine: Essai de Classification Positive* (Paris: Alcan, 1910)

Brunn, S. D. and K. A. Mingst, 'Geopolitics', in Michael Pacione (ed.), *Progress in Political Geography* (London: Croom Helm, 1985), pp. 41–76

Brush, Stephen G., 'Should the History of Science be Rated X?' *Science*, 183 (22 March 1974): 1164–72

Bryce, James, 'The Relations of History and Geography', *Contemporary Review*, 49 (1886): 426–43

——'The Migrations of the Races of Men Considered Historically', *Scottish Geographical Magazine*, 8 (1892): 401–25

Buck, Peter, 'Seventeenth-Century Political Arithmetic: Civil Strife and Vital Statistics', *Isis*, 68 (1977): 67–84

Bullough, Vern L., 'Varenius, Bernhardus', *Dictionary of Scientific Biography* (New York: Scribner's, 1970–81), vol. 13, pp. 583–4

Bunge, William, *Theoretical Geography* (Lund: Gleerup, 1962)

——*Fred K. Schaefer and the Science of Geography* (Harvard Papers in Theoretical Geography, Special Papers Series A, 1968)

——*Fitzgerald: The Geography of a Revolution* (Cambridge, Mass.: Schenkman, 1971)

——'The First Years of the Detroit Geographical Expedition: A Personal Report', in Richard Peet (ed.), *Radical Geography: Alternative Viewpoints on Contemporary Social Issues* (London: Methuen, 1978) (first published 1969)

——'Fred K. Schaefer and the Science of Geography', *Annals of the Association of American Geographers*, 69 (1979): 128–32

——'Perspective on *Theoretical Geography*', *Annals of the Association of American Geographers*, 69 (1979): 169–74

Burkhardt, Frederick and Sidney Smith (eds), *A Calendar of the Correspondence of Charles Darwin, 1821–1882* (New York: Garland Publishing, 1985)

Burrow, John W., *Evolution and Society. A Study in Victorian Social Theory* (Cambridge: Cambridge University Press, 1966)

Burton, Ian, 'The Quantitative Revolution and Theoretical Geography', *The Canadian Geographer*, 7 (1963): 151–62

Büsching, A. F., *A New System of Geography: In Which Is Given a General Account of the Situation and Limits, the Manners, History, and Constitution, of the Several Kingdoms and States of the Known World; And A Very Particular Description of their Subdivisions and Dependencies; their Cities and Towns, Forts, Sea-Ports, Produce, Manufactures, and Commerce*, 6 vols (London: A. Millar, 1762)

Butlin, Robin, 'George Adam Smith and the Historical Geography of the Holy Land: Contents, Contexts and Connections', *Journal of Historical Geography*, 14 (1988): 381–404

Buttimer, Anne, *Society and Milieu in the French Geographic Tradition* (Chicago: Rand McNally, 1971)

——*Values in Geography* (Association of American Geographers, Commission on College Geography, Resource Paper no. 24, Washington DC, 1974)

——'Charism and Context: The Challenge of *La Géographie Humaine*', in David Ley and Marwyn Samuels (eds), *Humanistic Geography: Prospects and Problems* (London: Croom Helm, 1978), pp. 58–76

——'On People, Paradigms, and "Progress" in Geography', in D. R. Stoddart (ed.), *Geography, Ideology and Social Concern* (Oxford: Blackwell, 1981), pp. 81–98

——(ed.), *The Practice of Geography* (London: Longman, 1983)

Büttner, Manfred, 'Kant and the Physico-Theological Consideration of the Geographical Facts', *Organon*, 11 (1975): 231–49

——'Bartholomäus Keckermann 1572–1609', in *Geographers. Biobibliographical Studies*, vol. 2, (London: Mansell, 1977), pp. 73–9

——'On the History and Philosophy of the Geography of Religion in Germany', Paper presented at the XVth International Congress of the History of Science, Edinburgh, 10–19 August 1977

——'Philipp Melanchthon 1497–1560', in *Geographers. Biobibliographical Studies*, vol. 3 (London: Mansell, 1979), pp. 93–7

——'The Significance of the Reformation for the Reorientation of Geography in Lutheran Germany', *History of Science*, 17 (1979): 139–69

——(ed.), *Carl Ritter: Zur Europaisch-Amerikanischen Geographie an der Wende vom 18. zum 19. Jahrhundert* (Paderhorn, FRG: Ferdinand Schoningh, 1980)

——and Karl H. Burmeister, 'Sebastian Münster 1488–1552', in *Geographers. Biobibliographical Studies*, vol. 3 (London: Mansell, 1979), pp. 99–106

Butzer, Karl W., 'Hartshorne, Hettner, and *The Nature of Geography*', in J. Nicholas Entrikin and Stanley D. Brunn (ed.), *Reflections on Richard Hartshorne's* The Nature of Geography (Washington, D.C.: Association of American Geographers, 1989), pp. 35–52

Cameron, Ian, *To the Farthest Ends of the Earth. The History of the Royal Geographical Society, 1830–1980* (London: MacDonald, 1980)

Campbell, J. A., *Some Sources of the Humanism of H. J. Fleure* (School of Geography, University of Oxford, Research Paper no. 2, 1972)

——'The Concept of "The Behavioural Environment", and its Origins, Reconsidered', in Frederick W. Boal and David N. Livingstone (eds), *The Behavioural Environment: Essays in Reflection, Application, and Re-evaluation* (London: Routledge, 1989), pp. 33–76

——and D. N. Livingstone, 'Neo-Lamarckism and the Development of Geography in the United States and Great Britain', *Transactions of the Institute of British Geographers* n.s. 8 (1983): 267–94

Campbell, Tony, 'Portolan Charts from the Late Thirteenth Century to 1500', in J. B. Harley and David Woodward (eds), *History of Cartography. Volume One. Cartography in Prehistoric, Ancient, and Medieval Europe and the Mediterranean* (Chicago: University of Chicago Press, 1987), pp. 371–463

Cannon, Susan Faye, *Science in Culture: The Early Victorian Period* (New York: Dawson and Science History Publication, 1978)

Capel, Horacio, 'Institutionalization of Geography and Strategies of Change', in D. R. Stoddart (ed.), *Geography, Ideology and Social Concern* (Oxford: Blackwell, 1981), pp. 37–69

Carozzi, Albert V. 'Guyot, Arnold Henri', *Dictionary of Scientific Biography* (New York: Scribner's, 1970–81), vol. 5, pp. 599–600

[Carpenter, Nathanael], *Philosophia Libera* (Oxoniae, 1622)

——*Geography Delineated Forth in two Bookes. Containing the Sphaericall and Topicall Parts Thereof* (Oxford, 1625)

——*Achitophel, or, the Picture of a Wicked Politician* (London, 1627)

Carter, H. B., *Sir Joseph Banks, 1743–1820* (London: British Museum of Natural History, 1988)

Castellani, Aldo, *Climate and Acclimatisation* (London: J. Bale and Danielsson, 1931)

Castlereagh, Duncan, *The Great Age of Exploration* (London: Reader's Digest, 1971)

Chalmers, A. F., *What is This Thing Called Science?* (Milton Keynes: Open University Press, 2nd ed 1982)

Chamberlain, M. E., *The Scramble for Africa* (Harlow: Longman, 1974)

Chapman, E. F., *Physical Geography in its Relation to Military Operations* (Aldershott: Aldershott Military Society, No. xxvii, 1890)

Chapman, Roger G. and Cleverland T. Duval (eds), *Charles Darwin, 1809–1882: A Centennial Commemorative* (Wellington, New Zealand: Nova Pacifica, 1982)

Charles, Havelock, 'Neurasthenia and its Bearing on the Decay of Northern Peoples in India', *Transactions of the Society of Tropical Medicine and Hygiene*, 7 (1913): 2–31

Cherry, G. E., *The Evolution of British Town Planning: A History of Town Planning in the United Kingdom during the 20th Century and of the Royal Town Planning Institute 1914–74* (Leighton Buzzard: Leonard Hill, 1974)

Chisholm, George G., 'Perplexities of Race: a Review', *Scottish Geographical Magazine*, 41 (1925): 300

Chorley, Richard J., Robert P. Beckinsale and Anthony J. Dunn, *The History of the Study of Landforms or the Development of Geomorphology. Volume Two: The Life and Work of William Morris Davis* (London: Methuen, 1973)

Christaller, Walter, *Die Zentralen Orte in Südeutschland* (Jena: Gustan Fischer, 1973)

Clark, John Willis and Thomas McKenny Hughes, *The Life and Letters of the Reverend Adam Sedgwick* (Cambridge: Cambridge University Press, 1890)

Clark, Robert T. Jr., *Herder: His Life and Thought* (Berkeley and Los Angeles: University of California Press, 1969)

Claval, Paul, *Essai sur l'Évolution de la Géographie Humaine* (Paris: Les Belles Lettres, 1976)

Cloke, Paul, Chris Philo and David Sadler, *Approaching Human Geography. An Introduction to Contemporary Theoretical Debates* (London: Paul Chapman, 1991)

Cobbe, Hugh, *Cook's Voyages and Peoples of the Pacific* (London: British Museum Publications, 1974)

Codere, Helen, *Kwakiutl Ethnography* (Chicago: University of Chicago Press, 1975)

Cohen, I. Bernard, *Revolution in Science* (Cambridge, Mass.: Harvard University Press, 1985)

'Columbus, Christopher', *Dictionary of Scientific Biography* (New York: Scribner's, 1970–81), supplement, pp. 87–91

Coleman, William, 'Science and Symbol in the Turner Frontier Hypothesis', *American Historical Review*, 72 (1966): 22–49

Cooke, Francis, *The Principles of Geometrie, Astronomie, and Geographie. Wherein is Breefely, Euidently, and Methodically Deliuered, Whatsoeuer Appertaineth unto the Knowledge of the Said Sciences. Gathered out of the Table of the Astronomicall Institutions of Georgius Henischius* (London, 1591)

Coones, Paul, *Mackinder's 'Scope and Methods of Geography' after a Hundred Years* (School of Geography, University of Oxford, 1987)

Copenhaver, Brian P., 'Natural Magic, Hermeticism, and Occultism in Early Modern Science', in David C. Lindberg and Robert S. Westman (eds), *Reappraisals of the Scientific Revolution* (Cambridge: Cambridge University Press, 1990), pp. 261–301

Cormack, Lesley, 'Non Sufficit Orbem: Geography as an Interactive Science at Oxford and Cambridge 1580–1620' (Ph.D. thesis, University of Toronto, 1988)

——'The Social Context of Geography at Oxford and Cambridge, 1580–1620'. Paper presented at the Joint Conference of the British Society for the History of Science and the History of Science Society, Manchester University, July 1988

——' "Good Fences Make Good Neighbours": Geography as Self-Definition in Early Modern England', *Isis*, 82 (1991): 639–61

Cosgrove, Denis, *Social Formation and Symbolic Landscape* (London: Croom Helm, 1984)

——'Geography and the Mathematical Arts: Considerations on Humanism, the Occult and Geography in the Late Renaissance'. Paper presented at the Annual Conference of the Institute of British Geographers, University of Leeds, 1985

——'The Geometry of Landscape: Practical and Speculative Arts in Sixteenth-Century Venetian Land Territories,' in Denis Cosgrove and Stephen Daniels (eds), *The Iconography of Landscape. Essays on the Symbolic Representation, Design and Use of Past Environments* (Cambridge: Cambridge University Press, 1988), pp. 254–76

C[ourtney], W. P., 'Carpenter, Nathanael (1589–1628?)', *Dictionary of National Biography*

Crane, Diane, *Invisible Colleges: Diffusion of Knowledge in Scientific Communities* (Chicago: University of Chicago Press, 1972)

Crawfurd, John, 'On the Effects of Commixture, Locality, Climate, and Food on the Races of Man', *Transactions of the Ethnological Society of London*, n.s. 1 (1861): 76–92

——'On the Connection between Ethnology and Physical Geography', *Transactions of the Ethnological Society of London*, n.s. 2 (1863): 4–23

Crone, G. R., *Modern Geographers. An Outline of Progress since AD 1800* (London: Royal Geographical Society, revised edn 1970)

Crosby, Alfred W., 'Ecological Imperialism: The Overseas Migration of Western Europeans as a Biological Phenomenon', in Donald Worster (ed.), *The Ends of the Earth. Perspectives on Modern Environmental History* (Cambridge: Cambridge University Press, 1988), pp. 103–17

Crosland, Maurice P., *Science in France in the Revolutionary Era* (Cambridge, Mass: Harvard University Press, 1969)

Cuningham, William, *The Cosmographical Glasse, Conteinyng the Pleasant Principles of Cosmographie, Geographie, Hydrographie, or Nauigation* (London, 1559)

Curtin, Philip, '"The White Man's Grave": Image and Reality, 1780–1850', *Journal of British Studies*, 1 (1961): 94–110

——*Death by Migration: Europe's Encounter with the Tropical World in the Nineteenth Century* (Cambridge: Cambridge University Press, 1989)

Cvijić, Jovan, 'The Geographical Distribution of the Balkan Peoples', *Geographical Review*, 5 (1918): 345–61

Dana, James D., 'Creation; or, the Biblical Cosmogony in the Light of Modern Science', in *Bibliotheca Sacra*, 42 (1885): 201–24

——'Biographical Memoir of Arnold Guyot', *Annual Report of the Board of Regents of the Smithsonian Institution for 1887* (Washington: Government Printing Office, 1889), pp. 693–722

Darby, H. C. (ed.), *An Historical Geography of England before AD 1800* (Cambridge: Cambridge University Press, 1936)

Darwin, Charles, 'The Structure and Distribution of Coral Reefs: Being the First Part of the Geology of the Voyage of the "Beagle", under the Command of Capt. Fitzroy, R. N., during the Years 1832 to 1836', *Journal of the Royal Geographical Society*, 12 (1842): 115–20

——*The Origin of Species by Charles Darwin: A Variorum Text*, edited by Morse Peckham (Philadelphia: University of Pennsylvania Press, 1959)

Davies, G. L., *The Earth in Decay. A History of British Geomorphology 1578 to 1878* (London: MacDonald, n.d.)

Davies, Wayne K. D., 'Theory, Science and Geography', in Wayne K. D. Davies (ed.), *The Conceptual Revolution in Geography* (London: University of London Press, 1972), pp. 31–41

Davis, William Morris, 'Geographic Classification, Illustrated by a Study of Plains, Plateaus and their Derivatives', *Proceedings of the American Association for the Advancement of Science (33rd Meeting Philadelphia)* (1885): 428–32

——'The Rivers and Valleys of Pennsylvania', *National Geographic Magazine*, 1 (1889): 183–253

——'The Development of Certain English Rivers', *Geographical Journal*, 5 (1895): 127–46

——'The Geographical Cycle', *Geographical Journal*, 14 (1899): 481–504

——'The Physical Geography of the Lands', *Popular Science Monthly*, 57 (1900): 157–70

——'Physical Geography in the High School', *School Review*, 8 (1900): 388–404

——'The Progress of Geography in the Schools', *National Society for the Scientific Study of Education. First Year Book* (1902), Part II, pp. 7–49

——'Systematic Geography', *Proceedings of the American Philosophical Society*, 41 (1902): 235–59

——'An Inductive Study of the Content of Geography', *Bulletin of the American Geographical Society*, 38 (1906): 67–84

——'The Progress of Geography in the United States', *Annals of the Association of American Geographers*, 14 (1924): 158–215

Dear, Michael, 'The Postmodern Challenge: Reconstructing Human Geography', *Transactions of the Institute of British Geographers*, n.s. 13 (1988): 262–74

Deason, Gary B., 'The Protestant Reformation and the Rise of Modern Science', *Scottish Journal of Theology*, 38 (1985): 221–40

——'Reformation Theology and the Mechanistic Conception of Nature', in David C. Lindberg and Ronald L. Numbers (eds), *God and Nature. Historical Essays on the Encounter between Christianity and Science* (Berkeley: University of California Press, 1986), pp. 167–91

Debus, Allen G., *Man and Nature in the Renaissance* (Cambridge: Cambridge University Press, 1978)

Desmond, Adrian, *The Politics of Evolution. Morphology, Medicine, and Reform in Radical London* (Chicago: University of Chicago Press, 1989)

Dickinson, Robert E., *The Makers of Modern Geography* (London: Routledge and Kegan Paul, 1969)

——*Regional Concept: The Anglo-American Leaders* (London: Routledge and Kegan Paul, 1976)

——and O. J. R. Howarth, *The Making of Geography* (Oxford: Clarendon Press, 1933)

Digges, Leonard, *A Prognostication Everlastinge of Righte Good Effecte Fruitfully Augmented by the Auctour, Contayning Plaine, Briefe, Pleasant, Chosen Rules to Judge the Weather by the Sunne, Moone, Starres, Comets, Rainebow, Thunder, Cloudes, with Other Extraordinary Tokens, Not Omitting Aspects of Planets, With a Briefe Judgement for Ever of Plenty, Lacke, Sickness, Death, Warres Ec. Opening Also Many Naturall Causes Worthy to be Known. To these and other now at the last, are ioyned divers generall, pleasant tables, with manye compendious rules, easye to be had in memory, manifolde ways profitable to al men of vnderstanding, published by Leonard Digges gentleman. Lately corrected and augmented by Thomas Digges his sonne* (London: Thomas Marsh, 1576)

Dillenberger, John, *Protestant Thought and Natural Science. A Historical Interpretation* (London: Collins, 1961)

Donovan, Arthur, 'James Hutton and the Scottish Enlightenment: Some Preliminary Considerations', *Scotia*, 1 (1977): 56–68

Downes, Alan, 'The Bibliographic Dinosaurs of Georgian Geography (1714–1830)', *Geographical Journal*, 137 (1971): 379–87

Draper, John William, *History of the Conflict between Religion and Science* (London: Henry S. King, 1875)

Driver, Felix, 'Henry Morton Stanley and his Critics: Geography, Exploration and Empire', *Past and Present*, 133 (1991): 134–66

——'Geography's Empire: Histories of Geographical Knowledge', *Environment and Planning D: Society and Space*, 10 (1992): 23–40

Dryer, C. R., 'Genetic Geography: The Development of the Geographic Sense and Concept', *Annals of the Association of American Geographers*, 10 (1920): 3–16

Dunbar, Gary S., 'Thomas Jefferson, Geographer', *Special Libraries Association, Geography and Map Division, Bulletin*, 40 (April 1960): 11–16

——*Elisée Reclus. Historian of Nature* (Hamden: Archon Books, 1978)

——'Elisée Reclus, an Anarchist in Geography', in David R. Stoddart (ed.), *Geography, Ideology and Social Concern* (Oxford: Blackwell, 1981), pp. 154–64

——'"The Compass Follows the Flag": The French Scientific Mission to Mexico, 1864–1867', *Annals of the Association of American Geographers*, 78 (1988): 229–40

Duncan, James, 'The Superorganic in American Cultural Geography', *Annals of the Association of American Geographers*, 70 (1980): 181–98

——and David Ley, 'Structural Marxism and Human Geography: A Critical Perspective', *Annals of the Association of American Geographers*, 72 (1982): 30–59

Durkheim, Emile, *The Elementary Forms of Religious Life*, translated by Joseph Ward Swain (London: Allen and Unwin, 1915)

Egerton, Frank N. III, 'Petty, William,' *Dictionary of Scientific Biography* (New York: Scribner's, 1970–81), Vol. 10, pp. 564–7.

Eijkman, C., 'Some Questions Concerning the Influence of Tropical Climate on Man', *The Lancet*, 206 (1924): 887–93

Elkins, T. H., 'Human and Regional Geography in the German-Speaking Lands in the First Forty Years of the Twentieth Century', in J. Nicholas Entrikin and Stanley D. Brunn (eds), *Reflections on Richard Hartshorne's* The Nature of Geography (Washington, DC: Association of American Geographers, 1989), pp. 17–34

Emery, F. V., 'Geography and Imperialism: The Role of Sir Bartle Frere (1815–84)', *The Geographical Journal*, 150 (1984): 342–50

Entrikin, J. Nicholas, 'Contemporary Humanism in Geography', *Annals of the Association of American Geographers*, 66 (1976): 615–32

——'Robert Park's Human Ecology and Human Geography', *Annals of the Association of American Geographers*, 70 (1980): 43–58

——'Carl O. Sauer, Philosopher in Spite of Himself', *Geographical Review*, 74 (1984): 387–408

——*The Betweenness of Place* (London: Macmillan, 1991)

Evans, E. Estyn, *Irish Heritage* (Dundalk: Dundalgan Press, 1942)

——*Irish Folk Ways* (London: Routledge and Kegan Paul, 1957)

——Review of *Land and Life*, by Carl O. Sauer, edited by John Leighly, *Geographical Review*, 54 (1964): 596–7

——*Mourne Country* (Dundalk: Dundalgan Press, 1967)

——*The Personality of Ireland* (Belfast: Blackstaff Press, 1981)

Evans, Ifor M. and Heather Lawrence, *Christopher Saxton. Elizabethan Map-Maker* (London: Wakefield Historical Publications and the Holland Press, 1979)

Eyre, S. R., 'Determinism and the Ecological Approach to Geography', *Geography*, 49 (1964): 369–76

Fahlbusch, Michael, Mechtild Rössler and Dominik Siegrist, 'Conservatism, Ideology and Geography in Germany 1920–1950', *Political Geography Quarterly*, 8 (1989): 353–67

Febvre, Lucien, *A Geographical Introduction to History*, translated by E. G. Mountford and J. H. Paxton (London: Kegan, Paul, Trench, Trubner, 1932)

Feigl, Herbert, 'Positivism in the Twentieth Century (Logical Empiricism)', in Philip P. Wiener (ed.), *Dictionary of the History of Ideas* (New York: Scribner's, 1973), vol. 3, pp. 545–51

Feingold, Mordechai, *The Mathematicians' Apprenticeship. Science, Universities and Society in England 1560–1640* (Cambridge: Cambridge University Press, 1984)

Feldman, Douglas A., 'The History of the Relationship between Environment and Culture in Ethnological Thought: An Overview', *Journal of the History of the Behavioral Sciences*, 11 (1975): 67–81

Felkin, Robert W., 'The Egyptian Sûdan', *Scottish Geographical Magazine*, 1 (1885): 221–38

——'Can Europeans Become Acclimatised in Tropical Africa?' *Scottish Geographical Magazine*, 2 (1886): 647–57

——'Uganda', *Scottish Geographical Magazine*, 2 (1886): 208–26

——'On Acclimatisation', *Scottish Geographical Magazine*, 7 (1891): 647–56

——'Tropical Highlands: their Suitability for European Settlement', *Transactions of the Seventh International Congress on Hygiene and Demography*, 10 (1892): 162

——*On the Geographical Distribution of Some Tropical Diseases, and their Relation to Physical Phenomena* (Edinburgh and London, n.d.)

Feyerabend, Paul K., *Against Method: Outline of an Anarchistic Theory of Knowledge* (London: New Left Books, 1975)

Fischer, Eric, Robert D. Campbell and Eldon S. Miller, *A Question of Place* (Arlington, Va.: R. W. Beatty, 1967)

Fleure, Herbert John, 'The Factors of Organic Evolution', *University College of Wales Magazine*, 24 (1901): 71–3

——'The Influence of Geographic Environment. A Review of Miss Semple's Work', *Geographical Teacher*, 35 (1911): 65–8

——'Ancient Wales – Anthropological Evidence', *Transactions of the Honourable Society of Cymmrodorion* (1915–16): 75–164

——'Régions Humaines', *Annales de Géographie*, 26 (1917): 161–74

——'The Racial History of the British People', *Geographical Review*, 5 (1918): 216–31

——'Human Regions', *Scottish Geographical Magazine*, 35 (1919): 31–45

——'The Teaching of Geography', in A. Watson Bain (ed.), *The Modern Teacher: Essays on Educational Aims and Methods* (London, 1921), pp. 173–94

——*The Peoples of Europe* (London: Oxford University Press, 1922)

———*The Races of England and Wales. A Survey of Recent Research* (London: Benn Brothers, 1923)

———*Wales and her People* (Wrexham: Hughes and Son, 1926)

———'The Nordic Myth: a Critique of Current Racial Theories', *Eugenics Review*, 22 (1930–31): 117–21

———'The Geographical Study of Society and World Problems', *Reports of the British Association for the Advancement of Science* (1932): 103–18

———'Ritual and Ethic: A Study of a Change in Ancient Religions about 800–500 BC', *Bulletin of the John Rylands Library*, 22 (1938): 435–54

———'Geographical Thought in a Changing World', *Geographical Review*, 34 (1944): 515–28

———'Geography and Evolution', *Geography*, 34 (1949): 1–9

———*A Natural History of Man in Britain, Conceived as a Study of Changing Relations between Men and Environments* (London, 1951)

———'Patrick Geddes (1854–1932)', *Sociological Review*, n.s. 1/2 (1953): 5–13

———'Racialism and Toleration', in E. Ashworth Underwood (ed.), *Science, Medicine and History. Essays on the Evolution of Scientific Thought and Medical Practice* (London: Oxford University Press, 1953), vol. 2, pp. 401–8

———'Recollections of A. J. Herbertson', *Geography*, 50 (1965): 348–9

———and E. Davies, 'Physical Character Among Welshmen', *Journal of the Royal Anthropological Institute*, 88 (1958): 45–95

———and T. C. James, 'Geographical Distribution of Anthropological Types in Wales', *Journal of the Royal Anthropological Institute of Great Britain and Ireland*, 46 (1916): 35–153

———and Harold Peake, *Apes and Man – The Corridors of Time Volume 1* (Oxford: Oxford University Press, 1927)

Flint, Robert, *Theism* (London: William Blackwood, 4th rev. edn 1883)

Forde, C. Darryl, 'Values in Human Geography', *Geographical Teacher*, 13 (1925): 216–21

———*Habitat, Economy and Society. A Geographical Introduction to Ethnology* (London: Methuen, 1934)

Foucault, Michel, *Power/Knowledge: Selected Interviews and Other Writings, 1972–1977* (Brighton: Harvester Press, 1980)

Fox, Cyril, *The Personality of Britain: Its Influence on Inhabitant and Invader in Prehistoric and Early Historic Times* (Cardiff: National Museum of Wales, 1932)

Freeman, T. W., *A Hundred Years of Geography* (London: Methuen, 1965)

———'The British School of Geography', *Organon*, 14 (1980): 205–16

———*A History of Modern British Geography* (New York and London: Longman, 1980)

———'The Royal Geographical Society and the Development of Geography', in E. H. Brown (ed.), *Geography Yesterday and Tomorrow* (Oxford: Oxford University Press, 1980), pp. 1–99

———'Herbert John Fleure, 1877–1969', *Geographers.: Biobibliographical Studies*, 11 (1987): 35–51

French, Peter J., *John Dee: The World of an Elizabethan Magus* (London: Routledge and Kegan Paul, 1972)

Frere, H. Bartle E., 'Presidential Address, Section E (Geography)', *Report of the 39th Meeting, British Association for the Advancement of Science, Exeter* (1869): 152–9

——'On Temperate South Africa', *Proceedings of the Royal Geographical Society*, n.s. 3 (1881): 1–26

Frisinger, H., *The History of Meteorology: to 1800* (New York: Science History Publications, 1977)

Fritsch, Gustar, 'Geographie und Anthropologie als Bundesgenossen', *Verhandlugen der Gesellschaft für Erdkunde zo Berlin*, 8 (1881): 234–51

Fuller, Thomas, 'Nathaniel [sic] Carpenter', in *The History of the Worthies of England* (London: Thomas Teff, new edn 1840), vol. 1

Fulton, John F., 'The Honourable Robert Boyle, F.R.S (1627–1692)', *Notes and Records of the Royal Society of London*, 15 (1960): 119–35

Gage, W. L., *The Life of Karl Ritter* (Edinburgh: Blackwood, 1867)

Galois, Bob, 'Ideology and the Idea of Nature: The Case of Peter Kropotkin', *Antipode*, 8, 3 (1976): 1–16

Galton, Francis, 'Address as President of Geography Section', *Annual Reports of British Association for the Advancement of Science*, 42 (1872): 198–203

——'Statistical Inquiries into the Efficacy of Prayer', *Fortnightly Review*, n.s. 12 (1872): 125–35

Garbarino, Merwyn S., *Sociocultural Theory in Anthropology: A Short History* (New York: Holt, Rinehart and Winston, 1977)

Geddes, Patrick, 'The Influence of Geographical Conditions on Social Development', *Geographical Journal*, 12 (1898): 580–7

——'Man and his Environment: A Study from the Paris Exposition', *International Monthly*, 2 (1900): 169–95

——'Nature Study and Geographical Education', *Scottish Geographical Magazine*, 18 (1902): 525–36

——'Civics as Applied Sociology. Part I', *Sociological Papers*, 1 (1905): 103–18

——'A Great Geographer: Elisée Reclus 1830–1905. An Obituary'. *Scottish Geographical Magazine*, 21 (1905): 552

——*Cities in Evolution. An Introduction to the Town Planning Movement and to the Study of Civics* (London: Williams and Norgate, 1915)

——*Town Planning in Kapurthala. A Report to H. H. the Maharaja of Kapurthala* (Lucknow: Murray's London Printing Press, 1917)

——*Town Planning Towards City-Development. A Report to the Durbar of Indore*, 2 vols (Indore: Holkar State Printing Press, 1918)

——and J. Arthur Thomson, 'Biology', *Chambers Encyclopedia* (London and Edinburgh: W. and R. Chambers, new edn 1925), vol. 2, pp. 157–64

Geikie, Archibald, *Elementary Lessons in Physical Geography* (London: Macmillan, 1886)

'Geography and the War Office', *Scottish Geographical Magazine*, 18 (1902): 423–5

George, H. B., *The Relations of Geography and History* (Oxford: Oxford University Press, 1901)

George, Wilma, 'Source and Background to Discoveries of New Animals in the Sixteenth and Seventeenth Centuries', *History of Science*, 18 (1980): 79–104

——*Darwin* (London: Fontana, 1982)

'German Colonisation in Tropical Africa', *Scottish Geographical Magazine*, 1 (1885): 263

Gerrish, B. A., 'The Reformation and the Rise of Modern Science', in Jerald C. Brauer (ed.), *The Impact of the Church Upon Its Culture* (Chicago: University of Chicago Press, 1968), pp. 231–75

Ghiselin, Michael, *The Triumph of the Darwinian Method* (Berkeley: University of California Press, 1969)

Giddens, Anthony, 'Positivism and its Critics', in Tom Bottomore and Robert Nisbet (eds), *A History of Sociological Analysis* (London: Heinemann, 1978), pp. 237–86

——*Central Problems in Social Theory: Action, Structure and Contradiction in Social Analysis* (London: Macmillan, 1979)

——*The Constitution of Society: Outline of the Theory of Structuration* (Oxford: Polity, 1984)

Gilbert, E. W., 'What is Historical Geography?' *Scottish Geographical Magazine*, 48 (1932): 129–36

——'Andrew John Herbertson 1865–1915. An Appreciation of his Life and Work', *Geography*, 50 (1965): 313–31

——*British Pioneers in Geography* (Newton Abbot: David and Charles, 1972)

Gilley, Sheridan, 'The Huxley–Wilberforce Debate: A Reconstruction', in Keith Robbins (ed.), *Religion and Humanism* (Oxford: Blackwell, 1981), pp. 325–40

Gilman, Daniel Coit, *The Launching of a University and Other Papers. A Sheaf of Remembrances* (New York: Dodd, Mead and Company, 1906)

Gitlin, Todd, 'Postmodernism Defined, At Last!' *Unte Reader*, 34 (1989): 52–61

Glacken, Clarence J., 'Count Buffon on Cultural Changes of the Physical Environment', *Annals of the Association of American Geographers*, 50 (1960): 1–21

——*Traces on the Rhodian Shore. Nature and Culture in Western Thought from Ancient Times to the End of the Eighteenth Century* (Berkeley: University of California Press, 1967)

Glick, Thomas F., 'History and Philosophy of Geography', *Progress in Human Geography*, 8 (1984): 275–83

Godlewska, Anne, 'Tradition, Crisis, and New Paradigms in the Rise of the Modern French Discipline of Geography 1760–1850', *Annals of the Association of American Geographers*, 79 (1989): 192–213

——'Napoleon's Geographers: Imperialists or Soldiers of Modernity?' in Neil Smith and Anne Godlewska (eds), *Geography and Empire*, forthcoming

Godlund, S., 'Bus Services, Hinterlands, and the Location of Urban Settlements in

Sweden, Specially in Scania', in *Studies in Rural-Urban Interaction, Lund Studies in Geography, Series B, Human Geography*, 3 (Lund: Gleerup, 1951), pp. 14–24

Goetzmann, William H., *New Lands, New Men. America and the Second Great Age of Discovery* (New York: Viking, 1986)

Goldie, George T., 'Geographical Ideals', *Geographical Journal*, 29 (1907): 1–14

Goldstein, Thomas, 'Geography in Fifteenth Century Florence', in John Parker (ed.), *Merchants and Scholars: Essays in the History of Exploration and Trade* (Minneapolis: University of Minnesota Press, 1965), pp. 9–32

——*The Dawn of Modern Science* (Boston: Houghton-Mifflin, 1988)

Golinski, Jan, 'The Theory of Practice and the Practice of Theory: Sociological Approaches in the History of Science', *Isis*, 81 (1990): 492–505

Golledge, Reginald G. and Douglas Amedeo, 'On Laws in Geography', *Annals of the Association of American Geographers*, 58 (1968): 760–74

——and Helen Couclelis, 'Positivist Philosophy and Research on Human Spatial Behaviour', in T. F. Saarinen, D. Seamon and J. L. Sell (eds), *Environmental Perception and Behavior: An Inventory and Prospect* (University of Chicago, Department of Geography, Research Paper no. 209, 1984)

——and G. Rushton (eds), *Spatial Choice and Spatial Behavior: Geographical Essays on the Analysis of Preferences and Perceptions* (Columbus, Ohio: Ohio State University Press, 1976)

——and H. Timmermans (eds), *Behavioural Modelling in Geography and Planning* (London: Croom Helm, 1988)

Goodman, David, 'Iberian Science: Navigation, Empire and Counter-Reformation', in David Goodman and Colin A. Russell (eds), *The Rise of Scientific Europe, 1500–1800* (Sevenoaks, Kent: Hodder and Stoughton, 1991), pp. 117–44

Gould, Peter R., 'Methodological Developments since the Fifties', in Christopher Board, Richard J. Chorley, Peter Haggett and David R. Stoddart (eds), *Progress in Geography. International Reviews of Current Research. Volume 1* (London: Edward Arnold, 1969), pp. 1–49

——'Geography 1957–1977: The Augean Period', *Annals of the Association of American Geographers*, 69 (1979), pp. 139–51

——'Signals in the Noise', in Stephen Gale and Gunnar Olsson (eds), *Philosophy in Geography* (Dordrecht: Reidel, 1979), pp. 121–54

——and Rodney White, *Mental Maps* (Harmondsworth: Penguin Books, 1974)

Gould, Stephen Jay, *Ontogeny and Phylogeny* (Cambridge, Mass.: Harvard University Press, 1977)

——'Morton's Ranking of Races by Cranial Capacity', *Science*, 200 (5 May 1978): 503–9

——'Darwin's Sea Change, or Five Years at the Captain's Table', in *Ever Since Darwin. Reflections in Natural History* (Harmondsworth: Penguin Books, 1980), pp. 28–33

——*The Mismeasure of Man* (Harmondsworth: Penguin, 1984)

Granö, Olavi, 'External Influence and Internal Change in the Development of Geography', in D. R. Stoddart (ed.), *Geography, Ideology and Social Concern* (Oxford: Blackwell, 1981), pp. 17–36

Graves, Norman J., 'Can Geographical Studies be Subsumed under one Paradigm or are a Plurality of Paradigms Inevitable?' *Terra* 93, 3 (1981): 85–90

Greely, A. W., 'Jefferson as a Geographer', *The National Geographic Magazine*, 7 (1896): 269–71

Greene, John C., 'Biology and Social Theory in the Nineteenth Century: August Comte and Herbert Spencer', in Marshall Clagett (ed.), *Critical Problems in the History of Science* (Madison, Wis.: University of Wisconsin Press, 1959)

——'Darwin as a Social Evolutionist', *Journal of the History of Biology*, 10 (1977): 1–27

——*American Science in the Age of Jefferson* (Ames: Iowa State University Press, 1984)

Gregory, Derek, *Ideology, Science and Human Geography* (London: Hutchinson, 1978)

——'The Ideology of Control – Systems Theory and Geography', *Tijdschrift voor Economische en Sociale Geografie*, 71 (1980): 327–42

——'Human Agency and Human Geography', *Transactions of the Institute of British Geographers*, n.s. 6 (1981): 1–18

——'Solid Geometry: Notes on the Recovery of Spatial Structure', in Peter Gould and Gunnar Olsson (eds), *A Search for Common Ground* (London: Pion, 1982), pp. 187–219

——'Suspended Animation: The Stasis of Diffusion Theory', in Derek Gregory and John Urry (eds), *Social Relations and Spatial Structures* (London: Macmillan, 1985), pp. 296–336

——'Environmental Determinism', in R. J. Johnston, Derek Gregory and David M. Smith (eds), *The Dictionary of Human Geography* (Oxford: Blackwell, 2nd edn 1986), pp. 131–3

——'Functionalism', in R. J. Johnston, Derek Gregory and David M. Smith (eds), *The Dictionary of Human Geography* (Oxford: Blackwell, 2nd edn 1986), pp. 165–7

——'Marxist Geography', in R. J. Johnston, Derek Gregory and David M. Smith (eds), *The Dictionary of Human Geography* (Oxford: Blackwell, 2nd edn 1986), pp. 287–92

——'Areal Differentiation and Post-Modern Human Geography', in Derek Gregory and Rex Walford (eds), *Horizons in Human Geography* (London: Macmillan, 1989), pp. 67–96

——'Presences and Absences: Time-Space Relations and Structuration Theory', in D. Held and J. B. Thompson (eds), *Social Theory of Modern Societies: Anthony Giddens and his Critics* (Cambridge: Cambridge University Press, 1989)

Gregory, J. W., 'Inter-Racial Problems and White Colonisation in the Tropics', *Scottish Geographical Magazine*, 40 (1924): 270

Gregory, S., 'On Geographical Myths and Statistical Fables', *Transactions of the Institute of British Geographers*, n.s. 1 (1976): 385–400

Gruffudd, Pyrs, 'Landscape and Nationhood: Tradition and Modernity in Rural Wales, 1900–1950' (Ph.D. thesis, Loughborough University, 1989)

Guelke, Leonard, 'An Idealist Alternative in Human Geography', *Annals of the Association of American Geographers*, 64 (1974): 193–202

——*Historical Understanding in Geography: An Idealist Approach* (Cambridge: Cambridge University Press, 1982)

Guyot, Arnold Henri, *The Earth and Man: Lectures on Comparative Physical Geography in its Relation to the History of Mankind* (1849; rep., New York: Scribner's, 1897)

——'Carl Ritter: An Address to the Society', *Journal of the American Geographical Society*, 2 (1860): 25–63

——'Cosmogony and the Bible; or, the Biblical Account of Creation in the Light of Modern Science', in Philip Schaff and S. Irenaeus Prime (eds), *History, Essays, Orations, and Other Documents of the Sixth General Conference of the Evangelical Alliance, held in New York, October 2–12, 1873* (New York: Harper and Brothers, 1874), pp. 276–87

——*Creation or the Biblical Cosmogony in the Light of Modern Science* (New York: Charles Scribner's Sons, 1884)

Hacking, Ian, 'Experimentation and Scientific Realism', in Jarrett Leplin (ed.), *Scientific Realism* (Berkeley: University of California Press, 1984), pp. 154–72

Haddon, A. C., *The Races of Man and Their Distribution* (Cambridge: Cambridge University Press, 1924)

Hägerstrand, Torsten, *The Propagation of Innovation Waves*, Lund Studies in Geography, Series B, Human Geography, 4 (Lund: Gleerup, 1952)

Haggett, Peter, *Locational Analysis in Human Geography* (London: Edward Arnold, 1965)

——and Richard J. Chorley (eds), *Frontiers in Geographical Teaching* (London: Methuen, 1965)

——and Richard J. Chorley, 'Models, Paradigms and the New Geography', in Richard J. Chorley and Peter Haggett (eds), *Models in Geography* (London: Methuen, 1967), pp. 1–41

Haines-Young, R. and J. R. Petch, 'The Methodological Limitations of Kuhn's Model of Science' (University of Salford, Department of Geography, Discussion Paper 8, 1978)

Hakluyt, Richard, *Principal Navigations* (9 vols, 1928), vol. 8, p. 440

Hale, John R., *Age of Exploration* (Netherlands: Time-Life Books, 1966)

——'A World Elsewhere', in D. Hay (ed.), *The Age of Renaissance* (London: Thames and Hudson, 1967)

Haller, John S. Jr., 'Nathaniel Southgate Shaler: A Portrait of Nineteenth-Century Academic Thinking on Race', *Essex Institute Historical Collections*, 107 (1971): 173–93

Haller, Mark, *Eugenics: Hereditarian Attitudes in American Thought* (New Brunswick: Rutgers University Press, 1963)

Hamilton, William R., 'Presidential Address', *Journal of the Royal Geographical Society*, 12 (1842): lxxxviii–lxxxix

Hanfling, O., *Logical Positivism* (Oxford: Basil Blackwell, 1981)

Hankins, Thomas L., *Science and the Enlightenment* (Cambridge: Cambridge University Press, 1985)

Harcourt, Robert, *A Relation of a Voyage to Guiana* (London: J. Beale for W. Welby, 1613)

Hariot, Thomas, *A Briefe and True Report of the New Found Land of Virginia* (London, 1588)

Harley, J. B., 'Meaning and Ambiguity in Tudor Cartography', in Sarah Tyacke (ed.), *English Map-Making. 1500–1650* (London: The British Library, 1983)

——'Maps, Knowledge and Power', in Denis Cosgrove and Stephen Daniels (eds), *The Iconography of Landscape. Essays on the Symbolic Representation, Design and Use of Past Environments* (Cambridge: Cambridge University Press, 1988), pp. 277–312

——and David Woodward (eds), *The History of Cartography. Volume One. Cartography in Prehistoric, Ancient, and Medieval Europe and the Mediterranean* (Chicago: University of Chicago Press, 1987)

Harris, Cole, 'Power, Modernity, and Historical Geography', *Annals of the Association of American Geographers*, 81 (1991): 671–83

Harris, Marvin, *The Rise of Anthropological Theory. A History of Theories of Culture* (New York: Thomas Y. Crowell, 1968)

Harrison, Richard T. and David N. Livingstone, 'Meaning through Metaphor: Analogy as Epistemology', *Annals of the Association of American Geographers*, 71 (1981): 95–107

Hartshorne, Richard, 'Upper Silesian Industrial District', *Geographical Review*, 24 (1934): 423–38

——*The Nature of Geography: A Critical Survey of Current Thought in the Light of the Past* (Lancaster, Pa.: Association of American Geographers, 1939)

——'"Exceptionalism in Geography" Re-Examinated', *Annals of the Association of American Geographers*, 45 (1955): 205–44

——'The Concept of Geography as a Science of Space, from Kant and Humboldt to Hettner', *Annals of the Association of American Geographers*, 48 (1958): 97–108

——*Perspective on the Nature of Geography* (Chicago: Rand McNally, 1959)

——'On the Role of Immanuel Kant in the History of Geographic Thought'. Paper presented to the Association of American Geographers Annual Meeting, 23 April 1975

——'William Morris Davis – The Course of Development of his Concept of Geography', in Brian W. Blouet (ed.), *The Origins of Academic Geography in the United States* (Hamden, Conn.: Archon Books, 1981), pp. 139–49

——'Hettner's Exceptionalism – Fact or Fiction?' *History of Geography Newsletter*, 6 (1988): 1–4

Harvey, David, *Explanation in Geography* (London: Arnold, 1969)

——'Revolutionary and Counter-Revolutionary Theory in Geography and the Problem of Ghetto Formation', *Antipode*, 4, 2 (1972): 1–13

——*Social Justice and the City* (London: Arnold, 1973)

——'Population, Resources, and the Ideology of Science', in Stephen Gale and Gunnar Olsson (eds), *Philosophy in Geography* (Dordrecht: Reidel, 1979), pp. 155–85 (First published in *Economic Geography*, 50 (1974): 256–77

——*The Limits to Capital* (Oxford: Blackwell, 1982)

——'On the History and Present Condition of Geography: An Historical Materialist Manifesto', *Professional Geographer*, 36 (1984): 1–11

——'The Geopolitics of Capitalism', in Derek Gregroy and John Urry (eds), *Social Relations and Spatial Structures* (London: Macmillan, 1985), pp. 128–63

——*The Condition of Postmodernity. An Enquiry into the Origins of Cultural Change* (Oxford: Blackwell, 1989)

Harvey, Milton E. and Brian P. Holly, 'Paradigm, Philosophy and Geographic Thought', in Milton E. Harvey and Brian P. Holly (eds), *Themes in Geographic Thought* (London: Croom Helm, 1981), pp. 11–37

Hassert, K., 'Friedrich Ratzel: Sein Leben und Wirken', *Geographische Zeitschrift*, 11 (1905): 310–25, 361–80

Haughton, Samuel, *Six Lectures on Physical Geography* (Dublin: Hodges, Foster and Figgis, 1880)

Hawkins, Richard, *The Observations of Sr. R. Hawkins in his Voiage into the South Sea 1593* (London: John Jaggard, 1622)

Hay, Alan M., 'Positivism in Human Geography: Response to Critics', in D. T. Herbert and R. J. Johnston (eds), *Geography and the Urban Environment: Progress in Research and Applications Volume 2* (Chichester: John Wiley, 1979), pp. 1–26

Hays, H. R., *From Ape to Angel. An Informal History of Social Anthropology* (New York: Knopf, 1958)

Heffernan, Michael J., 'From Knowledge to Power: The Geography of Geographical Knowledge in Late Nineteenth-Century France'. Paper presented at the Annual Conference of the Association of American Geographers, Toronto, April 1990

——'Militant Geographers: the French Geographical Movement and the Forms of French Imperialism, 1870 to 1920', in Neil Smith and Anne Godlewska, *Geography and Empire*, forthcoming

Helgerson, Richard, 'The Land Speaks: Cartography, Chorography, and Subversion in Renaissance England', *Representations*, 16 (1986): 51–85

Herbert, Sandra, 'Man in the Development of Darwin's Theory of Transmutation: Part 2', *Journal of the History of Biology*, 10 (1977): 155–227

Herbertson, Andrew John, 'Geography in the University', *Scottish Geographical Magazine*, 18 (1902): 124–32

——'On the One-Inch Ordnance Survey Map, With Special Reference to the Oxford Sheet', *Geographical Teacher*, 1 (1902): 150–66

——'Recent Discussions on the Scope and Educational Applications of Geography', *Geographical Journal*, 24 (1904): 417–27

——'The Major Natural Regions of the World: An Essay in Systematic Geography', *Geographical Journal*, 25 (1905): 300–12

——'The Social Factor in General Geography', *Educational Bi-Monthly*, 1 (1906): 137–8

——'Geography and Some of its Problems', *Geographical Journal*, 36 (1910): 468–79

——'Regional Environment, Heredity and Consciousness', *Geographical Teacher*, 8 (1916): 147–53

——and F. D. Herbertson, *Man and His Work. An Introduction to Human Geography* (London: A. and C. Black, 1920, first published 1899)

Herbertson, F. D., *The Life of Frédéric Le Play*, edited by V. Branford and A. Farquharson (Ledbury: Le Play House, 1946)

Herbst, Jurgen, 'Social Darwinism and the History of American Geography', *Proceedings of the American Philosophical Society*, 105 (1961): 538–44

Herskovits, Melville J., *Franz Boas. The Science of Man in the Making* (New York: Scribner's, 1953)

Heske, Henning, 'German Geographical Research in the Nazi Period: A Content Analysis of the Major Geography Journals, 1925–1945', *Political Geography Quarterly*, 5 (1986): 267–81

——'Karl Haushofer: His Role in German Geopolitics and in Nazi Politics', *Political Geography Quarterly*, 6 (1987): 135–44

Hesse, Mary, *Revolutions and Reconstructions in the Philosophy of Science* (Sussex: Harvester Press, 1980)

Hettner, Alfred, *Die Geographie: Ihre Geschichte, Ihr Wesen und Ihre Methoden* (Breslau: Hirt, 1927)

Hibbert, Christopher, *Africa Explored. Europeans in the Dark Continent, 1769–1889* (London: Allen Lane, 1982)

Higgins, Charles G., 'Theories of Landscape Development: A Perspective', in W. N. Melhorn and R. C. Flemal (eds), *Theories of Landform Development* (New York: State University of New York, 1975), pp. 1–29

Higham, John, *Send These to Me. Jews and Other Immigrants in Urban America* (New York: Atheneus, 1975)

Hill, Christopher, *The Intellectual Origins of the English Revolution* (Oxford: Clarendon Press, 1965)

Hills, E. H., 'The Survey of the British Empire', *Scottish Geographical Magazine*, 24 (1908): 505–19

Hodge, M. J. S., 'Darwin as a Lifelong Generation Theorist', in David Kohn (ed.), *The Darwinian Heritage* (Princeton, N. J.: Princeton University Press, 1985), pp. 207–43

——and David Kohn, 'The Immediate Origins of Natural Selection', in David Kohn (ed.), *The Darwinian Heritage* (Princeton, N. J.: Princeton University Press, 1985), pp. 185–206

Hodgkiss, A. G., 'The Ordnance Survey One Inch to One Mile Map – An Outline History, with Special Reference to the Early Editions', *Bulletin of the Society of University Cartographers* (1969–70)

Holdich, Thomas H., 'The Use of Practical Geography Illustrated by Recent Frontier Operations', *Geographical Journal*, 13 (1899): 465–80

——'Some Geographical Problems', *Geographical Journal*, 20 (1902): 411–27

——'The Progress of Geographical Knowledge', *Scottish Geographical Magazine*, 18 (1902): 504–25

——'Some Aspects of Political Geography', *Geographical Journal*, 34 (1909): 593–607

——*Political Frontiers and Boundary Making* (London: Macmillan and Co., 1916)

Hooson, David, 'Carl O. Sauer', in Brian Blouet (ed.), *The Origins of Academic Geography in the United States* (Hamden, Connecticut: Archon Books, 1981), pp. 165–74

Hooykaas, R., 'Science and Reformation', *Journal of World History*, 3 (1956): 109–39

——*Philosophia Libera. Christian Faith and the Freedom of Science* (London: Tyndale Press, 1957)

——*Religion and the Rise of Modern Science* (Edinburgh: Scottish Academic Press, 1972)

——'Puritanism and Science' in Open University, *Science and Belief from Copernicus to Darwin, Block 3, Unit 6: Scientific Progress and Religious Dissent* (Milton Keynes: Open University Press, 1974), pp. 9–32

——*Humanism and the Voyages of Discovery in 16th Century Portuguese Science and Letters* (Amsterdam: North Holland Publishing Company, 1979)

——'The Rise of Modern Science: When and Why?' *British Journal for the History of Science*, 20 (1987): 453–73

Howard, Jonathan, *Darwin* (Oxford: Oxford University Press, 1982)

Hoy, David Couzens (ed.), *Foucault: A Critical Reader* (Oxford: Blackwell, 1986)

Hudson, Brian, 'The New Geography and the New Imperialism: 1870–1918', *Antipode*, 9 (1977): 12–19

Hull, David L., *Darwin and His Critics: The Reception of Darwin's Theory of Evolution by the Scientific Community* (Cambridge, Mass.: Harvard University Press, 1973)

——'Darwinism as a Historical Entity: A Historiographic Proposal', in David Kohn (ed.), *The Darwinian Heritage* (Princeton, N.J.: Princeton University Press, 1985), pp. 773–812

——*Science as a Process. An Evolutionary Account of the Social and Conceptual Development of Science* (Chicago: University of Chicago Press, 1988)

Humboldt, Alexander von, *Cosmos: Sketch of a Physical Description of the Universe,* translated by Edward Sabine (London: Longman, Brown, Green, and Longmans, 1847)

Hunt, James, 'On Ethno-Climatology; or the Acclimatization of Man', *Transactions of the Ethnological Society of London*, n.s. 2 (1863): 50–79

Hunter, J. M., *Perspectives on Friedrich Ratzel's Political Geography* (Lanham: University Press of America, 1983)

Hunter, Michael, *Science and Society in Restoration England* (Cambridge: Cambridge University Press, 1981)

Huntington, Ellsworth, 'The Adaptability of the White Man to Tropical America', *Journal of Race Development*, 5 (1914): 185–211

——'Graphic Representation of the Effect of Climate on Man', *Geographical Review*, 4 (1917): 401–3

——*World Power and Evolution* (New Haven: Yale University Press, 1920)

——*The Character of Races, as Influenced by Physical Environment, Natural Selection and Historical Development* (New York: Scribner's, 1924)

——'Environment and Racial Character', in M. R. Thorpe (ed.), *Organic Adaptation to Environment* (New Haven: Yale University Press, 1924), pp. 281–99

Hutton, James, 'Theory of the Earth; or an Investigation of the Laws Observable in the Composition, Dissolution, and Restoration of Land Upon the Globe', *Transactions of the Royal Society of Edinburgh*, 1 (1788): 209–304

——*Dissertations on Different Subjects in Natural Philosophy* (Edinburgh: Strahan and Cadell, 1792)

Hyatt Marshall, *Franz Boas. Social Activist: The Dynamics of Ethnicity* (New York: Greenwood Press, 1990)

Jackson, Donald, *Thomas Jefferson & the Stony Mountains: Exploring the West from Monticello* (Urbana, Ill.: University of Illinois Press, 1981)

Jackson, Peter and Susan J. Smith, *Exploring Social Geography* (London: George Allen and Unwin, 1984)

Jacobsen, H.-A. (ed.), *Karl Haushofer: Leben und Werk*, vols 1 and 2 (Boppard-am-Rhein: Harald Boldt, 1979)

Jaki, Stanley L., 'Introduction', in Immanuel Kant, *Universal Natural History and Theory of the Heavens*, translated with Introduction and Notes by Stanley L. Jaki (Edinburgh: Scottish Academic Press, 1981), pp. 1–76

James, Preston E., *All Possible Worlds. A History of Geographical Ideas* (Indianapolis: Bobbs-Merrill, 1972)

——and Geoffrey J. Martin, *The Association of American Geographers: The First Seventy-Five Years, 1904–1979* (Washington: Association of American Geographers, 1978)

Jay, L. J., 'A. J. Herbertson: his Services to School Geography', *Geography*, 50 (1965): 350–61

Jensen, J. Vernon, 'Return to the Wilberforce-Huxley Debate', *British Journal for the History of Science*, 21 (1988): 161–79

Johnson, Douglas Wilson (ed.), *Geographical Essays by William Morris Davis* (Boston: Ginn and Co., 1909)

Johnson, F. R. and S. V. Larkey, 'Thomas Digges, the Copernican system, and the Idea of the Infinity of the Universe in 1576', *Huntington Library Bulletin*, 5 (1934): 69–117

Johnson, James, *The Influence of Tropical Climates on European Constitutions; Being a Treatise on the Principal Diseases to Europeans in the East and West Indies, Mediterranean, and Coast of Africa* (London, 1821)

Johnston, D., 'A Brief Description of the Ordnance Survey and Some Notes on the Advantages of a Topographical Survey of South Africa', *Scottish Geographical Magazine*, 22 (1906): 18–27

Johnston, H. H., *The Backward Peoples and Our Relations with Them* (Oxford: Oxford University Press, 1920)

Johnston, R. J., 'Paradigms and Revolutions or Evolution? Observations on Human Geography Since the Second World War', *Progress in Human Geography*, 2 (1978): 189–206

——'Paradigms, Revolution, Schools of Thought and Anarchy: Reflections on the Recent History of Anglo-American Human Geography', in Brian W. Blouet (ed.), *The Origins of Academic Geography in the United States* (Hamden, Conn.: Archon Books, 1981), pp. 303–18

——'A Foundling Floundering in World Three', in Mark Billinge, Derek Gregory and Ron Martin (eds), *Recollections of a Revolution. Geography as Spatial Science* (London: Macmillan, 1984), pp. 39–56

——*Philosophy and Human Geography. An Introduction to Contemporary Approaches* (London: Edward Arnold, 2nd edn 1986)

——*Geography and Geographers: Anglo-American Human Geography since 1945*, (London: Arnold, 4th edn 1991)

Johnston, Stephen, 'Mathematical Practitioners and Instruments in Elizabethan England', *Annals of Science*, 48 (1991): 319–44

Jones, Greta, *Social Darwinism and English Thought. The Interactions between Biological and Social Theory* (Brighton: Harvester Press, 1980)

Jordan, Terry G., *The European Culture Area. A Systematic Geography* (New York: Harper and Row, 2nd edn 1988)

Jordanova, L. J. and Roy Porter, 'Introduction', in L. J. Jordanova and Roy S. Porter (eds), *Images of the Earth. Essays in the History of the Environmental Sciences* (Chalfont St Giles: British Society for the History of Science, 1979), pp. v–xx

Kant, Edgar, 'Umland Studies and Sector Analysis', *Studies in Rural-Urban Interaction, Lund Studies in Geography, Series B, Human Geography*, 3 (Lund: Gleerup, 1951), pp. 3–13

Kargon, Robert and Elizabeth Hodes, 'Karl Compton, Isaiah Bowman, and the politics of Science in the Great Depression', *Isis*, 76 (1985): 301–18

Karsen, Sonja, 'Alexander von Humboldt in South America: From the Orinoco to the Amazon', *Studies in Eighteenth-Century Culture*, 16 (1986): 295–302

Kass, Amalie M., 'Dr Thomas Hodgkin, Dr Martin Delany, and the "Return to Africa"', *Medical History*, 27 (1983): 373–93

Keane, A. H., *Man. Past and Present* (Cambridge: University Press, 1899)

Kearney, Hugh, *Science and Change 1500–1700* (New York: McGraw–Hill, 1971)

Kearns, G., 'Closed Space and Political Practice: Frederick Jackson Turner and Halford Mackinder', *Society and Space*, 1 (1984): 23–34

——'Halford John Mackinder 1861–1947', in T. W. Freeman (ed.), *Geographers. Biobibliographical Studies*, vol. 9 (London: Mansell, 1985), pp. 71–86

Keating, M. W., 'Geography as a Correlating Subject', *Geographical Teacher*, 1 (1902): 145–9

Kellner, L., *Alexander von Humboldt* (London: Oxford University Press, 1963)

Keltie, John Scott, 'Geographical Education. Report to the Council of the Royal Geographical Society', *Royal Geographical Society, Supplementary Papers*, 1 (1882–5): 439–594

——'Thirty Years' Work of the Royal Geographical Society', *Geographical Journal*, 49 (1917): 350–72

——*The Position of Geography in British Universities*, American Geographical Society Research Series no. 4 (New York: Oxford University Press, 1921)

Kelves, Daniel, *In the Name of Eugenics. Genetics and the Uses of Human Heredity* (New York: Knopf, 1985)

Kemsley, Douglas S., 'Religious Influences in the Rise of Modern Science: A Review and Criticism, Particularly of the "Protestant-Puritan Ethic" Theory', *Annals of Science*, 24 (1968): 199–226

Kennedy, Dane, 'The Perils of the Midday Sun: Climatic Anxieties in the Colonial Tropics', in John M. MacKenzie (ed.), *Imperialism and the Natural World* (Manchester: Manchester University Press, 1990), pp. 118–40

Kennedy, J. Gerald, *The Astonished Traveler. William Darby, Frontier Geographer and Man of Letters* (Baton Rouge: Louisiana State University Press, 1981)

Kenzer, Martin S., 'Milieu and the "Intellectual Landscape": Carl O. Sauer's Undergraduate Heritage', *Annals of the Association of American Geographers*, 75 (1982): 258–70

——'Like Father, Like Son: William Albert and Carl Ortwin Sauer', in Martin S. Kenzer (ed.), *Carl O. Sauer. A Tribute* (Corvallis, Oregon: Oregon State University Press, 1987), pp. 40–65

——'Tracking Sauer Across Sour Terrain', *Annals of the Association of American Geographers*, 77 (1987): 469–74

Kepler, J., *Kepler's Conversation with Galileo's Sidereal Messenger*, translated by Edward Rosen (New York: Johnston Reprint Corp., 1965)

Kersten, Earl W., 'Sauer and "Geographic Influences"', *Yearbook. Association of Pacific Coast Geographers*, 44 (1983): 47–73

Kidd, Benjamin, *The Control of the Tropics* (New York: Macmillan, 1898)

King, Leslie J., 'Alternatives to a Positive Economic Geography', in Stephen Gale and Gunnar Olsson (eds), *Philosophy in Geography* (Dordrecht: Reidel, 1979), pp. 187–213

——'Areal Associations and Regressions', *Annals of the Association of American Geographers*, 69 (1979): 124–8

Kirk, John, 'The Extent to which Tropical Africa is Suited for Development by the White Races, or under their Superintendence', *Report of the Sixth International Geographical Congress, London 1895* (London, 1896): 526

Kirk, William, 'Historical Geography and the Concept of the Behavioural Environment', *Indian Geographical Journal*, Silver Jubilee Volume (1952): 152–60

——'Problems of Geography', *Geography*, 48 (1963): 357–71

——'The Road from Mandalay: Towards a Geographical Epistemology', *Transactions of the Institute of British Geographers*, n.s. 3 (1978): 381–94

Klaaren, Eugene, *Religious Origins of Modern Science* (Grand Rapids: Eerdmans, 1977)

Klein, J., 'Reflections on Geopolitics: From Pangermanism to the Doctrines of Living Space and Moving Frontiers', in C. Zoppo and C. Zorgbibe (eds), *On Geopolitics: Classical and Nuclear* (Dordrecht: Martinus Nijhoff, 1985)

Koelsch, William A., 'The Historical Geography of Harlan H. Barrows', *Annals of the Association of American Geographers*, 59 (1969): 632–51

Koestler, Arthur, *The Case of the Midwife Toad* (London: Hutchinson, 1971)

Kohn, David (ed.), *The Darwinian Heritage* (Princeton, N. J.: Princeton University Press, 1985)

Kolakowski, L., *The Alienation of Reason: A History of Positivist Thought*, translated by N. Guterman (New York: Doubleday, 1938)

Kolb, Albert, 'Ferdinand Freiherr von Richthofen, 1833–1905', *Geographers. Biobibliographical Studies*, 7 (1983): 109–15

Körner, S., *Kant* (Harmondsworth: Penguin, 1955)

Kost, Klaus, *Die Einflüsse der Geopolitik auf Forschung und Theorie der Politischen Geographie und Ihrer Terminologie unter besonderer Berücksichtigung von Militär- und Kolonialgeographie*, Bonner Geographische Abhandlungen 76 (Bonn: Ferd, Dümmler-Verlag, 1988)

——'The Conception of Politics in Political Geography and Geopolitics in Germany until 1945', *Political Geography Quarterly*, 8 (1989): 369–85

Koyré, A., *From the Closed World to the Infinite Universe* (Baltimore: Johns Hopkins Press, 1957)

Kropotkin, Petr, 'What Geography ought to be', *Nineteenth Century*, 18 (1885): 940–56

——'On the Teaching of Physiography', *Geographical Journal*, 2 (1893): 350–9

——*Fields, Factories and Workshops* (Boston: Houghton Mifflin, 1899)

——*Memoirs of a Revolutionist*, 2 vols (London: Smith, Elder, 1899)

——'Anarchism', *Encyclopaedia Britannica* (1910), vol. 1

——*Mutual Aid. A Factor of Evolution* (Harmondsworth: Penguin, 1939, first pub. 1902)

Kuhn, T. S., *The Structure of Scientific Revolutions* (Chicago: University of Chicago Press, 1962, enlarged edn 1970)

Kurzweil, E., *The Age of Structuralism* (New York: Columbia University Press, 1980)

Larson, James, 'Not Without a Plan: Geography and Natural History in the Late Eighteenth Century', *Journal of the History of Biology*, 19 (1986): 447–88

Latour, Bruno, 'Drawing Things Together', in Michael Lynch and Steve Woolgar (eds), *Representation in Scientific Practice* (Cambridge, Mass.: The MIT Press, 1990), pp. 19–68

Lattimore, Owen and Eleanor, (eds), *Silks, Spices and Empire* (n.p.: Delacorte Press, 1968)

Laudan, Rachel, 'The Recent Revolution in Geology and Kuhn's Theory of Scientific Change', in Gary Gutting (ed.), *Paradigms and Revolutions* (Notre Dame: University of Notre Dame Press, 1980), pp. 51–89

——*From Mineralogy to Geology. The Foundations of a Science, 1650–1830* (Chicago: University of Chicago Press, 1987)

Leclerc, G., *Anthropologie et Colonialisme: Essai sur l'Histoire de l'Africanisme* (Paris: Editions du Seuil, 1972)

Leighly, John, 'Methodologic Controversy in Nineteenth Century German Geography', *Annals of the Association of American Geographers*, 38 (1928): 238–58

——'Some Comments on Contemporary Geographic Methods', *Annals of the Association of American Geographers*, 17 (1937): 125–41

——'What Has Happened to Physical Geography?' *Annals of the Association of American Geographers*, 45 (1955): 309–18

——'Introduction', to Matthew Fontaine Maury, *The Physical Geography of the Sea* (Cambridge, Mass.: Harvard University Press, 1963)

——'Introduction', in John Leighly (ed.), *Land and Life. A Selection from the Writings of Carl Ortwin Sauer* (Berkeley: University of California Press, 1963), pp. 1–8

——'Carl Ortwin Sauer, 1889–1975', in *Geographers. Biobibliographical Studies*, 2 (1976): 99–108

——'Scholar and Colleague: Homage to Carl Sauer', *Yearbook, Association of Pacific Coast Geographers*, 40 (1978): 117–33

——'Ecology as Metaphor: Carl Sauer and Human Ecology', *Professional Geographer*, 39 (1987): 405–12

Lepschy, G. C., *A Survey of Structural Linguistics* (Oxford: Oxford University Press, 1982)

Lewis, Charles Lee, *Matthew Fontaine Maury, Pathfinder of the Seas* (Annapolis: US Naval Institute, 1927)

Lewis, G. Malcolm, 'Changing Emphases in the Description of the Natural

Environment of the Great Plains Area', *Transactions of the Institute of British Geographers*, 30 (1962): 75–90
——'Early American Exploration and the Cis-Rocky Mountain Desert, 1803–1823', *Great Plains Journal*, 5 (1965): 1–11
——'Regional Ideas and Reality in the Cis-Rocky Mountain West', *Transactions of the Institute of British Geographers*, 38 (1966): 135–50
——'The Origins of Cartography', in J. B. Harley and David Woodward (eds), *History of Cartography, Volume One. Cartography in Prehistoric, Ancient, and Medieval Europe and the Mediterranean* (Chicago: University of Chicago Press, 1987), pp. 50–3
Lewthwaite, Gordon, 'Environmentalism and Determinism: A Search for Clarification', *Annals of the Association of American Geographers*, 56 (1966): 1–23
Ley, David, *The Black Inner City as Frontier Outpost: Images and Behaviour of a Philadelphia Neighborhood* (Washington DC: Association of American Geographers, 1974)
——'Social Geography and the Taken-for-Granted World', *Transactions of the Institute of British Geographers*, n.s. 2 (1977): 498–512
——'Styles of the Times: Liberal and Neo-Conservative Landscapes in Inner Vancouver, 1968–1986', *Journal of Historical Geography*, 13 (1987): 40–56
——and Marwyn S. Samuels (eds), *Humanistic Geography: Prospects and Problems* (London: Croom Helm, 1978)
Libbey, William, 'The Life and Work of Arnold Guyot', *American Geographical Society*, 16 (1884): 194–221
Lindberg, David C. and Ronald L. Numbers (eds), *God and Nature. Historical Essays on the Encounter between Christianity and Science* (Berkeley: University of California Press, 1986)
Linke, M., 'Carl Ritter, 1779–1859', *Geographers. Biobibliographical Studies*, 5 (1981): 98–108
Linklater, Eric, *The Voyage of the Challenger* (London: John Murray, 1972)
Livingstone, David N., 'Some Methodological Problems in the History of Geographical Thought', *Tijdschrift voor Economische en Sociale Geografie*, 70 (1979): 226–31
——'Environment and Inheritance: Nathaniel Southgate Shaler and the American Frontier', in Brian Blouet (ed.), *The Origins of Academic Geography in the United States* (Hamden: Archon Books, 1981), pp. 123–38
——'Natural Theology and Neo-Lamarckism: the Changing Context of Nineteenth-Century Geography in the United States and Great Britain', *Annals of the Association of American Geographers*, 74 (1984): 9–28
——'The History of Science and the History of Geography: Interactions and Implications,' *History of Science*, 22 (1984): 271–302
——*Darwin's Forgotten Defenders: The Encounter between Evangelical Theology and Evolutionary Thought* (Edinburgh: Scottish Academic Press, 1987)
——'Human Acclimatization: Perspectives on a Contested Field of Inquiry in

Science, Medicine and Geography', *History of Science*, 25 (1987): 359–94

——*Nathaniel Southgate Shaler and the Culture of American Science* (London: University of Alabama Press, 1987)

——'Preadamites: The History of an Idea from Heresy to Orthodoxy', *Scottish Journal of Theology*, 40 (1987): 41–66

——'Science, Magic and Religion: a Contextual Reassessment of Geography in the Sixteenth and Seventeenth Centuries', *History of Science*, 26 (1988): 269–94

——'Geography, Tradition and the Scientific Revolution: An Interpretative Essay', *Transactions of the Institute of British Geographers*, n.s. 15 (1990): 359–73

——'Of Design and Dining Clubs: Geography in Britain and America, 1770–1860', *History of Science*, 29 (1991): 153–83

——'The Moral Discourse of Climate: Historical Considerations on Race, Place and Virtue', *Journal of Historical Geography*, 17 (1991): 413–34

——*The Preadamite Theory and the Marriage of Science and Religion* (Philadelphia: American Philosophical Society, 1992)

——'A Geologist by Profession, a Geographer by Inclination: Nathaniel Southgate Shaler and Geography at Harvard', in Clark A. Elliott and Margaret W. Rossiter (eds), *Science at Harvard University. Historical Perspectives* (London: Associated University Press, 1992), pp. 146–66. Also published by Lehigh University Press, Bethlehem.

——'"Never Shall Ye Make the Crab Walk Straight": An Inquiry into the Scientific Sources of Racial Geography', in Felix Driver and Gillian Rose (eds), *Nature and Science: Essays in the History of Geographical Knowledge* (Historical Geography Research Series, no. 28, 1992), pp. 37–48

——'Climate's Moral Economy: Science, Race, and Place in Post-Darwinian British and American Geography', in Neil Smith and Anne Godlewska (eds), *Geography and Empire* (Oxford: Blackwell), forthcoming

——'Darwinism and Calvinism: The Belfast-Princeton Connection', *Isis*, 83 (1992): in press

——and Richard T. Harrison, 'Immanuel Kant, Subjectivism and Human Geography: A Preliminary Investigation', *Transactions of the Institute of British Geographers*, n.s. 6 (1981): 359–74

——and Richard T. Harrison, 'Understanding in Geography: Structuring the Subjective', in D. T. Herbert and R. J. Johnston (eds), *Geography and the Urban Environment: Progress in Research and Applications*, vol. 5 (Chichester: John Wiley, 1982), pp. 1–39

Lochhead, Elspeth, 'The Emergence of Academic Geography in Britain in its Historical Context' (Ph.D. thesis, University of California at Berkeley, 1980)

——'Scotland as the Cradle of Modern Academic Geography in Britain', *Scottish Geographical Magazine*, 97 (1981): 98–109

——'The Royal Scottish Geographical Society: The Setting and Sources of its Success', *Scottish Geographical Magazine*, 100 (1984): 69–80

——'On Socio-Scientific Circles and the History of Geography', unpublished type-script

Lonergan, Bernard J. F., *Insight: A Study of Human Understanding* (London: Darton, Longman and Todd, 1958)

Lowenthal, David, *George Perkins Marsh. Versatile Vermonter* (New York: Columbia University Press, 1958)

——'Geography, Experience, and Imagination: towards a Geographical Epistemology', *Annals of the Association of American Geographers*, 51 (1961): 241–60

——and Martyn J. Bowden (eds), *Geographies of the Mind: Essays in Historical Geosophy* (New York: Oxford University Press, 1976)

——and Hugh Prince, 'Transcendental Experience', in S. Wapner, S. Cohen and B. Kaplan (eds), *Experiencing the Environment* (New York: Plenum, 1976)

Lowie, Robert H., *The History of Ethnological Theory* (New York: Holt, Rinehart and Winston, 1937)

Lucas, J. R., 'Wilberforce and Huxley: A Legendary Encounter', *The Historical Journal*, 22 (1979): 313–30

Ludmerer, Kenneth, *Genetics and American Society. A Historical Appraisal* (Baltimore, Md.: Johns Hopkins Press, 1972)

Lukermann, Fred, 'The "Calcul des Probabilités" and the École Française de Géographie', *Canadian Geographer*, 9 (1965): 128–37

——'*The Nature of Geography*: Post Hoc, Ergo Propter Hoc?' in J. Nicholas Entrikin and Stanley D. Brunn (eds), *Reflections on Richard Hartshorne's The Nature of Geography* (Washington, DC.: Association of American Geographers, 1989), pp. 53–68

Lurie, Edward, *Louis Agassiz. A Life in Science* (Chicago: University of Chicago Press, 1960)

Lynch, Michael and Steve Woolgar, 'Introduction: Sociological Orientations to Representational Practice in Science', in Michael Lynch and Steve Woolgar (eds), *Representation in Scientific Practice* (Cambridge, Mass.: The MIT Press, 1990), pp. 1–18

Lyotard, J. F., *The Postmodern Condition. A Report on Knowledge* (Manchester: Manchester University Press, 1984)

McConica, James, 'Elizabethan Oxford: The Collegiate Society', in James McConica (ed.), *The History of the University of Oxford. Volume III. The Collegiate University* (Oxford: Clarendon Press, 1986), pp. 645–732

McEachran, F., *The Life and Philosophy of Johann Gottfried Herder* (Oxford: Clarendon Press, 1939)

MacIntyre, Alisdair, 'Myth', in Paul Edwards (ed.), *The Encyclopedia of Philosophy*, vol. 5 (New York: Macmillan and The Free Press, 1967), pp. 434–7

——*After Virtue: A Study in Moral Theory* (London: Duckworth, 2nd edn 1985)

McKay, Donald Vernon, 'Colonialism in the French Geographical Movement 1871–1881', *Geographical Review*, 33 (1943): 214–32

Mackenzie, Donald, 'Eugenics in Britain', *Social Studies of Science*, 6 (1976): 499–532

——'Statistical Theory and Social Interests: A Case Study', *Social Studies of Science*, 8 (1978): 35–83

——'Eugenics and the Rise of Mathematical Statistics in Britain', in John Irvine, Ian Miles and Jeff Evans (eds), *Demystifying Social Statistics* (n.p.: Pluto Press, 1979), pp. 39–50

——*Statistics in Britain, 1865–1930: The Social Construction of Scientific Knowledge* (Edinburgh: Edinburgh University Press, 1981)

MacKenzie, John M. (ed.), *Imperialism and the Natural World* (Manchester: Manchester University Press, 1990)

Mackinder, Halford J., *Oxford University Extension Lectures. Syllabus of a Course on Geography. Course II: Man and His Environment* (n.p., 1886)

——'On the Scope and Methods of Geography', *Proceedings of the Royal Geographical Society*, 9 (1887): 141–60

——'Modern Geography, German and English', *Geographical Journal*, 6 (1895): 367–79

——*Britain and the British Seas* (Oxford: Clarendon Press, 1902)

——'The Geographical Pivot of History', *Geographical Journal*, 23 (1904): 421–37

——'The Teaching of Geography from an Imperial Point of View, and the Use which Could and Should be Made of Visual Instruction', *Geographical Teacher*, 6 (1911): pp. 79–86

——*Democratic Ideals and Reality* (Harmondsworth: Penguin, 1944, First pub. 1919)

MacLeod, Roy, 'On Visiting the "Moving Metropolis": Reflections on the Architecture of Imperial Science', *Historical Records of Australian Science*, 5 (1982): 1–15

——and Philip F. Rehbock (eds), *Nature in its Greatest Extent. Western Science in the Pacific* (Honolulu: University of Hawaii Press, 1988)

McMullin, Ernan, 'History and Philosophy of Science: A Marriage of Convenience?' in Robert S. Cohen and Marx W. Wartofsky (eds), *Methodological and Historical Essays in the Natural and Social Sciences. Proceedings of the Boston Colloquium for the Philosophy of Science, 1969–1972* (Dordrecht: Reidel, 1974), pp. 585–600

——'A Case for Scientific Realism', in Jarrett Leplin (ed.), *Scientific Realism* (Berkeley: University of California Press, 1984), pp. 8–40

McPherson, Thomas, *The Argument from Design* (London: Macmillan, 1972)

Maddison, R. E. W., 'Studies in the Life of Robert Boyle, F. R. S. Part VII. The Grand Tour', *Notes and Records of the Royal Society of London*, 20 (1965): 515–77

Maguire, T. Miller, *Outlines of Military Geography*, Cambridge Geographical Series (Cambridge: Cambridge University Press, 1899)

Mair, Andrew, 'Thomas Kuhn and Understanding Geography', *Progress in Human Geography*, 10 (1986): 345–69

Malin, James C., 'Space and History: Reflections on the Closed-Space Doctrines of Turner and Mackinder and the Challenge of those Ideas by the Air Age', *Agricultural History*, 18 (1944): 65–74

Mandrou, Robert, *From Humanism to Science, 1480–1700* (Harmondsworth: Penguin, 1978)

Manicas, Peter T., *A History and Philosophy of the Social Sciences* (Oxford: Blackwell, 1987)

Manuel, Frank E, *The Prophets of Paris* (Cambridge: Harvard University Press, 1962)

Markham, Clements, 'A List of the Tribes in the Valley of the Amazon, Including those on the Banks of the Main Stream, and of all its Tributaries', *Transactions of the Ethnological Society of London*, n.s. 3 (1865): 140–95

——'Address to the Royal Geographical Society, 1905', *Geographical Journal*, 26 (1905): 1–28

Marsh, George Perkins, *Address Delivered before the Agricultural Society of Rutland County, 30 September 1847* (Rutland, Vt.: Agricultural Society of Rutland County, 1848)

Martin, Geoffrey J., *The Life and Thought of Isaiah Bowman* (Hamden: Archon Books, 1980)

——'Paradigm Change: A History of Geography in the United States, 1892–1925', *National Geographic Research* (Spring, 1985): 217–36

——'On Whittlesey, Bowman and Harvard', *Annals of the Association of American Geographers*, 78 (1988): 152–8

——'*The Nature of Geography* and the Schaefer-Hartshorne Debate', in J. Nicholas Entrikin and Stanley D. Brunn (eds.), *Reflections on Richard Hartshorne's* The Nature of Geography (Washington, D.C.: Association of American Geographers, 1989), pp. 69–90

Martin, James Ranald, *The Influence of Tropical Climates on European Constitutions, Including Practical Observations on the Nature and Treatment of the Diseases of Europeans on their Return from Tropical Climates* (London: John Churchill, 1856)

Massey, Doreen, 'Towards a Critique of Industrial Location Theory', *Antipode*, 5, 3 (1973): 33–9

——*Spatial Divisions of Labour: Social Structures and the Geography of Production* (London: Macmillan, 1984)

——'New Directions in Space', in Derek Gregory and John Urry (eds), *Social Relations and Spatial Structures* (London: Macmillan, 1985), pp. 9–19

Mathewson, Kent, 'Sauer South by Southwest: Antimodernism and the Austral Impulse', in Martin S. Kenzer (ed.), *Carl O. Sauer. A Tribute* (Corvallis, Oregon: Oregon State University Press, 1987), pp. 90–111

Matless, David, 'Nature, the Modern and the Mystic: Tales from Early Twentieth Century Geography', *Transactions of the Institute of British Geographers*, 16 (1991): 272–86

Matthew, W. D., 'Climate and Evolution', *Annals of the New York Academy of Sciences*, 24 (1915): 171–318

Maury, M. F., *The Physical Geography of the Sea* (first pub. 1855, London: Nelson, 1874)

May, J. A., *Kant's Concept of Geography and its Relation to Recent Geographical Thought* (University of Toronto, Department of Geography Research Publications, 1970)

——'The Geographical Interpretation of Ptolemy in the Renaissance', *Tijdschrift voor Economische en Sociale Geografie*, 73 (1982): 350–61

Mayr, Ernst, 'The Nature of the Darwinian Revolution', *Science*, 176 (1972): 981–9

——*The Growth of Biological Thought: Diversity, Evolution, and Inheritance* (Cambridge, Mass.: Harvard University Press, 1982)

Meller, Helen, 'Patrick Geddes: An Analysis of his Theory of Civics, 1880–1904', *Victorian Studies* 16 (1973): 291–315

——'Cities and Evolution: Patrick Geddes as an International Prophet of Town Planning before 1914', in Anthony Sutcliffe (ed.), *The Rise of Modern Urban Planning, 1800–1914* (New York: St Martin's Press, 1980), pp. 199–223

——*Patrick Geddes. Social Evolutionist and City Planner* (London: Routledge, 1990)

Mercer, David, 'Unmasking Technocratic Geography', in Mark Billinge, Derek Gregory and Ron Martin (eds), *Recollections of a Revolution. Geography as Spatial Science* (London: Macmillan, 1984), pp. 153–99

Merrens, H. Roy, 'Historical Geography and Early American History', *William and Mary Quarterly*, 22 (1965): 529–48

Merton, Robert K., 'Science, Technology and Society in Seventeenth Century England', *Osiris*, 4 (1938): 360–632

Mikesell, Marvin W., 'Friedrich Ratzel', in David L. Sills (ed.), *International Encyclopedia of the Social Sciences* (New York: Macmillan and Free Press, 1968), vol. 13, pp. 327–9

'Military Geography: A Review', *Scottish Geographical Magazine*, 16 (1900): 138–60

Mill, Hugh Robert, 'The Development of Habitable Lands: An Essay in Anthropogeography', *Scottish Geographical Magazine*, 16 (1900): 121–38

——'On Research in Geographical Science', *Geographical Journal*, 18 (1901): 410

——'The Present Problems of Geography', *Geographical Journal*, 1 (1905): 1–17

——'Geography', *Encyclopaedia Britannica*, 14th edn (London: The Encyclopaedia Britannica Company, 1929), vol. 10

——*The Record of the Royal Geographical Society 1830–1930* (London: The Royal Geographical Society, 1930)

Miller, A. Austin, *Climatology* (5th edn London: Methuen, 1947. First pub. 1931)

Miller, Martin A., *Kropotkin*, (Chicago: University of Chicago Press, 1976)

Miller, Perry, *Errand into the Wilderness* (New York: Harper Books, 1956)

Miller, Samuel, *A Brief Retrospect of the Eighteenth Century* (New York, 1803)

Monk, William, *Dr Livingstone's Cambridge Lectures together with a Prefatory Letter by the Rev Professor Sedgwick, Edited with Introduction, Life of Dr Livingstone, Notes and Appendix* (London, 1858)

Montgomery, William M., 'Germany', in Thomas F. Glick (ed.), *The Comparative Reception of Darwinism* (Austin: University of Texas Press, 1974), pp. 81–116

Moore, James R., *The Post-Darwinian Controversies: A Study of the Protestant Struggle to Come to Terms with Darwin in Great Britain and America, 1870–1900* (Cambridge: Cambridge University Press, 1979)

——'"Engines of Empire, Energies of Extinction": Reflections on the Crisis of Faith'. Paper presented at a Conference on the Victorian Crisis of Faith, Victoria College, University of Toronto, November 1984.

——'Socializing Darwinism: Historiography and the Fortunes of a Phrase', in Les Levidow (ed.), *Science as Politics* (London: Free Association Books, 1986), pp. 38–80

Moorhead, Alan, *Cooper's Creek* (London: Hamilton, 1963)

Morgan, John, 'Puritanism and Science: A Reinterpretation', *The Historical Journal*, 22 (1979): 535–60

Morrell, Jack B., 'Individualism and the Structure of British Science in 1830', *Historical Studies in the Physical Sciences* (1971): 183–204

Morrill, Richard L., 'Recollections of the "Quantitative Revolution's" Early Years: The University of Washington 1955–65', in Mark Billinge, Derek Gregory and Ron Martin (eds), *Recollections of a Revolution. Geography as Spatial Science* (London: Macmillan, 1984), pp. 56–72

Morris, Rita M., 'An Examination of some Factors Related to the Rise and Decline of Geography as a Field of Study at Harvard, 1638–1948' (Ph.D. thesis, Graduate School of Education, Harvard University, 1962)

Mudie, Robert, *The Sea. A Popular View of the Phenomena of Tides; the Inhabitants and Uses of the Ocean* (London: Ward and Co., 1835)

Müller-Hill, Benno, *Murderous Science. Elimination by Scientific Selection of Jews, Gypsies, and Others, Germany 1933–45* (Oxford: Oxford University Press, 1988)

Mumford, Lewis, 'Introduction', in Jaqueline Tyrwhitt (ed.), *Patrick Geddes in India* (London: Lund Humphries, 1947), pp. 7–13

Murphy, David T., 'Space, Race and Geopolitical Necessity: A Critique of Geopolitical Rhetoric in German Colonial Revanchism, 1919–1933', in Neil Smith and Anne Godlewska (eds), *Geography and Empire*, forthcoming

Nelson, Gareth, 'From Candolle to Croizat: Comments on the History of Biogeography', *Journal of the History of Biology*, 11 (1978): 269–305

Newbigin, Marion I., *Modern Geography* (London: Williams and Norgate, 1911)

Nicolson, Malcolm, 'Alexander von Humboldt, Humboldtian Science and the Origins of the Study of Vegetation', *History of Science*, 25 (1987): 167–94

Nisbet, H. B., *Herder and Scientific Thought* (Cambridge: The Modern Humanities Research Association, 1970)

Nisbet, Robert, 'Conservatism', in Tom Bottomore and Robert Nisbet (eds), *A History of Sociological Analysis* (London: Heinemann, 1978), pp. 80–117

——*History of the Idea of Progress* (New York: Basic Books, 1980)

Nott, J. C. and George R. Gliddon, *Indigenous Races of the Earth* (Philadelphia, 1857)

Nowell, Charles E., *The Great Discoveries and the First Colonial Empires* (Ithaca, N. Y.: Cornell University Press, 1954)

O'Brian, Patrick, *Joseph Banks. A Life* (London: Collins Harvill, 1987)

O'Donoghue, Yolande, *William Roy 1726–1790. Pioneer of the Ordnance Survey* (London: British Library, 1977)

Oldroyd, David, *The Arch of Knowledge. An Introductory Study of the History of the Philosophy and Methodology of Science* (New York and London: Methuen, 1986)

O'Loughlin, John and Henning Heske, 'From "Geopolitik" to "Geopolitique": Converting a Discipline for War to a Discipline for Peace', in Nurit Kliot and Stanley Waterman (eds), *The Political Geography of Conflict and Peace* (London: Belhaven Press, 1991), pp. 37–59

Olsson, Gunnar, 'Social Science and Human Action or On Hitting your Head Against the Ceiling of Language', in Stephen Gale and Gunnar Olsson (eds), *Philosophy in Geography* (Dordrecht: Reidel, 1979), pp. 287–307

——*Birds in Egg/Eggs in Bird* (London: Pion, 1980)

Olwig, Kenneth Robert, 'Historical Geography and the Society/Nature "Problematic": The Perspective of J. F. Schouw, G. P. Marsh, and E. Reclus', *Journal of Historical Geography*, 6 (1980): 29–45

O'Neill, Henry E., 'East Africa, between the Zambesi and the Rovuma Rivers: its People, Riches and Development', *Scottish Geographical Magazine*, 1 (1885): 337–52

Osborne, Michael, 'The Société Zoologique d'Acclimatation and the New French Empire: The Science and Political Economy of Economic Zoology during the Second Empire' (Ph.D. thesis, University of Wisconsin-Madison, 1987)

Ospovat, Dov, 'Darwin after Malthus', *Journal of the History of Biology*, 12 (1979): 211–30

O'Sullivan, Dan, *The Age of Discovery 1400–1550* (London and New York: Longman, 1984)

Outram, Dorinda, 'Politics and Vocation: French Science, 1793–1830', *British Journal for the History of Science*, 13 (1980): 27–43

P., D., *Certaine Brief and Necessarie Rules of Geographie, Seruing for the Vnderstanding of Chartes and Mappes* (London: Henry Binneman, 1573)

Pagden, Anthony, ' "The Impact of the New World on the Old": The History of an Idea', *Renaissance and Modern Studies*, 30 (1986): 1–11

Parker, Geoffrey, *Western Geopolitical Thought in the Twentieth Century* (London: Croom Helm, 1985)

Parker, W. H., *Mackinder: Geography as an Aid to Statecraft* (Oxford: Clarendon Press, 1982)

Parry, J. H., *The Age of Reconnaissance. Discovery, Exploration and Settlement 1450 to 1650* (Berkeley: University of California Press, 1981)

Parsons, James J., 'Carl Ortwin Sauer, 1889–1975', *Geographical Review*, 66 (1976): 83–9

Parsons, Talcott, *The Structure of Social Action* (New York: McGraw-Hill Book Company, 1937)

Passmore, John, 'Logical Positivism', in Paul Edwards (ed.), *The Encyclopedia of Philosophy* (New York: Macmillan, 1967), vol. 5, pp. 52–7

Paterson, J. H., 'German Geopolitics Reassessed', *Political Geography Quarterly*, 6 (1987): 107–14

Patterson, Elizabeth C., 'Mary Somerville', *British Journal for the History of Science*, 4 (1969): 309–39

——'Somerville, Mary Fairfax Grieg', *Dictionary of Scientific Biography* (New York: Scribner's, 1970–81), vol. 12, pp. 521–5

Paul, Diane, 'Eugenics and the Left', *Journal of the History of Ideas*, 45 (1984): 567–90

Peet, Richard, 'The Development of Radical Geography in the United States', *Progress in Human Geography*, 1 (1977): 240–63

——'The Social Origins of Environmental Determinism', *Annals of the Association of American Geographers*, 75 (1985): 309–33

——(ed.), *Radical Geography* (London: Methuen, 1978)

Pelzer, Karl, 'Geography and the Tropics', in Taylor (ed.), *Geography in the Twentieth Century, A Study of Growth, Fields, Techniques, Aims and Trends* (London: Methuen, 1951), pp. 311–44

Pemble, William, *A Briefe Introduction to Geography* (Oxford, 1630)

Penck, Albrecht, 'Der Krieg und das Studium der Geographie', *Zeitschrift der Gellschaft für Erdkunde zu Berlin* (1916): 158–76, 222–48

Penniman, T. K., *A Hundred Years of Anthropology* (London: Duckworth, 2nd edn 1952)

Penrose, Boies, *Travel and Discovery in the Renaissance 1420–1620* (Cambridge, Mass.: Harvard University Press, 1952; 1967)

Pfeifer, E. J., 'The Genesis of American Neo-Lamarckism', *Isis*, 56 (1965): 156–67

Pfeil, Graf von and Klein Ellguth, 'On Tropical Africa in Relation to White Races', *Report of the Sixth International Geographical Congress, London 1895* (London, 1896), pp. 537–44

Philo, Chris (compiler), *New Words, New Worlds: Reconceptualising Social and Cultural Geography* (Department of Geography, St David's University College, Lampeter, 1991)

Pickles, John, *Phenomenology, Science and Geography: Spatiality and the Human Sciences* (Cambridge: Cambridge University Press, 1985)

Pigafetta, Antonio, *Magellan's First Voyage Around the World*, translated by Lord Stanley of Alderney (Hakluyt Society, 1st series, vol. 52, 1874)

Plantinga, Alvin C., 'The Reformed Objection to Natural Theology', *Christian Scholar's Review*, 11, 3 (1982): 187–98

Plewe, Ernest, 'Alfred Hettner, 1859–1941', *Geographers. Biobibliographical Studies*, vol. 6 (1982): pp. 55–63

Pocock, Douglas C. D. (ed.), *Humanistic Geography and Literature: Essays on the Experience of Place* (London: Croom Helm, 1981)

Popper, K. R., *The Logic of Scientific Discovery* (London: Hutchinson, 1968)

Porter, Roy, Review of *Empiricism and Geographical Thought*, by Margarita Bowen, *British Journal for the History of Science*, 15 (1983): 301–2

Porter, Theodore M., *The Rise of Statistical Thinking 1820–1900* (Princeton, N. J.: Princeton University Press, 1986)

Powell, J. M., 'Griffith Taylor Emigrates from Australia', *Geography Bulletin*, 10 (1978): 5–13

——'Thomas Griffith Taylor, 1880–1963', *Geographers. Biobibliographical Studies*, 3 (1979): 141–53

Pred, Allan, 'Place as Historically-Contingent Process: Structuration and the Time-Geography of Becoming Places', *Annals of the Association of American Geographers*, 74 (1984): 279–97

Price, A. Grenfell, *White Settlers in the Tropics*, American Geographical Society Special Publication no. 23 (New York: American Geographical Society, 1939)

Price, Geoffrey, 'Reductionism and the Differentiation of Consciousness', in Arthur Peacocke (ed.), *Reductionism in Academic Disciplines* (Surrey: Society for Research into Higher Education and NFER-Nelson, 1985), pp. 125–42

Prichard, [James Cowles], Review of *Crania Americana; or, a Comparative View of the Skulls of Various Aboriginal Nations of the North and South America: to which is Prefixed an Essay on the Varieties of the Human Species* by Samuel George Morton, *Journal of the Royal Geographical Society*, 10 (1841): 552–61

Proctor, Robert N., *Racial Hygiene. Medicine Under the Nazis* (Cambridge, Mass.: Harvard University Press, 1988)

Purchas, Samuel, *Purchas His Pilgrimage; or, Relations of the World and the Religions Observed in All Ages and Places Discovered, from the Creation unto this Present* (London, 1613)

Pyenson, Lewis, 'Astronomy and Imperialism: J. A. C. Oudemans, the Topography of the East Indies, and the Rise of the Utrecht Observatory, 1850–1900', *Historia scientiarum*, 26 (1984): 39–81

Rabinow, Paul (ed.), *The Foucault Reader* (New York: Pantheon, 1984)

Rae, J., 'On the Esquimaux', *Transactions of the Ethnological Society of London*, n.s. 3 (1865): 138–53

Rainger, Ronald, 'Race, Politics, and Science: The Anthropological Society of London in the 1860s', *Victorian Studies*, 22 (1978): 51–70

Ranger, Terence, 'From Humanism to the Science of Man: Colonialism in Africa and the Understanding of Alien Societies', *Transactions of the Royal Historical Society*, 5th series, 26 (1976): 115–41

Ratzel, Friedrich, 'The Territorial Growth of States', *Scottish Geographical Magazine*, 12 (1896): 351–61
——*The History of Mankind*, translated from the second German edition by A. J. Butler, 3 vols (London: Macmillan, 1896–8)
——*Erdenmacht und Völkerschicksal*, edited and introduced by Karl Haushofer (Stuttgart: A Kröner, 1940)
Ravenstein, E. G., 'Lands of the Globe Still Available for European Settlement', *Proceedings of the Royal Geographical Society*, n.s. 13 (1891): 27–35
——Discussion, *Report of the Sixth International Geographical Congress, London 1895* (London, 1896), p. 547
Reingold, Nathan, *Science in Nineteenth Century America* (New York: Hill and Wang, 1964)
Relph, Edward, 'An Inquiry into the Relations between Phenomenology and Geography', *Canadian Geographer*, 14 (1970): 193–201
——*Place and Placelessness* (London: Pion, 1976)
Renbourne, E. T., 'The History of the Flannel Binder and Cholera Belt', *Medical History*, 1 (1957): 211–25
——'Life and Death of the Solar Topi', *Journal of Tropical Medicine and Hygiene*, 65 (1962): 203–18
Rich, Paul B., *Race and Empire in British Politics* (Cambridge: Cambridge University Press, 1986)
Robson, Brian, 'Geography and Social Science: the Role of Patrick Geddes', in David R. Stoddart (ed.), *Geography, Ideology and Social Concern* (Oxford: Blackwell, 1981), pp. 186–207
Roger, Jacques, *Les Sciences de la Vie dans la Pensée Français du XVIIIe Siècle* (Parison: Armand Colin, 1963)
Rorty, Richard, *Philosophy and the Mirror of Nature* (Oxford: Blackwell, 1980)
——'Method, Social Science, and Social Hope', in *Consequences of Pragmatism. Essays: 1972–1980* (Sussex: Harvester Press, 1982)
Rose, Paul Lawrence, 'Keckermann, Bartholomew', *Dictionary of Scientific Biography* (New York: Scribner's, 1970–81), vol. 7, pp. 268–70
Rose, Steven, Leon J. Kamin and R. C. Lewontin, *Not in Our Genes: Biology, Ideology and Human Nature* (Harmondsworth: Penguin, 1984)
Ross, Emory, 'The Climate of Liberia and its Effect on Man', *Geographical Review*, 7 (1919): 387–402
Rössler, M., 'Applied Geography and Area Research in Nazi Society: Central Place Theory and Planning, 1933 to 1945', *Environment and Planning D: Society and Space*, 7 (1989): 419–31
Roxby, P. M., 'The Agricultural Geography of England on a Regional Basis', *Geographical Teacher*, 7 (1913–14): 316–21
Rudwick, Martin, 'Senses of the Natural World and Senses of God: Another Look at the Historical Relation of Science and Religion', in A. R. Peacocke (ed.), *The Sciences and Theology in the Twentieth Century* (Henley and London: Oriel Press, 1981), pp. 241–61

Russell, Colin, *Science and Social Change 1700–1900* (London: Macmillan, 1983)

Russell, P. E., *Prince Henry the Navigator: The Rise and Fall of a Culture Hero* (Oxford: Clarendon Press, 1984)

Russett, Cynthia Eagle, *Darwin in America. The Intellectual Response 1865–1912* (San Francisco: W. H. Freeman, 1976)

Sack, Robert David, 'Chorology and Spatial Analysis', *Annals of the Association of American Geographers*, 64 (1974): 439–52

——*Conceptions of Space in Social Thought: A Geographic Perspective* (London: Macmillan, 1980)

Said, Edward W., *Orientalism. Western Conceptions of the Orient* (London: Routledge and Kegan Paul, 1978)

Sambon, Luigi Westenra, 'Remarks on the Possibility of the Acclimatisation of Europeans in Tropical Regions', *British Medical Journal*, 1 (1897): 61–6

——'Acclimatization of Europeans in Tropical Lands', *Geographical Journal*, 12 (1898): 589–606

——'Tropical Clothing', *Journal of Tropical Medicine and Hygiene* (15 February 1907), pp. 67–9

Samuels, Marwyn, 'An Existential Geography', in Milton E. Harvey and Brian P. Holly (eds), *Themes in Geographic Thought* (London: Croom Helm, 1981), pp. 22–40

Sanderson, Marie, 'Mary Somerville: Her Work in Physical Geography', *Geographical Review*, 64 (1974): 410–20

——*Griffith Taylor: Antarctic Scientist and Pioneer Geographer* (Ottawa, 1988)

Sandner, Gerhard, 'Recent Advances in the History of German Geography 1918–1945. A Progress Report for the Federal Republic of Germany', *Geographische Zeitschrift*, 76 (1988): 120–33

——'The Germanic Triumphans Syndrome and Passarge's *Erdkundliche Weltanschauung*: The Roots and Effects of German Political Geography beyond *Geopolitik*', *Political Geography Quarterly*, 8 (1989): 341–51

Sauer, Carl O., 'The Morphology of Landscape', *University of California Publications in Geography*, 2, 2 (1925): 19–54

——'Geography, Cultural', in E. R. A. Seligman (ed.), *Encyclopedia of the Social Sciences* (New York: Macmillan, 1934), vol. 6, pp. 621–4

——'Friedrich Ratzel', in E. R. A. Seligman (ed.), *Encyclopedia of the Social Sciences* (New York: Macmillan, 1934), vol. 13, pp. 120–1

——'Ellen Churchill Semple', in E. R. A. Seligman (ed.), *Encyclopedia of the Social Sciences* (New York: Macmillan, 1934), vol. 13, pp. 661–2

——'Destructive Exploitation in Modern Colonial Expansion', *Comtes Rendus du Congrès International de Géographie*, 2 (1938): 494–9

——'Theme of Plant and Animal Destruction in Economic History', *Journal of Farm Economics*, 20 (1938): 765–75

——'Foreword to Historical Geography', *Annals of the Association of American Geographers*, 31 (1941): 11–24. Reprinted in John Leighly (ed.), *Land and Life: A Selection from the Writings of Carl Ortwin Sauer* (Berkeley: University of California Press, 1963, pp. 1–8

——Plant and Animal Exchanges between the Old and the New World: Notes from a Seminar Presented by Carl O. Sauer, at UCLA in 1961, edited by Robert Newcomb (privately printed, 1963)

——*The Early Spanish Main* (Berkeley: University of California Press, 1966)

——*Northern Mists* (Berkeley: University of California Press, 1968)

——'The Formative Years of Ratzel in the United States', *Annals of the Association of American Geographers*, 61 (1971): 245–54

——*Sixteenth Century North America: The Land and The People as Seen by the Europeans* (Berkeley: University of California Press, 1971)

Sayer, Andrew, *Method in Social Science. A Realist Approach* (London: Hutchinson, 1984)

Scargill, D. I., 'The RGS and the Foundations of Geography at Oxford', *Geographical Journal*, 142 (1976): 438–61

Schaefer, Fred K., 'Exceptionalism in Geography: A Methodological Examination', *Annals of the Association of American Geographers* 43 (1953): 226–49

Schlick, Manfred, 'Otto Schlüter, 1872–1959', in *Geographers. Biobibliographical Studies*, vol. 6 (1982): 115–22

Schneider, William H., 'Geographical Reform and Municipal Imperialism in France, 1870–80', in John M. MacKenzie (ed.), *Imperialism and the Natural World* (Manchester: Manchester University Press, 1990), pp. 90–117

Schöller, P., 'Die Rolle Karl Haushofers für die Entwicklung und Ideologie Nationalsozialistischer Geopolitik', *Erdkunde*, 36 (1982): 160–7

Schultz, Hans-Dietrich, *Die Deutschsprachige Geographie von 1800 bis 1970: Ein Beitrag zur Geschichte Ihrer Methodologie* (Berlin: Free University, 1980)

——'Fantasies of *Mitte*: *Mittellage* and *Mitteleuropa* in German Geographical Discussion in the 19th and 20th Centuries', *Political Geography Quarterly*, 8 (1989): 315–39

Seamon, David and R. Mugerauer (eds), *Dwelling, Place and Environment: Towards a Phenomenology of Person and World* (Dordrecht: Martinus Nijhoff, 1985)

Searle, G. T. R., *Eugenics and Politics in Britain, 1900–1914* (Leiden: Noordhoff International Publishing, 1976)

Secord, James A., 'Nature's Fancy: Charles Darwin and the Breeding of Pigeons', *Isis*, 72 (1981): 163–86

——'King of Siluria: Roderick Murchison and the Imperial Theme in Nineteenth-century British Geology', *Victorian Studies*, 25 (1982): 413–42

——'Darwin and the Breeders: A Social History', in David Kohn (ed.), *The Darwinian Heritage* (Princeton, N.J.: Princeton University Press, 1985), pp. 519–42

Semple, Ellen C., 'The Anglo-Saxons of the Kentucky Mountains: A Study in Anthropogeography', *Geographical Journal*, 17 (1901): 588–623

——*Influences of Geographic Environment on the Basis of Ratzel's System of Anthropo-geography* (New York: Henry Holt, 1911)

Seymour, Ian, 'The Political Magic of John Dee', *History Today*, 39 (1989): 29–35

Shafer, B., *Nationalism: Myth and Reality* (New York: Harcourt, Brace and World, 1955)

Shaler, Nathaniel Southgate, 'The Immigration Problem Historically Considered', *America*, 1, no. 30 (1888): 1–2

——*Nature and Man in America* (New York: Scribner's Sons, 1891)

——'European Peasants as Immigrants', *Atlantic Monthly*, 71 (1893): 646–55

——*The Interpretation of Nature* (New York: Houghton Mifflin, 1893)

——'What is Geology?' *Chautauquan*, 18 (1893): 284–7

——'Our Negro Types', *Current Literature*, 29 (1900): 44–5

——*The Neighbor: The Natural History of Human Contacts* (Boston: Houghton Mifflin, 1904)

Shapere, Dudley, 'The Character of Scientific Change', in Thomas Nickles (ed.), *Scientific Discovery, Logic, and Rationality* (Dordrecht: D. Reidel, 1980), pp. 61–116

Shapin, Steven, 'History of Science and its Sociological Reconstructions', *History of Science*, 20 (1982): 157–211

——and Barry Barnes, 'Darwin and Social Darwinism: Purity and History', in Barry Barnes and Steven Shapin (eds), *Natural Order: Historical Studies of Scientific Culture* (Beverly Hills: Sage Publications, 1979), pp.125–42

——and Simon Schaffer, *Leviathan and the Air-Pump. Hobbes, Boyle, and the Experimental Life* (Princeton, N.J.: Princeton University Press, 1985)

Sharpe, Alfred, 'The Geography and Economic Development of British Central Africa', *Geographical Journal*, 39 (1912): 1–24

Shaw, George Bernard, *Sociological Papers* (London, 1905)

Shaw, Martin and Ian Miles, 'The Social Roots of Statistical Knowledge', in John Irvine, Ian Miles and Jeff Evans (eds), *Demystifying Social Statistics* (n.p.: Pluto Press, 1979), pp. 27–38

Shea, William R., 'Galileo and the Church', in David C. Lindberg and Ronald L. Numbers (eds), *God and Nature. Historical Essays on the Encounter between Christianity and Science* (Berkeley: University of California Press, 1986), pp.114–35

Shklar, Judith N., *Montesquieu* (Oxford: Oxford University Press, 1987)

Sinnhuber, Karl A., 'Alexander von Humboldt, 1769–1859', *Scottish Geographical Magazine*, 75 (1959): 83–101

——'Carl Ritter, 1779–1859', *Scottish Geographical Magazine*, 75 (1959): 153–63

Skelton, R. A., *Explorers' Maps. Chapters in the Cartographic Record of Geographical Discovery* (London: Routledge and Kegan Paul, 1958)

——'The Origins of the Ordnance Survey of Great Britain', *Geographical Journal*, 128 (1962): 415–30

——'Ralegh as a Geographer', *The Virginia Magazine of History and Biography*, 71 (1963): 131–49

Skinner, Quentin, 'Meaning and Understanding in the History of Ideas', *History and Theory*, 8 (1969): 3–53

Slatter, John, 'The Kropotkin Papers', *Geographical Magazine*, 53, 14 (1981): 917–21

Smith, Bernard, *European Vision and the South Pacific* (New Haven and London: Yale University Press, 2nd ed 1985)

Smith, Neil, 'Isaiah Bowman: Political Geography and Geopolitics', *Political Geography Quarterly*, 3 (1984): 69–76

——' "Academic War over the Field of Geography": The Elimination of Geography at Harvard, 1947–1952', *Annals of the Association of American Geographers*, 77 (1987): 155–72

——'Geography as Museum: Private History and Conservative Idealism in *The Nature of Geography*', in J. Nicholas Entrikin and Stanley D. Brunn (eds), *Reflections on Richard Hartshorne's* The Nature of Geography (Washington, D.C.: Association of American Geographers, 1989), pp. 91–120

——'Shaking Loose the Colonies: Isaiah Bowman's Role in the U.S. Assault on the British Empire', in Smith and Godlewska (eds), *Geography and Empire*, forthcoming

Smith, Susan J., 'Practicing Humanistic Geography', *Annals of the Association of American Geographers*, 74 (1984): 353–74

Smith, W. D., 'Friedrich Ratzel and the Origins of *Lebensraum*', *German Studies Review*, 3 (1980): 51–68

Soja, Edward W., 'The Spatiality of Social Life: Towards a Transformative Retheorisation', in Derek Gregory and John Urry (eds), *Social Relations and Spatial Structures* (London: Macmillan, 1985), pp. 90–127

——*Postmodern Geographies: The Reassertion of Space in Critical Social Theory* (London: Verso, 1989)

Solot, Michael, 'Carl Sauer and Cultural Evolution', *Annals of the Association of American Geographers*, 76 (1986): 508–20

Somerville, Mary, *Physical Geography* (London: Murray, 1848; 4th edn, 1858)

Spate, O. H. K., 'Ellsworth Huntington', in David L. Sills (ed.), *International Encyclopedia of the Social Sciences* (New York: Macmillan and Free Press, 1968), vol. 7, pp. 26–7

Spencer, Herbert, *Social Statics: or, the Conditions Essential to Human Happiness Specified and the First of Them Developed* (London: Chapman, 1851)

Speth, William W., 'Carl Ortwin Sauer on Destructive Exploitation', *Biological Conservation*, 11 (1977): 145–60

——'The Anthropogeographic Theory of Franz Boas', *Anthropos*, 73 (1978): 1–31

——'Historicism: The Disciplinary World View of Carl O. Sauer', in Martin S. Kenzer (ed.), *Carl O. Sauer. A Tribute* (Corvallis, Oregon: Oregon State University Press, 1987), pp. 11–39

Spinden, H. J., 'Civilization and the Wet Tropics', *World's Work*, 45 (1922–3): 438–48

Spottiswoode, William, 'On Typical Mountain Ranges: An Application of the Calculus of Probabilities to Physical Geography', *Journal of the Royal Geographical Society*, 31 (1861): 149–54

Sprat, Thomas, *The History of the Royal Society of London for the Improving of Natural Knowledge* (London, 1687)

Stafford, Barbara Maria, *Voyage into Substance. Art, Science, Nature, and the Illustrated Travel Account, 1760–1840* (Cambridge, Mass.: The MIT Press, 1984)

Stafford, Robert A., 'Geological Surveys, Mineral Discoveries, and British Expansion, 1835–71', *Journal of Imperial and Commonwealth History*, 12 (1984): 5–32

——'Roderick Murchison and the Structure of Africa: A Geological Prediction and its Consequences for British Expansion', *Annals of Science*, 45 (1988): 1–40

——*Scientist of Empire. Sir Roderick Murchison, Scientific Exploration and Victorian Imperialism* (Cambridge: Cambridge University Press, 1989)

Stamp, L. Dudley, 'Major Natural Regions: Herbertson after Fifty Years', *Geography*, 42 (1957): 201–16

Stanley, Henry M., 'Central Africa and the Congo Basin. An Inaugural Address', *Scottish Geographical Magazine*, 1 (1885): 1–17

——*The Congo and the Founding of its Free State: A Story of Work and Exploration*, 2 vols (London, 1885)

Stepan, Nancy, *The Idea of Race in Science: Great Britain 1800–1960* (London: Macmillan, 1982)

Stern, Robert A. M., 'The Doubles of Post-Modern', *Harvard Architecture Review*, 1 (1980): 75–87

Stevenson, W. Iain, 'Patrick Geddes 1854–1932', *Geographers. Biobibliographical Studies*, 2 (1978): 53–65

Stewart, John Q., 'Empirical Mathematical Rules Concerning the Distribution and Equilibrium of Population', *Geographical Review*, 37 (1947): 461–86

——'Suggested Principles of Social Physics', *Science*, 106 (1947): 179–80

Stocking, George W. Jr., 'Lamarckianism in American Social Science: 1890–1915', *Journal of the History of Ideas*, 23 (1962): 239–56

——'On the Limits of "Presentism" and "Historicism" in the Historiography of the Behavioral Sciences', *Journal of the History of the Behavioral Sciences*, 1 (1965): 211–17

——'From Physics to Ethnology: Franz Boas' Arctic Expedition as Problem in the Historiography of the Behavioral Sciences', *Journal of the History of the Behavioral Sciences*, 1 (1965): 53–66

——'What's in a Name? The Origins of the Royal Anthropological Institute: 1837–1871', *Man*, 6 (1971): 369–90

——'From Chronology to Ethnology: James Cowles Prichard and British Anthropology, 1800–1850', in James Cowles Prichard, *Researches into the Physical History of Man*, edited and with an introductory essay by George W. Stocking, Jr. (Chicago: University of Chicago Press, 1973), pp. ix–cxviii

——'The Basic Assumptions of Boasian Anthropology', in George W. Stocking, Jr. (ed.), *A Franz Boas Reader. The Shaping of American Anthropology, 1883–1911* (Chicago: University of Chicago Press, 1974), pp. 1–20

——*Race, Culture and Evolution. Essays in the History of Anthropology* (Chicago: University of Chicago Press, 1982)

——*Victorian Anthropology* (New York: Free Press, 1987)

Stoddart, D. R., 'Geography and the Ecological Approach: The Ecosystem as a Geographic Principle and Method', *Geography*, 50 (1965): 242–51

——'Darwin's Impact on Geography', *Annals of the Association of American Geographers*, 56 (1966): 683–98

——'The RGS and the Foundations of Geography at Cambridge', *Geographical Journal*, 141 (1975): 216–39

——'Darwin, Lyell, and the Geological Significance of Coral Reefs', *British Journal for the History of Science*, 9 (1976): 199–218

——'The R.G.S. and the "New Geography": Changing Aims and Roles in Nineteenth-Century Science', *Geographical Journal*, 146 (1980): 190–202

——'Darwin's Influence on the Development of Geography in the United States, 1859–1914', in Brian Blouet (ed.), *The Origins of Academic Geography in the United States* (Hamden: Archon Books, 1981), pp. 265–78

——'Ideas and Interpretation in the History of Geography', in D. R. Stoddart (ed.), *Geography, Ideology and Social Concern* (Oxford: Blackwell, 1981), pp. 1–7

——'The Paradigm Concept and the History of Geography', in D. R. Stoddart (ed.), *Geography, Ideology and Social Concern* (Oxford: Blackwell, 1981), pp. 70–80

——'Geography – A European Science', *Geography*, 67 (1982): 289–96

——*On Geography and Its History* (Oxford: Blackwell, 1986)

——'"Geography and War": The New Geography and the New Army in England, 1899–1914', *Political Geography*, 11 (1992): 87–99

Sturrock, John (ed.), *Structuralism and Since: From Lévi-Strauss to Derrida* (Oxford: Oxford University Press, 1979)

Sulloway, Frank J., 'Geographic Isolation in Darwin's Thinking: The Vicissitudes of a Crucial Idea', *Studies in the History of Biology*, 3 (1979): 23–65

Surface, George T., 'Thomas Jefferson: A Pioneer Student of American Geography', *Bulletin of the American Geographical Society*, 41 (1909): 743–50

Swayne, E., 'British Honduras', *Geographical Journal*, 50 (1917): 161–79

Tatham, George, 'Geography in the Nineteenth Century', in Griffith Taylor (ed.), *Geography in the Twentieth Century* (New York and London: Methuen, 1951), pp. 28–69

Taylor, Charles, 'What is Human Agency?' in *Human Agency and Language. Philosophical Papers, Volume 1* (Cambridge: Cambridge University Press, 1985), pp. 15–44

——*Sources of the Self. The Making of Modern Identity* (Cambridge, Mass.: Harvard University Press, 1989)

Taylor, E. G. R., *Tudor Geography 1485–1583* (London: Methuen, 1930)

——*Late Tudor and Early Stuart Geography 1583–1650* (London: Methuen, 1934)

——*The Mathematical Practitioners of Tudor and Stuart England 1485–1714*

(Cambridge: Cambridge University Press for the Institute of Navigation, 1954).

——*The Haven-Finding Art. A History of Navigation from Odysseus to Captain Cook* (London: Hollis and Carter, 1956)

Taylor, Peter J., 'An Interpretation of the Quantification Debate in British Geography', *Transactions of the Institute of British Geographers*, 1 (1976): 129–42

Taylor, T. Griffith, 'The Control of Settlement by Humidity and Temperature', *Commonwealth Bureau of Meteorology. Bulletin No. 14* (Melbourne, 1914)

——'Climatic Cycles and Evolution', *Geographical Review*, 8 (1919): 289–328

——'The Evolution and Distribution of Race, Culture, and Language', *Geographical Review*, 11 (1921), 54–119

——'Racial Migration-Zones and their Significance', *Human Biology*, 2 (1930) 34–62

——'The Zones and Strata Theory: a Biological Classification of Races', *Human Biology*, 8 (1936) 348–67

——'Racial Geography', in Griffith Taylor (ed.), *Geography in the Twentieth Century* (New York: Philosophical Library, 3rd edn 1957), pp. 433–62

Theroux, Paul, 'Mapping the World', *The Hongkong and Shanghai Banking Corporation Annual Report* (1981), p. 12

Thomas, Keith, *Religion and the Decline of Magic* (London: Weidenfeld and Nicolson, 1971)

Thomson, J. Arthur and Patrick Geddes, *Life: Outlines of General Biology*, 2 vols (London: Williams and Norgate, 1931)

Thomson, Joseph, 'East Central Africa, and its Commercial Outlook', *Scottish Geographical Magazine*, 2 (1886): 17–31

——'Niger and Central Sudan Sketches', *Scottish Geographical Magazine*, 2 (1886): 577–601

'Thomson, Joseph', *Dictionary of National Biography,* vol. 56, 262–5

Thrift, Nigel, 'On the Determination of Social Action in Space and Time', *Environment and Planning D: Society and Space*, 1 (1983): 23–57

Thrower, Norman J. W., *Maps and Man. An Examination of Cartography in Relation to Culture and Civilization* (Englewood Cliffs, N.J.: Prentice-Hall, 1972)

Tooley, R. V., *Maps and Map-makers* (New York: Crown Publishers, revised edn 1970)

Toulmin, Stephen, *The Philosophy of Science* (London: Hutchinson, 1953)

Trewartha, Glenn T., 'Recent Thought on the Problem of White Acclimatization in the Wet Tropics', *Geographical Review*, 16 (1926): 467–78

Trigger, Bruce G., *A History of Archaeological Thought* (Cambridge: Cambridge University Press, 1989)

Trindell, Roger T., 'Franz Boas and American Geography', *Professional Geographer*, 21 (1969): 328–32

Troll, Carl, 'Halford J. Mackinder als Geograph und Geopolitiker', *Erdkunde*, 6 (1952): 177–8

——'The Work of Alexander von Humboldt and Carl Ritter: A Centenary Address', *Advancement of Science*, 64 (1959–60): 441–52

Tuan, Yi-Fu, *The Hydrological Cycle and the Wisdom of God: A Theme in Geoteleology* (Toronto: University of Toronto Press, 1968)

——'Geography, Phenomenology and the Study of Human Nature', *Canadian Geographer*, 15 (1971): 181–92

——*Space and Place: The Perspective of Experience* (London: Edward Arnold, 1977)

Turner, Frank Miller, 'Rainfall, Plagues and the Prince of Wales: A Chapter in the Conflict of Religion and Science', *Journal of British Studies*, 13 (1974): 46–65

Tyacke, Sarah and E. J. Huddy, *Christopher Saxton and Tudor Map-Making* (London, 1980)

Tylor, Edward B., 'Introduction', in Friedrich Ratzel, *The History of Mankind*, translated from the second German edition by A. J. Butler, 3 vols (London: Macmillan, 1896–8), vol. 1, pp. v–xi

Ullmann, Edward, 'A Theory of Location for Cities', *American Journal of Sociology*, 46 (1941): 835–64

——*Geography as Spatial Interaction*, edited by Ronald R. Boyce (Seattle: University of Washington Press, 1980)

Unstead, J. F., 'A System of Regional Geography', *Geography*, 18 (1933): 175–87

Van de Wetering, Maxine, 'Moralizing in Puritan Natural Science: Mysteriousness in Earthquake Sermons', *Journal of the History of Ideas*, 43 (1982): 417–38

Van Orman, Richard A., *The Explorers: Nineteenth Century Expeditions in Africa and the American West* (Albuquerque: University of New Mexico Press, 1984)

Vidal de la Blache, Paul, 'Rapports de la Sociologie avec la Géographie', *Revue Internationale de Sociologie*, 12 (1904): 309–13

——'Les Genres de Vie dans la Géographie Humaine', *Annales de Géographie*, 20 (1911): 193–212, 289–304

——'Les Caractères Distinctifs de la Géographie', *Annales de Géographie*, 22 (1913): 289–99

——*Principles of Human Geography*, translated by Millicent Todd Bingham (London: Constable and Company, 1926)

Vorzimmer, Peter J., *Charles Darwin: The Years of Controversy. The Origin of Species and its Critics* (Philadelphia: Temple University Press, 1970)

Wallis, Helen, 'Hakluyt, Richard', *Dictionary of Scientific Biography* (New York: Scribner's, 1970–81), vol. 6, pp. 20–1

Wands, John, 'The Theory of Climate in the English Renaissance and *Mundus Alter et Idem*', in I. D. McFarlane (ed.), *Proceedings of the Fifth International Congress of Neo-Latin Studies* (Binghampton, New York: Medieval and Renaissance Texts and Studies, 1986), pp. 519–25

Wanklyn, Harriet, *Friedrich Ratzel. A Biographical Memoir and Bibliography* (Cambridge: Cambridge University Press, 1961)

Ward, Robert DeC., 'A New Classification of Climates', *Geographical Review*, 8 (1919): 188–91

——'Fallacies of the Melting Pot Idea and America's Traditional Immigration Policy', in Madison Grant and Chas Steward Davison (eds), *The Alien in our Midst or 'Selling our Birthright for a Mess of Industrial Potage'* (New York: Galton, 1930), pp. 230–6

——'Can the White Race become Acclimatized in the Tropics?' *Gerlands Beiträge zur Geopolitik*, 32 (1931): 149–57

Warntz, William, *Geography Now and Then: Some Notes on the History of Academic Geography in the United States*, American Geographical Society Research Series no. 25 (New York: American Geographical Society, 1964)

——'Newton, The Newtonians, and the *Geographia Generalis Varenii*', *Annals of the Association of American Geographers*, 79 (1989): 165–91

——and Peter Wolff, *Breakthroughs in Geography* (New York: New American Library, 1971)

Washburn, Wilcomb E., 'The Meaning of "Discovery" in the Fifteenth and Sixteenth Centuries', *American Historical Review*, 68 (1962): 1–21

Waters, David W., *The Arts of Navigation in England in Elizabethan and Early Stuart Times* (London: Hollis and Carter, 1958)

——'Science and the Techniques of Navigation', in Charles S. Singleton (ed.), *Art, Science, and History in the Renaissance* (Baltimore: Johns Hopkins University Press, 1967), pp. 189–237

Watson, J. Wreford, 'The Sociological Aspects of Geography', in T. Griffith Taylor (ed.), *Geography in the Twentieth Century: A Study of Growth, Fields, Techniques, Aims and Trends* (London: Methuen, 1951), pp. 463–99

Watts, Isaac, *The Knowledge of the Heavens and the Earth Made Easy: or, The First Principles of Astronomy and Geography Explain'd by the Use of Globes and Maps: With a Solution of the Common Problems by a* Plain Scale and Compass *as well as by the* Globe (London, 3rd edn 1736)

Webster, Charles (ed.), *The Intellectual Revolution of the Seventeenth Century* (London: Routledge and Kegan Paul, 1974)

——*The Great Instauration. Science, Medicine and Reform 1626–1660* (London: Duckworth, 1975)

——*From Paracelsus to Newton: Magic and the Making of Modern Science* (Cambridge: Cambridge University Press, 1982)

——'Puritanism, Separatism, and Science', in David C. Lindberg and Ronald L. Numbers (eds), *God and Nature. Historical Essays on the Encounter between Christianity and Science* (Berkeley: University of California Press, 1986)

Weindling, Paul, 'Ernst Haeckel, Darwinismus and the Secularization of Nature', in James R. Moore (ed.), *History, Humanity and Evolution. Essays for John C.*

Greene (Cambridge: Cambridge University Press, 1989), pp. 311–53.

Weiner, Douglas R., 'The Roots of "Michurinism": Transformist Biology and Acclimatization as Currents in the Russian Life Sciences', *Annals of Science*, 42 (1985): 244–60

Wells, Edward, *An Historical Geography of the New Testament. In Two Parts... Being a Geographical and Historical Account of all the Places Mention'd, or Referr'd to, in the Books of the New Testament...*(London, 1708)

Westfall, Richard, *Science and Religion in Seventeenth Century England* (New Haven: Yale University Press, 1958)

Westman, Robert S., 'The Melanchthon Circle, Rheticus, and the Wittenberg Interpretation of the Copernican Theory', *Isis*, 66 (1975): 164–93

——'Nature, Art, and the Psyche: Jung, Pauli, and the Kepler-Fludd Polemic', in B. Vickers (ed.), *Occult and Scientific Mentalities in the Renaissance* (Cambridge University Press, Cambridge, 1984), pp. 177–229

——'The Copernicans and the Churches', in David C. Lindberg and Ronald L. Numbers (eds), *God and Nature. Historical Essays on the Encounter between Christianity and Science* (Berkeley: University of California Press, 1986), pp. 76–113

——and J. E. McGuire, *Hermeticism and the Scientific Revolution* (Los Angeles: William Andrews Clark Memorial Library, 1977)

Wheeler, P. B., 'Revolutions, Research Programmes and Human Geography', *Area*, 14 (1982): 1–6

Whewell, William, *Astronomy and General Physics Considered with Special Reference to Natural Theology* (London: William Pickering, 1834)

White, A. Silva, 'On the Comparative Value of African Lands', *Scottish Geographical Magazine*, 7 (1891): 191–5

White, Morton, *Science and Sentiment in America: Philosophical Thought from Jonathan Edwards to John Dewey* (New York: Oxford University Press, 1972)

Whittlesey, Derwent, 'The Horizon of Geography', *Annals of the Association of American Geographers*, 35 (1945): 1–36

Wiener, Philip P., *Evolution and the Founders of Pragmatism* (Cambridge, Mass.: Harvard University Press, 1949)

——'Some Problems and Methods in the History of Ideas', *Journal of the History of Ideas*, 22 (1961): 531–48

Wilford, John Noble, *The Mapmakers* (London: Junction Books, 1981)

Williams, Frances Leigh, *Matthew Fontaine Maury: Scientist of the Sea* (New Brunswick, N.J.: Rutgers University Press, 1963)

Williams, Michael, '"The Apple of My Eye": Carl Sauer and Historical Geography', *Journal of Historical Geography*, 9 (1983): 1–28

——'Sauer and "Man's Role in Changing the Face of the Earth"', *Geographical Review*, 77 (1987): 218–31

Williams, Raymond, 'Social Darwinism', in Jonathan Benthall (ed.), *The Limits of Human Nature* (London: Allen Lane, 1973), pp. 115–30

Wilson, A. G., 'Theoretical Geography', *Transactions of the Institute of British Geographers*, 57 (1972): 31–44

Winchell, Alexander, *Preadamites; or a Demonstration of the Existence of Men before Adam; Together with a Study of their Condition, Antiquity, Racial Affinities, and Progressive Dispersion over the Earth* (Chicago: S. C. Griggs and Company, 2nd edn 1880)

Winnik, Herbert C., 'Science and Morality in Thomas C. Chamberlin', *Journal of the History of Ideas*, 31 (1970): 441–56

Wise, M. J., 'The Scott Keltie Report 1885 and the Teaching of Geography in Great Britain', *Geographical Journal*, 152 (1986): 367–82

Withers, Charles W., 'Improvement and Enlightenment: Agriculture and Natural History in the Work of the Rev Dr John Walker (1731–1803)', in Peter Jones (ed.), *Philosophy and Science in the Scottish Enlightenment* (Edinburgh: John Donald, 1989), pp. 102–16

——'The Rev Dr John Walker and the Practice of Natural History in Late Eighteenth Century Scotland', *Archives of Natural History*, 18 (1991): 201–20

——'A Note on the Term "Historical Geography" in Diderot's *Encyclopédie*', unpublished typescript

Wittfogel, Karl, 'Geopolitics, Geographical Materialism and Marxism', trans by G. L. Ulmen, *Antipode*, 17, 1 (1985): 21–72

Woodbridge, William Channing, *A System of Universal Geography on the Principles of Comparison and Classification* (Hartford: Oliver D. Cooke and Sons, 1824)

Woodcock, G. and I. Avakumović, *The Anarchist Prince: A Biographical Study of Peter Kropotkin* (London: T. V. Boardman, 1950)

Woodcock, George, *Henry Walter Bates. Naturalist of the Amazons* (London: Faber, 1969)

Woodruff, Charles E., *The Effects of Tropical Light on White Men* (New York Rebman Co., 1905)

Woodward, David, 'Medieval *Mappaemundi*', in J. B. Harley and David Woodward (eds), *The History of Cartography. Volume One. Cartography in Prehistoric, Ancient, and Medieval Europe and the Mediterranean* (Chicago: University of Chicago Press, 1987), pp. 286–368

Wooldridge, S. W. and W. G. East, *The Spirit and Purpose of Geography* (London: Hutchinson, 3rd edn 1966)

Wren, Christopher, *Oratio Inauguralis, in Parentalia: or, Memoirs of the Family of the Wrens;... But Chiefly of Sir Christopher Wren, Late Surveyor-General of the Royal Buildings, President of the Royal Society... Compiled by His Son Christopher...*(London: Osborn and Dodsley, 1750, republished in 1965 by the Gregg Press)

Wright, John K., *The Geographical Lore of the Time of the Crusades: A Study in the History of Medieval Science and Tradition in Western Europe* (New York: American Geographical Society, 1925)

——'A Plea for the History of Geography', *Isis*, 8 (1926): 477–91

——Review of *the Nature of Geography* (Cambridge, Mass.: Harvard University Press, 1966)

Yates, Frances A., 'The Hermetic Tradition in Renaissance Science', in Charles S. Singleton (ed.), *Art, Science, and History in the Renaissance* (Baltimore: Johns Hopkins Press, 1967), pp. 255–74

——*Theatre of the World* (London: Routledge and Kegan Paul, 1969)

——*The Rosicrucian Enlightenment* (London: Routledge and Kegan Paul, 1986; first pub. 1972)

Yeo, Richard, 'William Whewell, Natural Theology and the Philosophy of Science in Mid-Nineteenth Century Britain', *Annals of Science*, 36 (1979): 493–516

Young, Robert M., 'Malthus and the Evolutionists: the Common Context of Biological and Social Theory', *Past and Present*, 43 (1969): 109–45

——'Darwin's Metaphor: Does Nature Select?' *The Monist*, 55 (1971): 442–503

——'Evolutionary Biology and Ideology: Then and Now', *Science Studies*, 1 (1971): 442–503

——'Why are Figures so Significant? The Role and Critique of Quantification', in John Irvine, Ian Miles and Jeff Evans (eds), *Demystifying Social Statistics* (n.p.: Pluto Press, 1979), pp. 63–74

——'Natural Theology, Victorian Periodicals and the Fragmentation of a Common Context', in Colin Chant and John Fauvel (eds), *Darwin to Einstein: Historical Studies on Science and Belief* (Harlow: Longman, 1980) pp. 69–107

——'Darwinism *is* Social', in David Kohn (ed.), *The Darwinian Heritage* (Princeton, N.J.: Princeton University Press, 1985), pp. 609–38

Zipf, G. K., *Human Behavior and the Principle of Least Effort* (New York: Hafner, 1949)

Index

Lightning Source UK Ltd.
Milton Keynes UK
UKOW05f2348110913

217005UK00002B/168/P

9 780631 185864